D0333560

STUDIES IN
BIBLIOGRAPHY

STUDIES IN BIBLIOGRAPHY

EDITED BY

FREDSON BOWERS

Associate Editor

DAVID L. VANDER MEULEN

Volume Forty-Four

Published for

THE BIBLIOGRAPHICAL SOCIETY OF THE UNIVERSITY OF VIRGINIA

BY THE UNIVERSITY PRESS OF VIRGINIA, CHARLOTTESVILLE

1991

THE UNIVERSITY PRESS OF VIRGINIA
Copyright © 1990 by the Rector and Visitors
of the University of Virginia

Virginia. University. Bibliographical Society.

Studies in bibliography; papers v.1—
1948/49—
Charlottesville.
v. illus. 26cm. annual.
Title varies: 1948/49—

1. Bibliography—Societies.   I.   Title.
Z1008.V55   010.6275549–3353 Rev.*

ISBN 0–8139–1316–0

The editors invite articles and notes on analytical bibliography, textual criticism, manuscript study, the history of printing and publishing, as well as related matters of method and evidence. Send manuscripts to Fredson Bowers, *Studies in Bibliography*, Route 14, Box 7, Charlottesville, Va. 22901.

All other correspondence, concerning membership, subscriptions, and other business should go to Penelope F. Weiss, Executive Secretary, Bibliographical Society, University of Virginia Library, Charlottesville, Va. 22903.

Contents

[Textual] Criticism and Deconstruction

by

D. C. GREETHAM

"DECONSTRUCTION JUST HAPPENS:" THUS JACQUES DERRIDA AT HIS annual City University of New York lecture in September, 1989. His point was to distinguish "deconstruction" (a philosophical disposition or a critical practice) from "deconstruction-ism" (an institutionalised or scholarly movement, and only one of the several -isms of contemporary American "Theory," which word Derrida now regards as a proper noun in its current American usage, and not as a "theory" in the conventional scientific sense). The distinction between deconstruction and deconstructionism may be very pertinent to any discussion of the nature and role of deconstruction in present-day scholarship, for the academic and political power of deconstructionism may have given a bad name to the actual critical practice of deconstruction, whether it be in literary or in textual criticism, a practice which is addressed in G. Thomas Tanselle's recent article "Textual Criticism and Deconstruction,"[1] to which this present essay is in part a response.

But if deconstruction "just happens," what exactly does it do, and how may we recognise it in action? Is it in fact really much different from many of the critical practices we are already familiar with? Is it indeed (as some of its detractors have suggested) no more than yet another, this time decadent and anti-humanist, survival of formalism, whose last incarnation was the "old" New Criticism? Such speculations cannot be fully addressed here—in part because my concerns are more textual than they are literary (in the narrow sense of that term)—but I raise them to emphasise that deconstruction is not a practice that was "invented" at the École Normale Supérieure by Derrida, then brought to this country by the "hermeneutical mafia" at Yale. As one of its major practitioners, J. Hillis Miller, insists: "The present-day procedure of 'deconstruction,' of which Nietzsche is one of the patrons, is not . . . new in our own day.

---

1. G. Thomas Tanselle, "Textual Criticism and Deconstruction," *Studies in Bibliography*, 43 (1990), 1–33. All subsequent references to Tanselle are, unless otherwise noted, to this article.

It has been repeated regularly in one form or another in all the centuries since the Greek Sophists and rhetoricians, since in fact Plato himself, who in *The Sophist* has enclosed his own self-deconstruction within the canon of his own writing."[2] Rather, deconstruction is an *attitude* towards the apparent structures embedded in works (and texts), and an attempt to interrogate those structures, initially by inverting the hierarchies which the structures represent. It thus brings to literary criticism a "suspicion" of texts similar to that long endorsed by most practising *textual* critics. Let us not forget that Eugene Vinaver, whose major editorial work on Malory was done before any formal "deconstructive" movement, insisted that "textual criticism implies a mistrust of texts."[3] And twenty-five years ago, Fredson Bowers was warning critics against the "sleazy editing" of the great English and American classics, and suggesting that a Vinaver-type suspicion would be salutary to critical awareness. In a justly-celebrated passage in *Textual and Literary Criticism*, he roundly condemned the passivity and gullibility of the literary establishment: "[I]t is still a current oddity that many a literary critic has investigated the past ownership of and mechanical condition of his second-hand automobile, or the pedigree and training of his dog, more thoroughly than he has looked into the qualifications of the text on which his critical theories rest."[4] Bowers was then calling for what has become known in critical circles as a "hermeneutics of suspicion," of which textual criticism and deconstruction are, in their different ways, exemplary. In one sense, therefore, the deconstructors have simply joined the textual party rather late.

However, it is only fair to acknowledge that the sort of suspicion or mistrust brought to literary criticism by deconstruction does not at first appear to be at all related to the critical attitude of the philological tradition. Theirs, the deconstructors', seems to be whimsical, idiosyncratic, undisciplined, destructive, and badly written; ours, the philologists', is structured, objective, disciplined, constructive, and closely argued. Theirs seeks to fragment texts and to prevent their ever becoming works by exposing their inevitable *aporia* (their "central knot of indeterminacy"); ours seeks to make works out of the corruptions of texts, and (at least in the eclectic tradition) to create "texts that never were," which ideally should be consistent and determinate—or such is the most frequently-endorsed editorial aim. How can textual criticism as we have

2. J. Hillis Miller, "The Critic as Host," in *Deconstruction and Criticism*, ed. Geoffrey Hartman (1979), p. 229. All subsequent references to Bloom, de Man, Derrida, Hartman, and Miller are, unless otherwise noted, to this volume.

3. Eugene Vinaver, "Principles of Textual Emendation," *Studies in French Language and Medieval Literature Presented to Professor M. K. Pope* (1939), pp. 351–369.

4. Fredson Bowers, *Textual and Literary Criticism* (1966), p. 5.

usually defined that enterprise share any ideals or practices with deconstruction, despite their similar reliance upon suspicion?

The first step in answering that large question is to show deconstruction in action, and I begin by pointing to two well-known critical acts that may be regarded as deconstructive—one textual and the other non-textual. The non-textual first: when Freud began formulating his theories of psychoanalysis, he inherited a series of structures arranged in neat hierarchical disposition—conscious/unconscious, presence/absence, spoken/unspoken, wakefulness/dreams, etc., with the first term in each pair being conceived as the primary, more valid, more reliable, or more important of the two, and with the second being defined by its distance or separation from, or negation of, the first. In each case, the effect of Freud's theories was to invert the inherited hierarchical structure, by, for example, declaring that it was the unconscious which controlled the conscious and not the other way round, and that access to the "real" nature of a psychical problem could be gained through "slips" or "lapses," and not through intended expression. Freud was "deconstructing" these hierarchies, setting them on their head, and demonstrating that the fixed, reliable relationship we had got used to was in fact unfixed and unreliable. Similarly, in the textual sphere, when Greg wrote his famous article on copy-text,[5] he had inherited a series of textual structures arranged in hierarchical disposition, the most significant of which were content/surface and early/late. The copy-text article was quite literally "revolutionary" because it turned these terms and concepts around—positing that editors interested in recovering authorial intention should be concerned more about the characteristic surface features (accidentals) of a text than the content (substantives) in selecting a copy-text, and that therefore they would probably do better to choose an early text showing these putative authorial forms rather than the latest, most "finished" (in both senses) of states as copy-text. Like Freud, Greg was "deconstructing" the received wisdom of textual criticism by inverting the received hierarchies.

If this is all deconstruction is, it may all seem rather tame, but it does not end there. The real reason for the deconstructive inversion of hierarchies is not to create other (inverted) hierarchies in their place, which will become the *new* received wisdom, but to question each new hierarchy as it appears, with the effect of for ever delaying or denying a fixed, reliable relationship. Deconstruction's prime *philosophical* agenda is thus to interrogate and repudiate any appeal to a "metaphysics of pres-

5. W. W. Greg, "The Rationale of Copy-Text," *Studies in Bibliography*, 3 (1950–51), 19–36, reprinted in *The Collected Papers of Sir Walter Greg*, ed. J. C. Maxwell (1966), 374–391.

ence," any claim that would ground a system of difference in such a fixed and unchallengeable authority. This process of continual interrogation is usually called "différance", a play (in French) on the terms for "differ" and "defer," and, given Derrida's concern for inverting the priority of speech over writing, a play which can only be *seen* (in writing) and not *heard* (in speech), for in French there is no phonemic difference between the *e* and *a* of "différence"/"différance." This play (a characteristic Derridean *jeu*) is a post-structuralist response to the structuralist arrangement of pairs of concepts into positives and negatives based on their "difference" (a concept derived through structuralism from Saussure's "phonemic"—i.e., differential—analysis of language, whereby each phoneme is recognised as potentially meaning-ful by speakers of a language by the fact that is *not* another phoneme, but is "different"). Thus "*cat*" is heard as different from "*mat*" because [c] and [m] are phonemes in English. The most important pair in this differential calculus of language was that composite of the "sign," made up of the "signifier" (the actual form, the surface features, of the word) and the "signified" (the concept or substance to which this form referred), with the signified as the more "real," the more "transcendental" of the two. As can be readily seen, this distinction, especially in the privilege given to the signified, is very similar to the "substantives"/"accidentals" difference which Greg inherited and inverted, just as later linguists (and psychologists) were to invert Saussure. If, therefore, these differences are not fixed but may be challenged—even if they seem to embody such apparently permanent truths as substance and accidence—then it may be that we will never arrive at a definitive "system" which can support a universally relevant series of hierarchical relationships. There will never be a permanent "metaphysics of presence"—and it is this persuasion that deconstruction insists upon.

But does the practice of deconstruction "just happen" (to revert to Derrida's assumption)? Consider briefly the two examples already cited—Freud and Greg. One of the hierarchies endorsed by Freud is neurotic/psychotic, with the former being adopted as the "norm" whereby the latter's "difference" is to be measured. In Deleuze and Guattari's *Anti-Oedipus*,[6] this hierarchy is indeed challenged—and inverted, with the neurotic replaced by the psychotic as the norm in their deconstructive system of psychoanalysis, so-called "schizoanalysis." Similarly, the male/female pair in Freud (with the female being seen as a defective "version" of the male—especially genitally) has been challenged and inverted by

6. Gilles Deleuze and Felix Guattari, *Anti-Oedipus: Capitalism and Schizophrenia*, tr. Robert Hurley, Mark Seem, and Helen R. Lane (1983).

some post-Freudian feminists, with the male now seen as a (genital) "version" of the female.[7] On the "textual" side, we can observe the same process of continual challenge, for while Gregian copy-text theory and the related concepts of eclecticism and intentionality have had a long and successful influence on the production of scholarly editions in the English-speaking world, some of the hierarchies of that theory have indeed been challenged and inverted. From within intentionalism, Hershel Parker has attempted to overturn the consistent/inconsistent and the whole/part pairs, declaring that Greg's rationale is "too rational" to allow "full intentionality" to be presented.[8] And from a position somewhere on the margins between intentionality and sociology, Jerome J. McGann has challenged the early/late, original/copy, author/reader, single/multiple pairs of Greg-Bowers textual criticism, preferring to regard the authorial "originary moment" of composition as only one among several in the full ontology of the work, and to deny any *special* privilege to this early, original, single entity.[9] No doubt other challenges will come to upset the new hierarchies created by Parker and McGann.

So deconstruction *may* "just happen," as Derrida suggests, and it does not need "deconstruction-ism" or deconstructors to make it happen. It is happening all around us: indeed, as I will suggest here, it has happened in the article by Tanselle which is the *raison d'être* of this one, and it will happen in the concluding section of my essay. It is perhaps fortunate that this is so, for it may be easier to "show and tell" about something actually occurring before our eyes as we read than it is to talk in abstractions about concepts which may appear remote from and inimical to the interests of textual critics.

And so at last I turn to "Textual Criticism and Deconstruction," to Tanselle v. Hartman et al., and to my own typographically peculiar title, "[Textual] Criticism and Deconstruction." In dealing with the function and form of such titles, I will thus have to concentrate on the "surface features" of the text—brackets, word order, and the like—and I am sure that an audience of textual critics brought up in a Gregian or post-Gregian dispensation will not have to be convinced that such concentration is quite proper in an article on textual criticism, and will appreciate that these "accidentals" are potentially very significant, for they may embody much of the "substance" of a critical argument. It is, rather

7. See Jonathan Culler, *On Deconstruction: Theory and Criticism after Structuralism* (1983), pp. 167–175 for a discussion of this component of feminist theory.

8. Hershel Parker, *Flawed Texts and Verbal Icons: Literary Authority in American Fiction* (1984).

9. Jerome J. McGann, *A Critique of Modern Textual Criticism* (1983).

appropriately, a concern shared by textuists and deconstructors (as the play on "différance" has already shown).

Titles, and the specific form of titles particularly, are thus very important to the deconstructors, as Tanselle notes (p. 13) in his comments on the "double" title (reflecting the similarly "double" essay) in Derrida's "Living On. *Border Lines*," which emulates the appearance of a typical textual page and apparatus/commentary, with continual reference back and forth between the top and bottom of the page, over the "border" separating the two. This concept of border, a thin line of difference dividing one idea from its opposite or one function from another, is central to the structuralist ethic from which deconstruction derives, and is obviously important (as Derrida's parody of the textual edition shows) to our own discipline. We like to know which is which—text or apparatus. The difference that lies at the heart of the identity of the phoneme in structuralist linguistics (*cat*/*mat* etc.) is thus redolent not only in structuralist anthropology and structuralist poetics, but in the very concept of the lemma and variant so familiar in the apparatus of critical editions. The lemma (reflecting the accepted lection in the edited text) is "correct," "authoritative," "true," "sincere," "original," whereas the variants listed after the lemma are "incorrect," "unauthoritative," "false," "corrupt," or "derived." This difference is usually exemplified in the apparatus by the half square bracket]. Elsewhere, the prevalent typographical device of difference is the slash /, an increasingly common method to show this play of difference in titles,[10] and perhaps best-known in the title of Barthes' famous *S/Z*, a late-structuralist phonemic analysis of Balzac's novella *Sarrasine*. The play of difference, however, while setting up apparent bipolar oppositions of form and value, inevitably acknowledges the potential similarities between the two opposed phonemes or concepts (they are perceived as different in a particular language or cultural system precisely because they could possibly be perceived as identical in another), and the textual critic's phonemic use of] in the apparatus has a similar ambivalence. The "rejected" readings have at some time been accepted by some readers (scribes or compositors) as part of the text, and their status as variants is therefore only ever contingent, just as is the status of the accepted reading in the lemma itself. I am reminded, for example, of E. Talbot Donaldson's witty (if some-

---

10. Examples include Toril Moi's *Sexual/Textual Politics*, George E. Haggerty's *Gothic Fiction/Gothic Form*, Arthur C. Danto's "Philosophy as/and/of Literature," in *Literature and the Question of Philosophy* (1987), Michel Foucault's *Power/Knowledge*, ed. Colin Gordon (1980), and J.-F. Lyotard's *Discours/Figure*. Other experiments in titles on the phonemic difference created by typography include the journal *Sub-Stance* and *The [M]other Tongue: Essays in Feminist Psychoanalytical Interpretation*, ed. M. Sprengnether S. N. Garner, and C. Kahane (1985).

what sexist) analysis[11] of the editorial acceptance of readings as rather like choosing a wife, with whom one might live happily enough for some time before becoming discontented and seeking out an alternative (reading and spouse) from among those that had originally been rejected. The border line of the lemma square bracket, like all such border lines (including marriage in Donaldson's analogy) is therefore temporary and contingent, and the lemma is thus "bracketed" (quite literally), in the manner that the phenomenologist Husserl suggested that all concepts must be while they were under debate. Thus the brackets around [Textual] in my title, and thus this digression on phonemic typography, for it is precisely this problem (what does "textual" mean and what is a text?) that is at stake in Tanselle's interrogation of the deconstructors. My title thus co-opts Tanselle's but acknowledges that we will need to bracket [text] and [textual] in the discussion rather than simply assume that we already know what these terms mean before the debate begins. As I shall show later, it is precisely because Tanselle assumes one specific "phonemic" difference between "text" and "work" (and no other) that his analysis of *Deconstruction and Criticism* is a formal deconstruction of it, a reversal of its hierarchies.

Tanselle's title ("Textual Criticism and Deconstruction") is itself a play on the title of the work (or text?) he is examining, for he reverses the ordinal value of Hartman et al.'s *Deconstruction and Criticism* by making "deconstruction" the *second* term in the title, to be read against the grain of the first, now amplified as *Textual* Criticism. A small matter, but one emblematic of the primacy of the structuralist relationship in such pairings—the "violent hierarchy" which deconstruction seeks to undo. It is no accident that the Bowers volume already quoted from is called *Textual and Literary Criticism* (not the other way 'round), for he insists throughout that it is the literary critics' duty to be aware of, and corrected by, the findings of textual criticism before the literary enterprise can even be begun. Empowerment is thus reversed in Tanselle's title, and he has thus committed a deconstructive criticism of *Deconstruction and Criticism* before even beginning his analysis, for he has inverted the values of the deconstructors, turned the "violent hierarchy" on its head, deconstructed the deconstructors. It is my contention that his entire essay is precisely this—a deconstruction of deconstruction— and that this begins at the beginning, with the co-option of the title.[12]

11. E. Talbot Donaldson, "The Psychology of Editors of Middle English Texts," in *Speaking of Chaucer* (1970), pp. 102–118.

12. For a discussion of the "master-slave" relationship in titles involving two disciplines (and for an examination of the "and" joining—or separating—them), see Shoshana Felman, "To Open the Question," in *Literature and Psychoanalysis* (1982), pp. 5–10.

There is one further typographic idiosyncrasy I must comment on (rather than employ) before showing Tanselle's deconstruction in action. When planning this essay, I had hoped not only to be able to "bracket" [textual] criticism, but to place it *sous rature,* or "under erasure," by striking through the term with a mark of erasure while still leaving it legible. This device, familiar to textual critics in the textual page diacritics and marks of erasure used in some genetic editions, and especially in transcripts of heavily-reworked manuscripts, is the usual deconstructive manner of showing that the concept under discussion (especially "philosophy") is still present in its "traces" while being absent from the terms of the current debate: the technique is, in other words, identical in signification and in form to the textual critic's marking the "present absence" of a rejected, earlier reading in the evolution of a genetic text, legible only in its orthographic "traces." It is again an example of a deconstructive method that has been predicted by perfectly orthodox textual techniques. Unfortunately, while rhetorically desirable, the *sous rature* mark was not possible in the normal letterpress of *Studies in Bibliography,* and I had to settle for the phenomenological bracket— enough to make the basic point.

I will now briefly indicate how Tanselle's commentary on *Deconstruction and Criticism* is itself a deconstruction of that book—in the various ways I have already alluded to. Tanselle's frequent quarrel with the deconstructors appears to be that they have appropriated, or perhaps misappropriated, his very discourse, and specifically the distinction he wishes to make between two terms, "text" and "work," and the different conceptions those two terms may represent.[13] And like Tanselle, I be-

13. Tanselle is quite open about his plan. He announces that his analysis will "look at the use of the word 'text' in the five essays of *Deconstruction and Criticism* . . . and consider the implications of that usage for the arguments they make" (p. 2). It is, however, his own terminological opposition between "text" and "work" that will be the operative one. It would not be difficult to demonstrate, on purely philological grounds, that this opposition is not the *only* one that common usage allows, and that "text" by itself need not always have the specific narrow meaning Tanselle endorses. Thus, while "text" has, from its first appearances in the language, always had a possible reference to the actual language of a document—sometimes in a very concrete sense (e.g., "Fyrst telle me þe tyxte of þe tede lettres")—it has also had, from these very early times, the sense of the "meaning" of a passage, as in "For to telle of þis teuelyng of his trwe knyӡtes / Hit is the tytelet, token, & tyxt of her werkkez." Similarly, while the word has always been applicable to a book or document as a physical artifact (and sometimes distinct from the *language* contained in that artifact), e.g., "Iesus Crist apperede to Patrik, and took hym a staf, and þe text of þe gospel þat beþ in þe contray in þe erchebisshops ward," it has also been more narrowly applicable only to a *part* of the document, in such oppositions as "text" and "gloss," e.g., "Þis was þe tixte trewly / þe glose was gloriously writen" or "And alle the wallys with colouris fyne / Were peynted, bothe texte and glose." The word has also had the more figurative meaning of a saying, extract, an axiom or proverb, derived no doubt from its association with the *textus* of biblical authority, or received wisdom (e.g., "Ich theologie the tixte know" or "He yaf

lieve that there is a useful distinction to be made here, but a distinction which is useful to textual criticism, not necessarily to criticism or deconstruction, and not really permanent or unchallengeable. Tanselle's book *A Rationale of Textual Criticism* (1989) is in large part concerned with offering a wide-ranging and highly sophisticated interdisciplinary discussion of the various textual ontologies of different disciplines—literature, music, painting, sculpture, film, and so on. To this end, the distinction he posits between "text" and "work" in this book is very apt: the former is the concrete, specific embodiment (document or other physical state) of the conceptual entity "work." As Tanselle quite properly notes throughout his *Rationale*, in some disciplines (e.g., painting and sculpture) the two may compete for the same space, for there is no separate "work" beyond the singularity of its concrete manifestation or "text"; but in other disciplines (e.g., literature), the "work" may be finally unknowable, precisely because the document/text is not necessarily identifiable (according to his division of the terms) with this conceptual "work" lying behind it and is certainly not to be confused with it.

However, this view of the nature and limitation of "text" and "work" is useful (and accurate) only if one shares the assumption that the physical manifestation (text) is not identical with the conceptual entity (work) in disciplines like literature. As Jerome McGann insisted in response[14] to

---

nat of that texte a pulled hen / That seith that hunters beth nat hooly men" or "What must be shall be / That's a certain text"). This sense of "authority" (as opposed to criticism or glossing) is often used from the earliest times as an appeal to truth, e.g., "But truly I telle as þe text sais" or "It be-tid on a tyme þe text me recordis." And, complementary to this sense of authority was the implication that texts might need commentary and criticism in order to be fully understood, e.g., "This texte is playner than that it needeth to be expounded"—implying that most texts *will* need such expounding—or "The art of opening, or rather of undoing a Text of Scripture (as the phrase is now) was usurped by all." My listing of such examples is not, of course, intended to assert that the opposition used by Tanselle—based on a specific meaning of "text"—is in some way invalid, but rather that, from the very earliest employment of "text" in the language, there have been several such oppositions possible, not all of which would completely parallel Tanselle's distinction in all regards. And while not endorsing the deconstructors' extension of "text" to mean "work" in the idealist sense Tanselle reserves for that term, I would contend that the range of historical meanings—from physical writing to import or meaning to motto or axiom to actual book—already encompasses a wider reach than that now suggested in such criticism by the use of "text" to mean "work."

14. Jerome J. McGann, "You quote this [distinction between concrete 'text' and ideal 'work'] as if it were a fact about Textual Scholarship that everyone working in the field, whatever their other differences, would assent to. In fact, it articulates one of the key points of the controversy: far from representing an 'alien' condition for messages, it seems to me that 'the physical' (whether oral or written) is their *only* condition. And of course much of consequence follows from those fundamentally different ways people have of imagining and thinking about texts." Correspondence, 20 December, 1989. Thus, even within the field of textual scholarship, the meaning and function of the ideal and the concrete, the work and the text, are sources of contention.

a recent essay in which I had posited this difference,[15] the apparent clarity
of Tanselle's orderly distinction does not hold if (like McGann) one
holds that the concrete is not only the way in which we may know the
work but *is* the work itself. Within the body of the textual discipline,
McGann would therefore offer another system of differences for these
terms, and not necessarily that suggested by Tanselle as a defence and
exemplification of what McGann sees as an untenable "idealist" position. But this disagreement over terms among the textual critics is not
my concern here, but rather the effect of the terminological distinction
in Tanselle's "reading" of *Deconstruction and Criticism*, for throughout
his "Textual Criticism and Deconstruction" essay he reads Hartman
et al. "against the grain" of his own book the *Rationale*, continually
upbraiding the deconstructors for having failed to make the same distinction that motivated the *Rationale*. Tanselle is very open about this
technique, directing the reader early in his essay (note 2) to the *Rationale*
for a discussion of the issues "at greater length." In this way, he reverses
the priorities of the two works (i.e., deconstructs the first through the
second), moving the "text"/"work" distinction of the *Rationale* into the
centre of the *Deconstruction* collection, and marginalising the other concerns of that volume. This is a "classic" deconstructive mode, and Tanselle does it with considerable facility. For example, he chides Hartman
for using "the word 'text' to mean 'work,' " (p. 2) asks "are we to conclude
that he is using 'text' as a synonym for 'poem' and 'work'?" (p. 3) and,
most tellingly, insists that his "text"/"work" distinction is "nevertheless
a central one" (p. 8) despite the deconstructors' misprision of the terms.
Perhaps equally telling for the displacement of one book by another is
his comment that "A place does occur . . . where a distinction between
'text' and 'poem' is made, but it is not the one *I am making*" (p. 6; emphasis added).

The same dissatisfaction, and the same determination to move "text"
/"work" to the *centre* of *Deconstruction and Criticism*, is repeated
throughout Tanselle's essay and is much too frequent a charge to be
chronicled fully here. Just a few examples will show the technique: "how
we define 'texts' is the crux of the matter" (p. 19; "his equating of versions of works with the texts that survive in documents" (p. 10); "It is
remarkable that a group of critics so preoccupied with theoretical matters should have failed to include in their discussions some recognition
of the difference between the stationary arts . . . and the sequential arts"
(p. 29). In these and many other such comments throughout the "Textual Criticism and Deconstruction" essay, Tanselle places his perfectly

15. D. C. Greetham, "Textual Scholarship," in *Introduction to Scholarship in the Modern Languages and Literatures,* ed. Joseph Gibaldi, 2nd ed. (forthcoming).

valid "phonemic" difference of "text" and "work" at the centre of *Deconstruction and Criticism* and judges the values of that book by its failure to codify its arguments around the same phonemic difference. *Deconstruction and Criticism* is deconstructed (figuratively disassembled into a series of inconsistent utterances, inadequate because of their cavalier ignoring of the "text"/"work" distinctions of the *Rationale*) in the construction of "Textual Criticism and Deconstruction."

These recognised terminological inadequacies in *Deconstruction and Criticism* lead Tanselle to a second type of deconstruction—the exposure of the *aporia* or "fundamental knot of indeterminacy" in the collection. This can be done by a reader-response demonstration of a reader's problematic encounter with the text, as witness the following: "the reader will have assumed that these matters are to be pursued as the essay develops. But . . ." (p. 3); "One thinks, at first, that Bloom is going to make this point. . . . Immediately, however . . ." (p. 5); "Hartman's vagueness here will be noted only by those who have thought about the difference between texts of documents and texts of works" (p. 20). In such cases, Tanselle acts as a Fishian innocent reader, continually surprised and jolted by the twists and turns of the writer's utterance, and shows how such a reader's expectations (expectations founded upon an acceptance of a specific definition of "text" and "work") are constantly disappointed by the *actual* expression of the authors of *Deconstruction and Criticism*.

The exposure of inconsistency can also be done by a direct analysis of the *aporia* itself, rather than by acting as innocent reader, as witness the following: "But the confusion of the opening sentence undercuts everything else" (p. 8); "he is using a metaphor that undercuts what he wishes to say" (p. 17); "Yet he seems to see no awkwardness in letting 'texts' also mean the 'scriptures' or 'poems' " (p. 22); "This oversight causes him to confuse . . . and, as a result, to write an unpersuasive brief for deconstruction" (p. 28). This method (particularly the last swipe, implying that deconstruction has been ill-served by the deconstructors) is again a perfectly acceptable deconstructive mode, for it does not claim to deconstruct, but merely to demonstrate how deconstruction has already happened in the body of the text. As Hillis Miller has remarked, "Deconstruction is not a dismantling of the structure of a text but a demonstration that it has already dismantled itself."[16] And that is what Tanselle achieves—a demonstration that because of the logical and terminological inadequacies of *Deconstruction and Criticism*, that book has already "dismantled itself."

A third (and related) way in which Tanselle deconstructs is to use

16. J. Hillis Miller, "Steven's Rock and Criticism as Cure, II," *Georgia Review*, 30 (1976), 341.

the dual dissatisfaction of failed expression and reader unease as grounds for an actual re-writing of the text of *Deconstruction and Criticism* where it is perceived to be lacking or defective. This editorial desire is quite proper, of course, but it is also an instance of Bloom's doctrine of "strong misprision" (the desire of the belated poet/critic to rewrite the precursor in order to subdue him). Tanselle's rewriting and strong misprision ranges from the optative—a desire that x should have done so-and-so—to an actual reconstruction of, and "correction" of the precursor. Witness the following: "If he had pursued this question, he might have . . ." (p. 9); "But what he might also have said is . . ." (p. 4); "How much richer the passage would be if it resonated with . . ." (p. 6); "The point that I believe Derrida wishes to make could be more coherently expressed as follows . . ." (p. 15); "Hartman's account . . . cannot/but seem thin compared to what it would have been if . . . had been a part of it" (pp. 22–23); "This question would perhaps be more interesting than the one he has chosen to discuss" (p. 23); "the sentence . . . is not well phrased (it could begin . . .)"; and here, Tanselle does actually re-write de Man's sentence [n14], as he does Derrida's on p. 15. Criticisms of omission are, of course, the common stock of reviewing, but Tanselle's consistent rewriting of the text of *Deconstruction and Criticism* is more than this—it is a co-option of that text, and (again) a deconstruction of it.

And finally, Tanselle deconstructs the text of *Deconstruction and Criticism* by "playing" with the text, by indulging in a Derridean *jeu*, a fanciful and amusing commentary on it according to the principles of his own discipline—textual criticism and editing. For example, he includes a humorous note on a possible textual "error" in de Man's essay: "I have placed 'like' in brackets because the word in the printed text is 'line.' It seems unlikely that de Man meant to say 'Is the status of a text line the status of a statue?', for a 'text line' would seem to mean a unit or building block of a text and would therefore not be parallel with 'statue,' a whole work. The matter must remain uncertain, however—as, indeed, the constitution of all texts of works is uncertain. This typographical error, if it is that, illustrates the necessity for deciding on the makeup of the text as a part of the act of reading. It also shows how documents can be unreliable witnesses to past intentions, even though we can never know with certainty the precise extent of that unreliability" (n16).

This is both salutary, and in its irony, very funny, a play with the text reminiscent of the elaborate textuality of Nabokov's *Pale Fire*. And entering further into the spirit of this editorial play on the text in the deconstructive essay, one could perhaps suggest that, according to the classical doctrine of *lectio difficilior probior est* ("the more difficult reading is the more moral"), the "text line" reading, because of its seeming opacity (but not complete implausibility) is more likely to be authorial than compositorial.

Another amusing example of such a Derridean *jeu* is Tanselle's footnote 29, on a Miller misquotation. Commenting on the source of the word "uncanniest," Tanselle conducts a (mock?)-bibliographical analysis of the possible (though unlikely) discrepancies in the various editions of translations of Heidegger, concluding with the speculation that "it seems unlikely that the copy Miller used had a different reading. Perhaps, instead, the change from 'strangest' to 'uncanniest' in Miller's quotation somehow springs from his knowing the association of 'uncanny' and 'unheimlich' in translations of and commentaries on Freud . . ." (n29). It is a beautifully articulated *jeu*, especially in its invocation of a Freudian "slip" on Miller's part, dependent on Miller's putative reading of a *Freudian* text. It is a textual game well played, and is another deconstructive turn against the text of *Deconstruction and Criticism*.

Thus, in these several ways, Tanselle's reading of *Deconstruction and Criticism* becomes an act of deconstruction itself. And most importantly for this present discussion, in his placing of his interpretation of "text" and "work" at the centre of his reading of *Deconstruction and Criticism*, Tanselle has changed and inverted the priorities of that book by reading it against the grain of his own work *A Rationale of Textual Criticism*. The relationship between *Deconstruction and Criticism* and "Textual Criticism and Deconstruction" via *A Rationale of Textual Criticism* is thus simply another example of Derrida's dictum that "deconstruction just happens" and is, moreover, a demonstration of Derrida's insistence that "One text reads another. . . . Each 'text' is a machine with multiple reading heads for other texts" (p 107).

One might argue that these methods used by Tanselle in his long review of *Deconstruction and Criticism* are really no different from the traditional criticism practised in such reviews. The reviewer's responsibility is to point out the omissions and obfuscations, the inadequacies and the failures of the book under review. It may even be within the reviewer's brief to suggest ways in which the book could be improved by rewriting, even perhaps to do some of that rewriting oneself. And, of course, we must expect that the reviewer's own work and persuasions will act as a *de facto* criticism of the infelicities discovered and described. All of this happens in Tanselle's essay, and the easy answer to the demurral that such criticism is not specifically (or only) deconstructive might simply be to accept Miller's claim that deconstruction is "analytic criticism" as such, (p. 252) and to assume therefore that all such analysis is deconstructive. However, "Textual Criticism and Deconstruction" is all this and more: it is not only analytical, but it is querulous of the

oppositional hierarchies (e.g., between literature and criticism, or between critic and text) set up in *Deconstruction and Criticism*, and insistent upon the importation of a rival set of hierarchies as the means of
criticism; further, in its dismantling of the logic and coherence (if such
they be) of the book and in its shift in empowerment (judging the effectiveness of a book of criticism by its conformity to another source of
critical power, and ironically playing with and emasculating the text by
employing the techniques of another discipline), Tanselle's essay moves
beyond the generally-accepted limits of "analytic criticism" and becomes
a witty, careful, and very effective piece of deconstructive criticism. The
deconstructors hoist with their own petard.

I hope it is therefore clear that I am not supposing that there is anything malicious, untoward, or *unheimlich* in Tanselle's having [mis]-
read *Deconstruction and Criticism*. On the contrary, as I have already
suggested, Bloom's theory of "strong misprision" would doubtless com-
mend such a [mis]reading, and Miller's insistence that deconstructive
readings merely expose the aporia that is already there, together with
Derrida's assurance that "deconstruction just happens" would both accept Tanselle's using his book to read theirs as a quite proper interpretative stance. However, the next stage of the deconstructive enterprise is
to show that such a [mis]reading does not arrest the [re]interpretation,
that another [mis]reading will produce another set of reversed priorities
—in other words, that there are no "metaphysics of presence" or "definitive editions" of works, editions that will never have to be revised, editions that contain in text and notes a permanent, fixed, hierarchical
arrangement of the values inscribed therein. For just as Greg could
deconstruct earlier belletristic textual criticism, and just as McGann
et al. can then deconstruct Greg, so Tanselle's re-editing (for such it is,
in form as well as intention) of *Deconstruction and Criticism* does not
close the process but invites further re-reading.

This is my final task in the *showing* of deconstruction in action. Can
I offer another re-reading of *Deconstruction and Criticism* that will deconstruct Tanselle's deconstruction, just as one edition re-edits another?
If I were to reverse Tanselle's hierarchies, and look for congruence
rather than difference, common cause rather than dissension, between
the deconstructors and the textual critics, what did Tanselle's reading
miss that might be of value to a textual critic looking to *Deconstruction
and Criticism* for evidence of such similarities between the two disciplines rather than the differences? This is a part of the project to "domes-
ticise" deconstruction, and to demonstrate that, with a shift in perspective, a quite different valuation may be put on the aims and practices of
the deconstructors. I now offer such a consensual reading—in the order

used by Tanselle, and by the authors of *Deconstruction and Criticism*.

Harold Bloom's essay "The Breaking of Form" is concerned with the function of form as an interpretative device, in charting "our awareness, however precarious, that the sequence of parts is only another trope for form. Form, in poetry, ceases to be trope only when it becomes topos, only when it is revealed as a place of intervention" (p. 2). These places of intervention are perceived by Bloom as critical or creative, but in both of these senses they are inevitably a part of the textual (and particularly the editorial) act and prerogative. For just as textual commentary has been seen as a series of interventions, even "guerrilla raids" upon a text,[17] so the breaking of the form of a text and the reconstitution of it in another form is the strongest imaginable intervention and a perfect exemplification of Bloom's "misprision." All editors, best-text or eclectic, are healthily guilty of this misprision of documents, a suspicion that their evidence is somehow suspect and must be remade according to a different ethic (authorial rather than scribal, shall we say?). Form is thus the means whereby the editor asserts that there has indeed been an intervention, and that form is indeed no longer simply a trope but has become the very means and subject of the editorial desire—its topos, repeated, as such topoi inevitably are (if they are to become topoi, recurrent motifs), over and over again. As editors, we therefore must agree, with Bloom, that "innocence of reading is a pretty myth" (p. 6) and that "critical reading [i.e. critical editing, which is the concrete manifestation of critical reading] aspiring toward strength *must* be as transgressive as it is aggressive" (p 7). It is transgressive in the strict sense, that it crosses borders, the borders between reading and [re]writing, between text and commentary (for the new constructed text is a commentary on the old one), and between literature and criticism (for, similarly, new texts of literature are both new literature and criticism of that literature at the same time, in an osmosis of "host" and "parasite" much more cohesive than that posited later in this collection by J. Hillis Miller).

Furthermore, Bloom's insistence that "I only *know* a text, any text, because I know a reading of it, someone else's reading, my own reading, a composite reading" (p. 8) will come as no surprise to those textual critics (most of us, I would guess) who have spent the bulk of their professional lives trying to overcome the naivety of students (and faculty) who do not realise that interpretations do indeed depend upon texts, and that it really does matter *which* text one has read. As Bloom rather obviously notes "*The* Milton, *the* Stevens, *the* Shelley, do not exist."

17. Anne Middleton, "Life in the Margins: Or, What's An Annotator to do?" New Directions in Textual Studies Conference, 1 April, 1989, University of Texas, Austin. Forthcoming in *Library Chronicle of the University of Texas at Austin*.

(p. 8) Precisely—they do not exist as authors independent of the texts in which their authorship is enshrined, and these texts are variable, not singular or monodic. As even the CSE emblem admits, there is no *the* to an "approved text" only the indefinite *an*.

The singularity of a text is as much a product of editorial *suppression* (of the "inauthentic" or "insincere"?) as it is of augmentation or construction of texts. In all editing, it is thus a concept similar to Hill's coinage "addomission"[18] (the joint principles of inclusion *and* exclusion in variation), which is used in producing editorial singularity; as Hill's ambiguous term suggests, an editor may not always be able to determine which is which in comparing one text to another. But by such suppression of evidence, by confirming one reading out of many as acceptable, most editors (or at least those editors trying to construct single-state, eclectic texts) are always trying to restrict meaning, to fence it in and circumscribe it. Thus, Bloom's talk of the "authentic poem" having achieved its "dearth of meaning by strategies of exclusion" (p. 15) can be seen as an expression of one aspect of the ideology of eclecticism, as opposed to, say, the ideology of geneticism, which in general seeks to expand meaning without such suppression. But even the genetic editor will be concerned at mapping the changes in meaning, in the exclusions made from one stage to another, so that Bloom's definition of the "strong authentic allusion" as observable in "what the later poem *does not say*, by what it represses" (p. 15) would be recognised by the geneticist. Now, I acknowledge that Bloom is speaking of different *works* rather than different *texts* of the same work (to adopt Tanselle's terminology for the moment), but as any student of Yeats or Auden (or Chaucer or Shakespeare or Wordsworth or Shelley or Emerson or Dickinson) can testify, the genetic growth from one text or state or version to another text or state or version, or the growth of versions even *within* a single text or document, can display a similar variability, and therefore a similar series of acts of repression as those observable in the sort of progression from work to work that Bloom is concerned about. The important point is that the principle of exclusion and repression, authorial or editorial, is already familiar to the textual critic: Bloom's deconstruction has already been domesticised.

There is another textual issue raised in the Bloom essay that needs some comment here. Bloom invokes the authority of the Stoic school of Pergamanian philology in defending his own interest in "the revisionary ratios that take place *between* texts" (p. 14). He notes: "Ratios, as a critical idea, go back to Hellenistic criticism, and to a crucial clash

18. Archibald Hill, "Some Postulates for Distributional Study of Texts," *Studies in Bibliography*, 3 (1950–51), 63–95.

between two schools of criticism, the Aristotelian-influenced school of Alexandria and the Stoic-influenced school of Pergamon. The school of Alexandria championed the mode of *analogy*, while the rival school of Pergamon espoused the mode of *anomaly*. The Greek *analogy* means 'equality of ratios,' while *anomaly* means a 'disproportion of ratios.' Whereas the analogists of Alexandria held that the literary text was a unity and had a fixed meaning, the anomalists of Pergamon in effect asserted that the literary text was an interplay of differences and had meanings that rose out of these differences. Our latest wars of criticism thus repeat battles fought in the second century B.C. between the followers of Crates of Mallos, Librarian of Pergamon, and the disciples of Aristarchus of Samothrace, Librarian of Alexandria" (p. 14). And I would contend that the repetition of battles observable among the literary critics can be seen in similar ideological or methodological battles still being fought among textuists. Thus, Bloom's reference to the presumed "unity" of a text to the Alexandrian librarians reinforces the supposition that the extensive collection of multiple copies of the same work by the Alexandrians was to assist in the formation of linguistic and authorial rules of analogy whereby norms of utterance could be formulated and then used to identify spurious usage in texts. This "collational" system of the Alexandrians, based on the assumption of an ideal authorial text of which the surviving documents were only corrupt remaniements, is, I believe, similar in its ideology and methods to that of modern eclectic editing, which also regards the extant texts as vehicles for the restoration of a putative authorial form. I would go further, and claim that, while the Alexandrians embraced the empirical methodology of Aristotle, the desire for an appeal to an absolute, an ideal beyond the capacity of an individual text to preserve, owes more to the Neoplatonism of Greek Alexandria than it does to a technical reliance on Aristotle. One should note, for example, that some of the Roman apologists for analogy went as far as demanding that actual contemporary grammatical expression be amplified by such "ideal" forms where these did not exist in the preserved language.[19] On the other, Pergamanian, side of the debate, I would hold that the linguistic doctrine of anomaly is similarly no philosophical accident in a city dominated by the Stoic assumption that all material remaniements are inevitably flawed and that it is therefore both impractical and impious to attempt an Alexandrian resuscitation of a grammatical or authorial ideal usage. Instead, the Pergamanians and their followers insisted on a description of language (and therefore au-

---

19. See Elaine Fantham, "The Growth of Literature and Criticism at Rome," in *The Cambridge History of Literary Criticism, vol. 1. Classical Criticism*, ed. George A. Kennedy (1989), p. 242.

thorial usage) based entirely on the aberrations of preserved documentary forms. And it is this same reliance that motivates best-text editing, an assumption that a putative ideal authorial form is not recoverable (or not testable given the inevitably corrupt evidence of surviving documents) and that the best recourse is therefore a fidelity to the system of individual utterance—aberration or anomaly—that one finds in a particular document. Bloom uses the analogy/anomaly opposition to reinforce his support of "uncanny," "anomalous" criticism of the deconstructive mode, criticism looking for the play of difference rather than the play of similarity. I see the same opposition as being useful in charting the philosophical oppositions between two very different approaches to editing. We have both been taken to task by Donald H. Reiman, who, in an unpublished lecture, "Anyone for Pergamon?," declares that there is little historical evidence to support the opposition in the terms suggested by Bloom. Reiman's attack on Bloom's critical history does not, however, impinge upon the relation I am now positing between Bloom's evaluation of the *current* terms of the opposition in criticism between "canny" and "uncanny" critics, analogists seeking unity and anomalists seeking difference, and the similar unity/difference schools of editorial work shown in eclecticism and best-text theory. The arguments for (and against) deconstruction are already paralleled in the dialectics of textual criticism.

And so with de Man. This essay appears to make some bibliographical/textual concessions by echoing one of the traditional aims of textual criticism, "the establishment of texts whose unreliability is at least controlled by more reliable means" (p. 40). The various scientific or technical pretensions of various editorial schools, or schools founded upon technical disciplines (say, new bibliography on analytical and descriptive bibliography, or textual analysis upon statistics and probability theory) might make it seem to an outsider like de Man that such relative or desired or even measurable reliability might be an inevitable rationale for textual work, and outsiders like the deconstructors therefore often translate this desire into certainty or confidence, without realising the contingency that is always acknowledged in all reconstituted texts.[20] Thus,

20. The finest statement of this contingency and the challenge it presents occurs in the conclusion to Tanselle's *Rationale*: "Our cultural heritage consists, in Yeats's phrase, of 'Monuments of unageing intellect'; but those monuments come to us housed in containers that—far from being unageing—are, like the rest of what we take to be the physical world, constantly changing. Verbal works, being immaterial, cannot be damaged as a painting or a sculpture can; but we shall never know with certainty what their undamaged forms consist of, for in their passage to us they are subjected to the hazards of the physical. Even though our reconstructions become the texts of the new documents that will have to be evaluated and altered in their turn by succeeding generations, we have reason to persist in the effort to define the flowerings of previous human thought, which in their inhuman tran-

de Man's opposition of the philological and bibliographical is based upon ignorance or blindness, and therefore sets up a false opposition. Indeed, much of the body of his essay repeats in different language Bloom's concern with the changes brought about by exclusion—this time with a vocabulary of "erasure," "effacement," and "disfiguration" (p. 46). He observes such erasures in a number of figures—of forgetting and remembering (pp. 50–51), of veiling and unveiling (p. 53), burial and archaeology (p. 67), but all such figures emblematise the same opposition of lost and found, known and unknown, original and changed, and most are (interestingly enough) a part of the traditional vocabulary of textual scholarship (e.g., memorial reconstruction, archetypal unveiling etc.) If de Man's language is similar to that of textual criticism, what of the concepts?

Consider this: "How can a positional act, which relates to nothing that comes before or after, become inscribed in a sequential narrative? How does a speech act become a trope, a catachresis which then engenders in its turn the narrative sequence of an allegory? It can only be because we impose, in our turn, on the senseless power of positional language the authority of sense and meaning" (p. 64). The expression is indeed somewhat arch and opaque, but the insistence on the forced imposition of order through invoking the supposed power of positional language is no more than a recognition of the sort of changes wrought, and the differing empowerment constructed, as a result of the various plays on titles I discussed earlier in this essay. The "disfiguration" that is de Man's subject is the conscious, unconscious, or completely accidental series of reinscriptions that mark all acts of copying, of reading, and, of course, of editing. Editing is a particularly powerful "disfiguration" of the documentary tradition, even when it seems to endorse it by the selection of a "best" text, for the selection of the "best" is itself a disfiguration of pure history, which is usually more arbitrary, less personal, and less monodic than best-text editing.

Even the best-text editors perform their tasks because of the acknowledged absence of the author to do the job for them (or even, perhaps, because of a distrust of authors as well as documents), and thus when de Man observes that "[i]n Shelley's absence, the task of thus reinscribing the disfiguration now devolves entirely on the reader" (p. 67), he is not only confirming Bloom's assertion that we can never know *the* Shelley,

---

quillity have overcome the torture of their birth. Textual criticism cannot enable us to construct final answers to textual questions, but it can teach us how to ask the questions in a way that does justice to the capabilities of mind. It puts us on the trail of one class of our monuments and helps us to see the process by which humanity attempts, sometimes successfully, to step outside itself" (93).

but also acknowledging the editorial prerogative, as the most empowered reader of a text, to commit the disfiguration on behalf of this absent originator. There is a paradox in this relationship, for while most textual critics have (until recently, anyway) invoked the "metaphysics of presence" as the rationale for editing (that is, they have appealed to the author's presence as the ground for their decisions), they have usually been dependent upon that very author's absence (through death or the commitment of inner speech to the public sphere of writing) for the reconstruction of the presence. Thus even intentionalist editors have all along anticipated a familiar piece of Derridean deconstruction, for one of Derrida's earliest and most typical acts of deconstruction was to deny the apparent primacy of speech (presence) over writing (absence), a primacy asserted by Saussure's privileging of a phonecentric system of phonemes, and to assert that the full value of the Saussurean sign was conceptually impossible without writing, which thus had primacy over speech. Thus, the intentionalists are employing the Derridean inversion of absence over presence in seeking to discover the present author who is manifest only through the marks or "traces" of absence in the documentary remains—in "writing," or *écriture*.

This paradox would, I am sure, have been recognised by de Man had it been pointed out to him, and he comes near to articulating another paradox of editing when he notes of *The Triumph of Life* that a reading of the text of this work "establishes that this mutilated textual model exposes the wound of a fracture that lies hidden in all texts. If anything, this text is more rather than less typical than texts that have not been thus truncated" (p. 67). The truncaton he is referring to is Shelley's accidental death, which left the poem as a "fragment," but while de Man thus percipiently sees this truncation as symptomatic of the "state" of texts, the implication is still that most critics and readers resist the acknowledgement of such a "fracture" in the construction of works and prefer to see them "whole" and "completed." He is probably right in this characterisation of the typical non-textual critic, but his assertion would be woefully inadequate in describing the versioning, fragmentalist, revisionary type of textual criticism represented by such contemporary textuists as Reiman, Gabler, Shillingsburg, McGann, Urkowitz, Taylor, Warren, and Foley, for whom the "fracture" is indeed the norm. Again, textual criticism has anticipated and domesticated the agenda of the deconstructors. Did de Man realise, I wonder, when he penned the following passage that he was wrting a (somewhat rhetorical) description of the aims of textual criticism? "And to read is to understand, to question, to know, to forget, to erase, to deface, to repeat—that is to say, the endless prosopopoeia by which the dead are made to have a face and a voice which tells the allegory of their demise and allows us to apostrophise them in our turn" (p. 69).

As already observed, Derrida's double essay "Living On. *Border Lines*" imitates (or parodies) in its very textual appearance the dual form of the page of a scholarly edition, with "text" above and "commentary" or "apparatus" below, in reduced type. Tanselle briefly comments on this device (pp. 13–14), but neither he nor (I would hazard) Derrida fully appreciates the inherent possibilities of the parody. Thus, the "lower" ("*Border Lines*") text is indeed quite properly concerned at first with discussing, allusively and figuratively, the relationship between the commentary/apparatus and "the text itself" above. Noting (in the text of "Living On") that the commentary is usually thought of as "only a textual supplement," an "in other words" for the text proper, Derrida nowhere takes up this frequent theme of the "other words" and applies it to the formal mechanism of an apparatus, which is constructed precisely to find a home for these "other words" of the text. The apparatus is nothing but the text in other words (rejected words), and Derrida demonstrates this by his continuous "and so on and so forth" (back and forth) from text to commentary, without ever drawing on the formal, textual link that would have confirmed this hypothesis. As is to be expected, Derrida attempts to subvert (or invert) the traditional primacy of text to supplement (a familiar thesis of his deconstructive criticism) by embedding authorial *instructions* in the supplement that should, if carried out, authorise the translation of the text appearing in the nominally superior, but actually dependent, position. But, through chance or ill-will on the part of the translators, these instructions from the author are reproduced but then ignored, thus simultaneously seeming to endorse Derrida's inversion while practically failing to carry out the necessary measures that would ensure it. Thus Derrida may characterise the commentary in "*Border Lines*" by such instructions (e.g., "My desire to take charge of the Translator's Note myself. Let them [the translators] also read this band as a telegram or a film for developing (a film "to be processed," in English?)" pp. 77–78), but when it comes to specific wishes or commands (e.g., "This would be a good place for a translator's note" [p. 79] or "To be quoted in its entirety" [p. 135]), the authorial will is countermanded, for the extract is *not* quoted in full as Derrida had demanded of the translators, who similarly do *not* insert a "translator's note" at the "good place" suggested by the author. So by what is the authorial will countermanded? Paradoxically, by the translator's desire for fidelity to the text and therefore fidelity to the authorial will. And so here is the double bind: the translator is the virtuous copyist or compositor who writes or sets only *litteratim* what the author's text had already inscribed, but in so doing, in being faithful to the letter not the spirit, fails to carry out authorial intention in its wider implications. Derrida is at one level (quite literally) making a statement about the inherent subservience and inferior status of apparatus, commentary, and supplement in our culture, but might there not also be an equally contentious statement about intention as well?

The problem with Derrida's commentary is its uniformity (as Tanselle briefly notes [p. 14]). A compositorial (or maybe an authorial) desire for equally-balanced openings has resulted in right and left, recto and verso, of each opening, having equal lines of commentary (seven lines of commentary on each page). This effectively breaks any substantive relation between text and apparatus by the imposition of a formal or aesthetic requirement, which is perhaps Derrida's idea—that substantive relations of this sort are illusory. But in employing a standard, all-too-uniform textual-page division, the essay misses an important point, and an important opportunity, about the power and reflexivity of text and commentary. We have all seen scholarly editions, particularly of works with multiple witnesses, in which the readings adopted by the editor in the text proper are sustained, (literally) supported, and empowered by the rejected readings listed and discussed in the apparatus and commentary below. Scholarly editors have indeed been occasionally reprimanded for the weight and freight of such voluminous charting of variance and of arguments for textual substantiation (the Kane/Donaldson edition of the B text of *Piers Plowman* is often cited in this regard in my own period, with a couple of lines of text supported by fifty-odd lines of apparatus and commentary). The paradox in this intertextual relationship —and the one to which Derrida *might* be allusively referring—is that the authentication of the "primary" text above is wholly dependent on the description and evaluation of the "rejected" readings below. The editors must successfully demonstrate the inadequacies of the lower text in order to convince the reader that the upper text is authentic. Thus textual empowerment passes from the lower to the upper, which is therefore (in Derridean terms) "supplementary" or "secondary" and not "original" or "primary." It is a deconstructive inversion with which all multiple-text editors are familiar (and presumably comfortable), but to the deconstructor it must look like a perfect exemplification of the paradoxically primary role of the supplement. It is my suspicion, however, that the formal exigencies of Derrida's text imply that this particular deconstructor has probably not fully appreciated, or fully articulated, the paradox.[21]

21. A better example of the formal relationship between text and commentary in contemporary literary theory occurs in the joint essay by Gerhard Joseph (Host Text—on plagiarism in Dickens) and Jay Fellows (Guest Text—on cannibalism in Pater), "Mixed

It is, I believe, this relationship which is the significant editorial theme of Derrida's essay, but he does touch upon other matters that have textual import. For example, he alludes to the "functioning of the title, the transformation of its relationship to the context and of its referentiality" (p. 117) in a manner similar to my discussion earlier in this essay. He speaks of the way in which "[o]ne text reads another, of how "e[ach] "text" is a machine with multiple reading heads for other texts" (p. 107), in an acknowledgement of the intertextuality of multiple-text works and, of course, of the sort of "reading" of one book by another that I have suggested occurs in Tanselle's reading of *Deconstruction and Criticism* through *A Rationale of Textual Criticism*. Furthermore, it is to my mind ironic that Derrida is forced to conduct his discussion of the deconstructive concept of "invagination" (and "double invagination") entirely at the figurative level, since the "border line" between his two essays does *not*, in fact, involve any of the folding or double folding that the figure represents, whereas our own discipline, particularly in the work of the analytical bibliographer, is directly concerned with the physical problems of folding and double folding in the imposition and format of printed books, especially as that can impinge upon the total "meaning" of the book. As Derrida notes, "Invagination is the inward refolding of *la gaine* [sheath, girdle], the inverted reapplication of the outer edge to the inside of a form where the outside then opens a pocket. . . . Like the meaning "genre" or "*mode*," or that of "corpus" or the unity of a "work," the meaning of version, and of the unity of a version, is overrun, exceeded, by this structure of invagination" (pp. 97, 102). Derrida's figurative language of folding as it acts upon meaning and genre or version is limited to the conceptual and metaphorical in his essay—and in deconstructive discourse generally—but the figure can find concrete exemplification in the conscious bibliographical control over meaning and genre exerted by authors such as Jonson and Pope in preparing the differing public and bibliographical appearance of their works in differing formats with different (en)foldings. Thus the publication in 1616 of Jonson's *Works* (i.e. plays) in folio rather than in quarto (the expected format for popular, ephemeral, vernacular entertainments

Messages in Mr. Pecksniff's Grammar School . . . or The Rift in Pater's Lute," in *Perspectives on Perception: Philosophy, Art, and Literature*, ed. Mary Ann Caws (1989), pp. 225–259, where the upper, "host" essay by Joseph is gradually subverted, overwhelmed, and digested by the lower, "guest" essay by Fellows. Joseph's "text" becomes smaller and smaller as the essay(s) progress, until eventually Fellows' guest essay has bibliographically consumed Joseph's, much in the manner that the textual apparatus and commentary of a scholarly edition may appear to consume the host text. The Joseph-Fellows essay is particularly apposite because its form (text and commentary) portrays the substance of Hillis Miller's essay on the osmosis between host and guest.

like the drama) was a deliberate *play* on the genre-defined limits of bibliographical format, and Jonson was thus trying to change the cultural "meaning" (and genre) of his *oeuvre* by the move from double to single folding ("invagination"). A similar point was being made in Pope's issuing of his Homer translations in varying formats dependent on the cultural level and expectations of the audience, for Pope astutely sensed that genre, and thus meaning, was in part created by the various audiences' expectations of bibliographical format. Another well-known example of how the effects of bibliographical folding can affect meaning and genre (this time without authorial involvement) is the problem of casting-off of copy in the imposition for the Shakespeare First Folio, where miscalculations in the amount of manuscript text that would fit into a particular gathering caused prose to be set as verse (to waste space) and verse to be set as prose (to save space) in the outer leaves of the gathering: in this case, the meaning dictated by the necessity of the text's fitting into the space created by the bibliographical folding was actually observable in a technical change of genre. I would doubt that Derrida had Jonson or Pope or Shakespeare in mind in his consideration of "invagination" and its effects, but the figure is nonetheless striking, and is again an example of how textual critics are already predisposed to a consideration of some of the complex issues of meaning and form that are only now beginning to animate other critics.

Geoffrey Hartman's essay "Words, Wish, Worth: Wordsworth" specifically takes up the previously-mentioned deconstructive theme of speech and writing, presence and absence, in his discussion of the figures of voice and sight in Wordsworth. "[T]he greatest deceit voice has practiced is to represent itself as repressed by the written word. Derrida argues that it is writing that really suffered the repression, by being considered a mere reduction or redaction of the spoken word" (p. 207). Hartman's vocabulary ("redaction" in particularly) confirms that the deconstructive relationship between speech and writing, and the editorial complicity in overcoming the limitations of apparent absence in writing, do have textual significance of the sort I have already discussed. A redaction is indeed perceived in the ideology of textual criticism as a "reduction" of the power of an original, even though there may not always be a net reduction in the actual text that undergoes redaction. Through the genealogical assumption of "divergent variation," a downward multiplication of corruption and a consequent loss of authority as one charts the transmission of a text in a stemma, each redaction buries the original voice of the speaker-author in a cacophony of rival voices, each of which questions the authority of this original in its act of reinscription (and transmission). Hartman speaks for the aims of the traditional Lachmannian textual critic using the genealogical method to arrive at an archetypal reading when he suggests that such an "interpreter zealously redeems the buried voice of the text" (p. 207). Classical Lachmannian textual criticism is indeed an attempt at a "redemption" of something lost, and the image of burial (along with that of archaeology, cleaning, and revivifying) is a familiar one for such textual work —from Erasmus through to the higher criticism of *Altertumswissenschaft*.

However, Hartman goes on to note that such interpreters engage in this type of archaeology "instead of understanding how texts eclipse voice and speak silence" (p. 207). This understanding is linked by Hartman to the similar awareness of "the deceptive relation between speech acts and being-in-time" (p. 206), for the very "utterance of human wishes ... reveals, through such phenomena as texts, an 'untimely,' that is, residual and deferred element" (p. 206). Again, such thoughts, which are clearly imagined to be disturbing or unsettling to the literary critic, who may be used to making an immediate correlation between the speaking voice of a text and the speaking voice of an author, should be quite familiar to textual critics, who have traditionally based their discipline upon an open acknowledgement of the "residual" and the "deferred" in a text's transmission. In fact, it might be argued that if there were no such deferral, and no residue of an original, in the subsequent stages of textual dissemination, then there would no reason for textual critics to practice at all. If each text, each redaction, of a work contained "timely utterance" rather than "untimely," then each text could presumably have potentially equal authority and there would be no need for the adjudication of the textual critic. Now, it might be suggested that it is an assumption such as this that has caused the textual critics to despair at the naivety of literary critics imagining that all texts are "timely" and all texts authoritative. How refreshing, then, to find a deconstructive critic who is eagerly pointing out to his colleagues in the literary establishment that the textual critics have been right all along, and that literary critics must now recognise the "deferral" and the "residue" which characterises the buried voice of written texts! As I suggested earlier in this essay, the hermeneutics of suspicion is a predisposition shared by the deconstructors and the textuists.

However, this particular sort of suspicion (of residue and deferral) is acknowledged, indeed traded upon, only by those textual critics of what one might call an "idealist" persuasion, critics who regard the "untimely" physical contingencies of a text's survival as a liability and at the same time as a challenge. Such critics are well represented in some of the beautifully articulated cadences of Tanselle's *Rationale*, where he wrestles with the problems of deferral and residue. Consider this passage, for example: "What every artifact displays is the residue of an unequal contest: the effort of a human being to transcend the human, an effort continually thwarted by physical realities. Even a document with a text of the sort not generally regarded as art—a simple message to a friend, for example—illustrates the immutable condition of written statements: in writing down a message, one brings down an abstraction to the concrete, where it is alien, damaged here and there through the intractability of the physical" (pp. 64–65).

Yes, indeed, says Hartman, alienation and deferral, damage and untimeliness, are the norms of the written mode, which is continually striving against its residual status. Hartman goes even further, in suggesting that "[t]here is no authentically temporal discourse, no timely utterance, except by *resolute acts of writing* (p. 207, emphasis added). What may make an act of writing "resolute" is unclear in Hartman's essay (except, perhaps, in its success in replicating the "light" and "insight" which is the other subject of the essay). I would therefore suggest, given the similar language and similar concerns of Hartman and Tanselle, that the most (perhaps the *only*) resolute act of writing is the reinscription which is the very process and product of textual editing. For only such scholarly editing is both aware of the fallen conditions of the deferred text and has the skill and insight (if practised with imagination and authority) to unbury the text and the authentic discourse which the redaction conceals. Such anyway is the most common aim of scholarly editing in these past two millenia or so.

But not quite. The "idealist" position articulated by Tanselle and endorsed by Hartman, whereby the deferred and the physical are contingent and unauthoritative, would be challenged by the sociological approach recently favoured by such textual critics as McGann and McKenzie. For such critics, Hartman's redaction and Tanselle's alienation are neither reduced nor alienated *versions* of something else (a "timely utterance" or an "original intention"); rather, the redactive and the alienated are the things themselves, not mere representations: it is not only the unfortunate condition of the text to be deferred, it is its necessity and its ontology as well. There is no other way of knowing the text, and no other way that its timeliness can ever be manifest. Paradoxically, therefore, it is the "traditional" textual criticism of the Greg-Bowers school and its apologist the idealist Tanselle that is closer to the deconstructive ethic of Hartman, and the more recent current social textual criticism of McGann and McKenzie that would disavow such a textuality.

The final essay in the collection, J. Hillis Miller's "The Critic as Host," offers an etymological, philosophical, and critical evaluation of the sort of relationship I have already described in the discussion of text and commentary/apparatus—that of guest and host. As is well-known to linguists, the two terms, "guest" and "host," are ultimately drawn from the same Indo-European root, and this etymological congruence emphasises and confirms the duality of the roles within the osmotic relationship, as I suggested in the evaluation of the dual source of empowerment between text and apparatus. As Miller puts it, "A host is a guest, and a guest is a host. . . . This subverts or nullifies the apparently unequivocal relation of polarity which seems the conceptual scheme appropriate for thinking through the system" (p. 221). As a deconstructive critic, an adherent to a discipline and approach frequently criticised for being parasitical on the body of "real" literature, Miller is inevitably concerned to *valorise* criticism and deconstruction by demonstrating that the rigid distinction which supposes that literature has primacy over and is always different from criticism is imperfect and itself open to criticism—and deconstruction.

What is interesting for the textual critic is that Miller must therefore confront a series of charges (that criticism is ancillary, potentially destructive like a virus, and practised by those who cannot write literature) that are uncannily similar to the charges often levelled against the work of textual critics. For example, Wayne Booth's attack on deconstructive criticism as denying the "obvious or univocal reading" (p. 217) is of a spirit with Edmund Wilson's and Lewis Mumford's attacks[22] on textual critics for having encumbered the texts they edit with the unnecessary recording of variants and multiplicities of meaning, for having placed their own purposes and scholarly desiderata above those of the simple reader of simple texts, who desires a monodic, single-state, authorised, "univocal" reading instead of the complex texts and apparatus of the eclectic or genetic editor. For Wilson and Mumford, the prevailing figure was barbed wire; for Booth, it is the parasite—for both, it is a conviction that criticism of this type keeps the reader away from the text rather than helping him to understand its "obvious or univocal reading."

So yet again, there might be common cause, or at least a common enemy, between the deconstructors and the textual critics, but there is more to it than a similar political [dis]advantage. And it is in Miller's essay that this commonalty appears most strikingly. This is largely because Miller chooses to concentrate on the mediating effects of deconstruction, on its calling into question the metaphysical assumptions of criticism, on its attempt "to resist the totalizing and totalitarian tendencies of crticism" (p. 252). The hermeneutics of suspicion practised by deconstructors and textuists (particularly the textual criticism of recent

22. Edmund Wilson, *The Fruits of the MLA* (1968), and Lewis Mumford, "Emerson Behind Barbed Wire," *New York Review of Books* (18 January 1968), 3–5, 23.

years) is inherently antipathetical to such totalisation, for both are primarily concerned with a continuous evaluation of evidence in order to
"reveal hitherto unidentified meanings and ways of having meaning in
major literary texts" (p. 252). Both deconstruction and the scholarly
editing of multiple texts proceed from the assumption that history has
failed to disclose or appropriate all the potential forms of meaning in a
work as it is manifest in those several texts; and even though genetic
editing may appear to offer a more overt acceptance of heterodoxy than,
say, eclectic or best-text editing, the recognition of the necessity to overcome the widespread acceptance of the unmediated univocal meaning
in texts is common to all editorial disciplines, otherwise there would
no need for editorial interposition and mediation in history. As Miller
notes, "The hypothesis of a possible heterogeneity in literary texts is
more flexible, more open to a given work, than the assumption that a
good work of literature is necessarily going to be 'organically unified' "
(p. 225). Now, it could be argued, and I have myself argued,[23] that the
need for organic unity in a work has been present in both the New
Criticism and its coterminous textual equivalent, new bibliography:
both found the figure of the "well-wrought urn" beguilingly attractive,
and both sought to resuscitate it out of the apparent ironies and complexities in the texts of works. But the characteristic *method* of the
eclectic editing arising out of the new bibliography was nonetheless to
display the multiplicities of meaning for the intelligent reader, and to
assume that the multiplicity and heterogeneity were not ancillary to,
or preparatory to, an understanding of the work, but were a necessary
part of the work's very texture. The ironies and variables of the text(s)
might *appear* to be reconciled in the eclectic edition, but such editions
did not deny, but rather gloried in, the potentially endless permutations
that the apparatus/commentary charted. This was the "barbed wire"
that Wilson and Mumford objected to. In Miller's language, what
scholarly editing does, even eclectic and best-text editing, is first of all
to refuse to acknowledge the unquestioned authority of the name of the
author "printed on the cover of a book entitled *Poetical Works*" (p. 243);
second, to acknowledge that all such books and such texts contained
therein are chains "of parasitical presences—echoes, allusions, guests,
ghosts of previous texts" (p. 225); and third, to demonstrate in the presentation of evidence, that "the critic's attempt to untwist the elements
in the texts he interprets only twists them up again in another place and
leaves them always a remnant of opacity, or an added opacity, as yet

23. D. C. Greetham, "Textual and Literary Theory: Redrawing the Matrix," *Studies in
Bibliography*, 42 (1989), 7.

unravelled" (p. 247). It is true that the fragmentalist and revisionist schools of textual criticism already alluded to would seem to offer the closest parallel to Miller's elucidation of the problems of the unravelling of the elements of a text, but let us not forget that the very word *text* (and *textual*) is a cognate of not only the Latin *textus*—the sense of "authority"—but of *textile* as well, the woven fabric whose threads are forever threatening to come unravelled, and whose identity as a total or coherent entity is entirely dependent on the skills of the weaver in seeming to hide the construction of the fabric. The successful textual critic is, like the successful deconstructor, one who can perceive both the ravelling and the unravelling, the singularity and the heterogeneity, the construction and the dissolution. In analysing the term *deconstruction*, Miller insists that "tying up is at the same time a loosening" (p. 251), and that [d]econstructive criticism moves back and forth between the poles of these pairs, proving in its own activity . . . that there is no deconstruction which is not at the same time constructive, affirmative. The word says this in juxtaposing "de" and "con" (p. 251).

It is my contention that textual criticism and scholarly editing have this same de/con/structive balance or bipolar opposition. We talk of reconstruction and resuscitation, of perceiving the whole out of the corruptions of the fragment, but our work is a continuous acknowledgement of the power of the corrupt and the fragmentary, and even our editions may lay bare the otherwise unnoticed and separate threads of the textual garment as much as they present a completed artifact for the reader.

In thus rereading *Deconstruction and Criticism* according to principles different from Tanselle's, and emphasising the points of similarity rather than difference, I have presented what is in effect a deconstruction of Tanselle's deconstruction of *Deconstruction and Criticism*. The very difference between my essay and Tanselle's is thus an example of deconstructive *différance* (the pun on differ and defer mentioned earlier), since it offers a "phonemic" difference which also promotes and represents a deferral of final meaning, just as Tanselle's essay, by questioning the values and terminology of the deconstructors, not only differs from them but also defers a final meaning to "text" and "work." Such a chain of related readings, one book being read against another, is only to be expected, and is in any case no different from the re-editing of works by differing editorial persuasions, each subsequent one deconstructing the assumptions of the former. Just as Johnson re-edits Shakespeare in part to undo Pope and Theobald, and just as the CSE/CEAA editions were undertaken in part to undo the belletristically-derived texts of the

nineteenth and early twentieth century, so one rereading both acknowledges and undoes the earlier one. If deconstruction is only "analytic
criticism as such" (as Miller insists), then it should come as no surprise
to discover that we are all doing it, willy-nilly, or that deconstruction
may not be as inimical to criticism, textual or otherwise, as we had
supposed.

Text as Matter, Concept, and Action

by

PETER L. SHILLINGSBURG

EXTUAL CRITICISM AND SCHOLARLY EDITING DO NOT OCCUPY CONspicuous positions on the cutting edge of literary theory. This is because theory and practice in these disciplines have seemed largely unaffected by several fundamental propositions underlying modern literary theory, and indeed, scientific theory and philosophy, as well. Consequently, textual criticism—the science or art of detecting and removing textual error, the discipline of establishing what the author wrote or final authorial intention, the work of purifying and preserving our cultural heritage—textual criticism, I say, has appeared to occupy an intellectual backwater concerning itself with goals and a methodology challenged or abandoned by modern communication theory, principles of relativity, and concepts about the nature of knowledge. If, to the traditionalists, modern literary theory seems to have lost its moorings in reality, to the literary theorists the textual critics seem moored to a chimera.

I propose to entertain three fundamental propositions underlying recent challenges to old certainties in relation to the materials, goals, and methods of textual criticism to see whether, taken seriously, they would effect a revolution, or totally marginalize, or simply reify textual critical theory and practice. Although I can be only referential and suggestive in what I say about fields other than textual and literary criticism, I think that excursions into related fields is a way of raising a series of questions, to a few of which I want to contribute potential answers.

The first fundamental proposition of modern theories relating to factual, historical, and scientific knowledge is that objectivity is a chimera and that statements about facts, history, and truth are relative—not actually "knowable"—because of the gap in perception between object and subject (an inability to verify correspondence between mental constructs and "real" objects). This is not a new idea, of course. The second proposition is the structuralist notion that language provides the vehicle

and imposes the limits for mental constructs of "reality"; therefore, recent investigations of the nature of "facts," "history," and "truth" have
been focused on the structuring effect of language. The relevance of
these fundamental propositions to any form of speech or writing is quite
obvious. In communication, whether or not the listener/reader receives
into understanding precisely what the speaker/writer sent from intention is problematical—not ascertainable, not verifiable. The third proposition is, then, that the reader, listener, or perceiver is the most important, or some might say the only important, functional authority for
meaning or understanding. That is, it is impossible to conceive of a work
of art apart from a perceiver's perception of it. *Moby-Dick*, for example,
as it "exists" between the covers of a closed book has no functional existence as a work of art, remaining potential until someone reads it.
These three propositions are, I think, closely related; they may even be
said to entail one another. The reading, which "creates" the functional
existence of the work, is subject to the perception gap and determined
by the structuring nature of language, as was the writing which created
the "potential" existence of the work.[1]

Now the question I wish ultimately to tease out is how these propositions, if taken seriously, would affect specific ideas about the materials,
methods, and goals of scholarly editing and scholarly reading, how they
would affect the making and using of scholarly editions. A few years ago
I asked two or three colleagues who claimed to have no expertise in bibliography but who were "up" on literary theory, as I was not, "What
difference does it make to a deconstructive reading what text the critic
starts with?" They either did not understand the question or found it
irrelevant, and from some points of view they were right, for deconstruction is a means of seeing how meanings are generated from any text, not
a means of detecting the "intent" of a specific text. But what follows does
attempt an answer to the question. Therefore, I begin with a survey of
some ways in which the principles of relativity, structuralism, and reading have affected the practice and theory of literary criticism. If textual
criticism and scholarly editing are to provide texts and insights that are
valuable to literary criticism, they must be conducted in the light of
what literary critics find valuable to do. It seems to me that a great deal
of the textual criticism of the past twenty years has been conducted in
the light of literary critical practices of the 1930s to early '60s. I begin

---

1. Perhaps it "goes without saying" that a commitment to the first of these propositions
prevents any attempt to "use" structuralism as a means of approaching objectivity. Post-
structuralists' supposed rejection of structuralism is, I believe, a reaction against such attempts and not a denial of the fundamental concepts of structural linguistics.

then with an attempt to characterize some of the fundamental ideas of modern literary theory, though that field is such a seething sea of conflict that no summary can be adequate. Crucial differences in the basic assumptions literary critics and textual critics hold about texts, however, will emerge.

I. LITERARY THEORY AND THE WORK

In literary criticism the indeterminacy of meaning was long seen as the problem; and, until acceptance of relativity changed the aim of criticism, it was the goal of historical criticism to develop means to interpret texts so that they would be understood as they were intended. When structural linguistics began affecting the practice of literary criticism, faith in recovering intended meanings through strenuous biographical, historical and philological study began to erode. The *word* no longer could be used as a stable semantic unit or as access to "reality," since the word (signifier and its component phonemes and morphemes) bore an arbitrary, not "natural," relation to the signified, which was itself a concept, not the "object in reality." Attempts to link the phonemic elements of language to physiology or neurology so as to demonstrate that they were not entirely arbitrary have not proven very fruitful. Structural relations between words (syntax) was seen to govern their meaning, and the structuring aspect of language governed what could be meant. The Author as Authority for meaning lost ground to "the text itself."

Rumblings about intentional and affective fallacies focused attention on the text's meaning as opposed to the author's meaning, for the latter was both inaccessible and perhaps subverted by a failure to achieve that which was intended, though the text might well witness the success of other perhaps unintended meanings.[2] Literary theorists abandoned the author by defining texts as acquiring "determinate meaning through the interactions of the words without the intervention of an authorial will."[3] The phrase or sentence replaced the word as the irreducible semantic unit, and the intentional fallacy became something to avoid or disguise carefully. However, faith in syntax as a reliable semantic unit continued, as is evident in Beardsley's definition, and "the text itself" seemed a stable and concrete object amenable to disciplined analysis, though authorial intention seemed remote and problematic. The idea that meaning is created by the relations between the words and by the perceived choices among words that could, grammatically, have been used instead

2. W. K. Wimsatt and Monroe Beardsley, "The Intentional Fallacy," *Sewanee Review* (1946), 468–488.
3. Monroe Beardsley, *The Possibility of Criticism* (1970), p. 30.

made texts seem even more complex and at the same time apparently more able to communicate successfully. Bakhtin's ideas about a dialogical interaction between/within texts and Claude Levi-Strauss's concept of "bundles" which included societal and behavioral elements in the "sets" which defined the choices by which differentiations in structural relations were identified and understood can be seen as means by which communication can work more effectively (by narrowing the appropriate range of possible meanings) or to increase the amount of slippage (by multiplying our awareness of oblique references—i.e., we become more aware of the potential counters *not* chosen). In either case, the need for an author is diminished.

With post-structuralism, and particularly with focus being placed on the creative act of reading, came a second wave of reaction against the author that exceeded the new critics' distrust of the intentional fallacy. The author was proclaimed dead because meaning was seen as located and created in the readers' interaction with the text, making any meaning the text "has" or "is witness to" functional only in reading acts —the intending acts of authors having receded, so to speak, into the inaccessible past. Thus, scholars' attempts to recreate the moment of authorship were seen as futile; historical criticism had beached itself like a disoriented whale. Furthermore, faith in the semantic stability of syntax became as problematic as the meaning of the word had become with the advent of structuralism.

A strong undercurrent of thought accompanying the wave of post-structuralism and deconstruction indicated that because the past was unknowable and because speech acts, writing acts, and reading and listening acts have (or create) their meaning *now* in a cultural or social setting fraught with power struggles, hegemonic structures, and political agendas—including very local, perhaps even domestic ones—therefore (A) the meanings we create for a text now matter more than the supposed original or historical meanings and (B) the way in which meanings are generated and the uses to which meanings are put are a more interesting study than are the texts or the authors or the meanings they may originally have tried to produce. Overtly political forms of literary criticism, particularly marxist and feminist criticism, have received a boost of energy from this line of reasoning. Such criticism focuses on the economic power structures at work in diction and syntax, the patriarchal and class assumptions and structures—both linguistic and social—that can be seen imbedded in texts. To some literary theorists it seemed logical to conclude that this line of thought totally set aside the major concerns of textual criticism and scholarly editing as they had been understood and defended traditionally, since the most interesting aspects of texts are not supposed authorial intentions but, rather, the unintended revelations the text is witness to.[4]

In very recent years new historicism, while profiting from the insights of structuralism and relativity theory, has resurrected some of the interests of historical criticism. The result is radically different from the old historicism, for in developing accounts of the past, the new historicist is very conscious of the absence of any means to validate the correspondence between the past (whatever it was) and the historian's account of it. Further, new historicists are often very much concerned with the structuring influences of language and the political, social, and mythological "realities" it framed. New historicism, though subject to abuses and unconvincing practice, provides several fruitful means of investigation. One is that the understanding of a text derived from even indeterminate historical investigations is often palpably different from "readings" that relate the text only to the present reader's experience. It suggests that the richness and complexity of a text (and of language) is more fully experienced by contrasting the text as a product of a partially known (that is, constructed) past with the text as free-floating in the present or as it seems to have been experienced at significant moments in intermediate times.

Another rationale for new historicism considers that structuralism's undermining of authorial autonomy and post-structural emphasis on the death, absence, or self-subverting of the author has taken the reaction against belief in objectivity about as far as it seems likely to go. Furthermore, by concentrating its efforts on the creative act of reading, deconstructive criticism provides a methodology that concerns itself with only half of the picture. A returned interest in the idea of texts "conveying meaning" from an "originator of discourse" and belief in the possibility of "fiduciary trust" between author and reader has been defended in several ways. First, it is a demonstration of interest in the workings of culture and tradition—an interest that does not necessarily entail belief in the objectivity of their reconstructions nor a nostalgic reactionary hope to "re-establish" or "restore" anything, but a genuine interest in roots and differences and a fascination with the malleability and tensile strength of histories and ideologies. Curiously, this approach considers both "history" and "the present" as current constructs, which are nevertheless useful as a means of exploring the sense of continuity and change

4. Lost in the discussion, often, is the notion that these revelations are about meanings unintended *by someone* and that the text is being treated as witness to a designated historical event. In other words, the current political agenda of the modern critic attempts to derive strength from contrast to a supposed historical "actuality" about which the writers in question were supposedly unaware.

in human feeling and thought. Second, some new historicists attempt to explore the concepts of utterance and discourse as functional links between the verbal text and its social, economic, and material contexts. The aim of the approach is to study behavior rather than to ascertain and pin down definitive meanings or interpretations. It is in this way that new historicism can emphasize the link between the text as a material object and the meanings created from its physical format, which is one of the focuses of this paper.[5]

Deconstruction has exploited the implications of relativity by recognizing the futility of regaining or understanding intention and has focused on the independent life of the text as it is confronted by actual readers (who might, in spite of themselves be trying to conform to the roles of implied readers). To this, deconstruction adds the concept of ideological influences (structured "realities")—mostly subconscious—which make texts self-subverting in ways probably contrary to authorial intention but nevertheless very important to the reader. One should note that this way of putting it suggests that deconstruction "reinstates" authorial intention as something that can and must be inferred in order that it might be "decentered"—i.e. authorial intention is identified but not treated as an authority for meaning.[6] It should further be noted that "decentered" meanings are not dislodged by nothing, but rather by other provisionally centered meanings, each of which must be justified before it can in turn be "decentered." Some marxist and feminist critics have capitalized on these two principles to read texts politically and to value or discard texts according to the ideologies revealed in the "subtexts." As we shall see, however, release from the bondage of an impossible objectivity is not an escape from the physical object, the

5. A particularly interesting new theory of a basic semantic unit is presented by Price Caldwell in "Molecular Sememics: A Progress Report," *Meisei Review*, 4 (1989), 65–86, in which meaning is seen as determined by the rhetorical "molecule' within which what is said is contrasted by speaker and listener alike to that which is not said within the limits of the molecule. This is a rejection of syntax as the primary meaning unit and acknowledges a context socially conventionalized and thus accessible to socialized speakers and listeners to insure reasonable success in communication. The structure of a molecule is similar to, but not identical with, Levi-Strauss's "bundle." One very attractive feature of molecular sememics is its ability to explore the richness of subtle usages such as irony, analogy, metaphor, and even rhyme and lies.

6. One asks what is being subverted when a text is described as self-subverting. Is it the author's apparent meaning or the text's apparent meaning that is subverted? In either case, how can a reader "know" that the *text* is subverting a meaning? What meaning is being subverted? How can the reader know that the subversion was *not* itself intended and, therefore, itself be the meaning of the text? Or is it that the *reader's* meaning is subverted by the text? The whole question of agency of meaning is, in spite of protestations to the contrary, central to deconstruction—one can hardly deconstruct what is not there.

book. Nor is it an escape from the consequences of using one edition or copy of the book rather than another.

The full impact of relativity, structuralism, and reader oriented theory has, as I averred, not affected textual criticism, but it has begun to rock the boat. Textual criticism and its "handmaidens," bibliography and paleography, have had a strong positivist tradition, which manifests itself from time to time in phrases like "the calculus of variants" and "definitive editions," and more recently as "determinate meanings" and "social contracts."[7] The fact is, however, that the discipline has made some accommodations to the "truths" of relativism: the concepts of "critical editions" and "eclectic texts" as Fredson Bowers and G. Thomas Tanselle have developed them are such accommodations, diminishing the positivist force of "solid historical research" which supposedly resulted in "established texts that will not have to be edited again." Likewise, recent discussions of multiple texts and problematic texts, which refer specifically to indeterminacy of the words and punctuation constituting the work of art in addition to acknowledging the indeterminacy of the meaning of the text, are accommodations of relativity. One could even say that the recent emphasis on "process texts" and "versioning," which Michael Warren, Donald Reiman, and Paul Eggert to name only a few have undertaken, is an accommodation of structuralism—though to my knowledge none of them has characterized it as such. The result has been a slight shift (to some editors it seems a great shift, perhaps even a sellout) in the aim of textual criticism from considering the text as an established (or establishable) locus of authoritative stability to a concentration on text as process.

What this means in practice is that the editor or critic declares an interest in multiple texts for each work rather than just in the one true or final text. It means authorial revision and production influences on texts are seen as having potential "integrity" as representations of the work at various stages in the process of composition, revision, and production. It has meant, moreover, that for some works the editor posits two or even more texts to be read and studied in tandem. It has also, however, meant that the concept of textual purity has been rescued by making it necessary to "edit" correctly each stage of the process or to make the process visible by some means that distinguishes between the various agents of change and evaluates the changes, not only according to the perceived effect made by the change but according to the "authority" of the agent of change. In short, "process editing" has not embraced decon-

7. These phrases are used by a variety of writers but were given currency, respectively, by W. W. Greg, Fredson Bowers, Hershel Parker, and Jerome McGann.

struction as an approach to texts. It retains the idea of the author and of authority, though in the theory and practice of some practitioners, process editing has loosened its grip on the text as sacred icon or as the well-wrought urn.

I would suggest, incidentally, that though a great deal has been published on these subjects, and although they have radically altered the way some post-modernist works are produced, scholarly publishing itself as a technical practice seems to have resisted any influence at all that these ideas about communication might have on the nature of publishing and on the notions that publishers have about what a book is and how it should be printed. Editions continue to be published (and read) as if written works were stable, achievable, objective, tangible substances, though these are the very concepts about "reality" that have been challenged by the propositions with which I began.

II. THE HOLE AT THE CENTER OF THEORY: TEXTUAL AND LITERARY

The weakness of much literary theory and textual criticism is that practice is based on insights which have not had the advantage of a clear taxonomy of texts. Textual critics have not had a clear enough vision of the varieties of viable answers to questions about who has the ultimate authority (or even the "functional authority") over what the text becomes, whether it is possible for a work to have a variety of "correct forms," and the extent to which the editor's decisions about the "authority" of textual variants is a function of "reader response" rather than evidence. Likewise literary critics have not had a clear enough vision of the problematic nature of physical texts and their assumptions about textual stability (e.g., that a work is a text and a text is a book and the book at hand is, therefore, the work itself).[8]

It seems to me from this survey that the "structure of reality of written works" implied by the three propositions with which I began places the writer, the reader, the text, the world, and language in certain relationships and locates the focus of experience of that reality in the reader.

8. I note for example that in "From Work to Text" Roland Barthes wants to talk about the work "at the level of an object" and distinguishes between "Work" (by which he most of the time means "Book") and "Text" (by which he sometimes means an area of play, sometimes the players in that area, sometimes the way the area plays with readers, and sometimes an object located at the intersection of propositions—in short a variety of "things" more or less abstract). But in fact, Barthes does not discuss the physical object in any sophisticated way at all, treating the Book (Work) as a single unproblematic given. He is apparently not interested in Work and does not see its relevance to Text except as a something to be decanted. I should add that I have no quarrel with Barthes's useful exploration of his term Text—though I prefer to use several different terms for the various things he denotes by the term Text.

This relationship has been mapped by a number of theorists, some of whom I shall discuss presently, but it seems to me that these maps reveal a gaping hole in our thinking around which swirls a number of vague and sloppily used terms that we pretend cover the situation. The lack of clear, focused thinking on this question can be seen graphically if we locate the physical materials of literary works of art in a center around which we visualize scholarly interest in Works of Art. To the West of this physical center we can place the scholarship of interest in creative acts, authorial intentions and production strategies, biography and history as it impinges on and influences authorial activities. To the East of the physical center we can place the scholarship of interest in reading and understanding, interpretation and appropriation, political and emotive uses of literature. To the North of the physical center we can place the scholarship of interest in language and speech acts, signs and semantics. All three of these segments of our map tend to treat the work of art as mental constructs or meaning units; the physical character of the work is incidental and usually transparent.[9] To the South we can place the scholarship of interest in physical materials: bibliography, book-collecting, and librarianship. Only in this last area do we detect the appearance of special attention on the Material Text, but because traditionally scholars in these fields have made a sharp distinction between the Material and the Text and because they have focused their attention on the Material as object, their work has seemed tangential to the interests of the West, North, and East.

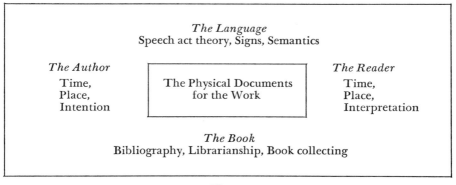

Chart 1

9. This map is adapted most immediately from two models by Paul Hernadi designed to illustrate the questions "What is a Work" and "What is Criticism," but the similarity to models of language by Roman Jakobson are apparent. (See Chart 2.)

In fact the "Southern" interest has traditionally been looked upon by the others as dull and supportive—we must have libraries and bibliographies—rather than as full-fledged fields of significant interest.[10] Textual criticism has tended to occupy itself with the concerns of the West (intention) and the South (documents), but if it took seriously the propositions underlying relativity and structuralism, it could be in the center of the "structure of reality" depicted in this graph, drawing upon all sides and informing all sides. It would not be self-defensive and apparently narrow-minded or subservient, as it has often appeared, clinging to questionable notions of objectivity and stability.[11]

It might be noted, by the way, that this particular "map" of textual concerns leaves out entirely what might be called the "data world" or that which in ordinary usage language is thought to refer to—the objective referents of language. It is because "knowledge" about that part of the picture has been removed or relativized or made objectively inaccessible by the perception gap and by the notion that knowledge of it is structured by or constructed through language. This "world view" may not be the "true" one, but it is the purpose of this paper to explore its implications to the concept of texts or works as attested by or extant in physical documents.

The specific questions I want now to raise for examination fall within a narrow band at the center of the related and interesting questions implied by this brief survey. I do not wish to be misunderstood as having raised them all or to have attempted answers to any outside that band. I am not, for example, raising any questions about what a particular text means, or what the author or other issuer of the text might have meant

10. G. Thomas Tanselle surveys a number of approaches to the problem of relating intention to texts in "The Editorial Problem of Final Intention," *Selected Studies in Bibliography* (Charlottesville: University Press of Virginia, 1979), 309–353, esp. 312–319; rptd. from *Studies in Bibliography*, 29 (1976), 167–211.

11. The degree to which textual criticism is breaking out of this narrow mold is probably not well known, for many edition users still look for a "standard" or "established" text to use uncritically, but there are new movements afoot. What I see as a problem is that proponents of the breakouts tend, unfortunately, to view their new insights as new, replacement orthodoxies—Jerome McGann, for example, bringing in and then overvaluing book production as the milieu of meaning, Hershel Parker bringing in the psychology of creativity and turning it into a determiner of text. The common problem appears to be that though textual critics are very well aware of the distinction between the Work and the Book, they have been obsessed with the notion that the Work should be reducible to a Book. My focus, however, is not upon what is wrong with textual criticism or textual critics but what a taxonomy of texts reveals about the connections between textual criticism and its related fields of interest and what it can show about the nature of Works of Art that might change our view of the aim of textual criticism and the way we treat the copies of works we use in our study regardless of our position, East, West, North or South.

by it, or even what a reader might have understood it to mean. I am supposing that the author and other purveyors of texts do mean something or somethings by them, and I am assuming that texts are understood by readers to mean certain things. The fact of these meanings is important but the meanings themselves are not my concern here. The answers to such questions lie to the West and East of my concerns. The questions I ask have to do with the mental and physical acts and the material results of acts attending the processes of composition, publication, and reception of written texts. And the questions I ask are about what these acts and results can be, not what they should be. Further, I assume that whether the author and reader understand the same thing by a text is not ascertainable. Moreover, I am not asking questions about whether an author's or publisher's "sense" of the work is individual or culturally determined, nor am I asking if the readers' reactions are culturally bound. At the moment I believe that, at least to some extent, and mostly unawares, they are. But I am not aware that any specific opinion about this notion bears significantly on the proposed taxonomy. Nor am I asking how the meanings of author and reader are generated and how they either succeed or go astray. The answers to these questions lie North of my concerns. On the other hand, I am not confining my interest to documents and books as items for bibliographical description or cataloguing for shelving.

The questions I raise are essentially those of textual criticism, but they involve all of these other fields at their margins, for texts—both as physical and mental constructs—lie at the center of any attempt to record or communicate any knowledge.[12] I wish to propose corollaries for two of the propositions that I proposed to entertain for their effects on textual theory: first, the perception gap that holds that our "knowledge" of the "real" world is restricted to our mental, inferred constructs, and, second, the view that language is the structuring tool through which "knowledge" is constructed. The corollaries of these propositions are: first, that the text of a work as found in a document (what I will call the Material Text) is the locus and source of every reader's experience of a written work of art and that regardless of what concepts of works are inferred from the evidence of the Material Text, there is no channel other than inference by which a reader may "reach out" to the mental forms of works as they may have been experienced by authors or other agents and originators of texts. The second corollary is that the mental construct of

12. All communication, that is, must pass through a physical medium as sounds or as signs to be seen, heard, or touched. Communications of any other sort are called telepathy, about which I have nothing to say.

the work derived by a reader from the Material Text in the act of reading (what I will call the Reception Text) is the only "thing" that a reader can refer to when making comments about a work.

These two fundamentals—the physical documents and the reading experience of decoding them—are the irreducible core of literary works. Without the reader, the physical documents are inert and inoperative; without the physical documents there is no reading.[13]

For most practical purposes the words "work of literary art," "book," and "text" are thought to be vaguely synonymous. But in fact there is a great deal of confusion about these words; whenever anyone means something specific by them, qualifications become necessary. So we talk about classroom texts, standard texts, established texts, inscriptions, or revised editions; and we add other concepts relative to production economics or reader response theory. It strikes me that even with these qualifications we do not have enough distinct terms for the concepts we use the words "text" and "work" for. Arguments about how to edit works are fueled by our confusions about what are or are not textual corruptions and about what aspects of book production are or are not legitimate "enhancements" of the work. And these confusions and controversies become heated to the extent that one or more parties believe there is a correct or optimum definition of "text" which is a guide to the desired good, correct, standard, or scholarly edition.

It has long seemed to me that the difficulty which we were not handling well was bridging the distance between concepts of works of art that are abstract, ideal, or mental with the material manifestations of or records of these concepts in paper and ink documents and books. One could try to put this in terms familiar to textual critics as an attempt to draw more clearly the relationship between intended texts and achieved texts, but that puts the question too narrowly (and too Westerly on my map). Or one could try to put it in the language of the English philosopher and linguist J. L. Austin as an exploration of the relationship between perlocution, illocution, and locution, but that tends to emphasize the Westerly and Northerly aspect at the expense of the physical center.[14] Most of the work upon the mental and abstract aspects of works

13. This is obviously not true of literary works held in the memory and that "live again" as they are remembered or recited without the aid of physical documents. I am perhaps being a bit literal when I define reading and writing in relation to physical documents, but textual criticism and scholarly editing seldom are able to concern themselves with memories and recitations. (See also note 29.)

14. *How to do Things with Words* (1962), pp. 99–130. Illocution, the way an utterance is used—as warning, advice, etc.—and perlocution, the effect aimed at by the utterance—as persuading one to respond appropriately—are just two of a number of possible ways to

of art is marred by vague or coarse notions of what the material texts are. And most of the work upon the physical materials of works of art has been marred by a parochial focus of attention or adherence to notions about objective reality.

Ferdinand de Saussure did explore the relation between mental concept and physical sound-image in speech, and a good deal of thought has been applied to that relation in linguistics; so what I am proposing to do for literary works is not entirely new. But confusion arises for at least two reasons when applying Saussure's model of speech to written works. First a speech act takes place in the presence of speaker and listener as a single event in time and in a shared space and physical context. Written works do not. Second, written works, contrary to folk tradition, are not stable, singular, verbal texts. They tend to change in "transmission" (to use one of textual criticism's least elegant terms) either by revision, by editorial intervention, or by accident. I will develop the implications of these two ·differences between speech acts and "write acts" in due course. For the moment, however, I would like to emphasize that the alleged similarity between the two has led many practitioners of literary and textual criticism and linguistics to treat the physicalness of the written text as unitary and unproblematic.

Theorists are, of course, greatly concerned with the complexities and problematics of "intention" and "interpretation," which precede and succeed the text, but the supposedly stable, unproblematic physical signifier between them, the written text, is simply missing from most diagrams of the problem. Paul Hernadi's adaptation of J. L. Austin's speech act theory is one of the most useful and enlightening of such diagrams. (See Chart 2.) He elaborates both ends of the author-work-reader equation and indicates relevant concerns about language as a communication system and its function in the "world as representable by verbal signs," but the center of Hernadi's chart identifies the "Work as verbal construct and locutionary act." As such it is the work of the author and a field of reader response and is described as *verbal*, not as *physical*. The *paper and ink* Work, as a repository of signs for the verbal construct and locutionary act, untethered from its origins does not exist on the chart.[15]

categorize the "intentions" that might constitute the thoughts and feelings preceding and leading to utterance, locution, or creation of a delivered text. See Appendix A for further analysis. The concept of "intention" is slippery and has been discussed in connection with literary texts by me and others elsewhere; see works cited below by Bowers, Tanselle, McGann, and McLaverty.

15. Paul Hernadi, "Literary Theory," in *Introduction to Scholarship in Modern Languages and Literatures*, Joseph Gibaldi, ed. (1981), pp. 103–105.

This physical absence (or transparency) is typical of speech act and literary critical formulations of the communication process. See for example Roman Jakobson's model:

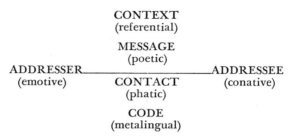

CONTEXT
(referential)

MESSAGE
(poetic)

ADDRESSER_____ADDRESSEE
(emotive)   CONTACT   (conative)
(phatic)

CODE
(metalingual)

What should, perhaps, be the physical text is apparently a straight line. That line, like Dr. Who's Tardis, may look small and ordinary from outside, but it is spacious and complex inside. From the outside, so to speak, written communication looks like spoken communication, but the differences are so startling as to make conclusions about speech seem simply inapplicable to writing. The problems can be easily demonstrated.

I was spring cleaning the family deepfreeze and came to three jars of frozen grape juice. The labels said: "This year's juice." When the person who canned and labelled the juice wrote the label, it was natural and perfectly unambiguous to say "This is this year's juice." Considered as a "speech act" rooted in time and place, the labelling had a "speaker," a "hearer," a place of utterance (the kitchen), a time (the year and moment of placing the juice in the freezer), a richness of social and physical context that identified the relevant "bundle" (Levi-Strauss's term) or molecule (Caldwell's term) that prevented any misunderstanding or sense of inappropriateness or inadequacy in the phrase, "This year's juice." Only when seen as a written message, a "write act," untethered from speaker, from moment and place of utterance, and from designated hearer, do we find it risible, inadequate, or frustrating to imagine this label as capable of signifying something specific at any time it happens to be read.

Another example: I was reading excerpts from some articles that had been photocopied and bound together for student use. One of the sources photocopied was itself a compilation of essays. At one point a cross-reference said: "See p. 33 of this book." When it was first written and printed "this book" was a phrase probably meant to distinguish the compilation from the original works being excerpted ("those books"). Now, in the photocopy for student use, the reference was inadequate and frustrating. The statement "This office will be closed until tomorrow" is perfectly

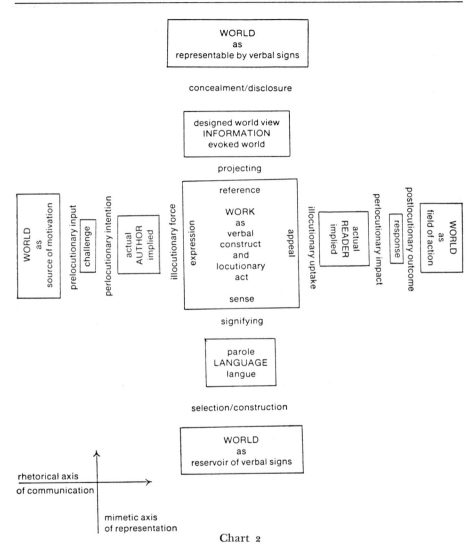

Chart 2

Reprinted by permission of the Modern Language Association of America from Paul Hernadi, "Literary Theory," *Introduction to Scholarship in Modern Languages and Literatures* (New York: Modern Language Association, 1981).

clear when announced to a waiting crowd, but totally ambiguous when posted on a locked door and read in the early morning. The "bundle" or "molecule" changes with reference to written material in ways never experienced in a speech act. The difference and ambiguity can be consciously exploited—as in the pub sign anouncing "free beer all day tomorrow." Thus, an exploration of the relation between mental concepts (signifieds) and physical texts (signifiers) for literary works leads to problems Saussure never discussed (that I know of) and will lead to descriptions of writing and reading acts in ways that clarify some of our disagreements about what they are and how they are. Perhaps it can also defuse some of the vehemence of our disagreements about what and how they ought to be.

III. A Taxonomy of Texts[16]

In 1984 I made an attempt to delineate the gradations of concepts from the ideal to the concrete, which I thought clarified the editorial materials and goals sufficiently so that disagreements among scholarly editors about editorial policies could be understood clearly and not result from vagueness or confusion.[17] Disagreements could thus be resolved or brought to a truce in which the parties at least knew why they disagreed. I have been gratified by the response to this effort from editors who expressed feelings of relief and release from conflicts between what their common sense inclined them to think was a desirable editorial solution and what standard editorial practice and principles seemed to dictate.

Now it seems profitable to raise the question again because the arguments about what constitutes the work of art rages not merely among textual critics, but among literary critics generally. I have found inspiration to continue my 1984 attempt in the writings of Jerome McGann, D. F. McKenzie, Joseph Grigely and James McLaverty.[18] My discussion

16. This is not really a taxonomy, for I am not classifying kinds of literary works; rather it is an anatomy, but only of a narrow band of what a literary work is. It is more accurately an ontology of texts, but a suggestive and tentative one. Most definitely it is a proposal for a partial nomenclature of textual criticism.

17. *Scholarly Editing in the Computer Age*, Occasional Paper #3 (English Department, Royal Military College, Duntroon, 1984); revised edition (Athens: University of Georgia Press, 1986). (An earlier, less developed presentation is in my "Key Issues in Editorial Theory," *Analytical & Enumerative Bibliography*, 6 (1982), 1–16.) Additional comments focused particularly on what might be called production texts or the sociology of texts are in my "An Inquiry into the Social Status of Texts and Modes of Textual Criticism," *Studies in Bibliography*, 40 (1988), 55–79.

18. Jerome McGann began elaborating his ideas about production versions of works in *A Critique of Modern Textual Criticism* (1984), but makes a clearer statement of them in "Theory of Texts," *London Review of Books*, 16 Feb. 1988, pp. 20–21. D. F. McKenzie explains his view of works as cultural artifacts with specific spatial and temporal appropriations and functions in the Panizzi lectures, *A Sociology of Texts* (British Library, 1987). In "The Textual Event," a paper for the Society for Textual Scholarship (STS) conference, New York, April 1989, Joseph Grigely presented his ideas of texts as occupying literal, historical and mental spaces and suggested a distinction between text and performance, which he did not elaborate. James McLaverty published two informative articles in 1984 ("The Concept

will take the form primarily of definitions. The distinctions between concepts, and the relations I will try to show existing between them, are designed first to provide a system for describing the range of materials that are commonly referred to vaguely as books or works of literary art, and second, to provide a ground for discussing the various sorts of acts (often characterized by confusion and conflict) undertaken in response to these materials. My purpose is to enable the conflicts to be focused more clearly on substantive differences of opinion and judgment rather than on confusions about what is being said. Although taxonomies are by definition logocentric and tend to pin down concepts or objects in a conventional way, the result of the taxonomy I propose is to suggest that the drive towards arresting and codifying Works of Art is futile. Instead, it suggests that the work is partially inherent in all "copies" of it. One might say the Work is neither this, nor that, but both and none. The Work is partially in the copy of the work but is not the copy. Works are known through proliferations of texts, not through their refinement or concentration. Nearly all experiences of works are, therefore, partial. This taxonomy helps reveal what parts remain unknown or unexperienced. I have adopted the convention of capitalizing the terms I have appropriated for definition. Since I use some of these terms before I have had a chance to define them, their capitalization is an indication that I will eventually define them.

A. *Methods of Classification*

It is customary to speak of a Work of literary art, such as *Moby-Dick* or *Dombey and Son*, as though such titles designated something definite. That they do not is easily demonstrated by asking, "If the *Mona Lisa* is in the Louvre in Paris, where is *Hamlet?*"[19] The term Work is used to classify certain objects, so that we can say "This is a copy of *Moby-Dick*, but this over here is a copy of *Dombey and Son*." The term Work and the title *Moby-Dick* do not refer to a thing, an object, but rather to a class of objects. We can see this by saying, "This is a copy of *Moby-Dick*, and this, too, is a copy of *Moby-Dick*." We might try to push the limits of

of Authorial Intention in Textual Criticism," *The Library*, 6, 121–138; and "The Mode of Existence of Literary Works of Art," *Studies in Bibliography*, 37, 82–105) on concepts of authorial intention, and at the STS conference in New York, 1989, he presented "Identity and Utterance in Textual Criticism," in which he suggested several concepts that might be used in identifying different forms of a work; these include identity, survival, function, and utterance. I am especially indebted to McLaverty for sparking off the ideas elaborated in this essay. I should add that conversations with my colleagues Paul Eggert and Jeff Doyle (at University College, Australian Defence Force Academy) have been influential in this paper in ways too numerous to point out.

19. The question has fascinated me since I first encountered it in James McLaverty's "The Mode of Existence of Literary Works of Art."

this insight by defining Work of literary art as that which is implied by and bounded by its physical manifestations.[20] This statement suggests both that a Work can have forms other than that of one of its physical manifestations, and that its potential forms are limited by the forms of its physical manifestations. It suggests, further, that a Work is in important ways both plural and fragmented. These are not simple or comfortable suggestions, and the reaction of some critics and editors is to limit their attention pragmatically to the physical manifestations of works, the book in hand, as if the Book and the Work were coeval and congruent. They are not interested in abstract notions of "intention" or in fragmentary forms of the work, which they would label "pre-utterance forms" or "pre-copy-text forms" or "shavings on the workshop floor." For them, the work *is* the book in hand. It is simple, it is practical; it is achieved by willfully ignoring certain sets of questions about the work.

But for those who stop to think that not all copies of a work are identical (which is particularly true of well-known, often reprinted, works), and that what person X says is the work (because he holds copy X in his hand) is different from what person Y says is the work (because she holds copy Y), there is a problem worth resolving, because what person X says about the work, referring to copy X, might be nonsense to person Y, checking the references in copy Y.[21] A fruitful approach to this problem is to examine the concept that the work is implied by and limited by its physical manifestations, rather than being identical with them. This examination requires that we contemplate, if only for argument, the idea that the work is an ideal or mental construct (or constructs) separate from but represented by physical forms. We can do this without arguing that the work is either the mental construct or that it is the physical form, and we need not argue that one or the other has a greater claim. Instead we might pursue the implications of defining the work as a mental construct that can be known only through its physical forms and the

20. This is probably not always true for the author who might consider "the work in his head" to be better than and independent from any of its physical inscriptions. As Marlowe notes of dreams in "Heart of Darkness," "no relation of a dream can convey the dream's sensation, that commingling of absurdity, surprise, and bewilderment and a tremor of struggling revolt, that notion of being corrupted by the incredible. . . ." It might also be untrue of readers who, having appropriated a work, rewrite it according to their own inspiration either as adaptations, abridgements, or retellings with augmentations. Most people would hesitate to include in their concept of the Work either what remains in the author's head or the lucubrations of others, but it is astonishing where some folks draw the line.

21. There are, of course, many other reasons why X and Y disagree, many of which are explored quite revealingly in works on reader response. I am here concerned with those disagreements arising from differences in the physical manifestations of works. (See also Chart 4.)

effects they create or allow.[22] Note carefully that I do not mean, by this distinction, the difference between a sign and its meaning or referent. I mean instead the difference between the physical sign sequence as recorded in copies of a work and the sign sequence a user of the copy of the work takes to be the work. The latter sign sequence is a mental construction deriving from the former with the added proviso that the user may consider the physical copy of the work to be marred by error or abridgement or to be partial by reason of revisions not recorded in that copy or even by reason of inappropriate packaging.

When two or more of these physical forms of a work disagree, it is patently obvious that, if the Work is a single ideal entity, they cannot both accurately represent it. Two possible explanations for differences between two physical manifestations of the work can be suggested. The first is that one is corrupt and thus misrepresents the Work (or both copies could be corrupt in different ways). The second is that the Work exists in two (or more) Versions each represented more or less well by one of the physical copies.[23] We can think of the Work, then, as existing in more than one Version and yet be one Work. This does not, however, help to resolve the problem of whether the Work or a Version of it is accurately represented by the physical copy held by person X or person Y.

Before pursuing that problem, there are some difficulties with the concept of Version to try to clarify. First, like the term Work, the term Version does not designate an object; it, too, is a means of classifying objects. In the same way that the Work *Dombey and Son* is not *Moby-Dick*, so too a first version is not a second, or a magazine version is not a chapter in a book, or a printed version is not a version for oral presentation. The term Version in these formulations is a means of classifying copies of a Work according to one or more concepts that help account for the variant texts or variant formats that characterize them. Second, it is not just the existence of different texts of the same Work which

22. I do not think that textual criticism is a "science" if by that term one implies something objective, but there is a pleasing similarity between the scientist operating as though photons and quarks exist, though he cannot see them, and a textual critic operating as though works exist, though he only has signs for them. I would distinguish in this way the relations between the concept of a work and sign for a work from the relation between Platonic ideals and realities, which seems more whimsical and better represented by, I believe, Christopher Morley's fiction about a limbo of lost works, a place where works continue to exist after all physical copies have been destroyed and forgotten.

23. It is theoretically possible with this concept to imagine that a work represented by only one physical copy in the whole world might be misrepresented by that copy. That is an important problem. We can imagine further that other Versions of the Work might have existed, but if we stick to our original proviso—that if the work is a mental construct it can be known only through its physical manifestations—we will spend little time with this possibility.

leads us to imagine multiple Versions of a Work. What we know about composition also suggests Versions. And to help distinguish various concepts relating to version, I would suggest the sub-categories Potential Version, Developing Version, and Essayed Version. These categories correspond to ideas we have about composition and revision. Potential Version refers to the abstract incipient ideas about the Work as it grows in the consciousness of the author. The Potential Version has no physical manifestation, but we judge from our own experience in composing that such a version exists at least in outline and we imagine this version capable of being developed, abandoned, or changed. The Potential Version is unavailable to us except as an idea. Developing Version refers to a process that does have physical outcomes. The Potential Version processed by thought and inscription produces, in the case of many authors, drafts or notes, which when added to more thought, more inscription, and perhaps some revision results in additional drafts. When the Developing Version has progressed sufficiently and been consolidated into an inscription of the whole, we have a physical representation of what I would call an Essayed Version.

The point at which the developing version reaches sufficient wholeness to be thought of as representing the first Essayed Version is, of course, a matter of opinion and, therefore, of dispute. This problem is another demonstration of the fact that the term "Version" refers to a means of classification, not to an actual stable object. The first Essayed Version can be thought about and revised and used as a basis for producing a second Version, etc. It might also be thought of as a provisional version or a finished version, but it is a version of the work in that it represents the work. Though the Essayed Version has physical embodiment in a text, it is not the physical text. We can imagine the Essayed Version in the author's imagination as more perfect than his or her ability to record it in signs which require compromise and are liable to inscription error. Even if there is only one physical copy of the Work, one could not say that the Version it embodied was the Work, for as soon as a new Version appeared the distinction between Version and Work would become necessary again.

We should pause for a moment here, suspended in the ethereal realm of ideal forms, to observe that the idea that "a Work is implied by a series of Versions" is based on ideas about composition, revision, and editorial interventions. That is, I have developed these ideas by imagining the processes of composition, not by starting with finished copies of the Work and inferring the processes "backward" from them. To think in this way about a work entails also believing that each new version has integrity or "entity" as an Utterance of the Work. If two copies of a work differ in ways that are explained by "infelicities in transmission" then one does not need a concept of Version to explain the differences. But if each is thought to be desirable or "authoritative" in its own way, then the concept of Version is useful for classification. One could think of a Version, then, as the conception or aim of the Work at a point of Utterance. But Version is a very complex and slippery concept I will define and discuss in detail later. Where there is a well-established convention for using the term Work to distinguish between *Vanity Fair* and *Jane Eyre*, there is not an established convention for distinguishing Versions of *Vanity Fair*.

Of the problems concerning the concept of Versions which must be discussed in detail later there are two which should be mentioned before moving on to definitions of Text and making clearer the connections between ideal concepts of works and their physical manifestations. The first is the problem of determining when the Essayed Version has stopped being the Developing Version so that it can be thought of as coalesced into a Version that can be identified and read as such. The second is the problem of determining if and when a second version has coalesced that should be considered as separate from the first. To discuss these problems we need several related concepts I will develop later: Time, Content, Function, and Material. One should also note that concepts of Intention and Authority are crucial to the idea of Versions; neither of these concepts is simple.[24] Needless to say, I think the idea of Versions is a very useful one, in spite of its problems.

B. *Texts: Conceptual, Semiotic, and Physical*

Although I have deferred discussion of some of the problems with the term Version, I need here to imagine the writer composing a Version of the Work in order to pursue the taxonomy through various concepts that are too often hidden in the use of terms such as Work or Version. One should note, then, that an Essayed Version is a conceptual entity not a physical entity; it is not equivalent with the physical embodiment of it, because its embodiment can be and usually is an imperfect representation of the Version. The contortions of that last sentence bear witness to the fact that Version is being used in two ways: it is a classification system for those texts that represent Version X as opposed to those that represent Version Y, and it is a Conceptual Text which copies of Version X or Y represent. This latter notion, the Conceptual Text, is not a system of classification but more like an ideal form of the Work. But it is not a Platonic ideal, for it develops and changes, and probably does not

24. I have discussed them elsewhere (*Scholarly Editing* chaps. 1 and 3, and "An Inquiry into the Social Status of Texts"), but I will return to these problems below, also.

"pre-exist" as an ideal, and it probably does not last very long either. The imperfections of physical texts are of various origins, including failures of creative imagination, failures of inscriptional skill or care, use of elisions and abbreviations to be filled in later, or unhappy interventions by scribal assistants. The Essayed Conceptual Text is always manifested in a physical form, but it is not a physical or Material Text, for the Conceptual Text that is Essayed remains (as the author's mental concept) invisible and probably not stable; but the embodiment of the Conceptual Text is visible and fixed in a material medium. The concept of "fixing" suggests another reason the Material Text may misrepresent or at least only suggest the work: Version (Potential, Developing, and Essayed) is fluid conceptual process, but the material text is physically static, fixed. However, since the Essayed Conceptual Text cannot be known except through a Material Text, people tend to equate them for practical purposes. But the Material Text can misrepresent the Essayed Conceptual Text and hence that equation is not exact. The ways in which the Material Text can misrepresent the Conceptual Text are many and often are indeterminate but some might be revealed in the drafts or by violations of syntax, grammar or orthography that cannot be justified as accurate representations of the ideal Version.[25]

It is common, at least among textual critics, to think of a text as consisting of words and punctuation in a particular order. I would like to call this concept of texts the Linguistic Text.[26] It refers to the semiotic dimension of Texts—the specific signs for words and word markers that stand for the Work (or the Version of the work). Linguistic Texts have three forms: Conceptual, Semiotic, and Material. The author's Conceptual Linguistic Text consisted of the signs he "intended to inscribe." A Semiotic Text consists of the signs found recorded in a physical form of the work. If a Version represents the conception or aim of the Work at a point of Utterance, the Linguistic Text is the execution or achievement of that Version, first as a Conceptual Text (thought) then as a Semiotic Text (sign), and then as a Material Text (paper and ink or some other physical inscription or production), at that point of Utterance. The Material Text is the evidence that a Conceptual Text was

---

25. See Fredson Bowers, *Bibliography and Textual Criticism* (1964) and *Essays in Bibliography, Text and Editing* (1975) for fuller discussions of means to detect and correct textual error.

26. This is Jerome McGann's term and corresponds to his distinction between Linguistic Texts and Production Texts. I prefer Material Texts to Production Texts, for it identifies an entity without regard to the agency responsible for its production. McGann, if I understand him, defines Production Text as the product of non-authorial book production procedures, but a Material Text is any union of a Linguistic Text with a physical medium which "fixes" it, whether it is a manuscript or a printed book.

formed and Uttered as a representation of a Version of the Work—in short, if there is no Material Text there is no Linguistic Text and hence no Version available to a reader. The Conceptual Text can be Materialized in spoken or written form, and it can be recorded in a mechanical or electronic way. It follows that the Linguistic Text can have more than one Semiotic form—spoken, written, electronic, and Braille, for instance. The Linguistic Text is not, therefore, physical; it is a sequence of words and word markers, conceived before spoken or written, and taking its semiotic form, when written, from the sign system used to indicate the language in which it is composed. We must also distinguish between the Linguistic Text and the Documents that preserve them, for as long as the sequence of words and markers is the same, the Linguistic Text is one, regardless of the number of copies or number of forms it is manifested in. All accurate copies, whether facsimiles, transcriptions, or encodings are the same single Linguistic Text. An inaccurate copy, however, is a different Linguistic Text for it is a different sequence of words and word markers, though it might still represent the same Version. The new Linguistic Text might represent the Essayed Conceptual Text more faithfully or less faithfully.

It should be noted that the Linguistic Texts representing an Essayed Version (the ideal aim of Utterance) run the risk of error at each transformation in production both through a failure of articulation (we've heard authors complain that they just couldn't put what they wanted into words) and because the author or a scribe failed to inscribe it accurately or completely. The Linguistic Text, therefore, corresponds to the Essayed Version only to the extent that its production was perfect. Editors (particularly "authorial intention" editors) have understood their job to be the production of a newly edited Linguistic Text that accurately represents the author's intentions for the final Version. Put in the terms defined here, the traditional "intention" of scholarly editing has been to create a new Material Text, the Linguistic Text of which coincides with the Essayed Conceptual Text. But because the author's Essayed Text is available to the editor only through material evidence for it, the editor can do no more than construct a new conceptualization of it (i.e., the editor does not in fact "recover" the author's Conceptual Text). The resulting edition is then a forward construction rather than a "backward" restoration.

To speak of the Linguistic Text as a sequence of words and word markers is to emphasize a distinction already made but that is of primary importance: that the Linguistic Text, being composed of signs, is a representation of the work and is not the work itself. It represents a Version, it is not the Version itself. It is the result of an encoding process undertaken by the author or the author and his assistants. The Linguistic Text is, therefore, a sign and not an object, though it is always manifested in an object. To speak this way about the Linguistic Text is also to emphasize the act of decoding which is necessary before another person can be said to have seen or experienced the work of art. It should be equally evident that such a decoding experience cannot take place without a physical manifestation of the text as a starting point.[27]

The word Document can be used to refer to the physical "container" of the Linguistic Text. It might be paper and ink or a recording of some sort, including for example a Braille transcript which can be just paper. Records, tape recordings, microforms, and computer disks are also documents, though decoding such documents requires mechanical or electronic equipment. Documents are physical, material objects that can be held in the hand. Each new copy of the Linguistic Text is in a new document. Two documents containing the same Linguistic Text are still two separate entities but only one Linguistic Text. This physical form not only provides a "fixing medium" (to borrow a concept from photography) but it inevitably provides an immediate context and texture for the Linguistic Text. It will be useful therefore to have a term for the union of Linguistic Text and Document. I call it the Material Text. It seems clear that a reader reacts not just to the Linguistic Text when reading but to the Material Text, though it be subconsciously, taking in impressions about paper and ink quality, typographic design, size, weight, and length of document, and style and quality of binding, and perhaps from all these together some sense of authority or integrity (or lack thereof) for the text. These aspects of the Material Text carry indications of date and origin, and social and economic provenance and status, which can influence the reader's understanding of and reaction to the Linguistic Text.[28] (See Chart 3.)

We should pause again for a moment, this time with our feet firmly planted in the material realm. A Material Text, any Material Text, is

27. It is interesting to note that the mistake of equating literary art with the printed representation of it is never made in music: a score is never confused wih the sounds it signals nor is a record or tape ever thought of as the music; every one knows it "must be played." However, recordings and scores share nearly all the textual problems which literary works have. The relationship between "playing it" for music and "reading it" for literature is very close.

28. The importance of the Material Text has been the special theme of much of Jerome McGann's and D. F. McKenzie's discussions of textual criticism and bibliography. McGann, by calling them "production texts," emphasizes the agents of production rather than the mere materiality of the texts. I believe he does so to help validate his contention that non-authorial agents of textual change and non-authorial creators of textual contexts have a legitimate role in making the Work of Art. The taxonomy presented here remains neutral on this point and is useful as a description of process and phenomenon regardless of what one thinks is "legitimately" the Work.

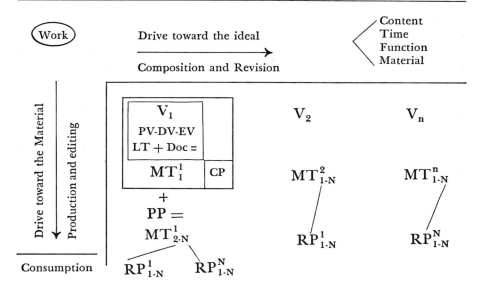

There are as many Versions (V) as the Receptor can convince himself were created.
There are as many Material Texts (MT) as there are copies of the work.
There are as many Reception Performances (RP) as there are Readings of the work.
Each Reception Performance is conducted in relation to one Material Text.
No Material Text is the equivalent of the Work but is one representative of it.

Chart 3

the reader's only access route to the Work. A Linguistic Text cannot
exist for anyone (who does not already hold it in memory) without a material medium;[29] the Linguistic Text and its medium are the Material
Text with all the implications of that union. Material Texts are the
production of Utterance. The first Material Text (says the manuscript)
is the first attempted union of the Essayed Version and a Document.
There might be a problem in distinguishing that first Material Text
from draft fragments, and it might be possible to "reconstruct" archaeo-
logically a Version buried in drafts in early manuscripts or in the cancelled and altered passages in a manuscript or typescript whose final
revisions represent Essayed Version one. Material Texts numbers 2-n
are transcriptions made by anyone including the author. These Material

29. This is true even if one hears a recitation produced by someone else's recollection
of the text, though the physical medium in such a case is air molecules vibrating in sound
waves rather than printed signs. One might add that any recitation, whether from memory
or from a written text, is a new production of the text susceptible to "transmission error" or
embellishment.

Texts might incorporate the results of revisions, editorial interventions, or errors, or they might be accurate transcripts.

It would appear from the concept of Material Texts that when an editor has extracted or edited the Linguistic Text which he believes best represents the Version he is editing, he must embody that Linguistic Text in a new document which will be a new Material Text with implications all its own. He cannot reincorporate a new Linguistic Text into an old Document to present a "restored" Material Text. The force of this idea came to me while reading Jerome McGann's explanation of the work as a product of social contract in which the production process was described as an integral and inevitable aspect of the concept of the work of art.[30]

C. Texts Again: Physical, Semiotic, and Conceptual

The terms Version, Text, and Document have brought us in the life of a literary work of art only through the down-swing of the pendulum from the "mind of the author" to the concrete manifestations of the work in Material Texts (i.e., books). And it should perhaps be emphasized once again that a Work may be "implied" by more than one Version and by more than one swing of the pendulum. But now we must face the Material Text in the absence of the Author and with a realization that as we approach the Material Text we are not before a verbal construct and that we cannot see prelocution, perlocution or illocution, or even intention or meaning. What we have before us is molecules compounded in paper and ink. Everything else must be inferred from that, beginning with the recognition of the sign shapes, which the ink shapes materially represent. I have mentioned that the Material Text is the starting point for further processes, the up-swing, necessary before the Work can be perceived, for the Material Text is not equivalent with the Work but is instead merely a coded representation or sign of the Work. Furthermore, the Material Text before us is only a single instance of many possible manifestations of the Work. Not all Material Texts are necessarily representative of the same Version of the Work, nor are they all equally accurate representatives of the Work. Nevertheless, a Material Text is where the reader begins the process of perceiving or experiencing the work of art. This process is one of decoding or dematerializing the Material Text into some mental construct of it. It is in this decoding process that the Work can be said to function.[31]

---

30. See my article "An Inquiry into the Social Status of Texts," p. 74.

31. Barthes says "the Text is not the decomposition of the work" ("From Work to Text," p. 56), which sounds like a contradiction of what I just said, but in fact we are saying the same thing. Barthes's "work" (my "Material Text") cannot be experienced until it be-

IV. TEXTUAL PERFORMANCES AS WRITE ACTS

It seems useful here to add the term Performance to our taxonomy of concepts related to Works of literary art.[32] Performance is an act, an event. Performances take place in time and space. They are not material objects, though they might produce results that are material and that can be used as records of the performance. However, these outcomes of performance are not the performances themselves. It will be useful to distinguish between at least three types: Creative Performance, Production Performance, and Reception Performance.

Creative Performance refers primarily to acts of authority over linguistic texts, determining what shall be encoded as the inscription representing a Version.[33] Creative Performance includes all that was indicated above by the terms Potential Version, Developing Version, and Essayed Version. Creative Performance is primarily inventive but usually involves some sort of mechanical work to inscribe through writing, typing or dictating. This mechanical aspect should perhaps more properly be called Production Performance, but when the author is inscribing new material it is clearly primarily a creative activity. One might say, however, that when the author makes a mechanical error in inscription, it might be a failure of production rather than of creation. To a casual reader this difference makes no difference, but to the editor who holds production authority over the work, it makes a significant difference, since he will correct a production error but not a creative failure (creative "errors" might, by the way, be creative innovations the editor has failed to understand).

Production Performance refers primarily to acts of authority over Material Texts, determining what material form the Linguistic Text shall have and re-inscribing it in those forms for public distribution. Production Performance can have a variety of methods and outcomes;

---

comes Barthes's "text" (my "Reception Text"). Since Barthes is interested only in the experience or play of Text, he would of course define the "real" aspect of the work of art as the experience of it. That experience of it (Barthes's Play begins with decoding or dematerializing the Material Text (Barthes says "decanting the work").

32. Joseph Grigely in "The Textual Event" uses the word "performance" to apply to those things people do when they engage with a copy or text of the work. He did not elaborate what he meant by the term. I will use the term to apply to authors and production crews, as well as to readers.

33. By the term "creative" I do not mean to imply that authors make something out of nothing. They may be manipulating givens or they may be manipulated by forces over which they have no control. The "nature of creativity" is not the issue here; rather, I am distinguishing acts of authority over linguistic texts (determining what words and punctuation and the order for them that will constitute the linguistic text) from other acts such as determining the format and design of productions or acts of interpretation or appropriation of meanings.

they can be nurturing or negligent, skillful or clumsy, well-intentioned and wise or well-intentioned but ignorant. Production Performance often affects the Linguistic Text and always affects the Material Text, but it differs from Creative Performance in that its primary purpose is the transmission and preservation and formal (not substantive) improvement of the Linguistic Text. It is a process of transcription, not one of revision. Creative Performance and Production Performance are often carried out simultaneously by the same person, but traditionally Creative Performance has been associated with authoring the Linguistic Text and Production Performance has been associated with manufacture and publishing the Material Text. In practice these two processes are not always easily separable, for authors occasionally perform production acts and publishers, printers, and editors quite often perform "authoring" acts. The results of these crossings are sometimes "happy" and sometimes not—often the judgment depends on who is judging.

Reception Performance refers to acts of decoding Linguistic Texts and "conceptualizing" the Material Text; that is what we do when reading and analyzing. Reception Performance differs from Production Performance in that its primary purpose is not the reproduction of the Linguistic Text in a new material form, but the construction of and interaction with the Linguistic Text in the form of a Conceptual Text. Readers do not normally distinguish consciously between the Material Text and their Conceptualized Text derived from it. They are also often unconscious of the ways in which the Material Text is more than just the Linguistic Text of the Work so that their Conceptual Text is formed under the influence of material contexts that did not attend the process by which the author materialized his Conceptual Text by inscribing it. To put this in a simple model, the author's Essayed Conceptual Text takes form as a Material Text which the reader uses to construct the Reception Conceptual Text. If we imagine, then, that the specific copy of the Work that reader X is using is Material Text X, that copy with its textual limitations and errors is *what* the reader is reading. It is a Material Text, not the Work, though the Work can only be known through a Material Text. It need not, however, be known through this particular copy; the imperfections of the particular Linguistic Text as well as the implications of the particular Material Text contribute to the uniqueness of this particular representation of the Work. Furthermore, it is not the Work itself that is known through the Material Text but the reader's reconstruction of the Work that is known, the "reader's Conceptual Linguistic Text as mediated by the Material Text," or, in short, the Reception Text. It should be noted that the Reception Text is still what Saussure calls a "signifier," for it is no more than the Linguistic

Text in internalized Semiotic form. It is then reacted to in a variety of ways and according to a variety of principles of interpretation which taken all together can be called the Reception Performance. The point to emphasize and then to elaborate is that these reactions are to the Reception Text not to the Material Text. (See Chart 4, where critics Q and R read the same copy of the Work and may disagree about interpretation because of their different skills in performing the Reception Text,

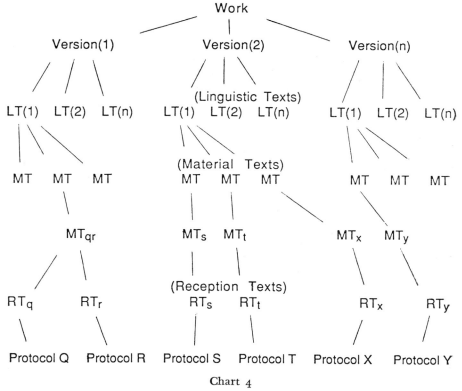

Chart 4

Critics Q and R disagree from the same copy of the Work.
Critics S and T disagree from different editions of a single Version of the Work.
Critics X and Y disagree from different Versions of the Work.

In part this is because Q, S, and X think the Work is Reception Text Q, S, or X
and R, T, and Y think it is Reception Text R. T, or Y.
(in a way each is right and wrong)

All that each critic knows of the Work is what finds its way into the Reception Text.
All that each critic can share with another reader is what finds its way into the Protocol.

because their experiences of life and reading differ, or because they employ different interpretational principles. Critics S and T, who read two different editions reproducing more or less well the same Version of the Work, may disagree about interpretation for any of the same reasons Q and R disagree, and because the Material Texts in which they encounter the Work differ. They may also, fortuitously, agree with each other if one or both have managed to ignore or "misread" the Material Text. Critics X and Y, who read different copies of the work, each representing a different Version, may disagree for any of the same reasons affecting Q, R, S, and T and also because the Linguistic Texts they are reading are different. To the extent that Q, R, S, T, X and Y think their copy of the work *is* the Work, their disagreements will seem unaccountable, irresolvable, or evidences of inadequacy in the others as critics.)

It might be useful to describe the process of Reception Performance by adapting some terms used by I. A. Richards to describe his experiments in practical criticism in the 1920s. Several "perusals" of a text at one sitting constituted an "attack" on the work of art. Several "attacks" spread over a short period of time, say a week, constituted a "reading." The reader's commentary on the work—the record of his reading and reaction—was called a "protocol." We sometimes call interpretations of works "readings," but the word is vague and overworked; we should call them something else such as protocols or records of the Reception Performance. I think it can be said that Richards was interested in this process as a process of interpretation of meaning, effect, and tone suggested by the words as grouped into sentences and paragraphs, and that he was not concerned with the problematic nature of the Material Texts he and his students used. Nor was he concerned with the problematic nature of the dematerialization of the text signs for words and punctuation. That is, he was interested in what the Text said, not in what the Work was. This is a common strategy of literary critics to avoid the problems of "authorial intentions." What I have called the Reception Text is in part the reader's decoding of the Linguistic Text as embodied in the Material Text at hand, but it also includes the reader's semiotic reconstruction or reading of the Material Text as a totality and to the environment in which the reader has undertaken the Reception Performance. Anything the reader says or writes about his experience of the work is a "protocol." The rules by which protocols are produced and judged are as numerous as there are games to be played in the Performance Field. (See summary of terms in Appendix B.)

We have in these three performances a key to why observations made about speech acts go awry when applied to writing. A speech act or spoken utterance is one event with three basic elements: the utterer's mental concept, the physical medium of utterance, and the listener's mental concept. These three elements always exist together in the context of time and place when and where the utterance is spoken. In written works all three of these elements exist also, but the context of time and place is fragmented, so that the writer's utterance takes place, so to speak, in the presence of an absent reader, and the reader's reception or construction of utterance takes place in the presence of an absent writer. Therefore, each utterance takes place in a context of time and place that is unknown to the other party and adventitious meanings are the highly likely result, for the "bundle" or "molecule" has been broken, modified or replaced. Finally, to complicate things even more, the writer's writing is seldom seen by the reader who usually has instead the printer's printing. So a written work entails at least three separate events (performances) whereas the spoken work is one event.[34] Experienced writers are, of course, aware of this and compensate by a multitude of strategies. That is one reason it is normal to think of writing as more formal and requiring more care than spoken communication. There are also many other reasons that written language must be made clearer, among them the fact that punctuation is a coarse substitute for intonation and gesture.

V. Hermeneutics or Theory

The terms and definitions provided thus far represent a "structuring of reality," which cannot be "true" but can perhaps be useful. It can be used in two fundamentally different ways that correspond to hermeneutics and literary critical theory. Photography again provides a good though not perfect analogy, since photographs can also be treated in these two ways. One could say that the Material Text is not the Work, but like a photograph, it represents the work, so that a person contemplating the Material Text (photograph) can create a mental construct corresponding to that which was photographed. There are, in this view of the matter, two reception images: one of the photograph or Material Text itself and another of that which was photographed or the "created world" in the work of art.[35] Another useful analogy to emphasize this hermeneutical use of the taxonomy is musical. The Material Text is like

34. This formulation does not apply to letters from one specific writer to one specific reader (addressee) in which, at least for the first reading of the letter, the event of writing and the event of reading are just two events.

35. Of course the reader may conjure up a number of mental representations including what he thinks was authorial intention, what should have been intended, what could have been intended, and what new uses or representations it could be made into. These might be whimsical or serious attempts to see the implications of differences.

the score of music; the Reception Performance is like the concert which created the musical event when the score is played. Thus the documentary musical score and the musical performances it enables are separate though related referents; likewise the Material Text and the Reception Performances it enables are separate though related. Reception Performances actually have two distinguishable parts—the first is the construction of a Reception Text, the second is the interpretation of and response to it. In the analogy with music, constructing the Reception Text is like an orchestra playing the music. Response to the Reception Text is analogous to listening to and responding to the played music. The reader is orchestra and audience rolled into one for a literary work. This distinction is readily seen as applicable to drama. Not only is there a difference between the written text of a play and the performances on stage—both of which precede Reception Performance by the audience in a theater—but there are often differences between the written text for performance and the written text for publication, the later intended to be performed as a reading (closet drama) rather than as a stage performance.[36] It is important to note that the reader's responses are not to the "work itself" but to the Reception Text. The quality of the Reception Text depends in part on the Material Text used as a basis and in part on the skill and quality of its rendition as performance; halting or inattentive readers are not likely to perform technically "good" Reception Texts, but this will not keep them from responding to them.

36. T. H. Howard-Hill develops the implications of these differences in "Modern Textual Theories and the Editing of Plays," *The Library*, 6th ser., 11 (June 1989), 89–115. After cogently arguing through the distinctions in aim and function of various possible versions and after justifying the critic's interest in works of shared authority, he concludes that, with renaissance plays, the theatrical version, completed where necessary by the editor into a theatrically satisfying work of art, is the (apparently one) legitimate goal of scholarly editing, for "to assign paramount importance to the existence of uncertainty is not a useful editorial principle. Least of all should an editor transfer to the reader the responsibility of adjudicating imperfect or conflicting evidence of authorial intentions, and never should he present the reader with a critical edition which he knows does not incorporate the author's intentions for the work" (pp. 114–115). Howard-Hill justifies this goal by defining the "writing of a book" as "a synecdoche: the full authorial intention is to write a work, a novel, a play, a poem" which he sees as very different from the intention to write an edition of a work— but this is to slough over the distinctions in the meaning and effects of intention by conflating the term into a single rather vague meaning. Howard-Hill is committed to the implications of his statement that "the product of a theory that interprets authorial intention primarily on the level of the document rather than on the level of the work is unacceptable for drama and perhaps, if it were my charge to examine the proposition here, unacceptable for poems and novels also" (p. 90). See section VII.B(2) for comments on the way the "four unities" are used to determine Versions—here Howard-Hill uses them to determine the Work. One can, of course, use with gratitude Howard-Hill's "theatrical" text for what it is (a representation of the theatrical version) without necessarily agreeing either that it is The Work or even that it is the best version of the work.

The taxonomy I have suggested, then, shows not only how interpretation or other protocols depending on a specific Material Text to reconstruct a Work might differ from other protocols depending on other Material Texts with the same title, but it shows how interpretations of the same Material Text by two persons or by the same person on two different occasions might also be different—each experience of the Work is based on a separately constructed Reception Text in a separate Reception Performance using a particular (and partial) representation of the work.

The second way of looking at this taxonomy is analogous to literary critical theory, focusing attention on the phenomenon of works embodied in Material Texts rather than focusing on the interpretation of those texts. In the analogy with photography, it is an examination of the photograph as photograph and photography as a process rather than seeing the photograph as representation of something else. The photograph becomes, in a way, an end in itself with its own meaning and ways of meaning regardless of any correspondence between itself and some other object or objects towards which the camera was aimed when the exposure was made. The critic's attention might be focused on technique, composition, texture and any number of other things relevant to the photograph as object and as result of process, all of which are unconcerned with "realism" or accuracy of representation. In photography each newly developed picture from a single negative is a material object which may be considered as a separate work; viewers of more than one copy might comment on the differences and prefer one to another for various technical and aesthetic reasons. We can use this taxonomy, therefore, to illuminate a variety of interests relating to process rather than to interpretation.

Literary critical theory has focused its attention primarily, though not exclusively on the portion of this taxonomy indicated by the terms Linguistic Text, Creative Performance, and Reception Performance. These correspond to the West, North, and East in the "map" of related interests described in section II. Literary critical theory has tended to neglect the portions indicated by Versions, Material Texts, and Production Performance. These correspond to the South and, astonishingly, the center of the "map." Marxist criticism has paid attention to Material Texts and Production Performance, but has tended to neglect or downplay Creative Performance and the mental constructs of Works and Versions. Textual criticism, until recently focused primarily on the Linguistic Texts and Creative Performance, has tended to neglect or deemphasize Production Performance and Reception Performance. To the extent that textual critics neglect Reception Performance, they turn a blind eye to the role of their own Reception Performance in "reconstructing" authorial intention.

VI. CONTEXTS AND CONVENTIONS

I round out this Taxonomy with three more terms in a somewhat cursory attempt to indicate the relevance of contexts and conventions to concepts of Text: Material Base, Social Context, and Performance Field.

Material Base—The world of sense data to which biological authors and readers and Material Texts (manuscript, book, etc.) belong. The Material Base includes all the raw materials of historicism. The term is used by J. Hillis Miller to refer not only to the book and earth and cities and to agricultural and industrial products, but he extends it to include institutions, conventions, and mores. He does so to present the view that there can be a visceral (i.e., physical) connection between "a people" and "the land" that is part of the textual complex.[37] Note that the Material Base is the "world" that the book and reader are a part of, not the "world" to which the work could be said to refer or to portray. Both of these worlds are, according to the "beliefs of the time" with which I began this paper, constructs or structured "texts of reality," but the "world the work refers to" is one construction removed from the Material Base.

Social Context—My preferred term for the complex of institutions, conventions, and mores whose expectations and habits are reflected in the Material Text and which form the extended field of inquiry along with the Material Base for new historicism. In particular with regard to Texts it should be noted that these conventions include relations and contracts and expectations between author and typists; author and publisher; publisher and editor, compositor, printer, binder, bookseller; and between author, publisher, bookseller and reader. I separate the Social Contexts from the Material Base because, as Thomas Carlyle pointed out in *Sartor Resartus* with more panache than originality, institutions, skills, and conventions are aeriform—they are constructs, not found objects. The principles of relativity and structuralism tell us that "found objects" are also constructs, but that insight does not smooth out the distinction between material constructs and social constructs.

Performance Field—This is where the Performance Text is "played" according to the rules of the reader's particular game of textual interaction and further limited by the performer's capabilities and resources. This is a term suggested by Roland Barthes's definition of Text, which he distinguishes from "Work" (by which he means Book or Material

---

37. See particularly Miller's "Presidential Address 1986. The Triumph of Theory, the Resistance to Reading, and the Question of the Material Base," *PMLA*, 102 (1987), 281–291.

Text) but which he does not distinguish from Linguistic Text or Performance Text. Performance Field is Barthes's field of play, though every reader performs or plays by the rules of his or her own league.

VII. PROBLEMS WITH CONCEPTS OF VERSIONS

A. *One Version or Several?*

Earlier, I passed rather quickly over two crucial but complicated issues to which I promised to return. The first was the question of how one determines whether an inscribed text accurately reflects the work it was meant to represent. The second, even more complex, had to do with determining, first, when a version had coalesced as a finished form and, second, when another version, differing from the first, can be distinguished as a separate entity.

Textual criticism from earliest times has been primarily concerned with the first of these problems; one might say its history has been one of obsession with the problem of textual corruption. I am not going to try to provide a primer on the subject here. What I said was that when two copies of a work, both bearing the same title and purporting to be the same work, contain variant Linguistic Texts, one explanation could be that one or both texts misrepresented the work. And, if the work was a single thing, then at least one of the variant texts had to be wrong. The point was that a work could be misrepresented by a copy of it. And it follows, therefore, that the work might be misrepresented by every copy of it. From this observation we must conclude that the work and the copies of the work are separate entities. It has been the business of textual criticism to do what it could about such misrepresentations. I will say no more here about how that can be done except to note that the textual critic's concept of Authority for the work is central to his task.[38]

The other explanation offered for textual variation between copies of a work was that the work might exist in two versions each represented by one of the variant copies each of which could be correct. Now it is a commonplace that authors revise their works, and mere revision has seldom been taken as proof that a separate version of the work exists. But if variant forms of the work are legitimate (i.e., not the result of corruption or inattention), and if reader X disagrees with reader Y because they are not reading identical texts, then something significant has oc-

---

38. More on this subject is in my *Scholarly Editing in the Computer Age*. See also G. Thomas Tanselle's *Textual Criticism since Greg, A Chronicle, 1950–1985* (1987), which provides a sensible evaluative guide to much theoretical and practical writing on editing; and Fredson Bowers, "Regularization and Normalization in Modern Critical Texts," *Studies in Bibliography*, 42 (1989), 79–102. Differing rather sharply with Bowers and Tanselle is Jerome McGann's *A Critique of Modern Textual Criticism* (1984).

curred, which impels us to think the concept of Versions of a Work
might be useful.

But for several reasons, the problem of Versions is not simple. Literary works of art come in Material Texts which are linear and single in
form. Variant texts, therefore, are difficult to present and assimilate;
they are not easily experienced simultaneously or side by side. Thus
most reading experiences are restricted to interaction with one Material
Text representing better or worse one Version of the Work. Publishers
are committed to perpetuating this form of experience and resist multiple text editions. Perhaps that is why there has been a tendency to consider revisions as a single continuum of creative efforts made to improve
the work. The process is said to be over only when the last revision is
made—and even then the process might have just stopped unfinished.
This is a fundamental principle for "final intention" editions. James
McLaverty calls this a Whig interpretation of revision, which often disregards meaning and effect in favor of a predisposition to credit revision
with improvement.[39] The "Whig" view is convenient, for it maintains
that the Work is singular and revisions are all part of a grand design
toward which the author works from beginning to end. Variant texts,
according to this view, either contain errors or represent incomplete revision. With this view it would be considered a reading Utopia if all
Material Texts in circulation were accurate renditions of the "final intention text"—a Utopia of logo-centrism.[40]

It is tempting to dismiss such views of the Work as oversimplifica-
tions, but not only do such views characterize most readers' habitual attitudes towards the texts they use, there are powerful influences in our
culture, at least in the present, to accept and even to enforce such a view.
The alternatives might be more honest or more sophisticated or more intellectually rigorous, but is it art? Is it the real thing? These are questions
about authority and authenticity. In painting, the questions are, Is it
a copy? Is it a fake? In literature one hardly ever thinks of a fake novel.
But we can say of a poem that it is "only a copy, and not a very good
one at that," by which we probably mean that its "authority" has been

39. "Identity and Function in Textual Criticism," STS paper.
40. A variant form of Whiggism is identified as "primitivism" by Jack Stillinger in
"Textual Primitivism and the Editing of Wordsworth," *Studies in Romanticism*, 28 (Spring
1989), 4–28, where he mounts considerable evidence to debunk the prevailing editorial attitude that every revision post-dating Wordsworth's first complete version is an evidence of
the poet's deterioration and growing heterodoxy. Unlike T. H. Howard-Hill (see note 36),
who opts for a logically superior text as the aim of editing, Stillinger concludes that Wordsworth's poems should be produced in editions of every version. He does not, however, offer
a guide for such a proliferation of texts, since his focus is on the Whiggery (my word, not
his) of current reductive editions and the determining and limiting effect they have on our
experience of Wordsworth's works.

compromised through textual variation from "unauthorized" sources. I have discussed the question of authority elsewhere, and so will not develop the idea here.[41] Suffice it to say that authority is not found *in* works but is attributed to them according to how the user defines authority. There are currently four common definitions of authority, some with a marvelous variety of subdivisions which feed astonishing controversies about which is the proper work of art and what is the proper goal of editing. Authority is a system of valuations relating to the Work for the purpose of distinguishing between what is the Work and what is not the Work.[42] In the hands of Whigs—those who want the Work to be one identifiable, real thing—authority is used to discountenance all Versions but the "true one." Exceptions are sometimes made for Works that have two or even more "true versions" such as Wordsworth's *Prelude* or Marianne Moore's "Poetry," but these are quite exceptional cases. Anyone who admits the possibility of more than one version, however, needs concepts other than "authority" to distinguish them. It stands to reason that if two people disagree on the definition or application of the concept of Authority, they will not be able to agree about Version. As we shall see, I think Version, like Authority, is not so much found in the textual material as it is put there. The ways in which Versions are identified, then, become an important matter to discover.

B. *Structuring Multiple Versions*

"Post-Whig" ways of gauging the significance (i.e., meaning and effect, and thence importance) of revision involve a concept of Versions identified or delimited with reference to one or more of "four unities": Time, Content, Function, and Material. The main point here is that a concept of Versions requires a way to identify something that can be "perceived" only through potentially misleading physical representations of it. A concept of Version has to be able to identify Version by distinguishing it both from other Versions of the Work and from the physical manifestations of it, which might be corrupt or which might actually mix text from more than one Version. It must also be able to distinguish between texts which differ because they represent different Versions and texts which differ merely because one or both contain errors. Unlike any of the distinctions between terms referring to the forms of Texts (Conceptual, Linguistic, Semiotic, Material, and Reception Texts), decisions about what constitutes a Version are matters of judg-

---

41. See *Scholarly Editing in the Computer Age*, pp. 11–106, and "An Inquiry," pp. 68–71.

42. Authority can be authorial, documentary, sociological, or aesthetic depending on whether greater value was placed on the author, the document, the "social contract" of production, or the "aesthetic integrity of the work itself" (*Scholarly Editing*, pp. 18–30).

ment and will depend entirely on the relative weight that the judge places on one or more of "four unities" in making that judgment.

(1) Utterances

Before discussing the "four unities" and how they have been used to identify Versions, we need to look again at the concept of Utterance, a term borrowed from speech act theory and literary theory.[43] The term is a problem, however, because it has been defined in several ways and applied to the acts of persons other than the author. Utterance can be the act of formulating the conception of the Work we call a Version into a Linguistic Text. If we define it so, however, we come very close to saying that each Utterance is a work of art and we might hesitate to accept this idea. Utterance can also be defined as the act of making a Version available or making it public. Here again, several acts can be referred to by the term. Making a Version available might be done by writing it down, or by giving it to a typist, or by submitting it to a publisher, or by reading and approving final proofs, or by publishing the printed book. Each of these acts might be thought of as a moment of Utterance which gives the Linguistic Text involved status as representing a distinct Version. Further, Utterance can be defined as what the author said or wrote, what the production process produced and published, or what the reader heard or read.

In order for Utterance to be a useful term we must not only distinguish it from Version and our other terms but show how it is helpful in describing or organizing them. We might say that Version is the aim of Utterance but that an Utterance might not succeed or might only partially succeed in its aim. But Utterance is not merely the production of a Material Text that might or might not accurately represent a Version. Utterance not only refers to the Performances of Works but to the circumstances, the contexts of those actions which influence and contain (i.e., keep from running wild) the meaning and help indicate what meanings are operable. This is a relatively simple concept in speech, as I have already noted, where the speaker and listener and circumstance are all together interacting at the moment of speech. But with written or recorded language, the Utterance of the author, of the various members of the production crew, and of the reader are each separated in time and circumstances so that meaning at every stage in the life of the written word is influenced by different milieux. It is not absurd, therefore, to

---

43. The appropriation of this term by textual criticism was first placed in its larger context, I believe, by G. Thomas Tanselle in "The Editorial Problem of Final Intentions," 309–353. McLaverty used it to good effect in "Identity and Utterance."

conceive not only of Creative Versions resulting from authorial acts (which has been the focus thus far) but of Production Versions (publication utterances), and Reception Versions (reader utterances). Now this would be complicated enough if the Work were one thing which could be rationalized into one universal text out of this proliferation of "versions" (which would not be true versions but simple imperfections). But, in fact, there is no agreement among scholars or artists about what one thing the Work is or ought to be (i.e., there is no universal definition of authority). Each person has a notion about what it ought to be, but the possibilities are quite numerous. Some concept of authority (to identify the authentic elements of the Work) and the four unities (to distinguish Versions of the Work) are the means by which readers impose order on this cacophony of utterances. That is, how an individual student of the Work understands Versions and how he reacts to Material Text X in his hand will depend on the specific Utterance selected and defined for use. And that selection and definition depends on the values given to the "four unities": Content, Time, Function, and Material. Needless to say, these values are usually selected and applied without conscious thought—in which case the Material Text becomes transparent and the only "text" that matters is purely and simply the Reception Text in the reader's Performance Field.

(2) Unities as Structural Glue

The unity of Content is the place to begin.[44] It is because the content, particularly the Linguistic Texts, of copy X and copy Y were not identical that this discussion began. If they had been identical there would appear to be no problem. The idea that one copy is accurate and the other inaccurate does not explain cases of revision. The idea that one copy represents an early incomplete stage of the work and the other represents a completed or improved stage does not explain cases where the revisions appear to mean contradictory things or to have palpably different but individually satisfying effects. But the problem here is to calculate first whether the content had a sufficient stability as an "entity" to be called a Version, and next to calculate how much of a change or what kind of change in content is required before a *different* Version, rather than an *improved* Version, results. The most radical answer to this question was offered by Hans Zeller, when he described the work as a network of relationships between its parts. He reasoned that any change

44. Content here refers to the make-up of the Linguistic Text. The word Content might suggest to some the substantive existence of the book or printed document. That concept will be taken up under the unity of Material.

in any part would change the nature of the network; and so, every textual change produces, logically, a changed work.[45] There is an empirical attractiveness in this view because it equates the work with the copy of the work; each variant copy is a new work, but there is an unsatisfying or disturbing implication in this view because it makes editing a work a nearly impossible task. A scholarly edition would have to incorporate whole texts of every authoritative source. G. Thomas Tanselle offers a compromise through his distinction between "horizontal and vertical" revision. Horizontal changes merely improve a presentation or intention already achieved more or less well in the original text; vertical changes alter the intention by changing the meaning or direction of the work.[46] In order to gauge the type of change, Tanselle uses also the unity of Function, so that not all changes in Content signal changes in Version. He suggests also that differences in the Time of revision might be a useful factor, but he does not anticipate the case of an accumulation of "horizontal" improvements having a "vertical" effect.[47]

The unity of Time derives from the idea that the person changes with time so that if an effort of creation is separated from an effort of revision it is likely or at least possible that the revision effort will reflect changes in the person and thus follow its own line of inspiration rather than that which informed the first. But the problem here is how to calculate how much time must elapse between engagements with the text for the lapse of time to be deemed significant and the resulting effort to be seen as a separate Version.[48] Among modern textual critics, the most radical view of Version that depends on the unity of Time is the one presented by Hershel Parker in *Flawed Texts and Verbal Icons* where he argues from a phychological model of creativity that authors lose their authority over a work after a certain period and that revision often not only violates the creativity of the original effort but can end in confusion which might make a text unreadable.[49] A good deal of my own 1984 recommendation concerning identification of Versions depends on the

45. Hans Zeller, "A New Approach to the Critical Constitution of Literary Texts," *Studies in Bibliography*, 28 (1975), 231–264.

46. G. Thomas Tanselle, "The Editorial Problem of Final Intention," 334–340.

47. A particular case is Samuel Richardson's *Pamela* where subsequent editions steadily improved Pamela's grammar till by 1800 she had lost most of the lexical roots of her rural past. See T. C. Duncan Eaves and Ben Kimpel, "Richardson's Revisions of 'Pamela,'" *Studies in Bibliography*, 20 (1967), 61–88.

48. A significant lapse of time may be the duration of a "lightning flash of inspiration" that alters a whole concept, or the time it takes for the "burning coal of inspiration to flame, flicker, and die," or the time it takes to "build the cathedral of art from foundation to capstone." The metaphors one uses for art often reflect, or perhaps even determine, what value one places on the "unities."

49. *Flawed Texts and Verbal Icons* (1983); see particularly the chapter on Mark Twain.

unity of Time. I would no longer rely so heavily on this one aspect. Even for an editor who is concerned with presenting only one somehow "best" version of the work, the unity of time is sometimes used to reject undesirable authorial revisions made later in time on the grounds that the passage of time had deprived the author of the inspiration (or at least continuity of thought or purpose) that informed the work now being revised without inspiration.

The unity of Function relates to the purpose for which the work is designed. Is it for a magazine; is it a chapter in a book; is it a play adaptation, a translation, a revised edition aimed at a new market? Each new function constitutes the potential for a new version. Revisions undertaken to adapt the work to a new function should not, according to this unity, be confused with revisions undertaken to enhance the success of the same function served by the unrevised text. This criterion requires that the revision be for a different purpose, not just a better fulfillment of an old purpose. Fredson Bowers has written considerably about this aspect of the identity of Versions, but in practice Bowers has tended to see new functions as superseding old functions (as long as they are authorial); so that, while he admits that the previous Versions have "authority" he tends to see new Versions as having "superior authority."[50] This is an example of what McLaverty calls the Whig interpretation of revision, the idea that revisions are better because it is absurd to think that an author would deliberately revise his work to make it worse.

The unity of Material relates to production efforts. In this concept the word Material means the physical object or document that bears the Linguistic Text. It equates, in effect, the concept of Version of the Work with the Material Text. The Material Text is, after all, the place where all the Performances and all the component aspects of a Work are brought together. The Creative Performance resulting in a Linguistic Text is united to the Production Performance resulting in a Material Text, which is where the Reception Performance must begin. The Material Text can be seen then as a social, economic and artistic unit and is the entity necessary for the full functioning of literary art. The primary proponents of this point of view are Jerome McGann and D. F. McKenzie.[51] The most obvious shortcoming of this position seems to be

50. See his "Multiple Authority: New Problems and Concepts of Copy-Text," *The Library*, 5th ser., 27 (1972), 81–115; and "Remarks on Eclectic Texts," *Proof*, 4 (1974), 13–58. Bowers is not wedded to this tendency, as he shows in his treatment of two versions of William James's reminiscences of Thomas Davidson (paper presented at the SAMLA convention, Washington, DC, November 1988).

51. See works by McGann and McKenzie cited above. I have reviewed the historical development and arguments for this view in "An Inquiry into the Social Status of Texts," also cited above.

its rigidity, its rather helpless acceptance of determinacy in the Material Text. There is a grand sense of coalescence in the view, but the Linguistic Text involved in many cases will strike some readers as having been over-determined or perhaps over-packaged. Production processes notoriously tamper with a Linguistic Text in ways both beneficial and detrimental to it as a representation of the Essayed Version. And it does not sit well with some people that the economic necessities and accidents of Production Performances should be allowed to shape (sometimes to shape out of existence) the subtleties of the Creative Performance.

VIII. THE READER AS AUTHOR

The conflicting claims of these four "unities" have been forcefully and amusingly presented in James McLaverty's rehearsal of the old analogy of Theseus' ship, except that the distinction between Content and Material is fudged.[52] Suppose that Theseus sets sail, says McLaverty, in a ship which after a while undergoes repairs. Say further that the ship eventually is so repaired as to have had all its material parts replaced. Is it still the same ship? The unity of Function would say yes, but the unities of Content, Material, and Time would say no. Suppose further, that someone gathered up the discarded parts of Theseus' ship and reconstructed the original ship; would the old reconstructed ship be Theseus' ship or the new repaired one? The unity of Function, if considered in the light of Continuity, would say the repaired one was the ship; but in the light of identity of Function it would say the old reconstructed ship had as good a claim. The unity of Material would support the old ship's claim, while the unity of Time would insist that three versions of Theseus' ship existed: the old one that had been Theseus' ship but which no longer exists, the repaired one Theseus now sails, and the reconstructed one which is not identical with the original ship though made of the same materials in the same configuration.[53] What happens if Theseus sells his ship and it becomes a cargo boat? Or what if a new owner also named Theseus uses it for the same purpose it originally served? Is that possible? Etc.

The main difficulty with the analogy is that in the case of the ship, the material being is the ship, while in the case of literary works, the physical document—the Material Text—is but a representation of the

52. McLaverty, "Identity and Utterance," STS presentation, 1989.

53. The most obvious difference between Theseus' original ship and the reconstructed ship made from the identical materials is not one of time but of production; the original ship was not a reconstruction or restoration and the restored ship is not an original construction. This difference can be seen as one in function, or it may point to the need to expand the four unities by adding other useful criteria.

Work. If Theseus were to say, "No, that ship reconstructed from old material is *not* my ship," we would believe him only if we vested authority for the naming of the ship in Theseus (the author, as it were). The Material Text—whether it is the Author's or the publisher's, whether it represents Version 1 or n, whether it is accurate or corrupt—is a necessary representation without which the Work cannot be experienced, but it is not identical with the Work, for no *particular* copy of the Work is needed for the Work to be experienced.

We see in this way of putting the problem the beginnings of an answer to the question, "What difference to a deconstructive reading of the Work does it make what Text is used?" For we see that the structure of the Work (that which the reader takes to be the work) depends upon the structure of the Material Text (the Linguistic Text in Semiotic form contained in a particular document). And we see further that the Material Text is not one unproblematic transparent "voice" but the "spoor" so to speak of a multitude of speakers working at various times and places combining their efforts in the Material Text. Which of these voices is to be centered in order that it may be decentered? Which self is to be focused on as self-subverting? The voice that is foregrounded by one particular Material Text may not be the same as that foregrounded in another. A deconstructive reader might not care for one reading more than another; indeed, he could not and remain true to his principles, but his understanding of the process of constructing meaning for a given text will depend to some extent on the particular Material Text he is exposed to. One can see, therefore, that a concept of authority underlies the way in which the Unities are employed to identify a "voice" or a "text" for the work by identifying an Utterance.

McLaverty, following the lead of James Thorpe[54] and Jerome McGann, places coalescence or Utterance of the work at publication, referring to stages of composition as moments of "pre-utterance." He is led to this, I believe, by the analogy of Theseus' ship. The parts of the boat removed and replaced are no longer the boat because they do not function as boat. And the boat does not function as boat until it is completed and launched. I suppose with boats, one knows if they function by putting them in the water. But works of literary art are not boats. The question of coalescence of a Work as a Version is a matter of opinion and judgment. Versions are not facts to be discovered about works; they are, rather, concepts created and put there by readers as a means of ordering (or as justification for valuing) textual variants. To say that an editor who had edited from the manuscripts a pre-publication version

54. *Principles of Textual Criticism* (1972).

(such as Hans Gabler's edition of Joyce's *Ulysses*) has prepared a "pre-utterance text" is to evaluate his work by a particular conjunction of the four unities and condemn it a priori. One may do that, but it is not a purpose of this taxonomy to encourage such judgments. Rather its purpose is to describe more accurately what judgments are being and can be made concerning the identity of copies of a work. Perhaps the most useful way to use the term Utterance is to say that each utterance has its intentions and its "social life" (i.e. the purpose for which it was released, and the context, moment and form in which it was designed and launched). Regardless of what decisions are made about the identity of a Version, when that tenuous issue is settled there remains the original question concerning works and versions: How accurately does the Material Text represent the Version or Work? Are there errors in the text?

All of this points, it seems to me, to an overwhelming conclusion concerning the concepts of Works and Versions—a conclusion that is consonant with the three fundamental propositions of this study. The concept of Work and, even more so, the concept of Version depend on Reception Performance just as much as on Creative Performance. If the reader must decide whether a Version is in fact a Version, its functional existence is determined by the reader. Creative performances, the idea of the Work as an Utterance of the author, and the idea of intended meanings are all Reader constructs. All the reader has is the Material Texts and whatever information about their provenance and alternative embodiments he has managed to scrounge up. The term Work helps him separate this mass of material from other masses relating to other works; the term Version helps him sort through this mass of material. He does so by classifying Material Texts according to the structure of Versioning that, to his perception, best accounts for the materials at hand. In short, the reader becomes the "functional authority" for the Work and its Versions. It would seem, therefore, that ideally the reader should have ready access to the evidence that would fully inform his or her decisions. Hence the importance of scholarly editions that foreground rather than submerge the evidence for Versions. T. H. Howard-Hill, contending that "uncertainty is a condition of mind and is not inherent in circumstances," recommends that "editors move with confidence and resolution like Tamburlaine," not like "Hamlets, shillying and shallying between this and that."[55] But if in his resolve an editor unwittingly stands in for all readers, making the decisions and producing a single reading text that purports to have reduced the Work to a book (the text that *is* the work), that editor has misrepresented the work, not refined and purified it.

55. "Textual Theories and Editing Plays," 113.

IX. Conclusions

This exercise in naming leads, I believe, to a number of conclusions about literary works of art.

One is that the word Work conveys both a singular and a plural meaning. A work is one thing: all the Versions of Henry James's *Roderick Hudson* are subsumed under this one title. Simultaneously a work is a thing of internal diversity. It exists wherever a copy of the work exists. Each copy is a more or less accurate representation of one Version of the Work.[56]

Another conclusion is that attempts to repair or restore original or pure texts of a work or to revise and improve them tend to proliferate texts rather than to refine them. If one thinks of proliferating refined copies, one must remember not only that the "unrefined" copies have not been changed but that, by the unities of Material, Time, and perhaps Function, the refined copies represent new and therefore different Material Texts, complete with all that that entails.

A further conclusion is that the crucial act in relation to a Work of literary art is not writing, or publishing, or editing it, but reading it. Of course, without the first of these there will be no reading, but without reading the first seems incomplete or lacks fulfillment. Several observations about reading arise from this taxonomy. First, to read Material Text X is to decode a Work (i.e., that which is implied by its various Versions) from interaction with only one of its many static forms. Reading, therefore, is almost always a partial interaction with the Work. Second, if Material Text X is taken as a transparent window on the Work, there is no question asked about Versions or about errors. Third, if Material Text X is taken as the result of a single, prolonged production effort, subject only to human error, there is no question asked about Versions, just about accuracy. Fourth, if Material Text X is taken "for what it is"—one of many representations of a version of a work—there are questions of both accuracy and Version. Questions of Version include questions about the agents of change (author, editor, etc.), and about time, function or motive, and material. Material Texts are not, in other words, transparent.

Since editing and publishing tend to increase the number of copies of a work, not just in numbers but in variant forms, it seems useful to devise a graphic system to identify and categorize the Material Texts which represent the work (see Chart 3). Thus when person X reads and remarks upon Material Text X and person Y evaluates those remarks in

56. A single copy might represent a mixture of readings from more than one Version. Such a copy is said to be eclectic or sophisticated, depending on whether one approves or disapproves of the mixture.

relation to Material Text Y, difficulties arise from several false assumptions: that both MTx and MTy contain the same Linguistic Text, that both are equivalent Material Texts, that a Linguistic Text as embodied in a document is a full rather than partial representation of the Work, and that the Work is represented adequately and equally well by any Material Text (or at least by MTx and MTy). Persons X and Y may disagree about the Work because they are not discussing a work but two unlike manifestations of the work. However, if X and Y understood the relation between the Material Text in hand and the Work, they might temper their judgments and remarks about it in the light of that understanding. Finally, if X and Y understand how each is developing a sense of Version by applying various mixes of the four unities, they might at least disagree with clarity about the issues in dispute.

For example, in the disputes between those who say the work of art is a social product finding its "true" form in the Material Text and those who consider the production process as unfortunately corrupting—but why be abstract? In the disparate views represented by Jerome McGann and Hershel Parker about the moment of coalescence for a work, McGann placing it in the Material Text and Parker placing it in the Linguistic Text at the moment of greatest creative control by the author, we have, I think, a disagreement that becomes clarified and a bit nonsensical. While many people have a gut feeling that "authorial authority" or Creative Performance is more interesting than "production authority" or Production Performance, the plain facts are that authors do some things badly and production does some things well.[57] If we take the view that the inscription which the author is finally satisfied to relinquish to a publisher is the closest representation of a Version, we are likely to take it as the basis for a new edition. But authors often show or relinquish manuscripts they know will be or must be changed. Would we be willing to say that the Essayed Version as embodied in the printer's copy (author's fair copy) is a form of the work which the critic can use as the basis for a "reading" of the work? Does the scholarly editor have a Production Performance task parallel to that given the work by its original publisher? It has seemed wise to say that the materials of the editorial project will dictate which answer is the most appropriate, but if that were true there would be no disputes. Disputes arise not only because, for example, McGann worked on Byron (who gratefully left the details of punctuation to those who cared and knew about such things)

---

57. Actually, these "facts" are no plainer than any other. The *judgment* of many people is that authors do some things badly and therefore need typists, editors and publishers to help them; likewise the judgment of many people is that these helpers do sometimes overstep their functions or perform them badly.

and Parker worked on Twain (who claimed to have telegraphed instructions to have a compositor shot for tampering with his punctuation), but because they define Version and Work by differing valuations of authority and of the "unities." I suppose the final irony is that any edition Parker produced would be, after all, a new production performance and that any edition McGann produced would undoubtedly be read by many as establishing the author's intentions. In short, the problem is not one of editors' shillying and shallying over uncertainties in their minds, but, first, of a cacophony of voices "in" written texts to be selected from, and, second, of a world of readers who habitually treat books as if they fully represented the one voice that matters (each reader, of course, identifying that voice as seems right in his own eyes).

Another conclusion that might be drawn, tentatively at least, is that the idea of "conveying meaning" might be a misleading way to think about how texts function. The processes of encoding meaning (by authoring) and repackaging the coding (by publishing) and decoding (by reading) are perhaps too complex and fraught with "noise" to allow for "conveying," and our experience is rife with instances of meaning being apparently misconveyed (misconstrued is a more accurate and more frequent term, as it should be) either by accident or by deliberate appropriation. This taxonomy suggests that texts influence, rather than control, Reception Performance. All the work of Creative Performance and Production Performance is ostensibly geared toward influencing Reception Performance.[58] The only chance that an author has to influence the Reception Performance is so to arrange the Linguistic Text that he will have the best chance possible of influencing the reading and thus be said to have been understood rather than to have been misconstrued. The Reception Performance is, however, influenced not only by the Linguistic Text but by a great deal besides, much of which is subconscious and fortuitous. When the Reader has produced a Reception Text, its coherence is usually considered satisfactory proof that the performance has succeeded. Dissatisfaction with that coherence can only come when a second reading or someone else's description of a reading appears more satisfyingly coherent. There is, of course, no way to verify any correspondence between Reception Performance and Creative Performance.

All of this seems to confirm a conclusion bruited among some literary theorists: that the community of scholarship (or any community of

58. That statement should be qualified by the possibility that some—and unfortunately perhaps all—production performance is geared toward influencing the *consumer* to *buy* rather than the *reader* to *comprehend*. But the surface intention of copy-editing, type design, proof reading, format and binding design is to "help the reader" apprehend the work. That the covert intention of production actually works is verified in every book purchased and shelved unread.

readership—our sense of cultural heritage and values) derives its power and cohesiveness from arbitrary agreements to use certain conventions as standards of behavior regarding the interpretation of works and the relevance of history and perceived hegemonic structures in commentaries upon literary works. All of these conventions and standards are convenient constructs, not natural truths, and are deemed convenient as long as we agree to find them so. I no longer find it convenient to consider the Material Text an original, stable, or transparent sign source for an entity called the Literary Work of Art.

APPENDIX A

Occasionally textual critics have referred to theories from related disciplines that seem suggestive as clearer explanations of some aspect of textual criticism or of some problem relevant to editorial practice. The following is intended as a tentative "commentary" on two of them: J. L. Austin and Michael Hancher.

J. L. Austin:
The following remarks arise from a reading of J. L. Austin's *How to do Things with Words*. The most frequent references by textual critics to Austin's theories are to the terms *illocution, perlocution,* and *locution*. These are thought to correspond to intention and execution, for illocution (the way an utterance is used—as warning, advice, etc.) and perlocution (the effect aimed at by the utterance—as persuading one to respond appropriately) are thought of as the intended force and meaning of the locution (the whole act of uttering something).

There are several problems with this appropriation of Austin's ideas. Austin writes of "constative utterances" which are statements that can be tested as logically or factually true or false, and he distinguishes them from "performative utterances" which are not true or false but by which or in which the speaker does something such as warn, advise, threaten, marry, or contract —that is, the speaker does something besides just "make an utterance" (which could be said of constative statements also). Just as constative statements can be true or false, the effect of performative utterances might be "happy" or "unhappy" depending on a number of factors including the sincerity of the speaker, his right to do the performative act, and the success of the utterance within the circumstances attending it.

One should note that most of Austin's remarks are particularly apropos to spoken, rather than written, utterances—which he says are "not tethered to their origin" as speech is. He admits written utterances if they are signed. This would seem to admit books which bear the author's name; indeed they nearly always bear the publisher's name, and sometimes that of the printer, book binder, and occasionally, on a sticker inside the cover, that of the bookseller. But it is difficult to apply Austin's categories to fiction because, for one thing, as an utterance fiction is usually multi-voiced; not only are the agents mentioned above in a sense the utterers of the work as a whole, there are the voices of the narrator (or narrators) and of each character in the book. Austin's categories seem more apropos when applied to the "speech acts" of a character than when applied to those of the author.

In addition, a book, a poem, a novel, is in a way not a single utterance but a whole string of utterances. Austin's categories apply to sentences, not to whole paragraphs. Second, though Austin develops the idea of performative utterances very interestingly, he sees them as but one kind of utterance in a range of possible kinds of utterances—"constative utterances" being one of them. Third, in developing the idea of performative utterances, Austin explains their occasional failure to succeed by listing a variety of "infelicities" which cause the utterance to "misfire" or to be "abused." Among the "abuses" of performative utterances are "insincerities" such as jokes and lying. He considers a speaker's authority and sincerity as essential elements for "happy" performative statements. That is to say, if the performative utterance is given with any other than its "sincere" surface "intention" it fails. Irony and parody, therefore, have no place in his scheme. Obviously, if Austin's scheme is to be applied to fiction or poetry, a whole range of new types of "felicities" would have to be elaborated, for there is no room in Austin's theory for an ironic utterance that succeeds in spite of itself by "intentionally" subverting its surface meaning, not in order to lie, but to convey "happily" a subsurface meaning that is expected to be understood. Austin himself considered fiction and poetry an "etiolated use of language."

Austin seems therefore an oddly weak reed to lean on in explaining the problems of textual criticism. His theories apply to single sentences uttered in spoken form. And he restricts his interests to certain types of sentences which exclude the majority of uses we associate with literary texts. Nevertheless, Austin's categories have been picked up and elaborated with some success for use with literature, in particular by Richard Ohmann, who modifies Austin's categories for analysis of jokes, irony and fiction as "happy" acts, by John Searle, who considerably extends Austin's notion of varieties of illocutionary modes and who emphasizes the importance of context in understanding the "functional" referentialness of words when that deviates from the "normal or expected" references, and by Quentin Skinner, who develops the idea of locutions as functional within circumstances and through conventions in such a way that a theory of "write acts" could be developed, except that he tends to treat the medium (sound waves and written text) as transparent vehicles.[59] Paul Hernadi drops Austin's divisions into constative and perfor-

59. Richard Ohmann, "Speech Acts and the Definition of Literature," *Philosophy and Rhetoric*, 4 (1971), 1–19, and "Speech, Literature, and the Space Between," *New Literary History*, 4 (1972–73), 47–63; John R. Searle, *Expression and Meaning* (1979); and Quentin Skinner, "Conventions and the Understanding of Speech Acts," *Philosophical Quarterly*, 20 (1970), 118–138. Skinner's distinctions, or very similar ones, have made their way into Wendell Harris's very useful book *Interpretive Acts: In Search of Meaning* (Oxford: Clarendon, 1988), though Skinner is not mentioned.

mative utterances, adds the terms prelocutionary (why the speaker decides to make the utterance) and postlocutionary (what reaction or outcome eventuates in the listener and reader), and divides perlocution and illocution into originating and receiving counterparts. Thus the text points back to authorial prelocutionary input, perlocutionary intention and illocutionary force and at the same time provides the basis for the reader's illocutionary uptake, perlocutionary impact and postlocutionary outcome.[60] This use of Austin's terms is somewhat loose but it applies better to literary utterances than Austin's original schema which was both more precise and more rigid.

Michael Hancher:

The most frequent references to Hancher are to "Three Kinds of Intention," *Modern Language Notes*, 87 (1972), 827–851. Hancher's three kinds of intention correspond roughly to Austin's analysis of performative utterances, except that Hancher applies his theories directly to literary texts. His terms are "active," "programmatic," "final."

By active intention, Hancher means "the act of meaning-something-by-the-finished-text." Here he subsumes Austin's idea of locution which corresponds roughly with "the-finished-text" and the idea of content or subject, "meaning-something." But it is not entirely clear whether Hancher is defining "meaning" in any other than the ordinary general sense of the word, which Austin has done a much better job of subdividing into types of meaning.

By programmatic intention, Hancher refers to the attempt to have a certain effect or elicit a certain response. Here Hancher incorporates what Austin calls perlocution and which Austin considers "happy" if it has the desired or intended effect. Hancher does not measure the "happiness" of programmatic intentions by their success, but he suggests that the motive power of "active intentions" might run counter to the motive power of "programmatic" intentions—as when the active intention to describe a scene with honesty and detail might run counter to a programmatic intention to satisfy the censors.

By final intention, Hancher means the author's intention, by the finished product, to cause a reaction or to make something happen.

It will be noted that these schemata treat the Linguistic Text as a totally transparent entity. That is, all the analysis is expended on intention to mean something and to cause effects on readers. They do not consider the Material Text as a focus or object of intention itself. They do not describe the author's intention to write a paragraph or spell a word or use a point of punctuation. The technical construction of the text is not seen as problematic. The result is that little attention is given to the particular characteristics of the Material Text in hand being subjected to analysis. Further, none consider the work of book-designers (type fonts, page formats, density of lines, width of margins, quality of paper and binding) or of price and methods of marketing

60. Paul Hernadi, "Literary Theory," in *Introduction to Scholarship in Modern Languages and Literatures*, Joseph Gibaldi, ed. (1981), pp. 103–105.

and distribution as "intentions" of Production Performances or as influences on the total "perlocutionary impact" of works.

APPENDIX B

Definition of Terms
Texts as Matter:
Material Text = The union of Linguistic Text and Document: A Sign Sequence held in a medium of display. The Material Text has "meanings" additional to, and perhaps complementary to, the Linguistic Text.
Document = The Material medium of display (paper, ink, etc.).
Protocol = A written or otherwise verbalized response to and commentary on a Work.
Texts as Concepts:
Work = That which is manifested in and implied by the material and linguistic forms of texts thought to be variant forms of a single literary entity. The term Work incorporates concepts of Versions (Ideations) which are made concrete or Material by a Production Performance and then reconceptualized by Reception Performance.
Version = A concept by which Material Texts (such as manuscripts, drafts, proofs, first editions, revised editions, etc.) are classified as representative of:
Potential—abstract conceptual texts in the mind of an author.
Developing—abstract conceptual texts as evidenced by trial drafts in some material form.
Essayed—finished (at least temporarily) versions as evidenced by completed manuscripts or revised texts.
Linguistic Text = A Sign Sequence for an Essayed Version displayed in a Document.
Reception Text = The Performed Text conceptualized by the reader in the act of reading; the decoded Material Text.
Conceptual Text = Any text that is "held" in the mind or contemplated by a person. Conceptual texts are the only kind that can be experienced, though Material Texts are where they begin.
Semiotic Text = The signs used to represent any given Linguistic Text.
Texts as Action:
Speech Act = The whole event of creation, production, and reception of a communication at a specified time and place.
Write Act = The complex, never closed, serial event encompassing the creations, productions, and receptions at any and all places and times in which a written work is created, produced and received.
Utterance = A whole Speech Act or a coherent selection of "speaker," medium, hearer, time(s), and place(s) employed with regard to a Write Act within which "an understanding" of the Work is achieved.
Creative Performance = The authorial development of Essayed Versions

resulting in Linguistic Texts as found in manuscripts and authorially revised texts.

Production Performance = The scribal and publication development of Material Texts resulting in typists' copies, proofs, and printed books.

Reception Performance = The development of a conceptualized Reception Text in the act of reading.

Texts as Units, the integrity of which is defined by:

Time—The Work as it existed at some significant time.

Content—The Work as represented by one Linguistic Text as opposed to variants of it.

Function—The Work as designed for a particular purpose or appearance.

Material—The Work as embodied in one or another particular physical format.

Textual Contexts:

Material Base = The world of sense data to which the Material Text (manuscript, book, etc.) belongs.

Social Context = The complex of institutions, conventions, and mores whose expectations and habits are reflected in the Material Text.

Performance Field = An ambiguously conceived abstraction that provides the illusion of stability or a "locus of meaning." It is where the Text is "played" according to the rules of the reader's particular game of textual interaction and limited by the performer's capabilities and resources. The "game" metaphor here accounts in a different way for the "play" or looseness in the "machine" model of interpretation, in which play is equivalent to tolerance, a concept about how much variation in interpretation is allowable before communication "breaks down."

Textual Criticism and Literary Sociology

by

G. THOMAS TANSELLE

I F ONE CONSIDERS SYSTEMATIC TEXTUAL CRITICISM TO HAVE BEGUN with the Alexandrian librarians of the third century B.C., then one can say that for twenty-two and a half centuries the ultimate goal of textual criticism was—almost without exception—the establishment of texts as intended by their authors. The controversy that has always characterized the field was concerned with how best to approach this goal, not with whether this goal was the proper one. Sometimes editors recognized that authors may have changed their intentions over time; but if there was some doubt about whether early or late intentions were to be preferred, the focus was still on authorial intentions. Even when editors of ancient writings stated that they were reconstructing the text of the lost common ancestor of the extant manuscripts, knowing that it could not be equated with the text intended by the author (if indeed there was a single author), they were nevertheless attempting to move backward in time with the aim of coming closer to the author's intended text (or the text intended by the various creators of the work) than anyone had previously come. Most editors of the past have simply assumed, without giving much thought to the matter, that the purpose of critical editing was to correct the texts that have survived in documents, so as to bring them more into line with what the authors of the works intended.

In recent years, however, several writers on textual criticism have questioned this assumption, and their arguments have been so widely noted and discussed that the issue can probably be regarded as the dominant one in current theoretical debates. The line of argument runs as follows: authors cannot normally bring their works to the public without the assistance of other persons, such as scribes, printers, publishers' editors, and publishers, who in various ways alter the texts that pass through their hands; literature is thus a collaborative art, the joint product of a number of people; a concern with what authors alone intended is therefore artificial, since works can only be produced in the forms (both linguistic and physical) that the social process of publication gives to them, and it is in those forms that readers encounter and respond to them (forms that keep changing over time as new publishers and new readers deal with them in different terms). This position shifts the emphasis from the individual creators of literary works to the social mechanisms for the dissemination and reception of particular texts of those works.[1] For the first time in twenty-three centuries, a significant segment of that body of individuals who consider themselves textual critics and editors are critically examining the place of authorial intention among the goals of editing. This is not to suggest that there has been any diminution in the proportion of editions focusing on authorial intention but only that more editors than ever before are cognizant of the reasons for considering an alternative approach.

This trend in textual theory is part of a larger movement in literary studies. During the same years, deconstruction, the "new historicism," and reader-response theory—among other approaches—have supported a turn away from the authorial and the canonical. Language is seen to betray those who attempt to express themselves through it, and meaning is found to emerge from historical contexts and from the encounter of readers with texts. Although there has always been little (far too little) interchange between textual and literary critics, they do inhabit the same intellectual world, and it is to be expected that the concerns of both groups should be touched by the same currents of thought. One of the effects on textual criticism has been a new emphasis on the instability of texts, on their indeterminate nature. In this context, some theorists have regarded the editorial aim of reconstructing an authorially intended text as a misguided attempt to fix a text in a single form, hiding rather than revealing the fluidity and openness that are characteristic of texts. The idea that texts are the ever-shifting products of converging social forces is compatible with those approaches to literature that elevate linguistic analysis, historical associations, and readers' responses over the effort to receive a communication from an individual in the past.

Editors of nineteenth- and twentieth-century literature have faced this set of issues for a longer time than some of them realize, and certainly before the time when a concern for social approaches to textual criticism was much in the air. The frequent survival of authors' manuscripts from these centuries has meant that editors dealing with this period have often had to decide between an author's manuscript and a first printed edition as the best choice for copy-text. When they chose

---

1. The fundamental distinction between the texts of works and the texts of documents, which will emerge at various points in the following pages, I have elaborated most fully in *A Rationale of Textual Criticism* (1989). (Cf. also note 63 below and my "Textual Criticism and Deconstruction," *Studies in Bibliography*, 43 [1990], 1–33.)

the first edition, their decision was generally made in the name of authorial intention, for they argued that the first edition contained the kinds of adjustments (especially in spelling and punctuation) that the author expected and desired the publisher to make. But whenever one speaks of an author's expectation that certain matters will be taken care of, one is involving other persons in the completion of the work and embracing a view of literary works as collaborative products. Although there can be instances in which an editor may decide that an author's uninfluenced intentions are best represented in a first edition, one can say in general that the choice between manuscript and first edition often reveals whether the editor's primary interest is in the product of an individual creative mind or of collaborative action. Greg's rationale of copy-text, favoring the former, has come in for considerable criticism in recent years by those who object to its orientation and thus to its wide influence. It is a healthy situation in any field for positions perceived as orthodoxies to be challenged, and the recent debates have unquestionably been useful in bringing increased recognition to the instability of texts and to the ways in which they are continually being shaped by society. An interest in the texts that emerged from the process of publication and were available to readers at given times is obviously one (but not the only) valid approach to the past, and it had not previously been altogether overlooked; nevertheless, its new visibility is welcome.

This attention would be more welcome, however, if the advocates of a socially oriented textual criticism wrote on its behalf with greater clarity and coherence. Unfortunately, many of the recent discussions are so carelessly presented that they could convince no one; but since thoughtful readers will understand in any case the value of looking at texts as social products, they may derive some new insights from these essays despite the illogical presentation. In what follows, I shall survey some of the theoretical writings on textual matters that have appeared during the second half of the 1980s, taking the social approach to textual criticism as the obvious theme.[2] I shall concentrate first on some

2. This is the fourth in a series of surveys covering the period since mid-century. The three earlier essays, originally published in *Studies in Bibliography* in 1975, 1981, and 1986, have been brought together as *Textual Criticism since Greg: A Chronicle, 1950–1985* (1987). (Any reference to these essays in the present piece provides the *SB* citation first, followed in brackets by the page reference to the 1987 book.) As in the earlier essays, I again focus on discussions of general theoretical significance in the English language and therefore do not mention many of the articles that concentrate on textual problems in particular authors' works and many of the reviews of specific editions.

During the period surveyed here, a useful volume of essays containing reflections on editorial history appeared in the series of Toronto Conferences on Editorial Problems: *Editing and Editors: A Retrospect*, ed. Richard Landon (1988), including essays on medieval Latin texts (Leonard E. Boyle), the Greek New Testament (Bruce M. Metzger), eighteenth-

recent work of D. F. McKenzie and Jerome J. McGann, whose writings in the late 1970s and early 1980s (discussed in my survey five years ago) had first brought significant attention to the social view and who are still generally regarded as its most prominent exponents (though their emphases are not identical). It will then be necessary to examine several writers who are concerned, in one way or another, with the integrity of individual versions of works. This concern is a manifestation of the same set of attitudes, for an emphasis on versions reinforces the idea of textual fluidity. And even when the emphasis is on prepublication versions, some writers (notably a group of French and German critics) view

and nineteenth-century writings (Donald H. Reiman), and American literature (David J. Nordloh). (The Toronto series has also recently included *Editing Early English Drama*, ed. A. F. Johnson [1987]; *Editing Modern Economists*, ed. D. E. Moggridge [1988]; and *Editing Greek and Latin Texts*, ed. John N. Grant [1989].) Three significant surveys of earlier editorial history are Richard W. F. Kroll, "Mise-en-Page, Biblical Criticism, and Inference during the Restoration," *Studies in Eighteenth-Century Culture*, 16 (1986), 3–40; Joseph A. Dane, "The Reception of Chaucer's Eighteenth-Century Editors," *Text*, 4 (1988), 217–234; and C. O. Brink, *English Classical Scholarship: Historical Reflections on Bentley, Porson and Housman* (1986). Some historical comments on the nineteenth- and twentieth-century editing of medieval manuscripts appear in J. A. Asher's "The Textual Criticism Connection," *Te Reo: Journal of the Linguistic Society of New Zealand*, 29 (1986), 305–311. And a surprisingly detailed narrative of the editing of American literature under the CEAA (with a glance at recent issues) occupies much of Guy Cardwell's "Author, Intention, Text: The California Mark Twain," *Review*, 11 (1989), 255–288.

Another historical account of the development of modern editing appears as the first chapter (pp. 1–29) of Mary-Jo Kline's *A Guide to Documentary Editing* (1987), prepared for the Association for Documentary Editing (ADE). Her account understandably emphasizes the editing of the texts of documents and the different traditions followed by editors of literary and historical figures; although she has conscientiously informed herself about the field of literary editing, she obviously speaks as one who has given more thought to historical annotation than to textual matters. (The bulk of the book deals with the routines and procedures for managing editorial projects; I have criticized its treatment of photocopies on pp. 39–41 of "Reproductions and Scholarship," *SB*, 42 [1989], 25–54. For a firm, yet generous, review of this book, see T. H. Howard-Hill, "Documentary Editing: Critical, Noncritical, Uncritical," *Review*, 10 [1988], 149–154.) More recently, the ADE has sponsored another volume, *Editing Documents and Texts: An Annotated Bibliography* (1990), by Beth Luey with the assistance of Kathleen Gorman. Although its goal is to cover both literary and historical editing, this checklist of about 900 entries, which are annotated with brief unevaluative comments, is slanted toward the editing of historical documents, for it cites many pieces from *Documentary Editing* on individual editions and omits many similar discussions, especially of literary editions, published elsewhere. But it is of course useful for the large number of references that it does bring together. (Joseph R. McElrath, Jr., in a brief historical description of recent editorial debates published in the journal of the ADE, emphasizes the divergence between "literary" and "historical" editors—unfortunately called "LITs" and "HITs" throughout—as if that were the meaningful dividing line; see "Tradition and Innovation: Recent Developments in Literary Editing," *Documentary Editing*, 10, no. 4 [December 1988], 5–10. This paper forcefully illustrates that the distinctions urged in Jo Ann Boydston's admirable ADE presidential address in 1985 have not been heeded, and she properly criticized several aspects of this paper in a letter to the editor; see her "The Language of Scholarly Editing," *Documentary Editing*, 7, no. 4 [December 1985], 1–6, and her letter in 11, no. 1 [March 1989], 28.)

such versions as evidence for assessing authors' attitudes (sometimes welcoming, sometimes apprehensive) toward the transition from private creativity to public professionalism. As for post-publication versions, one of the most interesting cases is drama, where the contrast between a text close to the playwright's manuscript and a text reflecting what occurred in performance epitomizes the dichotomy between uninfluenced authorial intention and the joint intention that emerges from the collaborative process whereby the playwright works with others to bring a performance into being. Finally, a brief overview of other recent essays, showing the prevalence of these issues, leads to a reconsideration of editorial apparatus, for not surprisingly this subject has surfaced repeatedly in the writings of the last few years: in many ways it lies at the heart of these debates and offers a means of reconciling the extreme positions that have been taken.

I

In 1985 the inaugural series of Panizzi Lectures at the British Library was delivered by D. F. McKenzie; published as *Bibliography and the Sociology of Texts* (1986), these lectures have reverberated through many of the subsequent discussions of textual matters.[3] Those familiar with McKenzie's writings of the previous ten years will recognize the ideas developed here; but unfortunately these lectures are often as confused in argument as his Wolfenbüttel piece on Congreve and lack the eloquence and power of his Bibliographical Society address.[4] The reason for the influence of these lectures is that their angle of approach is in tune with the intellectual temper of the times, not that particular ideas

3. Three thoughtful reviews, which should be read by anyone interested in pursuing the implications of McKenzie's general position, are those by Hugh Amory (*Book Collector*, 36 [1987], 411–418), T. H. Howard-Hill (*Library*, 6th ser., 10 [1988], 151–158), and Jerome J. McGann (*London Review of Books*, 18 February 1988, pp. 20–21). I share with Amory and Howard-Hill a feeling that these lectures are seriously flawed, but each of us emphasizes somewhat different matters (and, indeed, we are not always in agreement). Some comments on Amory and Howard-Hill appear in notes 5, 6, 7, 10, and 11 below; I discuss McGann's review in more detail at the beginning of part II below. An instance of the publicity that McKenzie's lectures have received is Roger Chartier's article ("Meaningful Forms") in the first number of *Liber* (October 1989; distributed to English-speaking readers with the *TLS* for 6–12 October 1989), pp. 8–9. Chartier considers the lectures "a brilliant manifesto in favour of an ambitious new definition of bibliography" and uses them uncritically to introduce the subject of "the effects on meaning produced by material forms." Chartier also cites McKenzie (p. 162) in "Texts, Printing, Readings," in *The New Cultural History*, ed. Lynn Hunt (1989), pp. 154–175; in this essay Chartier locates his field (as his tripartite title suggests) at "the crossroads of textual criticism, the history of the book, and cultural sociology" (p. 175)—yet no text exists, he claims, "outside of the support that enables it to be read" (p. 161).

4. I have discussed these two papers in *SB*, 39 (1986), 14–18 [122–126].

are offered with such rigor that the sheer force of the argument carries the day. Many of the principal points, when abstracted from their presentation, are in fact sound, and not particularly new. One can readily agree, for example, that bibliographical studies are historical studies (p. 3); that textual criticism encompasses the examination of texts transmitted in any form, not just in ink on paper or parchment (p. 4); that it is important to study "the social, economic and political motivations of publishing, the reasons why texts were written and read as they were, why they were rewritten and redesigned, or allowed to die" (p. 5); and that "the material forms of books, the non-verbal elements of the typographic notations within them, the very disposition of the space itself, have an expressive function in conveying meaning" (p. 8). None of these points is startling, and none, it seems to me, can be denied. Any cogent exposition of these matters would always be welcome and could provide a constructive point of reference for further discussion; McKenzie's lectures do not serve this function because the central points are not argued coherently and indeed are sometimes trivialized.

The opening pages of the first lecture ("The Book as an Expressive Form") reveal these weaknesses. McKenzie takes his first task to be a new definition of the scope of bibliography, and he begins by examining W. W. Greg's 1932 statement that bibliographers are concerned with printed texts as inked type-impressions on paper, as "arbitrary marks," not as groupings of words with meanings. McKenzie's style of thinking is represented by his first observation on this statement: "it remains in essence the basis of any claim that the procedures of bibliography are scientific" (p. 1). But surely what makes a procedure "scientific" (in the usual definitions of the term) is the method followed, not the exclusion (or inclusion) of a particular body of evidence (in this case the inked impressions as symbols for letters, which form words of a language). In any event, McKenzie finds Greg's statement "no longer adequate as a definition of what bibliography is and does" (p. 2). Because McKenzie is particularly interested in books as "expressive form," in book design as a purveyor of meaning to readers, he asserts that "bibliography cannot exclude from its own proper concerns the relation between form, function and symbolic meaning" (p. 2). But then he recognizes, a few paragraphs later, that bibliography has "consistently studied" book design, production, distribution, and collecting, as well as textual transmission: "no part of that series of human and institutional interactions is alien to bibliography as we have, traditionally, practised it" (p. 4). He further understands that "Physical bibliography—the study of the signs which constitute texts and the materials on which they are recorded—is of course the starting point." And then he adds, "But it cannot define the discipline" (p. 8). By this time the reader will wonder what the point of his criticism of Greg is. Greg obviously understood the interconnections among all these various "bibliographical" activities (as other parts of his essay show), and he practiced many of them himself; as an editor he took the meanings of words into account, but he felt, just as McKenzie does, that the physical evidence must be thoroughly investigated first. When he said that bibliographers regard letter forms as arbitrary marks, he was of course describing what McKenzie calls "physical bibliography" and not attempting to characterize the whole interrelated congeries of bibliographical studies. Greg and McKenzie would seem not to be at odds after all.[5]

What, then, is the basis for McKenzie's repeated worry about Greg's statement? Why, at the end of the lecture, does he say that "Greg's definition of what bibliography is would have it entirely hermetic" (p. 19)? One cannot believe that McKenzie is so literal-minded that he objects to Greg's use of "bibliography," in a context that makes clear what he meant, instead of "physical bibliography." Suppose, for the sake of argument, that Greg did wish only physical bibliography to be called "bibliography": what difference would that have made, since he plainly grasped the relationship between it and all the other aspects of textual study? If, as McKenzie acknowledges, the entire textual cycle, from composition by an author to response by a reader, has generally been understood to be linked together and deserving of integrated study, what does it matter whether it is called "bibliography" or something else? What difference does it make whether we think of that integrated study as a single field or as a group of related fields? Why is the label important if the substantive connections have been made? As it turns out, there is a reason—an embarrassing reason: "As long as we continue to think if it [bibliography] as confined to the study of the non-symbolic function of signs, the risk it runs is relegation. Rare book rooms will simply become rarer. The politics of survival, if nothing else, require a more comprehensive justification of the discipline's function in promoting new knowledge" (pp. 3–4). The phrase "if nothing else" does not accomplish its mission of making the point seem casual and subordinate.

5. Howard-Hill, in his review (see note 3 above) provides a fuller analysis of Greg's essay and McKenzie's distortion of it (pp. 152–153). John Barnard, in "Bibliographical Context and the Critic," *Text*, 3 (1987), 27–46, quotes (p. 28) a passage from the same 1932 essay of Greg's, stating that a text is a "living organism," which at each stage of "its descent through the ages" is "in some sense a new creation, something different from what it was for an earlier generation"—a point of view strikingly similar to McKenzie's. Barnard specifically aligns himself with McKenzie and McGann, asserting that "bibliography needs to widen its aims" (p. 40). (Greg's essay, "Bibliography—An Apologia," is available in his *Collected Papers*, ed. J. C. Maxwell [1966], pp. 239–266.)

To speak at all of the "politics of survival" trivializes the discussion beyond redemption. A "discipline" does not exist for the purpose of self-perpetuation; if it requires "justification" as a political strategy for survival, it had better be allowed to die.[6] McKenzie's politicizing of scholarship crops up again when he says that Greg's "confinement of bibliography to non-symbolic meaning, in an attempt to give it some kind of objective or 'scientific' status, has seriously impeded its development as a discipline" (p. 8). It is a misreading of history, as a strategy of "survival," to claim that Greg's statement, or the view it represents, impeded progress in any way. Bibliography, in the broad sense, has benefited immensely from the recognition of the role physical evidence plays in the study of textual transmission, and Greg was one of the scholars who established that field of study; it is understandable that, in addressing the Bibliographical Society in 1932 on its fortieth anniversary, he would emphasize physical bibliography, for the relation of physical evidence to literary study was the most far-reaching insight that had emerged under the aegis of the Society. Ten years later, in a fiftieth-anniversary paper, he stated that "the object of bibliographical study is . . . to reconstruct for each particular book the history of its life, to make it reveal in its most intimate detail the story of its birth and adventures as the material vehicle of the living word." Greg was thinking along the same lines as McKenzie—but thinking much more clearly: after pointing out that bibliographical and textual criticism were so interlocked that it was difficult to regard them as separate fields, Greg added, "This is not a matter on which I desire to lay stress, for it is largely a question of terms and therefore of relatively minor importance."[7]

What is of much more importance than deciding which activities we wish the term "bibliography" to cover is examining the attitudes we bring to our work. There can be no objection to thinking of bibliography as "a sociology of texts" (p. 8) if by that is meant an openness to all

6. The line "Rare book rooms will simply become rarer" is not only a poor joke; it is an incoherent intrusion. The implied connection between rare-book rooms as institutions and bibliography as a professional discipline cannot be taken for granted and would be difficult to support by a rational argument. Amory, in his review (see note 3 above), comments on this line of McKenzie's with characteristic flippancy, suggesting in his own way that intellectual pursuits have a higher aim than institutional self-preservation: "the prospect has its charms. Many a rare book room rests on the ruins of another, and a thoroughly [sic] reshuffling of the deck might advance bibliography more effectively than years of supine institutional possession" (p. 415).

7. "Bibliography—A Retrospect," in *The Bibliographical Society 1892–1942: Studies in Retrospect* (1945), pp. 23–31 (quotations from pp. 27, 30). Both Amory and Howard-Hill, in their reviews of McKenzie (see note 3 above), seem to me to be overly concerned with the question of how "bibliography" is to be defined; and by returning to this matter at the ends of their reviews, they both conclude with passages that are far from their strongest.

the kinds of research that bear on the history and influence of textual transmission. But McKenzie, despite his inclusive view of bibliography, has a curiously limited approach to historical investigation. His well-known skepticism about analytical bibliography[8] emerges here, as when he says that compositor studies have displayed "virtuosity in discerning patterns in evidence which is entirely internal, if not wholly fictional" (p. 7). If a pattern—or, more precisely, a conclusion based on a perceived pattern—is "entirely internal" (that is, unsupported by information in a document external to the book under examination), is it necessarily false or unworthy of serious consideration by historians? How does he think that facts (i.e., what we take to be facts until they are shown to be unsatisfactory) get established in the first place? Do we not search for patterns in external evidence, too, as part of the process of attempting to make sense out of a welter of data? He had earlier noted that bibliographical analysis "depends absolutely upon antecedent historical knowledge" (p. 2). But how is a body of "knowledge" built up if not by examining all kinds of evidence, and does not "antecedent" knowledge continually have to be revised as new pieces of evidence, or new interpretations of evidence, emerge? Analysis does not depend "absolutely" on antecedent knowledge, for the possibility must remain open that the results of analysis will overturn previously accepted views. When McKenzie later admits that physical bibliography is "the starting point" (p. 8), one has to wonder how sound a start it is if it excludes the kinds of analysis of physical evidence that are generally grouped under the term "analytical bibliography." More fundamentally, one has to worry about an approach to history that bans a basic category of evidence. Bibliography, he insists, is "the historical study of the making and the use of books and other documents" (p. 3). But his history, as it emerges, has a program, which is not hospitable to analytical bibliography; and by rejecting a large body of bibliographical evidence, he makes it impossible for readers to respect his approach as an open-minded search.

A major part of his program is to understand the physical book as "an expressive form"—and therefore to look at physical details not as evidence of the book-production process but as indicators of the cultural values surrounding that production and as determinants of readers' re-

8. Set forth most fully in "Printers of the Mind: Some Notes on Bibliographical Theories and Printing-House Practices," *SB*, 22 (1969), 1–75; see the responses by Peter Davison, in "Science, Method, and the Textual Critic," *SB*, 25 (1972), 1–28, and by me, in "Bibliography and Science," *SB*, 27 (1974), 55–89 (esp. pp. 73–78), reprinted in *Selected Studies in Bibliography* (1979), pp. 1–35 (esp. pp. 19–24). A recent brief assessment of the effect of McKenzie's essay appears in Robert Kean Turner, "Accidental Evils," in *Play-Texts in Old Spelling*, ed. G. B. Shand with Raymond C. Shady (1984), pp. 27–33 (see p. 33).

sponses. His principal illustration of this point, occupying the entire latter half of the first lecture, is the epigraph to W. K. Wimsatt, Jr., and M. C. Beardsley's famous 1946 essay "The Intentional Fallacy." Noting that the four lines quoted from Congreve's prologue to *The Way of the World* differ from the "authorized version" of 1710 in wording at one place, in punctuation at four places, and in capitalization at six, McKenzie argues that the 1946 readings alter the meaning of the passage to one that better suits Wimsatt and Beardsley's purpose. Whereas Congreve was asserting the rights of authors to establish their own meanings, he says, the 1946 quotation reverses the sense, encouraging "audience and readers to discount the author's meaning" (p. 14). This example of textual variation is not an apt illustration of all the points that McKenzie wishes it to demonstrate, and one wonders why he was content to offer it at length (unless for the amusing coincidence between the apparent content of the passage and the phenomenon it is cited to illustrate). It is in fact a much more conventional illustration than McKenzie seems to think, for what it demonstrates are the dangers of modernizing and of accepting any text that comes to hand. As McKenzie admits late in his discussion, Wimsatt and Beardsley in all likelihood took their quotation from a popular anthology, not from the 1710 edition; and although they presumably selected the passage because it seemed to support their argument, they were apparently not responsible for misquoting it to give it that meaning.[9] Furthermore, the changes in punctuation and in capitalization were no doubt made by the anthologists in an effort to modernize the text for students. The problems that unauthorized variants and modernized texts create for unwary critics have often been commented on; and it is no revelation to be shown that variant wording, punctuation, and capitalization are textual matters, for they are regularly regarded as such. What McKenzie's argument calls for is an illustration of the way in which format, type design, and layout can

9. Whether or not they misquoted it unintentionally is not clear. It is true, as McKenzie says (p. 18), that the substitution of "wrote" for "wrought" occurs in the anthology edited by George H. Nettleton and Arthur E. Case, *British Dramatists from Dryden to Sheridan* (1939); but that fact alone does not seem sufficient evidence from which to conclude that Wimsatt and Beardsley used this anthology. Their quoted passage differs in punctuation at six points from the Nettleton-Case text, whereas it agrees perfectly with the punctuation in two other popular American anthologies of the time: *Plays of the Restoration and Eighteenth Century*, ed. Dugald MacMillan and Howard Mumford Jones (1931); and the Modern Library *Twelve Famous Plays of the Restoration and Eighteenth Century*, introd. Cecil A. Moore (1933). These two anthologies do have "wrought" (and one of them—the 1933—differs from Wimsatt-Beardsley in the spelling "dulness" rather than "dullness"). But the question remains open whether greater weight is to be given to the agreement in punctuation on the one hand or the agreement in the reading "wrote" on the other.

convey meanings and are thus "textual." In his earlier Congreve essay he did cite such elements of design as integral parts of Congreve's intended texts, and it is puzzling that he does not do so here. He claims to have dealt with the signification of "the fine detail of typography and layout" (p. 16); but his discussion of Wimsatt and Beardsley scarcely touches on those matters, and the lecture therefore does not really engage its avowed topic, "the book as an expressive form."[10]

Despite the failure of the Congreve example to serve its requisite function, readers of the lecture are presumably willing in any case to agree in theory to many of McKenzie's conclusions, for there can be no question that the physical forms in which texts are presented to the public are the products of printers and publishers (and sometimes authors as well), that these forms reflect cultural influences, and that they in turn affect the interpretations of readers. One accepts these points as matters of common sense, not because McKenzie has provided any new insights into them.[11] Indeed, he confuses the issues because he does not coherently distinguish the procedure for locating authorial intention from that for assessing works as communal products. After pointing out that in reading contemporary editions of Congreve we must consider the contributions of the printer and the publisher to the "interpretation of Congreve's meaning" (p. 17), he asks, "Who, in short, 'authored' Congreve?" But this question (surprisingly) implies a single "Congreve," a single text, and does not recognize the distinction between the text of the printed artifact and the text of the literary work as intended by Congreve (or others). Yet earlier he had enumerated some of the issues in the history of the book as "What writers thought they were doing in writing texts,[12] or printers and booksellers in designing and publishing them, or readers in making sense of them" (p. 10). No single text can accommodate both the first (the authorially intended text) and the second (the text as published). Instead of asking who

10. Further shortcomings of this illustration are perceptively noted by Howard-Hill on p. 155 of his review (see note 3 above).

11. It is therefore surprising to find Amory, in his review (see note 3 above), saying that the current critical climate, reflected by McKenzie, places on libraries the "burden" of preserving "decaying reprints that in theory are primary sources—of something or other, anyway, if the literary theorists could only spit it out" (p. 417). Bibliographers, long before the current critical theorists, have repeatedly recognized that all printed items are primary sources for the history of printing and publishing and that "reprints" are primary sources for the study of authors' reputations. Amory is perfectly well aware of these points; yet for some reason he is willing to make the foolish statement, "There is such a thing as too much evidence."

12. Writers are really concerned to write *works*, of course, not *texts*, though in order to transmit those works they must produce specific texts, which may or may not faithfully represent the works.

"authored" Congreve's works, we have to ask whether we are interested in what Congreve himself "authored" or what he "authored" in collaboration with printers and publishers. There is of course a legitimate interest in both, as well as in the meanings that readers have derived at different times from the texts available to them. But McKenzie sums up this variety in a troublesome way: "My argument," he says, "therefore runs full circle from a defence of authorial meaning, on the grounds that it is in some measure recoverable, to a recognition that, for better or worse, readers inevitably make their own meanings" (p. 10). The sequence is hardly a "full circle," for readers' meanings can arise from any public text and do not necessarily derive from one intended by the author, if indeed such a text has ever been "recovered." And to justify the search for authorial meaning "on the grounds that it is in some measure recoverable" misstates the basis for historical research. We never know whether anything is recoverable, nor do we know when we have in fact recovered something; all we can do is attempt to move in the direction of recovering whatever we have decided is worth recovering.

Deciding that the past can be of interest or relevance is the crucial matter, not how recoverable it is; and McKenzie's naïve view of this question undercuts the peroration of his first lecture, as it has weakened all that went before. He says that critical movements from "New Critical formalism" to deconstruction "share the same scepticism about recovering the past" (p. 19). Of course they do—and they share it with all thinking individuals. What distinctively characterizes those movements is—in varying degrees—a lack of interest in the past, a rejection of the past as a useful concept. Whether a rejection of the past is a rejection of "human agency" is another question, and not one obviously to be answered in the affirmative, as McKenzie does. After all, the "critical self-absorption" that he sees in these approaches is also an example of the human effort to come to terms with the verbal artifacts that surround us. Our studies cannot so easily be robbed of humanity as McKenzie imagines, nor can bibliography so easily reinstate the human element by dealing with "discoveries as distinct from invented meanings" (p. 19). It would be far more understanding of humanity to recognize that discoveries *are* invented meanings, for they are known only through the exercise of human judgment. McKenzie has become so convinced of the idea that recent criticism is anti-humanistic that he reserves his last line for proclaiming that bibliography can correct this direction by showing "the human presence in any recorded text" (p. 20).[13] Leaving aside his assessment of

13. Bibliography, that is, in the broad sense. One of his earlier criticisms of analytical bibliography was its supposed exclusion of the human. Presumably one of the connections

contemporary criticism, one may question his vision in its own terms, for—despite his earlier inclusion of authorial intention among the concerns of bibliography—he now seems to exclude it. The emphasis on successive texts as recorded forms, he says, "testifies to the fact that new readers of course make new texts, and that their new meanings are a function of their new forms";[14] as a consequence, one approaches these texts "no longer for their truth as one might seek to define that by authorial intention, but for their testimony, as defined by their historical use" (p. 20). Why authorial intention is not one instance of human agency in the past is left unclear. McKenzie is waging an unnecessary battle if he thinks it will be difficult to convince anyone that texts as they change through time provide evidence for readers' changing responses; but the incoherence of his remarks about authorial intention and its place in historical study will nevertheless set up a barrier between him and his audience.

These problems persist through the second and third lectures: there is scarcely a paragraph not weakened by them. The second lecture, "The Broken Phial: Non-Book Texts," begins with several pages that continue the emphasis on expressive textual forms as "less an embodiment of past meaning than a pretext for present meaning" (p. 25). In other words, "Meaning is not what is meant, but what we now agree to infer" (p. 26). But one of the present meanings or inferences—though anyone is free not to be interested in it—is what we believe we can conclude about the meanings of a work at a given time in the past. Among those past meanings are the authorially intended ones; and a concern with authorial intention does not, as McKenzie seems to believe, contradict the idea of textual instability (p. 28), for authors' intentions shift with time, and our reconstructions of their intended texts can never be definitive. To say that the concept of the authorially intended text "has largely collapsed" (p. 28) is merely (and ineffectively) provocative (and indeed is at odds with the calmer—and true—statement, a few lines later, that it "no longer compels universal assent"). The ensuing statement that "The only remaining rule seems to be that we must not conflate any one ver-

---

he sees between analytical bibliography and the New Criticism (cf. p. 7) is that the former "has obscured the role of human agents" by ignoring the "inevitable dependence upon interpretive structures" (p. 8), just as the latter has eliminated "a concern for the complexities of human agency in the production of texts" (p. 19). Analytical bibliographers and textual critics in the Greg-Bowers tradition, however, have by no means been unaware of the fact that they were dealing with the actions of human beings in the past: one of the best illustrations of this point is Greg's classification of variants into substantives and accidentals as a way of reflecting the attitudes of Renaissance compositors toward their copy. (On the New Criticism and analytical bibliography, see also note 22 below.)

14. New meanings, of course, can also occur without new forms, as earlier editions are read in new contexts.

sion with any other" (p. 29) is simply incorrect. This "rule" is not in fact the only one—or the only respectable one—now being followed. And the implied connection between a declining interest in authorial intention and a rising distaste for eclecticism is not made clear; a connection can be made, but theoretically, of course, the arguments for and against eclecticism are relevant to any editorial goal.

The core of the second lecture is an examination of "non-book texts," and McKenzie takes up, in turn, landscape, maps, photographs and film, and theater. That texts in all media pose textual problems and that "textual criticism" encompasses all such problems are not new ideas.[15] Perhaps McKenzie is not claiming that they are, but he does seem to think he is exhorting "bibliographers" to broaden their outlook. What he is calling them to is unclear, however. His first illustration—the significance of landscape for the Arunta tribe—is meant to show how "the land itself" can be "a text" (p. 31), how topographical features can have "a *textual* function" (p. 32). But he confuses his point by explaining that these natural features "form the ingredients of what is in fact a verbal text, for each one is embedded in story . . . and supports . . . the symbolic import of a narration." In that case, he is talking about landscape as a visual supplement to, or embodiment of, a verbal text; but it is not the verbal narrative that makes the landscape a text, for the landscape is a text in its own right, a nonverbal text made up of physical objects, a text that can be read in the way sculpture can. McKenzie, here and later, does not clearly distinguish between, on the one hand, the nonverbal media in which communication can take place (as in painting, music, and dance) and, on the other, the various nonbook vehicles that are used to transmit works in the medium of language. He does, in some examples, deal with visual and kinetic texts;[16] but he never makes clear that

15. See, for example, Vinton Dearing's opening statement in the preface to *A Manual of Textual Analysis* (1959): "The method of analysis described in the following pages may be applied to the transmission and embodiment in any form of any idea or complex of ideas" (p. vii). In his expanded work *Principles and Practice of Textual Analysis* (1974), he opens his first chapter with the more explicit statement, "Messages are not confined to words or even to sound, but may consist wholly of visual images"; hence, "There is no limitation whatsoever in textual analysis on the type or types of transmitters. Textual analysis is . . . a completely general discipline of very wide specific applicability in the arts and social sciences." Dearing has recently summarized his distinction between the "genealogy of texts" (the subject of "textual analysis") and the "genealogy of media," in "Textual Analysis: A Kind of Textual Criticism," *Text*, 2 (1985), 13–23.

16. But sometimes puzzlingly. When he mentions television weather maps, he raises this question: "Should we not at least be asking . . . at which point one stops a kinetic image to keep a record for posterity?" (p. 38) The answer is obviously no: a single still image (or a number of still images) would falsify the record, since the text consists of moving images. Two pages later, after discussing a comic-strip rendering of Shakespeare, he says, "I hasten to add that I am not endorsing the form as a suitable one for Shake-

the relation of photographs, for example, to printed and manuscript books is of a different order from the relations among sound recordings, computer disks, and books as conveyors of verbal texts. His discussion is meant to argue for "the centrality of a textual principle in bibliography" (p. 43); but that principle is obscured by his failure to make these discriminations.[17] And would it not be more constructive to emphasize the centrality of textual criticism to all fields? Whether we define "bibliography" as essentially textual is less important than whether we understand the basic role that bibliographical and textual investigation plays in every field. Whether "bibliography" subsumes all such investigation is of less moment (except in academic politics) than whether the work gets done, and gets done by those who in each instance bring to it a knowledge of the field concerned.

The third lecture, "The Dialectics of Bibliography Now," showing little sense of progression, offers two more examples of the book as expressive form (drawing on Locke and Joyce) and one extended example of the textual study of a film (*Citizen Kane*). It is something of a letdown to find out that a principal point of the latter discussion is to demonstrate that films, like books, have "texts" and that "the word now has a meaning which comprehends them all" (p. 56). Obviously films and books (and all other physical objects) display patterns of details that we can agree to call "texts"—though whether we actually do call them that is a trivial matter, further trivialized by the insistent restatement that "the discipline [bibliography] comprehends them both [films and books]" (p. 59). As before, the more meaningful point is passed over: that films provide examples of textual problems in a different medium from literature, not just in a different form of transmission. Film is a different art from literature, whereas literature stored in a computer and literature stored in a book are not two different arts.[18] When Mc-

speare" (p. 40). What can this mean? The comic strip is of course not a theatrical performance; it is a work, inspired by Shakespeare, in another medium. Both these comments (like the treatment of landscape) suggest a reluctance on McKenzie's part to accept nonverbal texts on their own terms. I do not comment here on his brief account of drama (pp. 40–41) —which he begins by claiming, "The relation of textual criticism to the realities of theatrical production has always been one of embarrassed impotence"—because I take up the same issues (of the relation of play scripts to performance) in discussing Howard-Hill below (see note 63).

17. In his discussion of maps, he says that, "not as books but as texts, bibliographical principle embraces them [maps] too" (p. 37). What is "bibliographical principle"? If it is the "textual principle" that is central to bibliography, then the statement is merely a tautology.

18. The idea that a work of literature employs an intangible medium is not Platonic, as McKenzie seems to suggest in the second lecture (p. 24). One might more readily see as Platonic McKenzie's reference to "a kind of ideal-copy text, transcending all the versions and true to the essential intention of the 'work' " (p. 29), or his statement that "All

Kenzie says that bibliography is "committed to the description of all recorded texts" (p. 51), the term "recorded texts" glosses over an important question: whether it refers only to the concrete forms through which works in intangible media are primarily transmitted (that is, books, sound recordings, motion picture films, and so on) or whether it also includes works that exist in physical form (that is, paintings, sculptures, buildings, and so on). His imprecision in thinking about this question is illustrated by the observation that "Whereas libraries have held books and documents as physical objects, computer systems have been mainly concerned to retrieve content" (p. 60). But computer systems also inevitably hold their "content" in physical objects (tapes and disks); and librarians have generally been more concerned with "content" than with the preservation of objects, as their practice of replacing one edition of a work with a "reprint" (or microfilm) of it, or with another edition, shows. The two parts of the sentence are not parallel in focus, and the statement thus obscures, rather than illuminates, the relationship between books and computers.

The weaknesses of these lectures are epitomized in the opening sentences of this third lecture, when McKenzie summarizes his two contrasted "concepts of 'text' " in this way: "One is the text as authorially sanctioned, contained, and historically definable. The other is the text as always incomplete, and therefore open, unstable, subject to a perpetual re-making by its readers, performers, or audience" (p. 45). These two sets of attributes do not in fact distinguish the concept of the authorially intended text from that of the collaborative text (produced by publishers, readers, actors, and so forth, both contemporary with the author and later). What they actually describe is a very different dichotomy, that between texts of documents and texts of works. The text of a surviving document is "contained" and "historically definable"— though how it relates to the author's, or anyone else's, intention is a debatable question. The texts of works in intangible media must always be reconstructed from whatever physical and oral evidence comes to hand and inevitably reflect the predispositions of those doing the reconstructing; thus the texts of works—both authors' intended texts and the texts preferred by others—are "unstable" and "subject to a perpetual re-making." One of the summarizing statements in this lecture is the

---

the versions [performances of a play] imply an ideal form which is never fully realized but only partly perceived and expressed by any one" (p. 41). McKenzie does not seem to be grappling here with the intangible nature of the medium of verbal works, which makes the work itself always indeterminate. And he is certainly not suggesting that the ideal form is the one envisaged by the author. His argument does not require a concept of ideal form, and in the context of that argument these statements are incomprehensible.

assertion that "bibliography is of its nature . . . concerned specifically with texts as social products" (pp. 51–52); but McKenzie apparently fails to see that the attempt to reconstruct authorially intended texts is one of the many activities that readers can engage in as they evaluate the socially produced evidence that survives for their examination. These lectures would scarcely have warranted the space I have devoted to them here if they had not been written by McKenzie and had not, as a result, been given considerable attention by others. They do have some significance as an indication of a current direction in editorial thought, and it is disappointing that they cannot be greeted as an effective manifesto; but their laxity of argument makes them an unstable foundation on which to build.

II

Jerome J. McGann's prominence as a spokesman for the social approach to texts is largely due to *A Critique of Modern Textual Criticism* (1983),[19] though he has written a number of essays on editing, and his view of the nature of texts is of course evident in his many other writings. A basic statement of his position in the period under consideration here can be found in his review of McKenzie's lectures.[20] His general approach is substantially the same as McKenzie's, and perhaps for that reason he overlooks some of the flaws of those lectures. In any case, he serves McKenzie well, sometimes summarizing McKenzie's points more

19. I have discussed this book in *SB*, 39 (1986), 19–27 [127–135], along with several of his essays that have since been collected in *The Beauty of Inflections* (1985): "The Text, the Poem, and the Problem of Historical Method," "Shall These Bones Live?", and "The Monks and the Giants: Textual and Bibliographical Studies and the Interpretation of Literary Works." More recently, a linked pair of important criticisms of McGann's *Critique* has appeared: David J. Nordloh's "Socialization, Authority, and Evidence: Reflections on McGann's *A Critique of Modern Textual Criticism*," *Analytical & Enumerative Bibliography*, n.s., 1 (1987), 3–12; and Craig S. Abbott's "A Response to Nordloh's 'Socialization, Authority, and Evidence,' " *ibid.*, 13–16. Nordloh provides an admirable summary of Greg's position to show how McGann misunderstands Greg and Bowers, and he then argues that McGann's "notion of socialization introduces a dangerous vagueness" into editing (p. 7), making it no longer a "serious intellectual endeavor, circumscribed by evidence and limited by coherent, identifiable premises" (p. 12). He is correct to point out that McGann "seems less interested in fully defining the concept [of socialized textual authority] than in employing it as a weapon against other editorial principles" (p. 5); but Nordloh, in turn, does not go very far toward imagining the uses of a socialized approach by insisting that, "for intelligibility and for coherence, authority must be defined as precisely as possible in terms of active authorial creation" (p. 11). Abbott reinforces Nordloh's criticisms by noting that McGann "exaggerates the intransigence of Bowersian editing" (p. 13); and he predicts that the result of the current debates will be "a wider variety of editorial approaches, not the replacement of one approach with another" (p. 16). (Although neither Nordloh nor Abbott refers to McKenzie, their articles are joined under the heading "The Sociology of the Text.")

20. "Theory of Texts," *London Review of Books*, 18 February 1988, pp. 20–21.

effectively than McKenzie himself had done (despite his excessive reliance on fashionable jargon). There are two particularly valuable emphases in McGann's review. One is his insistence on the inseparability of the activities traditionally called "textual criticism" and "literary criticism." The other emerges from his understanding of the process of reading a good critical edition with apparatus: "a process by which the entire socio-history of the work—from its originary moments of production through all its subsequent reproductive adventures—is postulated as the ultimate goal of critical self-consciousness" (p. 21, col. 3).

There are some loose ends, however, that prevent his argument from being satisfying. He defines language to be "more properly conceived as an event than a medium," as "an extended field of communicative action"; one therefore "has to take the entirety of the language event as the object of interpretation" (p. 20, cols. 3–4). It follows that the same "text" will wear "different faces" in different situations (p. 21, col. 1). The problem arises in his accounting for these faces:

one might usefully distinguish "the text" (or the poem as a purely linguistic event) from the "version" (or the immediate and integral physical object "through which" the "text" is being executed), and make yet a further distinction of "text" and "version" from the "work" (the term to stand for some more global constitution of the poem). There is a "work" called *Paradise Lost* which supervenes its many texts and its many versions; to William Blake that work was one thing, whereas to William Empson it was something else; and of course to any one of us the work we call *Paradise Lost* can be, will be, reconstituted once again. (p. 21, col. 2)

This tripartite classification (of what?) into "text," "version," and "work" is too imprecise to be helpful. If we agree to consider "text" the name for the "purely linguistic event," we have to shift our definition from the one McGann proposed a few paragraphs earlier, where the "text" (almost always in quotation marks) is declared not to be a linguistic event (" 'The text' will not be located as the words on the page immediately before one's eyes"). Furthermore, why should "text," the linguistic event, be distinguished from "version," in McGann's sense of the physical object, if the point of the whole argument is that they are inseparable? "Text" and "version" are not two of the "faces" that a "text" (in a different sense) can wear; either the combination of "text" and "version" together (the words and their physical presentation) turns a different face to us under different circumstances, or else the "version" is the "face" that a "text" wears. In the latter case, the "text" (linguistic event) has an independent existence and would seem to be incongruent with the earlier definition of language as "an extended field of communicative action" (the extended field surely including the physical presentation). Even more surprising is the inclusion in this classification scheme of "work" as a "more global constitution of the poem." Presumably this vague phrase means that there is, after all, some meaningful sense in which a poem has an existence apart from its individual occurrences. If the "global" work "supervenes its many texts and its many versions" (note the "its"), how is it to be defined without conceiving of language as an intangible medium and depriving material texts of their postulated primary status? That to each of us "the work we call *Paradise Lost* can be, will be, reconstituted once again" suggests, as textual critics have traditionally thought, that the physical presentation of verbal texts offers us not the works themselves but the evidence out of which we "reconstitute" the works. This view does not contradict the idea that a document is "meaning-constitutive . . . in every dimension of its material existence" (p. 20, col. 2); but it subordinates that process of deriving meaning to the reconstitution of a work that has no tangible existence. McGann's concept of "the work" thus undercuts his larger argument and aligns him with an approach to texts that he seems at other times to find defective.[21]

This indecision is apparent in another passage as well. McGann identifies three kinds of reading, "linear" correlated with "text," "spatial" with "version," and "radial" with "work" (p. 21, cols. 2–3). But asserting that critical editions are "typically structured so as to enforce spatial and radial reading processes along with the linear process" once again paradoxically raises questions about the role of physical form in the creation of meaning. A critical edition has its own physical form; and the readings of other editions, reported in its apparatus, are a part of that form. If such an arrangement permits "radial" reading—that is, reading texts with the knowledge of other texts in one's mind—it can only do so on the "linear," not the "spatial," level, even if the physical features of the earlier editions are described, because no verbal description of visual effects (nor even a facsimile) can substitute for the actual visual presentation. It follows either that physical form is dispensable as an element in reading or that "radial" reading is not being posited as a full engagement with multiple texts.

The role of physical form is a central issue not only for literary sociology but also for traditional analytical bibliography, which McKenzie and McGann find too restrictive. McGann, seemingly with approval, summarizes McKenzie's "initial, critical remarks on theory of bibliog-

21. In the preface to his latest book, *Towards a Literature of Knowledge* (1989), McGann repeats this three-part classification of the "levels" of "operation" at which one can study the "social text" (p. ix).

raphy," particularly his criticism of Fredson Bowers for saying that "historical bibliography is not, properly speaking, bibliography at all" (p. 20, col. 1). McGann, like McKenzie, does not take into account the shifting usages of the word "bibliography" illustrated by such a quotation or seek to find a stable concept linking apparently divergent views of bibliography. The context of Bowers's statement (in his *Encyclopaedia Britannica* article on "Bibliography" in 1960) makes clear that he was distinguishing "analytical bibliography," the examination of physical evidence in books for clues to their production history, from historical studies of book-related topics, like type, paper, binding, printing, and publishing. He was certainly not implying that bibliography (i.e., analytical bibliography) was not a tool of historical research or that it did not draw on and contribute to historical studies of book production. Just how much of the whole realm of book history is to be called "bibliography" is unimportant, a mere matter of labeling. What is fascinating in this concern with the definition of bibliography is the downplaying of one kind of physical evidence and the elevating of another. Analytical bibliographers look at the physical evidence that can reveal information about production history; literary sociologists are concerned with the physical details that may have affected readers' responses (or that publishers—and sometimes authors—believed would affect those responses). The work of the analytical bibliographers is seen by the literary sociologists as feeding into an intentionalist view of literature, and as authorial intention loses favor, so must analytical bibliography do so. Although analytical bibliography was largely developed by editors interested in establishing authorially intended texts, it uncovers facts of printing history that are obviously not tied to any one editorial theory. What happens in the printing shop is part of the social process by which texts of works are disseminated and is of direct relevance to literary sociology. But McGann, like McKenzie, chooses to regard analytical bibliography as somehow inimical to history, as something now superseded by the "return to history" that has resulted from the sociological approach.[22]

22. McGann, following McKenzie, pairs the New Criticism with analytical bibliography (the "New Bibliography"), calling them, respectively, "versions of hermeneutical idealism and textual positivism" (p. 20, col. 2). Analytical bibliography may be considered positivistic, but not textually so. Nevertheless, McGann's succinct characterizations are more reasonable than McKenzie's strained comparison of the two. Analytical bibliography and the New Criticism, McKenzie believes, share a "view of the self-sufficient nature of the work of art or text" and "showed great ingenuity in discerning patterns" without concern for "precedent or subsequent processes" (p. 7). It is true of neither the New Criticism nor analytical bibliography that they have no regard for "precedent" (that is, history). In the case of analytical bibliography, Bowers, for one, emphasized what he called the "postulate of normality" in interpreting bibliographical evidence: that is, one must examine the evidence from a given piece of printing in the light of what is presently accepted—on the

In the course of his comments on critical editions, McGann cites "the excellent recent edition of *Ulysses* edited by Hans Gabler";[23] he had earlier written at length about this edition in an essay entitled "*Ulysses* as a Postmodern Text: The Gabler Edition,"[24] which offers further opportunity for examining his position on textual matters. The title under which he later collected the essay, "*Ulysses* as a Postmodern Work," is misleading, for it is not *Ulysses* but Gabler's edition of *Ulysses* (1984) that he sees as a "postmodern" work. The 1922 first edition is the "appropriate modernist *Ulysses*," whereas Gabler's *Ulysses* explains the work to us in "a peculiarly appropriate postmodern form" (p. 192). What makes it "postmodern" is its "synoptic text" (Gabler's term), full of variant readings and symbols aimed at showing the compositional development of the work. According to McGann this text is "distinctly postmodern" because "the style is impersonal and maintained in a surface mode ('languaged'); the procedure is intertextual and self-referencing; the form of order is stochastic" (p. 189). To the extent that this

basis of previous investigations—as the normal practice for the period or shop involved (see *Bibliography and Textual Criticism* [1964], pp. 64–77). As for the New Criticism, Cleanth Brooks says in the preface to *The Well Wrought Urn* (1947), a book often considered the epitome of the New Criticism, "If literary history has not been emphasized in the pages that follow, it is not because I discount its importance, or because I have failed to take it into account" (p. x); and in an appendix (after the body of the book has taken up a series of poems from Donne to Yeats in chronological order) he says, "I certainly have not meant to imply that the poet does not inherit his ideas, his literary concepts, his rhythms, his literary forms" (p. 197).

23. He quotes McKenzie's statement that the new edition could not "represent the physical form of *Ulysses* as it was first published." Then, after summarizing McKenzie's presentation of information provided by John Kidd, he observes, "This limitation turns out to be an important one, because Joyce appears to have used the page sequences and lay-out of the 1922 edition as part of the work's semiotic system" (p. 21, col. 3). According to McGann's theory of reading, however, would not such a limitation be important in any historical study, whether or not the author is known to have made use of the physical details of bookmaking?

24. *Criticism*, 27 (1985), 283–305; reprinted, with slight revisions and a new title ("*Ulysses* as a Postmodern Work"), in his *Social Values and Poetic Acts: The Historical Judgment of Literary Work* (1988), pp. 173–194. The latter text is cited here. My comments below on the Gabler edition are limited to points raised by McGann. For a detailed criticism of the Gabler edition, see John Kidd, "An Inquiry into *Ulysses: The Corrected Text*," *PBSA*, 82 (1988), 411–584. And for accounts of the much-publicized controversy over the Gabler edition, initiated by Kidd, see Robin Bates's "Reflections on the Kidd Era," *Studies in the Novel*, 22 (1990), 119–141, and two essays by Charles Rossman, also in *Studies in the Novel*, "The Critical Reception of the 'Gabler *Ulysses*': Or, Gabler's *Ulysses* Kidd-napped" (21 [1989], 154–181), and a sequel to be published in the fall 1990 number. Examples of the way in which the Gabler edition (as well as McGann's view of it) has prompted discussion of textual theory in general are Ira B. Nadel's "Textual Criticism, Literary Theory and the New *Ulysses*," in *Assessing the 1984 "Ulysses"*, ed. C. George Sandulescu and Clive Hart (1986), pp. 122–139; Patrick McGee's "Is There a Class for This Text? The New *Ulysses*, Jerome McGann and the Issue of Textual Authority," *Works and Days*, 5, no. 2 (1987), 27–44; and McGee's "The Error of Theory," *Studies in the Novel*, 22 (1990), 148–162.

characterization is accurate, it can be applied to any editorial apparatus (a point to which I shall return).[25] However "postmodern" the edition may be, one may wonder why it interests McGann, for Gabler's aim is to trace the history of the composition of the work, and thus the focus is on Joyce as author, not on the collaborative forces of the production process. But McGann does look at the edition itself as the product of a particular set of social forces: Joyce's text, he says, is "enmeshed within an editorial network" that reflects two sets of "determinants"—the viewpoint of "an internationally mobile scholar," with training at Virginia and access to computer facilities at Tübingen, and "the institutional history of Joyce scholarship up to the present time." The form of the edition "replicates the conditions of its production," and its details are "no less than a coded set of interpretive clues for understanding, and using, the work" (p. 188). This observation does not, however, provide a reason for singling out Gabler's edition, since any edition can be approached in this way. McGann himself immediately says, "The same is of course true for other literary works, whose meanings are a function of their material, institutional, and social histories."[26]

One must therefore look elsewhere for the distinctiveness of the Gabler edition, for the reason to discuss it in the context of those scholarly works that "immediately establish themselves as epochal events" or in relation to the "few seminal works" of modern textual study (p. 173). To say that the Gabler edition ought to be "a required object of study for every scholar working in English literature" (p. 174)[27] necessitates noting those features that set it apart from other editions. McGann's aim, accordingly, is "an exploration of the general methodological significance of the edition in its immediate historical context." The significances he points out can be summarized under four heads: (1) Gabler's focus on the composition process; (2) his handling of copy-text; (3) his

25. McGann also says that "Gabler's edition calls attention to a peculiar generic quality of modernist [postmodernist?] writing: that its subject is often the act and process of writing itself" (p. 182). But all editions with apparatus recording authorial revisions call attention to "the act and process of writing."

26. His switch to "literary works" here—when he had been talking about an edition of a work—is perhaps meant to suggest that the "work" is inseparable from the apparatus in which it is "enmeshed" in a given edition, the two becoming a single new entity.

27. And, he says, the availability of many documents in published facsimile (such as The James Joyce Archive and the Rosenbach facsimile) "has made it possible for any student anywhere in the world to follow Gabler's work in the most minute and exacting detail" (p. 174). That no facsimile can ever be trusted to this extent is set forth in my "Reproductions and Scholarship," SB, 42 (1989), 25–54, which includes some comment on the deficiencies of the Joyce facsimiles and on Gabler's excessive reliance on those facsimiles (p. 32). John Kidd (see note 24 above) has discussed this matter in detail (pp. 433–448); and Gabler's admission that he did not fully collate his transcription against the Rosenbach original appears in Robin Bates's article (also cited in note 24 above).

deployment of apparatus; and (4) the implications of the edition for critical analysis. In each of these areas McGann's reasoning is faulty, and in none of them does he succeed in showing how Gabler's edition is distinctive. His analysis does not finally serve to clarify the details of his "sociohistorical empiric" (p. 186).

As for the first matter—the focus on Joyce's composition—McGann appears to imply that Gabler's emphasis on distinguishing evidence of composition from evidence of transmission is a distinctive feature of the edition and thus is somehow different from what intentionalist editors have traditionally done. But there is nothing new, for example, in saying that "Joyce is sometimes merely his own scribe, a textual transmitter and not a textual maker" (p. 177); this statement is simply another way of saying that editors must be critical even of texts in the author's hand, since the author, like anyone else, can make mistakes in writing. McGann quotes, evidently with approval, Gabler's operational distinction between "documents of composition," in which " 'the text is held to possess full authority, unless it can be shown to be faulty,' " and "documents of transmission," in which " 'the text is held to be potentially faulty, unless it can be proved to possess authority' " (pp. 176–177). Gabler recognizes here that the texts of individual documents are often unlikely to be either exclusively compositional or exclusively transmissional.[28] But the lack of parallelism in the two parts of the statement ("to possess full authority, unless . . ." versus "to be potentially faulty, unless . . .") leads one to see that in fact the texts of both categories of document are potentially faulty and must be questioned at every point. The two-part classification of documents is more a hindrance than a help, since the texts of extant documents are unlikely to correspond exactly to stages of textual development: a single extant document may contain the only surviving clues to several compositional and transmissional stages of the text. In order to associate such stages with discrete documents, Gabler is sometimes led to citing hypothetical lost documents, containing in Joyce's hand the authoritative revisions that appear in extant transmissional documents (not in his hand). But having admitted that Joyce himself can be at times only a transmitter rather than a creator, Gabler cannot by this maneuver realistically postulate lost documents that are entirely compositional—and therefore it is hard to see how this approach is more than a confused way of stating

28. As he also does elsewhere. For example: "Since by their autograph overlay the typescripts and proofs partially acquire the status of documents of composition, the question arises of how far the authorial presence affects, and penetrates, their basic level of transmissional transcription" (p. 1893). This statement describes an issue that editors have always dealt with; Gabler's classification of typewritten and printed documents as essentially transmissional, however, proves to be an impediment to a clear exposition of the issue.

what editors have always understood. They have always assumed, of necessity, that some of the readings in extant documents first appeared in documents now lost. What else could editors focusing on authorial intention have done but to extract from extant documents the evidence for understanding the compositional history of a work? McGann's discussion actually adds some confusion not present in Gabler;[29] but what is more significant is that it fails to show how Gabler has made any new contribution to textual theory or practice in his concept of compositional and transmissional documents.

Regarding copy-text, McGann says that "the problem of copytext in this edition focuses attention upon everything in the edition which is most interesting and important" (p. 178). Despite his own misunderstanding of the concept as conventionally used,[30] McGann does see that Gabler's usage is unconventional, since in the *Ulysses* edition "copytext" means the eclectic text that Gabler has constructed, not the documentary text (or texts) serving as the basis for that construction. This pointless shift in definition cannot be what is important, however. Presumably what is claimed to be significant is the way in which Gabler has gone about constructing his "continuous manuscript text." McGann seems to think that the existence of a plethora of prepublication documents—a common situation for twentieth-century authors—necessitates a new editorial goal: "Whereas critical editors of earlier works tried to reconstitute some (now lost) state of the text—ideally, the earliest

29. A primary instance is McGann's contradictory description, within the space of one page (p. 176), of the authority of the 1922 first edition. He first notes that Gabler places the 1922 readings in the historical collation, not in the synoptic text, because "the first edition is prima facie a part of the 'full record of corruption' "; half a page later he calls the first edition "the 'ultimate stage of compositional development.' " The latter phrase is quoted out of context from Gabler and produces an inconsistency that was not present in Gabler's discussion: Gabler said, "The first edition admittedly represents the closest approximation to be found in one document of the work at its ultimate stage of compositional development" (p. 1894). Another misleading statement of McGann's is the following: "Because Gabler wants to assemble a text of the work's compositional development . . . and because he regards the act of composition as an entirely isolated and personal affair, he always sets a privilege on autograph manuscript texts. The typescripts, the proofs, and the first edition involve the intervention of other, purely *transmissive* authorities, and hence they fall outside the process of compositional development" (p. 177). This way of summarizing Gabler's procedure does not allow, as Gabler does, for the use of such documents as proofs and published editions as evidence of authorial revision in lost documents.

30. McGann's explanation of the "usual understanding" never mentions the distinction between substantives and accidentals and defines copy-text simply as "what an editor chooses to take as the text of highest presumptive authority" (p. 177); he thus ignores, in what he calls "the post-Greg context," Greg's primary contribution, the suggestion that one text may serve as the primary source for accidentals, another for substantives. Gabler's understanding of copy-text is similarly skewed: "By common consent, an editor chooses as the copytext for a critical edition a document text of highest overall authority" (p. 184). Greg's point was that no single document might have "overall authority."

possible or 'original' text—critical editors of modern works are already in possession of the kind of 'original' text which those other editors were trying to recover" (p. 179). Critical editors of earlier works, however, do not necessarily focus on "the earliest possible or 'original' text"; critical editors of later works, even when they have the author's fair-copy manuscript, still have to determine how it relates in every detail to the author's intention, if that is what they are interested in; and critical editors of all works seek to reconstruct the texts of works as they stood at particular past moments, texts that can never be assumed to coincide with those of any surviving documents. McGann is nevertheless correct in pointing out that the text Gabler arrives at by building up a text from a succession of prepublication documents is different from "a fully and systematically corrected edition of 1922" (p. 180): whenever any variants are regarded as indifferent, the choice of copy-text (in the conventional sense) determines some features of the critical text. But McGann's distinction between these two approaches to the choice of copy-text is puzzling:

> Gabler's is an imagination of Joyce's work and not its reconstitution. Gabler invents, by a process of brilliant editorial reconstruction, *Joyce's Ulysses* (as it were), a work that existed, if it ever existed at all, for Joyce the writer rather than Joyce the author. Gabler's edition does not give us the work which Joyce wanted to present to the public; rather, it gives us a text in which we may observe Joyce at work, alone, before he turns to meet his public. (p. 181)[31]

In the first place, critical editors—by definition—always produce an "imagination" or a "reconstruction" of a past text. Furthermore, is not the distinction between "Joyce the writer" and "Joyce the author" a way of talking about two kinds of intention? Editors have regularly distinguished between an author's prepublication or private or artistic in-

31. A few pages earlier, McGann had described Gabler's text as "the work of *Ulysses* as Joyce actually produced it in a continuous act of writing and rewriting" (p. 175). The word "actually" does not allow for the role of judgment and conjecture involved in producing "an imagination of Joyce's work" (or in imagining "a continuous act of writing and rewriting")—or, indeed, in preparing any critical edition. Furthermore, McGann should have questioned whether it is proper to imagine all intended readings as having appeared in Joyce's hand—that is, whether it is proper to imagine lost documents that present Joyce's intended readings without error. It is always possible that some intended readings may never have appeared in the author's hand (such as a typist's or printer's correction of an author's slip of the pen). Gabler is therefore holding an untenable position when he says that "the final state of the text's development is considered reached when it is last fully and correctly written out in the author's hand" (p. 1901). Given Gabler's focus on intended texts abstracted from documents, he is free to emend errors in extant documents and to imagine the *intended* texts of inferred documents; but he cannot claim that such intended texts were always "fully and correctly written out in the author's hand." His tying of intended readings to handwriting, and thus to documents (whether extant or inferred), is a central weakness of his whole approach.

tention and an author's more inclusive intention that incorporates various ways of accommodating the expectations or demands of others in the publication process. The two kinds of intention may indeed imply different choices of copy-text, but not necessarily; only the editor's judgment in assessing the nature of the surviving materials and the author's working habits can lead to a decision about copy-text (which may of course be a decision to choose different copy-texts for different parts of a work). McGann has not demonstrated that Gabler's treatment of copy-text is "interesting and important," if by that he means that it pushes forward our thinking about the concept.

McGann makes even higher claims for Gabler's presentation of textual evidence in the form of a "synoptic text" that incorporates the compositional variants, coded with diacritical marks and symbols. Gabler himself declared, "As a form of apparatus to be read and used as a text, the synoptic presentation of *Ulysses* in progress from manuscript to print is the innovative feature of this edition" (p. 1901). McGann goes further and says that Gabler's synoptic text "completely overhauls *the way we might think about the text as a whole*" (p. 181, italics his): by giving "priority of importance" to the synoptic text as a text for "seriatim reading" (p. 175), Gabler shows what is "entailed in the idea of textual instability" and allows a "number of different *Ulysses* . . . to occupy the space of critical possibility" (p. 181). There are no grounds for regarding Gabler's edition as pioneering in this respect, since an "inclusive" apparatus (incorporated in a running text) has been used by many editors to show manuscript revisions; the 1962 edition of *Billy Budd, Sailor*, edited by Harrison Hayford and Merton M. Sealts, Jr., is a famous earlier example of a genetic text accompanied by a reading text.[32] Whether Gabler's approach to apparatus is innovative is less significant in any case than the general question of what this kind of apparatus accomplishes. McGann's view at the time of this essay was apparently that the placement of superseded variants in a running text gives them greater prominence and offers the reader a better sense of the instability of texts. But everything that he says about Gabler's synoptic text could be applied as well to the kind of apparatus in which variants are listed at the foot of a page or the end of a text. Gabler's diacritics he calls "a grammar of an artificial language" (p. 181), and he believes that, when we have mastered it, "we shall have gone a long way toward understanding the nature of texts in general" (p. 182). The "surrounding diacritics"

---

32. In the case of *Billy Budd, Sailor* there is only one manuscript to report, but it is a complicated manuscript showing many revisions that reflect several stages of composition. On the differing significance of inclusive apparatus in a transcription of one document and a consolidated record of multiple documents, see note 91 below.

emphasize the "fragility" of the text, in which "one reading is marginalized by another"; we are "made conscious that this text is to be fundamentally characterized as a thing of many real and concrete details which are, at the same time, extremely fragile, and put together in strange, stochastic orderings" (p. 191). The alternative system of reporting variants in footnotes or lists is also a "language," and when its conventions are mastered it tells us the same things. Variants placed in a running text are not necessarily more prominent, or easier to read in context, than those placed elsewhere: it is all a matter of becoming familiar with a set of conventions. That McGann may have come to this opinion is suggested in his review of McKenzie when he includes critical editions among the productions that encourage "radial" reading, the reading of several versions of a work simultaneously. It is clear that he is not thinking only of editions with genetic texts because he describes how "one moves around the edition, jumping from the reading text to the apparatus, perhaps from one of these to the notes or to an appendix, perhaps then back to some part of the front matter which may be relevant, and so forth" (p. 21).[33] This positive description of how a critical edition "allows one to imagine many possible states of the text" makes admirably clear the way in which an appended apparatus can be just as stimulating and productive an aid to reading as an inclusive apparatus is. Gabler's *Ulysses*, then, is not particularly significant for its handling of apparatus.

Finally, McGann stresses one particular critical implication that he finds in the Gabler edition. He argues that those critics who see textual meaning as the product of readers are not inclined to be concerned with the kind of textual indeterminacy that arises from the existence of variant documents. They see texts as "angelic rather than human" (p. 185), as having an ideal existence apart from physical embodiments. If we view them as human products, however,

the interpretive act "constitutes meaning" (as we now say) only in terms that are licensed by the received sociohistory of the text. And that sociohistory, for *texts*, is constituted at its most elementary level as a set of empirical documents whose meaning is intimately bound up with the sociohistory of the documents. (p. 185)

33. More recently still, McGann has advocated a form of edition consisting of a printed reading text accompanied by a computer disk containing "the electronic hypertext"—that is, a record of all variants, accessible "through hypertext programs which would enable the reader to reconstruct any state of any particular text, and to organize those particular texts into any form or order within themselves or in relation to each other" ("Which Yeats Edition?", *TLS*, 11–17 May 1990, pp. 493–494). Although he does not use the term "radial reading" in this review, a computerized apparatus would clearly facilitate such reading.

McGann is making a valuable point if he is saying that reader-response critics overlook an important factor in readers' production of meaning when they do not take into account the physical features of documents. But how he wishes to link this observation, or some such observation, to the Gabler edition is not clear. "Gabler's edition," he says, "helps one to see the formal limits which always constrain the generation of texts" (p. 182). These "formal limits," this "sociohistory of the documents," cannot have much to do with the formal arrangement of text on pages or with the physical appearance of the documents, for the amount of information on such matters to be derived from the Gabler edition is not extensive (nor is it from any edition without facsimiles). We are left, then, with the text itself, encompassing alterations within individual documents and variants between one document and another; and if McGann is merely saying that the Gabler edition reports such alterations and variants, he is not distinguishing it from hundreds of other editions. "What Gabler's edition shows," he tries to explain, "is that unstable 'texts'—texts that are 'in process' or 'indeterminate'—always appear in material forms that are as determinate as the most 'stable' text one might want to imagine" (p. 186). But it is not true that texts "always appear in material forms": some texts exist only in the mind, and others have a public existence only in oral recitation. Furthermore, documents that no longer exist did have determinate texts when they existed, but their texts can now only be conjectured—and are therefore indeterminate, since no reconstruction can be certain. It is thus hard to see how McGann is stating anything more than the obvious fact that the texts of extant documents are determinate. His aim of incorporating the study of those documents within the process of literary criticism is laudable; but curiously his way of pursuing the point seems to reinforce the old separation of textual from literary criticism by suggesting that textual criticism and analytical bibliography set limits to be followed subsequently by literary criticism. Bibliographical analysis of a given document can indeed set limits on conjectures about the production of that document and hence sometimes about how the text of the document came to be what it is; but such analysis cannot operate on nonexistent documents, and any facts it seems to have established regarding extant documents cannot limit the emendations that may be proposed for reconstructing a text that does not at present exist. This limit is set by the informed judgment of the individual doing the reconstructing, and interpretation is thus tied to textual criticism in a more basic way than McGann's essay manages to make clear.[34] Gabler's edition is in any case

34. I am not claiming that McGann does not understand this point but that his prose fails to convey it.

no more appropriate for illustrating this line of argument than any other edition that records variant readings; indeed, it may be particularly inappropriate, for its citation of inferred documents as sources of readings de-emphasizes the distinction between existent and conjectured texts as underpinnings for critical editing.

McGann's discussions of Gabler and McKenzie offered two natural opportunities for him to clarify what was left confused in the *Critique*. But neither essay makes matters clearer, except possibly at one point: in the Gabler piece, he says that " 'genetic' texts . . . may be conceived either as mirrors of composition or mirrors of production" (p. 182). If this statement indicates a recognition that authorial intention and the results of the collaborative process of production are two independent (and in most instances mutually exclusive) goals of critical editing, it would mark a significant advance over the thinking reflected in the *Critique*. The statement in fact still displays some confusion by making " 'genetic' texts" rather than so-called reading texts its subject: the choices entailed in producing a clear (i.e., "reading") text cannot normally accommodate both goals simultaneously, but a "genetic" apparatus can be constructed to do so. Possibly McGann would have made this point if he had written the Gabler essay after the McKenzie review, where his account of apparatus seems more in line with it. But no further clarifications, so far as I am aware, have appeared in his other recent pieces on textual criticism,[35] although in a 1986 interview he explicitly amplified the *Critique* by accepting authorial intention as one of the editorial goals that can emerge from a study of the full compositional and production history of a work.[36] This development in his thinking

35. Such as two slight pieces for the Society for Textual Scholarship. The first, "Interpretation, Meaning, and Textual Criticism: A Homily," sums up his "socio-historical" approach to textual scholarship in terms of a "schematic outline" moving from the "originary textual moment" to the "immediate moment of textual criticism," via a series of "secondary moments of textual production and reproduction" (*Text*, 3 [1987], 55–62). The second, "The Textual Condition," restates his plea for "bringing about an end to the schism in literary studies" between textual and literary criticism (*Text*, 4 [1988], 29–37). One of his main points in the latter piece cannot be too often emphasied: "Scholarship is interpretation, whether it is carried out as a bibliocritical discourse or a literary exegesis" (p. 37).

36. The interview, effectively conducted by David Gorman in the fall of 1986, was published the next year as "An Interview with Jerome McGann on Textual Scholarship as Literary History and Ideology Critique," *Social Epistemology*, 1 (1987), 163–173 (see p. 165). His point here has a different emphasis (as he recognizes) from his statement in the *Critique* that author's intentions are "only one of many factors to be taken into account" and that they may sometimes "determine the final decision" (p. 128); cf. my discussion of this statement in *SB*, 39 (1986), 22–25 [130–133]. (McGann's awareness, in the interview, of "the possibility of different kinds of editions for different works and authors" is welcome, but how it "moves against certain currently dominant views and procedures in editorial method" is unclear.) Later, in the preface to *Towards a Literature of Knowledge* (1989), McGann speaks of "the network of intentionalities which constitute the field of the social text," a

is welcome because it will make more coherent his argument for an inclusive conception of textual criticism. Up to now, his effectiveness has been seriously undercut by a lack of rigorous thought, at least as reflected in his often careless prose. He has nevertheless played an important role in recent years by causing more textual critics than ever before to pay attention to other goals for critical editing than the construction of authorially intended texts and thus to define their activities in relation to a broad range of critical endeavor.

III

McGann's interest in Gabler's approach to editing illustrates how the genetic aspects of textual study can be seen to reinforce, and be congruent with, a sociological view of literary history. How authors inscribe and revise their private manuscripts can reveal their attitudes to the public world of literary publishing. The pre-publication growth of a work through various textual stages reflects the same openness and instability that are seen in the post-publication vicissitudes of texts; and every text, whether in an author's manuscript or a published edition, is obviously the product of a set of sociohistorical forces. Gabler sees his own work as growing out of a German and French movement that emphasizes the study of authors' manuscripts and the process of composition. Several European textual critics of this general orientation are becoming better known in the English-speaking world through the recent publication of some of their papers in English translation (although an essay by Hans Zeller, editor [1958–   ] of C. F. Meyer, has been available in English since 1975).[37] Through Gabler's efforts, this movement was well represented at a Charlottesville conference in April 1985 honoring Fredson Bowers on his eightieth birthday, and a few days later some of the same speakers participated in the biennial conference of the Society for Textual Scholarship in New York. As a result, eight papers by six French and German scholars appeared in the 1987 volume of *Text* and the 1988 volume of *Studies in Bibliography* (those from the

"field of intentions" made up of various "intentional structures or agents," none of which "will ever be equal to the entire set" (p. x); but he does not in this context comment on the editorial possibilities of focusing on particular intentional agents.

37. "A New Approach to the Critical Constitution of Literary Texts," *SB*, 28 (1975), 231–264. Zeller's emphasis on the integrity of every "version" of a work is linked with a social view of literary production: he believes that "uninfluenced artistic intentions" (p. 248) cannot be separated from the "play of forces from all sides" on the author (p. 244)—"the magnetic needle of the author's wishes is quivering in the field of non-aesthetic forces" (p. 245). I have commented on Zeller's article in "Problems and Accomplishments in the Editing of the Novel," *Studies in the Novel*, 7 (1975), 323–360 (see pp. 329–331) and more briefly in *SB*, 34 (1981), 30–31 [72–73].

STS conference in the former, the Charlottesville conference in the latter).[38]

Gabler's own contribution[39] makes no advance over his 1981 paper that set forth the rationale for his synoptic text of *Ulysses*,[40] but it does contain some sentences that concisely capture the underlying tenets of this approach. For example: "A work revised in successive stages signals the author's free intentional choices at any given textual stage, and the aggregate of stages may justifiably be considered to embody his final intentions with regard to the work as a whole" (p. 110). Thus "authorial rejection cannot be equated with editorial rejection" (p. 110): "The text in the determinate record of its instability falls to the editor therefore not for the fulfillment of its real or assumed teleology, but for the description and analysis of its documentary existence" (p. 111). Any apparatus of variants, of course, provides an account of documentary evidence, and Gabler's essential complaint about what he calls "the conventional model of the critical edition" is that its apparatus subordinates the genetic record to a "stable reading text of unquestioned privilege" (p. 107). Although some editors have no doubt been so foolish as to think that their critical texts commanded "unquestioned privilege," most editors—having laboriously worked through all the documentary evidence—recognize that any clear reading text is only one of the texts that can be derived from the evidence. And surely, after going to great pains to record variant readings, their intention is not to "annihilate" them—though Gabler believes that "What is near-to-annihilated . . . in the established critical edition is the superseded authorial variant, relegated as it is to apparatus lists in footnotes or at the back of the book, together with the bulk of rejected transmissional errors" (pp. 109–110). As in his earlier piece, Gabler reduces an interesting conceptual question—the nature of texts as reflections of works in process—to the practical level of methodology for reporting evidence. Some forms of apparatus may be better than others in certain situations, but the decision to record variants in appended lists does not imply that genetic study is unimportant. A more basic flaw, however, is Gabler's failure to distinguish clearly between texts of extant documents and stages in the development of a work. He does recognize that authorial revisions "leave a record when, though only in so far as, committed to paper"—and, he should have added, not all such pieces of paper have survived. But he

38. For the literature of this general movement, see (in addition to the editions referred to below) the documentation to Hurlebusch's *SB* essay (note 43 below).

39. "The Text as Process and the Problem of Intentionality," *Text*, 3 (1987), 107–116.

40. "The Synchrony and Diachrony of Texts: Practice and Theory in the Critical Edition of James Joyce's *Ulysses*," *Text*, 1 (1984 for 1981), 305–326; I have commented on this essay in *SB*, 39 (1986), 37–39 [145–147].

still can say that textual instability is, for the editor, "determinate," being "confined within the complex, yet closed system of the words and signs on paper" (p. 111). This statement can mean nothing more than the obvious point that editors with a historical orientation are not free (as authors are) to put whatever words they like into a text. It does not illuminate the imaginative role of the historical scholar in reconstructing from fragmentary physical evidence the growth of a work in an intangible medium.

Somewhat more useful as an introduction to *critique génétique* (as this approach has come to be called in France) are two essays by Louis Hay, founder of l'Institut des Textes et Manuscrits Modernes in Paris.[41] The one in *Text* sketches the history of modern editing in Germany and France, noting that "editing has always embodied the main ideological and cultural concerns of its day" (p. 117), and concentrates on the last half-century, when the attention has been on "a new kind of scholarly object: the text as it grows" (p. 118). Hay cites some illustrative editions, beginning with Friedrich Beissner's (1943–62) of Hölderlin, and describes a growing interest in the technology of examining manuscripts; but he leaves for his essay in *Studies in Bibliography* any real speculation about the nature of texts as implied by this work. That *SB* essay conveys some sense of the excitement experienced by this group of scholars as they began to explore the "avant-texte," the "pre-text"—that is, the versions preceding the published one.[42] But it is finally unsatisfactory in its attempt to explain the theoretical foundation of genetic criticism. Answering the question of his title, "Does 'Text' Exist?", obviously involves distinguishing various concepts of "text," and the question is of course meant to suggest that "text" as a fixed entity does not exist; but no clear concept of "text" emerges. Despite Hay's recognition (p. 69) that "The ink on the page is not the writing itself" (meaning, presumably, that texts of documents are not texts of works or versions of works), his discussion does not seem firmly grounded in this important distinction. "Pre-text," on which genetic critics focus, leads up to "text," which "is considered achieved when published," for "the author's intention . . . becomes manifest in the act of publication" (p. 71); even rough

---

41. "Does 'Text' Exist?", *SB*, 41 (1988), 64–76; "Genetic Editing, Past and Future: A Few Reflections by a User," *Text*, 3 (1987), 117–133.

42. After mentioning the varieties of apparatus employed by these scholars to show both "the genesis in its process and the final state of the text," Hay makes an odd observation: "they all mark their distance from the traditional apparatus of variants, abandoning the viewpoint of pure erudition for the problematic of the pre-text" (p. 70). The original French does say "l'érudition pure"; apparently "érudition" here carries the sense not of learning but of established and incontrovertible fact. See p. 152 of " 'Le texte n'éxiste pas': Réflexions sur la critique génétique," *Poétique*, 62 (April 1985), 147–158.

drafts can be promoted from "pre-text" to "text" by being published
(p. 72). This distinction seems superficial, for the act of publication does
not change the ontological status of physical texts; the texts of all documents, unpublished or published, may equally fail to reflect accurately
the intangible works of language that they purport to represent. In analyzing two versions of Paul Éluard's poem that became "Liberté," he
says that the "first, distinct work was one of the *possibilities* of the text,
though it was neither integrated nor subsumed in the second work. . . .
Perhaps we should consider the text as *a necessary possibility*, as one
manifestation of a process which is always virtually present in the background" (p. 75, italics his). The shifting meanings of "text" here (and
its unclear relation to "work") are symptomatic of the lack of sharp
focus throughout.

A similar slipperiness in the handling of concepts mars the two essays by Klaus Hurlebusch, coeditor of the Hamburg Klopstock edition
(1974–   ).[43] The far more substantial piece, in *Studies in Bibliography*,
attempts to contrast two "editorial concepts" that reflect two opposing
views of authorship, growing out of "the fundamental conflict between
an individual and a social identity" (p. 102). One concept, "reception-
oriented," regards the author as a "community being" (p. 125), primarily
concerned with a finished, public product to be received by readers; it
results in editions that emphasize an established text over an apparatus
of variants. The other, "production-oriented," sees the author as principally engaged in personal expression, developing ideas "as independently as possible of considerations for others, of readers' expectations"
(p. 124); it results in editions that emphasize genetic process. In the
former, "what the author ultimately intends is an imagined and affirm-
able idea of himself as a person, in relation to which his creative ability
of expression is secondary"; in the latter, "the identity of the author
whose perceptions continually change finds expression not so much in
the work as in the *process* of perception, i.e., the author's working
procedure" (pp. 122–123).[44] Hurlebusch is struggling here with a di-

43. "Conceptualisations for Procedures of Authorship," *SB*, 41 (1988), 100–135; " 'Relic'
and 'Tradition': Some Aspects of Editing Diaries," *Text*, 3 (1987), 143–153.

44. He offers two very different examples of the former category. Unquestionably the
selective recording of variants in the Weimar Goethe edition (1887–1919) reflects a lack
of concern for genetic study. But Friedrich Beissner's edition (1943–62) of Hölderlin contains detailed records of manuscript variants, and Hurlebusch places it in this category
because "the author is still granted the decision how his works are to be read" (p. 111), with
a final alteration "not seen as the last of several textual options, but as the 'only possible
form' or the 'consummate form' of expression" (p. 113). Hurlebusch regards Beissner's
presentation of a text representing the author's final intention as a sign of his subordination
of genetic process, despite the thorough genetic record. Karl Goedeke's edition of Schiller
(1867–76), on the other hand, is considered a "production-oriented" edition, even though

chotomy that all editors must give thought to, but his formulation of it is not helpful. For one thing, it assumes a sharp and recognizable distinction between "the productive function of writing" and "the revisional one" (p. 123), as if the operation of a "writer activating his powers" (p. 122) is separate from that of a writer engaging in the "redaction and revision of his own texts" (p. 125)—and as if revision is to be equated with a move towards conventional expression. Furthermore, it assumes that, after authors are classified according to this distinction (Hölderlin, for example, being "a primarily text-producing author" [p. 123]), the editorial emphasis to be accorded them follow naturally.[45] There is no recognition that every author may legitimately and usefully be provided both with critical editions (containing critically constructed texts, with records, however presented, of variant readings) and with reproductions of documents. Hurlebusch makes a strong case for the importance of some authors' manuscripts as visual objects, every detail of which is reflective of the creative process; but he does not indicate that all manuscripts can be approached in this way, even those by "reception-oriented" authors.[46] In addition, his comments on intention, like Hay's, fail to make careful discriminations. Authorial intention sometimes seems to mean intention to publish: "If the author has actually . . . released the contents and textual composition from his control and submitted it to . . . a publisher's, . . . it is true to say that this version is intended by the author" (p. 109). But then we are told that "every

---

its apparatus (like Beissner's) presents manuscript variants "according to the pattern of the apparatus criticus in classical philology" (p. 115), because the main text in each instance is the earliest one and the aim of the edition is to provide "a history of Schiller's mind" (p. 114). Hurlebusch sensibly does not make the form of the apparatus the determining characteristic here; but he might have noted that Beissner was not slighting the composition process simply because he wished to offer readers a text reflecting the author's final intention, for his edition illustrates how a study of the genetic record is essential to the construction (and critical reading) of such a text.

45. For example, he concludes his section on "reception-oriented" editions in this way: "As long as there are authors who sufficiently clearly lay down their decisions on the versions in which they wish their texts to be read, and as long as there are readers willing to submit their souls to authorial guidance, this editorial concept cannot be considered outdated" (p. 114). But an editor's decision to aim at an authorially intended text is independent of the degree to which the author has made the task easier—and, in any case, critical editors must evaluate for themselves every purported authorial decision (as must critical readers, even if they ultimately wish to "submit their souls to authorial guidance"). An "editorial concept" is valid or invalid (not "outdated") according to its own logic and coherence; it may fall out of favor (and seem "outdated"), however, as fashions in critical approaches to literature shift.

46. He invents an unnecessary dilemma when he asks, "Are they ['the writers' working procedures'] of interest merely by their workshop handling of texts and variants, and not also as the author's medium of expression?" (p. 124). That he sees these two as separable is shown by his answering the question affirmatively in regard to alterations that can be classified as "revision" (rather than "production" or creation).

state of a text . . . only represents the intended state *as a whole*, and not *in every detail*" (p. 110). It is hard to see how such a distinction can be productive, since textual intention must always be concerned with textual details and since any "state of a text" is given its character, "as a whole," by those same details. His other essay, an insignificant piece in *Text* on editing diaries, furthers the reader's puzzlement by observations that seem out of line with this essay.[47] One has to conclude that Hurlebusch, though clearly of a conceptualizing turn of mind, has been presented to English-speaking readers in essays that do not demonstrate clarity of thought and do not advance editorial theory regarding the nature of authorship.

Of the remaining three papers in this group of translations from European textual critics, the one by Gerhard Neumann, one of the editors of the Kafka edition (1982–   ), should be touched on here, for its concluding paragraphs serve to epitomize some of the conceptual problems common to the whole group.[48] After explaining how Kafka was a writer torn between the desire for intimate self-expression and the desire for public recognition, he sets forth "three fundamental concepts which all bear on what we have to understand by 'text' in the modern situation" (p. 98): "script," "work," and "a 'fluid composite' which is never wholly the one nor the other." "Script" (or "writing") reflects "the flow of creativity"; "work" reflects "the area of 'authorship' as an institution and the communicative function of literature as a social phenomenon"; and the "fluid composite" reflects the "intertextuality" that results from placing particular "textual units" in different arrangements and collections. It seems unwise to use the word "work" to refer to published texts (imputing to what an author publishes an unwarranted degree of tex-

47. He asserts, for example, that diaries "must be edited in a way which preserves their individuality and uniqueness as documents of non-intended transmission while maintaining as far as possible the conventions of text rendering and readability which belong to the area of 'tradition' documents" (p. 146). (A "tradition" document, in his terminology, contains a text intended for publication; a "relic" document contains a text not intended for publication.) Or again: "the task of the editor is twofold: on the one hand, he has to preserve the nature of the document and, on the other, he must present a readable text" (p. 148). The quite proper emphasis in the *SB* essay on the importance of the physical features and idiosyncrasies of private documents would seem to make the "conventions of text rendering and readability" irrelevant.

48. "Script, Work and Published Form: Franz Kafka's Incomplete Text," *SB*, 41 (1988), 77–99. The other two essays are Jean-Louis Lebrave's "Rough Drafts: A Challenge to Uniformity in Editing," *Text*, 3 (1987), 135–142; and Siegfried Scheibe's "Some Notes on Letter Editions: With Special Reference to German Writers," *SB*, 41 (1988), 136–148. Lebrave, who is working on computer systems for analyzing manuscript variants in Heine, believes that standard approaches to recording variants do not facilitate the analysis of the "genetic memory" (p. 135) embedded in rough drafts and other *avant-textes*. Scheibe, an editor of Goethe, Georg Forster, and Christian Gellert, discusses general guidelines for determining the contents of editions of letters.

tual authority); but Neumann's usage stems from the same tendency observed in the other writers to exaggerate the finality conferred by authorized publication and to compartmentalize creativity in the pre-publication stages—a tendency to stress the author's search for identity at the expense of sufficient consideration of the practical realities of the publishing world. Neumann's need to create a "fluid composite" category, however, shows that he sees, at least in some respects, how the private and public categories overlap. For Kafka, he says, "one has little choice but to bring out all three aspects in an edition." Once again there is the concern with how an edition can, through its formal arrangement, emphasize one or another characteristic of authorship and a seeming lack of understanding that—far from having "little choice"—an editor of any author might positively desire to "bring out" these conflicting aspects of authorship, recognizing their relevance in all cases. He is right, of course, to conclude that editing involves interpretation (being, he unfortunately adds, "no longer a mechanical task of unquestioning reproduction"); but when he says that interpretation is necessary "to do justice to modern concepts of author, work and text" (p. 99), one must wonder how this triad relates to the earlier one, where "work" was one of three categories of "text." This whole group of papers regrettably lacks rigor and thus makes no significant theoretical contribution to editorial thinking. But the attention now being given to prepublication material by European literary and textual critics is welcome in any case, for the importance of such material is unquestionable—as editors in English-speaking countries have also long recognized (witness the original manual of the Center for Editions of American Authors in 1967).[49]

An interest in textual genesis is inseparable from an interest in "versions" of works, and a number of English-speaking textual scholars have in recent years focused on "versions"—most conspicuously a group of Shakespeareans including Steven Urkowitz, Gary Taylor, Michael War-

49. See the paragraph containing the statement, "Cancellations in pre-copy-text forms will normally be fully reported" (*Statement of Editorial Principles*, p. 8). Robert Murray Davis has recently suggested that students of textual genesis and the creative process should draw on what composition teachers have learned about "recursion," a nonlinear, looping pattern characterized by pausing, moving backward, rewriting, and so on: see his "Writing as Process: Beyond Hershel Parker," *Literary Research*, 12 (1987), 179–186. His title of course implies that this understanding of composition is an advance over the concept of the determinate period of creativity presented in Hershel Parker's *Flawed Texts and Verbal Icons* (1984)—on which I commented in my previous survey (*SB*, 39 [1986], 27–34 [135–142]). (For two additional views of Parker, see James McLaverty in *Review*, 8 [1986], 119–138, and Don L. Cook in *Documentary Editing*, 9, no. 1 [March 1987], 5–8.) Parker has presented a summary of his position in " 'The Text Itself'—Whatever That Is," *Text*, 3, (1987), 47–54.

ren, and E. A. J. Honigmann.[50] One result of this movement has been the inclusion of two versions of *King Lear* in the new one-volume Oxford Shakespeare (1986) on the grounds that conflating the first quarto and the Folio texts (as customary in the past) mixes two discrete stages of Shakespeare's work on the play.[51] Such arguments for maintaining the identity of versions—whether by scholars writing in French, German, or

50. For references to their work, see my comments in the preceding survey, *SB*, 39 (1986), 36 [144], note 68. More recently, Steven Urkowitz has said that "today we confuse bibliographical expertise with textual omniscience," in " 'Well-sayd olde Mole': Burying Three *Hamlet*s in Modern Editions," in *Shakespeare Study Today*, ed. Georgianna Ziegler (1986), pp. 37–70 (see p. 68). And Stanley Wells, in "Revision in Shakespeare's Plays," in *Editing and Editors: A Retrospect*, ed. Richard Landon (1988), pp. 67–97, advises editors to "get out of the strait-jacket of attempting to provide texts that aspire to definitiveness and aim rather at a reasoned plurality" (p. 97). See also Grace Ioppolo, " 'Old' and 'New' Revisionists: Shakespeare's Eighteenth-Century Editors," *Huntington Library Quarterly*, 52 (1989), 347–361. Other scholars, reflecting experiences in other fields, have also taken up this matter. S. M. Parrish, for instance, thinks of each version as "a vertical slice cut through the continuum of text" (p. 346) and defends "the autonomy and the validity of each steady state of the text" (p. 349); see his "The Whig Interpretation of Literature," *Text*, 4 (1988), 343–350 (in which the "Whig" view disregards early versions as superseded by "an inner logic of inexorable growth" toward a final form [p. 349]). Another recent proposal for separate editions of versions comes from John T. Shawcross, in "Scholarly Editions: Composite Editorial Principles of Single Copy-Texts, Multiple Copy-Texts, Edited Copy-Texts," *Text*, 4 (1988), 297–317: "for certain works, particularly where multiple authoritative texts exist, a single version of the text is not sufficient for a scholarly edition; rather, significant texts should be offered as the disparate texts that they are" (p. 301). Edward Mendelson, in a piece entitled "The Fading Coal vs. The Gothic Cathedral or What to Do about an Author Both Forgetful and Deceased" (*Text*, 3 [1987], 409–416), distinguishes an interest in early versions from an interest in late versions by the two images of his title (but the "cathedral," despite its suggestiveness, is apparently not meant to imply collaborative effort). On the fundamental question of how to distinguish between versions to be presented separately and those (if any) to be incorporated into an eclectic text, see the references recorded in note 87 below.

51. See the editors' commentary volume, *William Shakespeare: A Textual Companion*, by Stanley Wells and Gary Taylor with John Jowett and William Montgomery (1987), pp. 16–19 (a general argument for Shakespearean revision) and p. 509 (an explanation of the "radical departure from traditional editorial practice" for *Lear*). (For assessments of this notable volume, see Peter Davison's review in the *Library*, 6th ser., 10 [1988], 255–267, and MacDonald P. Jackson's review in *Shakespeare Survey*, 41 [1989], 228–241.) Some of Taylor's statements in the general introduction—such as "Editorial controversy, like all other forms of discourse, is an instrument of power. . . . Editors are the pimps of discourse" (p. 7)— resemble those in his paper on "The Rhetoric of Textual Criticism" in *Text*, 4 (1988), 39–57, in which he links the "revisionist revolution in the editing of Shakespeare" to "a change in the rhetoric of textual criticism" (p. 53) and describes the "rhetorical strategy" that elevated the idea of two *Lears* from the status of an "iconoclastic heresy" to the position of being supported by an apparent "mass movement" (p. 46). He sets forth the revisionist position in "Revising Shakespeare," *Text*, 3 (1987), 285–304—where he sees it as "the new revisionist onslaught" against "the entrenched conflationist orthodoxy" (p. 302). A recent example of the revision theory in operation is John Jowett and Gary Taylor's "The Three Texts of 2 *Henry IV*," *SB*, 40 (1987), 31–50.

English—often founder on the question of what role critical editing can play in the production of editions of versions. No defense is needed for reproducing or transcribing the texts of documents (handwritten and printed) exactly as they stand: such texts are historical facts, and it is useful to have them made available. But some editors wish to purge those texts of readings—such as typographical errors—that were not intended. In departing from the texts of documents, they must face the question of defining what kinds of emendations are to be allowed; and no matter what categories are named (even if only typographical errors, which are of course not always obvious), there is the possibility that some instances will be detected only by noting the variants in other documents and deciding that some of them were the intended readings all along. One is not mixing versions simply by drawing readings from different documents, since the texts of documents cannot be equated with the texts of versions—a fact recognized in the original decision to present a critical text. After all, traditional critical editors interested in authors' final intentions are not trying to mix versions but to recreate one—one that is not present in satisfactory form in any surviving document. But recent discussions of the importance of versions have too often been guilty of a double fallacy: believing that eclecticism (drawing readings from different documents) necessarily involves the mixing of versions, and believing that critical editing can ever be other than eclectic.[52]

Donald H. Reiman published in 1987 a spirited defense of the production of scholarly editions containing versions,[53] but it does not entirely avoid these confusions. Reiman advocates what he calls "versioning" rather than "editing" (p. 169): "there are good reasons to redirect our energies away from the attempt to produce 'definitive' or 'ideal' critical editions and, instead, to encourage the production of editions of discrete versions of works" (p. 179).[54] This summary statement suggests

52. I have made these points about versions in *SB*, 34 (1981), 62–63 [104–105], note 75; *SB*, 39 (1986), 44 [152], note 85; and *A Rationale of Textual Criticism* (1989), pp. 79–82.

53. " 'Versioning': The Presentation of Multiple Texts," in his *Romantic Texts and Contexts* (1987), pp. 167–180. The first part of this book, entitled "Romantic Texts" (pp. 15–180), brings together (along with the first appearance of " 'Versioning' ") nine pieces that had previously appeared elsewhere, seven of them reviews and essays relating to specific editions of nineteenth-century poets and the other two being the valuable two-part historical survey of the editing of the Romantics that he published in 1982 (*Studies in Romanticism*) and 1984 (*Text*). See also "Textual Criticism in Nineteenth-Century Studies," *Nineteenth-Century Contexts*, 11 (1987), 9–21; and "Gentlemen Authors and Professional Writers: Notes on the History of Editing Texts of the 18th and 19th Centuries," in *Editing and Editors: A Retrospect*, ed. Richard Landon (1988), pp. 99–136. Another recent piece of his is "Gender and Documentary Editing: A Diachronic Perspective," *Text*, 4 (1988), 351–359—where he confusingly links "slips of the pen" with "indifferent educational opportunities" as two causes of unintended readings in the texts of documents (p. 352).

54. Whether his preference for single-version editions is a matter of principle or con-

that what he favors are unaltered documentary texts (facsimiles and transcriptions), as indeed he does for some purposes. But he also includes within the concept of "versioning" the presentation of texts in which the editor has corrected "any typographical errors" and perhaps some other errors: pointing and orthography may be emended, but not "in any wholesale way, lest what results is some version *other than* the one being advertised" (p. 178, italics his). He is thus not opposed to the critical editing of versions; but he does not address the question of how the process of editorial judgment entailed in recreating pre-final versions is different from the one required for recreating a finally intended version. He is in fact sanctioning for pre-final versions what he calls " 'definitive' or 'ideal' critical editions" when devoted to finally intended versions. Apparently it is not the judgment involved in critical editing that bothers him, but rather what he sees as its excessive concentration on final intention. Such a conclusion is surprising, however, in view of his sarcastic remarks about editorial judgment—as when he says that an editor who engages in "versioning" may not require "the preternatural power to divine the unstated moods or preferences of dead authors" (p. 178). He fills most of a page detailing how editing would be different in a world where "versioning" were standard. Among the points enumerated: "Editing might not always then require the detective skills to root out all the surviving evidence about the author's involvement . . . in a work throughout its entire textual history"; "there would be less need for the editor to hypothesize events and attitudes where the crucial evidence concerning the author's involvement in the text is lacking"; there would be no need to decide which variants "resulted from the author's grateful acceptance of the publisher's or compositor's suggestions and corrections and which ones resulted from reluctant acquiescence in, or unawareness of, each particular change" (p. 177). What is particularly troubling about this litany is the implication that non-"versioning" editors have engaged in a great deal of unnecessary work and idle speculation. On the contrary, the topics listed are relevant to any study of a work's textual history; and informed speculation is an essential ingredient in all historical reconstruction. Reiman seems to feel, paradoxically, that eclectic texts with full apparatus inhibit debate, whereas separate texts of individual versions encourage it.[55] It was not

venience is not entirely clear. At several points he complains about the difficulty of using lists, and once he even says that a critic could "learn more" from comparing discrete versions than "by trying to unravel a conflated eclectic edition" (p. 173). (One can disregard, however, his statement in his prefatory note that he has found some eclectic editions to be "untrustworthy" [p. 167]: there are no doubt scholars capable of producing untrustworthy editions of single-version texts also.)

55. "The surviving pertinent materials would be before the reader and critic, the

necessary in any case for him to attempt to denigrate eclectic texts as he promoted single-version texts: the value of the latter has never been in question, as his interesting survey of examples indicates.[56] But single-version editing has no doubt received less discussion, and Reiman's vigorous championing of it may serve to bring it further attention.[57]

A consideration of authorial versions in the context of the social or collaborative status of authorship eventually leads one to think of the theater, for the preproduction version of a play is likely to be different from the one that emerges from the production process, and the collaborative character of theatrical production raises in extreme form the question of how authorial intention in a work of language is to be conceived. Recently T. H. Howard-Hill has turned his attention to the implications for play-editing of the nature of drama as a genre, and the resulting essay, as one would expect, is impressive in its scholarship, its sharpness of insight, and its style of argument (although one may question some of its assumptions). "Modern Textual Theories and the Editing of Plays"[58] provides, first, a searching criticism of Greg's rationale of copy-text, and, second, a forceful statement of the view that playwrights' intentions can be fulfilled only in performance. The two matters are separable (and the second is the one directly relevant here), but the connection is clear: Greg's rationale leads toward the choice for copy-text of the text closest to the playwright's manuscript; but the text of a (later) document associated with the theater, which is likely to contain the playwright's revisions made during the course of production, may seem to reflect the playwright's intentions better than a preproduction text. Thus, for Howard-Hill, Greg's rationale "applies least suc-

---

teacher and student, who could participate in the debate over issues that really matter until a new consensus emerged, rather than wait passively for a new canonical text to be imposed from 'above' " (p. 177).

56. Yet he seems to believe that the great volume of writing about critical editing has led to "some prejudice against the 'uncritical' presentation of primary manuscripts or early published versions" (p. 176).

57. One of his suggestions should be heeded: the publication of photofacsimiles of printed texts emended with paste-over alterations in an appropriate type face (pp. 178–179). In fact, this procedure is not limited to single-version editions; many eclectic texts produced by full critical editing would not incorporate emendations of such quantity or kind that a resetting of the copy-text would be necessary.

58. *Library*, 6th ser., 11 (1989), 89–115. A related brief essay of his, "Playwrights' Intentions and the Editing of Plays," *Text*, 4 (1988), 269–278, covers much of the same ground as the latter half of the *Library* essay. In a somewhat earlier article—"The Author as Scribe or Reviser? Middleton's Intentions in *A Game at Chess*," *Text*, 3 (1987), 305–318—he made some of the same points, but it was evidently written before he had developed the position on indifferent variants taken in the *Library* essay (cf. p. 318, note 18, of the 1987 piece with the comments on indifferent variants discussed below).

cessfully to the genre that brought about its conception" (p. 89).[59] Since under Greg's procedure the alterations judged authorial from a later text could in any case be emended into an early text, the heart of Howard-Hill's criticism of Greg is the treatment of so-called indifferent variants (although the value of preserving an early copy-text's accidentals is also questioned). Howard-Hill's position is that, if some variants in a later text seem clearly authorial, then some (or all) of the indifferent variants in that text might be authorial, too, and they should not automatically have to yield to the readings of the (early) copy-text. Discussing this question does not seem very productive, however, since everything depends on how an editor in a particular situation decides which variants are to be called "indifferent."[60] What is of greater interest is the concept of dramatic authorship implicit in Greg's rationale. The choice of a copy-text close to the manuscript and the goal of reconstructing an inferential authorial fair copy show that Greg was interested in the form

59. A few sentences later he says that it may also be unacceptable for other genres. One fault he finds with it is that it "interprets authorial intention primarily on the level of the document rather than on the level of the work" (p. 90). How can one locate the work except through the evidence of the texts of documents?

60. Howard-Hill obviously wishes Greg had decreed in such situations that the later text carries presumptive authority for indifferent variants (which would have left him closer to McKerrow). (I am using "indifferent variants" to mean those variants that seem equally balanced to an editor, taking everything into account. Howard-Hill distinguishes two uses of the term, one—"the usual interpretation"—referring to the "significance or aesthetic value" of the readings themselves (p. 98), the other referring to the authority of the sources of the readings. The two must ultimately coalesce, however, for any inference regarding the source of a reading, or inability to infer one, is influenced by a critical evaluation of the reading itself, in the light of what is known of the author's habits of expression.) Howard-Hill accepts at face value Greg's statement that "there can be no logical reason for giving preference to the copy-text" in the choice between indifferent variants, and he proceeds several times to call the practice illogical (as on pp. 97, 99, 100). Actually, the whole drift of Greg's argument provides the reasoning: the copy-text is chosen for its genealogical proximity to the text of the author's manuscript, on the grounds that texts deteriorate as they are recopied or reset in type; thus those readings (substantives and accidentals) in later texts that differ from copy-text readings may be presumed to be nonauthorial, except when a case can be made that the variants result from authorial alteration or from repair (by someone) of the kind that the editor would have had to undertake anyway. One may disagree with this entire line of reasoning, but one cannot label as illogical the idea of retaining the copy-text readings in cases of indifferent variants, for it is a consistent part of the whole. In practice, one can decide in a given instance that the circumstances demand the conferring of presumptive authority on all the substantive variants of a later text (or certain categories of them); I am only trying to suggest why it is understandable that Greg did not state this position as a general rule. As for Greg's position leading—in the hands of some editors—to a "new 'tyranny of copy-text'" (p. 90), one can never hope to eliminate this danger (of which Greg was well aware), whatever one's approach. The art of critical editing has always centered on the delicate process of guarding against, on the one hand, excessive reliance on a favored text and, on the other, overconfidence in one's ability to improve it.

of plays as conceived by their authors working alone and that he wished
to exclude from critical texts the alterations introduced in the process
of staging. The appropriateness of this approach is indeed an important
subject for debate.

Howard-Hill believes that editors who follow Greg "reject the playwright for the author, the dramatic script for the literary manuscript"
(p. 103). Playwrights understand, he says, that their manuscripts are
"the raw material in a process of shaping a play for performance that
requires the collaboration of many contributors: theatre personnel, actors, directors, and the author himself" (p. 105). Thus the author writes
a manuscript "expecting (to various degrees) that the script will be
modified in the theatre" (p. 105). It follows that "a playwright's intentions are represented best (if perhaps not completely) in a manuscript
associated with the theatre" (p. 112), and any editor whose goal is to
reconstruct a preproduction manuscript "averts his face from the theatre
for which the dramatist wrote, and presses boldly backwards into the
primitive jungle of the author's drafts" (p. 108). That "jungle" has its
own interest, of course, as we have been reminded by the critics just
discussed, among others; and Howard-Hill would presumably agree that
there is always a value in editions that focus on preliminary versions.
But his particular concern is with works as finally intended by their
authors, and from his vantage point a rationale for play-editing that
purports to stress final intention and emphasizes preproduction documents is "textually-regressive" (p. 90), or "editorially regressive" (p. 101).
Part of this argument would be accepted by anyone: that a play does not
exist in its intended medium except in performance, and performance
is necessarily collaborative. No one can object to editions that attempt to
record the text followed in a play's initial (or some other) production,
for the versions that reached the public in performance are obviously of
historical interest. What is objectionable in Howard-Hill's presentation
is his insistence that the only legitimate critical texts for representing
playwrights' final intentions are those based on performance texts (or
such textual evidence as there is of what actually occurred in performance). His account is notably unbalanced in not sufficiently recognizing
that alterations made for performance (even if agreed to by the playwright) do not always please the playwright.[61]

61. In his concluding paragraph, he states his "most important" recommendation in
this way: "authorial intentions relinquished to the theatre by design and custom should
be completed by an editor in accordance with his understanding of the author's intentions
as reflected in surviving documents, and of the theatrical milieu in which the playwright
wrote" (p. 115). This statement does not clearly distinguish two possibilities. Aspects of a
play "relinquished to the theatre" were sometimes completed in ways that were not in
accord with the playwright's intention; but in that form they became part of the perfor-

It is indicative of a fundamental misconception underlying Howard-Hill's argument that he sees a meaningful opposition in "the dramatic script" versus "the literary manuscript," "the playwright" versus "the author." Presumably he means that the "author" of a "literary" piece like a novel or poem works alone, whereas the "playwright" of a "dramatic" piece must engage in the collaborative activity of production, and therefore an editor who uses a preproduction manuscript of a play as copy-text is behaving as if the work being edited were of a "literary" rather a "dramatic" genre. "Literary" authors, however, must participate in the collaborative (and altering) process of publication if their work is to reach the public, and thus the real opposition is not between "drama" and "literature" but between versions of works (of whatever genre) as intended by their authors alone and versions of works (of whatever genre) as they emerged from the collaborative efforts required to bring them to the public. The analogy between production and publication (of which Howard-Hill approves [p. 104]) is worth exploring further. There is an obvious way in which the analogy is inexact, for what a performance of a play offers is an actual work of drama, whereas what a book provides is not a work of literature (the medium of which is not paper and ink) but a set of instructions, a script, whereby one can re-create a work of literature through the act of reading. The publication of a play in print is directly comparable to the publication of a novel or poem: in both instances the printed text is the means by which works in intangible media can be transmitted. In the one instance, the work involves actors and props on a stage (and is thus a mixed-media work, using sound, movement, and visual effects as well as language); in the other, the work consists of language alone, and the recreation of the work can take place within the mind or in private recitation.[62] A more exact com-

mance text actually used. Howard-Hill earlier stressed the importance of the editorial adoption of such texts (as from promptbooks), because plays are collaborative products and playwrights expect changes to be made in their work. The emphasis in this statement, however, is on the editor's own emendations designed to produce a performance text in line with what can be known of the playwright's intention. A text reflecting the playwright's intention for performance is a very different editorial goal from a text reflecting the handling by theater personnel of details relinquished by the playwright.

62. A playwright who wishes to have a different text for the reading audience from one followed on the stage is of course creating two works, the one in print being like a novel (or a "closet drama") in employing only language as its medium. Even when the texts are the same, there may be features of the text, as in stage directions, that seem written primarily for the benefit of a reading audience; but as long as the text intended for the reading audience is the same as the text intended for performers, it is difficult to conclude that certain non-dialogue features of the text were meant to create a distinct work for the reading audience, since they also influence the performance of actors. The relations of reading text to performance are productively explored by Randall McLeod (writing as "Random Cloud") in "The Psychopathology of Everyday Art," *The Elizabethan Theatre*, 9

parison is with music: the first performance of a symphony constitutes its publication as a work of music (that is, publication in the medium in which it was meant to be experienced); the publication of its score on paper simply makes more widely available the instructions for recreating the work.[63]

Thus critical editors of drama are in a position no different from the editors of other works in intangible media (including literature): they all must rely on surviving documents (which are not the works themselves) and strive to reconstruct from them the texts that were intended by particular persons (whether authors alone, or authors in collaboration with others) at particular points in the past.[64] One of the basic

---

(1986), 100–168, which makes a similar point: McLeod argues against normalizing the irregular naming of characters in speech prefixes, for he believes that it (like punctuation) affects not only readers' responses but also actors' interpretations. (Cf. Philip Brett's discussion of the way in which the modernizing of musical notation affects performance, in "Text, Context, and the Early Music Editor," in *Authenticity and Early Music: A Symposium*, ed. Nicholas Kenyon [1988], pp. 83–114.)

63. Howard-Hill's argument is not helped by an eccentric use of the word "work," which does not in his definition encompass a play. He speaks of "the essential distinction between authors of works and playwrights" and explains, "The distinction I make is between an intention to publish by performance ('play'), and one to publish in print ('work')" (p. 108). My comments in this paragraph, and the definitions of "work" and "text" implicit in them, are derived from my *A Rationale of Textual Criticism* (1989), *passim* (on drama, see p. 85). (This paragraph and the next can also serve as my response to McKenzie's discussion of drama in his Panizzi Lectures, where he says, rather obscurely, that "the sociological dimension of production and reception . . . confirm[s] the textual nature of each element in a play" [p. 41].) My distinction between works and documents is entirely misunderstood by Margreta de Grazia in "What Is a Work? What Is a Document?", in *The New Historicism and the Editing of English Renaissance Texts* (photocopied papers, separately paginated, from the Renaissance English Text Society MLA panel organized by Thomas L. Berger, 1989): she believes that the traditional view (and mine) can be represented by such statements as "A work has an author, a document does not. A work is subject to critical interpretation, a document is not" (p. 1). It is no wonder that "this distinction is approaching collapse"— the "claim" of her paper, though a more challenging claim to prove would be that it ever existed. She somehow finds that attention to Shakespeare's plays as performed, along with the printing of multiple versions, shows an "indifference to a distinction ['the work/document distinction'] that was once basic" (p. 8); she does not see that every physical text is a documentary text and that every one of them is also an attempt to transmit a work. Another article, besides Howard-Hill's, that in my view fails to see the similarities between the texts of plays on paper and the tangible texts of works in other intangible media is John Glavin's "Bulgakov's Lizard and the Problem of the Playwright's Authority," *Text*, 4 (1988), 385–406. Glavin asserts that "the fusion of text and theatre . . . subverts the inscription that evokes it," and this "subversion radically fractures the relation between drama and other major literary genres" (p. 387)—as if fiction and poetry reach the public without intermediaries. Indeed, his statement that "The novel or poem is printed, read, and studied as written" seems oblivious to the fact that private and public texts of such works are so frequently different as to have given rise to the debate between intentionalist and social textual critics.

64. Even though a play exists as a work only in performance, historical research into the texts of plays—like playwrights' own composition—must rely on documents (i.e., on

choices any editor has is whether to concentrate solely on an author's intention or to focus on the combined intention of the group (including the author) overseeing public dissemination—for the two interests can almost never be satisfied by a single clear text. An editor who chooses as copy-text the fair-copy manuscript of a novel rather than the first edition set from it is doing the same thing as the editor of a play who selects the final preproduction manuscript as copy-text. In both cases emendations can be made from later texts if there are variants that seem to reflect the author's uninfluenced intention—which is, after all, the aim of these editors. The choice between authorial and collaborative intention and the crucial distinction between intention and expectation have been much discussed,[65] and it is in the context of those issues that the editing of plays should be viewed, for plays do not present a unique situation. Howard-Hill apparently wishes to be understood as believing that there is no historical validity to the concern for authors' (at least early playwrights') uninfluenced intentions: "To postulate amongst professional playwrights of the early period the romantic author pouring his inspiration into his early drafts which alone conveyed his intentions, having been afterwards corrupted by grubby theatre professionals, is the worst kind of historical error" (p. 106).[66] Even if it had been couched in less slanted language, this statement would have been unacceptable. Writers of all periods, as human beings with feelings and opinions, have had their own personal preferences regarding the form and content of their work, even if their status as professionals sometimes required them to accept or initiate alterations that seemed to them less desirable. And as long as anyone is interested in understanding the workings and accomplishments of minds of the past, the task of attempting to determine authors' own intentions and to reconstruct texts reflecting them is a valid activity of historical recovery. Howard-Hill's contrary position is weak-

---

instructions for performance). Thus an editor seeking to reconstruct the text of a play as intended by its author for performance need not be bothered by the fact (or possibility) that the play was never actually performed in that version. The play (as a work) may not have existed, but plans for it existed in the playwright's mind and, in greater or lesser degree, in the form of text on paper. Those plans or instructions (in the form of text) are the reality that such an editor is attempting to recover.

65. For my own comments, see *SB*, 29 (1976), 183–191 (reprinted in *Selected Studies in Bibliography* [1979], pp. 325–333), and *A Rationale of Textual Criticism* (1989), pp. 77–78.

66. The idea that an interest in the autonomy of the author is "romantic" (which has become fairly common in anti-intentionalist writing on textual criticism) is challenged by Tilottama Rajan in "Is There a Romantic Ideology? Some Thoughts on Schleiermacher's Hermeneutic and Textual Criticism," *Text*, 4 (1988), 59–77: "My own contention is that not only is the ideology of the author as sovereign subject that subtends much textual criticism a modern reconstruction that finds only partial authority in the Romantic period but that the origins of the contemporary questioning of this authority initiated by McGann are also to be found in the Romantic period" (pp. 59–60).

ened by his presenting it as the only defensible approach rather than as one alternative, as one of several paths to the past, each of which gives us a different perspective.

IV

The pervasive presence of textual and literary sociology (with its related challenges to authorial intention) in the current climate is indicated by the attention it receives in general assessments of the present state of textual studies. For example, Fredson Bowers, in his presidential address to the Society for Textual Scholarship at its biennial conference in 1985,[67] devoted half his time to a critical examination of McGann's approach, voicing his suspicions of "any overall theory that denigrates an author's intentions by sharing them with social milieu as a central fact" (p. 10) and concluding that "Critics who mistrust our developed conventional editorial theory do not seem to be fully aware of its flexibility when properly applied, its consciousness of the shift in the nature of problems and of the methods for dealing with them as the centuries pass" (p. 11). Two years earlier, Paul Oskar Kristeller's presidential address[68]—not published until 1987—had considered "traditional" textual scholarship to be on the defensive and argued that, although "economic, social, and political developments are necessary conditions for many or even all cultural or intellectual developments of the past," they are not "sufficient causes that would adequately explain the concrete texts and documents with which we are concerned, or their specific form and content" (p. 6). Both scholars affirm traditional approaches, not because they are unwilling to consider alternatives but because the recent challenges seem (as Bowers says) to be based on a misunderstanding of the traditional approaches and attempt (as Kristeller says) not only "to supplement traditional scholarship (which would be quite acceptable) but to discredit it and to replace it" (p. 2). Nevertheless, they both see the challenges as a central fact of the present moment.

The founder of the Society for Textual Scholarship, D. C. Greetham, has constructed a characteristically wide-ranging description of the situation at present by setting out a series of "ideological pairings" between

67. "Unfinished Business," *Text*, 4 (1988), 1–11. During the period under review here, Bowers has given particular attention in print to the complex issues of regularization: "Readability and Regularization in Old-Spelling Texts of Shakespeare," *Huntington Library Quarterly*, 50 (1987), 199–227; "Regularization and Normalization in Modern Critical Texts," *SB*, 42 (1989), 79–102; "The Problem of Semi-Substantive Variants: An Example from the Shakespeare-Fletcher *Henry VIII*," *SB*, 43 (1990), 80–95.

68. "Textual Scholarship and General Theories of History and Literature," *Text*, 3 (1987), 1–9.

textual and literary theories, showing that the various literary approaches emphasizing authors or texts or readers have their counterparts in textual theory.[69] Social textual criticism of course receives its due in this scheme as one of the reader-based theories, and Greetham says that it has become "a major focus for debate" (p. 23) as a result of McGann's *Critique*, which provides its "clearest statement in recent *textual* theory" (p. 11). In Greetham's earlier account of the state of editing medieval materials (which is in fact a lively treatment of issues involved in any editing),[70] McGann's approach and the related emphasis on versions are linked to "current critical positions—the death of the author, the primacy of the fragment, the deconstruction and aporia of the work as a consistent framing of one person's intention" (pp. 61–62). Greetham, in essays such as these, has been actively promoting greater understanding of the connections between textual and literary theory, and he was given a useful opportunity for furthering the cause when he was asked to serve as commentator on the papers delivered at a "Symposium on

69. "Textual and Literary Theory: Redrawing the Matrix," *SB*, 42 (1989), 1–24. This essay can in some respects be supplemented by Greetham's "A Suspicion of Texts," a provocative introductory essay for the general reader published in *Thesis: The Magazine of the Graduate School and University Center* (City University of New York), 2, no. 1 (Fall 1987), 18–25. Near the end of the essay he suggests some of the ways that theoretical orientations reveal themselves in published editions, and his final line is that "a suspicion of texts is in fact one of the fundamental requirements of the critical mind."

70. "The Place of Fredson Bowers in Mediaeval Editing," *PBSA*, 82 (1988), 53–69. Greetham's interest in placing medieval textual problems in the context of current debates in textual criticism is also illustrated in "Challenges of Theory and Practice in the Editing of Hoccleve's *Regement of Princes*," in *Manuscripts and Texts: Editorial Problems in Later Middle English Literature*, ed. Derek Pearsall (1987), pp. 60–86. He offers here a descriptive list of seven "theoretical options . . . available to the editor," ordered in "declining degrees of 'fidelity' to the documentary state and history of the work" (p. 62). The list begins with "the photographic facsimile" and ends with (in sixth place) "the Slavic textological model, with its emphasis on the potentially equal status of all remaniements as textual witnesses" and (in seventh place) "a 'social' textual theory such as that envisaged by Jerome McGann" (p. 68). (One may wonder whether these last two are in fact at the farthest extreme from photographic facsimiles in terms of " 'fidelity' to the documentary state and history of the work," for they both could be well—perhaps best—accommodated by the use of facsimiles. They are both at the opposite extreme from final authorial intention, but facsimiles do not necessarily represent authorial intention.) In the course of the essay he makes a statement that explains the form of a number of recent textual essays: "The conservative turned radical always seems to feel that his earlier conservative credentials need a greater demonstration of their frailty than do his new radical precepts, which can be regarded as articles of the revealed truth" (p. 70). Greetham here concludes that "a 'social' school of textual criticism is invalid where intention is recoverable" (p. 80); a detailed account of his method of reconstructing Hoccleve's intended text of *Regement of Princes* by incorporating into it Hoccleve's practice in accidentals, as established by analysis of holographs of other works, is provided in "Normalisation of Accidentals in Middle English Texts: The Paradox of Thomas Hoccleve," *SB*, 38 (1985), 121–150 (see p. 127, note 10, for his criticism of McGann's treatment of the relation between Lachmannian genealogical analysis and Gregian copy-text theory).

Textual Scholarship and Literary Theory," organized by the Society for Critical Exchange and held at Miami University (Ohio) in March 1987.[71] His even-handed remarks are firmly critical of literary theorists who see textual criticism as a static field intellectually unrelated to literary theory (a view represented at the conference); at the same time he takes for granted that the period when authorial intention had its "greatest practical influence" in textual criticism has passed.

Another textual conference, "New Directions in Textual Studies," was held in March–April 1989 at the Harry Ransom Humanities Research Center in Austin. On this occasion Ian Willison attempted a general survey of the connections between editorial theory and the history of the book, stating at the outset that as a historian of the book and authorship he is "obliged" to favor the social approach to textual matters represented by McGann and McKenzie.[72] It is surprising that a historian of books and authorship would see a necessity to choose between the social and the authorial approaches to editing, when each concentrates on a different aspect of the total picture and the two taken together might be thought to produce a more rounded view.[73] An earlier conference, one on "textual hermeneutics" held at Canberra in May 1982, produced some controversy that appeared in print over the next several years.[74] At the conference Stephen Knight attacked "old-fashioned positivist, text-and-author centered editing" (p. 44) and indicated that his own aim in editing Chaucer is to produce a text "with the fullest socio-

---

71. The papers from this conference and Greetham's response are to form a special issue of *Critical Exchange* (which, as of this writing, is not yet available). I am grateful to Professor Greetham for providing me with a copy of his commentary.

72. He adds that he finds support for his view from authors' statements of their own intentions—ignoring not only the difference between intention and expectation but also the historian's task of analyzing critically the motivations underlying statements made by individuals in the past. Willison's paper does in fact show the ubiquity, from medieval times to the present, of the split between authors of works and disseminators of texts. The papers from the Texas conference will be published in a special number of the *Library Chronicle of the University of Texas* (the collection is not yet available, as of this writing). I am grateful to Mr. Willison for giving me a copy of his paper.

73. Another historian of books and publishing, John Sutherland, has ridiculed the intentionalist approach and depicted those advocating the social approach as adversaries of a repressive establishment. See "Publishing History: A Hole at the Centre of Literary Sociology," *Critical Inquiry*, 14 (1988), 574–589; reprinted in *Literature and Social Practice*, ed. Philippe Desan, Priscilla Parkhurst Ferguson, and Wendy Griswold (1989), pp. 267–282. My response to this slight piece, which trivializes its subject by approaching the careers of McGann, McKenzie, and Robert Darnton in terms of academic politics, appears in *Literature and Social Practice*, pp. 283–287 ("Response to John Sutherland").

74. See Stephen Knight, "Textual Variants: Textual Variance," *Southern Review* [Adelaide], 16 (1983), 44–54; Harold Love, "Sir Walter Greg and the Chaucerian Force Field," *Bibliographical Society of Australia and New Zealand Bulletin*, 8 (1984), 73–81; Stephanie Trigg, "The Politics of Editing Medieval Texts: Knight's Quest and Love's Complaint," *ibid.*, 9 (1985), 15–22.

literary potency" and that he chooses between "equally possible variants" the one with "the maximum possible historical tension, the reading which loads the text most strongly with ideology" (p. 49). Harold Love later responded, with some sarcasm, on behalf of intentionalist editing;[75] and Stephanie Trigg then noted some of the deficiencies of both Knight's and Love's papers, accepting Knight's point that (in her words) "any edited text is an ideologically loaded construct" (p 20) but preferring to stress the reading audience as the locus for the production of meaning.[76]

Numerous other essays deal with these matters in one way or another. Peter Shillingsburg, for example, provides an exposition of the obvious considerations involved in the "social contract" approach to editing, sensibly affirming editorial pluralism;[77] James L. W. West III focuses on the "act of submission" as a key moment in the textual history of a work, a moment that serves to illuminate the contrasting attitudes of editors following authorial and social theories;[78] Leonard N. Neufeldt describes

75. He describes Knight's "distortions of Greg" as "a classical example of a Bloomian *tessera*—a 'strong misreading' of an anxiety-causing precursor designed to create imaginative space for the textual ephebe" (p. 76). More usefully, he points out that a social goal for textual criticism is "a matter of editorial philosophy which can be applied to any work of literature whatsoever" and is "not necessarily dependent on the work being the product of collective composition" (p. 79). But he muddles this point by asserting that, in choosing between indifferent variants, "Knight's principle is certainly no less logical than the idea that one should follow the reading of the 'best manuscript' or Greg's recommendation that one should accept the reading of the copy-text" (p. 80). If one can apply social textual criticism to any work, as of course one can, then one's method of handling indifferent variants must be consistent with it, and Knight's is more appropriate for this purpose than Greg's. No doubt Love had this in mind, but what he says does not make entirely clear that social and authorial emphases cannot sensibly be mixed in a single edited text— and thus he does not elucidate as much as he might the very real problem, in Knight's piece, of allowing authorial intention to guide some, but not all, editorial decisions. Love weakens his argument even further by suggesting at the end that an edition following Knight's rationale would be "a twentieth-century artefact, not a medieval one" (p. 80). Although he understands that all editors, including "traditional" ones, bring their own "ideologies" to their work, he does not proceed to recognize that texts constructed to reflect authors' intentions and those constructed to recreate the "dialectical tensions of the period of origin" are equally the products of the historical imagination of scholars living and working at particular times and inescapably imbued with the sensibility of those times.

76. She believes that "medieval texts, far from being the innocent victims of superimposed critical theories, or coloured by different editorial practices, are only produced as we read them" (p. 21).

77. "An Inquiry into the Social Status of Texts and Modes of Textual Criticism, *SB*, 42 (1989), 55–79. Shillingsburg says that "this survey of competing views of editing has convinced me even more that editing is a critical enterprise that not only involves criticism but is in fact a form of literary criticism." Like others before him who have made this discovery, he adds, "I believe no theorist should say that his method is the only responsible one, though I think it is possible to discover that some methods are irresponsible" (p. 74).

78. "Editorial Theory and the Act of Submission," *PBSA*, 83 (1989), 169–185. West concludes that an intentionalist editor can accept some of the alterations made in a text by persons other than the author if those alterations seem to reflect fulfillment of the author's

editorial work as the product of a specific time and place, influenced by
particular critical theories and all the other "forces of institutionaliza-
tion in the field of literature";[79] Hugh Amory criticizes an introductory
bibliographical and textual manual for its emphasis on the "obsoles-
cent" Greg-Bowers tradition and its neglect of McKenzie and McGann;[80]
and many studies of particular authors or fields explicitly confront (however effectively) the competing claims of the authorial and the social.[81]

---

active intentions (and the resulting edition is both "an act of literary criticism and of
biography" [p. 185]). He regards this position as intermediate between the strict intentionalist view, which would not allow any alterations not made by the author, and the social
view, which would favor the reproduction of the received text accompanied by notes of
"who did what during the compositional process" (p. 185). In this scheme, West believes that
the two extremes are "rigid," whereas his recommended intermediate approach "increases
the element of critical thinking in the creation of a scholarly text" (pp. 184–185). Some
"rigid" intentionalist editors probably do exist, but being strictly intentionalist requires
judgment, not rigidity. Any attempt to construct an authorially intended text demands
"critical thinking," and the decision to accord a delegated authority to some of the changes
made by authors' personal editors or publishers' editors does not necessitate a greater in-
fusion of it, but rather an application of it toward somewhat differently defined ends.
West has not proposed a new approach to critical editing but only another perspective on
where the line between intention and expectation falls.

79. "Neopragmatism and Convention in Textual Editing, with Examples from the
Editing of Thoreau's Autograph Journal," *Analytical & Enumerative Bibliography*, n.s., 1
(1987), 227–236 (quotation from p. 230). Neufeldt speaks for many other editors when he
says, "Recent and current speculation about literary theory, theory of language, theory of
discourse . . . has threatened a number of models that formerly offered a satisfactory starting point, *modus operandi*, and conceptual focus for editing texts. . . . Our eyes—including
our editorial eyes—are being retrained" (p. 227).

80. "New, Old, Anglo-American, Textual Criticism," *PBSA*, 80 (1986), 243–253 (quotation from p. 245)—a review of William Proctor Williams and Craig S. Abbott's *An Introduction to Bibliographical and Textual Studies* (1985). This often acute review misleadingly
depicts the "Anglo-American tradition of textual criticism" as an "immoveable orthodoxy"
resulting in "institutional and theoretical certainties" (p. 244)—ignoring, among other
things, the emphasis by many (perhaps most) of its practitioners on the lack of definitiveness
of its products. In contrast, he argues, "McKenzie's call for a deeper attention to the materiality of the text and McGann's appeal over the heads of Greg-Bowers to the precedents
of classical scholarship both entail a welcome return from the tyranny of method to
ratio et res ipsa" (p. 250).

81. See, for example, Gerald M. Maclean, "What Is a Restoration Poem? Editing a
Discourse, Not an Author," *Text*, 3 (1987), 319–346; David S. Hewitt, "Scott and Textual
Multiplepointing," *Text*, 4 (1988), 361–373; Herman J. Saatkamp, Jr., "Final Intentions,
Social Context, and Santayana's Autobiography," *Text*, 4 (1988), 93–108; and two essays by
Arthur F. Marotti, "Malleable and Fixed Texts: Manuscript and Printed Miscellanies and
the Tranmission of Lyric Poetry in the English Renaissance," in *Is the Typography Textual?* (photocopied papers, separately paginated, from the Renaissance English Text Society MLA panel organized by Carolyn Kent, 1988), and "Manuscript, Print, and the English
Renaissance Lyric," in *The New Historicism and the Editing of English Renaissance Texts*
(see note 63 above). Each of these essays refers to McGann on its first page and gives considerable attention to a socialized theory of textual criticism; none of the writers, however,
makes the point that both the authorial and the social approaches are independently applicable to every work. (Marotti comes close to doing so in the second paper but wishes—

I have cited all these essays to suggest how insistently the issue of social textual criticism has arisen in recent discussions and how frequently it has been linked with developments in literary theory. The connections between textual and literary theory have not as often been seen, however, from the other direction: writers who think of themselves primarily as literary theorists or critics have not been very cognizant of the related debates taking place among textual critics. McGann is of course an exception to this generalization, and so is David Gorman, whose essay "The Worldly Text" is a remarkable survey of current directions in literary and cultural theory, directions that are "worldly" because they go beyond the purely linguistic.[82] Gorman includes "textual studies" as one of three areas for detailed discussion, the others being "the theory of social action" and "the philosophical questions raised by historicism," each chosen because he believes it "suggests important new avenues of research in cultural history" (p. 183). The essay, which is well-informed and judicious, may possibly be the first survey from a literary theorist, addressed to an audience interested in literary theory, that takes adequate account of developments in textual criticism. He ends his section on textual critics by saying that "The level on which their theoretical debate is taking place is very high indeed, and one that should put many theorists of interpretive criticism to shame" (p. 198).

Nearly all of the essays I have mentioned, here and earlier in this survey, have touched—in more or less detail—on the matter of textual apparatus, on how textual evidence is to be reported in an edition; and some other essays, dealing exclusively with apparatus, have recently appeared. Although apparatus may seem a less intellectually interesting subject than theories about the nature of verbal texts, one can readily see why the form of apparatus has become a central concern at a time of challenge to traditional intentionalist editing, for the standard presentation

---

as he says in the first—to "dissociate" his work from "the usual textual and bibliographical program . . . that is informed by a textual 'idealism' that effectively eradicates those interesting socioliterary processes in which texts are historically embedded" [p. 1]. Saatkamp appends to his essay the naïve recommendation that "critical authorial editions" of living authors be undertaken, allowing the authors to determine their intended texts—as if the existence of such editions would alter in any way the scholar's task of assessing authorial motivation and reconstructing the texts intended at particular past moments.) These issues have also become prominent in the study of other arts. In music, for example, attention has been given to "authenticity," meaning fidelity not to composers' intentions but to the details of contemporary performance; see *Authenticity and Early Music*, which includes Philip Brett's excellent essay (see note 62 above) surveying the history and issues of music editing in the context of the theoretical debates among literary editors.

82. "The Worldly Text: Writing as Social Action, Reading as Historical Reconstruction," in *Literary Theory's Future(s)*, ed. Joseph Natoli (1989), pp. 181–220. The section on textual criticism, "Beginning with a Text" (pp. 190–198), deals largely with Hershel Parker, Jerome McGann, and me.

of a clear text with appended apparatus (on the same page or elsewhere)
has been interpreted as reinforcing the concept of a single, closed, definitive text. There are two levels on which discussions of apparatus can
take place, and they should be carefully distinguished, for they are often
intertwined in the same arguments. One level, the lower one, has to do
with readers' convenience, or the "usability" of an apparatus. Objecting
to an apparatus solely because it seems cumbersome, or because it can
be expected to discourage readers from using it, expresses a concern at
the practical level of clerical procedure, not at the conceptual level of
theory. All of us would like the books that we read and study to be convenient to use, but we put up with inconvenient ones all the time, because we have no choice but to use them as they are. It is unquestionably
a flaw in an edition to have an unnecessarily awkward apparatus, but not
nearly so severe a flaw as to have left out an essential category of information; at least the information is on record, even if it is less easy to retrieve
than one might wish. But objections to an apparatus can also be raised
on a more serious level, when arguments are made that a particular
presentation of material is substantively misleading, incompatible with
the historical situation being depicted or with the scholarly goals of the
editor. Although such arguments do necessarily involve a questioning
of formal conventions, their real concern is with the communication of
meaning through the modes of expression classified as apparatus.

Two recent articles illustrate these levels. Don L. Cook[83] surprisingly
challenges the assumption that "the more information we can give the
user of a critical edition about the genesis and evolution of a written
work, the more useful our volume will be" (p. 82). Certainly he is moving against the current trend represented by the European proponents
of genetic criticism. Few would disagree with his point that the publication of revisions in prepublication documents "should result only from
the thoughtful consideration of the service they can provide to the serious scholars who will be using the volumes, not from considerations of
respectability or continued funding" (p. 89)—or from the mechanical
following of some rule. But it is hard to see how such information would
ever be useless to scholars, and Cook recognizes that editors themselves
must always be aware of pre-copy-text alterations. The reason not to
publish the information, then, is on the practical level: such lists are
likely to be long, and therefore expensive (pp. 83, 87); they are also

---

83. In "Some Considerations in the Concept of Pre-Copy-Text," *Text*, 4 (1988), 79–91.
Cook has also written, during the period under review here, a skillful account of "Preparing
Scholarly Editions" for a general audience: see *Humanities* [National Endowment for the
Humanities], 9, no. 3 (May/June 1988), 14–17. (His comment on apparatus in this piece is
simply that an editor should record "fully the evidence on which the editorial decisions are
made, including all the variant readings.")

likely to be complex, and users may thus "become exhausted and finally disillusioned" in attempting to use them (p. 84).[84] To condone the withholding of avowedly important information on these grounds seems a counsel of despair.[85] Another article, by Ted-Larry Pebworth and Ernest W. Sullivan, II,[86] recommends that versions of works representing "markedly different semiotic entities" or independent textual traditions (p. 44) be presented as separate texts, each with its own apparatus. Although the authors do complain that some information may not be "easily discoverable or recoverable from the traditional lengthy and complex apparatus format" (p. 44) or that "some bibliographical training and considerable industry" is required to retrieve it (p. 47), this kind of problem is not their primary point—which is rather that a consolidated apparatus may in some cases misrepresent the textual history of a work by merging the histories of independent traditions and suggesting that the version printed as the text is more authoritative than the other independent versions (p. 46). They may have exaggerated the degree to which "traditional" editions are guilty of this practice; in any case one can say that there is another established tradition as well, in which separate editions are prepared for versions that are so different as to be judged distinct works.[87] Pebworth and Sullivan's proposal is a

84. Another reason, which Cook cites from the Indiana edition of Howells, is that serious scholars will wish to examine the manuscripts themselves; but this argument ignores both the usefulness of genetic information to a wide variety of readers and the scholarly contribution made by editors (experts in their authors' handwriting and working habits) in deciphering documentary texts, which are often complex or unclear.

85. Another scholar critical of standard apparatus is Barry Gaines, though the specific target of his attack is very different: in "Textual Apparatus—Rationale and Audience," in *Play-Texts in Old Spelling*, ed. G. B. Shand with Raymond C. Shady (1984), pp. 65–71, he contends that "no one is really interested in reconstructing the copy-text from the apparatus which accompanies a critical edition" and that, indeed, anyone would be foolish to try to do so when microfilm and other facsimile copies are available (p. 68); and the historical collation, he feels, is "simply a record of what the editor has endured to earn the right to proceed with the edition" (p. 69). The ineffectiveness of his argument is suggested by this false analogy: "When scientists publish their conclusions, they are not asked to include as an appendix all their worksheets" (p. 69).

86. "Rational Presentation of Multiple Textual Traditions," *PBSA*, 83 (1989), 43–60.

87. See, for example, my "The Editorial Problem of Final Authorial Intention," *SB*, 29 (1976), 167–211 (reprinted in *Selected Studies in Bibliography* [1979], pp. 309–353), especially the third section and the references cited there. An essentially similar approach to the one I proposed in some detail has been sketched in broad terms by Giovanni Aquilecchia in "Trilemma of Textual Criticism (Author's Alterations, Different Versions, Autonomous Works): An Italian View," in *Book Production and Letters in the Western European Renaissance: Essays in Honour of Conor Fahy*, ed. Anna Laura Lepschy, John Took, and Dennis E. Rhodes (1986), pp. 1–6: "I would maintain," he says, "that it is part of the critical editor's task to distinguish . . . between mere alterations which do not affect the structure of the work or a part of it on the one hand (to be recorded in the apparatus of a critical edition) and different versions of the work or part of it, sometimes amounting to different works altogether on the other" (p. 4). Fredson Bowers pursues this question further in "Mixed

refinement on this tradition, most valuable in its suggestions for handling versions of which only certain lines or passages require printing in
full. One should not, however, draw from their article the conclusion
that independent versions are printed separately *for the purpose of*
clarifying the apparatus; they are printed separately because the editor
judges them to be independent versions (or works) demanding such
treatment, and separate apparatuses follow as a matter of course. The
essential problem with a consolidated apparatus for independent versions is not that it is inconvenient but that it is a reflection of an inappropriate treatment of the texts.

These essays do not question the use of apparatus as an accompani-
ment to clear texts; but theorists who stress the indeterminacy of texts
often object to the "privileging" of any one selection of variant readings,
regarding a clear text with an appended apparatus as an inappropriate
elevation of certain readings and subordination of others. Many such
editors in recent years have argued strenuously for inclusive texts—
texts, that is, in which variant readings, or some categories of them, are
inserted directly into the linear text, accompanied by any necessary sigla
or diacritics. The essence of Gabler's rationale for his presentation of
the text of *Ulysses* is that he wishes to show the "diachrony" of the revisional stages of the work by placing each authorial variant in its "contextual relations" within the text; apparatus is the central concern, for
the traditional apparatus, he feels, results in "fragmentation" of the text
as a whole, the text conceived as the totality of all the author's revisions.[88]
A common theme among scholars of the genetic school, however different their actual handling of variants, is that the traditional apparatus
falsifies the historical situation by minimizing the significance of certain
variants, subordinating them to an editorial construct, instead of giving
them their due as equal partners in an inexorable chronological proces-
sion. A clash of editorial theories finds its battleground in the lists of
apparatus.

An awareness of the two levels of discussion about apparatus can

---

Texts and Multiple Authority," *Text*, 3 (1987), 63–90. After distinguishing "mixed authority" in a single-text tradition (produced by authorial revision) from "discrete multiple
authority" (produced by thorough rewriting), the former amenable to eclectic editing and
the latter not, he examines situations with "radiating multiple authority" (p. 74), compatible with eclectic editing but posing special problems because of the multiple "sets of independent documentary evidence," often of equal authority (p. 75). This essay supplements
his landmark essay on "Multiple Authority: New Problems and Concepts of Copy-Text,"
Library, 5th ser., 27 (1972), 81–118 (reprinted in *Essays in Bibliography, Text, and Editing*
[1975], pp. 447–487). On authority, see also his "Authority, Copy, and Transmission in
Shakespeare's Texts," in *Shakespeare Study Today*, ed. Georgianna Ziegler (1986), pp. 7–36.
    88. See "The Synchrony and Diachrony of Texts" (note 40 above); quotations from
p. 311.

help one analyze these arguments. One might at first assume that the objections of the genetic critics to traditional apparatus are on the more significant of the levels: they may seem to be saying that the traditional apparatus distorts the story they have to tell, that it reflects a misleading presentation, or fragmentation, of the text. But further reflection casts serious doubt on this assumption. The kinds of variants that genetic critics usually deal with are not the kinds Pebworth and Sullivan discuss: that is, students of textual genetics normally confront revisions made in a linear series, not variants that produce, or result from, independent traditions of transmission. Revisions that form a single sequence (and do not produce versions to be regarded as discrete works) lend themselves perfectly well to consolidated presentation; unlike variants that cluster into distinct groups, each telling a separate story, they form a continuous narrative.[89] If, then, a consolidated treatment of such revisions does not falsify (but rather clarifies) the picture of how the text developed, one must conclude that the choice between the two forms of consolidated treatment—texts with inclusive apparatus and texts with appended apparatus—is a decision on the level of efficiency and convenience for the user. Both forms bring together the evidence from separate documents to produce the editor's reconstruction of a historical process; neither one is inherently incompatible with that goal. The form the apparatus takes in these instances is not an unimportant matter, but it raises practical, not theoretical, issues.

Some of the editors who have opposed the appended style of apparatus have argued that it subordinates the readings thus recorded, taking them out of the context of the text as a whole, and complicates the reader's effort to see a continuous narrative. This position is often regarded as advanced or "radical," challenging the conservatism of an established tradition. In fact it is a traditional position, assuming the primacy of linear reading; the argument, on the other hand, that an appended apparatus does not subordinate material recognizes the more complex ways in which serious reading is performed. When we think of readers extractng all they can from books, reading intensely and productively, we do not picture them moving dutifully from one line to the next, but rather we see them jumping forward and backward, comparing one statement with another, bringing one point into the context of another—precisely the process McGann has effectively described as

89. Some genetic critics may wish to present facsimiles and transcriptions of any or all of the documents that preserve such revisions, simply because any text as it stands in a document is of interest, for it is what exists in physical form. But in these cases a consolidated presentation, showing the development of the text as reflected in a series of documents, is also always in order.

"radial reading."[90] Editors who construct "traditional" appended apparatuses expect serious readers to behave in this way. The form of the text that they choose to present in linear style no doubt reflects their priorities (as, indeed, does the form other editors choose for ordering the readings of inclusive apparatuses), but they are not trying to suggest, by placing the apparatus at the foot of the page or the end of the text, that it is not to be read in the process of trying to understand the text. The *Introductory Statement* (1977) of the Center for Scholarly Editions, rightly regarded as an endorsement of intentionalist editing, described the importance of having variant readings present within the same volume that contains the rest of the text:

> Textual scholars are not the only ones who use textual apparatus: any literary critic—indeed, any careful reader of the text—may, in considering a particular passage, wish to know whether any other versions of that passage have ever appeared. It may be vital to a particular interpretation to know what readings—if any—an editor has rejected as nonauthorial or superseded. If this information has to be searched out in the special-collections department of a particular research library, the matter may never be pursued. But if it is easily available in published form, such as a list in the edition that the critic is using or in a standard edition to be found in many academic and sizable public libraries, one can reasonably expect that the question is much more likely to be investigated. The ready availability of textual data, in other words, is likely to result in better-informed and more fruitful discussion of the writings involved. (pp. 3–4)

The case could be put still more strongly, but even here there is the recognition that apparatuses are to be used actively in reading. Whether one decides to insert variants into a running text or to record them in appended lists properly turns on the details of the individual situation, not on the preconceived notion that one or the other is necessarily easier for the reader to use. Each involves a set of conventions, and in general one can as readily become accustomed to the one system as the other. Some people have found Gabler's inclusive record of Joyce's revisions usable and effective, and others have not; some have been appreciative of Bowers's appended record of William James's revisions, and others have not. Readers, like editors, may disagree about which system should be used in particular cases; but it is not logical to regard one or the

---

90. And that theorists of reading and writing call "recursion," as Robert Murray Davis has pointed out (see note 49 above). This view of reading does not in itself make the contents of books a visual art, despite the similarity of the process to the way our eyes roam over a painting or a sculpture. The way in which we study the physical object containing a verbal text does not alter the status of the text: it may be a set of instructions for the recreation of a work of language, or it may be a visual work as well; but its classification in this regard is not determined by readers' techniques for perusing it.

other system as inherently more practical or convenient or informative for the consolidated presentation of readings from different documents.[91]

If both appended and inclusive apparatus can alternatively serve to present a conflated record of prepublication authorial revisions in a meaningful fashion, both can also be used effectively in presenting non-authorial alterations that emerge from the initial and later publication process. The idea that an apparatus gives readers access to differing texts of a work (while at the same time showing the evidence underlying editorial decisions) is of course the traditional reason for providing apparatus; and it may yet offer a means for reconciling the social and the authorial approaches to editing. In the presidential address mentioned earlier, Fredson Bowers, speaking as one who favors authorial intention, remarked, "If he makes proper use of the apparatus, a cultural historian may find what he needs to know from a thoroughly edited work" (p. 8).[92] An editor approaching texts from the other direction

91. An argument can be made, for example, that appended apparatuses have a particular advantage for texts intended for publication in that they allow for clear texts, and published texts are characteristically clear. The texts of private documents, on the other hand, are typically rough, with canceled and alternative readings; and one can argue that editions of individual private documents are especially well served by inclusive apparatuses, which retain the roughness in the linear text. This theoretical consideration no longer applies, however, when (as in Gabler's *Ulysses*) the readings of more than one private document are brought together in a single record. In such cases an inclusive apparatus produces a composite text, not a literal rendering of an individual documentary text; its primary purpose is thus to serve as a record, not to present a particular physical arrangement of words and punctuation, and the decision to use an inclusive rather than an appended apparatus to accomplish this purpose is a practical, not a theoretical, one. (I have made the argument to use appended apparatus for the texts of works intended for publication and inclusive apparatus for the texts of *individual documents* not intended for publication in, among other places, "Some Principles for Editorial Apparatus," *SB*, 25 [1972], 41–88 [esp. pp. 46–47]; reprinted in *Selected Studies in Bibliography* [1979], pp. 403–450 [see pp. 408–409]. I have also suggested, more than once, that practical considerations in certain situations may alter this recommendation, as in "Literary Editing," in *Literary & Historical Editing*, ed. George L. Vogt and John Bush Jones [1981], pp. 35–56 [esp. pp. 44–45].) Albert J. von Frank, in "Genetic versus Clear Texts: Reading and Writing Emerson," *Documentary Editing*, 9, no. 4 (December 1987), 5–9, takes a practical point of view in examining these alternatives for individual documents and advocates the production, on the computer, of both forms of apparatus. Robert H. Hirst, in *Mark Twain's Letters*, ed. Edgar Marquess Branch *et al.* (1988–   ), has developed a "plain text" system in which inclusive apparatus is used for some details and appended apparatus for others "in order to make the text as complete and informative as possible without destroying its legibility" (1, xlvi). Peter L. Shillingsburg (who believes, with Gabler, that authorial variants are part of the totality of a work but who does not object to appended apparatus) has addressed the separate question of indicating (or, perhaps one should say, nominating) the agent responsible for each variant: see his *Scholarly Editing in the Computer Age: Theory and Practice* (1986), pp. 111–113, which I have discussed (in its 1984 edition) in *SB*, 39 (1986), 40–41 [148–149].

92. See note 67 above. Bowers's basic statement of the requirements for an apparatus is "Notes on Editorial Apparatus," in *Historical & Editorial Studies in Medieval & Early Modern English, for Johann Gerritsen*, ed. Mary-Jo Arn and Hanneke Wirtjes, with Hans

could say that students of authorial intention can find what they need in the apparatus. As long as it is not realistic to imagine that many works can routinely be the subject of alternative critical editions, some means must exist for accommodating different critical approaches within the same volumes. Apparatus (both inclusive and appended) has obviously been the standard device for accomplishing this goal, and the recent dissatisfaction with traditional intentionalist editions has often been directed at an assumed subordination of the readings in apparatus (particularly appended apparatus). All critical editors, like all other critics, bring points of view to their work, and in that sense an emphasis is placed on one approach in each instance. There is no reason why editors cannot, when they choose, take the social instead of the authorial point of view and represent the other in the apparatus. The key is the recognition that apparatus (whether inclusive or appended) presents alternative texts that can be read without difficulty, once the conventions are understood. In a thorough edition, the editor's own point of view does not deprive readers of reading alternative texts. Surely serious readers are not thwarted by the practical necessity (which everyone faces all the time) of accommodating themselves to specific (and sometimes unfamiliar) conventions and routines. Jo Ann Boydston, who shrewdly chose "In Praise of Apparatus" as the title of her 1989 presidential address to the Society for Textual Scholarship, emphasizes how apparatus, far from being a form of subordination, is "the history of a text," recreating "everything that happened to a text, from the author's conception of it throughout its life"—"a story of suspense and discovery, a true textual drama." What one can find in an apparatus, she concludes, is "a stimulating and highly productive intellectual adventure."[93] When apparatus is viewed in this spirit, most of the quarrels over formal arrangements shrink into insignificance, and a fruitful understanding of the validity of alternative textual theories can prevail.

These considerations lead to the question of what a critical text constructed according to a social textual theory would amount to. One would select as copy-text the text that best reflects the intentions of those persons responsible for the public presentation of a work at a given time, and one would emend that text to correct readings not intended by them. Presumably the resulting text would not be very dif-

Jensen (1985), pp. 147–162—cited in my previous survey along with his earlier exchange with Paul Werstine (*SB*, 39 [1986], 37 [145], note 69). Bowers's most detailed examination of the apparatus for recording manuscript variants is "Transcription of Manuscripts: The Record of Variants," *SB*, 29 (1976), 212–264, which emphasizes clear text with appended apparatus but proposes a system of transcription equally applicable to inclusive apparatus.

93. This address is to be published in the fifth volume of *Text*. I am grateful to Professor Boydston for allowing me to have a copy of the paper as delivered.

ferent from the text of a published edition (or, for earlier periods, a scribal manuscript) that actually circulated, for the emendations in most cases would consist entirely of the correction of so-called typographical errors (or slips of a scribe's pen).[94] Theoretically, of course, one might choose to be interested in the intentions of one, rather than all, of the persons involved in the production process—focusing on the intentions of a publisher's editor, for example, and attempting to eliminate the alterations made by compositors and copy-editors. But it seems unlikely (except perhaps in the case of certain well-known editors, like Maxwell Perkins) that the interest in any one of these persons would outweigh the interest in the joint product of all of them. The question then arises as to whether an editorially constructed critical text has any advantage over facsimiles and transcriptions for the student of literary sociology. The critical text would weed out certain slips (such as typographical errors) that could not have been an intended contribution of the production process; but those slips, after all, were in fact one of the results of that process and were a part of the texts that were presented to the public. One wonders, therefore, whether it is worth while to prepare critical texts reflecting the collaborative process of publication, when facsimiles and transcriptions can come closer to showing what the readers of a given time actually had at their disposal.

This point of view is by no means novel: it is, indeed, a traditional one, and it brings us back to the most basic decision that all editors must make. Every editor must decide whether to present the texts of documents (and thus use a noncritical presentation, such as photographic facsimiles or literal—"diplomatic"—transcriptions) or whether to go beyond the documents and attempt to construct the texts of works as they were intended by one or more persons in the past (and thus use a critical presentation, in which documentary texts are emended to bring them closer to the intended forms as conjecturally established). Both approaches have long histories. When editors of the past chose facsimiles and transcriptions, they were no doubt thinking primarily of the value of making documentary evidence widely available; they naturally understood that the texts present in medieval manuscripts and later printed editions were the texts that had emerged from the publication process

94. Such texts are precisely what the Library of America series is producing in those instances in which the text of an already existing scholarly critical edition is not used; but the aim in so doing is not an emphasis on publishers over authors. The series is committed to texts that already exist (critically edited only to the extent of correcting typographical errors); but within that constraint it tries to choose the texts that best (if, inevitably, not fully) represent the auhors' intentions. Correcting typographical errors (which are always listed in the Library volumes) does bring published texts closer to their publishers' intentions—but of course to their authors' intentions as well.

and had been given to readers, but they did not always announce this point because (aside from its being obvious) it had not been made a prominent issue for discussion. Nevertheless, facsimiles and transcriptions do serve the interests of literary sociology and cultural history, and students of those fields do already have a great mass of editions appropriate to their needs. It is true that editors who have decided to produce critical texts have concentrated almost exclusively on authorial intention; but even those who gave little thought to other approaches were obviously aware of the existence of noncritical or documentary editions, serving other purposes, and realized that they had chosen one editorial path rather than another. There has always been an implicit understanding that the reconstruction of authorially intended texts is not the only possible approach to textual study, even if the alternatives were not so precisely delineated or so insistently advocated as they have been in recent years. And can one, in retrospect, blame critical editors for focusing on authorial intention? They may not have considered alternatives; but we, looking back, can see that any other goal for a critical edition generally makes less practical sense. If one is making the critical effort of constructing a text that recreates some moment in the textual history of a work, there is usually little to be gained by choosing any goal other than an authorially intended text—for authorially intended texts are rarely, if ever, to be found perfectly embodied in surviving documents, and their attempted recovery requires acts of informed critical judgment, whereas socially produced texts are available intact in documents that survive and are normally (at least in the era of printing) in no need of reconstruction.[95]

Textual and literary theorists can, and will, continue to debate the nature of texts, but editors have to face the practical question of how their procedures are affected by the theoretical positions they hold. When they examine the choices before them, they will see that their alternatives have not been changed by the debates. There is no escape from the eternal dilemma posed by works in the medium of language (or in any other intangible medium): do we accept the texts of artifacts,

95. Every surviving manuscript book from the pre-print period is a social product, but many manuscript books that contained significant texts no longer survive. A standard procedure among editors of early manuscripts, when faced with multiple texts of particular works, is to attempt the reconstruction of the common ancestor of the surviving texts. The result of this process is a critical text recreating a social product, not an authorially intended text (though the editors of such texts have assumed that they were moving in the direction of an authorial text, as some of their critical judgments in the process of recension make clear). For works primarily transmitted in printed form, there is less occasion for reconstructing socially produced texts; but when no copies of a particular edition are known, it might sometimes be feasible, from the evidence of earlier or later editions or manuscripts, to attempt reconstructing it.

which are primary evidence of the forms of works that were disseminated at particular times, or do we create new texts from that evidence, hoping through the trained historical imagination to come closer to what the authors (or other producers) of the works intended? Editors who have contemplated the conflicting demands of the social and the authorial theories of the production of texts are still confronted with the old choice between documentary and critical editions; and as a practical solution they may well decide, as editors before them have generally decided, to prepare critical texts if their primary interest is in authorial intention and to produce facsimiles or transcriptions if their primary interest is in surviving documents, either as records of the genetic history of texts or as the collaborative products of the publication process. If editing thus goes on as before, it nevertheless will not go unchanged, for the framework of thought within which editorial choices are made will have been more fully articulated as a result of the discussions of social textual criticism. The study of the past inevitably involves thinking about the role of individuals in history as against the role of social process. Both must be investigated: the intentions of individual creative minds will always be a valid subject for textual critics to pursue, as will the forms of texts that reached the public, shaped by the social forces of a given moment. The two are complementary, and any claims that one supersedes the other are obviously naïve. Partisanship is a natural element in attempts to revitalize what is perceived as a neglected concern, and exaggerated claims are a part of the process. But the lasting legacy of the recent debates, after the partisan controversy has taken its place as an episode in the history of scholarship, will be a greater awareness of the theoretical alternatives for textual study and a wider understanding of the position of textual criticism in intellectual life.

PRINTING AT FROBEN'S: AN EYE-WITNESS ACCOUNT

by

JOHAN GERRITSEN *

IT is the purpose of this study to present and discuss the earliest account known to date of the process of printing books from movable types. The account in question is a letter written on the first of July, 1534, from Dulmen near Munster, by the Frisian scholar and statesman Wigle fen Aytta fen Swigchem (1507–1577), Viglius (ab Aytta) Zuichemus to give him his usual Latin style. It was addressed to a friend and fellow-Frisian, Dooitzen Wiarda, and is not known to have been preserved. But Viglius kept the draft, which eventually came, with the rest of his correspondence and his judicial and political commentaries, to the college he had founded at Louvain. There it disappeared, but a copy survived till 1794, and was then lost when the College had French troops quartered in it.

If Viglius had remained merely a scholar, that would have been that. But he lived to become a major statesman and to play an important role in the imperial politics of Charles V, and so the historian, and Archpriest of Malines, C. P. Hoynck van Papendrecht found his correspondence of sufficient interest to print a selection of over four hundred letters in his *Analecta Belgica*, published at The Hague in 1743. Our letter is number 52 in volume 2, part I, and the title placed over it claims that it accurately describes the whole business of printing, its tools and its workmen. Besides the letters, the *Analecta* printed various other of Viglius' papers including his autobiography and his will, but these contain nothing further relating to printing.[1]

---

* The substance of this paper was read to the Bibliographical Society, London, on 15 December 1987. On a number of points it has benefited by the discussion with those then present.

1. The letter came to my notice through some queries relating to its meaning from a good friend and colleague, the historian E. H. Waterbolk, then quite unaware of the signal service he was thus doing to the history of printing. The status of the text is uncertain. It was in the last of a set of four folio volumes numbered V, VI, VII, VIII, of which only VI had a title. This stated that its contents were *descriptæ ex minutis per Feijonem Snecanum aº. 1560*; and the same may have held for the other three. How it came to Louvain is unknown; the Viglian College did at one time possess, through his bequest, folio volumes of drafts taken down from Viglius' dictation and generally checked and sometimes signed by him, but by 1743 many of these had already disappeared. The situation is fully described by Hoynck van Papendrecht, who gives evidence of having been a precise scholar (transcribing a MS title on *2ᵛ of vol. II.i, he refuses to expand but has the printer make shift to insert the marks of abbreviation of the original). The full (Latin) text of the letter is printed below as an appendix; there are no indications that it was manipulated in other respects than in the minutiae of presentation (such as the use of accents on some vowels).

To know Viglius' credentials to provide such a description we must look briefly at one or two elements from his early career. In August 1533 we find him leaving Padua, where he had lately been lecturing, to make for home after an absence of fourteen years, first as a student, then as a tutor, lecturer, and eventually professor at Louvain, Dole, Bourges and finally Padua. In 1532, while at Padua, he had discovered in the library of St Mark's in Venice an important Greek version of Justinian's *Institutes*, by Theophilus Antecessor. He had delivered a course of lectures on it, he had prepared an edition, and he had written a series of *Commentaries* on ten titles of the *Institutes*. Through the good offices of his friend Boniface Amerbach he had found the firm of Froben and Episcopius at Basel prepared to print these, and they acquired an imperial privilege for them dated October 1, 1533. The *Commentaries* carry a dedication to his friend and colleague from Louvain, now at Malines, Gerard Mulert, bearing that same date; the Theophilus carries a seventeen-page dedication to the Emperor Charles V dated May 31, 1533, that has become a classic in its field.

Viglius had sent the manuscript of the Theophilus ahead to Basel, but the *Commentaries* he brought along himself. Before coming to Basel he first visited Erasmus at Freiburg im Breisgau, but he must have arrived in Basel, with the manuscript, at some date in early November, for we have a letter to him from Erasmus, from Freiburg, dated on the eighth of that month. Replying early in December he reported that on his arrival he had found the Theophilus largely printed off, so that the emendations he had wanted to introduce from a second manuscript discovered and given to him by Baptista Egnatius had to go in an appendix. He added that he had given Froben the *Commentaries* to print, and that he was staying to assist Gelenius in correcting the proofs. According to the colophon the Theophilus was not completed till March (the *Commentaries* only give the year), but on January 7, 1534, Viglius returned to Freiburg.

In actual fact, when he arrived only sheets a–h of the Theophilus had been printed off: the heading to the emendations states that they have been incorporated except for the part already printed off, and the list ends with p. 96, i. e. signature h6^v. But though according to its colophon the book was not completed till March, and the *Commentaries* might therefore be thought to have been given precedence, Viglius was sending copies of the Theophilus to Bembo and Egnatius as early as 23 December.[2]

Viglius reached Friesland on March 12, and on May 4 he left again for Westphalia, where in the course of June he settled for a while at Dulmen. Thanks to the diligence of Hoynck van Papendrecht we therefore have almost exact information on his movements, and we have his own testimony, in the letter, that he stayed with Froben at Basel for two months, and that he did so to correct his proofs. Even without this letter, merely from what we know of his movements we should have come to the same conclusion, and we may accordingly feel quite certain that he did indeed have two whole months at

2. Hoynck van Papendrecht, I. i, 93–94.

Basel in which to find out from the inside how things were done at Froben's. We should therefore take what he has to report seriously. It was, moreover, not his first acquaintance with printing: in March, 1530, while studying under Alciati at Bourges, he had read proof for that scholar's *De Verborum Significatione*. Unfortunately, of course, he reports on what interests him, not on what interests us. What he relates is how it is done, but the technical details are beneath—or beyond—him. All the same the letter contains some significant material.

Viglius begins by recalling the circumstances that led to his writing the letter. For practical reasons I shall quote him mainly in English translation, but of course the Latin text is our primary source.[3]

The language aspect is not wholly unproblematic, and at one point, in fact, both German and Dutch will be invoked to make sense of what would otherwise seem extremely improbable in any language. Translation inevitably involves interpretation, and the hardest thing in trying to understand such a text is to avoid interpreting things into it. Therefore the body of the letter will be taken more or less paragraph by paragraph first, but some of the more problematic points will be set aside for discussion in the context of the whole, and some wider issues will be raised finally. To make the text more surveyable, some words and phrases have been capitalized as a guide.

Viglius begins by recalling to Wiarda how on his presenting him with a copy of the *Commentaries* the conversation turned to the art of printing, and how he had promised to supplement the description then given orally by an account in writing, i. e. the present letter.

We may be surprised that in 1534, roughly a century after the invention of the art, a gentleman of culture in Friesland should still require this information, but we should observe that, for all their reputation in early printing, the first printing press to be installed in the Netherlands North of Zwolle (an area including the whole of Friesland) was still half a century away.

What we should also observe is that Viglius presented Wiarda with a copy of the *Commentaries*. Not in itself surprising; but we should note the fact that it could be done at all. This is the book for which he carried the manuscript with him; and for him to be able to present Wiarda with a copy on getting home it must therefore have been completed in the two months he was at Basel. It is a 212-page folio, so totals fifty-three sheets, which implies a production rate of a sheet a day. Also, Viglius must have been at hand during its making from beginning to end. We do not, of course, know that proofs were not sent out to him, but what he has to say about the proofreading, as we shall see presently, ought to imply his attendance at the printing house for that purpose. This, in turn, implies a shop working to a fixed schedule.

But first the evidence. As on the earlier occasion, Viglius' plan is to discuss the printing process in terms of the functionaries engaged in it, in the

3. I am most grateful to my colleagues Drs L. J. Engels and B. L. Hijmans, both skilled in Renaissance Latin, for thorough help over my English rendering, as also to Dr F. Akkerman for his opinion on a further point. The ultimate responsibility naturally remains mine.

order in which they would be engaged on the production of a book, and then to give some details as required of their instruments.

First of all (he writes) there is at its head he whom we call the TYPOG-RAPHER, who is now so called by us, not because in the better shops he should be accustomed to perform any of those tasks (whence originally the title was derived) but because he is the Master of the shop, and sees to its finances, pays all the other workmen hired by him their wages, and super-vises them. For it is his major endeavour to search diligently for books that are worth printing and that are for sale, and for this end to earn the goodwill of learned men who might supply him with something of that nature. And although now the master printers perform hardly any other part of the work, it is yet probable that the first inventors of this art under-took and performed all parts. However, the size and number of the works and books to be printed has since effected that duties performed in the beginning by one and the same person were subsequently divided over many.

This should need little discussion. One might think that a printer would look for books that would sell, rather than for books that were for sale, but the Latin *venales* allows only the one interpretation, and saleability is pos-sibly more or less implied in *prælo dignos*, worth printing. That it matters, we learn at the letter's end. In a situation like Froben's, where practically every one of his books carries an imperial privilege, and several a royal French one as well, the point would be that a book has to be available for publica-tion in the first place. We may also note that, in another letter, Viglius relates with complete equanimity if not with some pride how at the end of that same year 1534, although the Theophilus is selling poorly, the *Commentaries* are already sold out and that Gryphius at Lyon is planning a new edition. The four years were not out, but the imperial privilege was the only one, and it did not run in France. Froben himself reprinted in 1542, and there were other reprints elsewhere. The point is perhaps also worth making that of the poorly selling Theophilus rather more copies seem to be about now than of the *Commentaries*.

Viglius continues:

Therefore, after the Typographer himself, they placed first of all the de-signer and CUTTER OF the actual TYPES. How great his importance is may easily be discerned by the fact that books printed in shapeless char-acters cost no less in labour and expense than those set in elegant type.

Accordingly the first thing the printer has to see to is to obtain the most elegant types possible, and particularly such as shall be able to satisfy not merely the sharp eye of youth but also the failing sight of advancing age. For letters that are too pointed offend the eye, but on the contrary those that are round and have been well designed, even when quite small, win the reader's approval. And from this skill Typography seems indeed first to have derived its origin.

As an account of the aesthetics of typography this is interesting, especially in its clear preference for roman over black letter. Needless to say, Froben's books by this time are generally in roman. But it should be equally clear that Viglius never saw anything of the punch-cutting and subsequent activities that eventually produce the matrices employed by the next workman discussed. The remark on the origins of typography, too, betrays no privileged knowledge, though he does single out the most essential element of the new art, the movable types.

> He is assisted by the FOUNDER OF these same TYPES, who is among the first necessaries in busy and well-equipped shops. For every day the types themselves decay, wear and break; and hence new ones must be substituted by the founder for those that are used up and thrown out. It is true, however, that his work is not such a necessary everyday requirement as that of the others of whom we shall speak hereafter, especially once a shop has been well equipped; nevertheless, just as they have supplied the instruments of the typographic art in the first place, so it is by them that these must be maintained, and as old types fail new ones must again be supplied in their stead.

It is again doubtful whether Viglius saw any typefounding done, but he makes it clear that it is a specialized job, and that in a well-furnished shop like Froben's it only takes place at intervals, a picture that accords well with what we find thirty years later in Plantin's records, where we see François Guyot and Laurens van Everbroeck visiting at intervals to cast type, apparently from matrices owned by Plantin and using matter bought by him.

With the next workman, however, we do at last seem to enter the realm of personal observation.

> They are followed by him whom they call the COMPOSITOR, whose job it is to assemble together the types themselves, which are arranged in their boxes according to the alphabet, and to compose them into groups of characters according to the custom of writing; and when the job has been finished to loosen these same types again and to put them back and distribute them into their boxes. And it is almost this man's chief usefulness and praiseworthy diligence, to compose the types themselves not only fast, but accurately as well. For as in writing those are praised who quickly and correctly take in and set down what is dictated, so also this compositor's diligence merits no less a praise. Those, however, among them who perform a just task are accustomed to deliver about two formes daily; the more diligent ones, three; those who deliver four are reckoned among the most excellent; they, however, who deliver only one are deservedly branded with lazyness. And indeed, if delay occurs here the work of all the other workmen suffers a hurtful delay. Accordingly printers are accustomed to look to it that the compositors in particular carry out their task diligently and complete their formes at regular intervals, by which these can once and again be placed under the press in order that thereby they may be produced

and printed more correctly and perfectly. In which their labour likewise is not small: for however careful they are, if they do not also have some erudition and judgment, they cause much work to the correctors, of whom we shall speak hereafter, and greatly hamper the other workmen and are of little use to their master printers.

The most remarkable statement here is that the lay of the case is alphabetical. It seems hazardous to dismiss such information out of hand: it is, after all, the earliest known statement on the matter, though on the other hand it is not very precise. It should be possible to keep the characters in alphabetical order and to vary merely the size of the boxes, but advancing this as an argument here would be playing devil's advocate, and not merely because of the carpentry that would be involved. Since the capitals at the top of the case are in fact in alphabetical order, unless one actually does some typesetting oneself, one may easily get the idea that the other characters would be the same. But we are also told that speed and accuracy of composition are valued, and they would undoubtedly demand an ergonomically justified arrangement capable of easy construction.

Another point we should dwell on for a moment is the comparison with scribal writing. Viglius takes it entirely for granted that scribal writing is done from dictation, a point that is interesting in its own right; but one may accordingly wonder whether he means to imply that composition is done the same way. It would then, however, be remarkable, given the avowed method of his description, that he makes no mention of a reader as a member of the team. It would thus seem that the point of the comparison is merely in the speed and accuracy of performance, and not in this external circumstance. The requirement of erudition in a compositor has only been dropped in our own day.

The PERFORMANCE DATA I propose to pass over for the moment: they deserve thorough discussion in the light of fuller information and will also require a look at the books themselves.

The letter continues:

This compositor, then, is followed by him whom we have called the COR-RECTOR. This function is generally entrusted to some scholar, who reads over the composed formes with understanding and checks whether all types and letters are correctly joined together, and all words and paragraphs properly separated. But this duty the master printers themselves, if they have any learning, sometimes undertake. And this task Erasmus of Rotterdam himself (to whom the Frobenian Printing-house owes its first fame) did not scorn to undertake: as a result of which his works saw the light all the more correctly. The same solicitude has also kept me at Basel for two months while publishing my commentaries, in order that this first birth should be the more perfect. And yet at that time the responsibility for this task so far as all other works were concerned was in the hands of Sigismund Gelenius, a famous scholar, and worthy of far better things. And although nearly all master PRINTERS STRIVE first of all AFTER PROFIT, unless they have a learned corrector of delicate taste, however elegant their types, and however much they applaud all else, yet they lose praise unless the corrector's care is apparent: for any student requires faultless books rather than handsome ones.

Before discussing this we should look at the next paragraph as well, without which the last one cannot be properly understood.

Working under the corrector there is he whom we call the READER. For COLLATION of the first printed forme WITH all THE EXEMPLAR is altogether necessary, and if it is to be done properly it requires two men's work. And in well-regulated shops it is customary for THREE PROOFS to be produced, and duly to be READ individually, by which faults and errors may be expurgated throughout.

We see a number of things here. First of all, there is a printer's reader whose job it is to collate the proof with the copy, and secondly there is a corrector. The corrector, we are told, must be a scholar and a man of taste; it is his task which Viglius apparently undertook for his own work instead of leaving it to Gelenius. About the qualifications required of the reader nothing is said, though we are told he works under the corrector. But we are also told that for the collation with the exemplar to be done properly, two men are needed, and the passage about the corrector is silent on the exemplar. This makes it likely that the proper interpretation of the passage about the reader is that the collation of proof with copy is done in the way that has always been accounted best, the reader reading out the exemplar aloud and the corrector checking the proof. Especially when done several times over (as personal experience has shown), it is the safest way there is.

This interpretation would also make sense of the often quoted passage from Zeltner, 1716, if we assume that Zeltner mistook the successive reading of three or four proofs for the simultaneous reading aloud of the text for three or four sheets. It is quite true that, as he observes, a reader's steady tempo would make it hard for the compositor to waste time in rêverie, but one may well doubt the efficiency of composition in a shop where three or four sheets were being read out simultaneously *sonora voce*, in a resounding or ringing voice, rather than, as Dr Gaskell translates, a *clear* one.[4]

If that (orthodox) interpretation of the reader's job is allowed, it follows that the three proofs next mentioned belong to successive stages of correction, i. e. mean proof and two revises. The three proofs are to be read individually, which should mean read completely, not merely checked for correction of what had been marked, but as we are told that collation with the exemplar is necessary for the *first* forme we may think that the process was repeated

4. *A New Introduction to Bibliography*, 1972, 49, note 32. The last sentence of the Latin needs no *sic*. The method appealed to Zeltner because it imposed a set speed and eliminated daydreaming.

reading the last corrected proof or revise aloud. We also find confirmed that it is the corrector's responsibility to watch over style, typographical probably as well as linguistic, if not literary. Another corollary of what we are told must be discussed when we return to the compositor.

Attention should also be drawn to two incidental remarks: nearly all master printers, we are told, strive first of all after profit, and the pulling of three proofs is customary in well-regulated printing-houses. In other words, to stay in business a printer must first of all be a hard-headed businessman, and secondly and no less importantly he must get his business properly organized. The remark is also characteristic of Viglius, whose own career as a statesman was based on corresponding principles.

Let us follow him to the next stage of the printing process.

And after this the PRESSMEN are free to print. One of them moistens the balls with ink and in turn strikes them together, by which the ink shall spread over them more conveniently; and with them he then wets the types all over; the other, however, puts the PREPARED PAPER under the press and then works the press itself, and the printed sheets having been taken off again puts new paper under. The paper cannot, however, be PRINTED except ON ONE SIDE of the sheet on a single day, BECAUSE IT MUST FIRST BE DRIED lest the ink runs and in order that it shall take the impression on the other side the more conveniently. For this reason some drying substances are even added to the ink, by which the printed sheets can more easily retain the fluid. For unless they have been well dried the printed letter-forms may easily disappear by beating when they are BOUND.

This presents the well-known picture of the two pressmen and their division of labour, but it does not give us much of an idea of the actual process. The matter of the drying, too, is ambiguous. Here again, it is wise to let matters rest for a moment, until we shall have all the relevant information that the letter contains. Its next sentence underlines this, but more is to come.

Last of all, to be sure, there is need for a FOLDER, whose duty it is to dry the printed sheets, next to fold them, and thereafter to arrange them in two's, three's or fours, as we now say; and then to collect those again into a complete volume and copy AS THEY ARE SOLD; the formes themselves, too, when the number to be printed is complete, and before the types are distributed again into their compartments, he must carefully RINSE, lest any black and viscous liquid sticks to the types, and (when new FORMES are to be prepared) they can for that reason, even when loosened, less easily be composed again; in addition he must WET the BALLS AND the PAPER, in order that it shall more easily receive the impressed letters, by means of some interposed DAMPENED LINEN CLOTHS, and also see to it that the INK is properly MADE. In performing these duties, though, the pressmen themselves sometimes take a part.

Whether the pressmen take a hand or no, this last of the printing-house op-
eratives has a complicated job. He must fold the sheets, but we are not told
unambiguously whether this means just doubling them up or folding them to
their final format. (Viglius may not have seen any books below folio format
printed or gathered; both his own were folios. Cf. the discussion of formes
below.) Next he must quire them, and then he must gather the quires into
complete copies, 'as they are sold'. I am not aware of instances from this
period, but cases seen or reported from the next century invariaby have been
folded to the correct format (though not necessarily quired correctly). For
folios, which is what the majority of Froben publications are, it does of
course come to the same thing. But the quiring before gathering is interesting.

What is also interesting is the addition of 'as they are sold', which very
clearly does not envisage binding or in fact any form of provisional sewing
(such as was common at least in the eighteenth century). It also, like the
whole account, implies a printer who is his own publisher and does not
normally work for others.

Further, he must rinse the formes prior to distribution by the compositor,
and he must dampen both the balls and the paper before printing, using
dampened linen cloths for the purpose. There is no mention of urine for the
balls. Finally, he must make the ink.

After the workmen, the instruments.

The principal tools of the printing house, however are the types, paper, ink,
balls and press.

About the TYPES nothing further need be said.

As to the PAPER it is unnecessary to explain how it is made from bruised
and softened linen cloths. It is usually distinguished into sheets, quires,
reams and bales, to use vulgar words where Latin ones are wanting. The
bale, then, contains ten reams, the ream twenty quires, the quire again
twenty-five sheets. When, however, a formless bale of paper sells for five
florins, when the print has been added it is usually estimated at nearly
twenty.

The 500-sheet ream is hardly remarkable for this area, but it is pleasant to
have the ten-ream bale as well. The final statement will draw some present
comment. A surprise is, however, in store for us with the next statement.

The INK, however, of books and printers is not much different from writing
ink, which is principally made of linseed oil and resin.

For printing ink the recipe is adequate enough (though the pigment is missing) but it produces what is known as 'varnish' and thus the statement about
writing ink is disturbing, the more so as Plantin in 1567 clearly says that the

two are not to be compared.[5] Did Viglius, as he wrote the letter, really think he was dipping his pen in linseed oil and resin?

The BALLS have a semicircular shape and consist of skin stuffed with hair. Because it easily wears it must frequently be changed.

This misses out the wooden base and handle, but is otherwise adequate. The translation, however, calls for a defence. The balls, Viglius says, *constant folio pilis suffulto*, and a *folium* is first of all a leaf, then a sheet of paper or parchment, then a number of other more specialized things, but never so far as I can find is it skin. Yet skin is what we have come to expect here, and though we must reckon with the possibility that in the early days things were done differently, none of the meanings of *folium* denotes a substance that could conceivably be of any use for inking. We should remember that it is wetted, too. For an explanation we must, I suggest, turn to Viglius' linguistic background, and we must assume that, habitually, he did not think in Frisian but in Dutch. Viglius scholars consulted, though they can give no certain enlightenment on this point, do not object. Viglius learnt, and for that matter also wrote, about printing, in what today at any rate we would term a German-speaking area. Now the German word for animal skin is *Fell*, a word that, as *vel, fel* also exists in Dutch and in Frisian. But the Dutch *vel*, unlike its German and Frisian cognates, can equate with *folium*, as in addition to the common *skin* sense it can denote a sheet: of paper, parchment, &c. We would have here, then, an extreme example of the well-known phenomenon that every vernacular has its own Later Latin.

The next statement is perhaps the most startling in the whole letter:

The PRESS has nothing special that merits explaining.

It seems plain that by this time the press could hardly have been much simpler than what we know from the early cuts, and in fact may not have differed much from what we find in the earliest first-hand drawing, Saenredam's of 1628.[6]

What Viglius' statement therefore ought to mean is: the press is like those presses that you know from your own everyday experience. In Friesland, oil and linen presses, if not wine presses, should at least have been known: they give the screw principle but hardly the hose &c. The basic mechanism of the

5. *La Première et la Seconde Partie des Dialogues François pour les Jeunes Enfans*, section *L'Imprimerie*: 'Ie laisse ce que nous auons de commun auec l'écriuain, comme le papier & l'encre, encore que nostre encre soit semblable à la sienne.'—'Quelle difference y a-il?'—'La difference est, que la nostre est faite de tormentine, huile, & fumée: aussi est-il necessaire qu'elle le soit.'

6. Reproduced by J. W. Enschedé, 'De drukpersafbeeldingen in Ampzing en Scriverius 1628', *Tijdschrift voor Boek- en Bibliotheekwezen*, 6 (1908) 265–268. This sequel to his substantial study of two years earlier in the same journal was unfortunately missed by Dr Gaskell. To the reference in his *New Introduction*, p. 123, note 3, should also be added pp. 262–277.

carriage was known from such instruments as the mangle; but this too is far from the whole story. Rather, the purely mechanical aspects of the technology would not seem to have interested Viglius, an observation that can be made at various other points in his account.

> The WAGES as well of pressmen and compositors as of other workmen of the printing house vary according to the conditions of the times and places and quality of the men.

We could have guessed.

This, my Dooitzen, is what I had to impart to you, &c.

With the full information contained in the letter now available, we can turn back to the points left out of the discussion so far. The principal of these are the performance data. According to Viglius, two formes a day is the norm, three is good, four is superb. Distribution is done by the compositor himself. Let us relate this to his own books. The Theophilus is something under 1,000 ems of Greek per page, the Latin *Commentaries* about half as much again, both without the side-notes. They are both folios, so the normal double-page forme would contain twice this amount of type, up to 3,000 ems without the sidenotes. This would give a daily production of over 6,000 ems (two formes) as the norm, over 12,000 (four formes) for a superb compositor. Moreover we are speaking of the delivery of formes, not of the rate of type-setting so that, assuming our superb compositor to be able to distribute at a rate commensurate with his type-setting prowess, he would have to set at the rate of about 16,000 ems per day, 1,300 to 1,600 ems per hour, depending on the length of his working day.

Let us now confront this with known data from the period. Beginning in October 1563, Plantin's best compositor, Cornelis de Molenaer, is on record for a great many years. Though the records are often insufficiently specific, his average rate can accordingly be calculated over fairly long periods, and then may reach about 5000 ems per day, as a rule in a rather smaller letter than in the Theophilus with its 20-line measurement of 109 millimetres (roughly *texte* or great primer) and one that would mostly have been faster to set. In a twelve-hour working day, with make-up and so forth done in the workman's own time but distribution in the boss's, that would mean about 550 ems per hour of actual setting.

For the 1565 Nonius Marcellus, set in *mediane* (roughly pica), Jan Strien set 25 formes in five weeks, a weekly average of 22,440 ems, just over 400 ems per hour, without the *gaillarde* side-notes. His colleague Gosuin Gouberi set 39 formes of the same book in eight weeks, which amounts to still less. Adding the work on the side-notes we get near to Cornelis' average.

These figures are of the same order of magnitude as those assembled by Dr Gaskell from the records of the Cambridge University Press, and we are thus almost inevitably led to the conclusion that the *forma* here must be the single folio page. This then naturally prompts the question whether that does also mean single-page formes, with single-pull printing on folded sheets such as we know from the early days of printing.

Haebler states that till c. 1470 the greater number of incunables were printed page by page, and that the representations of the press show that this practice could have continued till the end of the period, though that is no proof that it did so happen. Dr Needham states that 'By the mid-1470's, when setting and printing by formes on the two-pull press began to become common, conspicuously awkward textual joins, the result of carelessness and inaccurate casting off of copy, can easily enough be found' and cites Haebler (who does not, however, view the matter in quite that way).[7]

Tests for the method used are not hard to find: differential inking; identical material in forme-mates; incorrect alignment of forme-mates; differential perfecting of forme-mates; printing on folded paper evidenced by blind impression in forme-mate; red shift; and (just possibly) wrong impositions. They are not hard to imagine, but often quite hard to use. The problem is that most of the tests depend on things going wrong, and that responsible printers may therefore discard what could be evidence before it ever gets into a volume. Besides, some of the phenomena described are unlikely to show up in the average incunable. One is not surprised to find single-pull in a Koberger folio of 1477 so big that no other method could then have produced it; or to find it in the work of small men like the printers of the Delft Bible of the same year or like Jacob Bellaert at Haarlem as late as the eighties. But for a big firm like Froben's to have used it still in 1534 would be extremely surprising. It is therefore fortunate that it can be proved that in 1500, at least, Johann Amerbach and Johann Froben de Hammelburg used two-pull printing for their quarto *Decretum Gratiani* of that year. Printed in red and black, it has enough identical red shift in the two halves of the sheet to prove that these must have been printed together in one forme.

The point is emphasized because of the conclusion that the letter ought not here to be accepted at its face value. The word *forma* occurs seven times, all but one in the plural, but not all with the same reference. In four it is clearly the forme of type delivered by the compositors, in the other three it is as clearly the proof pulled from this by the pressmen. Viglius' *forma* cannot be the full, two-pull forme, but we can also rule out that Froben still practised single-pull printing. Where is the way out? It may lie in a well-known linguistic phenomenon, language lagging behind external reality. We have long been accustomed to green, and are even accustoming ourselves to white blackboards. 'Whiteboard' now seems to be gaining currency for the latter, 'greenboard' appears to have remained largely a dictionary word. The printer's forme, as it came into existence in the early days of printing, was the single

7. Konrad Haebler, *Handbuch der Inkunabelkunde* (1925), 65–67, 76–78; Paul Needham, 'Division of Copy in the Gutenberg Bible: Three Glosses on the Ink Evidence', *PBSA* 79 (1985), 411–426, p. 426.

folio page, printed at a single pull on a folded sheet. Plainly this is the sense in which Viglius uses the word, and he must be doing so because he has heard it used that way.[8] But equally plainly technology has advanced, and two of these 'formes' are now printed within a single chase, at two pulls. But that is technology, and of no interest to Viglius. The press has nothing special that merits explaining.

Another remark that should be dwelt upon further is what we are told about the compositors' key position in the shop. They in particular must

carry out their task diligently and complete their formes at regular intervals;

if they do not,

the work of all the other workmen suffers a hurtful delay;

and also if they have not sufficient erudition

they cause much work to the correctors . . . , and greatly hamper the other workmen.

What all this refers to is that unless the compositor works to schedule, the men coming after him stand to lose. They will have to be idle, and for the pressmen at least that means loss of income. This tallies precisely with what we see at another well-regulated establishment, Plantin's, where there is a system of fines for those causing delay, so as to reimburse those who suffer by it. Thus we see how the compositor composing the wrong forme has to reimburse the pressmen, the pressmen who deliver the wrought-off forme too late for distribution must reimburse the compositors. It is a good shop, so it does not happen often, but it happens, and gets recorded. And those who cannot meet its standards, such as Benedict Wertlaw, who beat too fat, are forced to leave while still owing five stivers for beer.[9]

There is no reason to quarrel with Professor McKenzie over what happened at the Cambridge University Press in the eighteenth century but, as I have suggested in print before, and as has been stated more recently by Dr Needham, the eighteenth century is no strict evidence for the seventeenth or earlier centuries any more than these earlier centuries are for the eighteenth. We have to work with generalizations, but they need not be the same for all times, and they must not be applied to specific cases without checking that they apply. A further instance will appear presently.

There may well have been (indeed, there probably were) printers who were proud of muddling through; there certainly were printers who stuck to fixed schedules. But workmen may fall ill, or may go on the tiles, equipment

---

8. It is evident that Viglius never considers formats below folio.

9. The precise fault quoted here is interpretation. Plantin was dissatisfied with his work and told him so. He claimed the paper was insufficiently sized, so Plantin gave him good Troyes paper, with which he could do no better. He lasted almost four months in 1564, having started up the third press. (Antwerp, Museum Plantin-Moretus, MS 31, *Journal des Ouvriers 1563–74*, fol. 3ᵛ.)

may break down, even in the best regulated shops. The smaller the shop, the more it hurts. Even at Plantin's one cannot be certain how things went on when, after the first few years, full records were no longer needed, and so were not kept, though such evidence as has been examined suggests that, if methods changed, method remained. But it is important to realize that this is then only a working hypothesis.

If the account so far is accepted, a problem attaches to the proofreading. This has to be done against the exemplar, which is reasonably simple if composition is continuous, but must also have been feasible when it was by formes (which such evidence as has been gathered suggests was the case with Viglius' *Commentaries*). When can the proofreading have been done? It is a fairly slow job, and it can mean more than merely checking the proofs: restarting in 1563 Plantin buys four thesauruses, seven dictionaries, two biblical concordances, a Latin Bible, and a Greek New Testament, to the tune of some sixty florins, 'pour le service de la correction'. Later, he buys more. Moreover, the corrector will have to deal with a number of compositors: in 1563 Plantin engaged Matthijs Ghisbrechts to correct the work of six men, all six of them setting by formes. What if they all produced their proofs and revises at the same time?

The answer could lie in an aspect of the matter that generally seems not to have had sufficient attention. Of course compositors are not composing the whole day; they are also distributing, dressing formes, etc. This could provide part of the answer. But there is something else. There has been repeated mention of a twelve-hour day, and that may have been correct for the Continent, though for England it may have been too long. But the twelve hours are not a solid block, any more than our present eight-or-fewer-hour day is: they are punctuated by what we would now call coffee, lunch and tea breaks, amounting to up to two and a half hours in England, and on the Continent perhaps even more. All in all this means that there are on average four or five hours every day when the compositor will not need the copy. It should also be added that when the working day starts (at five or six a.m.) the compositors start composing and the pressmen printing: any preparations needed have been made in their own time. There is a clear illustration in the later Plantin records, when the pressmen complain about the new doorman, who will not let them in early enough. Especially when printing in red and black they do not have enough time to start printing at six, when their working day starts.

In this sort of situation it makes no difference whether setting is continuous or by formes. Setting by formes must necessarily have been the earliest method, and printing house routine will accordingly have been based on it. With the full forme it can still be found throughout the seventeenth century, though it is hard to tell when it stopped. Dr Gaskell's statement that Plantin changed to continuous setting around 1565 rests on a misunderstanding.[10]

10. *New Introduction*, 42 and note 9; the reference must be to II, 303, where Dr Voet deals with this matter. Dr Gaskell then only knew his book in proof. A fuller discussion of

Dr Voet, whom he cites, merely states that Plantin then went over to having a book set by a single compositor instead of two, and even that is only a general but not a particular truth. But when he uses two compositors on a single book, each now usually (not invariably) has full sheets to set. When Plantin changed over to continuous setting I do not know, for I have no useful records beyond 1570, but at that date setting by formes was still there, and it is a fairly logical way of dealing with printed copy.

The next statement to return to is the one about selling price as a factor of paper price:

> When, however, a formless bale of paper sells for five florins, when the print has been added it is usually estimated at nearly twenty.

Plantin buys paper for the 1564 Virgil at 26 stivers/ream, for the Sambucus Horace at 23½ stivers/ream. On 26 February 1564 he sells 500 of either to Arnold Brickman & Co at the Fat Hen for 3 florins (sixty stivers) a ream. That is less than three times the cost of paper, but of course when the book reaches the retail customer it will cost more. Shortly after, on 5 March, he sells two copies of the Virgil at 3½ stivers each. The book is 19½ sheets, in an edition of 2500 copies; the paper used, with waste and proofs, was 101 reams. This amounts to a paper cost per copy of just over 1 stiver, so a retail price almost 3½ times the paper cost, not so far from what Viglius states, and again the sale is not to the ultimate user. The total cost per copy, incidentally, which Plantin works out correctly, is one and a half stivers.

He also sells two copies of the Horace at 3 stivers. This was 11 sheets in an edition of 1250, using 28 reams, so costing just over ½ stiver in paper, seven-eighths of a stiver in all, per copy to produce. This agrees precisely with Viglius. Of the very comparable Lucan (11½ sheets, 29½ reams, 1250 copies) Brickman buys 300 at again 3 florins a ream, and of this, too, two copies are sold at 2 stivers each. These are some of the earliest books for which we have records, and they are sold in Antwerp, thirty years after the letter. But they do bear out Viglius' words as a general statement.

Perhaps the most important point in the letter still remains, viz the matter of casting off:

> The paper cannot, however, be PRINTED except ON ONE SIDE of the sheet on a single day, BECAUSE IT MUST FIRST BE DRIED lest the ink runs and in order that it shall take the impression on the other side the more conveniently. For this reason some drying substances are even added to the ink, by which the printed sheets can more easily retain the fluid. For unless they have been well dried the printed letter-forms may easily disappear by beating when they are BOUND.

this and some related points is in my 'Plantin aan het werk—Het tweede begin,' *Het oude en het nieuwe boek, De oude en de nieuwe bibliotheek: Liber Amicorum H. D. Vervliet,* Kapellen (1988), 115–127.

We have here the only reference to binding, but that is not its main point, which is rather the statement that, because of the condition of the ink, only one side of the paper can be printed on a single day. Viglius is quite emphatic that it is because of the ink, and his mention of the addition of drying substances adds to his credibility here. But it is not so clear what he means by the disappearance of the ink during binding, a process of which this is the only mention. We may also note that quite soon after his 1563 restart, Plantin, who did not then do any binding himself, but who employed numerous binders to bind sufficient numbers of his books to suggest that they were bound on spec and not on commission, bought a big press for pressing unbound books. And why should the dried sheet take the impression on the other side the more conveniently? Is the problem offsetting? For it is a fact that in many early books partial offsets of the same or (sometimes) another sheet are frequently to be found. And should it then be necessary to wet the paper again for perfecting? For to take the ink properly a damp paper is required, and we are in fact told that drying the paper is the folder's duty. One thing seems certain: if for the normal book at least half a day had to pass before a sheet could be perfected, there would be every point in setting by formes.

Since Viglius is not more specific, answers to the questions just put must be tentative, but some observations can be made. The drying of the ink involves two processes, oxydation of the varnish and absorption by the paper, which must be balanced to make the pigment stick. If absorption is faster than oxydation, the pigment is no longer protected by the varnish, and may rub off. To avoid this a strong varnish is needed, but the problem is that the lampblack with which it is mixed considerably weakens the varnish.[11] It is therefore essential to ensure that the ink has dried properly before perfecting, and again before gathering.

To show that early printing and perfecting did in fact not take place on the same day proved more difficult. What is needed is a book that will allow of proper type and/or headline analysis (preferably both), and this is not easy to find when the quality of printing is high and headlines are frequently absent. Only a single case can be reported so far, viz *Die Cronycke van Hollandt Zeelandt ende Vrieslant* printed by Jan Seversz at Leiden in 1517. This is a fat folio of 284 formes, all but a few with headlines, set by two compositors from two different main fonts that were both sufficiently worn to make type analysis (just) possible. The quiring is a curious mixture of sixes and fours, and the division of labour between the two compositors (who each set full sheets) is equally curious, but both the headlines and the types make it evident that practice (for a run of sixes) was as follows.

The first forme through the press was the outer forme of the outer sheet, which was followed by the outer forme of the middle sheet. Next these two sheets were perfected in the same order, after which came the outer formes of the inner sheet and of the outer sheet of the next quire. These were then

11. Brugman, J. M., *Drukinkten in de praktijk*, Amsterdam (1951), 14–15.

similarly perfected, the middle and inner sheet of the second quire followed in the same way, after which the process started all over again.[12]

That Froben worked in precisely this way cannot be proved, but it is evident from what Viglius wrote that some such system must have been in operation, and the pattern of recurrence of the four-line ornamental E's, a fairly frequent feature in the *Theophilus,* suggests that it was not too dissimilar. It would seem to be a system that nobody would use who did not have to, but given the problem of the ink it is the most efficient way of meeting that.

To sum up: although the letter is the earliest document presently known on the subject, the art of printing with movable types was almost a century old when it was written. The technical information it supplies is severely limited; the process it describes is basically the process as we know it from later evidence, but the manner of proceeding partly differs. Of the prototypography it can tell us nothing: the few historical remarks it contains are clearly inferential. In its use of the word *forma,* however, it seems to retain an echo of an earlier state of affairs, when the 'forme' was coextensive with the imposed folio page. Just how long that state persisted in different places is not perhaps as evident as has been suggested; but it is probably only one reason why, as it would appear, composition long (but not exclusively) continued by formes. It would need further research into the composition of the inks to determine a date when perfecting and printing *might* have fallen on the same day, but it is doubtful if after four or five centuries the evidence remains. The main advantages of consecutive setting appear in setting prose from manuscript, and it may well be that it was first confined to this. But when the manuscript given to the compositor was a regularly written scribal copy, for which Plantin again provides early evidence, even this advantage was not considerable.

In its concentration on the workmen and the principal tools the letter gives us a precise listing of the functions in the shop and their distribution over individuals, though in the case of the compositors and pressmen it gives no numbers. There is clearly but one master, and one corrector with his reader; probably only one folder, considering the number of different tasks he is assigned. The reader is met here for the first time, and is part of the job Viglius specifically stayed in Basel for. How general his role was we cannot tell; there is no evidence for it at Plantin's.

Of the tools it is a pity more is not said.

APPENDIX
EPISTOLA LII.
DOTHIÆ WYARDÆ.
Omnem artis typographiæ rationem instrumentorum, operariorumque, accuratè describit.

Quum peracto studiorum meorum curriculo in Patriam reversum, multa (uti fieri solet) tum parentes ac propinqui inter quos te, mi *Dotia,* facile mei amantissimum

12. See my "Jan Severz prints a Chronicle," *Quærendo,* 21 (1991), forthcoming.

sum expertus, de anteactæ vitæ studiis, iisque rebus, quarum aliquam cognitionem longa experientia ac annorum quatuordecim continua absentia comparavissem, curiosè interrogaretis: ac tandem forte mentio incidisset artis Typographicæ, occasione nata ab exemplari commentariorum meorum in aliquot Institutionum *Justiniani* titulos, quos in meo ex Italia reditu Basileæ *Frobenianæ* officinæ imprimendos tradideram, tibique velut militiæ meæ tesseram dono obtuleram; non satis tunc tibi facere potui exponendo ea quæ ibidem observaram, nisi eadem quoque scripto me explicaturum reciperem. Et quanquam non ea cura singula notaram, ut de ipsis aliquid litteris me posse tradere considerem (quippe qui obiter, & quasi per transennam dumtaxat quæ in ea officina gerebantur conspexeram) extorsit tamen hoc ab mea verecundia tua authoritas, dum nihil tibi denegare ausus fui, ut ut plus promiserim, quàm præstando solvendoque essem. Et lubenter quidem silentio hanc obligationem dissimulassem, nisi tua tam crebra appellatio, me tandem calamum in manum assumere compulisset: fidem quidem lubenter impleturus, quatenus videlicet se mea extendit memoria. In quo si quid desiderabis, tibi imputa, qui a me potius, quàm a peritioribus ista cognoscere volueris. Sequar autem ordinem quem tunc tenebam singulosque officinæ Typographicæ ministros paucis recensebo.

Inprimis ei præest is quem Typographum nominamus, qui sic nunc a nobis vocatur, non quod ipse aliquid earum operarum in celebrioribus officinis soleat subire (unde principiò nomen desumptum est) sed quod officinæ Magister sit, sumptusque subministret, cæterisque operariis omnibus a se conductis mercedem exolvat, eisque superintendat. Nam hujus præcipuum est studium, ut libros prælo dignos venalesque conquirat, atque in id doctorum virorum, qui ejusmodi aliquid suppeditare ei possint, gratiam sibi comparet. Et quanquam nunc primarii Typographi nihil fere præterea operæ præstent, primos tamen ejus artis inventores, omnes partes subiisse explevisseque verisimile est. Verùm operum librorumque imprimendorum magnitudo, multitudoque deinceps effecit, ut munia ab uno eodemque principiò tractata in plures deinde dividerentur.

Igitur post ipsum Typographum proximo loco ponebant eum, qui ipsos litterarum typos effingit, sculpitque. Cujus quanta sit præstantia, ex eo dijudicari facile potest, quod non minus laboris sumptusque libri deformibus, atque alii bene elegantibus, characteribus impressi, constent. Proinde id inprimis Typographo studio esse debet, ut typos quàm elegantissimos conquirat, ac tales præsertim, qui non solum adolescentium perspicacitati; verum etiam senescentium labentibus oculis queant satisfacere. Nimium enim acutæ litteræ oculos offendunt, ac contra quæ rotundæ apteque concinnatæ sunt, etiamsi minutiores sint, lectori applaudunt. Et ab hoc quidem artificio, Typographia principiò originem duxisse videtur.

Cui adminiculatur eorumdem typorum fusor, qui operosis locupletibusque officinis cùm primis est necessarius. Quotidie enim ipsi typi litterarii labascunt, atteruntur, confringunturque: unde in consumptorum rejectorumque locum, novi per fusorem substituendi sunt. Verùm licet ejus non ita necessaria, quotidianaque, ut cæterorum de quibus postea dicemus, est opera, præsertim in officina semel bene instructa: attamen ut illi primi Impressoriæ artis instrumenta subministrarunt, ita per eosdem retinenda, & veteribus deficientibus typis in eorum locum novi rursus sufficiendi sunt.

Hos sequitur is quem Compositorem vocant, cujus officium est typos ipsos litterarios per loculos suos ordine juxta Alphabetum collocatos, secundùm materiam subjectam libri, operisque imprimendi, in unum componere, & in syllabas juxta scribendi consuetudinem colligere, opereque completo rursus postea eosdem typos dissolvere, inque suos loculos reponere, distribuereque. Et hujus quidem fere præcipuus est usus, commendabilisque industria, non solummodò ut cito, verùm etiam emendate typos ipsos componat. Uti enim in scribendo ii laudantur, qui & celeriter & correcte dictata recipiunt, describuntque: sic & hujus Compositoris diligentia, non minorem laudem meretur. Qui justam autem inter hos operam implent, solent fere duas formas quotidie exhibere: diligentiores, tres: qui quatuor, hi cum primis præstantes habentur: qui verò unam dumtaxat, ignaviæ meritò notantur. Atque hic quidem si cessatum fuerit, cæterarum omnium operarum labor damnosam patitur remoram. Itaque in hoc Typographi vigilare solent, ut ipsi Compositores suum officium diligenter expleant, formasque tempestivè absolvant, quò semel iterumque prelo subjici, ac sic correctius emendatiusque exire, ac imprimi queant. In quo itidem non parva eorum est opera: etenim quantumvis sint diligentes, nisi quoque aliquid eruditionis, judiciique habeant, Correctoribus de quibus postea dicemus, multum negotii facessunt, & cæteris operariis magnum impedimentum adferunt Typographisque officinæ Magistris parum sunt utiles.

Huic autem Compositori succedit is quem Correctorem vocavimus. Quod officium docto alicui viro fere committi solet, qui cum judicio formas compositas relegat, recenseatque num recte omnes typi litteræque sint conjunctæ, syllabæque ac orationes distinctæ. Ac hoc etiam officii ipsimet Typographi, si quid litterarum tenent, sibi nonnunquam assumere solent. Et hanc quidem operam ipse *Erasmus* Roterodamus (cui *Frobeniana* Typographia celebritatem primam debet) subire non gravabatur: quo opera sua eo emendatius in lucem exirent. Eadem solicitudo & me in commentariis meis edendis menses duos Basileæ detenuit, ut prima fœtura emendatior prodiret. Quanquam eo tempore hoc officii præstabat in cæteris operibus, quæ in eadem officina imprimebantur, *Sigismundus Gelenius*, vir insigniter doctus, & longe meliore fortuna dignus. Et cùm ipsi Typographi quæstum ferè omnes imprimis sectentur: nisi doctum emunctæque naris Correctorem habeant, quantumvis elegantes sint typi, cæteraque omnia applaudant: laudem tamen amittunt, nisi Correctorum diligentia appareat: cùm quilibet Studiosus libros magis emendatos, quàm elegantes requirat.

Correctori autem subservit is quem Lectorem vocant. Collatio enim primæ formæ impressæ cum exemplari, omnino necessaria est: & ut rectè fiat, duorum operam requirit. Solentque in bene institutis officinis tres confici formæ, ordineque singulæ relegi, quo omni ex partè mendæ vitiaque expurgentur.

Ac deinde Impressoribus libera imprimendi fit potestas. Ex quibus unus pilas atramento irrigat, easque invicem collidit, quo se atramentum commodius in eas dispergat: quibus deinde typos undique tingit: alter verò chartas ad id paratas prelo imponit, ipsumque deinde prelum subigit, ac sublatis impressis, novas iterum subjicit. Non possunt autem nisi in unum folii latus uno die chartæ imprimi quod prius exiccandæ sint, ne atramentum diffluat, & ut alterius lateris impressionem commodius suscipiant. Ideoque etiam siccativæ quædam materiæ atramento adduntur, quo impressa folia liquorem facilius retineant. Nam nisi bene siccatæ fuerint, tum quoque cùm religandæ sunt, impressæ litterarum figuræ pulsatione facile evanescunt.

Novissime verò Complicatore quoque aliquo opus est, cujus est officium impressas chartas exiccare, deinde complicare, ac postea in duerniones, terniones, quaterniones-ve (uti nunc loquimur) digerere: ac deinde eosdem in integrum volumen, ac exemplum quemadmodum vendi solent, colligere: formas quoque ipsas ubi numerus imprimendorum completus est, & antequam typi rursus in suos disponantur loculos, diligenter lavare, ne ater viscosusque liquor typis adhæreat, ac minùs commodè idcirco vel dissolutæ rursus (dum novæ conficiendæ sunt formæ) componi queant: adhæc etiam pilas papyrumque, quo facilius litteras impressas recipiat, interpositis quibusdam humectantibus linteolis madefacere, atque atramentum rite confici curare. In quibus tamen operis præstandis partem aliquam ipsi quoque impressores nonnumquam subeunt.

Potissima autem officinæ instrumenta sunt typi, papyrus, atramentum, pilæ, & prelum.

De typis nihil est opus amplius dicere.

Papyrus autem quomodo ex contritus commolitisque linteolis fiat, explicare non est opus. Hæc autem per folia, arcus, risas, ac balas, ut vulgaribus utar vocabulis (quando Latina deficiunt) distingui solet. Continet autem bala risas decem: risa arcus viginti: arcus rursus folia viginti quinquæ. Cùm autem bala papyri informis quinque florenis vendatur, ubi impressio accessit, viginti ferè æstimari solet.

Atramentum autem hoc librarium impressoriumque non multum a scriptorio differt, quod potissimum ex lini oleo glessoque conficitur.

Pilæ autem hemicycli formam habent, constantque folio pilis suffulto. Quod quia facile conteritur, mutare subinde necesse est.

Prelum autem nihil habet speciale, quod explicari mereatur.

Mercedes cùm Impressorum Compositorumque tum aliorum officinæ ministrorum pro temporum locorum hominumque qualitate variant.

Hæc, mi *Dothia*, habui quæ tibi impertirem, ex quibus nonnulla forte obscuriora tibi videbuntur, quàm, ut ex hac descriptione mea plenè queas intelligere. Verùm si penitius hanc artem cognoscere desiderabis, propriis ea tibi erunt perlustranda oculis: & mihi veniam dabis, qui hæc te compellente, qualitercumque explicare nisus sum. Bene vale Consobrine cumprimis chare. Datum Dulmaniæ. Calendis Juliis 1534.

TERMINOLOGY

As the subject has recently come in for a certain amount of attention, it may be useful to review briefly the terminology employed in the letter. It is mostly simple and unambiguous; there are only a few cases where different terms are used with apparently the same reference. The art of printing itself is variously *ars typographica, impressoria ars, typographia,* and the verb is *imprimere.* Paper is both *charta* and *papyrus,* but there is perhaps a distinction, *charta* being restricted to the sheets and *papyrus* being used more generally for the substance. It comes in *folia, arcus, risas et balas,* sheets, quires, reams and bales. It is made from *linteolum,* linen cloth, and the same material is also used as an interlay in the process of damping the heap. The printing house seems to be both *officina typographica* and *(Frobeniana) Typographia,* though in view of the use of *typographia* in the sense of *ars typographica* mentioned above, one might perhaps take it in that sense here. In two cases the term employed is the same as the present-day English one: *compositor, corrector,* and the meanings also appear to coincide, though the corrector operates in a strictly defined way, assisted by his *lector.* The compositor's job is, naturally, *componere,* and afterwards *distribuere,* and the types are in *loculi,* boxes, but no term is given for the cases. The copy he works from is the *exemplar.* The press, *prelum,* is operated by two *impressores,* pressmen, using *pilas,* balls, to distribute the ink, *atramentum,* an *ater viscosusque liquor,* over the forme. The term *forma* has been discussed in the text; it is perhaps proper to point out that when not referring to proofs it has a purely physical denotation, as is also primarily the case with the types, *typi,* or more fully *typi litterarii,* though when the most elegant must be selected, the images printing on the paper (the *impressæ litterarum figuræ*) are of course also thought of. The term for printing is the usual *imprimere.* Other team-members, finally, besides the *Typographus,* the master printer himself, are the *typorum fusor,* the typefounder, coming only now and then, and the *complicator,* the gatherer and folder, responsible as well for whatever else needs doing in the shop for which there is not a specialist. The punch-cutter remains too far out of sight to be given an appellation.

COPY-TEXT AND ITS VARIANTS IN SOME RECENT CHAUCER EDITIONS

by

JOSEPH A. DANE

THE purpose of the present paper is to examine the use of both the term and concept "copy-text" with reference to some recent Chaucer editions. The paper will be in two parts: the first deals with the concept of copy-text in general, based on a conservative reading of Greg's definition; the second deals with the use of this and related terminology primarily in the recent Variorum Chaucer volumes, the Riverside Chaucer, and Blake's edition of the *Canterbury Tales.*

GREG'S NOTION OF COPY-TEXT

In a recent book, Jerome J. McGann gives what seems to be a standard and unproblematic definition of copy-text: "In the post-Greg context, the term signifies what an editor chooses to take as the text of highest presumptive authority in the preparation of an eclectic, or critical, edition. . . . The copytext serves as the basis of the critical edition that is to be produced."[1] This definition is a clear one, but McGann associates the term with specific editorial procedures different from those assumed by Greg himself. As I shall discuss below, to invoke a copy-text in McGann's sense (with its reference to Greg) is to invoke potentially competing editorial theories. For Chaucerians, the problem is compounded by the assumption that medieval editors (scribes) and modern editors are analogous, and one Chaucer editor has used the term to mean what a medieval scribe (rather than a modern editor) might work from. N. F. Blake refers to the hypothetical exemplar for the Hengwrt manuscript of the *Canterbury Tales* as follows: "That all MSS are ultimately dependent upon Hg's copy-text will guide editorial practice; for it presupposes that there was only one copy-text."[2] That such uses of the term can be misleading is a point I shall be arguing in both sections of this paper. Here it is enough to note that what McGann and Blake refer to above as "copy-

---

1. *Social Values and Poetic Acts: The Historical Judgment of Literary Work* (1988), p. 177. By "post-Greg," I assume McGann acknowledges that this formulation is "different from" that of Greg. See the more extensive discussion in *A Critique of Modern Textual Criticism* (1983), "The Theory of Copy-Text," pp. 24–36. A similar definition is given by Philip Gaskell, *From Writer to Reader: Studies in Editorial Method* (1978), pp. 4ff.

2. N. F. Blake, "On Editing the *Canterbury Tales,*" in P. L. Heyworth, ed., *Medieval Studies for J. A. W. Bennett* (1981), p. 112. See also, N. F. Blake, *The Textual Tradition of the Canterbury Tales* (1985), p. 168.

texts" could be just as accurately and unambiguously referred to as "base text" and "exemplar" respectively.

Greg's definition differs from the understanding of the term both by his predecessors and by his followers. The copy-text is not necessarily (in Mc-Gann's words) "the text of highest presumptive authority." It is, rather, the version of a text the editor chooses to follow for "accidentals" as opposed to "substantives":

> whenever there is more than one substantive text of comparable authority, then although it will still be necessary to choose one of them as copy-text, and to follow it in accidentals, this copy-text can be allowed no over-riding or even preponderant authority so far as substantive readings are concerned. ("Rationale," pp. 384–385)

Substantives are lexical and grammatical elements; accidentals are what Greg calls "formal matters" (p. 385; the term "material matters" might paradoxically be more accurate). These include spelling and punctuation.[3] Thus the copy-text for Greg provides "guidance" in the editor's representation of accidentals in an edition (p. 384); it provides formal standards (e.g., spelling conventions) for the substantive changes an editor introduces ("editorial emendations should be made to conform to the habitual spelling of the copy-text," p. 386). But it also has a second function, not explicitly mentioned by Greg but certainly assumed, which is to serve as a "basis of collation."

In most practical instances of editing, the copy-text might well be accorded authority in substantive matters, and under certain editorial methods, it would necessarily have such authority. But an exemplar's status as copy-text has nothing to do with its potential authority on substantives, and on this Greg is explicit:

> The true theory is, I contend, that the copy-text should govern (generally) in the matter of accidentals, but that the choice between substantive readings belongs to the general theory of textual criticism and lies altogether beyond the narrow principle of the copy-text. ("Rationale," pp. 381–382)

Greg's parenthetical "(generally)" is worth noting. So reluctant is he to accept the authority of any single exemplar, that he allows the copy-text itself to be corrected in the matter of accidentals or even disregarded:

> Since the adoption of a copy-text is a matter of convenience rather than of principle . . . it follows that there is no reason for treating it as sacrosanct, even apart from the question of substantive variation. Every editor aiming at a critical edition will, of course, correct scribal or typographical errors. He will also correct readings in accordance with any errata included in the edition taken as copy-text. I see no reason

3. W. W. Greg, "The Rationale of Copy-Text," *SB*, 3 (1950–51), 19–36; rpt. *Collected Papers*, ed. J. C. Maxwell (1966), pp. 374–391 (my citations are to the reprint). The later attempts to map this distinction onto one between final and original intentions are generally inapplicable to medieval editions; see, however, D. C. Greetham, "Normalisation of Accidentals in Middle English Texts: The Paradox of Thomas Hoccleve," *SB*, 28 (1985), 121–150, esp. p. 127 n. 10. Greg's acknowledged point of departure for his discussion is McKerrow's 1904 edition of Nashe and his 1939 *Prolegomena for the Oxford Shakespeare* (see pp. 378–381).

why he should not alter misleading or eccentric spellings which he is satisfied emanate from the scribe or compositor and not from the author. If the punctuation is persistently erroneous or defective an editor may prefer to discard it altogether to make way for one of his own. (p. 385)

This implies that the copy-text can be an abstract rather than a material thing. For medievalists, this possibility would bear largely on questions of spelling and normalization, and would be of no more interest than Greg seems to give it. But the implication that the copy-text can be an abstraction realized only as an editorial construct has been more fully exploited in other areas (Gabler's *Ulysses* is an obvious example).[4]

Greg's distinctions have different value for the editing of texts from different periods. For an editor of classical texts, Greg's discussion is only partially applicable: classical editions are generally normalized. For most Greek texts, normalization to medieval standards is simply conventional; for classical Latin texts, the standard modern system of normalization is considered more representative of authorial spelling than what is found in any extant medieval exemplar. In either case, most accidentals are determined by the particular conventions of spelling the editor adopts. Once the editor has determined the system or rules governing accidentals, the only editorial decisions deal with substantive matters (lexical and grammatical), which, when combined with the system of normalization governing accidentals, will produce a normalized orthography and punctuation. Editorial decisions on punctuation (a period? or semi-colon?) must still be made, but such decisions regarding particular accidentals are to be made on the substantive level (grammar, lexicon) or even on a thematic or aesthetic level (theme, tone, etc.). What a classical editor might call a "copy-text" will thus not be selected for its presumed authority on accidentals. If one of its functions is to provide a basis of collation (or a set of preliminary line numbers) there might well be reason to choose as copy-text the *textus receptus*, however corrupt, or even a recent edition. But to call such a text a "copy-text" in Greg's sense would be misleading.[5]

Greg's article was speaking specifically to the problems associated with fifteenth- and sixteenth-century texts (p. 378). As in the case of classical texts, substantive matters can here be separated from accidental matters. But the editorial situation differs from that faced by the classical editor in two ways: (1) no standard system of punctuation and spelling exists, and (2) the earliest manuscript might well be contemporary (or nearly contemporary) with the author and thus could reflect authorial accidentals with some accuracy. Edi-

---

4. See, in particular, the review of Gabler's *Ulysses* by Antony Hammond, *The Library*, 6th ser., 8 (1986), 382–390, and McGann, *Social Values*, p. 265, n. 8. The distinction between the abstract copy-text (a text) and the physical printer's copy (a material object) is made by G. Thomas Tanselle, "The Meaning of Copy-Text: A Further Note," *SB*, 23 (1970), 191–196; see also, "Greg's Theory of Copy-Text and the Editing of American Literature," *SB*, 28 (1975), 202.

5. Greg denies that the "English" theory of copy-text (i.e., his own) has any relation to the classical editor's "best text" ("Rationale," p. 375).

tors of more modern texts face a different situation: the earliest edition is generally contemporary with the author and later editions may well be revised by the author. Thus the question of choosing a copy-text for the editor of nineteenth-century texts tends to involve substantive matters.[6] The editors of medieval texts draw on textual-critical theories and language from all these fields; but their situation is also different. They will not admit casually a modern system of normalization as do classical editors and as did the earlier editors for such series as the Société des Anciens Textes Français; but they are equally reluctant to accept the system offered by any single manuscript source unless that manuscript is also given credit for "presumptive authority" on substantive matters.

BASE TEXT AND BEST TEXT

Before proceeding to some of the implications of Greg's theory and finally to the problems of medieval editing, "copy-text" needs to be distinguished from related editorial terminology, "best text," "base text," and such non-technical terms as "basic text." The differences are not simply matters of definition. The terms "best text" and "base text" imply specific editorial procedures quite different from those implied by the terms "copy-text." The non-technical "basic text" owes its utility to the very absence of a restrictive definition.

Greg, as often noted, assumed a genealogical method of editing, and it was that system to which his terminology applied. Even though the editing of modern texts employs different methods, most of the interesting and productive theorizing on Greg has been based on situations where the language of the genealogical method still has some application. For example, the difference between early and later printed editions of a text (and consequently the choice of which to use as the basis of an edition) could be described as one of simple filiation, involving a single line of descent complicated by authorial variants. But medieval editing almost never confronts such a situation (most of the manuscript evidence post-dates the author), and the definition of "copy-text" in terms of an abstraction such as "authorial intentions" could apply to very few editorial situations. For medieval editions, the language of one editorial method is less easily transferable to another.

The types of editorial procedures implied by these terms are various, but in Chaucer editing, the three basic types of edition defined some eighty years ago by Eleanor Hammond can be used as a starting point: (1) the exact reproduction of single manuscript (Wright's 1848–51 edition); (2) eclectic (the editions of Tyrwhitt 1775–78 and Skeat 1894, 1899); (3) critical. By "critical," Hammond refers to a recension (or genealogical) edition; in 1908, there were

---

6. See esp. Fredson Bowers, "Greg's 'Rationale of Copy-Text' Revisited," *SB*, 31 (1978), 90–161, esp. pp. 94–97, outlining some of the different concerns of Greg and editors of modern texts. See further, p. 125: "what impels an editor of later works to concern himself with copy-text is the conviction that the accidentals are an inseparable whole with the substantives in transmitting the author's total meaning." (The Middle English *Ormulum* is one of few likely exceptions.)

no full-length Chaucer editions of this type, but the most notorious later attempt at such an edition is the Manly-Rickert.[7]

The three terms "best text," "base text," and "copy-text" can be matched with these three types of editorial procedure. Hammond's first type of edition relies on a single exemplar; and this exemplar is often called a "best text." The word "best" may be ill-chosen, since a "best-text edition" could certainly be made of any manuscript, even a manifestly inferior one (for this reason, I shall refer to so-called "best-text editions" as "single-text editions" below). But if the term is used, it implies a specific editorial theory or procedure.[8] In medieval studies, a so-called "best text" is simply the exemplar followed conservatively in a single-text edition. The term "base text," by contrast, refers to the exemplar(s) on which an eclectic edition is based. Such a base text might also be called a "foundation text" or "basic text"; the advantage of these latter terms is that they do not seem to have developed technical meanings or implications. In practice, an eclectic method would call for the use of a particular exemplar even if only as the base in which to admit corrections from a number of other sources (e.g., Skeat's use of El for his *Canterbury Tales*); in early editing (and even in some recent editing) the base manuscript might be an earlier edition (e.g., Tyrwhitt's apparent use of black-letter editions).[9] A "critical" edition in Hammond's sense (a recension or genealogical edition) would not necessarily have a base manuscript, since all manuscripts might be of equal authority; but it must have a copy-text or at least something to serve the various functions of a copy-text. That one of these functions in most practical editorial situations is to provide a basis for collation is generally simply assumed; McGann is one of the few textual-critical theorists to make it explicit (*Critique*, p. 24). In addition, that critical edition must take its spelling conventions from somewhere, since the genealogical methods that lead to a substantive authorial reading do not lead to the author's conventions on accidentals (this, of course, is on the assumption that scribes and early publishers distinguished substantives from accidentals as we might, and further that they felt responsibility only to retain the former as authorial). According to Greg, a copy-text can be chosen "irrespective of descent" (and thus irrespective of its authority on substantive matters). The exemplar Greg selects as copy-text in his edition of the Antichrist Play from the Chester Cycle is the earliest extant, but not the highest in the stemmata; that is, authority

7. Eleanor Prescott Hammond, *Chaucer: A Bibliographical Manual* (1908), pp. 106–107.

8. On the term "best," see George Kane, " 'Good' and 'Bad' Manuscripts: Texts and Critics," (1986), rpt. *Chaucer and Langland: Historical and Textual Approaches* (1986), 206–213. The difficulties involved in invoking the word "best" can be seen, e.g., in Skeat, 2: lxvii on the *Troilus* MS Cl. "This is a beautifully written MS., and one of the best; but it is disappointing to find that it might easily have been much better. The scribe had a still better copy before him, which he has frequently treated with supreme carelessness." Extant MSS are thus by definition worse than imagined ones. See further, 4:xvii: "Of all the MSS., E. is the best in nearly every respect. It not only gives good lines and good sense, but is also (usually) grammatically accurate and thoroughly well spelt." Walter W. Skeat, *The Complete Works of Geoffrey Chaucer*, 7 vols. (1894–1900).

9. Atcheson L. Hench, "Printer's Copy for Tyrwhitt's Chaucer," *SB*, 3 (1950), 265–266.

on substantives (genealogical priority) is independent of its authority on accidentals (here a matter of chronological priority).[10]

Greg's theory of copy-text deals specifically with genealogical editions. Thus, an edition that relies on a copy-text in Greg's sense does not necessarily give what McGann calls "highest presumptive authority" to a single manuscript or exemplar. An edition that does so rely on a single exemplar may characterize it more usefully as a "base text"; if this exemplar has even greater authority (overriding or preemptive authority), the editors are producing a variant of a single-text edition and can then legitimately refer to this exemplar as a "best-text" (see, however, n8 and discussion above).

Although there can be no justification for calling a base text a copy-text, there are still advantages for retaining the term, even in editions that do not use the genealogical methods of Greg. Under any editorial method, an exemplar can be copy-text in Greg's sense if it serves as an authority for accidentals and (as a practical matter) a basis for collation. The use of the term should force an editor to describe editorial procedures and in particular to articulate the nature of the authority possessed by an exemplar or manuscript. Surely a copy-text can serve as base text, and in a single-text edition the copy-text is generally best, base, and copy-text.[11] But the choice of a base text does not mean that the question of copy-text is closed; in addition, the choice of an exemplar as a basis for collation and an authority for accidentals (a copy-text) does not mean that a base text or best text must even exist.

There are further implications to Greg's theory; under a perhaps overly literal interpretation, the copy-text could be a text of *some other text*. (I am going to reject such a use shortly, for obvious reasons, but the theoretical possibility of it should be reckoned with.) For early modern texts, this theoretical possibility poses few practical difficulties. If a fifteenth-century text existed only, say, in an eighteenth-century print, it is difficult to imagine why an editor would wish to produce an original spelling edition or how that edition could be justified. But the edition would certainly be possible. To produce it, an editor might rely either on a selected system of normalization as do classicists or might choose in lieu of such a system of normalization *another* text, one that would be ignored in all substantive matters. In classical editions, a major function of the copy-text is served by the text (a dictionary or perhaps better a school-grammar) that contains the spelling and punctuation conventions the edition follows. As for the basis of collation, any earlier edition (or translation) can serve as well, whatever its authority; even a list of line num-

---

10. W. W. Greg, *The Play of Antichrist from the Chester Cycle* (1935), Introduction. Cf. the situation of authorial revision discussed in "Rationale," pp. 389–391. In these cases, a later edition could have presumptive authority on substantives while the copy-text would maintain both chronological and genealogical priority; for Jonson's *Sejanus*, "it would obviously be possible to take the [earlier] quarto as the copy-text and introduce into it whatever authoritative alterations the [revised] folio may supply" (390).

11. Exceptions could theoretically exist. If I wished to edit one *Canterbury Tales* MS (say El) showing particularly how it differed from another (say Hg), I might do a "'single-text" or "best-text" edition of El using Hg as copy-text (for spelling, line references, etc.).

bers could conceivably serve this function.[12] In these cases, there again is no reason to invoke Greg's copy-text, since all the explicit functions of a copy-text are served by texts with no authority in substantive matters. Greg's repeated denials that the copy-text has authority on substantive matters somewhat paradoxically implies that it has at least potential authority in such matters. And it is this potential authority that modern textual-critical theorists have strengthened by referring to "presumptive" authority.[13]

In many cases, the term copy-text might well be avoided, and its potential functions defined and dealt with separately. There is clearly no reason for a classicist to speak of a copy-text in relation to normalization. Nor is there any advantage to using the term if all it refers to is a "basis of collation"; the more explicit term is preferable. Moreover, a system of normalization or basis for manuscript collation that does not contain a version of the text to be edited cannot usefully be called a copy-text even if it serves the same function.[14]

Greg's article was a reaction against what he called "the tyranny of the copy-text" (p. 382). It was an attempt in part to reduce the functions of the copy-text, taking away from it the substantive authority that modern textual critics have begun to restore. A return to Greg's definition of the term might define the copy-text out of existence in many editorial situations. For medievalists, this might not be a bad thing. In practice, the difference between copy text, base text, and best text involves the relative authority granted a certain exemplar; the difference could be considered one of degree. But keeping the theoretical distinctions in view would lead to a more accurate assessment of that authority. Furthermore, a more conservative use of the term would avoid the confusion between the imagined tasks of a medieval "editorial office" and the real tasks of a modern one. Since we do not know in most cases the precise procedures or theories a medieval editor followed,

12. On the function of a copy-text in the production of lemmata, see n. 22 below.

13. G. Thomas Tanselle, "Classical, Biblical, and Medieval Textual Criticism and Modern Editing," *SB*, 26 (1983), 50: "Thus what underlies [Greg's] conception of copy-text is the idea of presumptive authority. . . ." On p. 64, Tanselle notes that "the idea of copy-text as presumptive authority" is a "natural extension of Greg's position." Gaskell, *From Writer to Reader*, p. 5, seems to attribute this position to Greg himself: "[Greg's "Rationale"] argued essentially that the earliest in an ancestral series of printed editions should be chosen as copy-text, and should be followed both in words (which Greg called 'Substantives') and in non-verbal details (. . . 'accidentals'), unless the editor believed that verbal variants from another source had greater authority."

14. That a copy-text must be a version of the text to be edited seems obvious enough, but there could be situations where this might not be the case, e.g., where a "version" of a text is regarded not as a "variant" but as a *different text*. The Folio *King Lear* could easily be edited with the Quarto functioning as copy-text, even by an editor who regards them as representing different plays; see Gary Taylor and Michael Warren, *The Division of the Kingdoms: Shakespeare's Two Versions of King Lear* (1983). See the distinction by Fredson Bowers, "Regularization and Normalization in Modern Critical Texts," *SB*, 42 (1989), 79–102, where the two methods of standardizing accidentals are distinguished on the basis of whether the system is taken from a version of the text to be edited (regularization) or from an external system (normalization); only "regularization" would involve the use of a copy-text.

there seems little point in describing them with technical vocabulary developed to apply to the twentieth-century editor.

RECENT CHAUCER EDITIONS I (SINGLE-TEXT EDITIONS)

One of the more striking aspects of recent Chaucer editions is the privileging of the Hengwrt manuscript (Hg) for the *Canterbury Tales*. Among the editors to have done this are Pratt, Blake, those involved in the Oklahoma Variorum project, and even Donaldson in his earlier normalized edition. The justification for the reliance on Hg is generally claimed to lie in the Manly-Rickert edition of 1940.[15]

The problems of using Manly-Rickert (a genealogical edition) in support of a single-text edition based on Hg have been pointed out before.[16] Manly-Rickert's prefaces are often baffling, and the varying stemmata constructed never show Hg in a position of supreme authority for O′ (the supposed common ancestor of all manuscripts that Manly-Rickert attempt to reconstruct). The conflation of competing and often antithetical editorial theories has led to confusion, both in the methods themselves and in the language used to describe them (e.g., best text, base text, copy text, basis of collation).[17]

Such conflation seems to be acknowledged in the Editor's Preface of the 1979 facsimile—the first volume produced by the Variorum Project:

The editors as a group made the important decision to adopt the Hengwrt manuscript as base text for the *Variorum Chaucer*. They further decided that the Hengwrt text would be utilized as a "best" text and that in the individual fascicles the editors would emend it cautiously and conservatively. . . . This text, we believe—and the labors of Manly and Rickert bear us out—is as close as we will come to Chaucer's own intentions for large parts of the *Canterbury Tales*. And, as Baker states below, the best-text method, modified for our purposes, provides a neutral text of the *Canterbury Tales* to which the commentary may be appended and referred.[18]

15. John M. Manly and Edith Rickert, ed., *The Text of the Canterbury Tales*, 8 vols. (1940). The volumes from the Oklahoma Variorum Edition cited below include Paul G. Ruggiers, ed., *Geoffrey Chaucer, The Canterbury Tales: A Facsimile and Transcription of the Hengwrt Manuscript, with Variants from the Ellesmere Manuscript* (1979) [hereafter, *Hg Facsimile*]; Thomas W. Ross, ed., *The Miller's Tale* (1983); Derek Pearsall, ed., *The Nun's Priest's Tale* (1984); Donald C. Baker, ed., *The Manciple's Tale* (1984); Helen Storm Corsa, ed., *The Physician's Tale* (1987); Beverly Boyd, ed., *The Prioress's Tale* (1987). Other editions are by N. F. Blake, ed., *The Canterbury Tales by Geoffrey Chaucer, Edited from the Hengwrt Manuscript* (1980); E. T. Donaldson, ed., *Chaucer's Poetry: An Anthology for the Modern Reader* (1958); Robert A. Pratt, ed., *Geoffrey Chaucer: The Tales of Canterbury (Complete)* (1966).

16. George Kane, "John M. Manly (1865–1940) and Edith Rickert (1871–1938)," in Paul G. Ruggiers, ed., *Editing Chaucer: The Great Tradition* (1984), pp. 207–229.

17. For the failure to distinguish different editorial procedures, see, e.g., Ross, "All modern editions have returned to a single manuscript as base-text" (p. 111). This is the lead sentence in a section entitled "Modern Editions" and listing Skeat, Robinson, Manly-Rickert, and Pratt. The different procedures (eclectic, recension, and single-text) are here regarded as the same. (In fairness to the Variorum Editors, only Ross's version of the introduction contains this statement.)

18. Editor's Preface, *Hg Facsimile*, p. xii; Donald C. Baker, "Introduction: The Relation of the Hengwrt Manuscript to the Variorum Chaucer Text" flatly calls the Ellesmere MS "the second-best manuscript" (*Hg Facsimile*, p. xvii).

According to this, a best-text method is used to provide a text to serve as the basis of commentary; but the supposedly "neutral" text that results is supposedly one that cannot be improved, that is, the best-text method yields the best edition.[19]

The Variorum Chaucer has dual purposes, and these lead to contradictions (both in tone and in substance) in the prefaces. In the General Editors' Preface (I quote here the version printed in Ross's *Miller's Tale*), the editors say that their purpose is "only to provide a text upon which the commentary should depend" (p. xv). But the conflicting claims of the 1979 Preface (to produce the best possible edition) are scattered through each volume. In his own introduction, Ross (perhaps following Pearsall p. 97) states: "The text of The Miller's Tale in this edition is in one way more ambitious than is the monumental work of MR.... The Variorum Edition may thus present *The Miller's Tale* as Chaucer wrote it, as nearly as our present knowledge and resources permit" (p. 61).[20] These inflated claims and attendant rhetoric are occasionally repeated in reviews. According to one reviewer, a recent Variorum editor gives "all the evidence necessary for establishment of a text which would probably be as near to the original as present knowledge and scholarship could make possible."[21] Pratt's earlier edition makes similar claims: "the present text represents as accurately as possible Manly's 'latest common original of all extant manuscripts' (O'), with the correction of all recognizable errors in the transmission to O' of Chaucer's own text (O).... In attempting to recreate the text as Chaucer wrote it ..." (p. 561).

The arguments of Pratt and the Variorum Editors seem to assert that Manly and Rickert's reconstruction of the latest common ancestor (O') of all MSS is itself not in question. All that remains to do is to correct the "manifest errors" in that reconstructed ancestor and we are as close to Chaucer's text (O) "as it is possible to get."

But how can Hg be used for what precedes Manly-Rickert's O' when O' is it itself constructed in part on the basis of Hg? The argument for this depends on a serious misrepresentation of Manly-Rickert's methods; Pearsall's statement is an example:

The present edition assumes that the unique authority of Hg enables us to recover with some degree of assurance the text of the author's original. This reliance on Hg is not unreasonable, given its freedom from accidental error and editorial improvement, and given too that the text that MR print, as established by the processes of recension, moves consistently from the text used as the basis for collation, Skeat's

19. See further Joseph A. Dane, "The Reception of Chaucer's Eighteenth-Century Editors," *Text*, 4 (1988), 217–236, on the equally uncritical and often amusing editorial rhetoric regarding the "worst" Chaucer edition.

20. I assume Pearsall's is the earlier text, although it was published later.

21. Florence H. Ridley, rev. Boyd, *Speculum*, 64 (1989), 684; cf. the more judicious review by A. S. G. Edwards in *SAC*, 11 (1989), 189–191. See also Baker, "Introduction," *Hg Facsimile*: "What we are attempting is the difficult task of providing at one time the text which is as near as it is possible to get to what Chaucer must have written (and we believe that for most of the *Canterbury Tales* it is that of the Hengwrt manuscript—as slightly emended—to a greater extent than that of the Manly-Rickert text)" (p. xviii).

Student Edition (MR, 2.5), that is, a text based predominantly on El, towards Hg. (Pearsall, p. 97; see also p. 122, quoted below)

The manifest circularity of the first part of this statement is not at issue here. What concerns me is only the failure to distinguish a "basis for collation" from "base text." Pearsall's reasoning, in a single-text edition, conflates the language of two competing methods. Manly-Rickert used Skeat's "Student Edition" as a "basis of collation" for their recension edition; Skeat's edition is itself based on El (it is eclectic). But Pearsall implies that Manly-Rickert took Skeat as their "base text," emending it in the direction of Hg; that is, he argues as if they were producing a different type of edition.

Manly-Rickert, in the section entitled "Manner of Collating" to which Pearsall refers, discuss only the method of collating manuscripts and the mechanical means of recording variants; as a "basis for collation," they used Skeat's Student's Edition (2:5). Its function was only to collate manuscripts and to aid in the construction of lemmata. The readings in that edition are of course irrelevant and unrecorded. As a text, it has no more authority than a translation, which could have served the same function. To ignore this is to assume that Manly and Rickert, whatever their failings as editors, after examining and describing all the *Canterbury Tales* manuscripts, did not recognize the difference between a manuscript authority and a modern edition. I am not certain what Pearsall means by his statement that the Manly-Rickert edition "moves consistently from the text used as the basis for collation . . . toward Hg." But if all this means is that in cases where Manly-Rickert differ from Skeat they tend toward Hg, I see nothing surprising in that. Had they used Hg as a basis for collation, similar results might have obtained. In cases where they differed from Hg, they might well "tend" toward something else, perhaps El, perhaps even Skeat.

A basis for collation is something used to collate manuscripts and produce lemmata, not a "base text" for an edition. As the Variorum Editors recognize, "The decision about what is a lemma is, of course, purely arbitrary" (Ross, p. 52). To choose a version of the text to be edited is wise from an economic standpoint only, since it would be tedious to set forth *every* manuscript reading as a variant of an arbitrary lemma. But two sets of lemmata must be distinguished. The preliminary lemmata produced while collating MSS (defined as variants of a "basis of collation") are not the same as those listed in the notes to an edited text (defined as variants of the edited text).[22]

---

22. What I call "preliminary lemmata can be based on any text; for the opening of the *Canterbury Tales*, "When that April with its showers sweet" might be a more economical basis of collation than "When April with its sweet showers"; the preliminary lemmata would differ but the textual-critical results would probably be the same. The lemmata printed in the final edition would differ only if the final line attributed to Chaucer differed. Kane, "Manly and Rickert," pp. 208–209, also criticizes Manly-Rickert's use of Skeat's Student's Edition. Kane's point, however, is that Manly-Rickert do not explain in detail the editorial procedures by which they postulate manuscript groupings, and that Skeat (which contains both original and unoriginal readings) cannot be used as a touchstone to identify "unoriginal" ones.

Manly and Rickert use a genealogical method, and as such, they have no base text at all. Pearsall acknowledges this, but then describes Manly-Rickert's "basis for collation" as a "copy-text": "It is noteworthy, therefore, that MR, though they use no base manuscript (the copy-text is SK), draw frequently toward Hg and away from El in their choice of readings" (p. 122).[23]

To speak of a copy-text for Manly-Rickert is misleading and unnecessary, even though certain texts can be identified as serving functions associated with a copy-text. The Student Skeat operates as a basis of collation only (it does not even provide line numbers). For matters of spelling, the function of copy-text is served by a system presumably based on a comparison of Hg and El:

Any attempt to include spelling and dialect forms would complicate the record to the point of uselessness. . . . (2:10)

The brief chapter on Dialect and Spelling very inadequately represents the large amount of attention which has been devoted to this subject by Miss Mabel Dean of our staff. Miss Dean first attempted to discover whether the more carefully written MSS of the first two decades of the fifteenth century showed any regularity or approximation toward a common standard, with a view to making use of these results in the spelling of our text. She discovered that there was strong evidence of the prevalance of common habits which, if systematized, approximated very closely the spelling found in the Hengwrt and Ellesmere MSS. This was accordingly adopted as our standard. (1:ix–x)[24]

In reference to the Hg-based texts themselves (the Variorum and the editions of Blake and Pratt), the notion of "copy-text" should be merely redundant (thus unnecessary), since "copy-text" is simply subsumed under the notion of "base text" and occasionally "best text." The usual way the Variorum Editors speak of Hg is as a "base text" (the Variorum is "based on/upon Hg."[25] But the term "copy-text" is sometimes used as a variation: "On the other hand, Hg omits two couplets, both of which are included in the present

---

23. Cf. Baker, *Manciple's Tale*, p. 72: "all subsequent editions collated except MR have used El as their copy-text (and usually base-text as well)." Baker then states that Manly-Rickert's "copy-text" is SK (the argument that Manly-Rickert "draw" away from El is of course irrelevant unless SK with its readings from El is Manly-Rickert's "base text"). That Manly-Rickert have no base text is also recognized by Corso, p. 85: "MR is not based on any particular manuscript or manuscripts." The abbreviation SK is misleading; Manly-Rickert chose the Student Skeat (a conveniently packaged, cheap physical object) as a means of collation, not the Oxford Skeat (a cumbersome, expensive scholarly edition).

24. The section on dialect and spelling is dealing primarily with the value of formal matters in determining MSS groups, as are the three pages dealing with spelling (Dialect and Spelling, 1:545–560; spelling is discussed directly only in pp. 557–560). Manly-Rickert show no great concern with spelling as authorial, a motive force behind Greg's notion of copy-text: "in close groups of MSS there is nothing to show that the spelling system of the lost original was preserved" (1:560).

25. See the section "The Present Edition" in the various *CT* volumes of the Variorum. See also, Donaldson, p. v: "I have followed the lead of Manly and Rickert by using Hengwrt as my base." I assume Donaldson means only that he has chosen his base text because of his interpretation of Manly-Rickert's results (not that Manly-Rickert also use such a base text). Since Donaldson normalizes spelling, there is no reason to distinguish a copy-text apart from his base text, Hg.

edition, though enclosed in brackets to indicate that they are not in the copy-text" (Ross, p. 54). Moreover, "copy-text" is also used to mean "the exemplar for a specific extant MS": "[Hg and El] were written from different exemplars at different times. . . . El's copytext had two extra couplets, which may have been Chaucer's . . ." (ibid.).

There is no question that Hg is the "copy-text" for the Variorum Edition, but to speak of it as such is merely to invoke textual-critical language that applies to a different editorial situation. Hg's function as copy-text is trivial, since it is also the base text and for these editors the best text. The Variorum is a simple variant of a single-text edition; Hg is "conservatively emended" from a number of manuscripts, selected on the basis of Manly-Rickert's groupings.[26] It thus has the potential for incorporating not only the virtues of the genealogical, eclectic, and single-text methods but their failings as well.

The arguments of N. F. Blake for the privileging of Hg are similar in many respects to those of the Variorum Editors. But Blake's editing theory gives greater authority to Hg, and provides as well a dynamic model of manuscript exemplars that complicates the entire enterprise of producing a static (i.e., printable) edition.[27] Blake's edition is, like the Variorum, a single-text edition, although Blake refers to Hg as "base MS": "in the light of our present knowledge it is safest to edit the poem . . . using Hg as the base manuscript and excluding anything not found in it" ("On Editing," p. 111). Blake acknowledges the convenience of an assumption of strict linear descent of MSS, an assumption that would turn any manuscript into an absolute authority for all posterior readings: "If we accept that there is a manuscript tradition which goes back to one manuscript, Hg., then there are three possible ways to edit the poem" (p. 105). Blake's purpose is to discard the notion of "authorial variants" and thus to simplify the editorial process; the assumption of lineal descent of all MSS from a single manuscript is a convenient polemical position. But the assumption Blake seems to have made is less radical. Blake assumes the descent of all MSS from an exemplar copied by Hg: "That all manuscripts are ultimately dependent upon Hg's copy-text will guide editorial practice, for it presupposes that there was only one copy-text" (p. 112); "later scribes used Hg's exemplar rather than Hg" (p. 113). This assumption, of course, challenges the absolute authority of Hg, since it acknowledges other lines of descent from O' (i.e., radial descent, rather than linear descent). If this is the case, Hg has no more authority *a priori* than any other MS., a difficulty Blake tries to overcome by allowing that other MSS may "suggest . . . how Hg may be emended or corrected" (p. 119), leaving open the question of whether they can do so with any authority.[28]

But let us look here at Blake's notion of copy-text, by which he means

26. Ralph Hanna III, rev. of Pearsall, *Analytical and Enumerative Bibliography*, 8 (1984), 184–197.

27. Blake omits the Canon Yeoman's Tale, not in Hg, an option not reasonably open to the Variorum editors, given the nature of their edition as a base for commentary.

28. See Blake, *Textual Tradition*, chap. 3, pp. 44ff.; Blake occasionally misrepresents Manly-Rickert's grouping of MSS (El is assigned to group *a*, p. 50).

the exemplar for Hg, "Chaucer's working copy" ("On Editing," p. 115).[29]
Blake claims that this hypothetical exemplar was constantly revised in an
"editorial office" (p. 115). As does Pearsall, Blake uses "copy-text" to mean
both an editor's copy-text as well as an historical exemplar for an extant
version of a text. This notion of copy-text is part of further terminological
slippage: "But if the exemplar (i.e., Chaucer's own fragments) was being
constantly emended in the editorial office, the good text would gradually
disappear under a host of corrections" (p. 116). Whereas Manly-Rickert
studied the extremely complex relations among real manuscripts in search of
a singular hypothetical origin (O'), Blake reverses this logic, dismissing all
complexities among real manuscripts as meaningless, and hypothesizing instead an equally complex (and less well-documented) history that produces
the single extant manuscript Hg. Thus, the problems associated with the
editorial copy-text (problems the very nature of a single-text edition should
solve) are reintroduced on a hypothetical, historical level, where such terms
as "exemplar," "Chaucer's own fragments," "copy-text," and "good text" exist
in some uneasy equation.[30] Blake's apparent reliance on a single authority,
an assumption that should simplify matters, in fact hypothesizes a situation
(a medieval editorial office) in which no single authority seems to exist or
can be articulated much less recovered. Thus Blake can dismiss as "the
rather uncertain art of literary criticism" ("On Editing," p. 103) all attempts
to recover editorially more than a group of Chaucerian fragments.

CHAUCER EDITIONS II (ECLECTIC EDITIONS, RIVERSIDE EDITION, WINDEATT'S
TROILUS)

Other recent Chaucer editions have been eclectic, and the language describing them is varied. Fisher, in what is primarily a student edition, uses
the language from a number of textual-critical schools:

The method of producing the text for this edition has been . . . to choose the best
manuscript . . . and adhere closely to the text and orthography. . . . In addition to
indicating all the substantive changes in the copy text, the textual notes in italics at
the foot of each page give a sampling of the more interesting variants from important manuscripts. . . . The text of the Canterbury tales in this edition is based on
the Ellesmere. Some recent editors have used the Hengwrt manuscript . . . as their
copy text. . . . Although Ellesmere and Hengwrt represent the earliest and two of
the best texts. . . .[31]

29. Hg is the ideal witness for this copy, since the Hg scribe "copied only what was in
front of him and took no liberties with the text and did not seek to edit the contents"
(*Textual Tradition*, p. 95).

30. *Textual Tradition*, pp. 165ff. ("A Matter of Copytexts"): "the hypothesis of a copy-
text, which itself was being modified, as the basis of many early manuscripts, appears to be
a more satisfactory solution [than Manly-Rickert's groups] to the textual problems of the
poem. . . . We may assume, therefore, that there was the basic copytext, which formed the
Chaucerian draft copy. . . ." To this copytext were added various glosses and "alternative
readings" (p. 168). Blake identifies this text used by various early scribes as "the author's
draft" (p. 169).

31. John H. Fisher, ed., *The Complete Poetry and Prose of Geoffrey Chaucer* (1977),
pp. 966–967 (the section on the text is unchanged in later editions). Fisher's opinion has

Fisher is clearly producing an eclectic edition using a base manuscript. There is no reason to refer to copy-text at all, either to describe his own or other editors' procedures, although the distinction Fisher implies here is that a copy-text in his sense (the status accorded Hg by other editors) has more "presumptive authority" than a base text.

Of more concern to me is the Riverside edition—an edition that like the Variorum attempts to serve a number of different purposes, some of which may be incompatible. The title page claims it is *The Riverside Edition, Third Edition*, "based on" the second edition of Robinson.[32] That bibliographical ambivalence is a reflection of the uncertainty and often contradictory nature of editorial procedures. Robinson has always been perfectly serviceable as a student edition, and the Riverside attempts (successfully) to maintain that serviceability. Yet Robinson's editorial procedures have been so often questioned that a more radical revision would certainly be required to maintain its status as a scholarly text (or reference text). The Riverside editors have not decided whether to depart absolutely from Robinson, and the result is that Robinson often functions as copy-text and perhaps as base text. The edition that by its very existence should supersede the authority of Robinson's earlier editions has paradoxically transformed Robinson's earlier text into a textual authority.

The Riverside edition and its individual editors have responded rationally to the problem of updating a standard edition. Individual editors are not forced to adopt a single system, nor to proclaim an unlikely unanimity on editorial procedures. The relative clarity of the descriptions of editorial procedures may well be a consequence. In general, the editors avoid the issue of copy-text, and speak in a non-technical vocabulary. An exception is the preface by Hanna and Lawler on *Boece*, where a very accurate indication of the opposing functions of base text and copy-text is implied: "The work has been previously edited, always with C1 or C2 as base. . . . In this edition we follow C1 as copy-text. We chose this manuscript because it is complete, tolerably consistent in its spellings, and one of three manuscripts most faithful to O' " (p. 1151). Following Greg's distinctions, C1 is chosen not because of its presumptive authority on substantives, but rather because of its accidentals (its spelling system) and its completeness. Elsewhere, the Riverside editors tend to avoid the term, even when they are warranted in using it: John Reidy, editing the *Astrolabe*, attempts to "establish an archetype" (p. 1194), and selects a MS (B11) specifically on the basis of its spelling conventions: Reidy does not refer to this as a copy-text, although it is so precisely

---

since changed; see "The Text of Chaucer," *Speculum*, 63 (1988), 779–793, noting "the excellence of the text of the Hengwrt manuscript in comparison with that of the Ellesmere," its "correctness" and "elegance of its expression" (p. 787). Fisher attributes the modern favoring of Hg over El to "the deconstructive temper of modern criticism" (p. 791). A better explanation might be his own (p. 787) and numerous other Chaucerians' involvement with the Variorum.

32. Larry D. Benson, ed., *The Riverside Chaucer* (1987); F. N. Robinson, ed., *The Works of Geoffrey Chaucer* (2nd ed. 1957).

in Greg's sense. John H. Fyler's edition of *House of Fame* is based on different editorial methods, which, however justifiable, are clearly described: "I
have made only a few changes in Robinson's text. . . . The many departures
from the base text, F, . . ." (p. 1139).

More complex is the text of the *Canterbury Tales*; here, the eclecticism
of the Riverside shows to advantage. In comparison to *Boece*, the *Canterbury
Tales* is hardly edited at all; but Hanna's notes make no claim to the contrary:

> For our textual presentation, we adopt the same eclectic (and perhaps not com-
> pletely consistent) procedures used in Robinson's second edition. The text of the
> *Tales* remains based, as was Robinson's, on El. . . . we believe the text we print still
> to be Robinson's; rather than switch copy texts or intercalate all possibly correct Hg
> readings, we prefer to present a hybrid. (p. 1120)

In this straightforward, non-technical paragraph (itself in contrast with the
trenchant description of the earlier history of editions in the same section),
Hanna acknowledges that Robinson functions as base text. More important,
he proves that it is still possible to produce a serviceable edition without reliance on a sudden and remarkable editorial consensus.[33]

In the textual notes to *Troilus*, written by Stephen A. Barney, Robinson
seems to serve a different function: that of copy-text. Barney begins with a
statement of editorial consensus: "Windeatt largely agrees with Robinson,
Pratt [Pratt previously made "much of the analysis of the variants and many
decisions about authentic readings"], and me about the appropriate methods
of establishing the text, and for that reason Windeatt's text and this one differ
little in substantial matters" (p. 1161). The base text is Cp: "The text here
presented, like Robinson's (and Donaldson's, Baugh's, and Windeatt's) is
based on Cp. When Cp is rejected or deficient, this edition prints the readings
of Cl or J, in that order" (p. 1162). But Barney's edition also makes use of
a copy-text: "The present edition is based on microfilm and other photographic copies of all the authorities, supplemented by reference to printed
editions and discussions of the text, primarily Root and Windeatt. The goal
has been to adopt the forms of Robinson's text, which is sensible and intelligent, while reconsidering "from scratch" the readings . . ." (p. 1161).[34] Bar-

33. See the criticism heaped on Robinson by Roy Vance Ramsey, "F. N. Robinson's
Editing of the *Canterbury Tales*," *SB*, 42 (1989), 134–152. Ramsey's attack on Robinson is
by implication criticism of the Riverside, an edition that competes with the Variorum with
which Ramsey himself is heavily involved. Ramsey argues that Robinson based his text not
as he claims on El but on the previous editions of Skeat and Manly. Ramsey is surely justified in criticizing the celebratory essay by George F. Reinecke, "F. N. Robinson (1872–
1967)," in *Editing Chaucer*, pp. 231–251. But that an eclectic edition should rely heavily on
previous editions should come as no surprise; that Robinson agrees with Skeat (the most
respected editor of Chaucer at the time) in cases where their texts diverge from El is to be
expected. Ramsey's supporting statistics are difficult to evaluate, and there are occasional
errors in his descriptions of them (e.g., p. 141; if the figures in Ramsey's chart are correct,
for "129 of 255 cases" read "140 of 255 cases"; the figure 129 is from a different column).

34. The statement on the next page is slightly different, but the first difference be-

ney's first claim makes an apparent distinction between "forms" and "readings." This is, I think, equivalent to Greg's distinction between accidentals and substantives (punctuation is not at issue here). What this statement implies, then, is that the copy-text (in Greg's sense) for this edition is Robinson's second edition. Such claims elevate Robinson to the status of independent authority on Chaucer's use of accidentals. Where Robinson himself spoke of his spelling system as one of normalization, that vocabulary has now disappeared.[35]

Earlier, I noted that there was simply no point in calling a "system of normalization" a copy-text, since such a system did not have to exist as a version of the text to be edited (see Bowers, "Regularization and Normalization," and above n. 14). The reason for that is obvious. Robinson's system of normalization is not simply that found in his text of *Troilus* but one that he constructed from his experience with Chaucer's manuscripts and his knowledge of standard descriptions of Middle English grammar. There is no reason for Robinson to speak of this as a copy-text, since among Chaucer texts it is represented only by his version. Barney disguises that system by allowing it to intrude into the text *as if* it were represented in a medieval copy-text. And for that reason, it would not only be legitimate for Barney to speak of Robinson as copy-text, but also advisable, since such terminology would warn readers of the extent to which Robinson's text serves as authority.

Windeatt's *Troilus* has a much different look, due in part to format (the printing of Boccaccio's *Filostrato* in a facing column, the double column of notes), and in part to Windeatt's decision to represent initial capital *F* graphically as *ff*.[36] But Windeatt also wishes to present a different type of edition:

The form of this edition presents the text of *TC* in the context of the corpus of variants, or "readings", from the extant MSS, not only because those variants can be of editorial value in helping to establish the text, but also because they are held to be of a positive literary value, to embody in themselves a form of commentary, recording the responses of near-contemporary readers of the poetry. (p. 25)

tween Robinson and Barney I find is a comma in line 57: "I have been slightly more conservative of Cp's forms than Robinson, but I have generally treated the spelling of the text as he did, altering some odd . . . or misleading . . . spellings of Cp and suppressing (and occasionally adding) final *-e* in accordance with Chaucer's usage, especially when its pronunciation would affect the meter" (p. 1162).

35. See Robinson, pp. xxxix-xliv: "throughout all Chaucer's works . . . the spellings of the manuscripts have been corrected for grammatical accuracy and for adjustment of rimes" (p. xxxix); "Skeat's general policy was to normalize both the spelling and the grammar of his text . . ." (p. xli); "in a library edition, like the present one, there seems to be no purpose in preserving two inconsistent systems of orthography. . . . The editor has consequently gone farther than any of his predecessors in removing such scribal, or ungrammatical, *-e*'s" (p. xliii); "the orthography of the *Legend* and a number of the minor poems has accordingly been freely normalized" (p. xliii). See also the textual notes to *LGW* by A. S. G. Edwards and M. C. E. Shaner (p. 1179); Prologue F is "normalized," apparently according to Robinson.

36. B. A. Windeatt, ed., *Geoffrey Chaucer, Troilus & Criseyde: A New Edition of 'The Book of Troilus'* (1984).

Manuscripts, thus, are not to be construed necessarily as evidence of authorial intentions, but rather as evidence of audience responses. This allows Windeatt to direct his discussion away from the question of the relative authority of manuscripts and to speak of manuscript relations as "various scribal traditions of copying the poem" (p. 37). It also allows him to define a copy-text:

> The copy-text of this edition is MS Cp, and its form has been treated conservatively. Cp's spelling conventions with regard to *ff*, *ʒ*, *i/j*, and *u/v* have been retained. Capitalisation is editorial, but with regard for Cp's practice. Cp's abbreviations are silently expanded. Punctuation is editorial, but has been kept reasonably light. (p. 65; see also p. 69)

Windeatt's naming Cp a copy-text rather than a base text (even though it arguably serves such a function) seems in line with his effort to reduce the authority of any single manuscript (representing authorial intentions) in favor of the extant manuscripts (representing the text's reception). That is, the edition is an attempt in some way to present an audience-based edition. The wisdom of this may be questioned, but it does allow Windeatt to limit the authority of his copy-text to formal matters.[37]

Yet in practical terms, Windeatt's edition is little affected by his theory. Like Blake, Windeatt simplifies editorial procedures by discounting authorial revision (in this case, the theory of three authorial versions of *Troilus*). Coherent authorial intentions can then be determined by manuscript relations (p. 41), and some manuscripts better reflect those intentions than others; the relative authority of manuscripts is of course implicit in his description of Cp and Cl (pp. 68–69). Windeatt's "copy-text" finally has as much authority over the substantives of the text as Barney's "base text."

KANE'S PIERS PLOWMAN

Without question, the most significant recent edition of a Middle English text is the Kane-Donaldson *Piers Plowman*[38]—a work that will probably influence future Chaucer editors as much as any of the specific Chaucer editions discussed above. I cite this in conclusion in hopes that its editorial language will prove as influential as its substance and tone. Kane's entire enterprise is directed against the possibility of a recension edition; thus, the terminology of Greg designed particularly for such an edition is not easily applicable. The language adopted by Kane, however, is instructive. In the edition of the A Version:

> The basic manuscript or copy-text is T. This was chosen for several reasons. First, it is one of the few A manuscripts without large omissions or physical imperfections. . . . The choice is thus between T and Ch, which are both complete and not demonstrably inferior copies. . . . (p 165)

---

37. See "The Scribal Medium," pp. 25–35; B. A. Windeatt, "The Scribes as Chaucer's Early Critics," *SAC*, 1 (1979), 119–141; and McGann's notion of a literary work as a social product (*Critique*, pp. 51–63). Cf. Kane's harsh criticism of Windeatt's evaluation of scribes: " 'Good' and 'Bad' Manuscripts," p. 208.

38. George Kane, ed., *Piers Plowman: The A Version* (1960, 1988); George Kane and E. Talbot Donaldson, ed., *Piers Plowman: The B Version* (1975).

The grammatical and orthographical forms of T have generally been preserved. . . . No attempt has been made to restore the morphology of the author's copy from manuscript evidence. (pp. 168–169)

T is as true a copy-text as could be possible in a non-recension edition, here serving to supply a system of regularization for accidentals. It is also a base text (although Kane does not so describe it), since the kind of edition Kane is engaged in must be called eclectic. Kane wishes to place himself in a direct line with Greg and Housman, and his primary target is the "tyranny of the copy-text"—the editorial procedure that would substitute a physical authority for editorial experience. I assume this is why he refers to T as a copy-text or (using non-technical terminology) as a "basic text." Since all changes from T are shown in square brackets, the degree to which T is the "highest presumptive authority" will reflect the editor's willingness to include such brackets in the text.

In the B Version, the textual-critical language becomes even more explicit, as does the reference to Greg:

The ideal basic manuscript or copy-text [ref. to Greg] is the one which first provides the closest dialectical and chronological approximation to the poet's language, and then second, most accurately reflects his original in substantive readings. It is because the function of a copy- or basic text is to furnish the accidentals of an edition that the first requirement is primary: the least corrupt manuscript will not necessarily fulfil it best. (p. 214)

Kane-Donaldson choose W as their "basic manuscript" (p. 216): "For one thing W's consistent spelling and systematic grammar afford a clear model for the many readings that have to be introduced into the text by emendation" (p. 215). The citation of Greg is significant, since the function of a copy-text becomes more limited as the editor's own intervention increases. The Kane-Donaldson edition is still an eclectic or base-text edition, and this is reflected in the language above. But the presumption of authority in substantive matters is secondary. Again, describing such a base manuscript in the language of Greg puts the editor under fewer constraints to follow it. And the difference between the B Version and A Version editions is in one sense a recognition of those implications.

Kane uses terminology only when its history has some import: thus his use of the term "copy-text." Elsewhere, non-technical terminology suffices (thus "basic-text" instead of the technical terms "best text" or "base text"). Furthermore, he uses technical terminology to reduce external authority, not to elevate it.[39]

---

39. Those who emphasize the authority of Kane's procedures seriously misrepresent his methods. Kane establishes principles by which scribes err, and error, by its nature, is not subject to infallibility. Patterson, in his review, however, seems to think it is: "As a system, this edition validates each individual reading in terms of every other reading, which means that if some of the readings are correct, then—unless the editorial principles have in an individual instance been misapplied—they must all be correct"; Lee Patterson, "The Logic of Textual Criticism and the Way of Genius: The Kane-Donaldson *Piers Plowman* in Historical Perspective," in Jerome J. McGann, ed., *Textual Criticism and Literary Interpreta-*

CONCLUSION

McGann's definition of copy-text seems to be a reasonable extension of Greg's notion, and certainly is useful in practice:

In the post-Greg context, the term signifies what an editor chooses to take as the text of highest presumptive authority in the preparation of an eclectic, or critical, edition. That is to say, after examining the surviving documents in which the text is transmitted forward, the editor chooses one of these—or sometimes a combination— as his copytext. The copytext serves as the basis of the critical edition that is to be produced. (*Social Values*, p. 177)

The rejoinder to this argument is that it provides an excellent definition of a "base text" (implying an eclectic edition), not a "copy-text" (implying a recension edition or what was once meant by the phrase "critical edition"). Furthermore, the argument assumes that editors must choose a text as their highest authority. Yet recension editions still exist, and Kane has proved that even a base-text edition can exist without attributing undue authority to the basic text itself.

Chaucerians, however, seem to be moving toward single-text editions, and Greg's inadvertent defense of such editions can certainly be taken at face value: "what many editors have done is to produce, not editions of their authors' works at all, but only editions of particular authorities for those works, a course that may be perfectly legitimate in itself, but was not the one they were professedly pursuing" (p. 384). Editions of Hg and editions of Chaucer are two different things, and there are certainly reasons to prefer the former (economics, editorial consistency in a project involving many editors, etc.). And editors might do well to portray legitimate, economically based decisions for what they are, rather than to obscure them with textual-critical jargon. This is the approach successfully taken by the Toronto Medieval Latin Texts series. Furthermore, editorial projects are not necessarily doomed because they have multiple (and possibly conflicting) purposes. Poiron's cheap student edition of the *Roman de la Rose* follows a single manuscript (allowing the reader to reconstruct it) while adding in brackets the lines of the *textus receptus* not included in it. In so doing, Poiron can incorporate earlier editions rather than condemn them.[40]

An obvious conclusion here would be for Middle English editors to drop the notion of copy-text altogether unless they are willing to define it precisely (as, say, Greetham, "Normalisation") and to speak directly to the problem of what the accidentals provided by such a text are supposed to represent

---

tion (1985), p. 69. Even disregarding the grim political implications of such reasoning, its logical and scientific invalidity should be noted. I could well apply a rule that every word in *Piers* was "In" and do so consistently; I would be right in some cases. Cf. Greg's critique of McKerrow that leads off his "Rationale": alterations of a particular exemplar must be "*of a piece* before we can be called upon to accept them *all*" (p. 381). But we cannot determine that without testing them individually.

40. George Rigg, "Medieval Latin," in A. G. Rigg, ed., *Editing Medieval Texts: English, French, and Latin Written in England* (1977), pp. 107–125; Daniel Poiron, ed., *Guillaume de Lorris et Jean de Meun: Le Roman de la Rose* (1974), see pp. 33–35.

or suggest: those of the author? or simply those of one of the author's near-contemporaries? Unless an editor is interested in grappling with such questions, I see little reason to invoke Greg's term. A statement such as "the base text for the edition is X (corrected), with forms normalized according to the edition of Robinson" makes perfect sense and can be easily justified. An edition will not (or should not) be condemned simply because it is selective in the issues it deals with. The use of the term "copy-text" for Middle English editions that are completely different from the type of edition on which Greg based his theory leads generally to confusion and to an obscuring of the often legitimate editorial procedures employed.

BIBLIOGRAPHICAL METHODS FOR IDENTIFYING UNKNOWN PRINTERS IN ELIZABETHAN/JACOBEAN BOOKS

by

ADRIAN WEISS*

THE functions of the descriptive bibliographer and textual editor vary somewhat in purpose and scope but both depend upon knowledge of essential bibliographical facts about a book. Of primary importance is the relation between the identity of the printer of a book and the circumstances of its production. Early books divide into three classes, each of which presents a special problem in this context. First, the need for printer identification is obvious in books which lack a signed imprint and mention of the printer in in the Stationers' Register entry. The second class consists of books whose printer is given in the imprint and/or a Stationers' Register entry but which actually were shared with one or more other printers. Although it has been generally assumed that such printer identifications are trustworthy, the many instances of previously undetected shared printing in this class of books is demonstrable cause for suspicion. As a result, it is necessary to verify these

* The research for this paper was supported by a generous grant from the National Endowment for the Humanities, Division of College Teachers, for which I am also indebted to Fredson Bowers, Peter Blayney, and Donald H. Reiman for their supporting recommendations. This paper would not have been possible without this support. I also thank Fredson Bowers for suggesting the approach of this paper and encouraging and guiding its progress, and Peter Blayney for sharing his vast knowledge of the subject. The staff of Reader Services and the Special Reading Room of The Huntington Library also deserve a note of appreciation for their cheerful and efficient assistance.

identifications in order to distinguish a third class consisting of books printed solely by the specified printer. Tentative printer identifications supplied in the revised *STC* upon the basis of ornamental evidence also must be subjected to this verification process. The significance of the identity of the printer(s) of a book and the distinction between shared and unshared books is self-evident. Descriptive bibliographers and textual editors should, as a consequence, settle these issues as completely as circumstances permit before proceeding with other aspects of description and analysis. However, they should approach the task with realistic expectations, given the unpredictability of the process of searching for an unidentified sharing printer.

The purpose of descriptive bibliography is to record two kinds of information about a book: its physical characteristics and corresponding inferences about its printing history; and other details which may contribute to the general understanding of early printing.[1] Hence, a bibliographer who is working on a specific project involving a group of books or is on the staff of a rare books collection should, as a matter of course, take a long-term perspective by examining every book for evidence of shared printing. Even if the sharing printer(s) cannot be identified, the divisions of labor should be recorded along with any data that may provide clues for the future identification of the

1. G. Thomas Tanselle's wide-ranging discussion in "The Use of Type Damage as Evidence in Bibliographical Description," *The Library*, 5th ser., 23 (1968), 329–351, includes an especially relevant comment: "By definition a descriptive bibliographer must describe; and description entails more than the notation of the minimum number of apparently 'significant' features for the bibliographical analysis of one work. The bibliographer is further obliged to contribute to a larger body of information, and any descriptive bibliography should be, in effect, a partial history of printing. Details which may turn out to be unimportant in analysing the printing of a particular book or determining the number of impressions it went through may nevertheless furnish important corroborative evidence to another bibliographer dealing with a different book of the same period," p. 336. In this context, the kinds of evidence which suggest or demonstrate shared printing of a book should be given special attention. Although Tanselle's observations on the importance of evidence from type damage for reconstructing the printing of an issue or edition are certainly sound, I have difficulty understanding how damage to specific types can be defined in a bibliographical description so that they would be recognizable in another book. This seems a bit too idealistic. The precise image of a damaged type as seen at high magnification is necessary for identifying its recurrence. No degree of precise verbal description or recording of measurements can serve the purpose.

This paper assumes a familiarity with concepts, principles, methods and examples presented in two earlier papers: "Reproductions of Early Dramatic Texts as a Source of Bibliographical Evidence" (hereafter "Reproductions"), *TEXT*, 4 (1989), 237–268; and "Font Analysis as a Bibliographical Method: The Elizabethan Play-Quarto Printers and Compositors" (hereafter "Font Analysis"), *Studies in Bibliography*, 43 (1990), 95–164 (see note 12, p. 152, for an explanation of my method of labeling specific fonts). Important background information about shared printing and typographical study is found in Peter W. M. Blayney, "The Prevalence of Shared Printing in the Early Seventeenth Century," *Papers of the Bibliographical Society of America*, 67 (1973), 437–442, and *The Texts of 'King Lear' and Their Origins* (hereafter *Texts*), vol. 1 (1981); Antony Hammond, "*The White Devil* in Nicholas Okes's Shop," *Studies in Bibliography*, 39 (1986), 135–176, and Hammond's review of Blayney's *Texts*, *The Library*, 6th ser., 6 (1984), 89–93; and Charlton Hinman, *The Printing and Proof-Reading of the First Folio of Shakespeare* (1963).

sharing printer(s). Similarly, evidence that confirms the identity of the assigned printer in unshared books is an essential component of a bibliographical description. Typographical evidence is of primary importance in printer identification. The bibliographical descripton of the typefaces found in a book has been discussed in some detail by Fredson Bowers.[2] Although limited to generic typographical characteristics (style of face such as roman, italic, or black letter, and 20-line height), such information can save valuable time otherwise wasted in surveying irrelevant books: a note that type of a specified style and size appears in a book as the text font or that it appears only as the emphasis font, or no mention of a particular type in the description (indicating that it does not appear at all), permits an immediate decision as to whether to examine the book for typographical evidence or simply disregard it. To this may be added the description of more specific information about the fonts found in a book consisting of "gross features" (easily observed font differentiae such as mixed capitals and/or the foul-case cluster). This category of typographical evidence provides the initial clues to the identity of a font and is of utmost importance in the printer-search process. A match-up of the foul-case letters found in a target font in a shared book with those listed

2. See discussion, *Principles of Bibliographical Description* (1949), pp. 300–306, 344–347. G. Thomas Tanselle, "The Identification of Typefaces in Bibliographical Description," *Papers of the Bibliographical Society of America*, 60 (1966), 185–202, is rather non-specific about early typography but establishes useful principles for including information about typefaces in a bibliographical description. Evolving knowledge should eventually produce a more specific basis for such descriptions. A potential problem exists in as much as W. Craig Ferguson's *Pica Roman Type in Elizabethan England* (1989), described as a "vital reference source," may be used unwittingly by bibliographers in the manner described by Bowers, e.g., "The font of type . . . should be identified by reference to books on printing types," p. 305. Ferguson's misconception of the actual complexity of typefaces and fonts underlies his overly simplistic method of typographical analysis which, as a consequence, lacks the precision needed for sorting out extremely similar letters in different typefaces and, moreover, eliminates from consideration most of the lower-case, all capitals except the 'M', and all ligatures and punctuation. In general, the magnitude and frequency of demonstrable errors and oversights that are found in *Pica Roman Type* disqualify it as a dependable reference for the identification of typefaces and specific fonts. Of particular concern are problems encountered in Tables 2, 3, 8, and 9 (all duplicated in Table 1 entries). For details, see my review (forthcoming in *Papers of the Bibliographical Society of America*, December, 1989) as well as comments included below. See "Font Analysis," note 10, pp. 151–152, for references to contemporary typeface specimens; and Frank S. Isaac, *English and Scottish Types 1535–58, 1552–1558* (1932).

My suggestion that bibliographers check the fonts in every book calls for a word of encouragement since a well-known bibliographer (who shall go unnamed) responded with what may be a typical reaction: "You can't expect someone to examine the type in over a thousand books." Indeed, this seems an enormous burden to impose upon an already devastatingly tedious task. However, once one learns to recognize typefaces by stylistic traits and differentiate fonts by easily observed "gross features," it becomes a simple matter to note typographical facts while paging through a book in search of ornamental stock, anomalies in signatures and/or pagination, and other kinds of bibliographical data that should be recorded as a matter of course. A method of learning typeface characteristics is described in "Reproductions," pp. 252–254. Special stylistic traits and variant letter-forms are discussed in detail in "Font Analysis," esp. pp. 97–119 and note 28.

in a bibliographical description can lead directly to the unknown sharing printer.

On the other hand, the textual editor is absolutely bound to resolve the issue of shared printing and to define the sections of a shared book before proceeding with the analysis of setting and presswork upon which inferences about the evolution of a text depend. A complete execution of editorial responsibility extends to the identification of the sharing printer(s), the key fact which links the evolution of a text to the production methods and personnel of particular shops and the known manner in which they can affect the textual transmission process. At minimum, a textual editor should attempt to identify the section(s) of a shared book printed by the primary printer, provided that he is identified by the book's imprint (or *STC* assignment) or can be inferred tentatively from ornamental stock appearing in the book.[3]

The process of settling the shared printing issue, distinguishing sections, and searching for the printers of a book can be a time-consuming, frustrating, and ultimately a sometimes futile effort. However, such an outcome need not reflect upon the calibre of the investigator, given the vagaries and erraticness of early printers' practices. While the search process itself should be guided by logic, the phenomena that it seeks to unravel are sometimes illogical, unpredictable, and off-the-cuff responses to a vacillating business situation. Early printers apparently were reluctant to turn a potential printing job back into the street; rather, part of the job went out the back door and down the alley to another printer who could take it on at a moment's notice. The search for unknown printers is facilitated by a systematic approach grounded in an awareness of the various irregularities that occur in the business and printing practices of early printers. This paper is intended to provide bibliographical scholars with a knowledge of the kinds of evidence which suggest shared printing, methods of avoiding pitfalls in interpreting that evidence, and methods of searching for and identifying sharing printers or printers of books lacking an imprint. For the most part, the principles and methods described in the following are derived from an analysis of the factors which contributed to demonstrable errors in printer assignments and oversights of shared printing as found in the bibliographical literature. As is typical of research limited to a quite small sample of the books printed before 1640, it can be assumed that the following discussion by no means exhausts the probable variations on the problem of printer identification and shared printing. Much work remains to be done. I hope that this paper will create an aware-

---

3. The unfortunate fact, however, is that during the past quarter century or so the "publish or perish" pressure in academia has left little leisure for this degree of editorial responsibility. The discipline must eventually recognize the futility of the continuing production of new editions of shared Elizabethan play-quartos which are treated as if they are the work of a single printer. The fact that the search for a sharing printer can require a considerable amount of time and end in failure is not a valid reason for avoiding the minimal task of detecting shared printing and identifying the primary printer's section(s) of a book.

ness of the intricacies of the problem so that bibliographical scholars, armed with the potent tool of font analysis, will eventually complete this sketch of what actually happened in early printing.

I

Several kinds of facts normally noted in the routine examination of a book suggest that the font(s) in which it is printed be analyzed in order to settle the issue of shared printing. Strictly speaking, such facts are not "evidence" of shared printing but rather should be viewed as "clues" to that possibility. In general, these clues represent disruptions in the regular patterns established earlier in a book in one or more aspects of printing style or method of imposition and almost always occur at the boundaries between sections of a shared book. Despite this coincidence, the analysis of the font(s) in the book provides the only entirely reliable evidence that the disruption is attributable to sharing rather than to some irregularity in normal shop procedure during the machining of the book.

(1)
A disruption in the sequence of signature alphabets usually occurs only in long shared books but is not a necessary adjunct of sharing. *Essays* STC 18041, for example, runs through continuous alphabets although Eld printed Book 3 at 2S–3C and Simmes resumed with Book 4 at 3D. A sharing strategy based upon the division of a text into units such as books or parts or some other form of sub-heading may invite a shift in alphabets that was not necessarily implemented even in shared books. Stafford printed the title, preliminaries and part of the text (L–O2) of Part 1 of *Essays* STC5775 (1600), while Read(?) did Part 2 about a year later. Despite the gap in production, Parts 1 and 2 are continuously signed with the split at O2/O3. However, the two books of *Treatise of Antichrist* STC7120 (1603) are separately signed. Eld printed the title and preliminaries and most of Book 2 while Braddock printed Book 1. The division into three sections in *An Apology* STC19295 is accompanied by shifts to new alphabets which reliably indicate the *general* pattern of sharing. The title (with Eld's imprint), preliminaries, and Book 1 are signed ¶–E, whereas Book 2 commences with a new alphabet at [F1] running 2A–O; then the third shared section begins with a third alphabet running 3A–N4. In this instance, Eld's sharing strategy was obviously based upon the natural divisions by books and the flexibility in production schedule offered by non-sequential signing. Jaggard's machining of Book 2, in effect, was temporally independent of Eld's work on Book 1. At some point, Eld took over Book 2 after Jaggard's long stint 2A–O and began the third alphabet.

Perfectly logical sharing strategies in Elizabethan printing, however, must be held suspect until confirmed by font analysis. In each of the foregoing examples, font analysis reveals further sharing within sections: the font Creede-3 appears in B–K of STC5775 Pt. 1; Creede-4 appears in STC7120 2H–M; and Jaggard's three fonts alternate in 3H–K of STC19295. In general, no irregularity in signing occurs in short texts requiring only one alphabet, although a few isolated instances can be found such as *Vertumnus* STC12555 where Okes printed A–C2v, and Eld began his section ²B–H with a repeated alphabet. It should be noted that both the preliminaries and first sheet of text are frequently signed A as a matter of course. Although fairly uncommon in quartos, a shift in pagination can provide a clue to a sharing division. For example, Islip paginates his first section of *De Missa* STC23456 1–325, and the sharing printer not only repeats the alphabet but also begins with the second page 1.

Signature-alphabet shifts occur sometimes in a particular class of books consisting of a primary title/text and an appended secondary title/text. It is not always clear whether the two (or more) texts were intended as sections of one work or as complementary works, or were simply printed together as a matter of expediency. Eld printed the first title (with his imprint) and preliminaries of *Remaines* STC4521 (1604), Simmes did the first text B–2H, and Eld the second title "Certaine Poems, or Poesies, Epigrammes . . ." and text accompanied by a shift to lower-case alphabet a–h. A simultaneous shift occurs from Simmes-S1 to Eld-Y1. However, shifts also occur in other instances involving only one printer. Jaggard appended *Genealogie of Vertue* with a repeated alphabet ²B–K to *Anatomie of Sinne* STC12465.5 [old 565] (1603) which ended at I2v; Jaggard-Y1a prints both texts. Finally, the theoretical possibility should be borne in mind that a shift between quarto printing in fours and eights could occur at boundaries of shared sections. For example, this occurs in *A Reformation* STC3906 after sheet P where the alphabet and pagination repeat along with shifts in the pica roman and italic emphasis fonts.

(2)

The sets of running-titles automatically change between shared sections of a book. Hence, running-title analysis is a fairly reliable method of detecting the possibility of shared printing, especially when a relatively large number of skeletons (e.g., four, five, and six) are found in a play-quarto, provided, of course, that the sets of titles and associated skeletons are correctly identified and charted. If fewer than four sets obtain, shared printing may nevertheless be suggested by a change in the method of imposition and number of skeletons.

In some instances, shared sections are immediately suggested by obvious differences in sets of running-titles. White's pica italic titles in EF of *Isle of Gulls* Q1–2 STC6212–13 are sandwiched between the large double-pica italic titles of A–D and GH. Irregularities in the style of capital letters in initial positions can be quickly noted. Braddock set an erect Granjon italic capital '*A*' in both initial positions in A–C of *An Answer* STC12988, while Short (D–G), Snodham (H–L), Field (M–P), and Harrison (Q–V) set a variety of combinations in the second position consisting of the Granjon erect '*A*' and swash '*A*', and lower-case '*a*'; an anomalous oversized swash '*A*' occurs in

Short's section at D4, E4, G4; and Harrison set a 96mm roman 'A' in both positions at R1 and S4. In other instances, the text of the running-title changes between sections.[4]

However, the tracker of running-titles in shared books faces a dangerous pitfall when the sharing printers set their running-titles in the same italic typeface. Unless the sequential sets of titles exhibit some abnormalities that permit differentiating them, they are easily confused.[5] In *Whore* Q1 STC6501, the titles of AB and CD can be thus differentiated. On the other hand, the titles of E–K cannot, inviting the incorrect assumption that the section was printed by one printer and the incorrect correlation of some titles in EF with others in G–K. Similarly, the titles of AB and EF in *Fools* STC4963 have been confused as well as the titles in other plays. In these examples, the detection of the boundaries of the shared sections depends upon subtle differences in the sets of titles which can easily escape the eyes of even seasoned bibliographers.[6] The fundamental value of font analysis as the initial step in examining a book is obvious here. In each instance, a glance at the type below the titles reveals a night-and-day difference that cannot be overlooked and needs no subtle analysis. Whereas the titles of *Whore* F4v and G1, for example, are actually indistinguishable at high magnification, the radically different typefaces in F4v (Stafford-EFb) and G1 (Eld-Y1) are brutally obvious both in regard to font composition and general appearance. The same is true in *Fawne* Q1–2 STC17483–84, D4v (Purfoot-Y2) vs. E1 (Windet-S1) and in many other instances.

In general, it seems that such fortuitous shifts in typefaces occur at boundaries of shared books in the great majority of cases. *Dutch Courtesan* STC 17475 is an exception that underscores the difficulty of distinguishing same-face fonts both in running-titles and text. Y-fonts appear in both A–E and F–H, so that the boundary at E4v/F1 is not obvious at first glance, although

---

4. See W. W. Greg, " 'The Honest Whore' or 'The Converted Courtesan,' " *The Library*, 4th ser., 15 (1935), 54–60; Fredson Bowers, "Notes on Running Titles as Bibliographical Evidence," *The Library*, 4th ser., 19 (1938), 315–338, and "The Headline in Early Books," *Essays in Bibliography, Text, and Editing* (1975), pp. 199–211.

5. See discussion in "Reproductions," pp. 242–244, and "Font Analysis," note 40. In addition, I should note that the font used in running-titles may suggest the identity of a suspected printer or lead to a rejection of him as a candidate. The font may contain unique discriminants sufficient to demonstrate ownership. On the other hand, a survey may reveal that the candidate printer never used the typeface seen in the titles. For example, STC14377 and STC14381 are assigned respectively to Simmes and Windet, but the running-titles are set in a Y-font which neither used elsewhere. Both conclude with the Read/Eld McKerrow 320b "Gilley flower" (I have seen only the final page of STC14381 in British Library copy 720.a.32(3)). STC14377 also uses a Read/Eld 'V' (A2) and 'A' (A6), and Eld-Y1 in the letter (A2–2v) and as emphasis in the black letter text.

6. The ingenious technique devised by Randall McLeod which employs transparencies of running-titles is a valuable improvement over the unaided eye. It seems that the added precision offsets the expenditure of time required to produce the transparencies. See "A Technique of Headline Analysis, with Application to *Shakespeares Sonnets*, 1609," *Studies in Bibliography*, 32 (1979), 197–210.

the first stage of font analysis can produce "gross features" evidence which leaves no doubt that a different Y-font (Jaggard-Y1b) prints F–H.[7] As a general rule, then, the most efficient and trustworthy approach in running-title analysis is first to compare the type fonts on the first and final pages of subsequent gatherings to ascertain whether the typeface itself is different on these facing pages. Overall, a leisurely execution of this procedure requires far less time than the frustrating tedium of sorting out units of, say, seventeen same-face italic letters on about sixty pages and then grouping them into sets of four or eight and charting their movement, including transpositions, through a book. Once a shift in typeface indicates a likely boundary such as at E4v/F1, the task of analysing the running-titles is considerably simplified because the hypothesis of sharing focuses efforts upon just two groups of titles in the two sections of the book.

(3)
    In shorter books such as play-quartos, the sections of a shared book almost inevitably exhibit some differences in the various details of layout and setting cumulatively termed "printing style." Compositorial and textual studies of shared play-quartos usually take note of such differences but overlook the possibility of sharing.[8] Caution must be exercised in interpreting such evidence, since it could merely imply a shift between two compositors in one shop. For example, the two Windet compositors who used the Windet-S1, and the Windet-S2 and -F cases differ in some aspects of printing style. Eld's compositors consistently sign all four leaves of play-quartos during 1603–1606 (as do Purfoot's compositors), but after late 1606, the practice changes to the more common signing of only three leaves in most dramatic texts.[9] None of the five printers of *An Answer* STC12988 (1603) signs the fourth leaf, but Snodham's section (H–L) is the only one signed with roman numerals (H, Hii, iii), an easily recognized clue to the sharing in his section. Such peculiarities of printing style may seem, at first glance, to be potential clues to a printer's work in shared books. However, other factors could be responsible. In printing two of Jonson's dramatic quartos (*Sejanus* STC14782, 1605; *Volpone* STC14783, 1607), for example, Eld set the speech prefixes with an initial

    7. As a matter of course, correct procedure entails moving from the general to the more specific in stages. Having ascertained that the Y-face appears throughout, the next step involves a quick survey aimed at detecting obvious "gross features" differences, beginning with the capitals, punctuation, and foul-case cluster. The font of A–E contains both Y- and S-face capitals throughout, while F–H uses Y-capitals exclusively. This in itself indicates the strong probability of two same-face fonts. Further weight is added by a survey of foul-case italic capitals that yields different clusters which overlap in just a few sorts. By this point, there can be little doubt that a boundary marked by a shift in fonts occurs at signatures E/F and implies the possibility of shared printing.
    8. See recent studies noted in "Reproductions" and "Font Analysis" as well as studies of the shared play-quartos noted below.
    9. See, for example, *Devil's Charter* STC1466, *Byron* STC4968, *T. Travailes* STC6417, *Northward Hoe.* STC6539, *Westward Hoe!* STC6540, *Volpone* STC14783, *What You Will* STC17487, *A Tricke* STC17896, *Hamlet* Q3 STC22277, *Troilus* STC22331.

pica roman capital followed by small roman capitals, a rare deviation from the standard use of itaic in speech prefixes. The same setting style also appears in Braddock's printing of *Poetaster* STC14781 (1602) and Snodham's *Alchemist* STC14755 (1610). Thus it seems more probably attributable to Jonson's direct involvement in the printing of these plays than to a shop's practice. The two could be confused and lead to the erroneous suspicion that Eld printed sheets CD of *d'Olive* STC4983 (1606), given the possibility that Eld-Y1 and Eld-S1, used previously in Eld's books, could have been mixed to produce the font in CD (the fact that Braddock did not use an S-font eliminates him from consideration). Compositorial preferences are a primary consideration. Both Simmes's and Jaggard's compositors periodically switched to a lower-case initial letter in italic speech prefixes possibly because of shortages in the capitals, and/or they punctuated alternately with colons or commas instead of periods. The appearance of the former atypical practice in *Isle of Gulls* STC6212 (1607; see H) and *Dutch Courtesan* STC17475 (1605; see H3v-4) provides a preliminary clue to the possibility of Jaggard's involvement; Simmes is easily rejected since his pica roman font is in the wrong face.

II

A different kind of frustration characterizes the reliance upon ornamental stock as a means of identifying printers and detecting shared printing. Despite the fact that ornamental stock has long served as the primary evidence of a printer's work, a comprehensive catalogue has yet to be published and probably never will be. Hence, scanning the standard references to identify the owner of a particular ornament frequently (or usually, in my experience) ends in failure.[10] This seems to have happened to *STC* researchers as well since, in some instances, a printer has not been supplied for books in which ornamental stock appears. Likewise, shared printing has been overlooked when the stock of a second printer appears along with that of the printer given in the imprint. Furthermore, the reliability of ornamental stock as evidence of printer identity is somewhat lessened by the common practice of borrowing and the existence of duplicate castings and copies. The printer assignments in new *STC* that are based upon the identification of ornamental stock are thus considered tentative and are cited in brackets; these must eventually be verified by font identification.

Oversights of shared printing and incorrect identification of printers in the new *STC* seems reason enough to discuss in detail the difficulties associated with the reliance upon ornamental stock. The basic flaw in previous printer-research has been the *sole* reliance upon ornamental stock.[11] How-

10. References that reproduce and identify ornamental stock are given in *Texts*, pp. 458–459, largely duplicated in "Font Analysis," note 1; see also notes 11 and 15 below. I follow Blayney's method of citing these references, e.g., the author of the reference separated by a slash "/" either from the owner of an ornament or the title of the reference; McKerrow's identifications in *Printers' and Publishers' Devices* are cited simply by number.

11. The back-and-forth process of comparing ornaments and searching for printers is reflected in Katherine V. Pantzer's apt selection of the title "The Serpentine Progress of the

ever, a more accurate and trustworthy conclusion both about the sharing issue and the identity of a sharing printer can result if the appearance of ornamental stock is understood as an initial clue to the possibility of shared printing that must be followed up by font analysis and identification. A discussion of the various patterns of ornamental appearances seen in shared books will contribute to a more effective use of this kind of evidence.

(1)

In general, the usefulness of ornamental evidence increases with the length of a book and the opportunities presented by the kind of text for the insertion of ornamental stock. Unfortunately, no predictable relationship obtains between the various patterns of sharing and the appearances of ornaments. Many short texts such as play-quartos and theological pamphlets present no opportunity for the insertion of sharing printers' ornaments after the preliminaries and beginning of the text, although this is not an inviolable pattern. The first section of a short shared text could in fact be given to a sharing printer while the printer cited in the imprint (usually accompanied by his ornamental stock in the title and preliminaries) completes the text without the insertion of ornamental stock. Thus Creede's initial Yamada/Creede T6 begins the octavo text of *Essays* Pt. 1 STC5775 while Stafford prints the final section (L–O); and Eld's rarely used 'W' begins the text of *Malcontent* Q1–2 STC17479–80 while Simmes prints the second section (F–H). Shorter texts consisting of two sub-titles or a major title and sub-title present the opportunity for the insertion of ornamental stock. In the octavo *Of the Calling of the Ministerie Two Treatises* STC19733 (1605), Roberts's imprint and ornaments appear in the preliminaries and his two fonts alternate in the first treatise in [1]BC. "The Second Treatise" shifts to a repeated alphabet with Yamada/Creede initial I1 in [2]B1 heading the text in [2]B–K which is printed in Creede-4.[12]

STC Revision" for her report in *Papers of the Bibliographical Society of America*, 62 (1968), 297–311, which includes reproductions of six initials and one factotum (p. 303) and valuable discussion of the search process, pp. 299–309, ending with a confession: "I like catching the printers with their ornaments and initials showing; a bibliographical Peeping Tom, so to speak." For the average bibliographer who lacks access to the *STC* office's resources for identifying ornamental stock, the peeping-tom analogy leaves something of a bitter taste since the initial glimpse is sometimes the last, as if the shade were pulled or the lights switched off.

12. Ferguson's oversight of identifiable ornamental stock at divisions between shared sections here and in other works such as *Antichrist* STC7120 and *Essays* STC18041 is puzzling, but the end result is that the shared printing is overlooked. More puzzling is his comment on STC19733: ". . . sheet C is neatly divided between C4v and C5r, the centre of the sheet. The division in sheet B is not so neat: the Lyon(b) was used on B1r, the Lyon(a) was used to the middle of page B5r, and then the use of the Lyon(b) fount recommenced at a new paragraph. There is no evidence of mixing *later in the book* [my emphasis] so the seven and a half pages of Lyon(a) must have been carefully distributed back into its own cases. One can answer the question of whether compositors sometimes stuck to their own cases and distributed back to them in the affirmative," *Pica Roman Type*, p. 15. In fact, Roberts's final section is sheet C, and the rest of the book is printed in Creede-4, so quite naturally the type from sheet C would not be mixed in with the type seen "later in the

In longer texts, divisions by books and chapters frequently occasion a shift in ornamental stock between shared sections which is almost inevitably accompanied by a shift in fonts except in instances of borrowing. Printers sometimes concluded intermediate shared sections with a favorite ornament to fill space even though the text continued in the next section. In general, it is therefore advisable to check for a shift in fonts before and after the textual appearance of an ornament or initial even when the piece is identified in the references. This approach usually clarifies whether a boundary between shared sections obtains. In some instances, the divisions of shared sections do not coincide with the points at which ornaments appear. For example, it seems clear that a decision to begin each chapter with an initial accompanied the jobbing out of *An Answer* STC12988 with the result that each of the six printers had the opportunity to insert at least one initial. However, only Braddock's 'H' (Chapter 1, A1) and Harrison's 'Y' (Chapter 8, Q1) appear coincidentally at the beginning of sections and chapters. Other initials are buried within sections (E2, H1v, K4, N4, P1v). The ornaments in the preliminaries and text of *Seven Deadly Sinnes* STC6522 (1606) present a confusing situation which can only be resolved by identification of the contextual fonts. Allde's imprint and ornaments appear in the title (McKerrow 207; see *STC* description of four states of the title), the dedication (McKerrow/Allde ornament 15 and an 'I' in ^{1}A3), then two of Stafford's pieces (McKerrow 295b, Lavin/Danter initial I2) head the Induction ^{2}A1–4r which is printed in Stafford-EFb; the short letter "Reader" in an unsigned, apparently extra, leaf begins with an unidentified factotum (similar to Woodfield/Field Fac. 1), is printed in Allde-S2, and concludes overside with an identified Allde piece (McKerrow/Allde 4). Examination of the papers reveals that Staf-

---

book." Creede's 1605 reprint of the book (19733a), moreover, also uses the same Yamada/Creede I1 initial and prints in Creede-4. This should have been enough to occasion a closer look at the fonts in BC and ^{2}B–K, provided Ferguson checked 19733a. There is the outside possibility that we looked at two different issues, one printed entirely by Roberts, but the presence of Yamada/Creede I1 in a hypothetical second issue hardly could have escaped detection by *STC* researchers since it appears so frequently in Creede's books. Since Ferguson consistently fails to provide essential information as to *which* copy of a book he means, the hypothesis of two issues is left hanging as an improbability. In fact, one fatal weakness of *Pica Roman Type* as a reference work is the absence of information about the books that were actually examined in the surveys of the various printers. The reader is left with the task of surveying a specific printer's books from a particular year to determine just where "in 1602 another pica was used." Beyond that, it is clear that oversights of three kinds undercut the reliability and usefulness of *Pica Roman Type*: (1) pica roman books listed in Morrison's *Index* were overlooked; (2) although some pica roman books in Morrison were checked for possible reassignment in the new *STC*, many others were not; and (3) the new *STC* was not searched as a whole for newly assigned or reassigned pica roman books. As a result, errors in font identifications are compounded by the omission from the Tables of both identified fonts and at least a dozen unidentified fonts from 1595–1610. Aside from such deficiencies, the proposed printer-search method (see pp. 18–19) using the Tables and facsimiles cannot substitute for reliable empirical methodology. On the one hand, no system of typographical analysis, however sophisticated, can identify a font on the basis of the evidence seen in a single page reproduction. Conversely, recurrent-types which are required for conclusive identification of a font can be absolutely identified only in originals.

ford's preliminary gathering was mistakenly bound in between ^{1}A3–4 of Allde's preliminaries. The text (^{2}B1–O4) in black letter begins with an unidentified headpiece and Lavin/Danter I2 followed by a factotum similar to Woodfield/Wolfe Fac. 3 on C2v. The appearance of an identified piece in each of this sequence of sections would seem to suggest that Stafford then continued with the entire text. However, a special problem (see later discussion, note 41) arises in distinguishing the shared sections in the remainder of the book since it prints in black letter with pica roman as the emphasis typeface.

In unshared long books, external identification of ornamental stock is frequently unnecessary since some pieces recur throughout the book. However, a change in the manner of heading chapters and the appearance of new ornamental stock could be misinterpreted. Bearing Jaggard's imprint, *Badges* STC889 is continuously signed B–2G; each of the four textual units (Books 1–3 and "A Corollary") contains numerous chapters, each headed by an initial. A mixed setting style is established in Book 1 comprised of factotum 1 (C1, E1, F5, F8v, K2), and initial T1 (E4, F3v, F7, G6v, H5v, H7, I4v), with the remaining chapters headed by unornamented, large (7mm) roman capitals. The appearance of previously unseen initial A1 at N4 in Book 2; the shift to setting large roman initials almost exclusively in 20 chapters of Book 3 except for the previously unseen I1 at Q2 and a problematic initial T2 on 2C2v which seems identical to T1 except that single rather than double rules enclose it, making it seem a different initial (it actually is); and factotum 2 in Book 4 (2E1) should cause no difficulty because of the recurrence of previously seen ornamental stock and the mixed setting style. Ornament 1 begins both Book 1 and 2, T1 continues in Book 2 (O7, O8), and factotum 1 appears twice in Book 3 (Q2, R5v). Book 4 raises the possibility of sharing with its new factotum 2 and different printing style, but that can easily be attributed to the change in the kind of text. Moreover, the font which prints the whole book is easily recognized as Jaggard-Y1b.

In some long quartos, sharing may be hinted at by an apparent shift in ornamental stock, although a common problem is that usually too few pieces appear to permit such an insight. Hence, the erratic appearance of ornamental stock somewhat lessens its usefulness as a means of detecting shared printing since pieces may be scattered about in a book without much of a recognizable pattern or with just a few appearances across several gatherings. Furthermore, the intermittent appearance of ornamental stock at likely boundaries between shared sections can create the impression of a sharing pattern less complex than that which actually occurs in a book. Eld's stock and Eld-Y2 appear in Book 1 of *An Apology* STC19295, followed by Jaggard's stock and fonts in the first half of Book 2. However, a shift to a third alphabet reintroduces Eld-Y2 up to and after 3H–L, where Jaggard's fonts appear.

Even when a pattern of recurrence or the appearance of identified pieces is encountered in a shared book, it may not provide a basis for precise differentiation of sections, especially if the two printers print in alternate groups of gatherings instead of in a simple division into long self-contained sections. *De Missa* STC23456 (1603) illustrates these difficulties. Bearing Adam Islip's imprint, the text of Books 1–3 is continuously signed B–$2T3$ but a repeated alphabet is prematurely introduced at [$2T5$] with the beginning of Book 4. The simultaneous shift from easily distinguished Islip-EFb, which uses Guyot capitals exclusively, to a Y-font suggests, at first glance, a simple division by books. However, the distribution of fonts in Book 4 reveals the actual sharing pattern: the Y-font prints ^{2}A–L, ^{2}P–R, ^{2}T, and ^{2}X; Islip-EFb prints ^{2}M–O, ^{2}S, and ^{2}V. It is illuminating to consider the ornamental evidence against this background. The ornamental stock in Books 1–3 is extensive, including two identified head-pieces and one identified factotum in six appearances, nineteen initials in forty-seven appearances, and three factotums in single appearances. Together with the shift in signature-alphabets, a group of twelve new pieces in ^{2}A–L easily points to a sharing division marked by six recurrent pieces (repeated alphabet assumed in the following): factotum 1 recurs at K2, L7v; 'S' at A1, E1; 'A' at A4v, C5, D4v, G2; 'I' at B1v, H1, K4; 'Q' at C1, D6v, I7v; and 'P1' at C5v, I1v, and R5. In addition, six other initials occur once: 'V' at A8v; 'D' at B5v; 'C' at B3; 'R' at E5v; 'F' at H4; and 'B' at L2v. However, the ornamental evidence is clear only about the ^{2}A–L section of Book 4. Relatively few initials occur after ^{2}A–L, leaving little to go on as to the precise division of sharing. The recurrence of 'P1' at ^{2}R5 (previously seen at ^{2}C5v and ^{2}I1v) links ^{2}R to the sharing printer of ^{2}A–L; otherwise three additional initials appear in his later sections: the 'T' at ^{2}P6; 'E' at ^{2}T8; and 'V' at ^{2}X1. The latter could possibly be confusing since another 'V' appears at ^{2}A8v; it might suggest a third printer rather than one who possesses and uses two different 'V' in the same text. The recurrences of five initials from Books 1–3 permit the assignment of three gatherings of Book 4 to Islip and clearly indicate that the division of labor was not a simple "by books" job; rather, Islip alternated with the sharing printer in Book 4.[13] Overall, internal ornamental evidence clarifies the divisions of labor for most of the book with B–$2T$, ^{2}N, ^{2}O, and ^{2}S assigned to Islip, and ^{2}A–L and ^{2}R to the sharing printer. "Gross features" font analysis is adequate for settling the assignment of the remaining six gatherings (^{2}M, V to Islip; ^{2}PQ, T, X, to the sharing printer) and confirming the rest.

In general, the appearance of previously identified ornamental stock in alternating gatherings of a shared section such as Book 4 of *De Missa* STC 23456 provides a short-cut to the assignment of some gatherings. All five recurrent initials noted above belong to Islip, so that a charting of initials through Books 1–3 to establish a recurrence pattern is unnecessary in this instance. However, this is possible only if a previous survey of a printer's work has established that such initials are part of his stock. A rather quick survey of long books (especially folios if available) in the proximate period by

13. These initials include: the M5 at ^{2}N7, from ^{2}G2v, ^{2}K2, ^{2}R8v; the Fish-S at ^{2}O8, from ^{1}D5v, I4v, ^{2}D2, ^{2}G1, ^{2}R3; the Winged-Horse-E at ^{2}S1, from ^{1}O6v, S6v, ^{2}B1v, ^{2}C6v, ^{2}E2v; the 'V' at ^{2}S4, from ^{1}D4, P1v, Q4v, ^{2}I6; the N5 at ^{2}S5v, from ^{1}A5, ^{2}A5, ^{2}C4; and a 'V' from ^{1}D4 recurs at ^{2}S4.

the printer given in the imprint of a shared book will usually locate at least a few pieces which can tentatively establish his sections in the latter. However, in Islip's case, this approach is thwarted by an anomaly in the output from his shop (see later discussion).

Long folios generally contain many pieces so that an internal grouping of ornamental stock exclusive of external identifications frequently can provide an initial clue to the alternation between two printers and sometimes the actual boundaries of sections, provided that the sections are long enough for the recurrence of one or more pieces, or of several initials that belong to a particular alphabet. The latter situation merely hints at ownership by one printer, but is a valuable initial clue to the identity of some printers. For example, an initial from Islip's Blayney/Alphabets 4 and 5 rarely (if ever) appears alone in books which use several initials. Similarly, the Robinson/ Braddock stock included at least eight (A B F H I O T S) large (41mm) initials enclosed by two outer rules separated from an inner frame by ringlets (see Plomer T158, F161, H163; Purfoot also used a similar 'T'; see *Romish Spider* STC5963.5, B1). A second Robinson/Braddock alphabet is characterized by human subject-matter on a filled black background. An appearance of a few initials from these recognizable alphabets calls for a check of the contextual font(s). Moreover, the shift in a long book to previously unseen stock calls for a comparison of the fonts at the previous border between gatherings. Adam Islip and George Eld are identified in the imprint (an extremely rare gratuitous clue) of *A General Historie* STC12374 (1608) so that the identification of their respective sections should be nothing more than a "mop-up" operation. The new *STC* assigns to Eld sections O–2D, 3A–3P, 4I–5F, and 5X–6C, with the rest to Islip. The error in the assignment of the first section is puzzling and illustrates the need for consideration of the pattern of ornament appearance as well as font shifts. Islip's ornaments and initials from his Alphabets 4 and 5 appear up to K5. A different set of five initials appears between L1–N. Then Eld's Mermaid head-piece (30mm x 150mm) and a large 'I' (48mm x 45mm) appear on O1. As far as I know, the Horseman-L at L1 and the "Honi Soit"-A at L3v do not appear previously in an Eld book, but the three others do, including the Monkey-D at L5, the Demon-W at M5v, and Scholar-T at N4v. Nonetheless, two recur in later sections assigned to Eld: the "Honi Soit"-A appears later in the first section at V2, in the second section at 3M6 along with the Scholar-T at 3I7, and in the third section at 4X5. These appearances overlap with 15 other of Eld's initials in the correctly assigned sections,[14] a fact that should be easily noted and interpreted as evidence of Eld's work in L–O. Moreover, a shift in fonts occurs at L1 along with the introduction of the new set of initials; why this was overlooked is puzzling, given the fact that other boundaries were detected in the absence of ornamental stock. The shift to Islip's font at 2E1 occurs fairly close to the

---

14. For example, the Vine-I at T6, Lute-G at X5, the Vine-T at Z6, 3H3 and 4K1, the Stag-C at Q2v and 4X5, the Rabbit-W at 4Y2v, the Standing Cherub-M at S6, 3H5v,6, and 4I6v, and the Satyr-D at 3A1 and 3F2v.

appearance of his Mermaid head-piece (34mm x 126mm) and initials P5 at
2E4 and K5 at 2E5v. However, font shifts without ornamental stock occur at
3Q1 [3M6], 5X1, and 6C1 [5P2] at some distance from the previous appearance of ornamental stock (in brackets). In short, it is not necessary to know a
printer's entire ornamental stock in many instances if proper attention is
given to the pattern of appearances and contextual fonts.

(2)

In general, printer identifications rely upon the recognition of ornamental stock previously identified in the references, or by the appearance of pieces
in the context of a printer's other identified ornaments. Peter Blayney's discussion of "the pitfalls awaiting the unwary ornament-hunter" (Texts, pp.
491–497) documents the difficulties created by the common practices of the
borrowing and the passing of ornamental stock among printers. The existence of duplicate castings and copies likewise can cause confusion. In one
extraordinary instance, eight of Eld's ornaments and initials were specially
forged for a pirated edition.[15]

Several strategic factors can impede the discovery of the owner of a given
ornament when the piece is not identified in the references. With luck, a survey of the suspected sharing printer's books sometimes turns up other appearances of the ornament. However, in many instances, a given ornament was
used very rarely, with appearances separated by a decade or more, so that
such a survey can be quite time-consuming and futile, ending in an erroneous
rejection of the suspected printer. Moreover, an appearance of the ornament
may be found in a shared section whose printer is unidentified. The 'W' that
begins Eld's section of Malcontent Q1–2 STC17479–80 (1604), for example,
does not appear again until 1608, and not since 1598 when Gabriel Simson
owned the shop. These appearances are obviously beyond the reach of a proximate survey of Eld's (and Read's) books so that my search for this initial was
a dead-end.[16] An appearance of a borrowed ornament creates a similar confusion. The large "THE" logo frequently shared by Simmes and Eld, for
example, was lent to Creede for London Prodigal STC22333 (1605), its only
appearance noted by Yamada in Creede's books. The appearance of this
unique logo in the title of Prodigal, its total absence in other Creede books,
and its frequent appearance in Simmes's and Eld's books could lead one to
doubt the veracity of the imprint of Prodigal. The suspicion that either Eld or
Simmes ghosted the book, however, is laid to rest by the fact that Creede-4
printed the text. Once another tentative appearance has been located, the
two ornaments must then be confirmed as being the same piece rather than
duplicate castings or copies. When an ornament or its contextual stock have
been verified as identical to those in the references and ownership thus established, the issue of whether the actual owner used the ornament in a given

15. See William A. Jackson, "Counterfeit Printing in Jacobean Times," The Library,
4th ser., 15 (1934), 364–376, with reproductions of the forged items at p. 367 and pp. 368–369.
16. I am indebted to Peter Blayney for pointing out appearances of this 'W' in STC
18230 (1598), A2, and STC7188 (1608), B1.

book can be settled only by the identification of his font(s) as the context of the ornament's appearance. If an ornament appears several times in the context of a given printer's font(s), it is reasonable to assume ongoing possession of the ornament whether or not the printer actually owned it.

For purposes of identification, ornamental stock falls into two categories: (1) duplicate castings which are basically identical and thus must be distinguished by damage; and (2) more or less faithful copies distinguished by major or minor design differences. Differences due to design and damage can usually be detected through direct comparison of simple pieces such as most initials and xylographics. For example, Simmes and Eld frequently used nearly identical title page xylographic ornaments. Small leaves project inward at top-center from the volutes (large scrolls). Eld's right leaf (shaped somewhat like a parrot's beak) is oversized and the tip extends markedly below the left leaf (see *Fools* STC4963); Simmes's leaves are nearly symmetrical with the tips aligned (see *Malcontent* Q1–3 STC17479–81). Failure to note this fairly obvious difference probably occasioned the incorrect new *STC* assignment of *Siege of Ostend* STC18895 (1604) to Simmes, whereas it is Eld's version that appears in the title, followed by his Goat-head head-piece at ^{2}A1, three of his initials, his pica italic, and Eld-Y1 at ^{1}A2v–3. Jaggard also used the Simmes version of these xylographic ornaments as the outer portions of a head-piece in a folio setting (*Foure-footed Beastes* STC24123, 1607, ¶6, 2¶5). This particular head-piece (similar to Plomer 52) seems identical to the one used by Eld (see below). Large duplicates and copies like this sometimes exhibit major design differences that can be detected by a brief comparison of the pieces. Three versions of Plomer head-piece 52 were in use. In all versions, the centered cherub's head rising from a cluster of three fishes is flanked by two dolphin-like creatures. These are flanked by feeding rabbits in Simmes's version, but by feeding squirrels in the versions used by Eld, Jaggard, A. Hatfield (*Maison* Q2 STC10548, 1606), and Melchisadech Bradwood (*A Copy* STC6164, 1606, C4v; *Concerning* STC24719, 1607, A2; *A Preamble* STC18191, 1608, ¶3). The latter can be distinguished in part by the cherub's head detail. The left cheek is straight and forms an angle with the jaw in Hatfield/Bradwood/Plomer 52, whereas the cheek is chubbier and rounded in the Eld/Jaggard version. The tips of the curved leaves flanking the head nearly touch the halo-like protrusions from the head in the Eld/Jaggard version, while they are spaced about a halo's width from the haloes in the Hatfield/Bradwood/Plomer 52 version. Concentration on these two areas of details is adequate for distinguishing the three versions of the head-piece. However, large pieces with no such major design differences present more of a challenge.[17]

17. An effective method of comparing similar ornaments or initials, especially large complex ones, employs transparencies produced on a Xerox machine, provided that the machine permits a continuous adjustment of the reproduction ratio so that the two images can be reproduced at an identical size. When the transparencies are placed one on the other on a sheet of glossy white paper (or a light-table if available), differences attributable to design, flawed copying or damage usually are easily detected.

In general, ornamental stock is especially prone to a variety of damage because of the complexity of even simple designs. Straight borders and linear elements exhibit bends, gaps created by missing sections, or sheared sections bent away from the original line. In addition, curved elements typically exhibit flattening or wavy damage. Some comment about the differences in the initials of Alphabets 4 and 5 reproduced by Blayney (*Texts*, pp. 446–447) is useful for illustrating the difficulty of sorting out duplicate castings in a particular style. The best method for comparing two similar initials depends on the nature of the ornamental design. Ornamentation with recognizable subject matter such as human figures, animals, birds, and objects provides clearly defined areas within the initial for comparison (see Blayney W2, E7, H8, N13, C15 etc.). However, abstract, stylized arrays ("arabesques") of vines and leaves such as Blayney/Alphabets 4, 5, 9, and 12 lack recognizable forms for judging symmetry and proportions. It is best to examine a section at a time (e.g., the top third, the lower-right quadrant etc.) for discontinuities, gaps, bends, extra buds, shoots, tendrils, leaves and vines. For example, the diagonal vine passing through the bottom-left section of the upper counter of Blayney B4 shows a short stem or shoot that is lacking in B5. At the upper right corner, the tips of the two leaves touch on the extreme right border in B4, but not in B5. In addition, the letter in B4 is slightly smaller. Note also that the leaf directly beneath the left base-serif of N4 is notably smaller than in N5. Differences in size can be detected by measurements of the rules enclosing a letter (height, width, diagonal) and the spacings between points in the design. If the two initials are identical duplicate castings, the objective of a comparison is to detect damage, usually quite minor, that differentiates the two initials. For example, if B4 and B5 actually were identical, the two could be distinguished by damage at the extreme lower-right, where B4's vine exhibits a sinuous bend and is separated from the leaf. Note also the damage illustrated in States 1 and 2 of T4 (p. 450) and the missing outer section of the leaf at 10mm down and to the right of H5. The differences created by damage in some Alphabet 5 letters owned by Okes (17 letters) and Islip (at least 15 letters) can be noted by reference to Blayney's reproductions.[18] The dates of appearance are important in deciding whether these examples repre-

18. The differences are as follows:

A5: upper-right corner, detail in a rectangular area 10mm down, 4mm in: damage in Islip's A5 produced a 1mm gap between the berry and base of the leaf; the nearly horizontal portion of the vine at the bottom of the area is blunted and prints quite bold. Okes's A5 is undamaged. See Islip's A5: STC17291 (1598), D8, L4v, L8; STC13200 (1601), T5; STC15170 (1602), Y4v.

I5: the vine splits into a flaring double-line 2mm below the junction with the top leaf (extreme upper right); the outer line is sheared at the bifurcation point and is pushed away from the inner line in Islip's I5. Okes's I5 is normal. See Islip's I5: STC11196 (1599), A2; STC23456 (1604), P8; STC5504 (1605), A2.

T5: the vine above the left edge of the cross of Islip's T5 (see enclosed area of T4 State 2, p. 450) is straightened to form a wide-angle inverted 'V'; the vine above the right portion of the cross exhibits a 1mm gap at 7.5–8.5mm in from the right edge. See Islip's T5: STC5493 (1600), Q1v; STC13200 (1601), O2; STC17291 (1598), B3v.

sent two states of the respective initials (as with Blayney T4). In general, damage is progressive and irreversible. The damage to Islip's initials precedes the appearance of Okes's undamaged initials by several years, a fact which settles the issue.

Since damage is progressive and cumulative, an earlier appearance may lack some damage seen in a later state. A comparison of early and late states of an Islip factotum (Blayney/A3r) illustrates the point. Blayney reproduces a 1607 state (*Texts*, p. 492) in which two gaps appear in the top border, one large gap at the lower left, and three gaps in the bottom border. Only the gap at the top-left corner is present in the 1600 state (*Les Reports* STC5493, at *3, A1). Such damage to the rules enclosing a piece is not the firmest kind of evidence, but establishes a strong probability of identity. Hence, this gap, along with most of those seen in Blayney's reproduction, leave little doubt that the factotum at A2 of *Six Books* STC3193 (1606, Islip) is the same. Islip also possessed what appears to be an identical duplicate casting of this factotum (Blayney/A3r #1) that illustrates one kind of confusion caused by duplicates and copies. The two factotums are virtually indistinguishable except for the fact that A3r #2 is enclosed in double rules and is in much better condition. Both appear in *Six Books* STC3193 with the inner enclosing rules (the only rules in A3r #1) in obviously different condition: the rules are undamaged in A3r #2 (see *Six Books*, B1, 2M5v, 2S4v; also *De Missa* STC 23456 (1603), A2, B1, Z7v, 2F2v; *Christian's Sanctuarie* STC7113 (1604), B1, K1; and *A General Historie* STC12374 (1608), C4).[19] Similarly, Jaggard owned the duplicate castings T1 and T2 (noted earlier) which can be differentiated by single vs. double rules; both are characterized by the strange bulge of the whole arabesque array in the upper right quadrant which possibly could be explained in terms of the uneven depth of the mold. Again, simultaneous appearances in one book with differentiating damage leaves no doubt that two pieces are involved (see *Foure-footed* STC24123, T1 at B3v, T2 at P5, Q6; also *Badges* STC889 noted earlier).

Large copies and duplicates that exhibit only minor design differences are especially troublesome when the issue is borrowing vs. sharing. An assignment crux arises from the appearance, in the context of identified ornamental stock of one printer, of pieces that are extremely similar to or identical to those known to have been used by another printer. The two samples must be painstakingly compared for differences produced by design or because of the imperfect copying of the original version. In some instances, such differences are so clearly due to design that the issue of damage is irrelevant. However, the absence of distinct progressive damage can leave the question hanging if the ornaments are duplicate castings. These problems are exemplified in

19. The internal frame of a factotum into which an ordinary initial was inserted was especially vulnerable to damage incurred during insertion. Framing rules are frequently missing; in factotums lacking internal framing rules, the portions of the design abutting the frame are frequently damaged or obliterated. This area of a factotum can sometimes be quite useful for distinguishing castings but seems rather unreliable on the whole for identification purposes.

the preliminaries at ¹A1–4v of *An Answer* STC12988 (1603) where the Eliot's Court ornament McKerrow 352 appears on the title page, followed by three ornaments which seem identical to those used by Read and then Eld. This raises the questions: did Eliot's Court lend McKerrow 352 to Eld specifically to be included in the title, with Eld then filling in ¹A3,4,4v with his three ornaments and an 'M' initial, or did Eliot's Court own duplicates of all four Eld pieces, or were the pieces borrowed from Eld? The *STC* assignment of the preliminaries to Eliot's Court is based upon either of the two latter options.

Two of the head-pieces are faithful copies, each with more than one known version. The Eld/Jaggard version of Plomer 52 appears at ¹A3; as noted earlier, Bradwood, who joined the Eliot's Court group in 1602, and Hatfield used the Plomer 52 version at least four times. Eliot's Court could have owned both versions, or replaced an earlier Eld/Jaggard version with the Plomer 52 version by 1606.[20] In any event, progressive damage along the upper half of the left edge strongly suggests that the piece in STC12988 is the same as that used by Eld.[21] The initial 'M' seen at ¹A3 STC12988 undoubtedly is the same that appears in Eld's books.[22] Damage to two of three areas of the Turk's Head tail-piece in the state seen in ¹A4v of STC12988 leaves little doubt that it also is the same piece used by Eld.[23] Finally, the second head-piece, a Goathead flanked by feeding-squirrels and grotesques, exists in two nearly identical versions differentiated by quite minor design

20. I must note that a comprehensive survey is needed to determine whether both versions were used in books produced by the Eliot's Court group. I have not performed the survey at this time but serendipitously stumbled onto the appearances in STC6164, STC 10548, STC24719 and STC18191.

21. It can be noted in Plomer's reproduction that the outer half and tip of the leaf leaving the stock at 11mm down from the top is intact. This leaf and the first leaf above the bulb (larger in the Eld/Jaggard version than in Plomer 52, another difference from imperfect copying) have been sheared along a straight-line drawn from the outer edge of the top-most leaf through the outer edge of the bulb (13mm down). This state obtains in STC 12988 and an early Eld book (*Darius* STC 350, A1, late 1604). The left edge of the top leaf is blunted inward and the terminating curl of the tendril immediately below is lost in a slightly later state (*Obedience* STC25633, A2 and B3, early 1605). In addition, the tip of the second leaf at the top-right corner has been blunted with a slight cut above the tip.

22. At bottom center, the tip of the leaf is severed from the long center petal with a precise cut; the entire left edge has been blunted or sheared downward and the tip of the middle leaf has been compressed to a vertical line about 1mm in length; a gap in the line from the center occurs prior to the first leaf at the top-right; and an extraneous 1mm line extends beyond the left top-serif. Additional progressive damage is seen in *Spider* STC5693.5: the leaf tips at the upper right are sheared or blunted. (See also *De Vnione* STC13951, 1604; *Times Anatomie* STC20342, 1606).

23. The STC12988 state lacks the gap in the outer line forming the mustache at the junction with the left frame. STC12988 was entered 7 April 1603, a few months before the gap appears in a Read/Eld book (*Isahaacs* STC25643, B4v) which was entered 16 June 1603, suggesting progressive damage; it remains in later appearances (see *Darius* STC350, 1604, A4; *Ostend* STC18895, 1604, 2G3v; and in *Fools* STC4963, 1605, A3v. Damage to two other areas is identical. The bold line forming the underside of the leaf at the lower-right seems to have been depressed so that a portion prints thinly. A wide gap appears in the outer line of the frame just to the right of the right mustache.

details. Eld's version can be differentiated from that used by Barker and Islip on the basis of at least six such details. On the other hand, design and damage are identical in Eld's version and that which appears in [1]A4 of STC12988.[24]

In short, the preliminaries of STC12988 contain one unquestionable Eliot's Court ornament and four pieces which, for all intents and purposes, cannot be distinguished from those used continuously over a long period of time by Eld. So, while ornaments are usually more easily recognized and identified than fonts and frequently lead directly to the correct printer, assignment cruxes do arise that ultimately must be settled by the identification of the contextual font(s). Since A3–3v are set in a Guyot double-pica roman titling font almost never used in texts because few printers owned enough of this type for this purpose, the discovery of samples by either Eliot's Court or

24. A smaller version of the Goat-head flanked by feeding-squirrels is reproduced in Woodfield/Field #10; although it exhibits major design differences, the general concept is the same. Version #1 appears in *An Answer* STC23451 (1595) at B3, with the imprint "Deputies of R. Barker"; and in *Les Reports* STC5493 (1600), A1, with the imprint "in aed. T. Wight" but reassigned in the new *STC* to A. Islip on the basis of ornamental stock, an assignment which can be confirmed by the appearance of many ornaments in the context of Islip's fonts in other books. Version #2 appears in *An Answer* STC12988 (1603), [1]A4; and frequently in Eld's books, including *A Panegyric* STC12061 (7 June 1603), B1; *Darius* STC 350 (1604), B1; *Ostend* STC18895 (1604), A1, 2G3; and *Fools* STC4963 (1605), A3. Absolute design differences differentiate the two versions as follows:

1. Leaves of the top right flower: in #1, the first small petal to the outside is a short nib; it is longer in #2 with a curved tip. This difference cannot be due to progressive damage, since elements can be shortened but not lengthened.

2. The third vine 9mm in from the left bottom corner is formed by three lines (double lines form the top) in version #1; it is formed by two lines in #2.

3. Area at top left, 27mm in, 9mm down: in #1, a 1mm gap separates the short, blunt leaf from the large scroll structure; the leaf is larger and pointed in #2 and touches the scroll.

4. At left center: in #2, the beak of the grotesque animal figure touches the leaf to the left; the two are separated by a 1mm gap in #1.

5. Upper left corner, 15mm in, 7mm down; the small tendril ends in simple curl in #2, but in #1 terminates in a four-loop bud.

6. Upper right corner: in #1 the coiled tendril is formed with distinct first and second loops, a compressed third loop, and terminates like a monkey-tail hanging down; in #2, the termination is a simple, thin vine which could conceivably be a remnant of the monkey-tail structure following damage, except that the overall structure of the tendril suggests otherwise.

Some differences that could result from damage should be noted; these details also suggest that Eld's #2 appears in STC12988.

7. The outer line of the first loop of the coiled tendril (noted immediately above) exhibits a 1mm gap in #2 not in #1.

8. Upper right corner: #1 has a short curled leaf to the right of the stem at the base of the flower bulb; its absence in #2 could be due to blunting or shearing damage.

9. Bottom of outermost right vine: #1 shows a downward thorn or petal that is absent in #2; damage is highly unlikely as a perfectly clean cut exactly parallel to the line would be required.

10. Bottom center: three hairs extend from the tip of the beard downward: in #1 they flare and terminate at the same level; in #2, the left hair is longer than the right.

11. Bottom center: in #1, a two-leaf cluster extends below the arches which support the squirrel on both sides of the goat head; the left leaves are lacking in #2 (they could have been cut away).

Eld is a project clouded with potential futility. (As luck would have it, Eld used his Guyot double-pica roman [140mm; see Vervliet, Fig. 185, p. 248] to also set the epistle "From the King" in B1–2v of *Obedience* STC25633. The small size of the two samples is balanced by the small quantity of type in the font so that a dozen identifiable types recur in STC12988 and STC25633, and at least four recur in the two formes of STC25633.) In many instances that involve the more common pica and 96mm roman fonts, it seems more efficient to hunt after a printer's fonts since they are likely to appear with greater regularity than a printer's ornaments.

III

The identification of a printer's font in a sample text provides the only absolute evidence that he printed all or part of a book. The process of verifying a printer's ownership of a font in a shared book involves a survey of books in the proximate period by suspected printers in order to locate candidate fonts, followed by a comparative analysis to settle upon the most likely candidate. The target font in question and the candidate font are then examined for recurrent identifiable types which provide absolute evidence of the identity of the two fonts and thus establish the identity of the unknown printer of an unsigned book or a section of a shared book. The process is encumbered with pitfalls created by the seemingly inexhaustible inconsistencies in early printing. Sharing strategies frequently defy common-sense logic so that anomalous sharing patterns can be expected as the norm. Furthermore, the patterns of font usage varied widely among printers, a factor which frequently confuses the font ownership issue. Finally, the ownership question can be left hanging because of variations in shop output in the particular size of typeface in question during the proximate period.

In general, the process of sorting out the printers in a shared book usually begins with an initial clue as to the identity of one printer: a signed imprint, an identified ornament, or an entry in the Stationers' Register usually implies the assigned printer's ownership of one or more of the fonts found in the text although this assumption cannot be trusted categorically. In some instances, the printer specified in the imprint did only the title or the title and preliminaries. Moreover, some books lack such initial clues so that the search for the printer(s) begins in a vacuum with nothing more to go on than the fonts found in the book. For example, *Whore of Babylon* STC6532 (1607), tentatively assigned to Eliot's Court in *STC*, contains no initials or ornamental stock, but prints in two fairly distinct pica fonts in the classic two-section A–B sharing pattern (A4–G, H–L1). Except in longer books which permit insertion of ornamental stock, this situation obtains with shared sections nearly always in shorter books and invariably in play-quartos. Cancel titles and/or preliminaries in reissued or remarketed books present another kind of problem which must be settled by font analysis since the clues are sometimes confusing. Supplemental evidence provided by the distribution of papers (identified by watermarks) in a book (or books) frequently clarifies the situation. For example, Islip's imprint appears in the cancel title on A2 (A1 blank) of the long *Lectures* STC7118, but a Dawson initial appears on A3 and the book prints in Dawson-EFc. Half-sheets A1–2 and A3–4 are printed on different papers. Islip clearly farmed out the entire book to Dawson but reserved the title for printing at half-sheet. *Seven Sinnes* STC6522 is an extreme case since the title page is found in four different states, each exhibiting a different printer's ornament (see *STC* description). The setting of the preliminaries is identical in at least two states, although changes occur in the title setting. The improper binding of ^{2}A between ^{1}A3–4 in the Huntington copy may provide a clue to the circumstances that produced this anomaly. In general, nothing can be trusted implicitly except an identified font; thus assignments based upon evidence in the title and preliminaries must be verified as a matter of course.

The survey process focuses upon books produced in the proximate period by either an assigned printer or the suspected sharing printer(s) in order to enhance the probability that a candidate font is the one in current use in the shop and in the same state as the target font.[25] Two kinds of books are

25. The survey process will benefit immensely when P. G. Morrison's outdated *Index to Printers* is superseded by the appearance of Volume 3 of the revised *STC* in late 1990 or early 1991. Scholars attracted to printer research by its inherent sense of mystery (not to mention the flush of sublime fulfillment that accompanies each identification of an unknown printer) will no longer have to "read the *STC*" in search of newly assigned books by a suspected sharing printer. (Incidentally, I must note that my research was guided primarily by Morrison's *Index* and supplemented by searches of portions of the new *STC* that promised new leads; it can be assumed that I have inevitably overlooked assignments that will emerge in Volume 3.) Katharine V. Pantzer has graciously supplied information about the format and contents of Volume 3, which is an accumulation of an incredible amount of information relevant to early printing. Two indexes are most pertinent to printer research. "Index 1: Printers and Publishers" lists printers and publishers identified in new *STC* in alphabetical order, each headed by supplemental information garnered from numerous references followed by a chronological list of books by STC number. "A Chronological Index" rearranges STC books by author's surname and STC number for each year to 1640. Items with erroneous, conflicting or multiple dates are re-entered under each date. The compiler of "A Chronological Index," Philip R. Rider (University of Northern Illinois), richly deserves the gratitude of the scholarly community for accomplishing this monumental task.

The survey process begins by compiling from Index 1 a list of proximate books that are assigned to a suspected printer. The books are then checked for samples of a font in the correct size and style that matches the target font. In general, it is wise to continue until two or three font samples are located in order to confirm tentatively that the printer used the candidate font more than once. Comparative analysis leads either to the rejection of the printer or to the final stage of locating recurrent-types and confirming his work in the target book.

The search process can sometimes be more narrowly focused by the consideration of circumstantial factors. The kind of text can lead to the elimination of potential candidates who would otherwise be surveyed because of their use of a correct style and size of font. For example, Robert Barker used a Y-font but never printed a play-quarto. Or again, Islip frequently printed privileged legal texts courtesy of Wight's patent and then for the Stationers' Company after September 1605. A glance at *STC* entries for theological authors such as Matthew Sutcliffe or Henry Smith can suggest potential printers for this type of

encountered in a survey. First, signed books printed in a single font imply ownership of the font in the absence of evidence to the contrary. Signed books printed in two or more fonts must be approached with an awareness of the possibility of shared printing although some printers used two fonts simultaneously. The survey process is affected by fluctuations in shop production. A decrease in overall production may be real, but in some instances is an indication that the shop was involved in printing unidentified sections of shared books. Moreover, the printing of books requiring other sizes of type can depress the use of the candidate font during the proximate period. In either case, the number of samples of a candidate font can drop dramatically. The varied patterns of font ownership and usage that are characteristic of Elizabethan printing thus can complicate a survey aimed at locating a candidate font in a suspected printer's proximate books. Three classes of font ownership and usage occur, each with its own set of subtle variations occasioned by the frequency, methods, and period of usage of the specific fonts that are encountered in a shop's output: (1) the use of a single font for an extended period, or a sequence of single fonts during shorter periods; (2) the use of more than one font either long-term or during transitional replacement periods; and (3) the continuous use of a font which was transformed at some point through replenishment, mixing or fouling.

---

book. In contrast, trade printers such as Allde, Braddock, Creede, Eld, Jaggard and Purfoot seem to have printed anything that came through the door and are likely candidates in any case, provided that the fonts match. Format sometimes suggests candidates. Islip seems to have favored folios after about 1605. Similarly, Eld undertook some heavily illuminated and illustrated folio texts that were remarkable challenges (see especially *Birth of Mankinde* STC21161 and *Admirable & Memorable Histories* STC12135). Many of the trade printers produced play-quartos: see the repeated involvement of the group in *STC* sections on playwrights such as George Chapman, Ben Jonson, John Marston, Thomas Middleton, Shakespeare and others. Translations form another class of books that might focus a search; Eld, for example, printed several translations by Edward Grimeston. In this area, Virginia Renner, Reader Services Librarian at The Huntington Library, is currently working on a bibliography of *STC* translations extending to over a thousand items; once completed, the relationships among translators, publishers and printers that emerge should be a valuable resource in printer research. (See also Julia G. Ebel, "A Numerical Survey of Elizabethan Translations," *The Library*, 5th ser., 22 (1967), 104–127, which is limited to items in the unrevised *STC* for 1560–1603.) Similarly, the publisher-printer relationship has not received much attention to date, but quite valuable information and analysis is found in Gerald D. Johnson, "Nicholas Ling, Publisher 1580–1607," *Studies in Bibliography*, 38 (1985), 203–214, and "John Busby and the Stationers' Trade," *The Library*, 6th ser., 1 (1985), 1–15; and Blayney's *Texts*. Known sharing relationships provide another network of cooperation. For example, William Aspley and Edmond Blount published books with either Eld or Simmes as primary printer, several of which were shared between the two. Then again, Eld as primary printer shared with Braddock, Creede, Jaggard, Purfoot, Simmes, Stafford and White, Purfoot with Jaggard and Windet, Creede with Windet, and so on. Other printers such as Felix Kingston seem not to have taken much to sharing.

Overall, a printer search is pure detective work and unpredictable. The sometimes radical variations in shop output imply one disturbing factor whose significance cannot even be estimated, namely, the probability that some portion of the books produced in the period are no longer extant.

(1)

The demonstration of ownership is a straightforward matter if the target font belongs to the class of printer who used a single font in a large number of books over an extended period of time in conjunction with his imprint and/ or ornamental stock or entries in the Stationers' Register. Simmes-S1, for example, was the primary font used in this manner in Simmes's shop from 1594–1606. Similarly, White-M was White's primary font from 1597 until about 1608 when it was replaced with White-S1. Although Stafford-EFb appeared in a lower proportion of the books printed by Stafford between 1599– 1607?, it nonetheless is the only pica roman font that he used. Creede-3 appeared in a large number of signed books 1594–1602. Given an initial clue such as an imprint or identified initial, a check of a few proximate books by such printers usually will produce a candidate font sample. For example, a survey of a few of Simmes's books from 1604 as suggested by his imprint and xylographic (opposed scrolls) in the titles of *Malcontent* Q1–2 STC17479–80, Q3 STC17481, and *Whore* STC6501 quickly leads to the identification of Simmes-S1 in his sections of these shared books (sigs. F–H, B–G, and AB respectively).

However, this ideal situation is fairly uncommon since most pica fonts were replaced at intervals of about 2–4 years, a factor which can present a problem. The survey of the suspected printer's books can yield samples of the wrong font in the sequence used by the correct printer if a font was replaced during the proximate period of the target book. If the sequence involves fonts in different faces, an extension of the survey beyond the proximate period is usually adequate to establish that a replacement occurred and when. The shifts from mixed Creede-3 to S-face Creede-4 (1603) to hybrid Creede-5 (1609) or from Allde-M to Allde-C2 (1591) to Allde-Y1 (1597) are easily established by an extended survey. In contrast, a sequence of two same-face fonts requires closer scrutiny since it is possible to confuse them as a single font in continuous use. For instance, Braddock printed regularly with his sequence of Braddock-Y1,2a from 1598–1601, 1602–1605, with a slight decrease in pica roman output 1601–1602. Y-font samples before and after this transitional period are common enough. Although Braddock-Y1 is easily distinguished by its foul-case cluster, failure to perform this stage of analysis could lead to the erroneous assumption that any Braddock Y-font book 1598–1605 uses the same font. Hence, a comparison of a target font (Braddock-Y1) predating the replacement point of 1602 with a later book (Braddock-Y2a) would lead to the rejection of Braddock as a potential sharing printer. (Further discussion of same-face sequences follows below.)

(2)

The appearance of two or more fonts in an assigned proximate book(s) by a candidate printer raises the possibility of shared printing so that the intermediate issue of his ownership of more than one font must be settled before work proceeds on the target text. In such a case, the pattern of font usage in

assigned books in the proximate period usually provides evidence of ownership. Ideally each font appears separately in a single-font book which can be
unquestionably assigned to the printer. Otherwise, proximate books usually
provide evidence of the simultaneous use of two or more fonts, especially
when the fonts appear in an alternating pattern within gatherings or lesser
units. A survey of proximate books should yield books to establish ownership
in uncommon instances of a printer's two fonts alternating in sections consisting of gatherings in the manner typical of shared printing. Finally, an
extended survey is sometimes necessary to establish the ownership of a replacement sequence of two fonts used simultaneously for a short period before the
old depleted font was discarded.

In general, two situations occur: the long-term use of two fonts or the
simultaneous use of two sequential fonts during a transitional period. In
either instance, the simultaneous use can lead to transformations in font composition that affect the font identification process. Such transformations are
usually progressive and irreversible. Reverse transformations through decontamination seem not to have happened except through purging of foul-case
italic letters.[26] Hence, a commonsense assessment of the changes necessary to
transform a font from suspected early to late states usually suffices to settle
the issue. The possibility of the total replacement of individual sorts should
be considered in the context of the number of affected sorts. It is conceivable that a printer decided to jettison entire 'a k y ?' sorts and replace
them with newly-cast type. However, at this point, there seem to be no examples of this having occurred. When the balance or proportions are observed to
shift dramatically to new replenished types in a sort, remnants of the original
types are inevitably present. The transformation issue is sometimes critical
in establishing the sequence of fonts in a shop during one printer's tenure
or in deciding whether a font passed to a new printer along with a shop. In
the matter of identifying a sharing printer, a target font in a shared section
can be compared to either state of a transformed candidate font. If it can
be established that the font was transformed at some point, text samples in
the earlier state will contain recurrent-types that can establish the identity of
the font in the later state in a target text (or vice versa).

In ideal situations, the ownership of two fonts is easily demonstrated by
the interwoven use of two fonts in bibliographical units that eliminate shared
printing. New Simmes-S2 prints most of *Eliosto* STC13509 (1606), but old
Simmes-S1 appears at D3–E4v. Such a pattern argues against sharing because
of the mutual appearance of the two fonts in the respective halves of a gathering. Ballard took over the two fonts and used them in a similar fashion in
Merry Devil STC7493 (1608). Shop lineage, in this instance, provides added
evidence of ownership of the two fonts. The alternation of Kingston-Y1 and
-EFc, both used simultaneously for a few years, in *T. Workes* STC12316 (1601)

26. For discussion of the impact of several classes of foul-case letters upon the purging
process, see "Font Analysis," pp. 131–134.

was probably occasioned by the demands of the large folio setting, although alternating compositorial stints are plausible, and leaves no doubt about ownership. For example, EFc sets 3D1–1v, Y1 sets 3D2:1–49, followed by EFc from 3D2:50–3D2v:38 with Y1 completing the page (:39–54). The shift to EFc on 3D3:1–26 is accompanied by mixing in of some Y1 sorts until Y1 takes over from 3D3:27–47, then EFc sets a long section 3D3:48–3D4:17, Y1 from 3D4:22–D5:34, and EFc concludes the gathering 3D5:35–D6v. The intricate interweaving of two fonts within page-length units in this manner is infrequent but valuable typographical evidence of ownership. The observation of the minor transformation of Kingston-EFc by the fouling with Y1 sorts in 3D3:1–26 provides additional internal evidence of the identity of EFc.

In some instances, the transformation is more extensive, consisting either of a partial or a complete mixing of two fonts in different faces. This kind of phenomenon is usually accompanied by the transitional use of the two in an alternating pattern which leaves no doubt as to ownership and transformation. The mixing of a replacement font into the previous font is illustrated by the creation of Creede-3. Creede-1 (S-face) is used to D in *Selimus* STC 12310a (1594), at which point Creede-2 (C2-hybrid) takes over; the two alternate, then are promiscuously distributed and fully mixed by the end of the book. The new mixed font Creede-3 immediately begins its appearances in a long sequence of signed books to 1602. The transformation of one case of Windet-S1 into Windet-S2 from 1605 by fouling with Windet-F letters (A D G H M O T a b g k w x y z) has been noted previously.[27] The process can be observed in *Fawne* STC17483 (1606) where Windet-F and -S2 alternate

---

27. See "Font Analysis," pp. 133–134, for discussion of the process of contamination affecting one case of Windet's S-font (Windet-S2). Incidentally, at no point was Windet-F mixed wholesale into Windet-S1,2 as claimed by Ferguson, i.e., "In 1607 a fifth fount [5] was created by mixing together the recast Garamond [F-hybrid] and the Lyon(c)," *Pica Roman Type*, p. 32. The process of low-density contamination of Windet-S2 dates from at least as early as 1605, was nearly up to peak levels by March 1606, and therefore was not a new phenomenon in 1607. The level of contamination seen in Plate 164 which purports to reproduce the "new" "Windet-5" is essentially the same seen, for example, in *Fawne* Q2 STC17484 (12 March 1606) G3, G4v, or *Sophonisba* STC17488 (17 March 1606) B3–4, D1,2, especially D2v–3, F2,3,4,4v. Furthermore, the mis-identified "Garamond" typeface and fonts (Tables 2, 9) is actually a hybrid which combines Haultin's Y-face capitals and '?' with a second lower-case long-since attributed also to Haultin (see Dreyfus, *Type Spec. Facs.* Vol. I, notes for facsimile 14, specimen 393, and facsimile 15, specimen "Mediaen Romeyn, No. 1"). It was used as early as the 1550's in Venice by Paulo Manuzio and Angelo Gardano, and in Holland throughout the 17th century. Similarly, the mis-labeled "Le Be" typeface and fonts (Tables 8, 9) do not match Le Be's Garamond punches/matrices, but are hybrids which combine sorts from dissimilar sets of non-Garamond punches. Actually, one mis-labeled "Tavernier" font (Sutton-1, Plate 142) is the only example (as far as I know) of a Garamond pica roman (see *Type Spec. Facs.* Vol. II, "Index 1567" and "Le Be" specimens 12, 13) to appear in England during the period (excepting in imported books by R. Schillers, Middelburg); nor is Bynneman-4 (Plate 29) a Tavernier, but simply the Haultin Y-face whose first (?) appearance in *A Dictionarie* STC6832 (1570) predates Jerome Haultin's arrival by four years. Shipment directly from the Haultin establishment at La Rochelle seems the inevitable inference.

by formes in Q1, but in the resetting of pages for Q2, they alternate within pages accompanied by some cross-contamination.[28] With the further contamination of Windet-S1 in *Sophonisba* STC17488, the clear distinction between Windet-S1 and -S2 becomes somewhat obscured by the low-density mixing of these and additional Windet-F capitals (E F P S) into Windet-S1, an increase in the proportions of these capitals in Windet-S2, and the mixing of Windet-F 'g w' into both fonts. However, Windet-S1 remains relatively free of Windet-F lower-case sorts. Though difficult, it would be possible to sort out the alternating stints of the two fonts in many pages of a later text such as *1 Henry 4* Q5 STC22283 (1608) and *Romeo & Juliet* Q3 STC22324 (1609) if the need arose in a compositorial analysis.

The transformations in the sequence of three fonts used by Eld 1603–1609 occur in the context of a simultaneous transitional use of Eld-Y1 to Eld-S1 and Eld-S1 to Eld-Y2 in interwoven settings during both transitions. The resulting cross-contaminations yield foul-case clusters in Eld-S1 and Eld-Y2 that aid in potential recognition of the two fonts if encountered in shared sections. Eld clearly planned ahead in acquiring new fonts, but for some reason pushed the old fonts to the brink of depletion, thereby occasioning the transformations of the new fonts. Although his compositors were quite careful, it seems that interweaving a depleted font with a new one presented an impossible distribution situation. Each of the fonts appears separately in signed books; nonetheless, Eld's ownership is clear from the use of the respective pairs of fonts in alternating patterns which eliminate the possibility of shared printing. Put into use in 1603?, Eld-Y1 was the only pica roman that appeared in books from the shop until early 1605, when Eld-S1 appeared in *Survey* (STC6201, 22 January 1605) with Eld's imprint and thereafter in several others (*An Answer* STC26002 etc.) to 1608?. The low-density S-capitals that appear in Eld-Y1 early on are possibly remnants from Simson/Read-S1; this suggests that part of Simson/Read-S1 was in the shop until replaced by Eld-Y1 in 1603? If so, it either was not used at all, or only in shared sections, although this seems unlikely because of the overall production of the shop during Read's tenure, which seems to have included but a few short ephemera and no books of noteworthy length after 1601. However, the fouling of Eld-Y1 with additional S-capitals and then with lower-case sorts begins

28. See "Reproductions," pp. 250–251, and "Font Analysis," note 57, for a description of the patterns of alternation. Incidentally, Ferguson cites *Edward 3* STC7502 (1599) as an example of "irregular," or alternating, stints (p. 16), and later offers an explanation based upon STC7502 for the composition of Stafford-EFb which he considers "very much a jumble": "behind the mixture probably lay some Haultin [Y-face] sorts and some Lyon(a) [C2-hybrid] which were used more or less unmixed in printing parts of the 1599 edition of [*Edward 3*] STC7502, into which was mixed some Lyon(c) [S-face] as time went on," p. 31. Assuming (again) that STC7502 exists in only one state represented by The Huntington's copy, it can be noted categorically that the text prints entirely in Stafford-EFb and nothing else. See "Font Analysis," pp. 122–125, and Appendixes III and IV, pp. 145–148, for an exhaustive analysis of Stafford-EFb's actual composition.

an upswing in the proximate period of the acquisition of Eld-S1.[29] Unfortunately, the actual transitional period is obscured by several factors, including discrepancies between imprint and entry dates, a common problem in sorting out font sequences.[30] During the nebulous transitional period, Eld-Y1 and Eld-S1 alternate in an anomalous pattern in *Eastward Hoe!* Q1 STC 4971.[31] Moreover, the sequence of *Eastward* Q1–2 provides a unique additional kind of evidence of ownership. Standing type in Eld-Y1 from Q1 migrates across page and gathering boundaries into Q2. In the process, lineation is disrupted as the measure is expanded to 100mm in HI to accommodate the transferred type.[32] Tied-up standing type could conceivably be transported between shops, but that unlikelihood is completely dismissed by the dovetailing of standing vs. reset type in *Eastward* Q2. Eld-Y1 makes a final appearance in two pages (E1v, F3v) of Q3 along with Eld-S1. The period of transition from Eld-S1 to Eld-Y2 likewise is somewhat nebulous due to uncertainty about the date at which Eld-Y2 began use, but Eld's ownership of the two fonts is clear from alternating patterns within gatherings. Eld-S1 appears heavily fouled with Eld-Y1,2 capitals at F2, G1v–2, H4v, I1–2, I4v, K3v–4v, L1v–2, M4–4v of *Lingua* STC24104 (23 February 1607) and at I(i), K2, M1, M3v–4v, N2v–3 of *Volpone* STC14783 (imprint: 1607; entry: 3 October 1610). The progressive fouling suggests that Eld-S1 was considerably depleted in the upper-case at the end of its lifetime; the lower-case was contaminated with Y-sorts throughout its lifetime. The process left Eld-Y2 contaminated with S-face sorts (A B C D2 E1 G2 H I L M O P R S T V Y b1 f1,4 g1 k1 n3,4 p1 x2; ligatures: ct fl2 fi fl ft; and '?') in varying low-density proportions. There seems to be a concentration of fouled sorts in sections of later texts such as *Troilus* STC22331 (1609) which may be useful in compositorial analysis.

29. See "Font Analysis," pp. 135 and 139, for discussion of this phenomenon which implies a printing sequence of *Whore* Q1–2 STC6501–6501a, *Malcontent* Q3 STC17481, *Fools* STC4963, *Eastward* Q1 STC4971.

30. For example, *Sejanus* STC14782 was entered twice (first entry 2 November 1604, re-entered 10 August 1605) and bears an imprint of 1605. *Fools* STC4963 bears an imprint of 1605 but was not entered; the performance at Court in January 1605 suggests the earliest printing date possible. This leaves the problem of dating the printing of *Malcontent* Q3 STC17481 (entered 5 July 1604; imprint: 1604) and of *Eastward* STC4970–73 (entered 10 September 1605; imprint: 1605).

31. The distribution pattern of Eld-S1 and -Y1 in *Eastward* Q1 STC4971 is: Eld-Y1: A2, A3, A4v–B2, B4v–C2v, D4v–E2, E4v, F2v–3v, H2v–4, I1–2; Eld-S1: the rest including I2v–4v. Note the typographical error in the last line of the table in "Reproductions," p. 248, reading "F2v–F3r" instead of "F3v".

32. The migration of standing type from *Eastward* Q1 STC4971 to Q2 STC4972 is as follows: E4v:1–32 to E2:12–36 [stick Q1 = 92mm, Q2 = 96mm]; E4v:33–37 to E2v:1–5; H2v: 3–30 to G3:17–37; H2v:30–37 to G3v:1–5 [G3v:6–37 reset in Eld-S1]; H3v:2–H4:7 to G4:1–37 [speech prefixes mostly reset]; H4:8–37 to G4v:1–27 [28–37 reset in Eld-S1; stick = 100 mm]; I1:1–23 to H1:22–37; I1:24–39 to H2:1–14; I1v:1–29 to H2:15–39; I2:1–38 to H2v:9–39 [H2v: 1–8 reset in Eld-S1; 38 lines of Q1 are crammed into about 30 lines in Q2 with turn-overs etc.].

Transformations in fonts usually occur offstage. Unless the process is observed in progress, it must be inferred from the demonstrable ownership of the two fonts either in long-term or transitional simultaneous use. This is the case with the two states of Jaggard-Y1. Jaggard-Y1a appeared in at least three books before transformation: *T. Anatomie* STC12465.5 (1603), *T. Triumphs* STC18279 (1605), and *T. Lamentation* STC7606 (1605). At some point in 1605, Y1a was transformed into Y1b by the addition of C2-hybrid sorts. Two factors obscure the time and source of contamination. Jaggard-Y1b's first appearances in signed books occurs in 1606: *Essays* STC1139, and *T. Badges* STC889. However, Jaggard used the font earlier in his section (F–H) of *Dutch Courtesan* STC17475, entered 26 June 1605. The most likely source of the contaminating sorts was Jaggard-C2. However, the date of Jaggard's acquisition and first use of this font is unclear, but it seems to have been later than 1605. The date of its appearance in *Westward Hoe* STC6540 is confused by the contradiction between the crossed-out Stationers' Register entry of 2 March 1606 and the imprint of 1607. An alternative possibility is that, in order to extend the life of the font, Jaggard replenished Y1a with C2 sorts from the same foundry that supplied Jaggard-C2 before acquiring the latter. In any event, ownership of Y1b and Jaggard-C2 is not an issue because of Jaggard's practice of alternating these fonts within gatherings along with a third font, Jaggard-S1. Jaggard's section (A–G; Eld-Y2 in H–I2v) of *Westward Hoe*, for example, prints in Jaggard-Y1b except for Jaggard-C2 in D4 and F1, and Jaggard-S1 in B2v–3, C1, C2v–4v, E1–3, E4v, F1v–4v and G2v–3. The three fonts alternate in Jaggard's sections of *An Apologie* STC19295, shared with Eld, and Jaggard-C2 and -S1 alternate in *T. Miseries* STC25635 (1607).[33] The two were used at least once in alternating fashion as the emphasis fonts (*T. Deade Tearme* STC6496, 1608). Just why Jaggard acquired and used the three fonts is a mystery since Jaggard-Y1b was still adequate in 1606 for setting the long (B–2G) *T. Badges* STC889. Even so, the use of the three is confined to 1607, suggesting a transitional waiting period until Jaggard-Y2 was delivered in 1608 (*Jesuites* STC1824). The fonts may have been used more extensively than we know. The practice of alternating seems to have gone amuck and fouled one case of Jaggard-S1 in *Sermons* STC15882 (1607) where a mixture of Y1b, C2 and S1 sorts occurs in R6,7,8, S1,2v,3,4v and later. The font is largely uncontaminated in the short text in A2–A3v:15 of *Ruine of Rome* STC6641 (1607), but this probably is attributable to the use of the uncontaminated case. A transient phenomenon confined to 1607, the three fonts seem to occur always in alternating fashion and thereby provide a unique kind of font identification composite consisting of the pattern and the cross-contamination.

One circumstance is shared by the Islip-Y1a,b and Jaggard-Y1a,b transfor-

---

33. The pattern of alternation in *T. Miseries* STC25635 (1607): Jaggard-S1 at A2–4v, B(i), C, D1v–3, E, F1–2v, G, H1–2, I1–2v, I3:25–36, I3v–4v, K1,2v,3–4; Jaggard-C2 at B(o), D1,3v–4v, F3–4v, H2v–3v [4–4v lacking], I3:1–24, K1v,2,4v.

mations. The contamination respectively with EFc and C2 sorts occurs in rough proximity with the acquisition of a new font. In both instances, a similarity in the nature of the transformation and the lapse between the introduction of the new font perhaps implies something about supply sources, that is, replenishment from a local source which supplied a particular hybrid set of letters. Islip-Y1a appears uncontaminated in 1598 in *A Treatise* STC 17291, but by 1599 exhibits the replenished EFc sorts in *Prenobilis* STC11196. Meanwhile, Islip-C2 makes its final(?) appearance in the same year (see *T. Love* STC19540). Islip-EFb first appears in 1600 in *EMOH* STC14767, which establishes its first date of usage and not necessarily its date of acquisition. Its appearance in the incorrectly assigned and dated (A. Jaffes, c1585) *Articuli* STC4584 (see *Pica Roman Type*, Plate 76, Jaffes-1) probably predates *EMOH* (8 April 1600). The fact that two versions of the EF-hybrid are involved raises a question about the connection between the two acquisitions, implying perhaps that two supply sources were involved, one of which supplied the EFb-hybrid with Guyot capitals. Perhaps the replenishment of Islip-Y1a was an attempt to extend the life of the font, and once completed, Islip decided to order the new font Islip-EFb. This is plausible in view of the fact that Islip had obtained Islip-S1 by 1602. The font was used along with, but independent of, Islip-EFb until 1604; similarly, Islip-Y1b continued in use until 1602. Overall, a pattern emerges in which a sequence of three fonts was acquired and used separately during two-year overlapping periods, although this degree of precision may be illusory.

In general, the continuous use of a single font in two states can be demonstrated by recurrent-types in the early and late states. In some instances, a font is already contaminated in what seems to be its earliest appearance. Circumstances may indicate the plausible source of contamination. For example, Allde-Y1 appeared in 1597 (*R & J* Q1 STC22322; and *Granados* STC 16902, 1598) with a low-density wrong-face mixture in place, including S-face sorts (A1 D1 G H O T; low-riding C F1 G2 H I L M P; a d2 f1 h2 p1 u1; ligatures: ct fi2 fl2; and '?') and C2-hybrid sorts (b2 k1 g2), all of which are probably from Allde-C2 which last appeared in 1596. However, Jaggard-Y2 appears with oversized capitals (2.95–3.15mm) already in place which do not seem to come from Jaggard-S1 (A B C D G H I K M O P R S T V; see *T. Pathway* STC898, 1609).

The transformation issue can be clouded when the similarity exhibited by a sequence of fonts is such that transformation seems the logical explanation. The general principle that transformations are progressive usually permits settling the issue. Sorting the sequence of fonts in Purfoot's shop 1598–1607? is complicated by the fact that three same-face fonts are involved (see also later discussion of Robinson-Y1a,b). The sparse known output during the transitional periods between Purfoot-Y1, -Y2, and -Y3 forces an extension of the survey across 1601–1606 in order to locate samples of each font. The five-year period represents sufficient time for major transformations to have occurred. The early font, Purfoot-Y1 (last seen in 1601?) exhibits mixed Y- and

S-capitals, an obvious characteristic of Purfoot-Y2 (first seen in 1605?), inviting the inference that the two are the same.[34] A closer examination reveals that whereas Purfoot-Y2 exhibits an uncontaminated lower-case, Purfoot-Y1 exhibits a variety of moderate-density oversized wrong-face roman letters: (S-face: b3, p1; C2-hybrid: k1; B-face: a b1,2 c d e h i m n o p q r u; Guyot 'w'; o15). Although the dearth of output eliminates the opportunity to observe the transformation of Y1 into Y2, the hypothesis that Purfoot-Y1 capitals were mixed in with a new Purfoot-Y2 to produce the apparent continuity in the capitals can be rejected on the basis of the new condition of the latter. There is no doubt that the rest of Purfoot-Y1 was discarded since its contaminated state precludes the kind of modification that would be necessary to permit mixing the lower-case into Purfoot-Y2. Furthermore, the acquisition of uncontaminated Purfoot-Y3 during the four-year interval separating the use of Purfoot-Y1 and -Y2 clearly indicates a strategy of total replacement of Purfoot-Y1. On the other hand, the sequence of uncontaminated Purfoot-Y3 in 1603–5, followed in 1605 by Purfoot-Y2 with mixed S-capitals, looks like an internal transformation of one case of Purfoot-Y3 by replenishment with wrong-face capitals. The two-year period could conceivably deplete the upper-case of Purfoot-Y3, but the replenishment of just one case is improbable. The fact that both Purfoot-Y2 and Purfoot-Y3 were adequate for setting prose quarto texts in the same year (1605: *Spider* STC5963.5, *Papisto-Mastix* STC 17913, *Downefall* STC1819 etc.) as well as play-quartos contradicts the depletion hypothesis. The issue can be settled with finality on the basis of the general principle: if a seminal font is split into two through replenishment or mixing, recurrent-types will remain in both states. Recurrent-types first seen in 1603 are still in Purfoot-Y3 in 1605, but absolutely no sharing of recurrent-types with Purfoot-Y2 is detectable.

(3)

    A fairly common problem arises if proximate books were printed during a transition in shop ownership, raising the question of whether a font passed to the new owner. On the one hand, a survey may reveal a gap of several years in the use of what seems to be a single font in intermittent use in a shop. In some instances, the interval is such that common sense rejects the notion that a single font is involved. Font analysis usually can confirm this view, especially if a significant transformation in the composition of the suspect font(s) would have been necessary. For example, a seven year gap occurred between Middleton's last use of a Y-font (1581), which was extensively contaminated with wrong-face letters, the passing of the shop to Robinson, and

---

34. See Ferguson's explanation that a single Y-font, obtained in 1582, "was used through 1610. . . . From 1594 there was a mixture of 'M's in at least one case of the Haultin, but Purfoot kept at least one case unmixed," *Pica Roman Type*, p. 29. Twenty-eight years of usage would indeed be remarkable. Incidentally, Plate 117 purporting to reproduce Purfoot-2 ("unmixed") is actually Jaggard-Y1b. See also the explanation of the Middleton-3 to Robinson-2 to Braddock-1 lineage, 1579–1610, pp. 29 and 30.

the introduction of Robinson-Y1 (1588?). The fact that at least thirty lower-case letters and ligatures and most capitals had to be purged to transform the former into the latter leaves no doubt that these are different fonts. The four-year interval separating the last use of Read-S1 (1601) and the appearance of Eld-S1 (1605) is not as great, but only a transformation through a highly improbable decontamination could have produced the latter.[35] Read-S1 is contaminated with Y-face letters: the high-density 'a' (about 30%) and 'k' (about 40%) variants and low-density 'A D E F I M P p', and the low-density crimped 'w', which is not seen elsewhere at this time. Eld-S1 is uncontaminated in its first three appearances in 1605 and does not exhibit Y-face fouling until its use in *Eastward Hoe!* Q1. Moreover, fundamental differences are seen in the S-face composition of the two fonts. For example, Read-S1 contains worn t1,2 and moderate-density oversized t3 whereas the new t1 is exclusive in Eld-S1; the old worn S–k1 is dominant in Read-S1 except for moderate-density replenished S–k2 and fouled Y-face 'k' variants; Eld-S1 sports new S–k2 and no Y-face 'a k p' variants, capitals or ligatures. Read-S1's capitals are correctly cast and justified; the miscast D2 and G2 are exclusive in Eld-S1; and Eld-S1's punctuation sorts are new and uncontaminated. In addition to these and other compositional differences, Eld-S1 is, in sharp contrast to Read-S1, a crisp clean font in 1605. In short, the differences between the two fonts preclude any possibility of transformation.

Settling the issue of ownership from shop lineage is a relatively simple matter if the production of books in the font size in question was consistent before and after the change in shop ownership. This is true even in instances where overall production was consistently low as long as a few books in the given font can be found. For example, shop output was sparse both during Simson's, Widow Simson's, and Read's tenures. Nonetheless, the lineage of Simson-S1 to Read-S1 is easily demonstrated. The font is used in combination with ornamental stock in proximate books before and after the passing of the shop to Read.[36] The unmistable composition of the font bridges the transition without modification. The passing issue is more difficult to resolve if the fonts used before and after the passing of a shop are in the same-face and lack such significant differentiae. In general, a recurrent-types survey must be employed to resolve the same-face passing issue in this situation.

Two factors present a problem in determining whether Robinson-Y1b

---

35. Ferguson concluded that Read-S1 passed to Eld-S1 along with the shop and explained: "When Eld obtained the materials [Read-S1] he discarded those letter forms which did not belong, and produced an 'i' with the dot a trifle higher," *Pica Roman Type*, p. 30. This proposition ignores the virtual impossibility of a compositor sorting through the approximately 1000–3000 types in a sort (see Blayney's sort-counts, *Texts*, pp. 145–148) and attempting visually to distinguish wrong-face pica types and discard them. See also discussion of purging in "Font Analysis" (see note 25 above).

36. Widow Simson, *AElohim-triune* STC5329 (2 January 1601). Read, *Ten Learned Personages* STC1074 (16 January 1601); *A Sermon* STC1454 (imprint: 1601; entered 18 March 1600); *Contemplations* STC4662 (18 October 1601); *Cynthia's Revels* STC14773 (23 May 1601).

passed to Braddock in 1598. Because of the lack of books from the shop in the preceding year, Braddock-Y1 of 1598 must be compared to the Robinson-Y1b seen in at least four books in 1595–96: in the text of *Salomon* STC18194, 1596; the preliminaries (¶2–3v) and sheet P of *The Discoverie* STC20634, 1596; long quotations in *A Comparison* STC4098, 1595; and as the emphasis font in *The Second Time* STC18246, 1596. Furthermore, Braddock-Y1 exhibits a more extensive contamination with wrong-face sorts than Robinson-Y1b, giving it a different overall appearance. However, the limited foul-case cluster present in Robinson-Y1b (S-face A P S; italic *I O S*; turned 'p'; 108mm ',') is consistent with that seen in Braddock-Y1. Progressive contamination through fouling and replenishment during 1597–1598 is a plausible explanation for the expansion of the cluster since the transformation requires no elimination of sorts found in Robinson-Y1b. In this instance, the large font samples from 1596 and 1598 create a favorable situation for a successful recurrent-types survey to either confirm or reject identity. The passing and continuous use of the font is demonstrated by recurrent-types from the 1595–96 Robinson-Y1b in Braddock-Y1 from 1598–1600.[37]

(4)

The failure to locate recurrent-types that positively confirm the identity of the same-face fonts in samples from before and after the suspected passing must be viewed as negative evidence and interpreted with caution. The simple

---

37. The distinction between Robinson-Y1a (1590–1594) and -Y1b (1595–1597) as possible states of one font ignores the probability that two fonts as a whole are involved. However, the relationship between the two is not entirely clear at this point since some sorts of Y1a could have been transferred to Y1b. Adequate samples of both are available and reveal that a major decontamination was necessary to transform Y1a into Y1b, including the purging of oversized capitals (A C D2 E4 H I M O P R S T V), Guyot 'L S', a few low-density lower-case S-face sorts (d1 g1 f1 n1 x2), and over-sized 'e h o r', and discarding the entire, new S-face 'ft' ligature. The presence of the latter can be attributed to almost total replenishment since a very few original Y-face 'ft' ligatures still remain in Y1a. In addition, the proportion of damaged sorts drops radically when Y1b appears in 1595 in *A Comparison* STC4098 and the oversized capitals have been reduced to the 'A P S'; the presence of these capitals is not significant in itself as evidence of identity with Y1a since several Y-fonts in the 1590's seem to have been purchased or replenished almost immediately with an assortment of these capitals which range from 2.85–3.15mm in height. (This phenomenon requires further study, but it is worth noting that the cluster of oversized capitals was expanded in Braddock-Y1 after 1598 along with the addition of moderate-density new S-face 'ft' ligature, although the lower-case remained uncontaminated). However, the appearance of eleven S-face 'ft' ligatures as well as the 'R' on L1v–2 suggests the possibility that Y1a had not yet been discarded and was used to set this final Y-face passage. Moreover, a search of 45 prose pages of *Tetrastylon* STC25701 (1593) revealed only three battered types with any probability of recurrence in Y1b. Of these, only the 'w' at p. 37:25 of STC25701 is almost certainly that seen in *Salomon* STC18194 (D4:16, O1:26, P1v:36) and *Two Treatises* STC12322 (1598) (B2:16, D2v:29), but another recurrence or two in STC25701 would be helpful. The same holds for the 'a' at p. 32:3 of STC25701 and O4:18 of STC12322. Overall, the issue of the identity of Robinson-Y1a,b is left hanging, but the general principle implied by the unsuccessful recurrent-types survey is clear: a sample text in Robinson-Y1a cannot be used to establish his ownership of a target font if that font happens to be Robinson-Y1b.

fact is that two reasonably adequate samples of one font will eventually yield recurrent-types. The length of the samples must increase proportionately with the interval separating them to adjust for the on-going process of purging battered types, a factor which varies among shops. In general, samples consisting of several quarto gatherings at both ends of a long interval (three years or more) are usually adequate for the purpose, provided that the font is reasonably battered to start with. The variables that must be weighed in interpreting the failure of the survey include (1) investigator oversights, (2) a less-than-thorough search for recurrent-types, and (3) the possibility that each sample text was set from a different case thereby precluding recurrence of identifiable types. The first clue to the latter possibility is that recurrent-types appear in both formes of a gathering, a fairly certain indication that only one case was used in setting the text.[38]

The lack of adequate font samples during a transitional period can produce an ownership crux that can be resolved tentatively at best. For instance, shop lineage is established by Read's inheritance of Simson-S1 along with the shop's ornamental stock, which then passed to Eld. The situation is complicated by the assumption, based upon the first appearances of Eld's imprint, that he took over the shop in 1604.[39] The appearances in 1601, 1602,

---

38. See below, note 48.

39. In this instance, circumstances of the Read/Eld shop's history invite speculation that makes some sense of the situation. The transfer of the shop to Read occurred in January 1601, bounded by Widow Simson's *AElohim* STC5329 with the shop's McKerrow 320a "Gilley flower" ornament (the initials "G[abriel]. S[imson]." still in place) on the title page and the text in Simson/Read-S1, used also in 1601–1602 Read books *Ten Learned Personages* STC1074, *Revels* STC14773, *Contemplations* STC4662, as emphasis in C–E of *Sermon* STC 1454 (18 March 1601), and in Read's section (H–M2v) of *EMIH* STC14766 (1601). McKerrow 320b with the initials "G. S." effaced appears as well in STC1454 (E1v), *Essayes* Pt. 2 STC 5775 (O3), *Tragedies* STC26076 (title), *A Dialogue* STC18892 (title), and *Cromwell* STC 21532 (title). If *Essayes* STC5775 Pt. 2 (October 1601) was actually printed in Read's shop, it marks the virtual cessation of production until *Cromwell* (11 August 1602) since *Epitaph* STC3415 and *A Dialogue* STC18892 are such negligible, short emphemera. In general, it is difficult to reject the probability that Eld took over the shop in early 1603. Eld served his apprenticeship (1592–1600) to Robert Bolton in Richard Jugge's old shop at the sign of The Printers Press in Fleet Lane (as did Read), but his activities during 1600–1603 are unknown. Read apparently trainferred Simson's materials from The White Horse to The Printer's Press address when he took over. According to the title pages of *Revenger's Tragedy* STC24149 (1607) and *A Trick* STC17896 (first issue, 1608), and the Stationers' census of 1615, the shop remained at this location.

The appearance of Eld-Y1 in *Nero* STC12551 (entered 23 February 1603) commences a dramatic shift from the relative dormancy of Read's shop during 1602 to the consistently high output of Eld's mainstream printing activies during the subsequent two decades. Overall, 1603 production included at least fourteen titles (STC1117, 6260, 7120, 7594, 10800, 11086, 12061, 12551, 14377, 14381, 18292, 24041, 24343, 25643; and as sharing printer: 18041, Book 3). Volume 3 of revised *STC* may reveal other books assigned to Read. It is interesting to note the coincidental first appearance (as far as I know) of Eld's favorite title page xylographic ornament (the opposed scrolls described earlier) in *T. Opinion* STC24343 along with other stock; unfortunately, *T. Opinion* was not entered, so the date of printing is unclear, although a survey of papers in 1603 would probably establish this book's position in the shop's output.

and 1603 of Y-fonts in suspected Read books, and then Eld-Y1 in signed books in 1604, create the appearance of the continuous uninterrupted use of a single Y-font and raise the possibility that it passed to Eld along with the shop. Overall, these font samples exhibit no significant differentiae that would raise suspicion about their identity. Two Y-font appearances in early 1602 contribute to the appearance of the continuous use of a single font, but the sample is less than minimally adequate in both instances. The Y-font that appears in one quarto-page (B2v) of verse in *Epitaph* STC3415 (entered 24 February 1602) is considerably worn and battered; the Y-font seen in speech headings in *A Dialogue* STC18892 (entered 25 February 1602), a very short quarto, is in distinctly better condition. This observable difference in condition is a reasonable basis for rejecting the identity of the two. It is plausible that the font of *A Dialogue* STC18892 is that seen in the other books but the amount of type in *A Dialogue* is simply too limited to provide the evidence needed to establish identity. On other hand, the consistent appearance of Read/Eld stock in pages set in a Y-font in the octavo text of *Essayes* Pt. 2 STC5775 (entered 19 October 1601) and *Tragedies* STC26076 (1601, not en-

A second remarkable change occurs in shop activity with respect to the initiation of business relationships with a new group of publishers. As far as we know, Read printed 1601–1602 for J. Brome, W. Burre, M. Law, W. Jones, and E. Mattes, a small group that reflects the sparse output from the shop. It seems significant that none of these publishers is included in the group commencing with *Nero* STC12551 (23 February 1603) and extending through 1609. The obvious inference is that a kind of radically new marketing environment emerged in 1603 which, in business circles, is usually attributed to new management. It seems safe to assume that publishers "shopped around" for the best deal then just as they do now, and furthermore, that printers had a choice either of passively waiting for business to walk through the door or of aggressively marketing their services. The latter is suggested by the fact that, in 1603 alone, nine publishers without prior involvement contracted printing jobs (W. Aspley, E. Blount, C. Burby, F. Burton, G. Chorlton, J. Harrison IV, J. Norton, T. Pavier, G. Seton). Of these, Aspley and Blount remained frequent customers, while Burton brought only two other books (1604, 1606) to Eld. During 1604–1608, Eld printed four or more editions for T. Adams (5), W. Aspley (8, and four others as sharing printer), E. Blount (7), T. Thorpe (7), S. Waterson (4), and J. Wright (8).

Furthermore, a new business strategem emerges in the form of Eld's activity as a sharing printer, first with Simmes in *Essayes* STC18041, a relationship that would endure for at least two years. It is inconceivable that the veteran Simmes, backed by the equally astute publisher Edmund Blount, would approach a printer with Read's track record to undertake the printing of Book 3 of *Essayes* STC18041, an investment risk of the first magnitude for which no expense seems to have been spared. This job alone represents a large multiple of the total known output of Read's tenure. Blount and Cuthburt Burby also contracted other large jobs in 1603. Parts of Burby's *Antichrist* STC7120 (entered 22 April 1603), moreover, were then farmed out to Braddock and Creede, an unprecedented move that probably indicates that the shop's resources were pushed to the limit for the first time. One wonders, finally, what in Read's track record led Blount to feel confident about bringing the latin text of *Nero* STC12551 to the shop. In short, everything points to an Eld takeover of the shop in early 1603. It should be borne in mind that ownership of the shop passed to Eld via marriage to Widow Read, probably after a respectable mourning period. Perhaps the plague of 1603 removed Read from active involvement in the shop's operation, but this is pure ungrounded speculation of the kind so frequently encountered in hypothetical dating efforts and should be treated as such until a church record of Read's interment adds the essential fact that can settle the issue.

tered), and two later dramatic quartos suggests a single font. However, two factors prevent reaching a definite conclusion about the identity of these font samples in this instance. As sometimes happens, the practical reality of limited library holdings can present an obstacle: since The Huntington lacks an original copy of *Cromwell* STC21532 (entered 11 August 1602), it is impossible to perform a recurrent-types survey which could link *Essayes* Pt. 2 to the first demonstrable appearance of Eld-Y1 in *Nero* STC12251 (entered 23 February 1603) via identifiable types in *Cromwell*. *Cromwell* could be an important source of evidence given the quite good condition of the type in *Essayes*, *Tragedies*, and *Nero*, a factor which makes it difficult to locate identifiable types in the latter books. In general, some identifiable types remain in a font throughout its lifetime. However, the probability of locating recurrences of specific types is affected by the random recurrence phenomenon and hence is directly proportional to the number of such types in a font. Although the interval between *Essayes/Tragedies* and *Nero* is hardly enough in itself to explain the apparent absence of recurrent-types in the two books, the relatively few identifiable types in each compounds the problem presented by the interval. A third set of identifiable types in *Cromwell* would dramatically increase the chances of finding overlapping recurrences if the fonts are actually the same. It is also possible that repeating the recurrent-types survey of *Essayes/Tragedies* and *Nero* would eventually yield evidence of identity. Nonetheless, the ornamental evidence in combination with the composition of the complementary Granjon pica italic font points to a single font in *Essayes/Tragedies*, *Cromwell*, and *Nero* although specific typographical evidence is lacking.[40] In general, the suspicion about ownership raised by the

---

40. In the absence of an original copy which could yield identified recurrent-types in the target font, the composition of the complementary italic font used for emphasis, speech prefixes and stage directions in dramatic quartos such as *Cromwell* STC21532 sometimes provides corroborative evidence that the target font is being used by the suspected printer (see discussion, "Font Analysis," pp. 126–127, and notes 42–46). The cogency of such evidence, which usually consists of wrong-face letters in the font, depends upon the uniqueness and longevity of the mixture. This evidence must be approached with caution since mixing of italic capitals is such a common phenomenon. In this instance, the mixed composition of the Read/Eld Granjon pica italic font is fairly distinct and long-term and consistently recurs through *Nero* STC12551 but not later in *Isahaacs* STC25643 (entered 16 June 1603). Prose texts such as *Ten Learned* STC1074 and *Essayes* Pt. 2 STC5775 place minimal pressure on the italic font, but most capitals appear at least a few times in each so that opportunity exists for the random recurrence of the set of Guyot italic letters (see Vervliet, Fig. 231, specimen IT10, p. 301). Mixed into the Granjon italic are Guyot capitals (swash-*A* swash-*B C E F G H N* swash-*R S T*) and Guyot lower-case '*v w*'. The '*C E T*' are present in moderate-density proportions and appear in STC1074, *Cynthia's Revels* STC14773, STC5775, STC26076, STC21532 and STC12551. The '*N*' appears in all but STC1074 and STC26076; the swash-'*B*' skips STC5775 and STC12551; the swash-'*A*' appears only in STC14773, STC 26076, and STC5775; the '*F*' only in STC14773 and STC21532; the '*G*' in STC1074 and STC14773; the '*H*' in STC14773, STC21532, STC26076, and STC12551; and the '*S*' in STC 1074, STC5775, STC26076, and STC12551. Oddly enough, the Guyot swash-'*R*' appears only in STC5775 (T7v:18). The lower-case '*v*' appears in all except STC26076 while the '*w*'

failure to locate recurrent-types in reasonably battered candidate and target fonts from the proximate period is usually a sound indication that a search for a sharing printer is necessary.

Finally, the ownership crux is unresolvable if a font appears in only one assigned book but in the absence of an interwoven setting which could demonstrate ownership. The presence of identifiable ornamental stock in such an instance is inadequate to prove the ownership of the font because of reasons discussed earlier. On the other hand, ownership can be assumed if the single appearance of the font occurs in combination with an identified complementary font (e.g., italic, black letter) in quantities and patterns such as preclude sharing. Very short settings that are inserted into a text which is set before and after in another font style or size present a special problem since transportation from another shop is not unrealistic. The page of short verse noted above in *Epitaph* STC3415 is such an instance. Page-length prose epistles or dedicatory verses in preliminaries seem to be another class of settings to approach with caution. It seems wise to require a verifiable second appearance of a font in these instances before concluding ownership. The need for such caution can be illustrated by two cases involving books signed by Roberts. His infrequently used 76mm Guyot pica roman appears in three short settings in the context of identifiable fonts and ornamental stock. The passages at B4–4v and I3–3v of *Scourge of Villanie* STC17485 (1598) are inserted in a text in Roberts-S1. The epistle in A3–3v of *A True Discourse* STC7293 (1604) shares A3 with a Guyot pica italic such as Roberts used and Roberts-S1 serves as the emphasis font in the black letter text A4–D3. Similarly, the epistle on A2–4 of *Euphues* STC17075 (1597) is headed by Roberts's Trumpets-T, followed by a Granjon italic in A4v–B1v such as he used elsewhere, and Roberts-S1 on B2–B2v headed by his Angel-G, followed by Roberts-S1 as emphasis font in the black letter text B3–2F2.[41] In these instances, the contextual materials and their pattern of appearances would be sufficient

---

skips the latin emphasis of STC5775 and latin text of STC12551. An additional discriminant is provided by the normal tall-'*C*' and swash-'*I*' which appear frequently in all. Overall, these appearances conform to the pattern of random recurrence that is to be expected in the context of sort-pressure generated by the kinds of texts involved. There can be little doubt that the Read/Eld italic font appears in *Cromwell* STC21532.

41. The minimal font sample found in emphasis appearances presents a special problem that merits comment. The emphasis use in long quotations such as Short-Y1 in *English Secretary* STC6404 and Robinson-Y1b in *A comparison* STC18246 or in catechetical dialogues such as Read-S1 in *Contemplations* STC4662 and Purfoot-Y1 in *Caesar's* STC18432 usually permits a complete analysis of composition and possibly the discovery of recurrent-types that lead to the identification of a font. However, an emphasis use limited to names and the like often results in such a limited typographical sample that it is impossible to define a font's composition completely. It is possible to sort out shared sections on the basis of this limited evidence in some cases if different typefaces are used by two or more sharing printers. For example, Stafford-EFb can be distinguished from Allde-S2 in *Seven Deadly Sinnes* STC6522 in emphasis appearances of the former in sheets BC and O, with Allde-S2 in D–N. Similarly, Jaggard-C2 can be distinguished in *T. Deade Tearme* STC6496

to allay any doubts about Roberts's ownership of the Guyot pica roman. Fortunately, Roberts used the Guyot pica at least two other times as the text font, leaving no doubt of ownership (See *Englands Heroicall* STC7196 [4th ed., 1600], STC7197 [5th ed., 1602]; not checked: STC7193 [1st ed., 1597] and STC7195 [3rd ed., 1599]). However, two appearances of Y-fonts in books signed by Roberts are deceptive and lead to an erroneous inference of ownership. The minimal sample of a Y-font seen in the few speech heads and emphasis in the black letter text (A2–C3v) of *Clim of Clough* STC1808 (1605) lacks distinguishing features (except for the odd use of the 'fl' ligature in setting "Cloudesse" which may indicate a lack of the 'ff' ligature in the font) and would be cause for suspicion of sharing if it was the only appearance of a Y-font in a book signed by Roberts. However, the entire text of *Scourge* STC 17486.5 (1599) (Folger 17486a; British Library C.39.b.43) also prints in a Y-font which, despite the gap of five years and the minimal sample in STC1808, would seem adequate to demonstrate ownership. Furthermore, Roberts-S1 accumulates an extensive foul-case set of Y-face capitals from about 1600 on, a factor which suggests the use of a Y-font in the shop. However, the Y-font of STC17486.5 exhibits an extensive foul-case cluster that makes it easily identifiable (even a single-page reproduction such as Plate 124, *Pica Roman Type*, contains highly suggestive evidence of identity). Roberts actually farmed out STC17486.5 to Braddock and the font is Braddock-Y1 in a state similar to that seen in *Midsummer Night's Dreame* Q1 STC22302.[42] Finally, a short

---

in D3,4v, E3, F2, G1,2v from Jaggard-S1 in A3–4v, BC, D1–2v,3v, E1–2v,3v–4v, F, G1v,2,3,3v and in many pages of *Sermons* STC15282 so that the alternating pattern serves as evidence of ownership. If these were shared books, the evidence would be adequate to point a search in the direction of a printer who simultaneously used the two typefaces. Otherwise, the usefulness of emphasis appearances is defined by the quantity of "gross features" evidence that can be located. Read-S1's differentiae, for example, can be noted (along with ornamental stock) in C–E of *Sermon* STC1454, but an unfamiliar head-piece and factotum appear at B1 along with a shift to 96mm roman emphasis that indicates a second printer. The quite limited Y-font emphasis appearance in *A Dialogue* STC18892, on the other hand, reveals a few S-face sorts that are not seen in Eld-Y1 until much later. In some instances, the uniqueness of composition is suggestive. Given the mix of Windet-F sorts in Windet-S2, especially the short second-stem 'w' and condensed 'fh' ligature, an appearance in short preliminaries or as the emphasis font should produce enough evidence to suggest a look at Windet-S2 and thence to a comparison of the target book's font to Windet's equivalent font. For example, several books previously assigned to William Stansby contain short samples of Windet-S2 (see *T. Jesuites Play* STC21514, A3).

42. *Scourge* STC17486.5 illustrates the potential impact of undetected font samples hidden in ghosted books or shared sections upon font analysis and bibliographical analysis. Despite the imprint of 1599, the actual date of the printing of *Scourge* STC17486.5 is unclear. Given the fact that the first edition (STC17485) was entered 8 September 1598 and Roberts printed another edition dated 1599 (STC17486), it seems safe to assume that STC 17486.5 was printed sometime later than 1599. The foul-case cluster of Braddock-Y1 in STC 17486.5 suggests a transitional state between earlier works and *MND* Q1 STC22302 (see "Font Analysis", p. 140 and Table 5, p. 149). First, the resident S-face cluster is consistent throughout 1598–1600 with most sorts appearing in STC17486.5 (A E H I M Q R S V; lacking: P). A similar consistency is seen in the proportion of the damaged 'ff' ligature fouling the 'fl' ligature sort. The italic foul-case cluster is substantially the same seen in earlier

passage printed in a font distinguished by such "gross features" can sometimes suggest the identity of the printer of a section in another font style or
size. For example, the appearance of 18 lines of Stafford-EFb at D1 in the
96mm roman text font of sheets CD in *T. Whole Magnificient Entertainment*
STC6513 (1604) suggests the assignment of the section to Stafford.

(5)

The practice of sharing sometimes diminished the known output from a
shop and created gaps in the use of a given font because it was used in unknown sections of shared books. The current state of knowledge about this
phenomenon is by no means exhaustive. The stages of progress reflected in
the expanded list of sharing printer assignments added to Morrison's *Index*
and old *STC* in new *STC*, and the assignments yet to be added on the basis
of typographical evidence, suggest that a significant portion of the output
from printers with known sharing activity may lie buried in shared sections.

---

works (*A B E H I L P S T*) and in approximately the same proportions, previously unseen
letters (swash-*B D F O*) appear at low-density levels, and several low-density sorts (*C G N Q*)
do not occur, primarily due to low sort-pressure, but purging also is possible. However, the
state of Braddock-Y1 in *Downefall of Robert* STC18269 and *Death of Robert* STC18271 (both
entered 1 December 1600 after *MND* Q1), two other texts from 1601 not listed in Morri-
son/*STC*, indicates that purging did not occur. Although Braddock-Y1 is used here only
as the emphasis font in speech prefixes and stage directions, the complete S-face and italic
(excepting '*C G O*') clusters occur. In addition, prefixes pull italic '*K R*' into the font. It is
clear from the increase in the density of italic cluster members that Braddock-Y1 was
severely depleted in the upper-case.

The transitional state between 1599–1601 is clear from the presence of two portions of
the cluster. My ignorance of the hidden sample of Braddock-Y1 in STC17486.5, 18271, and
18269 led to the erroneous conclusion that the 96mm 'C' were purged at the same time as the
96mm 'T' ("Font Analysis," p. 140). Although the 96mm 'T' is absent and presumably was
purged, the 96mm 'C' seen in *A Short Forme* STC12312 (imprint: 1599; see 2D3v, 2E4v, 2G1,
2I2) is still resident in STC17486.5 (see A4, C6v, C7, D7v) and *Death* (see G1v). In fact, the
96mm 'C' were not purged after *A Short Forme* but simply skipped *MND* Q1. Furthermore,
the presence of a new portion of the cluster in STC17486.5, along with the residence of
the 96mm 'C', provides important evidence about the printing of *MND* Q1. As I noted in
"Font Analysis," viewing the occurrences of small capitals '*A H I T*' as "repeated responses
to newly developed shortages in these sorts (transient fouling) totally distorts the picture
of presswork that emerges, if, in fact, these foul-case letters are resident in the font, i.e.,
already in the respective sort compartments before setting began" (p. 129; see also note 46).
The small capitals '*A H I T*' appear in STC17486.5 at roughly the same proportions as in
MND Q1, although comparing densities in quarto vs. octavo settings is difficult. In addition,
a small capital 'M' appears twice in STC17486.5 but not in *MND* Q1, although the non-
appearance is to be expected if but a single type is involved (as seems to be the case). *Death*
and *Downefall*, however, exerted heavy pressure on the depleted 'M' sort and required as
many as seven small capital 'M' per page (see B4v of *Downefall*). In addition, small capitals
'*F P*' appear. The black letter colon likewise appears with the low frequency seen in *MND*
Q1 A and C so that the deluge of 20 such colons in B clearly represents transient fouling
that was deliberately purged during the distribution of B (see discussion of a similar foul-
ing/purging process by Short's compositors, "Font Analysis," p. 131). *Death* and *Downefall*
are ambiguous in this context since no colons were required. (I should note that STC17438
is incorrectly listed as "17483" in Table 4 and Table 5.)

Two factors affect the practical implications of this possibility: (1) these sections may actually constitute a large portion of the pica (or other sizes) output from a shop; and (2) since font identification requires recurrent-types identified in original copies, a virtual shortage may occur because the library at which one is working lacks a copy of the key assigned book in which the critical font sample is found. The unknown output in Eld-Y1 provides an informative example. The six books assigned to Eld in Morrison/*STC* for 1604 include two Eld-Y1 texts: *Epigrames* STC5672 (four octavo sigs.), and *A Loyal Subjects* STC25760 (9 quarto sigs.), equivalent to eleven quarto gatherings (plus one minimal use as emphasis font in *Palladis* STC26014). New *STC* adds three Eld-Y1 texts (*Supplication* Q2–3 STC14429.5, 14430.5, ten quarto sigs.; Q4 STC14430, one sig. [only] standing from Q3 [see later discussion]) comprising eleven quarto prose gatherings. In addition, Eld-Y1 printed *Malcontent* Q1–2 STC17479–80, B–E (eight sigs.); Q3 STC17481, HI (two sigs.); *Whore* Q1–2 STC6501,6501a, G–K (eight sigs.); and two pages in *Siege* STC18895, or slightly more than eighteen gatherings. Overall, the fact that eighteen of a total of forty gatherings for 1604 are hidden in unidentified shared sections obviously is a significant factor in a survey for Eld-Y1 samples in 1604. Similarly, one Eld-Y1 appearance in a Read book in 1603 is found in Morrison/*STC* in the tentative assignment of *Antichrist* STC7120; new *STC* assigns 2A–G to Read (seven sigs.) as well as *Nero* STC12551 (eighteen sigs.) for a total of twenty-five gatherings. In addition, Eld-Y1 appears in Book 3 of *Essayes* STC18041, an enormous Eld-Y1 sample in a prose folio in sixes which dwarfs the previously known output.

A different kind of problem is encountered in a survey of Eld's 1605 books. Both Morrison/*STC* and new *STC* assign *Survey* Q1–2 STC6200,6201 to Eld. Q2 prints in Eld-S1, while Q1 prints in a Y-font which could be easily misinterpreted as a healthy eight gathering sample useful for identifying Eld-Y1 in a shared section of another book. However, it is not Eld-Y1. Papers used in Q1 are shared with *An Apology* STC19295 (1607) and do not seem to appear in any other Eld or Simmes book 1603–1608. In private correspondence, Peter Blayney suggests a 1607 piracy. The 1607 dating of Q1 is unquestionable, but the issue of piracy can only be settled by the identification of the Y-font. Given a list of about 100 identified Eld-Y2 types which recur in half-dozen 1607 books by Eld, whether Eld-Y2 prints STC6200 could be easily settled, but The Huntington lacks a copy, a situation which amounts to a virtual gap in shop output and leaves the issue hanging upon another research trip (note also previous discussion of *Cromwell* STC21532). Nonetheless, the question remains: how is it that papers concurrently used by Eld in 1607 would find their way into a pirated text bearing Eld's imprint and a false date of 1605? Adam Islip's 1598–1605 output represents an extreme case that probably is unique but is worth mentioning since more moderate cases may occur. Pica roman output is lacking in 1599–1601 books bearing the Islip imprint and listed by Morrison/*STC*. New *STC* reassignments to Islip of books bearing the Thomas Wight (and/or Bonham Norton) imprint reveal the reason for the apparant lack of pica roman output: Islip-Y1a,b appears in at least seven such books 1598–1601. Islip-S1 appears at least in one Islip book 1602–1604, but in at least six Wight books.[43] The impact of new *STC* reassignments such as this will become clear once Volume 3's "Index of Printers" appears.

(6)

The detection of shared printing is often aided by the fortuitous accident that sections of a shared book print in dissimilar fonts. The alternating pattern of dissimilar fonts in units of a gathering or more provides an obvious clue to the possibility of sharing and reveals the possible divisions of labor. The divisions are usually obvious in a book shared in the classical two-section A–B pattern. For example, it is impossible to overlook the fact that Eld-Y1 appears in *Malcontent* STC17479 Q1 B–E with Simmes-S1 in F–H; or Creede-4 in A–2D and Windet-F in 2EF of *Regiment* STC1827. The same holds for books shared in three or four sections so long as a sequence of dissimilar fonts emerges, as, for example, in *Honest Whore* STC6501, where Simmes-S1 prints AB, Creede-4 prints CD, Stafford-EFb prints EF, and Eld-Y1 prints G–K. In such instances, the dissimilar typefaces or obvious "gross features" differentiae are easily detected in the initial seriatim font analysis. However, a crux frequently emerges in books of more than two sections when two of the sections print in same-face fonts separated by one intervening section (or more) in a dissimilar font. This raises the intermediate issue of whether the two separated same-face fonts are the same and therefore indicate one printer as opposed to two printers using same-face fonts. In instances involving separated appearances of a font distinguished by "gross features" or obvious differentiae, the matter can be easily decided. Creede-3's unique mixture, for example, appears in *Parnassus* STC378 (1600) at B–S and 2G–K, separated by Purfoot-Y1 at T–Z and Simmes-S1(?) at 2A–F. Purfoot-Y1 could be as easily distinguished in a split appearance because of its unique composition. However, instances such as the appearance of Windet-S1 in EF and HI of *Fawne* Q1 STC17483 present a problem.

Same-face fonts lacking obvious differentiae usually can be identified in separated appearances only by a recurrent-types survey. Perfectly practical and logical assumptions about sharing strategies cannot be trusted in such instances.[44] For example, the appearances of same-face fonts in widely sepa-

43. Noted Islip-Y1a,b appearances: *A Treatise* STC17291 (1598), *T. Dialogues* STC21576 (1598), *La Nowel* STC10964 (1598), *Prenobilis* STC11196 (1599), *A Booke* STC3345 (1600), *Four Bookes* STC13200 (1601), and *Le Necessarie* STC4719 (1601). Noted Islip-S1 appearances: *Abrahams* STC18538 (1602), *Eirenarcha* STC15170 (1602), *A Booke* STC3346 (1603), *Sanctuary* STC7113 (1604), *Lytylton* STC15753.4 (1604), *T. Duties* STC15155 (1604).

44. See comment in "Font Analysis," pp. 122–123, regarding sharing patterns (note as well the alternating pattern of Islip-EFb and the unidentified Y-font in *De Missa* STC23456 discussed earlier). For example, it makes sense that, in *Fools*, Eld would print AB (Eld-Y1) and farm out the two-gathering sections CD (White-M), EF (Stafford-EFb) and GH (Eld-Y1) to printers 2, 3, and 4, the final full gathering I (White-M) to printer 5, and do half-sheet K himself. What actually happened makes very little sense: he resumed printing with GH, but then gave I to White, and finished with half-sheet K. The many instances of sharing in

rated sections of long books invites the erroneous assumption that, given the length of the book and individual sections, a sequence of printers were involved. A second factor frequently contributes. Printing quality and appearance easily change (sometimes due to different job lots of papers) in long books, leading to the suspicion that a second font appears in a later section. The font distribution in *An Apology* STC19295 (1607) is complicated by the fact that this quarto in eights was the work of two printers who respectively used two and three fonts during the proximate period. The major difficulty involves determining whether a single Y-font appears in widely separated sections in Book 1 (¶, B–E), 3A–G, and 3L–N. The low-density foul-case S-face sorts in this state of Eld-Y2 (A C D M S T Y b1 g1 k2; 'fl' ligature) do not recur in these isolated sections with the frequency and consistency needed to infer a single font so that evidence of recurrent-types is necessary to establish that Eld-Y2 indeed is the font. Sorting the remaining fonts is assisted by the font distribution. Although Eld was using Eld-S1 at the time, the alternating pattern of fonts in Jaggard's section, which includes Jaggard-S1, eliminates the possibility that Eld-S1 was involved. The combined appearances of Jaggard's three fonts in several gatherings clearly indicate a single printer in those sections;[45] individual full-gathering appearances in Book 2 of Jaggard-C2 (2D, 2G, 2K, 2O) and Jaggard-S1 (2LM) can be resolved by an analysis of cross-contamination. The combined appearances by halves of Jaggard-Y1b and -S1 in 3H and 3K separated by Jaggard-C2 in 3I repeat the pattern of Book 2 and furnish the evidence necessary for assigning the section (3H–K) to Jaggard.

Although shared printing is usually implied by a sequence of fonts in units of a gathering or more, the possibility exists that a printer with two fonts used them in this manner, which is typical of shared printing. The alternation of Lownes-S1 and -Y1 in *A Modest* STC5882 (1604) invites the inference that three printers were involved as suggested by an S-font in R–2C between Y-fonts in B–Q and 2DE.[46] As in STC19295, the widely separated

anomalous divisions and separated sections suggests that flexibility was more important than tidy logic in Elizabethan sharing strategies. The seriatim order of analysis should be followed as a matter of course.

45. In Book 2 of STC19295, for example, Jaggard's fonts alternate within gatherings as follows. In sig. 2B, Jaggard-C2 appears in 1, 2v, 3v–6, 7, 7v; Jaggard-Y1b in 1v; Jaggard-S1 in 2, 3, 6v, 8, 8v. In sig. 2I, Jaggard-S1 appears in 1–2v, 5v, 6, 7–8v; Jaggard-C2 in 3–5, 6v.

46. New *STC* tentatively assigns the book to Lownes, Kingston, and East (in that order). However, Kingston did not use an S-font (section 2) nor did East use a Y-font (section 3). The alternation of Roberts-S1 and -C2 in *Hamlet* Q2 STC22276 in units of a gathering or more (Roberts-C2: B–D, F, I, N–O2v) creates the appearance of sharing. The only other noted use of Roberts-C2 is in *Of the Calling* STC19733 where it alternates within gatherings (see note 12 above), a pattern which usually indicates ownership. In general, several appearances of a font in signed books are desirable and should be expected. In this case, supplemental evidence from running-titles could be decisive. In "The Printing of *Hamlet* Q2," *Studies in Bibliography*, 7 (1955), 41–50, Fredson Bowers describes an anomalous movement of running-titles across the boundaries established by the alternating fonts: title V moves from I1 (C2) to O1 (C2) to M1 (S1), VII moves from I3 to M4, VIII moves from I2v to M4v, XII moves from L2 (S1) to N4 (C2), XIII moves from L3 to N3, and XIV moves from

fonts in B–Q and 2DE seem different because of printing quality. Nonetheless, recurrent-types indicate that Lownes-Y1 printed both sections with Lownes-S1 in R–2C. The rationale underlying this in-shop division of labor between two fonts is unclear, but the similarity to Jaggard's alternation of Jaggard-C2 and -S1 in STC19295 is obvious. Both may be related to compositorial stints.

The sequence of four editions of *A Supplicatione* culminates in an undesirable kind of same-face crux: the Eld-Y1 and Simmes-S1 sections of Q3 are reset in Q4 in a second Y-font except for one standing gathering in Eld-Y1 and a few pages in Simmes-S1. Q1 STC14432 prints entirely in Simmes-S1 (incorrectly assigned to the English Secret Press in new *STC*). Both Q2 and Q3 are in the two-section A–B sharing pattern. B–E is in Eld-Y1 and F–O is in Simmes-S1 in Q2 STC14429.5. In the resetting for Q3 STC14430.5, F of Q2 shifts to Eld-Y1 with Simmes-S1 printing G–O. The redistribution of labor and the sections of standing type seen in Q4 STC14430 provide one clue to the sequence of editions.[47] The complex sharing pattern constructed around standing Eld-Y1 in F and standing Simmes-S1 in M4 and O1–2v would be impossible except in a line-for-line resetting of a text previously containing the standing sections. The pattern exemplifies the problems associated with separated appearances of same-face fonts. White-M with its mixture of nearly complete S- and Y-fonts is easily distinguished in D and G of Q4. Creede-4 could possibly be confused at first with the minimal sample of Simmes-S1 in the latter's standing section; moreover, the separated appearances of Creede-4 could also suggest two more sharing printers; however, Creede-4's differentiae permit verification of separated appearances in BC, H, and L. Another major pitfall is created by the appearance of Y-fonts in the remainder of the pica roman sections of text. The previous use of a same-face font in a section(s) of an earlier edition creates a predisposition to assume that it appears in the same section (or part thereof) in the later edition. Given the fact that Eld-Y1 appears in B–E of Q2 and B–F of Q3, it is easy to assume that Eld-Y1 therefore appears in EF, I, N and M3v of Q4. The analysis of "gross features" and composition is frequently inadequate to distinguish same-face fonts in these situations: the few wrong-face capitals in Eld-Y1 in Q3 B–F (B E L P S, Guyot 'S') seem consistent with the 'E P' in Q4 E (E2v:1, 3), the 'P' with the crimped bowl (Q4, E4:9, I:13, N2v:16) seems at first glance consistent with that seen in Eld-Y1 in Q3 (B2v:15, B3:25, C1v:35, D1v:3, E3v:3), and the few fouled italic 'P S' seen in Q4 could easily be attributed to transient fouling. A recurrent-types survey of Q4 is necessary to identify Eld-Y1 in standing F and distinguish it from the second Y-font. The remainder (E, I, M3v, N) was reset (very prob-

---

L4v to N4v. If Bowers's identifications are correct, they indicate setting in one shop and hence confirm Roberts's ownership of the C2 font.

47. Incidentally, new *STC* lists Q3 and Q4 in reverse order on the basis of the corrected signature B3 in 14430.5 (missigned C3 in 14430) which is taken as the later state and thus the later edition. 14430.5 is actually Q3. 14430.5 Q3 is printed on the same job lot of papers found in 14429.5 Q2 except for sheet H while Q4 is printed on entirely unrelated papers. Q4 presents a rare instance in which a short section (bottom half of M3v) had to have been reset in Braddock's shop and transported (or vice versa, M4 transported from Simmes's shop).

ably) in Braddock-Y2a. The correct sequence of 14430.5 and 14430 is implied by the fact that the final sections of Q3 in Eld-Y1 (F) and Simmes-S1 (M4, O1–2v) wēre undistributed and hence remained standing for Q4. Similarly, resetting patterns in the absence of standing type may provide useful evidence as to a sequence of editions. For instance, the font distributions shift between the two editions of *Pericles*. Q2 STC22335 is set in the classical A–B pattern, with White-S1 in A–D and Creede-5 in E–I3v. In Q1 STC22334, however, sheet E is printed by White and sheet B by Creede so that the resulting distribution is: White-S1: A, C–E; Creede-5: B, F–I. In general, the simple two-section pattern usually occurs in the first edition while the disrupted pattern occurs in a line-for-line resetting in the second edition.

The most treacherous crux consists of the appearances of two same-face fonts in contiguous sections of a shared book. If other clues to sharing are present, the possibility of two fonts should be tested immediately. The shift of ornamental stock in Book 2 of *Antichrist* STC7120, for example, calls for a comparative analysis of the Y-fonts in Books 1 and 2 in order to differentiate Braddock-Y2a from Eld-Y1. Although an uncommon case, the *Dutch Courtesan* STC17475, a book bearing Purfoot's imprint and printed in two Y-fonts, epitomizes the various complications that can confound the search for sharing printers. Some aspects of printing style and the running-titles shift between A–E and F–H. Purfoot's ownership of both Purfoot-Y2 and -Y3 is a complicating factor in detecting shared printing in this instance. The S-capitals and italic foul-case cluster in A–E leave little doubt that Purfoot-Y2 printed the section. However, the Y-font in F–H exhibits a deceptive similarity to Purfoot-Y3. The italic foul-case cluster in F–H is consistent with that seen in Purfoot-Y3 although the two overlap in only a few sorts. This difference could be attributed to progressive fouling and/or purging. The presence of the turned 'p q' and the oversized 'b' and 'ct' ligature in F–H, Purfoot-Y2 and -Y3, in contrast, suggests cross-contamination and renders the inference of identity more difficult to dismiss. In any event, this obvious evidence is ambiguous. The recurrent-types survey of F–H produces another complicating factor: several positively identifiable types appear in both formes of sheet F,[48] indicating one-case setting with distributions after each forme, a sound basis for inferring that only half of the font appears in F–H. In turn, this undermines the conclusiveness of the failure of a recurrent-types survey of F–H and Purfoot-Y3 to yield identified types in both fonts. The identity of the target font in F–H, in short, can be determined only by the discovery of a candidate font which yields recurrent-types. The obvious differentiate exhibited by the F–H font lessens the difficulty of settling upon a suitable candidate such as Jaggard-Y1b. If it is the correct candidate, recurrent-types usually emerge

48. See: k1: F2:15, F4v:21; b1: F1v:32, F4v:1; y1: F1v:11, F3:7; C1: F1:20, F2:1; M1: F1:31, F3v:9; W1: F1v:6, F4v:31. A similar recurrence situation is seen in *Fools* STC4963 where embossing evidence indicates that the inner forme was first through the press: b1: B1:9, B1v:21; d3: B1v:30, B2v:30; f1: B1v:29, B3:36; f6: B2v:25, B4:34; l3: B1:3, B1v:9; r4: B2v:9, B4:7; w1: B1v:12, B2v:5; y4: B3:6, B4:35; (a7: B2:11, B3v:18?).

rather quickly. However, the search process seems destined to failure when a target font lacks obvious differentiae, and worse yet, exhibits minimal to virtually no damage and wear. For example, identified Eld-Y2 types recur throughout *Byron* STC4968 (B–O, QR) except in sheet P, where a Y-font in virginal condition appears. This font is entirely uncontaminated, almost all types print with crisp clean edges, and only a few types exhibit minor damage that could support positive identification in recurrences. Identification of this font would be a tenuous procedure even if the correct candidate font were located. The Y-font alternating with Islip-EFb in *De Missa* STC23456 is a similar instance but not quite as extreme.

(7)
    Although concluding on such a negative note seems poor rhetorical strategy, it nonetheless is indicative of the psychological experience that sometimes results from a futile search for a sharing printer. The commitment to printer research assumes a willingness to endure such frustration. The discovery of sharing, however, is important in itself and is a source of satisfaction. In fact, shared printing is the only area where new discoveries in relatively large numbers are within easy reach, given the high probability that we have found all the extant manuscripts of plays by important Elizabethan/Jacobean authors. Beyond that, an enormous amount of work remains to be done by employing font analysis to verify the tentative assignments in new *STC* that are based upon ornamental stock. A practical problem exists in regard to the recording and dissemination of the new information that will be generated by typographical analysis. Detailed evidence that affects our understanding of the transmission of early texts should find its way into print as a matter of course. However, the overwhelming majority of early books probably do not merit such treatment although typographical information about them can be extremely valuable in the context of printer identification. Publication of such information in printed format is obviously out of the question: the *Short Title Catalogue* with its abbreviated descriptions exemplifies the practical limits both in terms of economics and dedication (bibliographers cannot help feeling a sense of gratitude to Katharine V. Pantzer every time the revised *STC* is consulted). The creation of on-line computer databases, however, offers the exciting prospect of instant (or nearly so) dissemination of current bibliographical information that can be expanded and updated as the need arises. The proposal by Henry L. Snyder (University of California, Riverside), Director of the Eighteenth-Century Short Title Catalogue for North America, to include the *STC* in the on-going project of converting the *ESTC* to an electronic database has, in fact, been underway for some time.[49] Although the abbreviated entries of the revised *STC* serve as the basic records for the database, Snyder envisions expanding them "so that they

49. See "A Proposal: The English Short Title Catalogue", *Papers of the Bibliographical Society of America*, 82 (1988), 333–336.

would be comparable to *ESTC* records in fullness, content, and format." The possibility of adding to the database once it is completed should provide additional motivation for bibliographers to record routinely the kinds of evidence that are pertinent to shared printing and printer identification.

RECONSTRUCTION AND ADAPTATION IN Q *HENRY V*

by

KATHLEEN IRACE

IN recent years Gary Taylor's analysis of the "bad" quarto of *Henry V* has sparked new interest in this First Quarto version of the play. Taylor, believing that Q *Henry V* preserved a deliberate theatrical abridgment, later reconstructed by reporter-actors, incorporated some of the adaptations of the Quarto in his two Oxford editions of *Henry V*, based primarily on the Folio.[1] Though his decision was courageous, my own analysis of the Quarto shows that his basic assumption was incorrect, for my study shows that the Quarto was reconstructed from the reporters' recollections of a version similar to the Folio, which they apparently abridged as part of a single process of reconstruction and adaptation. Rather than reconstructed from an intermediate theatrical abridgment, the First Quarto of *Henry V* was created from a version linked to the Folio, by actors intent on putting together an abridged version of the play—perhaps for a tour outside London, perhaps as a reading text for a patron or friend of the actors.[2] Whatever the first

1. See Gary Taylor, ed., *Henry V* (1982) and *Henry V* in Stanley Wells and Taylor, eds., *William Shakespeare: The Complete Works* (1986). Taylor developed his views in *Modernizing Shakespeare's Spelling, with Three Studies in the Text of "Henry V,"* Stanley Wells and Gary Taylor (1979). Several have disagreed with certain details of Taylor's position, including, for example, Annabel Patterson in "Back by Popular Demand: The Two Versions of *Henry V*," *Renaissance Drama*, 19 (1988), 29–62. Patterson suggests that Q, rather than originating as a touring script for a reduced cast (Taylor's view), "may very well be closer than the Folio to what the London audiences actually saw on the stage at the absolute turn of the century" (p. 32). See also Patterson's *Shakespeare and the Popular Voice* (1989), pp. 71–92.

2. Certain features of Q point toward a simpler production appropriate for touring; for example, the "Scaling Ladders" (TLN 1082) specified in F for the scene at the gates of Harfleur (3.1) are omitted in Q. The Quarto also seems to require a smaller cast, as Taylor has pointed out in "We Happy Few: The 1600 Abridgment," in *Three Studies* (1979). Further research is needed, however, into the requirements of companies on tour. A recent

purpose of Q *Henry V*, its connection to the Folio version rather than an intermediate adaptation is a key finding of this study.

My analysis of Q *Henry V* is based on a parallel text, assembled from photocopies of the two versions in facsimile, and a computer analysis, designed from the handmade parallel text. Section 1 presents the results of my computer-assisted analysis of possible memorial reconstruction in Q *Henry V*. This analysis provides clear and quantitative evidence of the memorial reconstruction theory, identifying the most likely reporters and demonstrating their knowledge of a version related to the Folio rather than an intermediate abridgment. Sections 2 and 3 consider the possibility of deliberate adaptation in Q *Henry V*, for though the computer-aided analysis shows that the Quarto must have been reconstructed by actors familiar with a script linked to F, key differences between the two texts suggest that Q might have been deliberately abridged, perhaps at the same time as it was reconstructed. Section 2 discusses the unusual number of reattributions—80 lines in Q *Henry V* —persuasive evidence of intentional adaptation by the reporters or their colleagues. Section 3 focuses on a series of arguably intentional omissions in Q as well as key structural alterations in the plot. Significantly, many of these alterations corroborate an important result of the computer-assisted analysis in reinforcing the connection of the Quarto to a script linked to the Folio version rather than an intermediate theatrical abridgment.

SECTION 1: Memorial Reconstruction in Q *Henry V*

To seek verifiable evidence for or against memorial reconstruction, I designed a computer-assisted analysis to help compare the two versions of *Henry V*.[3] My analysis is based on the fluctuating quality of Q, observed by

report by researchers with the Records of Early English Drama project, U. of Toronto, suggests that tours were much more regular and widespread than earlier research had indicated, implying a level of sophistication in audiences that might match that of London audiences. These findings were presented at the 1990 Shakespeare Association of America meeting (Philadelphia), in a session devoted to touring entitled "Horses, a Wagon, and Apparel New-Bought," with Roslyn Knutson, J. A. B. Somerset, Sally-Beth MacLean, William Ingram, Paul Werstine, and Laurie Maguire. Early results of the REED project indicate that some tour stops may have been lengthy enough for players to reconstruct a play they might not have brought with them, in response to a special request. Or Q may have been designed as a reading rather than a playing text even though stage directions in Q *Henry V* are almost always confined to simple entrances and exits: detailed stage directions like those in certain other "bad" quartos, such as Q1 *Hamlet*, are missing from Q *Henry V*. Peter Blayney ("Shakespeare's Fight with *What* Pirates?" The Folger Institute, May 11, 1987) drew attention to Moseley's advertisement for the Beaumont and Fletcher Folio (1647), which implies that private transcripts reconstructed by actors may have been common: "When these Comedies and Tragedies were presented on the stage, the actors omitted some scenes and passages (with the author's consent) as occasion led them; and when private friends desired a copy, they then (and justly too) transcribed what they acted." It is possible that another person later adapted and abridged the reconstruction, but I believe, as the Moseley quotation implies, that experienced actors could have made the changes without the help of a playwright/adapter or "hack poet."

3. I have described this analysis in more detail in "Shakespeare on a Spreadsheet: Design for a New Analysis of the "Bad" Quartos," SAA Research Seminar "Using the Com-

many scholars, for the parts of certain characters seem to correspond more closely to F than others; the analysis is designed to isolate the lines with the highest correlation in the two versions and to identify both the speakers and the characters whose actors witnessed these closely parallel lines.

To implement the analysis, I first underlined each matching word in corresponding segments of my handmade parallel text, then marked each line with a code reflecting the degree of correlation. If every word in the line appears in the parallel segment of the other text (ignoring word order, lineation, and spelling), I marked the line "A" (for all). If more than half of the words correlate, the code is "M" (for most); if half or fewer words match, I marked the line "S" (for some). Lines that paraphrase the content of a parallel segment—but contain no matching words—were marked "P" (for paraphrase), and lines with no correlation were marked "X". Next, using computer typescripts of Q and F, I transferred the correlation codes from my parallel text to the computer texts. I also marked each line with codes to identify the speakers and the characters on stage.[4]

For each of the two texts, I used a database program to isolate and count the lines that each character speaks and the lines his or her actor witnesses while on stage. In addition, I determined the degree of correlation between the two texts for these spoken and witnessed lines, using the five correlation categories, A through X. Tables A, B, C, and D in the appendix record this basic information. Then I organized the data with the help of a spreadsheet program.[5]

Tables A and B in the appendix, which record the number of lines of each character in various correlation categories, show that actors playing 26 of the 51 roles are very unlikely candidates for a reporter. Even if a reporter

---

puter in Shakespeare Studies," April 1990. See also my "Origins and Agents of Q1 *Hamlet*," in *The "Hamlet" First Published (Q1, 1603)*, Thomas Clayton, ed. (U. of Delaware Pr., forthcoming).

4. The computer typescript of the Folio is from the Oxford University Computing Service, 13 Banbury Road, Oxford OX2 6NN; most of the quartos are also available from Oxford, though I needed to type Q *Henry V* myself. Since I returned to the photocopies of the facsimiles for detailed analysis of the text, any undetected errors in individual lines of the typescripts did not affect my analysis. It was sometimes difficult to decide whether to mark a line with P or X; similarly, the difference of a single word could determine whether a line would be marked P or S, S or M, or even M or A. But because of the large number of lines, the system allowed a good measure of the degree of correlation for various speakers and the lines they witnessed. Lines spoken by a different character in each version were also marked to identify reattributions discussed in Section 2; stage directions were coded as well, for retrieval by the database program.

5. Discrepancies between Tables A and B are the result of differences in lineation in the two texts, making the number of lines in the FA category of Table A, for example, different from those in the QA category of Table B. The database program I used is the textbase component of Nota Bene, version 3.0, from Dragonfly Software. The program allows me to isolate and examine any combination of coded lines, including, for example, lines in the "A" category of either text spoken by Exeter when Gower is on stage. The spreadsheet I used is Microsoft Excel, version 2.1 for IBM compatibles, essentially a sophisticated calculator.

had doubled in some of these roles, there is often too little information to draw any conclusions about his part in a possible reconstruction. Beaumont, Berri, and the Second French Ambassador have no lines in either version, making them the first to be eliminated. Clarence, Gebon, and the Lord have no lines in F; most of the lines spoken by them in Q are spoken by other characters in F, making them equally unlikely reporters. The Chorus, Ely, Westmorland, Isabel, MacMorris, Grandpre, Jamy, Bedford, Britanny, Rambures, Erpingham, and the English Herald have no lines in the Quarto version, though some lines have been reassigned. Court has one line in Q, only 2 in F, while the French Messenger and Salisbury each speak only 3 lines in Q (7 and 9 lines respectively in F); parallels between the lines in F and Q for each are not striking. The roles of the Dauphin, Bourbon, and Burgundy are radically different in Q, eliminating them as likely reporters. The Dauphin's role is reduced from 117 lines in F to 22 in Q; Bourbon is assigned some of these lines, as his role expands from 9 in F to 29 in Q. Burgundy's role is trimmed from 68 lines in F to only 4 in the Quarto. Warwick's and Gloucester's much smaller parts are also altered in Q: Warwick has 1 line in F, a line that does not appear in Q, but is reassigned 7 lines spoken by others in the Folio; Gloucester's part includes 5 lines in F, 11 in Q, again reassigned from the roles of other English lords in F. Thus these 26 unlikely candidates have been eliminated as possible reporters.

Table 1 shows the percentage of lines in the Folio with a high correlation to parallel lines in Q, for lines spoken and witnessed by the remaining 25 characters. We would expect that a reporter—if one existed for Q *Henry V* —would have remembered his own lines more accurately than those he witnessed, for it seems likely that an actor would recall his own part more fully than the words of others on stage with him. Using this criterion, I have eliminated as possible reporters the 14 characters listed toward the bottom of Table 1, for in each case the lines witnessed in the two texts are more closely parallel than those spoken by their actors. The only possible exception among this group may be Mistress Quickly, for the difference in correlation between spoken and witnessed lines is very slight. I believe her actor is an unlikely reporter, however, because of the relatively low proportion of lines in the "A" category and because her spoken lines are not more accurately rendered than those her actor witnessed.

In addition to remembering his own lines more fully than those he witnessed, we would expect a likely reporter to recall his own role with an accuracy greater than the average, shown near the center of Table 1. Orleans is at the median whereas Alice and Kate fall below both median and mean (average), making their actors unlikely reporters.

This leaves eight possible reporters out of the 51 characters: Exeter, Gower, Pistol, Nym, Scrope, the Governor of Harfleur, York, and Williams. I believe Williams is an unlikely reporter, for the proportion of his lines in the "A" category is considerably below the mean. York has only two spoken lines and witnesses only three others in F; because of the small amount of data, it is difficult to determine if his actor was a reporter, although one of

Table 1: Folio Spoken & Witnessed Lines with a High Correlation to Q
(expressed as a percentage of the character's total F lines)

	Folio spoken A + M	Folio witnessed A + M	Folio spoken A	Folio witnessed A
Exeter	84%	49%	57%	22%
Gower	61%	55%	40%	21%
Pistol	65%	55%	35%	22%
Nym	67%	53%	22%	20%
Scrope	100%	55%	62%	28%
Governor	100%	0%	57%	0%
York	100%	67%	50%	33%
Williams	43%	39%	11%	13%
MEAN (AVERAGE)	39%	39%	17%	17%
MEDIAN	33%	33%	10%	10%
Orleans	33%	25%	22%	9%
Alice	30%	13%	19%	4%
Kate	25%	22%	15%	7%
- - - - - - -	- - - - - - -	- - - - - - -	- - - - - - -	- - - - - - -
Quickly	59%	60%	22%	24%
French Amb.	65%	88%	24%	43%
Grey	50%	59%	8%	32%
Fluellen	48%	60%	10%	31%
Canterbury	45%	59%	24%	26%
Henry	42%	48%	19%	22%
Cambridge	40%	60%	27%	31%
Montjoy	33%	75%	13%	40%
Boy	29%	43%	12%	17%
Constable	28%	35%	10%	18%
Bardolph	27%	62%	10%	22%
French Soldier	20%	60%	0%	30%
Bates	18%	21%	6%	3%
Charles	14%	31%	2%	16%

the reporters certainly could have doubled as York. The case for the Governor of Harfleur is similar, for though his 7 lines in F are closely parallel to his role in Q, his actor witnesses no lines in the Quarto; one of the reporters could easily have doubled as the Governor, but without lines witnessed by this character in Q, there is too little evidence to evaluate.

Five characters, then, remain as major candidates for reporter—Exeter (obviously the most likely possibility), Gower, Pistol, Nym, and Scrope—perhaps also doubling the smaller roles of the Governor and York. Table 1 shows why Exeter is often mentioned as a likely reporter, for well over half of his spoken lines are virtually identical in the two versions, while 84% are closely parallel.[6] Lines spoken by the other likely reporters show less correspondence,

6. H. T. Price in *The Text of "Henry V"* (1920) first proposed that the actors playing Exeter, Gower, and the Governor of Harfleur were in part responsible for Q. He believed that they supplied their parts to a scribe in the audience who used shorthand to record the

though still considerably more than either the median or the mean. Equally important, the proportion of closely parallel lines witnessed by all five is also well above average, a key indication that Q did not begin simply as a transcript of these players' parts.

No single actor could have played all five of these roles in *Henry V*: although some doubling is certainly possible, each of the five appears with at least one of the others. Exeter could double Pistol or Nym, but this seems unlikely (apart from casting difficulties), because Exeter's scenes are generally more accurately rendered in Q than Pistol's and Nym's. Gower could double both Nym and Scrope; Pistol could also double Scrope, and any but Exeter could double the Governor and York. Three actors, then, could have reconstructed the Quarto: the actor playing Exeter, along with the actors playing Pistol and Gower, doubling Nym, Scrope and possibly the Governor and York. Thus Table 1, based on a quantitative analysis of possible candidates, verifies the widely-held impression that Exeter, along with one or two others, was responsible for reconstructing *Henry V* from his memory of performances, a significant confirmation of the memorial-reconstruction theory. This result is particularly important in light of the recent healthy skepticism of Steven Urkowitz and Paul Werstine, among others, concerning the validity of the theory of memorial reconstruction.[7]

Just as significantly, Table 1 indicates that the version the reporters apparently knew was a script linked to the Folio rather than to an intermediate abridgment. The proportion of closely parallel lines spoken by Exeter, Scrope, and the Governor suggests that the reporters attempted to reconstruct a version similar to the Folio, apparently abridging sections of it at the same time or shortly thereafter. Exeter's part in Q retains some 84% of his Folio lines with considerable accuracy, as noted above, while all 13 of Scrope's Folio lines and all seven of the Governor's reappear with equal accuracy. The Quarto, with 1629 spoken lines, includes only 50% as many lines as does the Folio (3253 spoken lines). If the reporters had known only an abridgment, their lines presumably would have been cut in such an abridgment in roughly the same proportion as the rest of the play. But Exeter's crucial part in particular is remarkably full as well as unusually accurate, a key indication that he was working from his memory of a longer, Folio-linked script. Though the Quarto version has obviously been abridged, probably deliberately, Table 1 presents

---

rest of the play. G. I. Duthie's *Elizabethan Shorthand* (1949) laid to rest the shorthand theory. Duthie supported the view that actors playing Exeter and Gower reconstructed the play from memory in "The Quarto of Shakespeare's *Henry V*," *Papers Mainly Shakespearean* (1964), pp. 106–130; see also Alfred Hart's *Stolne and Surreptitious Copies* (1942); J. H. Walter's Arden edition of *Henry V* (1954), p. xxxv; Gary Taylor's 1982 edition, pp. 22–23, and especially Taylor's "Corruption and Authority in the Bad Quarto," in *Three Studies* (1979), pp. 129–142.

7. See, for example, Urkowitz's "Good News About 'Bad' Quartos," in Maurice Charney, ed., *"Bad" Shakespeare* (1988), pp. 189–206; and Werstine's "Narratives About Printed Shakespearean Texts: 'Foul Papers' and 'Bad' Quartos," *Shakespeare Quarterly*, 41 (1990), 65–86. I was equally skeptical concerning memorial reconstruction before I completed my analysis.

significant new evidence that the reporters began with performances directly related to the Folio version rather than to a lost intermediate abridgment.[8]

SECTION 2: Reattributions

Perhaps the strongest indication of deliberate adaptation in the Quarto is the remarkable number of reattributed lines, a very unusual feature of Q *Henry V*.[9] In the Quarto, some 80 lines have speech headings different from the parallel lines in the Folio—not including 21 lines in 4.8 mistakenly assigned to Exeter in Q. Many of these 80 lines reattributed in Q may have been intentional alterations, made by the reporter/adapters when they reconstructed the text.

However the assignment of the 21 lines in 4.8 to Exeter rather than Henry is an obvious error in Q rather than a deliberate reattribution. In Q, the reading of the list of the dead at Agincourt is assigned to Exeter, as a continuation of his four lines that seem to begin a reading of the list. But the sequence beginning "This note doth tell me" (F3r, TLN 2799) must be Henry's, as F indicates, for the next speech in both versions belongs to Exeter.[10] The Quarto includes a double speech heading for Pistol in 4.1

8. Such an abridgment is not impossible, however; my preliminary studies of Q1 *Romeo* and the *Contention* suggest that these two early quartos may have been reconstructed from intermediate abridgments of scripts linked to the familiar texts.

9. The earliest scholar to suggest that Q had its origin as a stage adaptation or abridgment was P. A. Daniel; see his introduction to Brinsley Nicholson's edition, *"King Henry V": Parallel Texts of the 1600 Quarto and 1623 Folio* (1877), pp. x–xii. Daniel believed that the Quarto may have been "vamped up from notes taken during the performance," presumably of an abridged version. Barbara Damon Simison ("Stage Directions: A Test for the Playhouse Origin of the First Quarto of *Henry V*," *Philological Quarterly*, 11 [1932], 39–56) suggested that Q was derived from the promptbook of a theatrical abridgment. Alfred Hart (1942) also saw deliberate abridgment as a factor (along with memorial reconstruction) in Q's origin; Hart concluded that each of the "bad" quartos was a "garbled abridgement of an acting version made officially by the play adapter of the company from Shakespeare's manuscript" (p. 437). Greg noted in 1955 that Q "is certainly an abridgement," but found that whether the report or the abridgment came first was "not immediately apparent," though he favored the view of Q as a shortened report rather than the report of an abridgment; see *The Shakespeare First Folio*, p. 282. Duthie (1964, p. 124) concluded that actor-reporters apparently reconstructed the Folio version, "and that their manuscript was probably abridged after they had originally written it out." Gerda Okerlund ("The Quarto Version of 'Henry V' as a Stage Adaptation," *PMLA*, 49 [1934], 810–834) had been more emphatic in her view of Q as a deliberate adaptation. Like W. J. Lawrence ("The Secret of the Bad Quartos," *Criterion*, 10 [1931], 447–461) and Hardin Craig ("The Relation of the First Quarto Version to the First Folio Version of Shakespeare's *Henry V*," *Philological Quarterly*, 6 [1927], 225–234), Okerland rejected the theory of memorial reconstruction in favor of deliberate adaptation, a view also shared by Robert E. Burkhart, *Shakespeare's Bad Quartos* (1975), pp. 70–74; Burkhart believed that the "bad" quartos were authorized abridgments for use by Shakespeare's company in the provinces. The most recent supporter of deliberate abridgment is Gary Taylor, especially in his *Three Studies* (1979). Taylor argues that Q is a memorial reconstruction of an abridged performance version, a view shared by many. J. H. Walter (1954, p. xxxv), for example, commented, "the Q version may well be based on a cut form of the play used by the company for a reduced cast on tour in the provinces."

10. Act and scene numbers correspond to traditional divisions. F through-line numbers correspond to Charlton Hinman's edition of *The First Folio of Shakespeare* (1968). Signa-

(D3v); the second heading for Exeter's "Tis wonderful" could be a similar error. Instead, it seems more likely because of the sense of the passage (with its emphasis on God's hand in the English victory), as well as F's speech heading, that the omission of the speech heading to begin Henry's speech in Q is the error. In two other cases Q omits speech headings, once in 1.2 (A2v) when the Bishop's heading at the top of the page is missing (but present as a catchword on the previous page), once in 4.3 (E2v) when Henry's speech heading is similarly missing from the top of the page, but present in the catchword. In 4.8, however, the omission occurs near the bottom of the page, with no catchword to serve as a correction.

The remaining 80 reassigned lines in Q *Henry V* are not obvious errors (like the misattribution in 4.8); some are significant indications of purposeful adaptation in the Quarto. The most obvious and important include the reassignment of all of the Dauphin's lines in the French nobles' scenes at Agincourt. Table 2 lists the reattributions in scenes involving the French nobles.

Table 2: Reattributions in French Nobles' Scenes

Act & scene	Folio TLN	Quarto Sig. #	Description
2.4	956–7	C1v	F, French Messenger; Q, Constable
2.4	1039	C1r	F, Exeter; Q, French King
3.5	1384–5, 1388	C3v–4r	F, Dauphin; Q, Constable
3.5	1389–93	C4r	F, Brittany; Q, Bourbon
3.7	1632–3, 1645–7	D2v	F, Dauphin; Q, Bourbon
3.7	1667	D2v	F, Orleans; Q, Constable
3.7	1669–70	D2v	F, Dauphin; Q, Bourbon
3.7	1687–8, 1692	D2v	F, Dauphin; Q, Bourbon
3.7	1706–7	D2v	F, Dauphin; Q, Bourbon
3.7	1711–12	D2v	F, Rambures; Q, Orleans
3.7	1715	D3r	F, Dauphin; Q, Bourbon
3.7	1716	D3r	F, Orleans; Q, Gebon
3.7	1717	D3r	F, Rambures; Q, Orleans
4.5	2459	E3r	F, Constable; Q, Gebon
4.5	2460	E3r	F, Orleans; Q, Bourbon
4.5	2461	E3r	F, Dauphin; Q, Constable
4.5	2478–80	E3r	F, Orleans; Q, Constable
4.5	2482	E3r	F, Bourbon; Q, Constable

The Quarto omits one of the French nobles' scenes (4.2, except for the final 2 lines retained for the end of 3.7, as discussed in detail below). In 3.7, in which the nobles banter about mistresses and horses, the Dauphin is replaced in Q by Bourbon, a change consistent with his father's order in 3.5 that the Dauphin stay in Rouen. Several critics have suggested other theories for this alteration, but whatever the reason, it seems a deliberate, systematic change, accounting for 18 of Q's 80 re-attributed lines.[11]

---

ture numbers for Q are from facsimiles in Michael Allen and Kenneth Muir's *Shakespeare's Plays in Quarto* (1981).

11. See especially Taylor (1982), pp. 24–26.

Three of the Dauphin's other Folio lines are assigned to the Constable in 3.5, significantly reducing the Dauphin's part in his final appearance in Q. The Constable in Q also delivers the two lines spoken by the French Messenger in F's 2.4 (eliminating a speaking role in Q), two of Orleans's lines in 3.7, and five additional lines in 4.5, one spoken in F by the Dauphin, three by Orleans, and one by Bourbon. Some of these changes may have been intentional, as the Constable's role is significantly altered in Q, but others were probably inadvertent, for one of the Constable's Folio lines in 4.5 (TLN 1167) is given to Gebon in Q. This is especially interesting because "Gebon" —perhaps the name of an actor—speaks no lines in F, two in the Quarto.[12] In another change, Q assigns four of Brittany's (Folio) lines to Bourbon in 3.5, where he appears in F but has no lines. This change introduces Bourbon, preparing the audience for his expanded role in Q, and eliminates one speaking part, Brittany's; the lines are consistent with Bourbon's usual character in the Quarto, boastful, bantering, and colloquial.

One of the reassignments in 2.4 is an intriguing anomaly: in this scene, Q moves forward a line spoken by Exeter in the Folio, TLN 1039, and attributes it to the French king, in a segment parallel to TLN 899–901.[13] In F, Exeter warns the French that Henry "is footed in this Land already" (TLN 1039), in a four-line passage omitted from Q at the end of the scene. In the Quarto, the line appears instead at the beginning of the scene, as part of the French king's first speech: "he is footed on this land alreadie" (C1r). Because such anticipations are extremely rare in Q *Henry V*, and because this case involves one of Exeter's lines, I believe it was an intentional change, although we can only speculate about the reporter/adapter's reasons. Perhaps the actor who played Exeter salvaged a line from an omitted section to fill out a scene he remembered with difficulty. In any case the reattributed and moved line is another indication that the reporters were familiar with a version related to the Folio rather than an intermediate abridgment, for the transferred line is part of a neat cut of four lines not otherwise present in Q.

Other reassignments—none of them altering the impact of the scenes— include three lines in 3.7 (one changed from Orleans to Gebon, two from Rambures to Orleans) and one line in 4.5 (changed from Orleans to Bourbon). Speech headings in 4.5 in particular seem almost random in both texts, as the French lords move from despair to a show of bravery. The Constable, for example, is as miserable as any, in contrast to his earlier courage, while Bourbon (in F the Dauphin) is uncharacteristically bold, with his call to arms and its graphic reference to rape. Scene 4.5 calls into question the view that either text—especially Q—is consistent in its characterization of the individual French lords, casting a shadow on Taylor's decision to use Q's substitution of Bourbon for the Dauphin in both of his Oxford editions.

12. P. A. Daniel (1877, pp. xiii–ix) first suggested that Gebon might be the name of an actor; E. K. Chambers also mentioned this possibility in *William Shakespeare* (1930), I, 392.

13. Taylor (1979, pp. 137–138) pointed out this reattribution and transposition; Duthie (1964, pp. 110–111) had also discussed it.

In all, the scenes involving the French nobles account for 40 of the 80 lines reattributed in the Quarto. Surprisingly, the group of scenes with the next highest number of reassigned lines—29—includes the scenes with the English nobles, as shown in Table 3.

Table 3: Reattributions in the English Nobles' Scenes

Act & scene	Folio TLN	Quarto Sig. #	Description
1.2	148	A2r	F, Westmorland; Q, Exeter
1.2	313–19	A3v	F, Ely; Q, Lord
1.2	628	B2v	F, Bedford; Q, Gloucester
2.2	635–8	B2v	F, Exeter; Q, Gloucester
4.3	2243	E1v	F, Westmorland; Q, Warwick
4.3	2253–4	E1v	F, Bedford; Q, Clarence
4.3	2255	E1v	F, Exeter; Q, Clarence
4.3	2259–61	E1v	F, Westmorland; Q, Warwick
4.3	2312–13	E2r	F, Salisbury; Q, Gloucester
4.3	2316	E2r	F, Westmorland; Q, Warwick
4.3	2319–20	E2r	F, Westmorland; Q, Warwick
4.7	2650	F1v	F, Exeter; Q, Fluellen
5.2	3086	G1r	F, Isabel; Q, French King
5.2	3323–4	G3v	F, Westmorland; Q, French King

Because Exeter witnessed all of these reassigned lines—and spoke a few of them himself—some of Table 3's reattributions may have been deliberate. The largest block, the 7 lines spoken by Ely in the Folio (1.2, TLN 313–319) and assigned to a Lord in Q (A3v), eliminates a speaking part, if the Lord's lines are spoken by, say, Gloucester or Warwick.[14] Other reassignments in Q systematically eliminate Westmorland's role (19 lines in F). Nine of his lines are omitted entirely in Q, the other 10 reattributed: Exeter takes one (TLN 148), while Warwick replaces Westmorland in 4.3, where 7 of these lines appear as Warwick's 6 lines. One reason for this change may be that Warwick, not Westmorland, is included in Henry's brief list of heroic soldiers in both versions (TLN 2296–98, E2r). But this list in F also includes Talbot, who does not appear in the play, and omits Erpingham (as does the list in Q), although Erpingham is mentioned in F's entry direction for 4.3. Q alters the list to include York instead of Talbot, but omits Salisbury, though Salisbury is included in Q's stage direction (E2r). In F Henry addresses Westmorland twice by name (TLN 2263 and 2278); Q alters the first direct address to Warwick (E1v), an indication that the change from Westmorland to Warwick was deliberate, but omits the second. Westmorland's last 2 lines, TLN 3323–24, are paraphrased by the French king in Q. Though the evidence is mixed, I think it favors deliberate substitution of Warwick for Westmorland in the Quarto.[15]

14. Taylor (1982, p. 108), believing that Q has it right, assigns the lines to "A Lord" in his editions, since Ely's function is to second Canterbury, not contradict him; he sees Exeter as one of the two reporters, responsible for the accuracy of this scene and unlikely to forget the speaker here, since Exeter takes up his point in the next speech.
15. Taylor uses Q's Warwick throughout this scene in his editions.

Bedford is also eliminated from Q as a speaking role. Six of his 9 Folio lines are cut in Q, while his other 3 lines are divided between Gloucester (TLN 628, which is set in Q as two lines) and Clarence (TLN 2253–54). But not all of the reattributions in these scenes eliminate speaking roles: Clarence has no lines in F but 3 in the Quarto, including two of Bedford's lines just mentioned and one of Exeter's (TLN 2255), which precedes these lines in the Quarto version. Other reattributions include 4 lines transferred from Exeter to Gloucester and two from Salisbury to Gloucester. Gloucester's role may have been deliberately expanded, as he has 5 lines in the Folio, 11 in Q—and 4 of these are spoken by Exeter in F. In 4.7 Fluellen is reassigned another of Exeter's lines. This seems almost certainly intentional, for the line is altered to fit Fluellen's tone in Q: in F, Exeter tells Williams, "Souldier, you must come to the King" (TLN 2650), while in Q Fluellen, more roughly, says, "You fellow come to the king" (F1v).[16] One other reattribution in scenes involving the English nobles paraphrases Isabel's sentiment in 5.2 (TLN 3086) in one of the French king's speeches, as part of Q's systematic elimination of lines by Isabel.

Table 4: Other Reattributions

Act & scene	Folio TLN	Quarto Sig. #	Description
2.1	532	B1v	F, Bardolph; Q, Nym
2.1	543	B1v	F, Bardolph; Q, Quickly
2.3	828	B4v	F, Pistol; Q, Bardolph
2.3	850	B4v	F, Bardolph; Q, Boy
2.3	856–7	B4v	F, Boy; Q, Nym
3.2	1139–40	C2v	F, Pistol; Q, Nym
3.4	1131	C3v	F, Alice; Q, Katherine
4.1	2034–5	D4v	F, Williams; Q, Bates
4.1	2056	E1r	F, Williams; Q, Henry
4.1	2057–8, 2066	E1r	F, Henry; Q, Williams

Of the remaining 13 lines reassigned in Q, shown in Table 4, only 3 are especially significant. In the Folio (4.1, TLN 2056–58, 2066), Williams asks Henry how their quarrel should be renewed at a more appropriate time; Henry suggests the exchange of gloves. But in Q, the King asks, "How shall I know thee?" to which Williams throws down his glove and suggests the challenge, a marked difference. In the Quarto version, Henry seems more detached from the quarrel than he does in F, partly because of the omission of his line "I embrace it [the quarrel]" as well as other omissions. Henry's aloofness in Q is perhaps consistent with his true identity; the challenge seems rather childish, more in keeping with Prince Hal's behavior than King Henry's. Even so, the device of the glove is appropriate for a nobleman; coming from Williams it almost parodies the chivalric convention. Thus it is

16. Duthie (1964, p. 119) also noted the reattribution of some of Exeter's F lines and suggested that the alterations "may well reflect, not inaccurate reporting, but rather a rearrangement made in the course of an abridgement."

difficult to judge if the change was deliberate, especially since none of the likely reporters takes part in this scene.

Earlier in 4.1, Bates delivers a sentiment assigned to Williams in F (TLN 2034–35), a rather insignificant change. Equally indifferent reattributions include one of Alice's lines (TLN 1331) to Kate and the reassignment of 8 lines in the two Eastcheap scenes. Though some of these might have been intentional, the differences do not affect either the casting or the impact of the scenes.

Of the 80 lines attributed to different characters in the two versions, most seem to be deliberate changes, especially those involving Exeter's lines, the Dauphin-Bourbon substitution, and those that reduce the number of speaking roles (such as Westmorland's). Though some of the reattributions are indifferent, as a few lines seem assigned almost at random in the scenes with the French and even the English nobles, and others are difficult to judge, like the lines concerning the exchange of gloves, the majority of the reattributions support the view that the reporters deliberately altered certain roles as they reconstructed *Henry V*.

SECTION 3: Omissions and Alterations

Other indications of intentional adaptation include alterations in plot structure and a series of arguably intentional omissions that shape the Quarto as well as simply abridging it.

Table 5: Scene by Scene Comparison of Q and F

Q scene	Q signature	F Act, Sc., TLN	Capsule description
		(1.0, 1–35)	(Chorus)
		(1.1, 36–142)	(Canturbury & Ely conference)
1	A2r–B1r	1.2, 143–461	Court; decision re: French war
		(2.0, 462–504)	(Chorus)
2	B1r–B2v	2.1, 505–626	Pistol, etc.; Falstaff's illness
3	B2v–B4r	2.2, 627–822	Henry with three traitors
4	B4v–C1r	2.3, 824–884	Pistol, etc; Falstaff's death
5	C1r–C2v	2.4, 885–1042	French nobles; Exeter as messenger
		(3.0, 1043–1080)	(Chorus)
		(3.1, 1081–1118)	("Once more unto the Breach")
6	C2v–C3r	3.2, 1119–1258	Pistol, etc.; Fluellen, Gower (F only: Jamy & MacMorris)
7	C3r	3.3, 1259–1319	Henry at gates of Harfleur
8	C3r–C3v	3.4, 1320–1377	French lesson
9	C3v–C4r	3.5, 1378–1448	French nobles; Dauphin to stay at Rouen
10	C4r–D2v	3.6, 1449–1623	Gower, Fluellen, Pistol; Henry, Montjoy
11	D2v–D3r	3.7, 1624–1787	French nobles; Bourbon, not Dauphin in Q
		(4.0, 1788–1843)	(Chorus)
12	D3v–E1v	4.1, 1844–2164	Henry & soldiers on eve of Agincourt

		(4.2, 2165–2236)	(French nobles; 2 lines only in Q 3.7/sc. 11
13	E1v–E3r	4.3, 2237–2383	English prepare for Agincourt
14	E3r	4.5, 2457–2482	French nobles near defeat
15	E3v	4.4, 2385–2456	Pistol and French soldier, Boy
16	E3v–E4r	4.6, 2483–2523	Exeter re. end of battle; Henry orders prisoners killed
17	E4v–F2v	4.7, 2524–2712	Gower, Fluellen; Henry, others; Montjoy's surrender for French
18	F2v–F3v	4.8, 2713–2848	Conclusion of glove challenge; list of dead
		(5.0, 2849–2896)	(Chorus)
19	F3v–F4v	5.1, 2897–2983	Gower, Fluellen, Pistol: leek
20	F4v–G4r	5.2, 2984–3382	English & French courts; wooing scene (F only: epilogue)

Table 5 summarizes major differences in plot structure between Q and F. As indicated in Table 5, three scenes are missing from Q (along with the Choruses): 1.1 (over 100 of Canturbury's and Ely's lines), 3.1 (Henry's 35-line "Once more unto the Breach"), and 4.2 (around 70 lines spoken by the French nobles.)[17]

Only two lines remain from the end of 4.2, which were moved to the end of Q's parallel to 3.7. Following the messenger's warning in 3.7 that the English are very close to the French camp (1500 paces in F, only 100 paces in Q), the Quarto scene ends quickly with Constable's "Come, come away. / The Sun is hie, and we weare out the day" (D3r). The Folio's 3.7 ends with Orleans's "It is now two a Clock: but let me see, by ten / Wee shall haue each a hundred English men" (TLN 1786–87). At first glance the lines in Q may appear to be a minor substitution like those common in all of the "bad" quartos, for, as noted, a few lines earlier Q had substituted 100 paces for 1500. But in fact these two lines appear at the end of 4.2 in the Folio (TLN 2235–36), spoken by the Constable—the only lines of this scene retained by the Quarto version. Presence of this tiny bit from an omitted scene is a significant piece of evidence that the reporters knew a script linked to the Folio rather than an intermediate lost abridgment.[18]

Unfortunately, moving these lines forward from the later French nobles' scene seems to make the sun rise at midnight in Q's 3.7, which immediately precedes Henry's nocturnal visits to his soldiers in (Q's) 4.1.[19] At the end of 4.1 the reporter/adapters introduced another apparent error—one that, like the transposition, again links Q to the version preserved in the Folio. In a

17. Though F's 4.2 has no parallel in Q, Taylor, in both of his editions, assigns the Dauphin's lines to Bourbon in 4.2, as in Q's 3.7 and 4.5.

18. Taylor (1979, pp. 145–148) noted the transposition of the final two lines of 4.2; he acknowledged, "the adapter must have had access to a text of the full version," but made "little use of it."

19. P. A. Daniels (1877, p. xii) remarked on this transposition, seeing the couplet as evidence that the two scenes were deliberately combined by an adapter who failed to notice his blunder, which "brought in the sun at midnight!" Greg found Daniel's view "outrageously improbable" and credited the alteration wholly to the "dull reporter"; see *Shakespeare's "Merry Wives of Windsor"* (1910), p. xix.

skillful transition that masks the removal of 4.2 from the Quarto and pre-
pares for 4.3, in which the English make their final preparations for Agincourt, Gloucester enters (E1v, as in 4.1, TLN 2159) just after Henry's prayer
on the eve of battle, to remind the King that his soldiers are awaiting him.
However some 15 lines earlier, between the soldiers' exit and Henry's solitary
prayer, Q inserts "Enter the King, Gloster, Epingam, and Attendants" (E1r).
Erpingham enters in F for a brief exchange with Henry before the prayer
(4.1, TLN 2135), but the Quarto version eliminates this conversation—and all
the rest of Erpingham's role. The King of course is already on stage in Q,
Gloucester has a second entrance in the Quarto after the prayer, as noted,
and the attendants enter, also with an appropriate stage direction in Q, a
few lines after Gloucester. Except for the mention of Erpingham, this stage
direction could be merely a reporter's error, anticipating the entrance of
Henry's nobles in 4.3. But because Erpingham has no role in Q, this erroneous stage direction provides an important clue that the reporters knew a
longer, Folio-linked version rather than an intermediate abridgment preceding the Quarto.[20]

The Quarto's Act 4 also switches the order of F's 4.4 and 4.5, for in Q the
scene with the four defeated French lords occurs before Pistol's scene with
his French prisoner. The Q reversal of 4.4 and 4.5 may not have been intentional; either order could be effectively staged. At the end of Q's 4.4, however, Pistol leaves the stage, only to return immediately in 4.6, along with
Henry and his train. This quick reentry is another clue that the reporters
were adapting a version linked to the Folio, for such reentries are exceptional
in Shakespeare's scripts.[21] In the Folio version staging, Pistol may also have
entered with Henry and his train, as his presence in Q's 4.6 suggests. But only
Q mentions him by name—and even gives him the last word, "Couple gorge,"
a transposition from 2.1 (B2r, TLN 573) and certainly a clever addition here.[22]

Table 6 charts other possible evidence of purposeful abridgment as well
as additional evidence of memorial reconstruction. This table shows the relative number of lines in Q and F of each of the key characters. For example,
Henry speaks 53% as many lines in Q as he does in F, just above average
(50%). But Exeter speaks 85% as many lines in the Quarto as in the Folio,
a key indication that the actor playing Exeter knew his complete Folio-linked
role rather than an abridgment of it. Parts of the other likely reporters, Pistol
(77%) and Gower (67%), are also represented more fully than the average,
although some of these lines, as Table 1 indicated, do not correspond as

---

20. Duthie (1964, pp. 126–129) also discussed this stage direction, coming to a similar
conclusion.

21. For a discussion of the "law of reentry" that apparently governed entrances and
exits, see Irwin Smith, "Their Exits and Reentrances," *Shakespeare Quarterly*, 18 (1967),
7–16; Smith dismisses sixteen possible reentries (out of 750 scenes in Shakespeare's plays).
Andrew Gurr discusses the only likely reentry, occurring in *The Tempest*, as evidence of act
divisions in that play; see "*The Tempest*'s Tempest at Blackfriars," *Shakespeare Survey*, 41
(1989), 93.

22. Taylor discussed this Q addition (1982, pp. 65–66). He includes Pistol's line in both
of his editions.

Table 6: Comparison of the Number of Q to F Lines by Role
(expressed as a percentage of Q to F)

Scrope	100%	Alice	59%
Governor	100%	Kate	53%
York	100%	Henry	53%
Nym	87%	AVERAGE	50%
Exeter	85%	Montjoy	48%
Quickly	85%	Canterbury	48%
French Amb.	82%	Cambridge	47%
Pistol	77%	French Soldier	47%
Fluellen	72%	Constable	45%
Bates	71%	Grey	42%
Gower	67%	Boy	43%
Bardolph	67%	Charles	34%
Williams	64%	Orleans	31%

closely in Q and F as do Exeter's; the case is similar for Nym. Scrope's, the Governor's, and York's Folio-version roles—as Table 1 confirms—are reproduced almost exactly in Q. Table 6 shows Fluellen's role as unusually complete, because of his presence on stage with one or more of the reporters; Hostess Quickly, Bardolph, and the French Ambassador also habitually appear with at least one of the likely reporters. Bates's part at first seems unusually full, but a look at Tables A and B in the appendix reveals that though he speaks twelve lines in Q and seventeen in F, his lines in the two versions are quite different. Thus Table 6 lends further support to the conclusion that three actors—playing Exeter, Pistol, and Gower (doubling Nym, Scrope and possibly the Governor and York)—reconstructed lines from a Folio-linked script to fashion Q.

Table 6, along with Tables A and B in the appendix, also contributes evidence to the view that the reporters deliberately abridged a version related to the Folio as they reconstructed it, for Table 6, Table A, and Table B all indicate potentially intentional omissions from F.

The Chorus—223 lines, 7% of the Folio—is the most obvious omission. Because of other evidence that the reporter/abridgers were working from performances linked to the Folio, I believe this was an intentional cut: three actors experienced enough to recall so much of their own parts—and the parts of others—would not simply forget so important a role as the Chorus. Even if the Chorus's part was simply read at performances rather than memorized by one of the players, the reporters would still have heard these lines delivered, as they did other lines in the play. It is possible, as some have suggested, that the Choruses were added to the text underlying F after the publication of the Quarto in 1600.[23] In one case, however, the omission of a

23. G. P. Jones argued that the Choruses may have been designed for court performances, while a shorter version—like Q, without choruses—was meant for the Globe; see " 'Henry V': The Chorus and the Audience," *Shakespeare Survey*, 31 (1978), 93–104. For other views see esp. W. D. Smith, "The *Henry V* Choruses in the First Folio," *Journal of English and Germanic Philology*, 53 (1954), 38–57; R. A. Law, "The Choruses in *Henry the Fifth*," *University of Texas Studies in English*, 35 (1956), 11–21; Lawrence Danson, "*Henry V*: The King, Chorus, and Critics," *Shakespeare Quarterly*, 34 (1983), 27–43; and Annabel Pat-

Chorus in Q creates a minor staging difficulty, an indication that the Choruses were cut in the Quarto rather than added to the version underlying the Folio between 1600 and 1623. In both texts, 4.8 ends with Fluellen (and presumably Gower) leaving the stage with Henry and the others. Omitting the Chorus introducing Act 5, Q opens the next scene (5.1) with Fluellen and Gower immediately returning to the stage, chatting about Fluellen's leek and his planned revenge on Pistol. This quick reentry, like the one noted above for Pistol (in Q's 4.6), is so uncommon in Shakespeare's plays that it is a significant clue that the Choruses must have been omitted in Q rather than added to the Folio, perhaps in order to speed the action, eliminate a long speaking role, or remove the references to the Globe, especially if Q was designed for production outside London.

The entire sequence involving Jamy and MacMorris (almost 75 lines from 3.2) is also missing in Q, thus eliminating the need for two more actors (in addition to Fuellen) who needed to be proficient in dialects, another likely theatrical cut reasonable for a less ambitious production. Ely (33 lines), Westmorland (19 lines), Isabel (24 lines), Grandpre (18 lines), Bedford (9), Britanny (9), Rambures (9), Erpingham (8), and the English Herald (2) are also eliminated as speaking roles in Q (as shown in Table A in the appendix), though some of their lines are reassigned to others. But most of the 138 Folio lines spoken by these characters have been cut in the Quarto, allowing Q to eliminate nine more speaking roles. These nine characters have no lines in Q—but three others who do not speak in F, Clarence, Gebon, and the Lord, have a few lines in Q as a result of various cuts and rearrangements, as noted above. The net result, however, is seven fewer speaking parts in Q than F, including the elimination of the Chorus.[24]

---

terson (1988, 1989). The consensus of most editors and scholars is that the Choruses were cut in Q rather than added to F.

24. Gary Taylor (1979, esp. 94 and 106–108) devoted two of his *Three Studies* to the view that Q is a memorial reconstruction of a deliberately abridged intermediate version, not a reconstruction based on a script linked to the Folio version, supporting his view with evidence that each key difference between the two texts is related to Q's need for a reduced touring cast of 11 players. His theory works well except for one important role: Bourbon. Taylor must conclude that in order to avoid a twelfth actor, Bourbon was played by two actors, one in 2.4, where he has no lines, and a different actor in the later scenes with the French nobles, highly unusual theater practice, as Taylor himself admits. William A. Ringler, Jr. ("The Number of Actors in Shakespeare's Early Plays," in *The Seventeenth-Century Stage*, Gerald Eades Bentley, ed., 1968), found that F can be played by "14 men and 2 boys, or 12 men and 4 boys" (p. 123). Thomas L. Berger ("The Disappearance of MacMorris in Shakespeare's *Henry V*," *Renaissance Papers*, 1985/6, pp. 13–26) found evidence of cast-cutting in even the Folio version; he expanded his argument in "Casting *Henry V*," *Shakespeare Studies*, 20 (1988), 89–104. Two very recent studies cast doubt on the view that the "bad" quartos were adapted for a reduced company, presumably for touring: Scott Mc-Millin's "Casting the *Hamlet* Quartos: Longer is Smaller" in *The "Hamlet" First Published*, and Thomas J. King's study of casting requirements, both forthcoming. But without more information on the practices of companies on tour, it is difficult to tell if cast estimates of 12 players (as in McMillin and Taylor) would have precluded Q1 *Hamlet* or Q *Henry V* from use on tour.

Perhaps even more significant are omissions in scenes involving the French nobles. In what is almost certainly a deliberate change, as discussed above, the Dauphin is replaced by Bourbon in 3.7 and 4.5; the Dauphin's role is reduced from 117 lines in the Folio to 22 in the Quarto, while Bourbon's role increases from 9 in F to 29 in Q. Table 6 indicates the significant cuts in the roles of the other French nobles, including Constable (124 lines in F, 56 in Q), Charles (95 in F, 32 in Q), and Orleans (49 in F, 15 in Q); all three roles are pruned more than the average, especially those of Charles and Orleans.

Above average reductions in at least three other roles may also have been deliberate, for Exeter was present for all of these lines: Montjoy (52 in F, 25 in Q), Cambridge (15 in F, 7 in Q), and Grey (12 in F, 5 in Q). Although Montjoy's lines in 3.6 are rather fully represented in Q, some eight lines are neatly cut from his part in 4.3, another nine consecutive lines from 4.7. Similarly, the lines spoken by Cambridge and Grey in 2.2 are well represented—except for a neat cut of eleven consecutive lines (TLN 784-794), six spoken by Cambridge in F, five by Grey.

Table 6 also shows above average omissions in the roles of the Boy and the French soldier (Pistol's prisoner), some of them possibly intentional. The actor playing Pistol witnessed their Folio-version lines, but only thirty of the Boy's sixty-nine F lines and seven of the French soldier's fifteen remain in Q. Nearly all of the Boy's lines in 2.1 and 2.4 reappear in Q (though Nym paraphrases one of them), but thirteen lines are neatly cut in the beginning of his long speech in 3.2 (when Pistol is still on stage in Q), and all eleven lines in his final speech (4.4), delivered as Pistol exits. Other lines in 4.4—the scene with the French prisoner—are also cut, perhaps deliberately, including sequences of six, seven, and seven lines, shared in F by the Boy, Pistol, and the French soldier.

Nine of these lines omitted from 4.4 are in French—and a glance at the other scenes with patches of French shows that the reporter/adapters of Q were not completely fluent in French. Even so, as Table 6 indicates, the scenes with Katherine and Alice are not reduced more than the average in Q: though the grammar is sometimes odd and the spelling usually phonetic, these scenes are not cut more than the rest of the play.

But the Quarto is cut drastically, reducing the Q text to only half the length of the Folio. The FX (F Only) column of Table A in the appendix shows that 1593 of the 3253 lines spoken in F are missing in the Quarto, which includes only 55 lines unique to the shorter version (QX, Table B). Of the lines missing in Q, by far the largest number have been cut from Henry's part: 474 lines or almost 15% of the Folio.

Since Henry is almost always on stage with either Exeter, Pistol, or Gower, many of these cuts may have been deliberate. Indeed the reporters often reproduced Henry's lines with considerable accuracy (see the QA and QM entries for Henry in Table B in the appendix). As with other omissions mentioned above, many of the cuts in Henry's part are in long sequences: missing in the Quarto are 2.2, TLN 734-770 (37 lines) from Henry's speech to the three traitors; 3.1, TLN 1083–1118 (35 lines), the famous "Once more unto the Breach" sequence; 3.3, TLN 1270–1300 and 1311–18 (38 lines), his bloodiest threats to the city of Harfleur; 4.1, TLN 1845–80 (35 lines), his conversation with Gloucester, Bedford, and Erpingham; and 4.1, TLN 2079–2140 (60 lines), his soliloquy concerning the burdens of kingship and his brief chat with Erpingham. Though Exeter is not on stage for the soliloquy or the conversations with the nobles, I think even these omissions may have been deliberate, for the next lines, Henry's solitary prayer to the "God of Battles" and the brief sequence with Gloucester (4.1, TLN 2141–63), are well represented in Q (E1v–E1r).

The wooing scene is also considerably shorter in Q, although cuts in this scene may not have been intentional: no likely reporter was present, and the scene is rearranged in a way unusual for Q *Henry V*, as if the reporters had had difficulty recalling this scene. Yet in spite of its differences from F, the scene is perfectly coherent in Q and even contains a charming alteration of the F version: in Q, Henry explains in English (as in F, TLN 3164–65),

> When France is mine
> and I am yours,
> Then France is yours,
> And you are mine. (G2v)

He then goes on to repeat each phrase in French, mirroring the Folio version. But in the Quarto only, Kate translates to English after each phrase, creating a sweet and intimate exchange between the two. Following the stolen kiss (in both versions), the nobles reenter for the final sequence, very abbreviated and more domestic in Q, as the Quarto omits all of the rather crude byplay between Burgundy and Henry (as well as Isabel's formal prayer for a successful marriage); only 4 of Burgundy's 68 Folio lines remain in the Quarto's 5.2. Six lines—an unusually long addition to Q—are unique to the Quarto at the end of the scene (G4r), as Q substitutes a domestic wish for joy in the marriage of Henry and Katherine for the more political good wishes in F: characters in Q hope for love between the two spouses while those in F wish for peace between the two kingdoms. This seems to be a deliberate change, as the six-line addition to Q appears soon after a speech by Exeter that is closely parallel in the two versions.

Other possibly deliberate alterations or omissions involve lines spoken in F by the likely reporters but missing from Q. Of Exeter's 12 lines omitted in the Quarto, 8 occur in patches of two or three lines. One of these, TLN 269–271, is embedded in a twenty-one-line cut that does indeed seem deliberate, as Q omits a long sequence in 1.2 (TLN 262–282), in which Canterbury, Exeter, and Westmorland (eliminated entirely from Q) urge Henry to wage war on France.

Of the thirty-five Folio lines spoken by Pistol but omitted from Q, some twenty-three may be deliberate cuts, as they occur in passages of four or more lines omitted in the Quarto. Though in general Pistol's lines (and those his actor witnessed) are not so well reported as those of Exeter or even Gower, some of these omissions may have been deliberate.

Among Gower's twenty-three Folio lines omitted in the Quarto, twenty occur in long passages that must have been deliberate cuts. Ten of these lines appear in the seventy-five-line passage involving Jamy and MacMorris, 3.2, TLN 1183–1258. Ten other lines were apparently cut from 5.1, TLN 2965–74, in which Gower scolds Pistol for cowardice and deceit; with two likely reporters on stage, this seems an especially good example of a deliberate cut, for it seems improbable that both would simply forget all ten of these lines.

Table 7: Key Passages Missing in Q

# of lines	F Act, Sc. TLN	Capsule Description	Evidence passage pre-dates 1600?
223	(See Table 5)	Choruses	yes
102	1.1, 36–142	Canturbury & Ely conspire	
21	1.2, 262–282	Exeter, others urge French war	
37	2.2, 734–770	Henry with traitors	
35	3.1, 1083–1118	"Once more unto the Breach"	yes
75	3.2, 1183–1258	Jamy & MacMorris	yes
38	3.3, 1270–99, 1311–18	Henry before Harfleur	
40	4.1, 1845–80, 2135–40	Henry with Erpingham	yes
55	4.1, 2079–2134	Henry & burdens of kingship	
71	4.2, 2165–2236	French nobles	yes
11	4.4, 2446–2456	Boy's final soliloquy	
10	5.4, 2965–2974	Gower scolds Pistol	
82	5.2, 3022–54, 3271–319	Burgundy (and others)	
23	5.2, 2999–3007, 3080–3, 3380, 3350–59	Queen Isabel	yes

Key omissions in Q are summarized in Table 7. Some of these omissions are so neat—and so lengthy—that at first glance they may seem to support the hypothesis that an early script of the play might have been substantially expanded and revised after Q was printed, a variation of the once widely-held view that Q represents (or is a reconstruction of) an early Shakespearean draft.[25] But a closer look at the omissions listed in Table 7 shows that this theory is untenable. According to this hypothesis, certain passages missing in Q might have been added to an early script at some time between 1600 and 1623 (or at least 1616), making the Quarto a witness to a short early draft of the play. Given recent interest in the likelihood that Shakespeare, like other writers, sometimes revised his work, this hypothesis might at first seem pos-

25. The early-draft theory, supported by many until this century, has largely been discredited in favor of memorial reconstruction and theatrical abridgment. For a representative discussion of the early-draft theory, see Brinsley Nicholson, "The Relation of the Quarto to the Folio Version of *Henry V*," *Transactions. New Shakspere Society*, 1880–1882, 1, pp. 77–102. Pollard and Wilson suggested that the "bad" quartos were based on a pirate's recollections of Shakespeare's early drafts (A. W. Pollard and J. D. Wilson, "The 'Stolne and Surreptitious' Shakespearian Texts. *Henry V* [1600]," *Times Literary Supplement*, 13 March 1919, p. 134.). In his recent studies of some of the "bad" quartos, Steven Urkowitz, dismissing memorial reconstruction, has again raised the possibility that the flawed quartos might have originated as early drafts of the plays; see esp. "Good News About 'Bad' Quartos" (1988).

sible, for in several plays with two "good" versions, it is often difficult to determine if a passage was added to one or cut from the other.[26] Similarly, some of the omissions in Q *Henry V* might conceivably have been later additions to a short early version otherwise similar to F, creating an expanded Folio text after Q was published. For a generation familiar with renderings of *Henry V* as dissimilar as the adaptations by Laurence Olivier and Kenneth Branagh, proliferating versions of the play might seem quite natural. But, like the equally appealing theory that Q is based on an authorized abridgment, the hypothesis that Q's omissions might be additions in F is seriously flawed.

The Chorus, as noted above, might seem to be a possible late addition to the version underlying F. But apart from other objections raised over the years by various critics, the immediate reentry of Fluellen and Gower in 5.1, discussed earlier, signals the removal of a Chorus from Q, undercutting the view that the Choruses were added after 1600. The next three omissions listed in Table 7, from 1.1, 1.2, and 2.2, could be, potentially, either omissions in Q or additions to F, for there is no internal evidence in Q either way. But the next long omission, Henry's famous "Once more unto the Breach" must have been cut in the Quarto version, for both Q and F include Fluellen's amusing echo of the speech, as he urges Pistol and the others, in Q's rendition, "Godes plud vp to the breaches" (C2v).

It seems likely that the Jamy/MacMorris segment was also cut for the Quarto version rather than added after 1600. Though the presence of the Scotsman Jamy might appear to be a kind of compliment to King James, added, perhaps, after his accession in 1603, the King was certainly not amused by the use of a Scots accent in *Eastward Ho* (1605); it would have been safer to cut the passage for Q, even perhaps as early as 1600, than to add it later to the text underlying F.[27]

Omissions in 3.3, Henry's long sequences before the gates of Harfleur, as well as his soliloquy on the cares of kingship in 4.1, might have been either neat cuts or later additions, as far as we can tell from Q, but the sequences involving Erpingham must have been omitted in Q. Though Q cuts all of Erpingham's 8 Folio lines and the long sequence in 4.1 in which he appears, the erroneous stage direction in Q's 4.1 is an important clue that Erpingham was a character in the version known by the reporters, as pointed out earlier. Similarly, the presence in the Quarto of the last two lines in F's 4.2, moved

26. For detailed discussions of possible revision in *Lear*, see *The Division of the Kingdoms*, Gary Taylor and Michael Warren, eds. (1983). Concerning *Hamlet*, critics are still divided on the question of whether the "Denmark's a prison" and the "War of the Theatres" passages in F (2.2) were added to the Folio version or deleted from the Second Quarto. See Harold Jenkins, ed., *Hamlet* (1982), p. 44, and George Hibbard, ed. *Hamlet* (1987), p. 110, for representative opposing opinions; the view that these passages were added to F is favored by most.

27. As Taylor notes (1982, p. 15), King James ordered the imprisonment of two of the authors of *Eastward Ho*, Chapman and Jonson; Taylor also points out that James was high on the list of successors to Elizabeth by 1599 or so.

forward to Q's 3.7, is unmistakable evidence that 4.2 was not a later addition to the Folio text.[28]

The next three examples listed in Table 7 left no traces in Q, but the last, including most of Isabel's lines, must have been the result of cuts in Q, for the Quarto entry direction for 5.2 specifies "Queene Katherine" (F4v), apparently a vestige of the Folio-linked staging in which both Queen Isabel and Princess Katherine entered at this point.

Thus of the passages listed in Table 7 as potential additions to F, there are significant indications that several were present in the version the reporters had performed, and no signs that any of the others were later additions, thus casting very serious doubts on the hypothesis that some of the omissions reflected in Q might have been late additions to the text underlying F. Equally significant, evidence in the Folio suggests that F was based on Shakespeare's foul papers: additions as extensive as those listed in Table 7 presumably would have created a very different sort of base text.[29] These passages, then, must have been omitted by the reporter/adapters as part of the reconstruction and abridgment that resulted in the First Quarto.

Implications

A fresh look at the two versions of *Henry V*, in part aided by a computer analysis, contributes substantial new evidence to the view that Q *Henry V* originated as both a deliberate abridgment and a memorial reconstruction by actors who had taken part in the play. But my study reverses the commonly held view of the order of these two processes, for the players must have based their reconstruction on performances linked to the Folio version, not an intermediate and possibly authorized abridgment. The obvious signs of deliberate abridgment, then, were incorporated in the reporter/adapters' reconstruction, not derived from a (possibly authorized) theatrical abridgment that might have preceded the Quarto.

The implications are especially significant for editors, theater historians, and directors. As Gary Taylor pointed out in "Corruption and Authority in the Bad Quarto" (1979), the fluctuating correlation between Q and F helps identify the most likely reporters; it also allows an editor to evaluate which variants are likely to have authority in Q, for variants in closely parallel segments of Q may represent Shakespeare's intentions. If Q was reconstructed directly from a script linked to the Folio, these sections take on greater authority than if Q were based on an intermediate abridgment, making them even more useful to editors. Staging details in the Quarto, of particular interest to theater historians and directors, may preserve elements of the Globe staging rather than that of an abridgment, increasing the value of the Quarto.

28. The transposition is a strong indication that the quarto was ultimately based on a version similar to the Folio rather than on an early draft preceding the Folio version, for it seems unlikely that Shakespeare would bother to write a new scene to accommodate a two-line reference to the (wrong) time of day.

29. For discussions of F as based on foul papers, see Greg (1955), pp. 285–287; and Taylor (1982), pp. 12–18. See Werstine (1990) for an opposing view.

The cuts and other alterations in Q—probably the first deliberate abridgment of Henry V, designed, perhaps, as a promptbook for use in performances outside London—could also be of considerable interest to directors who themselves may need to prune the text for a particular theatrical purpose.

But at the same time, the authority of the alterations in Q decreases if the Quarto was reconstructed and abridged by actor/adapters. Gary Taylor, believing that Q may preserve a theatrical abridgment used by Shakespeare's company, argued that it contained a number of features that might have been approved by Shakespeare himself, including the substitution of Bourbon for the Dauphin in the Agincourt scenes, the replacement of Westmorland by Warwick, even the addition of Pistol's "Coup'la gorge" at the end of 4.6.[30] He incorporated each of these features of the Quarto (and others) in his two recent Oxford editions of *Henry V*. If, instead of Shakespeare, reporter/adapters were alone responsible for these and other alterations in Q, their authority clearly diminishes. Although these changes are intriguing and significant since they characterize a version of *Henry V* printed in England in Shakespeare's time, they may be inappropriate in the text of an edition of *Henry V* that seeks to communicate Shakespeare's intentions.

30. See esp. Taylor (1982), pp. 23–26, and 1987, p. 375.

Appendix

Table A: *Henry V* Folio Spoken Lines in Various Correlation Categories

	FX (F Only)	FA (All)	FM (Most)	FS (Some)	FP (Para-phrase)	F Total
All characters	1593	560	693	380	27	3253
Henry	474	198	239	118	11	1040
Fluellen	67	27	105	71	5	275
Canterbury	114	53	48	8	0	223
Chorus	223	0	0	0	0	223
Pistol	35	53	45	15	2	150
Constable	78	13	22	11	0	124
Exeter	12	73	34	8	0	127
Dauphin	74	11	24	8	0	117
Charles	67	2	11	13	2	95
Williams	22	8	23	18	1	72
Boy	38	8	12	10	1	69
Burgundy	64	0	0	4	0	68
Gower	23	27	14	3	0	67
Katherine	29	9	6	16	0	60
Montjoy	24	7	10	11	0	52
Orleans	32	11	5	1	0	49
Nym	9	10	21	6	0	46
Quickly	4	9	15	13	0	41
Ely	26	3	3	1	0	33
Bardolph	8	3	5	14	0	30
Alice	13	5	3	6	0	27
Isabel	23	0	0	0	1	24
MacMorris	19	0	0	0	0	19
Westmorland	9	1	6	3	0	19
Grandpre	18	0	0	0	0	18
Bates	10	1	2	4	0	17
Fr. Ambassador	0	4	7	3	3	17
Cambridge	8	4	2	1	0	15
French Soldier	8	0	3	3	1	15
Scrope	0	8	5	0	0	13
Grey	6	1	5	0	0	12
Jamy	11	0	0	0	0	11
Bedford	6	1	2	0	0	9
Bourbon	1	1	4	3	0	9
Britanny	4	0	3	2	0	9
Rambures	6	2	1	0	0	9
Salisbury	4	0	5	0	0	9
Erpingham	8	0	0	0	0	8
Fr. Messenger	3	1	3	0	0	7
Governor	0	4	3	0	0	7
Gloucester	3	1	0	1	0	5
Court	0	0	1	1	0	2
Eng. Herald	2	0	0	0	0	2
York	0	1	1	0	0	2
Warwick	1	0	0	0	0	1
Beaumont	0	0	0	0	0	0
Berri	0	0	0	0	0	0
Clarence	0	0	0	0	0	0
Second Fr. Amb.	0	0	0	0	0	0
Gebon	0	0	0	0	0	0
Lord	0	0	0	0	0	0

Table B: *Henry V* Quarto Spoken Lines in Various Correlation Categories

	QX (Q Only)	QA (All)	QM (Most)	QS (Some)	QP (Para- phrase)	Q Total
All characters	55	624	735	183	32	1629
Henry	14	215	266	44	11	550
Fluellen	6	39	109	36	7	197
Canterbury	0	55	48	3	0	106
Chorus	0	0	0	0	0	0
Pistol	4	64	42	6	0	116
Constable	2	19	26	9	0	56
Exeter	1	70	35	2	0	108
Dauphin	0	9	10	3	0	22
Charles	5	4	12	6	5	32
Williams	1	11	23	10	1	46
Boy	2	11	15	2	0	30
Burgundy	1	0	1	2	0	4
Gower	0	29	15	1	0	45
Katherine	6	6	9	11	0	32
Montjoy	1	10	12	2	0	25
Orleans	1	5	5	4	0	15
Nym	2	12	20	6	0	40
Quickly	0	12	15	7	1	35
Ely	0	0	0	0	0	0
Bardolph	0	3	9	6	2	20
Alice	2	2	5	6	1	16
Isabel	0	0	0	0	0	0
MacMorris	0	0	0	0	0	0
Westmorland	0	0	0	0	0	0
Grandpre	0	0	0	0	0	0
Bates	4	1	5	2	0	12
Fr. Ambassador	0	3	8	1	2	14
Cambridge	0	6	1	0	0	7
French Soldier	0	1	2	2	2	7
Scrope	0	10	3	0	0	13
Grey	0	1	3	1	0	5
Jamy	0	0	0	0	0	0
Bedford	0	0	0	0	0	0
Bourbon	0	7	16	6	0	29
Britanny	0	0	0	0	0	0
Rambures	0	0	0	0	0	0
Salisbury	1	0	1	1	0	3
Erpingham	0	0	0	0	0	0
Fr. Messenger	0	2	1	0	0	3
Governor	0	4	3	0	0	7
Gloucester	1	3	5	2	0	11
Court	0	1	0	0	0	1
Eng. Herald	0	0	0	0	0	0
York	0	1	1	0	0	2
Warwick	1	2	3	1	0	7
Beaumont	0	0	0	0	0	0
Berri	0	0	0	0	0	0
Clarence	0	1	1	1	0	3
Second Fr. Amb.	0	0	0	0	0	0
Gebon	0	1	1	0	0	2
Lord	0	4	3	0	0	7

Table C: *Henry V* Folio Witnessed Lines in Various Correlation Categories

	FX (F Only)	FA (All)	FM (Most)	FS (Some)	FP (Para-phrase)	F Total
All characters	1593	560	693	380	27	3253
Henry	266	155	185	101	7	714
Fluellen	99	111	104	45	1	360
Canterbury	58	48	61	16	3	186
Chorus	0	0	0	0	0	0
Pistol	63	58	85	46	7	259
Constable	193	60	59	25	2	339
Exeter	463	252	311	124	8	1158
Dauphin	160	49	45	27	2	283
Charles	185	50	49	31	2	317
Williams	79	30	59	56	4	228
Boy	40	20	31	26	2	119
Burgundy	83	7	17	14	2	123
Gower	139	111	177	92	4	523
Katherine	100	13	26	36	2	177
Montjoy	14	45	39	14	0	112
Orleans	141	17	33	9	0	200
Nym	35	31	51	34	3	154
Quickly	20	21	31	11	3	86
Ely	145	98	106	23	3	375
Bardolph	36	38	67	26	3	170
Alice	147	7	17	18	2	191
Isabel	124	7	17	18	1	167
MacMorris	45	0	0	0	0	45
Westmorland	177	200	197	52	3	629
Grandpre	7	1	0	1	0	9
Bates	54	4	21	35	5	119
Fr. Ambassador	0	21	22	6	0	49
Cambridge	55	48	45	7	0	155
French Soldier	22	25	25	11	1	84
Scrope	63	44	42	8	0	157
Grey	57	51	42	8	0	158
Jamy	53	0	0	0	0	53
Bedford	433	222	220	69	5	949
Bourbon	41	20	44	39	2	146
Britanny	100	45	40	24	2	211
Rambures	167	26	37	10	0	240
Salisbury	18	30	22	5	0	75
Erpingham	58	42	40	18	0	158
Fr. Messenger	79	2	1	1	0	83
Governor	8	0	0	0	0	8
Gloucester	435	253	309	130	9	1136
Court	64	5	22	38	5	134
Eng. Herald	30	35	36	23	0	124
York	0	1	1	1	0	3
Warwick	274	153	214	97	7	745
Beaumont	66	1	0	1	0	68
Berri	62	41	31	17	1	152
Clarence	309	183	222	96	9	819
Second Fr. Amb.	0	25	29	9	3	66
Gebon	0	0	0	0	0	0
Lord	373	147	182	92	6	800

Table D: *Henry V* Quarto Witnessed Lines in Various Correlation Categories

	QX (Q Only)	QA (All)	QM (Most)	QS (Some)	QP (Para-phrase)	Q Total
All characters	55	624	735	183	32	1629
Henry	22	178	190	40	8	438
Fluellen	2	119	114	14	1	250
Canterbury	0	46	63	6	2	117
Chorus	0	0	0	0	0	0
Pistol	5	60	91	29	8	193
Constable	2	59	56	16	4	137
Exeter	19	265	326	47	8	665
Dauphin	1	39	40	7	4	91
Charles	6	56	54	14	1	131
Williams	6	34	81	16	5	142
Boy	0	24	33	14	3	74
Burgundy	9	12	15	8	2	46
Gower	7	124	185	40	5	361
Katherine	15	30	59	32	5	141
Montjoy	0	48	36	5	0	89
Orleans	3	68	61	20	3	155
Nym	0	41	50	17	3	111
Quickly	0	21	35	5	2	63
Ely	0	100	111	9	2	222
Bardolph	2	50	61	17	1	131
Alice	18	31	57	28	4	138
Isabel	10	12	16	10	2	50
MacMorris	0	0	0	0	0	0
Westmorland	0	0	0	0	0	0
Grandpre	0	0	0	0	0	0
Bates	3	12	28	13	5	61
Fr. Ambassador	0	18	24	3	0	45
Cambridge	0	50	43	2	0	95
French Soldier	2	26	25	6	0	59
Scrope	0	46	41	2	0	89
Grey	0	55	41	1	0	97
Jamy	0	0	0	0	0	0
Bedford	0	13	5	0	0	18
Bourbon	4	58	53	14	4	133
Britanny	0	0	0	0	0	0
Rambures	0	0	0	0	0	0
Salisbury	3	45	42	6	0	96
Erpingham	0	0	0	0	0	0
Fr. Messenger	0	3	1	0	0	4
Governor	0	0	0	0	0	0
Gloucester	21	205	200	35	6	467
Court	7	12	33	15	5	72
Eng. Herald	1	15	24	5	0	45
York	4	44	42	7	0	97
Warwick	16	106	156	32	6	316
Beaumont	0	0	0	0	0	0
Berri	1	43	34	9	3	90
Clarence	20	271	317	45	9	662
Second Fr. Amb.	0	21	32	4	2	59
Gebon	3	29	31	15	0	78
Lord	16	195	219	36	8	474

JONSON'S AUTHORIZATION OF TYPE IN *SEJANUS* AND OTHER EARLY QUARTOS

by

JOHN JOWETT

WHEN Hugh Perry, original publisher of Henry Chettle's *Tragedy of Hoff-man*, gave the play to the reading public in 1631, he took the extremely unusual step of dedicating the play to a patron, Richard Kilvert. In assuming this prerogative of the author, Perry describes the play as '*wanting both a Parent to owne it, and a Patron to protect it*', and sets out to remedy both wants. He is '*fayne to Act the Fathers part, and pray you to be a God-father ... vnder whose wings it flyes for harbour and protection*'; he adds further on, '*I doubt not, but from you it shall receiue a kind of new birth*'.[1] In the play's first life it passed over the stage '*with good applause*'; now the publisher himself brings it into a new world of arts and learning.[2] The author of this popular stage play is absent by default, and in his absence the stationer offers himself as a substitute, an adoptive parent. Perry presumes that, given decent family connections, a play should be able to gain acceptance as a work of literature, and so, no doubt, redeem its original sin of sub-literate popularity. He takes it for granted that a stage play needs an author as a prerequisite for its publication in print. As such, his Dedication is a sure measure of Ben Jonson's success in establishing plays as valid works of literature. Jonson's innovative expansion of the author function had firmly taken root.

In the title-pages of earlier printed drama the author was usually absent —with the significant exception of translated classical plays, where stage performance could be bypassed altogether and the text inhabited an altogether more elevated literary environment. The virtue advertised on the title-pages of other plays printed in the 1560s and '70s was their suitability for performance. Inferably, it is exactly because the text's origins lay in a tradition of stage enactment that the author was redundant and so unnamed.

A major change in the circumstances of performance came in the late

---

1. This wording is found in the final of five variant versions of the Dedication. For '*harbour and protection*' Perry first wrote '*harbour*', then changed it to '*a new birth*', then '*protection*', then '*harbour and protection*'. When '*a new birth*' became '*protection*', Perry altered the original '*a kinde welcome*' to '*a kind of new birth*'. He only added '*and pray you to be a God-father*' when '*protection*' was expanded to '*harbour and protection*'. Thus Perry gradually and painstakingly develops the image of baptism. See Harold Jenkins, 'The 1631 Quarto of *The Tragedy of Hoffman*', in *The Library*, 5th Series, 8 (1951), 88–99, pp. 89–93, and Jenkins's Malone Society Reprint of the play, 1950 (1951), pp. x–xi.

2. In the fourth version of the Dedication, Perry calls Kilvert '*a true Friend to Artes and Learning*'.

1580s, when permanent theatre buildings and relatively stable acting companies were established. These developments encouraged a body of professional playwrights to come into being, but in the first place merely allowed them the status of artisans. For instance, most of Chettle's dramatic work was written in collaboration, most of it never found its way into print, and much of the printed material, including *Hoffman*, would be unattributable were it not for Henslowe's financial records in his Diary. Similar considerations apply to John Day, William Haughton, William Hathaway, Wentworth Smith, and others, all of them prolific writers.

The requirement for an increased output and range of play-texts could, of course, be met in ways other than Henslowe's favoured method of team writing on a piece-work basis. Bentley distinguishes a small group of 'attached or regular professionals' who had long-term exclusive attachments to particular theatres. Their enhanced status in relation to the theatre company, however, prevented them from advancing the status of their plays as literary texts, for they were normally obliged not to publish in print plays written for the company.[3] Nor did circulation of plays in 'literary' manuscripts offer a viable alternative. There is no evidence for literary transcripts of plays from the public or private theatres until after 1616, the year of Jonson's printed *Workes*.[4] Plays are long and require considerable time to transcribe; moreover, the drama simply did not belong to an élite culture in the sense that metaphysical poetry did. As authored literature, plays needed to claim a readership that, despite excluding the illiterate, bore some relation to the stage audience; they had to be able to circulate freely amongst artisan and gentry.

Long before 1616, Jonson established himself as the pioneer amongst a small group of freelance dramatists whose independence of the acting companies enabled him to bring plays into print. He began his career as dramatist with the Admiral's Men; his work for them, like most of Chettle's, was never published. Jonson's first play to appear in print, *Every Man Out of His Humour* (Quarto, 1600), was written, like *Every Man In His Humour*, before it, for the Lord Chamberlain's Men. It is perhaps incidental that this was Shakespeare's company, and that it organized its playwrighting along lines distinctly different from the Admiral's Men. There may be equal significance in the fact that Jonson did not stay with the Lord Chamberlain's Men; the next two plays he wrote after the *Every Man* pair were for the Chapel Chil-

3. Gerald Eades Bentley, *The Profession of Dramatist in Shakespeare's Time, 1590–1642* (1971), p. 30; see also pp. 264–292. The case of the 'university wits' perhaps demands further consideration. It may be noted here that the names of Greene and Marlowe appeared on play title-pages only after the authors' notorious deaths.

4. W. W. Greg suggests that manuscripts of this kind are not likely to date from before 1624, when the scandal of *A Game at Chess* provoked a flurry of transcriptions, in *The Editorial Problem in Shakespeare: A Survey of the Foundations of the Text* (1942; rev. ed., 1954), p. 45. If this is true, the manuscripts underlying Webster's *Duchess of Malfi* (1623) and a number of plays in the 1623 Shakespeare First Folio (not all in Ralph Crane's hand) must have been prepared specifically as printers' copies, for they would certainly have been 'literary' in style.

dren in 1601. Jonson's lack of obligation to the Admiral's Men and all other companies must be taken as the primary external factor that enabled him to become a publishing dramatic author.

Every Man Out of His Humour stands apart from all previously printed drama. This is appropriate, for the work is itself a kind of personal manifesto and, moreover, a theorized stage work alienated from its audience by the 'Grex'. The title-page proclaims the writer with an emphasis such that he is felt as an active hand behind the usually neutral and anonymous wording: '*The Comicall Satyre of* / EVERY MAN / OVT OF HIS / HVMOR. / *AS IT WAS FIRST COMPOSED* / by the AUTHOR B. I. / *Containing more than hath been Publickely Spo-/ken or Acted.* / With the seuerall Character of euery Person. / *Non aliena meo pressi pede si propius stes* / *Te capient magus & decies repetita placebunt.*' As the child is father of the man, the text brings forth its author. B. J. tumbles onto the title-page begotten in a tautology: 'composed by the author'. Neither term had previously been seen on the title-page of a play. In the Horatian motto Jonson even manages, by the sleight of hand of quotation, to insert the first-person pronoun '*meo*' into the title-page's usually neutral third-person space.[5] And so, even though it does not belong to the same fiction as the play, the very title-page becomes textual in the particular sense of being subjected to an author function.

On this title-page Jonson suggests that the play was cut for performance and/or was revised and expanded for publication. It was always a selling point to advertise theatrical 'new additions', but the gambit of offering a *non*-theatrical text had not been tried before. Though it was to be occasionally imitated by others, it is in spirit peculiarly Jonsonian. He was to make the same gambit, with renewed emphasis, in bringing *Sejanus* into print. It is part of a general and programmatic elevation of public plays into authored works, involving a forceful declaration of the author's interest in details of book design and typography. Except in the cases of *Every Man In His Humour*, which was brought to the press by the theatre company, and *Eastward Ho!*, which was written in collaboration, his hands are on the very forceps that give each text its new birth. Trespassing in the opposite direction to Perry,[6] Jonson has appropriated functions of the stationer and printer. He harnesses for himself the work of the compositor to establish the equivalent of a house style and a standard which bear his own distinctive birthmark.

As he scorns the common auditors, Jonson often implies that they missed a predetermined meaning. And indeed the vagaries of performance inevitably ensure that a theatrical text's meaning is insecure and incomplete. Jon-

5. Jonson's one precedent for heading a play with a Latin tag is Robert Greene. His case is complicated by the fact that the tag appears on the title-page of the posthumously published *James IV*. The Latin tag may be a quirk of Greene's dramatic manuscripts, or the stationer Thomas Creede may have recognized '*Omne tulit punctum*' as a distinctive motto associated with Greene from its appearance (in this or expanded form) in the title-pages of any of seven earlier works and the explicit of *Friar Bacon and Friar Bungay*.

6. Or for that matter Chettle, who may have at least partly rewritten *Greene's Groatsworth of Wit* (1592) in the course of editing it for the stationer John Danter.

son's efforts to preserve meaning intact take him along diverging paths towards stage platform and stationer's shop.[7] Ironically, the act of publishing in print in itself commits him to further diversification of the text. That fixed and stable entity the underlying text is in each manifestation marked by its absence; both performance and printed book are adumbrations, translations. In this situation the performance text can have no theoretical priority over the printed book. Each is a distinct phenomenon emerging from that deferred centre. And the book itself cannot be regarded as a neutral framework for an embodied text which arrives in it from elsewhere, for it has itself been textualized. Details of authography, typography, and page design are ostentatiously presented to be noticed and 'read'. Jonson makes the books overtly printerly; the type becomes (so to speak) a token.

Jonson's idiosyncrasy in matters of spelling and punctuation is apparent from the earliest play quartos. His punctuation painstakingly etches out the various nuances of phrasing, and as such works upon the text so as to stabilize its interpretation. However, it eschews the modern ideal whereby the pointing is most successful where it is least noticed: no small part of its function is precisely to be noticeable. This style of punctuation admittedly does not belong exclusively to the print medium, for Jonson and others (notably Ralph Crane) were frequently to adopt a similar style in manuscripts. But here we should recognize that the formalities of early Jacobean, especially Jonsonian, manuscripts and printed books could be cross-referential. Presentation manuscript copies of masques or plays might ape the layout of the printed book; conversely, a book might appear more 'printerly' precisely because of its imitation of sophisticated scribal practices. As we have seen, however, there was probably no such thing as a literary transcript of a play in 1605. And it was usually a matter of course for printed books to be more heavy, formal, and consistent in their punctuation than manuscripts. It may well be that the sophisticated manuscript style that later emerged as an end in its own right began in the restricted circumstance of the transcript prepared as printer's copy—which brings us back to Jonson himself.

Similar considerations apply to Jonson's spelling. In that it is regularized, it tends to consolidate word boundaries and the semantic units they enclose; but, by its inclusion of distinctive and pseudo-classical forms, it too becomes an element in the page's textual typography. Once again, any suggestion of a style based on the conventions of formal manuscripts and therefore alien to print will serve only to draw the actual medium of print more obviously into view; but once again it is more likely that the copy manuscript anticipates the printed document rather than referring to a tradition of similar manuscripts.

It is no accident that *Poetaster* (Quarto, 1602), Jonson's first play set in imperial Rome, should anticipate *Sejanus* (Quarto, 1605) in using 'massed'

7. Timothy Murray examines Jonson's use of the printed book to establish a stabilized, authored, and authoritative text, in 'From Foul Sheets to Legitimate Model: Antitheater, Text, Ben Jonson', *New Literary History*, 14 (1983), 641–664.

stage directions and marginal annotations in the printed text—though the annotations in *Poetaster* are confined to three literary sources and four commentary notes.[8] In each book the turn away from the visual semblance of a text deriving from acted drama converges with the text's historical authentication in classical works. By thus validating the work, the marginal notes also question its mimetic operation: in what way does a representation of ancient Rome represent aspects of the world as Jonson and his readers knew it? As Livor (Envy) says in the prologue to *Poetaster*, 'I am preuented; / All my hopes are crost, / Checkt, and abated . . . *Rome: Rome*? O my vext soule, / How might I force this to the present state?' The immediate humour is at the expense of Envy, with Rome being presumed different from the present state; but contextually the lines make the audience expect a correspondence, provokingly uncertain in extent yet certain in its presence.

Both plays got their author in trouble with the authorities; both quartos include in their authorial texts statements that the plays were taken as defamatory, and that the published text has required alteration. In *Poetaster*'s postscripted note 'TO THE READER' Jonson claims to have been '*restrain'd . . . by Authoritie*' from printing his Apology from the Author; in the epistle to the readers prefixed to *Sejanus* he blames the marginal notes themselves on 'those common Torturers, that bring all wit to the Rack' and have forced him to show his 'integrity in the *Story*'. The ground is in each case more discretely negotiated in the 1616 Folio. The begrudging afterword to *Poetaster* has been replaced by the dramatic epilogue in which Jonson famously explains his satirical method as 'To spare the persons, and to speake the vices'; in *Sejanus* the marginal notes and the explanatory address 'To the Readers' have been dropped—along with much of the commendatory verse and the Quarto's defensive but implausible addendum to the Argument, in which, as we shall see, the person of the king requires a very particular sparing.

Though there are analogies to various features of the *Sejanus* Quarto in various academic tragedies,[9] in many respects Jonson's immediate model was another of his own publications: the previous year's '*B. JON | King James* his Royall and Magnifi- | *cent Entertainement through his* | Honorable Cittie of London' (Quarto, 1604). This text is a monument to, and a literary celebration of, a prestigious dramatic spectacle that was itself firmly located in a historical moment. But here too Jonson is not content to remember; instead he refashions the presumptive text into a new and altered work. Here too the efforts of a collaborator (Dekker) have been deleted, and the remaining Jonsonian text has been supplemented. The Quarto includes other speeches celebrating James's accession to the English throne and the *Entertainment at Althrop*. Furthermore, the text of *The King's Entertainment* has extensive marginal notes and other kinds of typographical display that an-

8. On sigs. A4 (Ovid), D2ᵛ (Horace), and K3ᵛ–4 (Virgil and commentary notes).
9. See, for instance, the preliminary material, act headings, and lists of speakers in William Alexander's *Darius* (Edinburgh, 1603, and London, 1604), and the preliminary material and irregularly set marginal notes in Matthew Gwinne's *Nero* (1603).

ticipate those found in *Sejanus*. In both books Jonson seeks a style of page layout which will enhance the classicism of his subject. His technique is to monumentalize the dramatic text. There are obvious affinities between the printed text of the entertainment and the occasion of its performance, where triumphal arches would have quite literally framed the spoken words. The book can in this instance be regarded as a translation of the event. In the case of *Sejanus*, something more radical is involved, for the book breaks with the conventions of printing the kind of dramatic work that *Sejanus* is.

What Jonson offers his reader in the Quarto of *Sejanus* is far from a typical play-text with a border of annotation. *Sejanus* perpetuates the neoclassical entries and scene divisions of earlier Jonson play quartos. It is indeed the first to develop them to a consistent and even exaggeratedly austere classicism, and the first to print all the character names at the head of scenes in capitals. It is by far the most extreme in its quantities of prefatory matter (fourteen pages of it), its inscriptional effects, and its excessively formalized authography. In its physical make-up, the book consistently obtrudes itself between text and reader. We may see it as a greater text, itself layered, which holds, qualifies, or quotes the inner. And the address 'To the Reader' in the outer text asserts that the inner text itself has been revised; the book as a whole therefore both occludes and draws attention to the original collaborative work that had been performed on stage two years earlier.

Repression of the stage play is just one part of a larger endeavour to intensify and narrow the readers' response to the inner text. Any accusation of mere eccentricity will be tempered when the dangers of Jonson's situation are taken into account. The stage play had been regarded, not surprisingly, as a subversive work. According to Drummond, Jonson 'was called befor ye Coũncell for his Sejanus & accused both of popperie and treason' by Jonson's 'mortall enimie' Northampton.[10] Philip J. Ayres suggests that the specifically treasonable aspect of the play was the trial of Caius Silius, in which unhistorical details of Jonson's treatment would have suggested an analogy with the trial of Essex.[11] Jonson's Catholic leanings came to official attention once again as a consequence of the Gunpowder Plot: in November of 1605 (the year *Sejanus* was published) the Privy Council engaged him as a minor government spy against those associated with the conspiracy. Earlier in the year he had spent time in prison, not for his religious beliefs but for his part in the anti-Scottish *Eastward Ho!*. Though already established as the Court's leading writer of masques, Jonson was beseiged with danger.

The admonition printed after the Argument makes a clear reference to King James's preservation from the Gunpowder Plot. It thereby draws the author into prominent view as one who anxiously dissociates himself from

---

10. Ben Jonson, *Works*, edited by C. H. Herford and Percy and Evelyn Simpson, 11 vols (1925–52), 1:141.
11. 'Jonson, Northampton, and the "Treason" in *Sejanus*', in *Modern Philology*, 80 (1983), 356–363.

the Catholic conspirators. The expense incurred is that he imposes a con-
spiculously unfitting interpretation on his own play:

> This do we aduance as a marke of Terror to all *Traytors*, & *Treasons*; to shewe how
> iust the *Heauens* are in powring and thundring downe a weighty vengeance on their
> vnnatural intents, euen to the worst *Princes:* Much more to those, for guard of whose
> Piety and Vertue, the *Angels* are in continuall watch, and *God* himselfe miraculously
> working.

Instead of the customary disclaimer of topical intention, this passage asserts the definitive and correct topical reading; like such disclaimers, it should
not be trusted at face value.[12] This clearly is not, however, a persuasive account
of *Sejanus*. In its providential view of the play's events and their application
to the present, it sits very uneasily below the Argument, which is neutral and
factual to the point of being cryptic. A similar absence of concord is indicated
by the very appearance of the printed page. It is the seven lines of the coda,
not the thirty-one lines of the Argument itself, that are printed in standard
pica type. In contrast, the Argument appears in much smaller long primer.
The Argument is thus in a smaller typeface than any other part of the book
except for the marginal notes themselves. It looks as though the type size of
the Argument has been reduced specifically to fit the coda on the same page,
and to print it in the same type-size as was originally intended for the full
Argument. In other words, the coda appears to have been added on the spur
of the moment after the book's layout had been determined, and was given
priority over the Argument itself. A simple calculation proves that the page
could indeed result from this sequence of events. If the Argument without
its afterword had been set in pica it would have conveniently fitted the single
page.

My concern here is to note, not that certain events can reasonably be
inferred, but that a visible impression of them is given. The page layout
signals it, whether fictively or not. We should, I suggest, see the layout as
polemical, and a consistent part of Jonson's larger project in bringing *Sejanus*
into print. The text's allusions to Jonson's personal situation as a Catholic
and as a suspect traitor for writing *Sejanus* itself mediate between history and
the printed book. In so doing they generate the author in a historical context as a dimension of the text.

The marginal notes to *Sejanus* are another deeply ambiguous denial of
any intention towards political satire, and, as we have seen, Jonson drew
particular attention to this aspect of them. Physically, they constitute a distinct block of smaller print forming an intermittent column alongside the
play within. The type on the page gives a material representation of the way
the notes metaphorically frame and defend the play—how they contextualize
it and uphold its integrity. The dramatic work has entered a new literary
environment which is expressed in type through the conventions of page
layout. Compared with the normative play quarto in which the distribution

---

12. See Annabel Patterson, *Censorship and Interpretation: The Conditions of Writing
and Reading in Early Modern England* (1984), p. 57.

of space on the page still owes something to the layout of the theatrical manuscript, the shape of type-masses on the *Sejanus* page has been fundamentally altered. In the normative quarto the theatrical manuscript's four vertical columns are squeezed to fit the page size: the speech-prefix column is thus replaced by indents from the left-hand margin; the right-hand column is considerably reduced, so that long verse-lines fill the measure or even overflow it. However, that typical play quarto retains some features of the manuscript. It too is visibly variegated between verse and prose; its speech units are distinctly marked off from each other; theatrical stage directions, highlighted in italic type, are interspersed through the dialogue with relative frequency; and white spaces intrude from both left and right margins to break the text into units of dramatic articulation. None of this is true of *Sejanus*. Instead, prose is reserved for special inscriptional effects; no theatrical stage directions are to be found; new speeches are not indented; and the verse-line, where split between speakers, is printed on a single type-line, preserving the metrical unit at the expense of the theatrical speech unit. The flanking notes confine the dramatic text to a particularly narrow column, so that the play is presented as an elongated but solid and relatively unbroken oblong of type. The layout is again a polemic in its own right.

A particular example of the layout's textual significance may be found on sigs. K3ᵛ–4, where the play represents Sejanus' ritual appeal to the goddess Fortune for oracular knowledge of his future. One may suspect that a sententia marked in italics immediately before the entry on K3ᵛ and a mid-scene entry direction (exceptional in a text using 'massed' entrances) are just two initial excuses for the kind of typographical display in which these pages freely indulge. A tendency that runs right through the Quarto here becomes acute: to sacrifice textual clarity in favour of typographic virtuosity. In the third type-line after the entry on K3ᵛ, the stage direction (here a misleading term) is accordingly split into two distinct levels: a presumptively archaic 'TVB. TIB.', in capitals as if to replicate an inscriptional source, and the glossarial explanation on the same line, in lower case with conventional capital initials, 'These sound, ᵈ while the *Flamen* washeth.' This gloss in turn receives extensive comment in the marginal note signalled by the superscript 'd'.

The formula is repeated, but more expansively and intelligibly, on the opposite page, K4 (see illustration). The first two type-lines once again deploy an unusual range of types. What distinction is being made between roman capitals and the usual roman lower case, between either and italic? Do these different type-styles denote varying degrees of textual authority? There are no clear answers, and the marginal note 'a' again complicates the effect. But the note itself adds a radically new dimension to the page's typographical layout. It spills leftwards from the right-hand margin to occupy the entire measure for three lines. Then comes the amplification of 'TVB. TIB . . .', and the detailed account of the Flamen's ritual acts. After this description, the note signalled 'b', like 'a' before it, intrudes across the full width of the page, forming a barrier between the ritual and the dialogue that

SEIANVS.

Prae. [a]Favor It With Yovr Tongves.
Min. *Be present, and propitious to our vowes.*

[a] *Quibus, in clausu, populus vel*

cœtus à præconibus fauere iubebatur. id est bona verba fari. Talis enim altera huius formulæ interpretatio apud Briss. *lib.* 1. *extat.* Oui. *lib.* 1. *Fast. Linguis animisq; fauete. Et* Metam. *lib.* 15.—*piumque Æneadæ præstant & mente, & voce fauorem.*

Tvbicines. Tibicines.

While they found againe, the *Flamen* [b] takes of the Honey,
with his finger, and tasts ; then ministers to all the rest : so of
the [c] Milke, in an earthen vessell, he deales about; which done
he sprinkleth, vpon the Altar, Milke ; then imposeth the Honey ; and kindleth his Gummes, and after cenSng about the
Altar, placeth his Censer thereon, into which they [d] put seuerall branches of Poppy, and the musique ceasing, say all,

[c] *Accept our Offring, and be pleas'd great* Goddesse.

[b] *Vocabatur hic Ritus Libatio. lege.* Rosin. *Ant. lib.* 2. Bar. Briss̃o. *de form. lib.* 1. Stuchium. *de Sa-*

crif. Et Lil. Synt 17. [c] *In sacris Fortunæ lacte, non vino libabant.* ijsdem Test. *Talia sacrificia ἄοινα, & νηφάλια dicta. Hoc est sobria, & vino carentia.* [d] *Hoc reddere erat, & litare, id est propitiare, & votum impetrare : secundum* Nonium Marcellum. *Litare etiam* Mac. *lib.* 3. *cap.* 5. *explicat, sacrificio facto placare numen. In quo sens. leg. apud* Plaut. Suet. Senec. &c. [c] *Solennis formula, in donis cuius numini offerendis.*

Ter. See, see, the Image stirres. Sat. And turnes away.
Nat. *Fortune* [f] auerts her face. Fla Auert you *Gods*
The prodigie. Still ! still ! Some pious Rite
We haue neglected. Yet ! Heau'n, be appeas'd.
And be all tokens false, or void, that speake
Thy present wrath. Sei. Be thou dumbe, scrupu'lous Priest:
And gather vp thy selfe, with these thy wares,
Which I, in spight of thy *blind Mistresse,* or
Thy iugling *mystery, Religion,* throw
Thus, scorned on the earth. Nay, hold thy looke
Auerted, till I woe thee turne againe;
And thou shalt stand, to all posterity,
Th'eternall game, and laughter, with thy neck
Writh'd to thy taile, like a ridiculous Cat:

[f] *Leg.* Dio. *Rom Hist. lib.* 58. *pag.* 717. *de hoc sacrificio.*

Auoid

follows.[13] The passage of non-dialogue is therefore surrounded on three sides by incursive annotations. What we witness here is not a record of dramatic action. The moment and place of the stage have been bypassed: the original ritual is itself re-enacted, so to speak, in typography.

Jonson's annotations, nowhere more excessive, as always serve to validate facts; but here their particular function is to endorse the ceremony and decorum of the events they gesturally enclose. Their length is no mere encumbrance but a purposeful device. It is precisely where the semblance of ordinary dramatic dialogue is suspended that the marginal notes make their repeated inroads into the space of the play text. The annotations go beyond their usual function of holding the text from unmediated contact with the outside world. They here seal off one special part of the text, the ritual, from contamination with another, the dialogue. Thus they become an encapsulating vessel in which the ritual is physically, typographically, held.

If this marks an erasure of the stage, it erases the historical present as well; for if it were not for the vigorous historicising within the Roman context, would not some details of the ceremony seems suspiciously Catholic in flavour? But all sanctimony is scandalously emptied when Sejanus, calling religion a blind mistress or a juggling mystery, throws the priest's wares scorned on the earth. The words '*blind Mistresse*' and '*mystery, Religion*' appear lower on the same page, in an unannotated passage otherwise printed in conventional roman type; they are printed in italic, so as to visibly pick out the dangerous juggling with words. A maze of possibilities stands between this moment and Jonson's interrogation on his *Sejanus* and his papistry.

Later in Act 5, Tiberius' letter to the Senate, which in the play is the device on which the denouement hangs, in the printed book provides another occasion for some extravagantly formal inscriptional effects. On M1^v a centred heading is printed in brevier capital lettering with pica for initials, and the opening greeting below it appears in brevier capitals with points between words. In the main part of the letter, which is conventionally printed in italics, the repeated words '*CONSCRIPT FATHERS*' are set in spaced long primer italic capital letters and the words 'HONORABLE FATHERS' in pica and brevier Roman capitals. For dramatic purposes the contents of the letter exist only in speech, but Jonson seizes on the print medium in order to reproduce the letter's supposed graphic features in all their *Romanitas*. Here Jonson moves beyond the tabulation of sources, beyond the purely literary technique of modified implantation, to give, as it were, a type facsimile of a key document that has been incorporated into the text. Insofar as the text relates to stage production, the inscriptional effect is a fiction; but the typographical style is particularly similar to that of *The King's Entertainment*, which repeatedly quotes and represents the inscriptions of the actual tableaux, and indeed gives a large 22-line facsimile of a Latin inscription. In *Sejanus* Jonson acknowledges a source that may have influenced the enter-

13. In *The King's Entertainment* long marginal notes similarly flow into the full measure, but only at the foot of a page.

tainment as well: the examples of inscriptions reproduced in Barnabé Brisson's *De Formulis et Sollemnibus Populi Romani Verbis* (Paris, 1583).[14] Jonson cites *De Formulis* at three significant points: on E4; in a note keyed to the formulaic opening of the senate's meeting in 3.1, where Varro's words are printed in two lines of capital and italic type; and again on K3ᵛ-4 and M1-1ᵛ, the pages bearing the ceremony with the flamens and the opening of the inscriptional letter.[15] There could be no clearer mandate to regard the text as an object whose physical attributes are themselves invested with textuality.

Elsewhere I have further related this strange and extraordinary quarto to the play's oppositional qualities, the practical risks of publication, and the apparent contradictions in Jonson's ideological stances.[16] Another critical line of enquiry would begin by describing the play as mannerist (in line with Arnold Hauser's use of the term), as regards its verbally signified features of tone, imagery, and structure: its satirical waywardness from high tragedy, its preoccupations wth voyeurism and the statuesque, the schism between Tiberius and Sejanus as central figures. The same art-historical term can be applied to the text's typographical features: its problematization of historical space in the physical space of page layout, the ostentatious stylization of classical effects.[17] The critical implications are therefore far-reaching in various directions, and they emphasize the need for the reader of *Sejanus* to take into account the Quarto's typography. Needless to say, I am not satisfied by the common editorial position which regards the Quarto as superseded by the 1616 Folio text. I suspect, with Greg and Bowers, that an eclectic text should properly be Quarto based,[18] but the whole thrust of my argument is against an eclectic text in the first place. If it comes to a choice between Quarto and Folio, each printing is of such high authority that the purely textual sense of that word ceases to be sole arbiter. In the Folio, though it is essentially a modified reprint, the most distinctive features of the Quarto are weakened, abandoned, or dispersed. The Quarto is in various senses more textually significant; it is also more culturally significant, more Jonsonian.

To put the same point another way, the Jonson quartos sketch out an evolving history of interaction between performance and print, text and

14. See Philip J. Ayres, 'The Iconography of Jonson's *Sejanus*, 1605: Copy Text for The Revels Edition', in *Editing Texts: Papers from a Conference at the Humanities Research Centre, May 1984*, edited by J. C. Eade (Humanities Research Centre, Australian National University, Canberra, 1985), 47–53 and plates i–v.

15. *De Formulis* is also cited on sigs. F2, F2ᵛ, K2ᵛ, and L3ᵛ.

16. ' "Fall before this Booke": The 1605 Quarto of *Sejanus*', *TEXT*, 4 (1988), 279–295.

17. For mannerism, see Arnold Hauser, *Mannerism: The Crisis of the Renaissance and the Origin of Modern Art*, translated by Eric Mosbacher, 2 vols. (1965); John Shearman, *Mannerism* (1967); Claude-Gilbert Dubois, *Le maniérisme* (1979), and Cyrus Hoy, 'Jacobean Tragedy and the Mannerist Style', *Shakespeare Survey 26* (1973), 49–67. Dubois usefully identifies mannerism as a pole rather than a definitive style. Ralph Berry, in *The Art of John Webster* (1972), follows Shearman's more restricted and asocial application of the term 'mannerism' as based on *maniera*, 'stylish style', and describes Webster's art as baroque.

18. W. W. Greg, 'The Rationale of Copy-Text', *Studies in Bibliography*, 3 (1950–51), 19–36, pp. 34–35; Fredson Bowers, 'Greg's "Rationale of Copy-Text" Revisited', *Studies in Bibliography*, 31 (1978), 90–161, pp. 112–119.

author, author and society. There are good reasons why the author should most virulently announce himself, and be most severe in displacing the theatrical text, when he presents a play that has already put him in conflict with the state. Jonson sounds embattled, and is. The Jonsonian author cannot, however, be simply equated with the man himself. He depends on the capacity of the text to invoke a writer who proclaims the text his and addresses it to the world; he depends on the text's capacity to generate an authorial presence. This figure is a rhetorician, and the book's typography and layout are elements in the rhetoric. He is also a good parent. He defends the text; or rather, makes it ready to defend itself. And he creates a space for it to exist in. These manoeuvres take place in the text itself, and Jonson's transcription and revision of the stage play mean that it is impossible, even if it were desirable, to separate off the stage work from the penumbra of print. The text is the whole book, with its typographical as well as verbal semantics. It is a vehicle for the self-created author, that voice within the text who hails its readers and directs it to them. This voice emerges because it has specific work to do. It defines itself because the text, and the extratextual, biological, and historical author, existed in the real world.

'TRAVELLING WEST-WARD': THE LOST LETTER FROM JONATHAN SWIFT TO CHARLES FORD

by

CLIVE PROBYN

As Swift turned his back on London on 1 June 1713 neither he nor the Tory party was in a healthy state. The former still suffered from shingles, and both from fits of dizziness. Moreover, as his biographer has remarked, 'The fifteen months of European suspense over the peace negotiations were to be almost coterminous with Swift's suffocating humiliation over his preferment.'[1] At least the professional uncertainty was now over. Accompanied as far as St Albans by his good friend John Barber (1675–1741), Printer to the City of London since 1710, and printer of Swift's own *The Examiner*, Swift covered

1. Irvin Ehrenpreis, *Swift the Man, his Works, and the Age*, 3 vols., London, 1962–83, II, 622. For Swift's own account of the journey and stay in Dublin, see *Journal to Stella*, ed. Harold Williams, 2 vols. (1948), II, 670–671, and *The Correspondence of Jonathan Swift*, ed. Harold Williams, 5 vols. (1963–65), I, 360–361, 364–367, 372–374.

180 miles to Chester in six days. He missed the ships for Ireland by just one day, and so had the inn at Chester to himself for two nights, with time to catch up on his correspondence. He then proceeded via Holyhead to Dublin, arriving there at 9 o'clock on the evening of Wednesday 10 June. Three days later he was installed Dean of St. Patrick's, the permitted limit of his ecclesiastical ambitions.

Swift initially thought the journey to Chester would restore his health. On 31 May he had assured Vanessa that he would 'ride but little every day.'[2] In the event, he set a cracking pace, arriving at Chester thoroughly weary; his head felt 'something better,' yet his account book records a payment of 16s. 11d. to an apothecary (Saturday 6 June).[3] On the same day (6 June) he wrote to Vanessa's mother, referring her to Erasmus Lewis (Harley's Under-Secretary of State) for an account of his largely uneventful journey. On the Sunday, he wrote a short letter to his close and confidential friend Charles Ford (1682–1743) at his Whitehall office, where, through the influence of Swift, he had been appointed editor of *The London Gazette* on 1 July 1712.

In 1935 David Nichol Smith's edition of *The Letters of Jonathan Swift to Charles Ford* appeared, containing the sixty-nine extant letters from their joint correspondence of 'well over a hundred' (Nichol Smith's estimate). Fifty-one of the letters are from Swift to Ford. The fourth in chronological sequence, dated 7 June 1713, is a mere fragment: "If dissolving the Union could be without ill consequence to the Ministry, I should wish for it with all my heart. But I have been too long out of London to judge of Politicks.'[4] Nichol Smith's source for this fragment was the Christie's sale catalogue of 4 June 1896. The letter was offered but not sold at auction and subsequently disappeared; thus Harold Williams could reproduce only the fragment in his five-volume edition of Swift's *Correspondence* in 1963.[5] Apparently, when the fifty-one Swift letters in the original series were broken up in 1896, ten letters were randomly selected and dispersed at auction. Nichol Smith was able to locate nine of them (most of these being in the Pierpoint Morgan Library; forty-three others between Swift and Ford were in the Rothschild Library), and published them all. Until now, the only letter not published in full was the letter to Ford of 7 June.

The complete letter, now in the Swift Collection of Monash University, is reproduced below and in Plate 1. It is addressed: 'To Charles Ford Esqr, / at His Office at White-hall / London.'[6]

2. *Correspondence*, I, 360 (correctly ascribed to Mrs. Vanhomrigh in the second impression of Vols. I–II [1965]).

3. *The Account Books of Jonathan Swift*, transcribed and with an Introduction by Paul V. Thompson and Dorothy Joy Thompson (1984), p. 154.

4. David Nichol Smith, *The Letters of Jonathan Swift to Charles Ford* (1935), p. 11. Information on Charles Ford also from this source.

5. *Correspondence*, I, 367 (Williams's transcription is accurate).

6. Reproduced here by permission of the Librarian, Monash University, Victoria, Australia. The letter was purchased at Sotheby's sale of 14 December 1989. It is inscribed on a single quarto leaf, with address on verso, Chester postmarks '–XS|TER' within a circle and 'IV|—|12' within a circle, a scribbled-over numeral 8, and a wax seal. The same seal is repro-

Chester. Jun. 7. 1713.

Mr Lewis will tell you of my Journy and wearyness, and the prodigious dispatch I made in six days to this Place. How came it, I did not see you before I left London. Pray take Care of my Writing table, as you value me or my Lady Orkney. How dare you name the Gentry before the Clergy in your Addresses. I will cutt off Barber's Ears if he does not correct that Stile. I wish your L^d T^r comes off as well about his Commerce as he did about the Union. He puts me in mind of two Verses of Marvels. Blith as a Hare that had escaped the Hounds; The House prorogu'd the Chancellour rebounds. I have not these two years been a week out of pain while the Parlm^t was sitting. For my own Part. If dissolving the Union could be without ill Consequence to the Ministry, I should wish for it with all my Heart. But I have been too long absent from London to judge of Politicks—Pray have some Mercy on your Money, that you may not be reduced to live within eight miles of me, when Times change.

I go to morrow towards Holy head, and dread the Journy, When you and I went to London it was nothing to what I have suffered. There is something very disagreeable in travelling west-ward.—Tis late, and I am going to the Cathedrall; Adieu

This concise and allusive letter brings together several of Swift's pressing social and political concerns, as well as a number of his closest friends. It was Swift who had brought Ford and Lewis together for the first time, on 9 December 1710.[7] John Barber and Benjamin Tooke printed Ford's *The London Gazette* until Ford was tipped out of office (22 September 1714), and Barber was to be proceeded against for printing Swift's own *Publick Spirit of the Whigs* (advertised 23 February 1714).[8] Erasmus Lewis (1670–1754), of course, was Swift's intimate friend at the centre of Harley's administration since 1704, 'a Cunning Shaver, / And very much in HARLEY's Favour' ('Part of the Seventh Epistle of the First Book of Horace Imitated,' 1713, ll. 7–8). He was also Swift's trusted postman for his confidential letters to both Stella and Vanesssa.

The 'Writing table' had been the very personal gift of Elizabeth Villiers (1657?–1733), Countess of Orkney ('the most intrested joyner that ever made a thing of this natuer'[9]), and the circumstances of its construction and arrival are described by Swift in a letter to Stella of 28 October, where she is called 'perfectly kind, like a mother', and (in an earlier letter) 'the wisest woman I ever saw.'[10] Swift's letter to the 56-year-old cast-off mistress of William III (21 November), ten years his senior, is crammed with playful banter and some sexual innuendo. The gift clearly had been left in Ford's keeping, and

---

duced in *Journal to Stella*, ed. F. Rylands (1908), *The Prose Works of Jonathan Swift*, 12 vols., ed. Temple Scott (1897), II, facing page *xxii*. I have gratefully adopted some suggestions from David Woolley. His 'Note to the Corrected Impression' of *Correspondence*, IV (1972), xix, points out that Swift 'did not care overmuch whether he wrote a comma or a full stop, the sense not being in doubt'. Thus, after 'Part' Swift has written a full point, where a comma is retrospectively intended, and after 'Journy' in the last paragraph the reverse situation applies (comma written, full point intended).

7. *Journal to Stella*, I, 128.

8. For new light on this episode, see John Irwin Fischer, 'The Legal Response to Swift's *The Public Spirit of the Whigs*', in *Swift and his Contexts*, eds. J. I. Fischer, H. J. Real, J. Woolley (1989), pp. 21–38.

9. *Correspondence*, I, 320 (Orkney to Swift, 21 November 1712).

10. *Journal to Stella*, II, 569–570, 558.

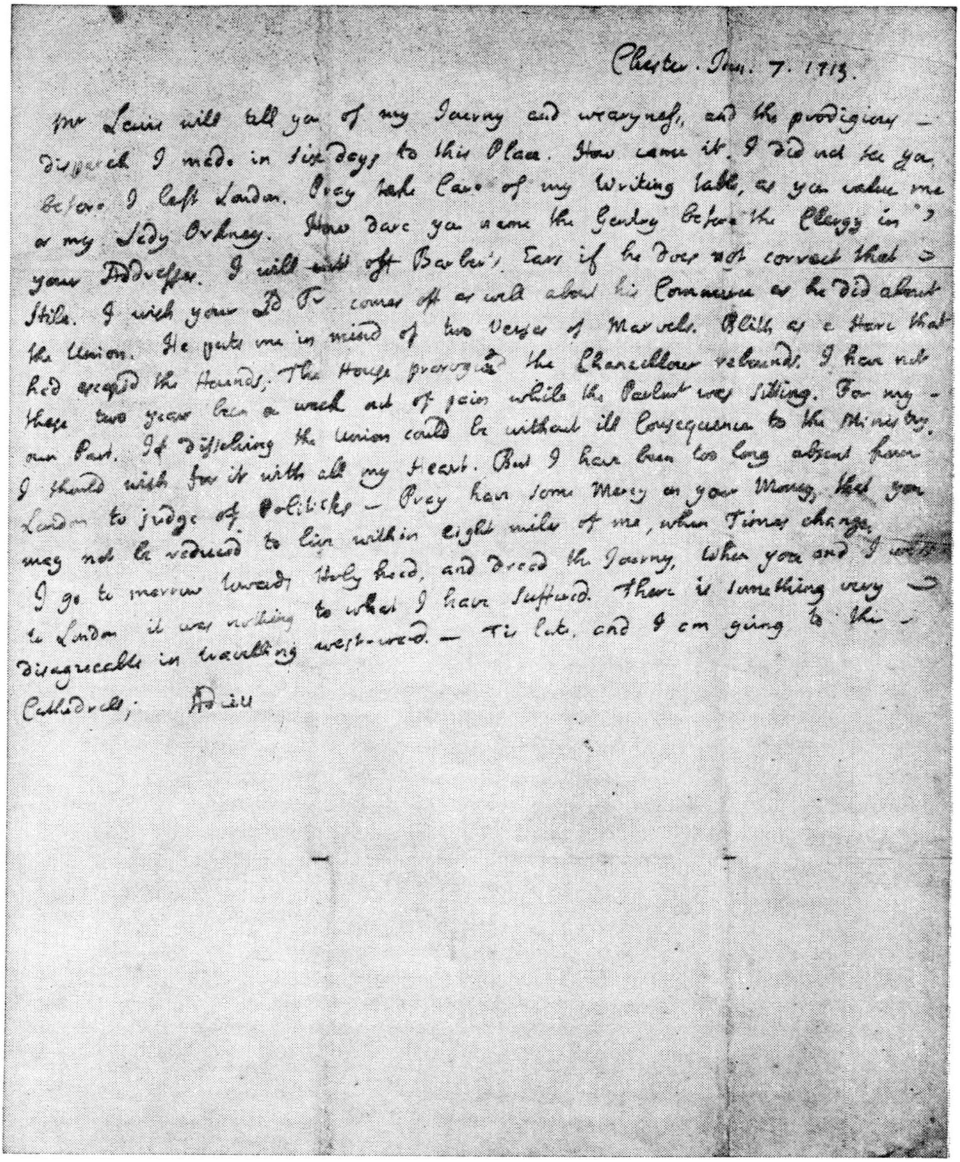

Plate 1: Jonathan Swift to Charles Ford, Chester, 7 June 1713. Published by permission of the Librarian, Monash University: Monash Swift Collection.

the threat to Barber no doubt referred to a 'blunder' of protocol in a recent issue of Ford's *Gazette*.

Of greater interest is Swift's quotation of a couplet from Marvell's *The Last Instructions to a Painter* (composed c. 1667: published 1689; ll. 335–336). Overt allusions to Marvell are exceedingly rare in Swift's works, the one to Marvell's *Answer to Parker* in the Apology to *A Tale of a Tub* being the most familiar. There are none to his poetry. Even so, here is confirmation that Swift, like almost everybody else in the period, was aware of Marvell's best-known poem. Marvell's coruscating attack on Charles II's parliament may perhaps lie behind Swift's savage attack on the Irish House of Commons in *The Legion Club* (1736). Certainly, Swift's poem has a strong if unrecognised claim to be considered as part of the poetic 'Advice to a Painter' genre first popularised in England by Waller. Swift owned the 1664 octavo edition of Waller's poems.[11] Denham's celebrated 'Advices' continued the Marvellian theme, and mimickry of the former's well-known lines in 'Cooper's Hill' is specifically forbidden in Swift's—and/or Mary Barber's—'Apollo's Edict' (ll. 46–49: 1721). Being no Court-poet, Swift enjoyed neither access to pane-gyrical limners nor acquaintance with those visual artists as expert as himself in grotesque engraving: thus *The Legion Club* concludes with the following apology:

> How I want thee, humorous *Hogart*?
> Thou I hear, a pleasant Rogue art;
> Were but you and I acquainted,
> Every Monster should be painted;
> You should try your graving Tools
> On this odious Group of Fools;
> Draw the Beasts as I describe 'em',

11. *A Catalogue of Books, The Library of the late Rev. Dr. Swift* [1745], ed. Harold Williams (1932), item 452. Swift annotated his 1672 octavo of *The Rehearsal Transpros'd* (the first edition): item 302. In his biography of Swift, Ehrenpreis alludes to Marvellian 'Advice' parallels in Swift's 'To Mrs Biddy Floyd' (1708), noting *Tatler* No. 3 as a cognate discussion, and in 'Directions for a Birthday Song' (1729): *Swift*, II, 308 and III, 641. In *Swift's Landscape* (1982), Carole Fabricant suggests 'echoes' of 'Upon Appleton House' in Swift's 'Vanbrug's House' and 'An Epistle upon an Epistle' (pp. 117, 119, 151). None is as likely as *The Legion Club*: cf. Swift's lines quoted above with Marvell's ll. 863–865: 'Dear *Painter*, draw this *Speaker* to the foot: / Where Pencil cannot, there my Pen shall do't; / That may his Body, this his Mind explain.' For Marvell, Denham, and the 'Advice' tradition, see H. M. Margoliouth, et al., *The Poems and Letters of Andrew Marvell*, 2 vols., 3rd edition (1971), I, 347–350; Brendan O'Hehir, *Harmony from Discords: A Life of Sir John Denham* (1968), pp. 210–229; and Mary Tom Osborne, *Advice-to-a-Painter Poems 1633–1856. An Annotated Finding List* (1949).

Swift quotes Marvell's lines from memory. The poem first appeared in *The Third Part* of the *Collection of Poems on Affairs of State* (1689), and thereafter in such collections as *Poems on Affairs of State: from the Time of Oliver Cromwell, to the Abdication of K. James the Second* (1697: Wing P2719, Case 188 [3]), where the (correct) lines are: 'Blither than Hare that hath escap'd the Hounds, / The House prorogu'd, the Chancellour rebounds.' Swift identified Marvell as (in Burnet's words) 'the liveliest droll of the age' in his copy of the latter's *History of his own Times* (1742–43), p. 260: see *Prose works of Jonathan Swift*, ed. Herbert Davis and others, 16 vols. (1939–74) V, 273.

Form their Features, while I gibe them;
Draw them like, for I assure you,
You will need no *Car'catura*;
Draw them so that we may trace
All the Soul in every Face.[12]

The immediate, and to Swift himself the least pleasant, context of this letter is political, i.e. the motion in the House of Lords on 1 June to bring in a Bill to dissolve the Union with Scotland. Harley's necessarily strenuous defence of the Union carried most, but not all Tories with him. The reference to the Treaty of Commerce, a section of the Treaty of Peace establishing trade with France (Bolingbroke's pet project, voted upon 18 June) was also defeated. This Whig triumph, Vanessa believed, would have been prevented if Swift had been in London rather than in Dublin.[13] In the general election in the following August and September, a Tory government was again returned. By 8 July, however, Swift was ostentatiously preferring the pastimes of 'a Country Vicar', hedging, ditching and expelling cows rather than 'driving out Factions and fencing against them.'[14]

Ford had inherited his modest paternal estate at Woodpark, Co. Meath, in 1705; its 100 acres lay between Dublin and Trim, and although it provided Swift with many hours, and Stella and Rebecca Dingley with many weeks, of pleasant relaxation (commemorated in 'Stella at Wood-Park, A House of Charles Ford, Esq; eight Miles from Dublin', 1723), Ford ('Don Carlos') had the tastes of a bon vivant, scorned Dublin society, and preferred to satisfy them in London. Swift's caution to Ford against financial profligacy characteristically reflected his own anxiety that the financial burdens which he would assume as Dean in a week's time would be beyond his means.

12. *Poems*, III, 839 (ll. 219–230). On this poem's authorship, see Pat Rogers, ed. *Jonathan Swift: The Complete Poems* (1983), p. 710.
13. *Correspondence*, I, 368 (Esther Vanhomrigh to Swift, 23 June 1713), and note 2.
14. *Correspondence*, I, 373.

ATTRIBUTIONS OF AUTHORSHIP IN THE *GENTLEMAN'S MAGAZINE*, 1731–77: A SUPPLEMENT TO KUIST

by

EMILY LORRAINE DE MONTLUZIN

WHEN James M. Kuist published *The Nichols File of* The Gentleman's Magazine: *Attributions of Authorship and Other Documentation in Editorial Papers at the Folger Library* (Madison: U of Wisconsin P, 1982), he provided scholars of the periodical press with an indispensable resource: the identification of authorship of almost 13,000 hitherto anonymous articles, reviews, poems, and other items appearing in the *Gentleman's Magazine*. Kuist's list, though breathtaking in its accomplishment, is designedly limited in scope. Confined as it is to the handwritten attributions of authorship entered by the *GM*'s long-standing editor, John Nichols, members of his family, and their associates into the office copy of the *Gentleman's* (now housed at the Folger Library), Kuist's list necessarily makes no use of a wealth of other sources. It does not incorporate, for example, attributions found in Nichols's two massive sets of miscellaneous material on the eighteenth-century world of letters, the nine-volume *Literary Anecdotes of the Eighteenth Century* (1812–15) and the eight-volume *Illustrations of the Literary History of the Eighteenth Century* (1817–58). Neither does it include attributions of authorship for articles bearing known pseudonyms or initials. Nor does it incorporate lists compiled by C. Lennart Carlson, Donald F. Bond, and Albert Pailler of the authors of poetry appearing in the early volumes of the *GM*.[1] Likewise Kuist, with two exceptions, makes no attempt to include Samuel Johnson's contributions to the *Gentleman's* in *The Nichols File*.[2] Furthermore, though Kuist's list is voluminous for the period from the 1780s to 1856, when John Nichols and his descendants dominated to varying degrees the history of the *GM*, it is predictably short of material for the pre-Nichols epoch, the period from the founding of the *GM* in 1731 through the 1770s.

Since *The Nichols File* made its appearance in 1982, Arthur Sherbo has twice updated Kuist's list with a substantial number of additional attributions of authorship.[3] The following list is designed to serve as a further update

1. C. Lennart Carlson, *The First Magazine: A History of* The Gentleman's Magazine (1938); Donald F. Bond, "The Gentleman's Magazine," *Modern Philology* 38 (1940): 85–100; Albert Pailler, *Edward Cave et le* Gentleman's Magazine *(1731–1754)* (2 vols.; Lille: Atelier Reproduction des Thèses, 1975).

2. For Johnson's contributions see Donald Greene and John L. Abbott, *A Checklist of Writings Attributed to Samuel Johnson* (New York: AMS, forthcoming).

3. "Additions to the Nichols File of the *Gentleman's Magazine*," *Studies in Bibliography*

of Kuist, covering the period before 1778, the year John Nichols became a principal proprietor of the *Gentleman's Magazine* and thus took the first step in the assumption of personal control over the *GM* that would last nearly five decades. As very few of Kuist's approximately 13,000 attributions fall within the pre-1778 epoch, the resultant addition of 859 attributions of authorship involving some 41 contributors should provide important information about the *GM's* early years. In addition, the following list includes the first full tabulation of approximately 300 reviews signed "X.," which appeared from April 1767 through March 1773 and which have been proven to have been the work of John Hawkesworth.[4] The complete "X." list has never before appeared in print and is included here in order to make the present compilation as comprehensive as possible.[5]

To be of maximum service to scholars, the following update of Kuist's list is designed to be accessible by article as well as by author. It therefore retains Kuist's valuable device of cross-listing material, permitting readers to look up an article by means of its chronological listing in order to determine who wrote it, as well as to look up an author by name in order to see a synopsis of his contributions. Shortened titles of articles appear throughout, and entries carry the following designations:

> L: letter to Sylvanus Urban
> A: article, note, or query
> R: review
> V: poetry
> O: obituary
> S: staff item of editorial content

In the chronological table the source of each attribution appears in brackets following the contributor's name. Those attributions assigned on the basis of the use of known signatures bear the designation "Sig.," followed by the relevant pseudonym or initials. Abbreviated titles used in the chronological listing of additions to the Kuist list are as follows:

---

37 (1984): 228–233; "Further Additions to the Nichols File of the *Gentleman's Magazine*," *Studies in Bibliography* 42 (1989): 249–254.

4. Donald D. Eddy, following up on a claim in Charles Harold Gray's *Theatrical Criticism in London to 1795* (1931) 171–172, was the first to publish convincing evidence that Hawkesworth wrote the "X." reviews. (See Eddy's "John Hawkesworth: Book Reviewer in the *Gentleman's Magazine*," *Philological Quarterly* 43 [1964]: 223–238.) G. J. Finch ("John Hawkesworth, 'The Gentleman's Magazine', and 'The Annual Register,'" *Notes and Queries* 22 [1975]: 17–18) and James F. Tierney ("Edmund Burke, John Hawkesworth, the *Annual Register*, and the *Gentleman's Magazine*," *Huntington Library Quarterly* 42 [1978]: 57–72) corroborate Gray's and Eddy's claim, as does Arthur Sherbo in his unpublished study, "Counting Words: The Prose Styles of Samuel Johnson and John Hawkesworth."

5. Only 20 of the approximately 300 "X." reviews are listed in John Lawrence Abbott's *John Hawkesworth: Eighteenth-Century Man of Letters* (1982). No other Hawkesworth attributions in Abbott are duplicated in the present list. Likewise, the update here presented does not incorporate any of the identifications of authors found in Carlson's, Bond's, and Pailler's lists.

Brett-James   Brett-James, Norman G. *The Life of Peter Collinson*. London:
            Dunstan, [1926].
GM   *Gentleman's Magazine.*
Illust.   Nichols, John. *Illustrations of the Literary History of the Eigh-
            teenth Century*. 8 vols. London, 1817–58.
Lit. Anec.   ——. *Literary Anecdotes of the Eighteenth Century*. 9 vols.
            London, 1812–15.
Med. Trans.   *Medical Transactions.*
Phil. Trans.   *Philosophical Transactions.*

ADDITIONS TO KUIST'S *NICHOLS FILE*:
CHRONOLOGICAL LISTING IN THE *GM*

2 (1732): 822.   V: "Week's Occurrences." Edward Cave. [*GM* ns 2 (1857):
    386]
5 (1735): 734–736.   V: Chronicle of the month in verse. Edward Cave. [*GM*
    ns 2 (1857): 386]
7 (1737): 631.   V: "Roberto Freind." Robert Lowth [?]. [*Lit. Anec.* 5: 88]
16 (1746): 545–546.   L: Inscription. Samuel Pegge the Elder. [*GM* 66–ii
    (1796): 979]
17 (1747): 180.   L: Inscription. Samuel Pegge the Elder. [*GM* 66–ii (1796):
    979]
19 (1749): 288.   S: Parag. re 2 preceding pamphlets. Edward Cave. [*Lit.
    Anec.* 1: 591]
19 (1749): 311–312.   L: "Rusticlericus's Answer." John Jones. [*Lit. Anec.* 1:
    586]
19 (1749): 413n.   S: Note re *Free and Candid Disquisitions*. Edward Cave.
    [*Lit. Anec.* 1: 591]
20 (1750): 68–69.   L: On fungi. Richard Pulteney. [*Lit. Anec.* 8: 196]
20 (1750): 135.   V: "To a favourite Dog." John Hawkesworth [?]. [Sig.:
    "J.H."]
21 (1751): 111–112.   L: "Poaching defined." Samuel Pegge the Elder. [*GM*
    66–ii (1796): 979]
21 (1751): 151.   A: "Weather and Diseases." John Fothergill. [*Lit. Anec.* 9:
    738, 740]
21 (1751): 195–196.   A: "Weather." John Fothergill. [*Lit. Anec.* 9: 738, 740]
21 (1751): 230.   V: Trans. of "Tableau de Jugement Dernier." John Hawkes-
    worth [?]. [Sig.: "X."]
21 (1751): 243–244.   A: "Weather." John Fothergill. [*Lit. Anec.* 9: 738, 740]
21 (1751): 254–255.   A: "Inscription explained." Samuel Pegge the Elder.
    [*GM* 66–ii (1796): 979]
21 (1751): 293.   A: "Weather." John Fothergill. [*Lit. Anec.* 9: 738, 740]
21 (1751): 323.   L: J.S.'s Ode enclosed. John Loveday the Elder. [Sig.: "Aca-
    demicus"]
21 (1751): 344.   A: "Weather." John Fothergill. [*Lit. Anec.* 9: 738, 740]
21 (1751): 390.   A: "Weather." John Fothergill. [*Lit. Anec.* 9: 738, 740]
21 (1751): 422.   L: "To Cato" enclosed. John Hawkesworth [?]. [Sig.: "J.H."]
21 (1751): 440.   A: "Weather." John Fothergill. [*Lit. Anec.* 9: 738, 740]
21 (1751): 488.   A: "Weather." John Fothergill. [*Lit. Anec.* 9: 738, 740]

21 (1751): 551–552.   L: Addison vindicated. William Warburton. [*Lit. Anec.* 2: 443–444]
21 (1751): 561.   L: "North American Plants." Peter Collinson. [Brett-James 227]
21 (1751): 577–578.   A: "Weather." John Fothergill. [*Lit. Anec.* 9: 738, 740]
22 (1752): iii.   S: Preface. Edward Cave. [*GM* ns 2 (1857): 9]
22 (1752): 5–6.   A: "Weather." John Fothergill. [*Lit. Anec.* 9: 738, 740]
22 (1752): 56.   A: "Weather." John Fothergill. [*Lit. Anec.* 9: 738, 740]
22 (1752): 75.   L: "Sima-rouba." John Fothergill. [*Lit. Anec.* 9: 740]
22 (1752): 102.   A: "Weather." John Fothergill. [*Lit. Anec.* 9: 738, 740]
22 (1752): 151–152.   A: "Weather." John Fothergill. [*Lit. Anec.* 9: 738, 740]
22 (1752): 202.   A: "Weather." John Fothergill. [*Lit. Anec.* 9: 738, 740]
22 (1752): 235.   V: "Ode on May." John Loveday the Elder. [Sig.: "Academicus"]
22 (1752): 252.   A: "Weather." John Fothergill. [*Lit. Anec.* 9: 738, 740]
22 (1752): 300.   A: "Weather." John Fothergill. [*Lit. Anec.* 9: 738, 740]
22 (1752): 346.   A: "Weather." John Fothergill. [*Lit. Anec.* 9: 738, 740]
22 (1752): 396.   A: "Weather." John Fothergill. [*Lit. Anec.* 9: 738, 740]
22 (1752): 401.   L: "Antient Coins." Samuel Pegge the Elder. [*GM* 66–ii (1796): 979]
22 (1752): 443–444.   A: "Weather." John Fothergill. [*Lit. Anec.* 9: 738, 740]
22 (1752): 459–461.   A: "Shakespeare's Falstaff." Philip Thicknesse [?]. [Sig.: "P.T."]
22 (1752): 497–498.   A: "Weather." John Fothergill. [*Lit. Anec.* 9: 738, 740]
22 (1752): 515–516.   L: "Roman Inscription." Samuel Pegge the Elder. [*GM* 66–ii (1796): 979]
22 (1752): 554–556.   L: "Disproof of Miracle." Samuel Pegge the Elder. [*GM* 66–ii (1796): 979]
22 (1752): 560–561.   A: "New Electrical Experiment." Benjamin Franklin. [*GM* ns 2 (1857): 383]
22 (1752): 590–591.   A: "Weather." John Fothergill. [*Lit. Anec.* 9: 738, 740]
23 (1753): 8.   A: "Weather." John Fothergill. [*Lit. Anec.* 9: 738, 740]
23 (1753): 12–13.   L: "Rebus." Samuel Pegge the Elder. [*GM* 66–ii (1796): 979]
23 (1753): 63.   A: "Weather." John Fothergill. [*Lit. Anec.* 9: 738, 740]
23 (1753): 66–67.   L: "Mistake in Cambden [sic]." Samuel Pegge the Elder. [*GM* 66–ii (1796): 979]
23 (1753): 92.   L: Verses ("The wicked cry") enclosed. John Duncombe. [Sig.: "Crito"]
23 (1753): 112.   A: "Weather." John Fothergill. [*Lit. Anec.* 9: 738, 740]
23 (1753): 143.   V: "On a D——." John Loveday the Elder. [Sig.: "Academicus"]
23 (1753): 158.   A: "Weather." John Fothergill. [*Lit. Anec.* 9: 738, 740]
23 (1753): 209.   A: "Weather." John Fothergill. [*Lit. Anec.* 9: 738, 740]
23 (1753): 226.   L: James I's letter enclosed. Philip Thicknesse [?]. [Sig.: "P.T."]
23 (1753): 260.   A: "Weather." John Fothergill. [*Lit. Anec.* 9: 738, 740]
23 (1753): 267–268.   L: "Old Proverb." Samuel Pegge the Elder. [*GM* 66–ii (1796): 979]

23 (1753): 305. A: "Weather." John Fothergill. [*Lit. Anec.* 9: 738, 740]
23 (1753): 331–332. L: "Ancient Inscriptions." Samuel Pegge the Elder. [Sig.: *GM* 66–ii (1796): 979]
23 (1753): 354–355. A: "Weather." John Fothergill. [*Lit. Anec.* 9: 738, 740]
23 (1753): 401. A: "Weather (conc.)." John Fothergill. [*Lit. Anec.* 9: 738, 740]
23 1753): 401. A: "Weather." John Fothergill. [*Lit. Anec.* 9: 738, 740]
23 (1753): 411–412. L: Roman gem. Samuel Pegge the Elder. [*GM* 66–ii (1796): 979]
23 (1753): 412–413. L: "Virgil misunderstood." John Duncombe. [Sig.: "Crito"]
23 (1753): 421–423. L: Homer, Shakespeare, Virgil, and Milton. John Duncombe. [Sig.: "Crito"]
23 (1753): 453–454. A: "Weather." John Fothergill. [*Lit. Anec.* 9: 738, 740]
23 1753): 465. L: "Text and Gloss." Samuel Pegge the Elder. [*GM* 66–ii (1796): 979]
23 (1753): 502. A: "Weather." John Fothergill. [*Lit. Anec.* 9: 738, 740]
23 (1753): 553–554. A: "Weather." John Fothergill. [*Lit. Anec.* 9: 738, 740]
23 (1753): 568. L: "Passage in Horace." Samuel Pegge the Elder. [*GM* 66–ii (1796): 979]
23 (1753): 601–602. A: "Critical Remarks on Virgil." Samuel Pegge the Elder. [*GM* 66–ii (1796): 979]
24 (1754): 8. A: "Weather." John Fothergill. [*Lit. Anec.* 9: 738, 740]
24 (1754): 58. A: "Weather." John Fothergill. [*Lit. Anec.* 9: 738, 740]
24 (1754): 66–67. A: "Proverbial saying." Samuel Pegge the Elder. [*GM* 66–ii (1796): 979]
24 (1754): 106. A: "Weather." John Fothergill. [*Lit. Anec.* 9: 738, 740]
24 (1754): 109–111. L: "Antique Inscription." Samuel Pegge the Elder. [*GM* 66–ii (1796): 979]
24 (1754): 151–152. A: "Weather." John Fothergill. [*Lit. Anec.* 9: 738, 740]
24 (1754): 157–160. L: "Antient Inscription." Samuel Pegge the Elder. [*GM* 66–ii (1796): 979]
24 (1754): 161–162. L: "Antient Syrinx." Samuel Pegge the Elder. [*GM* 66–ii (1796): 979]
24 (1754): 204. A: "Weather." John Fothergill. [*Lit. Anec.* 9: 738, 740]
24 (1754): 211–212. L: "Proverb explained." Samuel Pegge the Elder. [*GM* 66–ii (1796): 979]
24 (1754): 212. L: "Derivation of the Word cate." Samuel Pegge the Elder. [*GM* 66–ii (1796): 979]
24 (1754): 256. A: "Weather." John Fothergill. [*Lit. Anec.* 9: 738, 740]
24 (1754): 282. L: "Anglo-Saxon Fragment." Samuel Pegge the Elder. [*GM* 66–ii (1796): 979]
24 (1754): 303. A: "Weather." John Fothergill. [*Lit. Anec.* 9: 738, 740]
24 (1754): 305–306. L: "A strange Bird." Samuel Pegge the Elder. [*GM* 66–ii (1796): 979]
24 (1754): 309. L: "Antient Inscription." Samuel Pegge the Elder. [*GM* 66–ii (1796): 979]
24 (1754): 310–311. L: "Lord's Prayer." Samuel Pegge the Elder. [*GM* 66–ii (1796): 979]

24 (1754): 352. A: "Weather." John Fothergill. [*Lit. Anec.* 9: 738, 740]
24 (1754): 363. L: Further discussion of the Lord's Prayer. Samuel Pegge the Elder. [*GM* 66–ii (1796): 980]
24 (1754): 400. A: "Weather." John Fothergill. [*Lit. Anec.* 9: 738, 740]
24 (1754): 407–408. L: "Antient Motto and Inscription." Samuel Pegge the Elder. [*GM* 66–ii (1796): 980]
24 (1754): 408. L: "Antient Motto." Samuel Pegge the Elder. [*GM* 66–ii (1796): 980]
24 (1754): 413–415. L: "A Learned Taylor [Robert Hill]." John Hawkesworth [?]. [Sig.: "J.H."]
24 (1754): 415–416. L: "English Proverb." Samuel Pegge the Elder. [*GM* 66–ii (1796): 980]
24 (1754): 445–446. A: "Weather." John Fothergill. [*Lit. Anec.* 9: 738, 740]
24 (1754): 459–460. L: "Ancient Seal." Samuel Pegge the Elder. [*GM* 66–ii (1796): 980]
24 (1754): 475. L: "Bolingbroke's Philosophy." John Hawkesworth [?]. [Sig.: "H.J."]
24 (1754): 493–494. A: "Weather." John Fothergill. [*Lit. Anec.* 9: 738, 740]
24 (1754): 494–495. L: "Antient Inscription." Samuel Pegge the Elder. [*GM* 66–ii (1796): 980]
24 (1754): 508. A: "French Word." Samuel Pegge the Elder. [*GM* 66–ii (1796): 980]
24 (1754): 546–548. L: Further discussion of the Lord's Prayer. Samuel Pegge the Elder. [*GM* 66–ii (1796): 979]
24 (1754): 594–595. L: "Swearing." Samuel Pegge the Elder. [*GM* 66–ii (1796): 980]
25 (1755): 6. L: Warburton's *Macbeth*. Samuel Pegge the Elder. [*GM* 66–ii (1796): 980]
25 (1755): 6–7. A: "Weather." John Fothergill. [*Lit. Anec.* 9: 738, 740]
25 (1755): 7. A: "Weather." John Fothergill. [*Lit. Anec.* 9: 738, 740]
25 (1755): 25–29. L: "Wolsey." Samuel Pegge the Elder. [*GM* 66–ii (1796): 980]
25 (1755): 55. A: "Weather." John Fothergill. [*Lit. Anec.* 9: 738, 740]
25 (1755): 59–61. A: "Fire-eating Art." Ellis Farneworth [?]. [*Lit. Anec.* 2: 391–392]
25 (1755): 84. V: Elegy. Joseph Robertson. [Sig.: "Eusebius"]
25 (1755): 103. A: "Diseases." John Fothergill. [*Lit. Anec.* 9: 738, 740]
25 (1755): 106–108. A: "Case of Charles Brandon." Samuel Pegge the Elder. [*GM* 66–ii (1796): 980]
25 (1755): 108. L: "Female Impostor in France." David Henry [?]. [Sig.: "D.Y."]
25 (1755): 152. A: "Diseases." John Fothergill. [*Lit. Anec.* 9: 738, 740]
25 (1755): 197. A: "Weather [for March]." John Fothergill. [*Lit. Anec.* 9: 738, 740]
25 (1755): 197. A: "Weather [for April]." John Fothergill. [*Lit. Anec.* 9: 738, 740]
25 (1755): 197–198. A: "Weather for May." John Fothergill. [*Lit. Anec.* 9: 738, 740]
25 (1755): 211. L: "Immur'd Skeleton." Samuel Pegge the Elder. [*GM* 66–ii (1796): 980]

25 (1755): 212–213. L: "Critical Explanations." Samuel Pegge the Elder. [*GM* 66–ii (1796): 980]

25 (1755): 246. A: "Weather." John Fothergill. [*Lit. Anec.* 9: 738, 740]

25 (1755): 265. L: "Genesis xiv. 6." Samuel Pegge the Elder. [*GM* 66–ii (1796): 980]

25 (1755): 272–274. L: "Maiden-Way." Samuel Pegge the Elder. [*GM* 66–ii (1796): 980]

25 (1755): 299–302. A: "Wolsey." Samuel Pegge the Elder. [*GM* 66–ii (1796): 980]

25 (1755): 321. L: Exod. 9. 31–32. Samuel Pegge the Elder. [*GM* 66–ii (1796): 980]

25 (1755): 321. L: "Pontopidan." Samuel Pegge the Elder. [*GM* 66–ii (1796): 980]

25 (1755): 343. A: "Weather." John Fothergill. [*Lit. Anec.* 9: 738, 740]

25 (1755): 345–347. L: "Wolsey." Samuel Pegge the Elder. [*GM* 66–ii (1796): 980]

25 (1755): 394–395. L: "Antient and fabulous History." Samuel Pegge the Elder. [*GM* 66–ii (1796): 980]

25 (1755): 438. L: "Answer to Lasenbiensis." Samuel Pegge the Elder. [*GM* 66–ii (1796): 980]

25 (1755): 439. A: "Weather, for September." John Fothergill. [*Lit. Anec.* 9: 738, 740]

25 (1755): 439. A: "Weather for October." John Fothergill. [*Lit. Anec.* 9: 738, 740]

25 (1755): 451–452. A: "To Lasenbiensis." Samuel Pegge the Elder. [*GM* 66–ii (1796): 980]

25 (1755): 494. L: "Of antient Mythology." Samuel Pegge the Elder. [*GM* 66–ii (1796): 980]

25 (1755): 495. L: "Pierce [sic] Plowman." Samuel Pegge the Elder. [*GM* 66–ii (1796): 980]

25 (1755): 503–504. L: "White-pine." Peter Collinson. [Brett-James 228–229]

25 (1755): 541–542. L: "Pibley Dam." Samuel Pegge the Elder. [*GM* 66–ii (1796): 980]

25 (1755): 550–551. L: "American Pine." Peter Collinson. [Brett-James 228–229]

26 (1756): 16. A: "American Firr-tree." Peter Collinson. [Brett-James 228–229]

26 (1756): 17–18. L: "Case of Chanticleer." Samuel Pegge the Elder. [*GM* 66–ii (1796): 980]

26 (1756): 71–72. L: "Cruelty of terrifying weak Minds." Samuel Pegge the Elder. [*GM* 66–ii (1796): 981]

26 (1756): 113–114. L: "Cultivation of Exotics." Peter Collinson. [Brett-James 228–229]

26 (1756): 131. L: "Virgil Illustrated." Samuel Pegge the Elder. [*GM* 66–ii (1796): 981]

26 (1756): 164–165. L: "Northern Lights." Samuel Pegge the Elder. [*GM* 66–ii (1796): 981]

26 (1756): 172–173. A: "To Granticola." Samuel Pegge the Elder. [*GM* 66–ii (1796): 981]

26 (1756): 223–225. L: "*Albumazar.*" Samuel Pegge the Elder. [*GM* 66–ii (1796): 981]

26 (1756): 229–230. L: Ancient customs. Samuel Pegge the Elder. [*GM* 66–ii (1796): 981]

26 (1756): 330–332. L: "Sect of Philosophers." Samuel Pegge the Elder. [*GM* 66–ii (1796): 981]

26 (1756): 486. L: "Land and Sea Officers." Samuel Pegge the Elder. [*GM* 66–ii (1796): 981]

26 (1756): 559–560. L: "Antique Figure." Samuel Pegge the Elder. [*GM* 66–ii (1796): 981]

27 (1757): 58. L: "Militia Bill." Samuel Pegge the Elder. [*GM* 66–ii (1796): 981]

27 (1757): 59–60. A: "Passage in Juvenal." Samuel Pegge the Elder. [*GM* 66–ii (1796): 981]

27 (1757): 123–124. L: "Coluber of Virgil." Samuel Pegge the Elder. [*GM* 66–ii (1796): 981]

27 (1757): 127–128. A: "Gemsege's Reply." Samuel Pegge the Elder. [*GM* 66–ii (1796): 981]

27 (1757): 215–216. L: "Passage of Virgil." Samuel Pegge the Elder. [*GM* 66–ii (1796): 981]

27 (1757): 256. L: "Critical Remark on Horace." Samuel Pegge the Elder. [*GM* 66–ii (1796): 981]

27 (1757): 305–306. L: "Anglo-Saxon Coins." Samuel Pegge the Elder. [*GM* 66–ii (1796): 981]

27 (1757): 487–491. A: "Dean Swift." John Hawkesworth [?]. [*Illust.* 5: 380]

27 (1757): 498–499. L: "Tradesmen's Tokens." Samuel Pegge the Elder. [*GM* 66–ii (1796): 981]

27 (1757): 559–560. L: "Excisemens [sic] Widows." Samuel Pegge the Elder. [*GM* 66–ii (1796): 981]

27 (1757): 560–561. L: "Violin." Samuel Pegge the Elder. [*GM* 66–ii (1796): 981]

28 (1758): 20–21. L: "New military Establishment." Samuel Pegge the Elder. [Sig.: "T. Row"]

28 (1758): 21–22. L: "Thoresby's Coin." Samuel Pegge the Elder. [*GM* 66–ii (1796): 981]

28 (1758): 173–174. L: "Country dance." Samuel Pegge the Elder. [*GM* 66–ii (1796): 981]

28 (1758): 210–211. L: On serpents. Samuel Pegge the Elder. [*GM* 66–ii (1796): 981]

28 (1758): 211. A: "Question to the Naturalists." Samuel Pegge the Elder. [*GM* 66–ii (1796): 981]

28 (1758): 261–262. L: "Sleep of Plants." Samuel Pegge the Elder. [*GM* 66–ii (1796): 981]

28 (1758): 312–313. L: "Bull's blood." Samuel Pegge the Elder. [*GM* 66–ii (1796): 981]

28 (1758): 320. L: "Oracles." Joseph Robertson. [Sig.: "Eusebius"]

28 (1758): 321. L: "Passage in Martial." Samuel Pegge the Elder. [*GM* 66–ii (1796): 981]

28 (1758): 418. A: "Decency in the Repositories of the Dead." Joseph Robertson. [Sig.: "Eusebius"]

28 (1758): 422.   L: *Ars Poetica*. Samuel Pegge the Elder. [*GM* 66–ii (1796): 981]

28 (1758): 435.   V: On Count of Gisors. Matthew Maty. [*Lit. Anec.* 3: 258]

28 (1758): 465–466.   L: "Obsolete Latin Word." Samuel Pegge the Elder. [*GM* 66–ii (1796): 981]

28 (1758): 477.   L: "On Cemeteries." John Hawkesworth [?]. [Sig.: "X."]

28 (1758): 570–571.   L: "Passage in Virgil." Samuel Pegge the Elder. [*GM* 66–ii (1796): 982]

29 (1759): 15–16.   L: "Rustic Philosophy." Samuel Pegge the Elder. [*GM* 66–ii (1796): 982]

29 (1759): 65–68.   A: "Stone Coffin." Samuel Pegge the Elder. [*GM* 66–ii (1796): 982]

29 (1759): 115–117.   L: "Sealing Deeds." Samuel Pegge the Elder. [*GM* 66–ii (1796): 982]

29 (1759): 164–165.   L: "Wives of Prelates." Samuel Pegge the Elder. [*GM* 66–ii (1796): 982]

29 (1759): 211–212.   L: "*Cicero de Senectute* corrected." Samuel Pegge the Elder. [*GM* 66–ii (1796): 982]

29 (1759): 270–272.   L: "Bumper." Samuel Pegge the Elder. [*GM* 66–ii (1796): 982]

29 (1759): 326–327.   L: "Stature of Jesus Christ." Samuel Pegge the Elder. [*GM* 66–ii (1796): 982]

29 (1759): 407–408.   L: "Roman Inscription." Samuel Pegge the Elder. [*GM* 66–ii (1796): 982]

29 (1759): 481–482.   A: "Incident in *Careless Husband*." Samuel Pegge the Elder. [*GM* 66–ii (1796): 982]

29 (1759): 571.   A: "Geographer of Ravenna." Samuel Pegge the Elder. [*GM* 66–ii (1796): 982]

29 (1759): 587.   V: "The Year Fifty-Nine." John Duncombe. [*Lit. Anec.* 8: 276]

29 (1759): 593.   V: "To a Great Minister." John Duncombe. [Sig.: "Crito"]

30 (1760): 337.   V: "To Col. Clive." John Duncombe. [*GM* 56–i (1786): 451]

30 (1760): 382.   V: "Herefordshire Grove." John Duncombe. [*GM* 56–i (1786): 452]

30 (1760): 382.   V: "O Rus." John Duncombe. [Sig.: "Crito"]

30 (1760): 501–502.   L: "Narrow Streets in London." Charles Rogers. [*Illust.* 8: 453]

30 (1760): 514–515.   L: "Remarkable Cavalcade." John Duncombe. [Sig.: "Crito"]

31 (1761): 38.   V: "My lov'd Boscawen dead!" John Duncombe. [Sig.: "Crito"]

31 (1761): 125.   L: "Stone Coffin." John Duncombe [?]. [Sig.: "J.D."]

31 (1761): 374.   V: "Happy the man." John Cowper. [*Lit. Anec.* 6: 615]

31 (1761): 376.   V: "Arrival of the intended Queen." John Hawkesworth [?]. [Sig.: "X."]

31 (1761): 456–459.   L: "Management of the French." David Henry [?]. [Sig.: "D.Y."]

32 (1762): 35.   L: Anecdote of Virgil. John Duncombe. [Sig.: "Crito"]

32 (1762): 54–55.   L: "Enabling Fellows of Colleges to Marry." John Loveday the Elder. [Sig.: "Academicus"]

32 (1762): 87. A: "From the Latin of M. Huet." John Duncombe. [*Lit. Anec.* 8: 277]

32 (1762): 567–569. L: "Christmas Festivals." Samuel Pegge the Elder. [*GM* 66–ii (1796): 982]

33 (1763): 12–15. L: "Sorcery and Witchcraft." Samuel Pegge the Elder. [*GM* 66–ii 1796): 982]

33 (1763): 81–82. L: "Passage in *P. Mela.*" Samuel Pegge the Elder. [*GM* 66–ii (1796): 982]

33 (1763): 160–162. A: "Passage in *Othello.*" Samuel Pegge the Elder. [*GM* 66–ii (1796): 982]

33 (1763): 223–224. L: "Criticism on the *Short Introduction to English Grammar.*" Samuel Pegge the Elder. [*GM* 66–ii (1796): 982]

33 (1763): 230–234. L: "Harrison's Time-Piece." John Nichols [?]. [Sig.: "Nauticus"]

33 (1763): 340. L: "Remarkable Inscription." John Hawkesworth [?]. [Sig.: "J.H."]

33 (1763): 395–396. L: "Festival of St Paul." Samuel Pegge the Elder. [*GM* 66–ii (1796): 982]

33 (1763): 441–442. L: "Ducarel's *Repertory.*" Samuel Pegge the Elder. [*GM* 66–ii (1796): 982]

33 (1763): 480–481. L: "Progress of the Sciences." Samuel Pegge the Elder. [*GM* 66–ii (1796): 982]

33 (1763): 486. L: "Method to recover drowned Persons." John Nichols [?]. [Sig.: "Nauticus"]

33 (1763): 585–586. L: "Holy Places at Jerusalem." Samuel Pegge the Elder. [*GM* 66–ii (1796): 982]

33 (1763): 598–601. L: "Character of King Charles the Second." David Henry [?]. [Sig.: "D.Y."]

34 (1764): 85–86. L: "Tasso's *Jerusalem.*" Samuel Pegge the Elder. [*GM* 66–ii (1796): 982]

34 (1764): 111. L: "Republic of Babine." John Hawkesworth [?]. [Sig.: "J.H."]

34 (1764): 329–330. L: "Fairfax's Translation of Tasso." Samuel Pegge the Elder. [*GM* 66–ii (1796): 982]

34 (1764): 361–363. L: "Further Remarks on Fairfax's Translation of Tasso." Samuel Pegge the Elder. [*GM* 66–ii (1796): 982]

34 (1764): 464. L: "Passage in Virgil." Samuel Pegge the Elder. [*GM* 66–ii (1796): 982]

34 (1764): 522–526. L: "Improvements in Agriculture." David Henry. [Sig.: "D.Y."]

34 (1764): 537. L: On Gen. 30. 37, 39. John Duncombe. [Sig.: "Crito"]

34 (1764): 537. L: West Country clergyman. John Duncombe. [Sig.: "Crito"]

34 (1764): 607–608. L: "Cross in Cheapside." David Henry [?]. [Sig.: "D.Y."]

34 (1764): 632. L: Agricultural improvements. David Henry. [Sig.: "D.Y."]

35 (1765): 6–7. A: Trans. from *Huetiana.* John Duncombe. [*Lit. Anec.* 8: 277]

35 (1765): 72–73. L: "Grave Stones." Samuel Pegge the Elder. [*GM* 66–ii (1796): 982]

35 (1765): 112–114. A: "Anecdotes from Huet." John Duncombe. [*Lit. Anec.* 8: 277]

35 (1765): 159–160.   A: "Sycamore." Peter Collinson. [Brett-James 231]
35 (1765): 212.   A: "Physic Garden." Peter Collinson. [Brett-James 235]
35 (1765): 335.   V: "Spring." John Nichols. [*Illust.* 8: xiii]
35 (1765): 511–514.   A: "Rattle-Snakes." John Bartram. [Brett-James 234]
36 (1766): 160.   L: "Foul Salt." David Henry. [Sig.: "D.Y."]
36 (1766): 175–177.   L: "Improvements in Husbandry." David Henry. [Sig.: "D.Y."]
36 (1766): 186.   L: "April Fool." Samuel Pegge the Elder. [*GM* 66–ii (1796): 982]
36 (1766): 203–204.   A: "Bishop of St. Davids." William Dodd [?]. [*Illust.* 5: 766]
36 (1766): 260.   L: "Robin Hood." Samuel Pegge the Elder. [*GM* 66–ii (1796): 982]
36 (1766): 282.   L: Insect nest. David Henry. [Sig.: "D.Y."]
36 (1766): 301.   L: Papers re Spanish trade in Jamaica enclosed. David Henry [?]. [Sig.: "Y.D."]
36 (1766): 331.   L: "Chestnut-Tree." Peter Collinson. [Brett-James 233]
36 (1766): 421–423.   A: "Political Anecdotes." John Hawkesworth [?]. [Sig.: "J.H."]
36 (1766): 424–425.   A: "Political Anecdotes." John Hawkesworth [?]. [Sig.: "J.H."]
36 (1766): 569–570.   A: "*Metempsychosis* Illustrated." Samuel Pegge the Elder. [*GM* 66–ii (1796): 982]
37 (1767): 106–107.   A: "Regalls." Samuel Pegge the Elder. [*GM* 66–ii (1796): 982]
37 (1767): 171–172.   R: *Quarantine*. John Hawkesworth. [Sig.: "X."]
37 (1767): 172.   R: *Letter to the proprietors of India stock*. John Hawkesworth. [Sig.: "X."]
37 (1767): 172–173.   R: *The Ghost*. John Hawkesworth. [Sig.: "X."]
37 (1767): 173–174.   R: *Elegies*. John Hawkesworth. [Sig.: "X."]
37 (1767): 174–178.   R: *History of civil society*. John Hawkesworth. [Sig.: "X."]
37 (1767): 178–180.   R: *Belisarius*. John Hawkesworth. [Sig.: "X."]
37 (1767): 243–244.   L: "*Montego*." Samuel Pegge the Elder. [*GM* 66–ii (1796): 982]
37 (1767): 256–257.   L: "Elephants." Samuel Pegge the Elder. [*GM* 66–ii (1796): 982]
37 (1767): 262.   R: *The Buck*. John Hawkesworth. [Sig.: "X."]
37 (1767): 262.   R: *Poetical Epistles* and *Tunbridge epistles*. John Hawkesworth. [Sig.: "X."]
37 (1767): 262.   R: *Dearness of provision*. John Hawkesworth. [Sig.: "X."]
37 (1767): 262.   R: *Crito*. John Hawkesworth. [Sig.: "X."]
37 (1767): 262–264.   R: *Cries of Blood*. John Hawkesworth. [Sig.: "X."]
37 (1767): 264–265.   R: *New topic of conversation*. John Hawkesworth. [Sig.: "X."]
37 (1767): 265–266.   R: *Great events*. John Hawkesworth. [Sig.: "X."]
37 (1767): 266.   R: *Scheme to pay off the national debt*. John Hawkesworth. [Sig.: "X."]
37 (1767): 266–268.   R: *Tables and Tracts*. John Hawkesworth. [Sig.: "X."]

37 (1767): 268–269. R: *Letters on the British Museum.* John Hawkesworth. [Sig.: "X."]
37 (1767): 307. A: "Passage in Virgil." Samuel Pegge the Elder. [*GM* 66–ii (1796): 982]
37 (1767): 309–313. R: *Original Genius.* John Hawkesworth. [Sig.: "X."]
37 (1767): 313–314. R: *Method of inoculating.* John Hawkesworth. [Sig.: "X."]
37 (1767): 314–315. R: *Idylliums of Theocritus.* John Hawkesworth. [Sig.: "X."]
37 (1767): 315–316. R: *Works of Metastasio.* John Hawkesworth. [Sig.: "X."]
37 (1767): 316–317. R: *Medical Advice.* John Hawkesworth. [Sig.: "X."]
37 (1767): 317. R: *Manners of the Times.* John Hawkesworth. [Sig.: "X."]
37 (1767): 317–318. R: *Letter to the people.* John Hawkesworth. [Sig.: "X."]
37 (1767): 318–319. R: *Remarks on Rousseau.* John Hawkesworth. [Sig.: "X."]
37 (1767): 319–320. R: *Henry the Second.* John Hawkesworth. [Sig.: "X."]
37 (1767): 346–347. L: "Achilles." John Duncombe. [Sig.: "Crito."]
37 (1767): 357–358. L: "Passage in Homer." Samuel Pegge the Elder. [*GM* 66–ii (1796): 982]
37 (1767): 361–362. R: *Dorando.* John Hawkesworth. [Sig.: "X."]
37 (1767): 362–365. R: *Diseases.* John Hawkesworth. [Sig.: "X."]
37 (1767): 365. R: *Two Letters.* John Hawkesworth. [Sig.: "X."]
37 (1767): 365–366. R: *History of Nourjahad.* John Hawkesworth. [Sig.: "X."]
37 (1767): 366–368. R: *Letters of Lady M——y W——y M——e* [*Mary Wortley Montagu*]. John Hawkesworth. [Sig.: "X."]
37 (1767): 368–372. R: *Examination of Doctor Benjamin Franklin.* John Hawkesworth. [Sig.: "X."]
37 (1767): 372–373. R: *Amaranth.* John Hawkesworth. [Sig.: "X."]
37 (1767): 408. L: "Richard Plantagenet." Samuel Pegge the Elder. [*GM* 66–ii (1796): 982]
37 (1767): 409–410. R: *Prospect of Liberty.* John Hawkesworth. [Sig.: "X."]
37 (1767): 411–412. R: *Address to the Public.* John Hawkesworth. [Sig.: "X."]
37 (1767): 412. R: *A sleepy sermon.* John Hawkesworth. [Sig.: "X."]
37 (1767): 412. R: *Short animadversions.* John Hawkesworth. [Sig.: "X."]
37 (1767): 412–413. R: *Comparative observations.* John Hawkesworth. [Sig.: "X."]
37 (1767): 413. R: *Letter to the Marquis of Granby.* John Hawkesworth. [Sig.: "X."]
37 (1767): 413. R: *Growth of popery.* John Hawkesworth. [Sig.: "X."]
37 (1767): 413. R: *A caution.* John Hawkesworth. [Sig.: "X."]
37 (1767): 413–415. R: *Treating small-pox.* John Hawkesworth. [Sig.: "X."]
37 (1767): 415. R: *London Merchant.* John Hawkesworth. [Sig.: "X."]
37 (1767): 415–416. R: *Miracles of the Gospel.* John Hawkesworth. [Sig.: "X."]
37 (1767): 416. R: *Speeches of the Lords of Council and Session.* John Hawkesworth. [Sig.: "X."]

37 (1767): 441–442.   L: "Origin of a common Phrase." Samuel Pegge the Elder. [*GM* 66–ii (1796): 982]

37 (1767): 443–444.   L: "Antiquities." Richard Gough. [*Lit. Anec.* 6: 271]

37 (1767): 453–456.   A: Trans., *Life of Huet.* John Duncombe. [*Lit. Anec.* 8: 277]

37 (1767): 458–460.   R: *Tour to the East.* John Hawkesworth. [Sig.: "X."]

37 (1767): 460–462.   R: *Narrative of the Proceedings.* John Hawkesworth. [Sig.: "X."]

37 (1767): 462–464.   R: *A Dialogue.* John Hawkesworth. [Sig.: "X."]

37 (1767): 464–467.   R: 2 pamphlets re Harrison's watch. John Hawkesworth. [Sig.: "X."]

37 (1767): 468.   R: *Health.* John Hawkesworth. [Sig.: "X."]

37 (1767): 488.   A: *Huetiana* (trans.). John Duncombe. [*Lit. Anec.* 8: 277]

37 (1767): 498.   L: "Coin of Vespasian." Samuel Pegge the Elder. [*GM* 66–ii (1796): 982]

37 (1767): 505–507.   R: *Affairs of Ireland.* John Hawkesworth. [Sig.: "X."]

37 (1767): 507–508.   R: *Narrative of Facts.* John Hawkesworth. [Sig.: "X."]

37 (1767): 508–510.   R: *Answer to a Pamphlet.* John Hawkesworth. [Sig.: "X."]

37 (1767): 510.   R: *Remarks on the Answer.* John Hawkesworth. [Sig.: "X."]

37 (1767): 511.   R: "Y."'s remarks on Langton. John Hawkesworth. [Sig.: "X."]

37 (1767): 511–512.   R: *Trials of James Brownrigg, and John his Son.* John Hawkesworth. [Sig.: "X."]

37 (1767): 512–514.   R: *Letters of Montesquieu.* John Hawkesworth. [Sig.: "X."]

37 (1767): 514–515.   R: *Letter to the Lord-Mayor.* John Hawkesworth. [Sig.: "X."]

37 (1767): 529–531.   S: "Price of Provisions." David Henry. [Sig.: "D.Y."]

37 (1767): 542.   L: "Contusions in Elephants [sic] Teeth." Samuel Pegge the Elder. [*GM* 66–ii (1796): 982]

37 (1767): 548.   L: "Coin." Samuel Pegge the Elder. [*GM* 66–ii (1796): 982]

37 (1767): 549.   L: Vine's illustration. Richard Gough. [Sig.: "D.H."]

37 (1767): 553.   R: *Poems by Dr. Dodd.* John Hawkesworth. [Sig.: "X."]

37 (1767): 553–554.   R: *Psalms of David.* John Hawkesworth. [Sig.: "X."]

37 (1767): 554–556.   R: *Manner of inoculating.* John Hawkesworth. [Sig.: "X."]

37 (1767): 556–558.   R: *Cause of Fevers.* John Hawkesworth. [Sig.: "X."]

37 (1767): 558–560.   R: *Considerations* [re *Welsh benefices*]. John Hawkesworth. [Sig.: "X."]

37 (1767): 560–561.   R: *Douglas Cause.* John Hawkesworth. [Sig.: "X."]

37 (1767): 561.   R: *Priest in Rhime.* John Hawkesworth. [Sig.: "X."]

37 (1767): 561–562.   R: *Peep behind the Curtain.* John Hawkesworth. [Sig.: "X."]

37 (1767): 572.   A: "Eruption of Mount Vesuvius." David Henry [?]. [Sig.: "Y.D."]

37 (1767): 580–581.   L: "Reading Romances." Samuel Pegge the Elder. [*GM* 66–ii (1796): 982]

37 (1767): 591–592.   R: *Letter to Madan.* John Hawkesworth. [Sig.: "X."]

37 (1767): 592–594.   R: *Aldwinckle.* John Hawkesworth. [Sig.: "X."]

37 (1767): 594. R: *National Establishments*. John Hawkesworth. [Sig.: "X."]

37 (1767): 594. R: *Doubts concerning the Confessional*. John Hawkesworth. [Sig.: "X."]

37 (1767): 595–596. R: *Venereal Disease*. John Hawkesworth. [Sig.: "X."]

37 (1767): 596. R: *Essay on Manilius*. John Hawkesworth. [Sig.: "X."]

37 (1767): 596. R: *Letter to Lord Clive*. John Hawkesworth. [Sig.: "X."]

37 (1767): 596–599. R: *Price of Provisions*. John Hawkesworth. [Sig.: "X."]

37 (1767): 599–600. R: *Widowed Wife*. John Hawkesworth. [Sig.: "X."]

37 (1767): 600–601. R: *Patriotism*. John Hawkesworth. [Sig.: "X."]

37 (1767): 601. R: *Hortonian Miscellany*. John Hawkesworth. [Sig.: "X."]

37 (1767): 640. R: *Collection of Poetry*. John Hawkesworth. [Sig.: "X."]

37 (1767): 640. R: *Cooper's Well*. John Hawkesworth. [Sig.: "X."]

38 (1768): 5–6. L: "Journey into Wales." Richard Gough. [Sig.: "P.Q."]

38 (1768): 18–20. A: *Huetiana* (trans.). John Duncombe. [*Lit. Anec.* 8: 277]

38 (1768): 23–24. L: "Suttonian Secret." Samuel Pegge the Elder. [*GM* 66–ii (1796): 1081]

38 (1768): 28. R: *Conversation, a Poem*. John Hawkesworth. [Sig.: "X."]

38 (1768): 28–29. R: *Britannia*. John Hawkesworth. [Sig.: "X."]

38 (1768): 29–31. R: *Revelation of St. John*. John Hawkesworth. [Sig.: "X."]

38 (1768): 31. R: *Memoirs of the Seraglio*. John Hawkesworth. [Sig.: "X."]

38 (1768): 31. R: *Apology for Lord Baltimore*. John Hawkesworth. [Sig.: "X."]

38 (1768): 31–32. R: *Royal Merchant*. John Hawkesworth. [Sig.: "X."]

38 (1768): 32–34. R: 2 pamphlets re living of A——w——le. John Hawkesworth. [Sig.: "X."]

38 (1768): 34–35. R: *Thoughts, Essays, and Maxims*. John Hawkesworth. [Sig.: "X."]

38 (1768): 35–36. R: *Temple of Gnidos*. John Hawkesworth. [Sig.: "X."]

38 (1768): 36. R: *Dearness of Provisions*. John Hawkesworth. [Sig.: "X."]

38 (1768): 38. V: "To the Earl of Chesterfield." Walter Harte [?]. [*Illust.* 5: 791]

38 (1768): 57–61. A: *Huetiana* (trans.). John Duncombe. [*Lit. Anec.* 8: 277]

38 (1768): 63. L: Registers of births and deaths. David Henry [?]. [Sig.: "Y.D."]

38 (1768): 78–82. R: *False Delicacy* and *Goodnatured Man*. John Hawkesworth. [Sig.: "X."]

38 (1768): 82–85. R: *Apology for the Catholicks*. John Hawkesworth. [Sig.: "X."]

38 (1768): 109. L: "Vulgar Error." Samuel Pegge the Elder. [*GM* 66–ii (1796): 1081]

38 (1768): 121–122. L: Ton of gold. Samuel Pegge the Elder. [*GM* 66–ii (1796): 1081]

38 (1768): 127–131. R: *State of the Differences*. John Hawkesworth. [Sig.: "X."]

38 (1768): 131–132. R: *Gout*. John Hawkesworth. [Sig.: "X."]

38 (1768): 132–133. R: *Battle of the Wigs*. John Hawkesworth. [Sig.: "X."]

38 (1768): 133. R: *Poetical Works of Lady M——y W——y M——e* [*Mary Wortley Montagu*]. John Hawkesworth. [Sig.: "X."]

38 (1768): 133. R: *Siege of the Castle.* John Hawkesworth. [Sig.: "X."]
38 (1768): 133. R: *Annabella.* John Hawkesworth. [Sig.: "X."]
38 (1768): 133. R: *No Rape.* John Hawkesworth. [Sig.: "X."]
38 (1768): 150–151. L: Crow. Samuel Pegge the Elder. [*GM* 66–ii (1796): 1081]
38 (1768): 172–177. R: *Account of Corsica.* John Hawkesworth. [Sig.: "X."]
38 (1768): 177–180. R: *Future life of Brute Creatures.* John Hawkesworth. [Sig.: "X."]
38 (1768): 180–187. R: *Trial of Lord Baltimore.* John Hawkesworth. [Sig.: "X."]
38 (1768): 188. R: *Sermons to Asses.* John Hawkesworth. [Sig.: "X."]
38 (1768): 188. R: *Modern Chastity.* John Hawkesworth. [Sig.: "X."]
38 (1768): 208. L: "Rhinoceros." Richard Gough. [Sig.: "H.D."]
38 (1768): 212–213. L: Rousseau and Saurin. David Henry [?]. [Sig.: "D.Y."]
38 (1768): 213–215. A: *Huetiana* (trans.). John Duncombe. [*Lit. Anec.* 8: 277]
38 (1768): 218–219. L: "Discontented Mariners." John Hawkesworth [?]. [Sig.: "J.H."]
38 (1768): 233–236. R: *John Byron.* John Hawkesworth. [Sig.: "X."]
38 (1768): 237. S: Reply to "A.B." John Hawkesworth. [Sig.: "X."]
38 (1768): 269–270. L: "Virtual Representation." David Henry. [Sig.: "D.Y."]
38 (1768): 283–284. L: "To run a muck." Samuel Pegge the Elder. [*GM* 66–ii (1796): 1081]
38 (1768): 289–290. R: *Defence of my Uncle.* John Hawkesworth. [Sig.: "X."]
38 (1768): 290–292. R: *Adventures of Telemachus.* John Hawkesworth. [Sig.: "X."]
38 (1768): 292–293. R: *Power of Alienation.* John Hawkesworth. [Sig.: "X."]
38 (1768): 293. R: *Letter from a Farmer.* John Hawkesworth. [Sig.: "X."]
38 (1768): 313–316. L: "Insects." David Henry. [Sig.: "Y.D."]
38 (1768): 326–327. L: "Assassin." Samuel Pegge the Elder. [*GM* 66–ii (1796): 1081]
38 (1768): 327. L: "Clark's *Cromwell.*" Richard Gough. [Sig.: "D.H."]
38 (1768): 333–335. R: *Customs of Italy.* John Hawkesworth ["X."]. [*GM* 38 (1768): 389]
38 (1768): 335–336. R: *Expostulation.* John Hawkesworth ["X."]. [*GM* 38 (1768): 389]
38 (1768): 336. R: *Man of Forty Crowns* and *Princess of Babylon.* John Hawkesworth ["X."]. [*GM* 38 (1768): 389]
38 (1768): 336. R: *British Liberty.* John Hawkesworth ["X."]. [*GM* 38 (1768): 389]
38 (1768): 336–338. R: *Lectureships.* John Hawkesworth. [Sig.: "X."]
38 (1768): 338–340. R: *Free Address.* John Hawkesworth. [Sig.: "X."]
38 (1768): 340. R: *British Empire.* John Hawkesworth. [Sig.: "X."]
38 (1768): 355. L: Gen. Amherst. Michael Wodhull. [Sig.: "L.L."]
38 (1768): 356. A: More on Gen. Amherst. Michael Wodhull. [Sig.: "L.L."]
38 (1768): 373–376. A: *Huetiana* (trans.). John Duncombe. [*Lit. Anec.* 8: 277]

38 (1768): 382–383. R: *Gardening*. John Hawkesworth. [Sig.: "X."]
38 (1768): 383. R: *Letter to Shelburne*. John Hawkesworth. [Sig.: "X."]
38 (1768): 383–384. R: *Free Trade*. John Hawkesworth. [Sig.: "X."]
38 (1768): 384. R: *Inflammations*. John Hawkesworth. [Sig.: "X."]
38 (1768): 386. R: *Things as they are*. John Hawkesworth. [Sig.: "X."]
38 (1768): 386–388. R: *Letter from T. Harris*. John Hawkesworth. [Sig.: "X."]
38 (1768): 388–389. R: *Ralph Hodgson*. John Hawkesworth. [Sig.: "X."]
38 (1768): 403. L: Rapin's *History*. David Henry [?]. [Sig.: "Y.D."]
38 (1768): 426. L: Apostle-spoons and peg-tankards. Samuel Pegge the Elder. [*GM* 66–ii (1796): 1081]
38 (1768): 431–434. R: *T. Harris Dissected*. John Hawkesworth. [Sig.: "X."]
38 (1768): 434. R: *Account of Denmark*. John Hawkesworth. [Sig.: "X."]
38 (1768): 434–436. R: *Essay on Diseases*. John Hawkesworth. [Sig.: "X."]
38 (1768): 436. R: *Seasonable Letter*. John Hawkesworth. [Sig.: "X."]
38 (1768): 436–437. R: *Principal Monarchies*. John Hawkesworth. [Sig.: "X."]
38 (1768): 437. R: *Caricatura*. John Hawkesworth. [Sig.: "X."]
38 (1768): 459–460. L: "Brightness of the Northern Hemisphere." Samuel Pegge the Elder. [*GM* 66–ii (1796): 1081]
38 (1768): 462–464. A: *Huetiana* (trans.). John Duncombe. [*Lit. Anec.* 8: 277]
38 (1768): 464. L: "Assassin." Richard Gough. [Sig.: "H.D."]
38 (1768): 475. A: "Peg-Tankard." Samuel Pegge the Elder. [*GM* 66–ii (1796): 1081]
38 (1768): 478–479. R: *Account of Italy*. John Hawkesworth. [Sig.: "X."]
38 (1768): 479. R: *Judgment of Paris*. John Hawkesworth. [Sig.: "X."]
38 (1768): 479–481. R: *Predestination*. John Hawkesworth. [Sig.: "X."]
38 (1768): 481–483. R: *History of Chess*. John Hawkesworth. [Sig.: "X."]
38 (1768): 483–484. R: *Philosophical Essays*. John Hawkesworth. [Sig.: "X."]
38 (1768): 484–485. R: *Passage in Homer*. John Hawkesworth. [Sig. "X."]
38 (1768): 515–516. L: "Virgil defended." Richard Gough. [Sig.: "H.D."]
38 (1768): 523. L: "Secker's Death." Samuel Pegge the Elder. [*GM* 66–ii (1796): 1081]
38 (1768): 526. R: *Gout*. John Hawkesworth. [Sig.: "X."]
38 (1768): 526–529. R: *Phil. Trans.* John Hawkesworth. [Sig.: "X."]
38 (1768): 529–532. R: *State of the Nation*. John Hawkesworth. [Sig.: "X."]
38 (1768): 532–533. R: *Case of William Penrice*. John Hawkesworth. [Sig.: "X."]
38 (1768): 533. R: *Modern Gallantry*. John Hawkesworth. [Sig.: "X."]
38 (1768): 533. R: *Corsica*. John Hawkesworth. [Sig.: "X."]
38 (1768): 574–576. R: *Grand Instructions*. John Hawkesworth. [Sig.: "X."]
38 (1768): 576–579. R: *Phil. Trans.* John Hawkesworth. [Sig.: "X."]
38 (1768): 579–581. R: *Cyrus*. John Hawkesworth. [Sig.: "X."]
38 (1768): 581. R: *Complaint of Liberty*. John Hawkesworth. [Sig.: "X."]
38 (1768): 605–607. A: "Inscription." David Henry [?]. [Sig.: "Y.D."]
38 (1768): 608–609. L: "Ancient Barrows." Richard Gough. [Sig.: "D.H."]
38 (1768): 619–620. R: *Hypocrite*. John Hawkesworth. [Sig.: "X."]

38 (1768): 620–621. R: *Cobleriana*. John Hawkesworth. [Sig.: "X."]
38 (1768): 621. R: *Masquerade*. John Hawkesworth. [Sig.: "X."]
38 (1768): 621–623. R: *Phil. Trans*. John Hawkesworth. [Sig.: "X."]
38 (1768): 623–625. R:*Massachuset's* [*sic*] *Bay*. John Hawkesworth. [Sig.: "X."]
39 (1769): 5. L: "Bones." Samuel Pegge the Elder. [*GM* 66–ii (1796): 1081]
39 (1769): 19–21. A: *Huetiana* (trans.). John Duncombe. [*Lit. Anec*. 8: 277]
39 (1769): 38–40. R: *Thoughts on Government*. John Hawkesworth. [Sig.: "X."]
39 (1769): 40–44. R: *Zingis*. John Hawkesworth. [Sig.: "X."]
39 (1769): 44–45. R: *Acids*. John Hawkesworth. [Sig.: "X."]
39 (1769): 45. R: *Art of Living in London*. John Hawkesworth. [Sig.: "X."]
39 (1769): 86–87. L: "Bones." Samuel Pegge the Elder. [*GM* 66–ii (1796): 1081]
39 (1769): 94–98. R: *Britain and America*. John Hawkesworth. [Sig.: "X."]
39 (1769): 98–100. R: *Reynolds' Discourse*. John Hawkesworth. [Sig.: "X."]
39 (1769): 100–101. R: *Verses in memory*. John Hawkesworth. [Sig.: "X."]
39 (1769): 101–102. R: *Phil. Trans*. John Hawkesworth. [Sig.: "X."]
39 (1769): 115–119. L: "Sir F. Goodwyn." David Henry [?]. [Sig.: "Y.D."]
39 (1769): 145–149. R: *Essay on Guiana*. John Hawkesworth. [Sig.: "X."]
39 (1769): 150–152. R: *Frederick and Pharamond*. John Hawkesworth. [Sig.: "X."]
39 (1769): 152–154. R: *State of the Nation*. John Hawkesworth. [Sig.: "X."]
39 (1769): 122–126. A: *Huetiana* (trans.). John Duncombe. [*Lit. Anec*. 8: 277]
39 (1769): 180–181. A: "Tobacco." Samuel Pegge the Elder. [*GM* 66–ii (1796): 1081]
39 (1769): 199. R: *School for Rakes*. John Hawkesworth. [Sig.: "X."]
39 (1769): 199. R: *Wit's Last Stake*. John Hawkesworth. [Sig.: "X."]
39 (1769): 199–200. R: *The Sister*. John Hawkesworth. [Sig.: "X."]
39 (1769): 200. R: *Fatal Discovery*. John Hawkesworth. [Sig.: "X."]
39 (1769): 200–205. R: *History of an Atom*. John Hawkesworth. [Sig.: "X."]
39 (1769): 247–248. L: "Wallis' *Antiquities*." Richard Gough. [Sig.: "D.H."]
39 (1769): 252. L: "Song of Solomon." Samuel Denne [?]. [Sig.: "S.D."]
39 (1769): 254–255. R: *State of the Nation*. John Hawkesworth. [Sig.: "X."]
39 (1769): 255–260. R: *Life of Pope*. John Hawkesworth. [Sig.: "X."]
39 (1769): 279. L: Killing caterpillars. David Henry. [Sig.: "Y.D."]
39 (1769): 281–284. A: *Huetiana* (trans.). John Duncombe. [*Lit. Anec*. 8: 277]
39 (1769): 288–289. L: "Curious Experiment." David Henry. [Sig.: "Y.D."]
39 (1769): 302–304. R: *Gout*. John Hawkesworth. [Sig.: "X."]
39 (1769): 304–306. R: *British Education*. John Hawkesworth. [Sig.: "X."]
39 (1769): 306–309. R: *Election for Middlesex*. John Hawkesworth. [Sig.: "X."]
39 (1769): 309. R: *Serious Considerations*. John Hawkesworth. [Sig.: "X."]
39 (1769): 309. R: *Question stated*. John Hawkesworth. [Sig.: "X."]
39 (1769): 325–328. L: "Middlesex Election." David Henry. [Sig.: "Y.D."]
39 (1769): 328. A: "Family of Ellis." John Spicer [?]. [Sig.: "C——o"]

39 (1769): 345. L: Virgil. Richard Gough. [Sig.: "H.D."]
39 (1769): 345–348. A: *Huetiana* (trans.). John Duncombe. [*Lit. Anec.* 8: 277]
39 (1769): 350–353. R: *Historical Anecdotes*. John Hawkesworth. [Sig.: "X."]
39 (1769): 353–355. R: *Biographical History*. John Hawkesworth [?]. [multi-part rev.; cont. signed "X."]
39 (1769): 382–385. A: *Huetiana* (trans.). John Duncombe. [*Lit. Anec.* 8: 277]
39 (1769): 390–391. L: "Gout." Samuel Pegge the Elder. [*GM* 66–ii (1796): 1081]
39 (1769): 398. R: *Yorick's Journey*. John Hawkesworth. [Sig.: "X."]
39 (1769): 398–400. R: *American Traveller*. John Hawkesworth. [Sig.: "X."]
39 (1769): 401–403. R: *Influence of Opinions*. John Hawkesworth. [Sig.: "X."]
39 (1769): 403–404. R: *Biographical History*. John Hawkesworth. [Sig.: "X."]
39 (1769): 419–420. L: "Seed Wheat." David Henry. [Sig.: "Y.D."]
39 (1769): 425–427. L: "British Zoology." Richard Gough. [Sig.: "D.H."]
39 (1769): 427. L: "Frogs." Samuel Pegge the Elder. [*GM* 66–ii (1796): 1081]
39 (1769): 443. L: "Clark's *Cromwell*." Richard Gough. [Sig.: "D.H."]
39 (1769): 446–447. R: *An Ode*. John Hawkesworth. [Sig.: "X."]
39 (1769): 447. R: *Shakespeare's Garland*. John Hawkesworth. [Sig.: "X."]
39 (1769): 447–450. R: *Conduct of Chatham*. John Hawkesworth. [Sig.: "X."]
39 (1769): 450–452. R: *Animal Reproductions*. John Hawkesworth. [Sig.: "X."]
39 (1769): 494. R: *Mirrour for the Multitude*. John Hawkesworth. [Sig.: "X."]
39 (1769): 494–498. R: *Travels*. John Hawkesworth. [Sig.: "X."]
39 (1769): 498–499. R: *Animal Reproductions*. John Hawkesworth. [Sig.: "X."]
39 (1769): 499–500. R: *A Refutation*. John Hawkesworth. [Sig.: "X."]
39 (1769): 500–502. R: *The Patriot*. John Hawkesworth. [Sig.: "X."]
39 (1769): 527. L: "Inscription." Richard Gough. [Sig.: "D.H."]
39 (1769): 542–546. R: *Speech on Wilkes*. John Hawkesworth. [Sig.: "X."]
39 (1769): 546. R: *Some Observations*. John Hawkesworth. [Sig.: "X."]
39 (1769): 576–579. A: *Huetiana* (trans.). John Duncombe. [*Lit. Anec.* 8: 277]
39 (1769): 591–594. R: *Travels*. John Hawkesworth. [Sig.: "X."]
39 (1769): 594–596. R: *The Brothers*. John Hawkesworth. [Sig.: "X."]
39 (1769): 596–598. R: *Letter to Hillsborough*. John Hawkesworth. [Sig.: "X."]
39 (1769): 598–599. R: *Letter to Grenville*. John Hawkesworth. [Sig.: "X."]
40 (1770): 8. L: Constantine. John Loveday, Elder or Younger. [Sig.: "Academicus."]
40 (1770): 12–16. A: *Huetiana* (trans.). John Duncombe. [*Lit. Anec.* 8: 277]
40 (1770): 16. L: "Want of Character." Samuel Pegge the Elder. [*GM* 66–ii (1796): 1081]

40 (1770): 21–23.   L: "Berkley Castle." Richard Gough. [Sig.: "D.H."]
40 (1770): 29–32.   R: *Important Question*. John Hawkesworth. [Sig.: "X."]
40 (1770): 32–36.   R: *False Alarm*. John Hawkesworth. [Sig.: "X."]
40 (1770): 57–59.   A: *Huetiana* (trans.). John Duncombe. [*Lit. Anec.* 8: 277]
40 (1770): 70–71.   L: "Controversy." John Duncombe. [Sig.: "Crito"]
40 (1770): 78–80.   R: *Letter to Johnson*. John Hawkesworth. [Sig.: "X."]
40 (1770): 80–83.   R: *Posthumous Works*. John Hawkesworth. [Sig.: "X."]
40 (1770): 83.   R: *Deserter*. John Hawkesworth. [Sig.: "X."]
40 (1770): 83–84.   R: *Phil. Trans*. John Hawkesworth. [Sig.: "X."]
40 (1770): 115–119.   A: *Huetiana* (trans.). John Duncombe. [*Lit. Anec.* 8: 277]
40   1770): 125–126.   R: *Timanthes*. John Hawkesworth. [Sig.: "X."]
40 (1770): 126–129.   R: *Mungo Campbell*. John Hawkesworth. [Sig.: "X."]
40 (1770): 129–131.   R: *A Discourse*. John Hawkesworth. [Sig.: "X."]
40 (1770): 131–133.   R: *Phil. Trans*. John Hawkesworth [?]. [multi-part rev.; earlier part signed "X."]
40 (1770): 133.   R: *Account in Rings*. John Hawkesworth. [Sig.: "X."]
40 (1770): 162–163.   L: "Remarks on the *Huetiana*." Samuel Pegge the Elder. [*GM* 66–ii (1796): 1081]
40 (1770): 168–171. A: *Huetiana* (trans.). John Duncombe. [*Lit. Anec.* 8: 277]
40 (1770): 174–177.   R: *Trial of William and John Spiggott*. John Hawkesworth. [Sig.: "X."]
40 (1770): 177–180.   R: *Peter Collinson*. John Hawkesworth. [Sig.: "X."]
40 (1770): 180–181.   R: *Whole proceedings*. John Hawkesworth. [Sig.: "X."]
40 (1770): 183.   V: "To Mrs. S——." Richard Gough. [Sig.: "Q."]
40 (1770): 201–203.   *Huetiana* (trans.). John Duncombe. [*Lit. Anec.* 8: 277]
40 (1770): 203–204.   L: "Of Swallows." John Duncombe. [Sig.: "The Translator of the *Huetiana*"]
40 (1770): 222–223.   R: *Present Discontents*. John Hawkesworth. [Sig.: "X."]
40 (1770): 223–225.   R: *Letters from Voltaire*. John Hawkesworth. [Sig.: "X."]
40 (1770): 225–227.   R: *Word to the Wise*. John Hawkesworth. [Sig.: "X."]
40 (1770): 227–229.   R: *Phil. Trans*. John Hawkesworth [?]. [multi-part rev.; earlier part signed "X."]
40 (1770): 251–254.   A: *Huetiana* (trans.). John Duncombe. [*Lit. Anec.* 8: 277]
40 (1770): 256–259.   L: "Air of Italy." Richard Gough. [Sig.: "Q."]
40 (1770): 259.   L: "Correction of Virgil." Richard Gough. [Sig.: "D.H."]
40 (1770): 262.   L: "*The Novelist*." John Duncombe. [Sig.: "Crito"]
40 (1770): 271–273.   R: *Deserted Village*. John Hawkesworth. [Sig.: "X."]
40 (1770): 273–275.   R: *Sermons by a Lady*. John Hawkesworth. [Sig.: "X."]
40 (1770): 275–277.   R: *Phil. Trans*. John Hawkesworth [?]. [multi-part rev.; earlier part signed "X."]
40 (1770): 280.   V: "To John Gurney." John Duncombe [?]. [Sig.: "Crito"]
40 (1770): 290–292.   L: "Harduin's Hypothesis." Richard Gough. [Sig.: "D.H."]
40 (1770): 295.   L: "Gunnery." Samuel Pegge the Elder. [*GM* 66–ii (1796): 1081]
40 (1770): 307–310.   A: *Huetiana* (trans.). John Duncombe. [*Lit. Anec.* 8: 277]

40 (1770): 310–311. L: "Rouse mistaken." John Duncombe. [Sig.: "Crito"]
40 (1770): 320. L: "Astronomers Royal." John Duncombe. [Sig.: "Crito"]
40 (1770): 321–323. R: *Critical Observations*. John Hawkesworth. [Sig.: "X."]
40 (1770): 323–324. R: *A Journey*. John Hawkesworth. [Sig.: "X."]
40 (1770): 324–325. R: *English Language*. John Hawkesworth. [Sig.: "X."]
40 (1770): 353. L: "Progress of the Arts." John Duncombe [?]. [Sig.: "J.D."]
40 (1770): 355–357. A: *Huetiana* (trans.). John Duncombe. [*Lit. Anec.* 8: 277]
40 (1770): 376–378. R: "Baretti's Travels." John Hawkesworth. [Sig.: "X."]
40 (1770): 378–382. R: *Lame Lovers*. John Hawkesworth. [Sig.: "X."]
40 (1770): 382–383. R: *Address to the Judges*. John Hawkesworth. [Sig.: "X."]
40 (1770): 407. S: Headnote to "Celebrated Entertainment." John Duncombe. [Sig.: "Crito"]
40 (1770): 415–416. L: "Duke of Essex." John Duncombe. [Sig.: "Crito"]
40 (1770): 426–428. R: "Baretti's Travels." John Hawkesworth. [Sig.: "X."]
40 (1770): 428–430. R: Guthrie's *Grammar*. John Hawkesworth. [Sig.: "X."]
40 (1770): 430–431. R: *Age of Lewis the XVth*. John Hawkesworth. [Sig.: "X."]
40 (1770): 431. R: *Duke of Cumberland*. John Hawkesworth. [Sig.: "X."]
40 (1770): 449–452. A: *Huetiana* (trans.). John Duncombe. [*Lit. Anec.* 8: 277]
40 (1770): 454–457. A: "Prévot's Novelists." John Duncombe. [Sig.: "Crito"]
40 (1770): 464. L: Voltaire's works. John Duncombe. [Sig.: "Crito"]
40 (1770): 468. L: Passage in Virgil. Richard Gough. [Sig.: "D.H."]
40 (1770): 470. R: *Imprisonment for debt*. John Hawkesworth. [Sig.: "X."]
40 (1770): 470. R: *Automaton*. John Hawkesworth. [Sig.: "X."]
40 (1770): 470–474. R: *The Proceedings*. John Hawkesworth. [Sig.: "X."]
40 (1770): 474–476. R: "Baretti's Travels." John Hawkesworth. [Sig.: "X."]
40 (1770): 476. R: *Thoughts English and Irish*. John Hawkesworth. [Sig.: "X."]
40 (1770): 479. V: "Sent to a Young Lady." John Duncombe. [Sig.: "Crito"]
40 (1770): 501–505. A: *Huetiana* (trans.). John Duncombe. [*Lit. Anec.* 8: 277]
40 (1770): 505. L: Archbishop Laud. John Duncombe. [Sig.: "Crito"]
40 (1770): 510–511. L: "Translation of antient Authors." John Hawkesworth [?]. [Sig.: "X."]
40 (1770): 527. R: *Press Warrants*. John Hawkesworth. [Sig.: "X."]
40 (1770): 527–528. R: *Letter to Mansfield*. John Hawkesworth. [Sig.: "X."]
40 (1770): 528. R: *Two Speeches*. John Hawkesworth. [Sig.: "X."]
40 (1770): 528–530. R: "Baretti's Travels." John Hawkesworth. [Sig.: "X."]
40 (1770): 530–531. R: *Plutarch's Lives*. John Hawkesworth. [Sig.: "X."]
40 (1770): 566–568. L: "Gift from the Clergy." John Duncombe. [Sig.: "Crito"]
40 (1770): 578–582. R: *It is Well it is no Worse*. John Hawkesworth. [Sig.: "X."]
40 (1770): 616–617. L: "Plautus." John Hawkesworth [?]. [Sig.: "X."]
41 (1771): 9–12. A: *Huetiana* (trans.). John Duncombe. [*Lit. Anec.* 8: 277]
41 (1771): 30–31. R: *Choir Gaur*. Richard Gough. [Sig.: "D.H."]

41 (1771): 73–76. A: *Huetiana* (trans.). John Duncombe. [*Lit. Anec.* 8: 277]
41 (1771): 77–80. R: *Fevers*. John Hawkesworth. [Sig.: "X."]
41 (1771): 82–84. R: *Temple of Compassion*. John Hawkesworth. [Sig.: "X."]
41 (1771): 84. R: *Natural Paper*. John Hawkesworth. [Sig.: "X."]
41 (1771): 115–116. L: "Great." Samuel Pegge the Elder. [*GM* 66–ii (1796): 1081]
41 (1771): 120–121. L: Inscription. Richard Gough. [Sig.: "D.H."]
41 (1771): 124–127. R: *West Indian*. John Hawkesworth. [Sig.: "X."]
41 1771): 127–128. R: *Almeida*. John Hawkesworth. [Sig.: "X."]
41 (1771): 128–130. R: *Critical Observations*. John Hawkesworth. [Sig.: "X."]
41 (1771): 130. R: *Speeches at large*. John Hawkesworth. [Sig.: "X."]
41 (1771): 153. A: "Osney Abbey." William Huddesford. [*Illust.* 4: 456]
41 (1771): 154–156. A: *Huetiana* (trans.). John Duncombe. [*Lit. Anec.* 8: 277]
41 (1771): 166. L: Princes called "the Great." John Duncombe. [Sig.: "Crito"]
41 (1771): 173–177. R: *Shipwreck*. John Hawkesworth [?]. [multi-part rev.; conc. signed "X."]
41 (1771): 177–180. R: *Historical Extracts*. John Hawkesworth. [Sig.: "X."]
41 (1771): 204. L: Osney Abbey. William Huddesford. [*Illust.* 4: 456]
41 (1771): 206–207. S: Freedom of conscience. John Hawkesworth. [Sig.: "X."]
41 (1771): 219–221. R: *Shipwreck*. John Hawkesworth [?]. [multi-part rev.; conc. signed "X."]
41 (1771): 221–222. R: *Minstrel*. John Hawkesworth. [Sig.: "X."]
41 (1771): 222–224. R: *State of Musick*. John Hawkesworth. [Sig.: "X."]
41 (1771): 225–227. R: *Medea and Jason*. John Hawkesworth. [Sig.: "X."]
41 (1771): 252–255. A: *Huetiana* (trans.). John Duncombe. [*Lit. Anec.* 8: 277]
41 (1771): 257. L: "Antiquities of Sarum." Mr. Haxman [?]. [Sig.: "Ignotus"]
41 (1771): 257. L: Hospital at Newton. Richard Gough. [Sig.: "D.H."]
41 (1771): 262. L: "Curious Leonine Verses." Samuel Pegge the Elder. [*GM* 66–ii (1796): 1081]
41 (1771): 268–271. R: *Shipwreck*. John Hawkesworth. [Sig.: "X."]
41 (1771): 271–274. R: *Gout*. John Hawkesworth. [Sig.: "X."]
41 (1771): 274–277. R: *An Address*. John Hawkesworth. [Sig.: "X."]
41 (1771): 277. R: *Essay on Townshend*. John Hawkesworth. [Sig.: "X."]
41 (1771): 300–301. L: "Avarice." Samuel Pegge the Elder. [*GM* 66–ii (1796): 1081]
41 (1771): 315–317. R: *Historia*. Richard Gough. [Sig.: "D.H."]
41 (1771): 321–323. R: *A Discourse*. John Hawkesworth. [Sig.: "X."]
41 (1771): 323. R: *History of France*. John Hawkesworth. [Sig.: "X."]
41 (1771): 323–325. R: Camoens' *Lusiad*. John Hawkesworth. [Sig.: "X."]
41 (1771): 344. L: "George's Island." John Duncombe. [Sig.: "Crito"]
41 (1771): 350–351. A: *Huetiana* (trans.). John Duncombe. [*Lit. Anec.* 8: 277]
41 (1771): 352–353. A: "Stature and Figure of Old People." Samuel Pegge the Elder. [*GM* 66–ii (1796): 1081]

41 (1771): 363–366. R: *Hermit of Warkwork*. John Hawkesworth. [Sig.: "X."]
41 (1771): 366–369. R: *Book of Job*. John Hawkesworth. [Sig.: "X."]
41 (1771): 369–370. R: *Doctor Dissected*. John Hawkesworth. [Sig.: "X."]
41 (1771): 370. R: *The Debauchee*. John Hawkesworth. [Sig.: "X."]
41 (1771): 401–402. L: "Cruelty of Aurelians." John Nichols [?]. [Sig.: "Eusebia"]
41 (1771): 410–414. R: *Chemistry*. John Hawkesworth. [Sig.: "X."]
41 (1771): 414–415. R: *Address to Cadogan*. John Hawkesworth. [Sig.: "X."]
41 (1771): 415–416. R: *Hermit Converted*. John Hawkesworth. [Sig.: "X."]
41 (1771): 439–443. A: *Huetiana* (trans.). John Duncombe. [*Lit. Anec.* 8: 277]
41 (1771): 446. L: "Clarendon's History." John Duncombe. [Sig.: "Crito"]
41 (1771): 459–460. L: "Lunar Hypothesis." Richard Gough. [Sig.: "Q."]
41 (1771): 461–464. R: *Properties of the Blood*. John Hawkesworth. [Sig.: "X."]
41 (1771): 464–466. R: *Chemistry*. John Hawkesworth. [Sig.: "X."]
41 (1771): 468. V: "Epigram." Richard Gough. [Sig.: "Q."]
41 (1771): 496. L: Scottish Antiquities. Richard Gough. [Sig.: "D.H."]
41 (1771): 499–500. L: Reply to "A Confessionalian." John Loveday, Elder or Younger. [Sig.: "Academicus"]
41 (1771): 500–501. L: Dido. Samuel Pegge the Elder. [*GM* 66–ii (1796): 1081]
41 (1771): 509–512. R: *Journal of a Voyage*. John Hawkesworth. [Sig.: "X."]
41 (1771): 512–514. S: *Histoire et Memoirs* [sic]. John Hawkesworth. [Sig.: "X."]
41 (1771): 534–535. L: "Saxon Heroine." Samuel Pegge the Elder. [*GM* 66–ii (1796): 1081]
41 (1771): 543–546. L: "List of Inns." Richard Gough. [Sig.: "D.H."]
41 (1771): 547–548. L: "Royal Marriage." John Duncombe. [Sig.: "Crito"]
41 (1771): 557–560. R: *Travels through Louisiana*. John Hawkesworth. [Sig.: "X."]
41 (1771): 606. L: "Brass Plate." John Nichols [?]. [Sig.: "Nauticus"]
42 (1772): 13–14. L: "Pestilential Winds." Samuel Pegge the Elder. [*GM* 66–ii (1796): 1081]
42 (1772): 29–30. R: *The Theatres*. John Hawkesworth. [Sig.: "X."]
42 (1772): 30–33. R: *Imprisonment for Debt*. John Hawkesworth. [Sig.: "X."]
42 (1772): 60–61. L: "Latin Parody." John Duncombe [?]. [Sig.: "J.D."]
42 (1772): 78–80. R: *English Garden*. John Hawkesworth. [Sig.: "X."]
42 (1772): 80–81. R: *Fashionable Lover*. John Hawkesworth. [Sig.: "X."]
42 (1772): 81–83. R: *Zobeide*. John Hawkesworth. [Sig.: "X."]
42 (1772): 119–120. A: "Sirnames [sic]." Samuel Pegge the Elder. [*GM* 66–ii (1796): 1081]
42 (1772): 120–121. L: "Killing Game." David Henry. [Sig.: "Y.D."]
42 (1772): 134–135. R: *Nowel's Sermon*. John Hawkesworth. [Sig.: "X."]
42 (1772): 137–139. R: *Grecian Daughter*. John Hawkesworth. [Sig.: "X."]
42 (1772): 169. L: "Cure for the Stranguary." David Henry [?]. [Sig.: "Y.D."]
42 (1772): 170–172: L: "Cause of Dearth." David Henry. [Sig.: "Y.D."]

42 (1772): 175. L: Misc. corrections for *GM.* Richard Gough. [Sig.: "D.H."]

42 (1772): 182. R: *Capital Punishment.* John Hawkesworth. [Sig.: "X."]

42 (1772): 182–185. R: *A Discourse.* John Hawkesworth. [Sig.: "X."]

42 (1772): 185–186. R: *Historia.* Richard Gough. [Sig.: "D.H."]

42 (1772): 186–188. R: *Med. Trans.* John Hawkesworth [?]. [multi-part rev.; cont. is signed "X."]

42 (1772): 208. L: "Letter from Francis I." Richard Gough. [Sig.: "D.H."]

42 (1772): 219–221. L: "Ancient History." John Duncombe. [Sig.: "Crito"]

42 (1772): 231–232. R: *Christian Minister.* John Hawkesworth. [Sig.: "X."]

42 (1772): 232–233. R: *Wensley-Dale.* John Hawkesworth. [Sig.: "X."]

42 (1772): 233–234. R: *Men-Midwives.* John Hawkesworth. [Sig.: "X."]

42 (1772): 234–235. R: *Med. Trans.* John Hawkesworth [?]. [multi-part rev.; cont. is signed "X."]

42 (1772): 253–254. L: "Sirnames [sic]." Samuel Pegge the Elder. [*GM* 66–ii (1796): 1081]

42 (1772): 254. L: "Property of Iron." David Henry [?]. [Sig.: "Y.D."]

42 (1772): 255–256. L: "Passage in Juvenal." Richard Gough. [Sig.: "D.H."]

42 (1772): 256. L: Answers to "Q." John Duncombe. [Sig.: "Crito"]

42 (1772): 257–258. O: "Mrs. Catharine [sic] Talbot." Sarah Duncombe. [*Lit. Anec.* 9: 769]

42 (1772): 273–275. A: "Extracts from *British Topography.*" John Duncombe. [*Lit. Anec.* 6: 271–272]

42 (1772): 278–280. R: *Sermons to the Rich.* John Hawkesworth. [Sig.: "X."]

42 (1772): 280–281. R: *Med. Trans.* John Hawkesworth [?]. [multi-part rev.; cont. is signed "X."]

42 (1772): 281. R: *Theodore Agrippa D'Aubigné.* John Hawkesworth. [Sig.: "X."]

42 (1772): 281–284. R: *Dissenting Ministers.* John Hawkesworth. [Sig.: "X."]

42 (1772): 284–285. R: *Senators.* John Hawkesworth. [Sig.: "X."]

42 (1772): 305. L: "Dividing Parishes." S. Watson. [*GM* 44 (1774): 161]

42 (1772): 311–312. L: "Introduction of Cherries." David Henry. [Sig.: "D.Y."]

42 (1772): 318–320. L: "Surnames." Samuel Pegge the Elder. [*GM* 66–ii (1796): 1081]

42 (1772): 324–325. R: "Foreign Intelligence." John Hawkesworth. [Sig.: "X."]

42 (1772): 325–326. R: *Abolition of Slavery.* John Hawkesworth. [Sig.: "X."]

42 (1772): 327–328. R: *Med. Trans.* John Hawkesworth. [Sig.: "X."]

42 (1772): 328–329. R: *Oeconomy of Beauty.* John Hawkesworth. [Sig.: "X."]

42 (1772): 367–368. A: "List of Surnames." Samuel Pegge the Elder. [*GM* 66–ii (1796): 1081]

42 (1772): 371–372. L: "Sir Thomas Bodley." John Loveday, Elder or Younger. [Sig.: "Academicus"]

42 (1772): 406–407. L: "A singular Character." S. Watson. [*GM* 44 (1774): 161]

42 (1772): 413.   L: "Battle of Blore-heath." S. Watson. [*GM* 44 (1774): 161]
42 (1772): 419.   L: "Wild Pine of Jamaica." David Henry [?]. [Sig.: "Y.D."]
42 (1772): 468–470.   L: "Sirnames." Samuel Pegge the Elder. [*GM* 66–ii (1796): 1081]
42 (1772): 510–511.   L: "English Sirnames." Samuel Pegge the Elder. [*GM* 66–ii (1796): 1081]
42 (1772): 517–518.   L: "Westminster Abbey." John Duncombe. [Sig.: "Crito"]
42 (1772): 520.   L: Life of Newton enclosed. Richard Gough. [Sig.: "D.H."]
42 (1772): 523.   L: Query re inscription. Richard Gough. [Sig.: "D.H."]
42 (1772): 528–532.   R: *Irish Widow.* John Hawkesworth. [Sig.: "X."]
42 (1772): 562–565.   A: Church organs. William Ludlam. [*Lit. Anec.* 3: 639]
42 (1772): 573.   L: "Inscription." Samuel Pegge the Elder. [*GM* 66–ii (1796): 1081]
43 (1773): 8.   L: "Reply to Mr. Row." Richard Gough. [Sig.: "Q."]
43 (1773): 15–16.   L: "Tradesmen's Daughters." John Nichols. [Sig.: "J.N."]
43 (1773): 17.   L: "Epitaph." Richard Gough. [Sig.: "D.H."]
43 (1773): 19.   L: "Of the Leviathan." Samuel Pegge the Elder. [*GM* 66–ii (1796): 1081]
43 (1773): 31–32.   R: *Conscience.* John Hawkesworth. [Sig.: "X."]
43 (1773): 32–33.   R: *Med. Trans.* John Hawkesworth. [Sig.: "X."]
43 (1773): 33–34.   R: *Case of James Sommersett.* John Hawkesworth. [Sig.: "X."]
43 (1773): 34–35.   R: *Poetical Epistle.* John Hawkesworth. [Sig.: "X."]
43 (1773): 35.   R: Earl of Carlisle's *Poems.* John Hawkesworth. [Sig.: "X."]
43 (1773): 61–63.   L: "Pig of Lead." Samuel Pegge the Elder. [*GM* 66–ii (1796): 1081]
43 (1773): 66–68.   L: "Prices of Provisions." David Henry. [Sig.: "Y.D."]
43 (1773): 82–86.   R: *A Discourse.* John Hawkesworth. [Sig.: "X."]
43 (1773): 122–123.   L: "Hume's Account of Quakerism." John Loveday, Elder or Younger. [Sig.: "Scrutator"]
43 (1773): 123–124.   L: "Voltaire's Misrepresentation." S. Watson. [*GM* 44 (1774): 161]
43 (1773): 134–136.   R: *Orlando Furioso.* John Hawkesworth. [Sig.: "X."]
43 (1773): 136–137.   R: *Agreeable Companion.* John Hawkesworth. [Sig.: "X."]
43 (1773): 137–140.   R: *Alonzo.* John Hawkesworth. [Sig.: "X."]
43 (1773): 172–173.   L: "Church of Rome." S. Watson. [*GM* 44 (1774): 161]
43 (1773): 182–184.   L: "Similies [sic] in Pope." Richard Gough. [Sig.: "Q."]
43 (1773): 211–212.   L: Northern lights. John Nichols. [Sig.: "J.N."]
43 (1773): 223–224.   L: "Fact corrected." John Duncombe. [Sig.: "Crito"]
43 (1773): 281–282.   L: Severn blockage. S. Watson. [*GM* 44 (1774): 161]
43 (1773): 283–284.   A: Bishop Burnet's description of destruction of Pleurs enclosed. Stephen Weston. [Sig.: "S.W."]
43 (1773): 319.   L: "Remark on Pliny." Richard Gough. [Sig.: "Q."]
43 (1773): 324–325.   L: "Voltaire's Vindication." S. Watson. [*GM* 44 (1774): 161]
43 (1773): 369.   L: P. Du Moulin's MS enclosed. John Duncombe. [Sig.: "J.D."]

43 (1773): 384–385. L: "St. Blase." Samuel Pegge the Elder. [*GM* 66–ii (1796): 1081]
43 (1773): 438. L: "Additional Anecdotes." John Duncombe. [Sig.: "Crito"]
43 (1773): 439. L: "Serpent destroyed by Regulus." Samuel Pegge the Elder. [*GM* 66–ii (1796): 1081]
43 (1773): 480. L: "Monstrous Serpent." David Henry [?]. [Sig.: "Y.D."]
43 (1773): 483–484. L: "Cromwell family." John Loveday, Elder or Younger. [Sig.: "Scrutator"]
43 (1773): 484. L: "Letter proved spurious." John Duncombe. [Sig.: "Crito"]
43 (1773): 499–500. L: "Anecdotes." John Duncombe [?]. [Sig.: "J.D."]
43 (1773): 547. L: Corrections for *GM*. S. Watson. [*GM* 44 (1774): 161]
43 (1773): 581. L: "Parliamentary Anecdote." Richard Gough. [Sig.: "R.G."]
43 (1773): 584. L: Creases on vellum. John Nichols [?]. [Sig.: "Nauticus"]
44 (1774): 62. L: Bacon's plan enclosed. David Henry. [Sig.: "Y.D."]
44 (1774): 75–76. L: "Ferguson's Principles." Henry Lemoine [?]. [Sig.: "H.L."]
44 (1774): 76. L: "Shakespeare's Description." Henry Lemoine [?]. [Sig.: "H.L."]
44 (1774): 77. L: "Pope's Translation." John Duncombe. [Sig.: "Crito"]
44 (1774): 122–123. L: "Journey of Innocent IV." Samuel Pegge the Elder. [Sig.: "T. Row"]
44 (1774): 153. L: "Fragment of History." David Henry [?]. [Sig.: "Y.D."]
44 (1774): 165. L: "Wild-Cats." Samuel Pegge the Elder. [*GM* 66–ii (1796): 1081]
44 (1774): 166. L: Barré's speech enclosed. David Henry. [Sig.: "Y.D."]
44 (1774): 247. A: Commentary on "Auncient Ordre." Richard Gough. [Sig.: "D.H."]
44 (1774): 249. L: "Voltaire." John Duncombe. [Sig.: "Crito"]
44 (1774): 249–250. L: "Art of Healing." David Henry. [Sig.: "Y.D."]
44 (1774): 252–253. L: "Names retained." Samuel Pegge the Elder. [*GM* 66–ii (1796): 1081]
44 (1774): 314–316. L: "Names retained [cont.]." Samuel Pegge the Elder. [*GM* 66–ii (1796): 1081]
44 (1774): 328. V: "A Thought at the Grave." John Duncombe [?]. [Sig.: "J.D."]
44 (1774): 351–352. L: "Planting Wheat." David Henry. [Sig.: "Y.D."]
44 (1774): 361–362. L: "Explanation of Antiquities." Samuel Pegge the Elder. [*GM* 66–ii (1796): 1081]
44 (1774): 402–403. L: "Pre-existent State of Christ." John Nichols. [Sig.: "J.N."]
44 (1774): 403–404. L: "Caesar's Landing." John Duncombe. [Sig.: "Crito"]
44 (1774): 406–407. L: "Names retained." Samuel Pegge the Elder. [*GM* 66–ii (1796): 1081]
44 (1774): 407–408. L: "Dr. Johnson." David Wells [?]. [Sig.: "Observator"]
44 (1774): 409. L: "Joseph of Arimathea." Stephen Weston. [Sig.: "S.W."]
44 (1774): 409. L: "Ancient Inscription." Richard Gough. [Sig.: "Q."]
44 (1774): 456. L: "American Advertisement." David Henry [?]. [Sig.: "Y.D."]
44 (1774): 456. L: "Wisbech Inscription." Richard Gough. [Sig.: "D.H."]

44 (1774): 459. L: "Rider's *History*." John Duncombe. [Sig.: "Crito"]

44 (1774): 462. L: "Bon-Mot." John Duncombe. [Sig.: "Crito"]

44 (1774): 465. L: "Bryant's *Mythology*." Stephen Weston. [Sig.: "S.W."]

44 (1774): 508–510. L: "Baptisteries [sic]." Samuel Denne. [Sig.: "W. and D."]

44 (1774): 519–520. L: "Interesting Story." Samuel Pegge the Elder. [*GM* 66–ii (1796): 1081]

44 (1774): 553–554. L: Herculaneum plates. George Ashby. [*Illust.* 7: 396–397]

44 (1774): 560. L: "Humourous Story." S. Watson. [*GM* 44 (1774): 161]

44 (1774): 563–564. A: "Flight of Henry de Bourbon" (trans.). Samuel Pegge the Elder. [*GM* 66–ii (1796): 1081]

44 (1774): 619–620. A: "Flight of Henry de Bourbon" (trans.). Samuel Pegge the Elder. [*GM* 66–ii (1796): 1081]

44 (1774): 627. L: "Miscellaneous Remarks." John Loveday, Elder or Younger. [Sig.: "Academicus"]

45 (1775): 14–16. A: "Flight of Henry de Bourbon" (trans.). Samuel Pegge the Elder. [*GM* 66–ii (1796): 1081]

45 (1775): 24. L: "Critical Remarks." Richard Gough. [Sig.: "Q."]

45 (1775): 65–66. L: "Private Judgment." Joseph Robertson. [Sig.: "Eusebius"]

45 (1775): 66–69. A: "Flight of Henry de Bourbon" (trans.). Samuel Pegge the Elder. [*GM* 66–ii (1796): 1081]

45 (1775): 113–115. A: "Flight of Henry de Bourbon" (trans.). Samuel Pegge the Elder. [*GM* 66–ii (1796): 1081]

45 (1775): 132. L: "Cruelties of Discoverers." Richard Gough. [Sig.: "H.D."]

45 (1775): 169–171. A: "Flight of Henry de Bourbon" (trans.). Samuel Pegge the Elder. [*GM* 66–ii (1796): 1081]

45 (1775): 178–180. L: "Punishing monks." Samuel Denne. [Sig.: "W. & D."]

45 (1775): 232–234. A: "Flight of Henry de Bourbon" (trans.). Samuel Pegge the Elder. [*GM* 66–ii (1796): 1081]

45 (1775): 273. L: "Moderation of K. William." John Nichols. [Sig.: "J.N."]

45 (1775): 273–274. L: "Yorick and Eliza." Richard Gough. [Sig.: "D.H."]

45 (1775): 274. L: "Seal." Samuel Pegge the Elder. [*GM* 66–ii (1796): 1082]

45 (1775): 326. L: "Late Occurrences." Richard Gough. [Sig.: "D.H."]

45 (1775): 326–327. L: "Critique on Horace." Samuel Pegge the Elder. [*GM* 66–ii (1796): 1082]

45 (1775): 327. L: "Arms of Archbishops." Richard Gough. [Sig.: "Q."]

45 (1775): 364–365. L: "Antiquities of Rochester." John Loveday, Elder or Younger. [Sig.: "Academicus"]

45 (1775): 392–393. L: "Snails." Samuel Pegge the Elder. [*GM* 66–ii (1796): 1082]

45 (1775): 480. L: "Mitre." Samuel Pegge the Elder. [*GM* 66–ii (1796): 1082]

45 (1775): 481. L: Chandler's description of Sigeum enclosed. Stephen Weston. [Sig.: "S.W."]

45 (1775): 513–516. L: "Wine made in England." Richard Gough. [Sig.: "R.G."]

45 (1775): 529–530. L: "Gostling's Walk." John Loveday, Elder or Younger. [Sig.: "Academicus"]

45 (1775): 629. L: "Hearne's Epitaph." John Loveday, Elder or Younger. [Sig.: "Academicus"]

45 (1775): 632–633. L: "Culture of Vines." Richard Gough. [Sig.: "H.D."]

45 (1775): 633. L: "Copland's *Herbal*." Richard Gough. [Sig.: "D.H."]

45 (1775): 633–634. L: "St. Paul's Shipwreck." John Duncombe. [Sig.: "Crito"]

46 (1776): 8. L: "Queries." John Loveday, Elder or Younger. [Sig.: "Academicus"]

46 (1776): 57–59. L: "Cathedral of Canterbury." Samuel Denne. [Sig.: "W. & D."]

46 (1776): 63–64. L: "Extraordinary Princess." John Duncombe. [Sig.: "Crito"]

46 (1776): 64. L: "Pompey the Little." John Duncombe [?]. [Sig.: "J.D."]

46 (1776): 105–106. L: "Diamonds." George Ashby. [*Illust.* 7: 399–400]

46 (1776): 110–111. L: "Divinity of our Saviour." John Nichols. [Sig.: "J.N."]

46 (1776): 116. L: "Christ-Church, Canterbury." John Loveday, Elder or Younger. [Sig.: "Academicus"]

46 (1776): 154. A: Preface to a sermon. Samuel Pegge the Elder. [*GM* 66–ii (1796): 1082]

46 (1776): 157–158. L: "Shakespeare." George Ashby. [*Illust.* 7: 397–399]

46 (1776): 167–168. L: "Homer's Geography." J. Greene [?]. [Sig.: "Fidus"]

46 (1776): 208–210. L: "Reply to Academicus." Samuel Denne. [Sig.: "W. & D."]

46 (1776): 210–211. L: "Creation of Peers." John Duncombe. [Sig.: "Crito"]

46 (1776): 355. L: "Head-Ach [sic]." Richard Gough. [Sig.: "H.D."]

46 (1776): 356–357. L: "Thomas-a-Kempis." Richard Gough. [Sig.: "H.D."]

46 (1776): 396. L: Jerry Markland. John Duncombe. [Sig.: "Crito"]

46 (1776): 401. L: "Vindication of Addison." Richard Gough. [Sig.: "H.D."]

46 (1776): 416. L: "Reply to W. & D." John Loveday, Elder or Younger. [Sig.: "Academicus"]

46 (1776): 446–447. L: "Hutchinson's Remarks." Richard Gough. [*Lit. Anec.* 8: 700–701]

46 (1776): 448. L: *Ars Generalis Ultima*. Samuel Pegge the Elder. [*GM* 66–ii (1796): 1082]

46 (1776): 461. S: Headnote re Critique on Bryant. Richard Gough. [*Illust.* 7: 437]

46 (1776): 461–463. A: Critique on Bryant. George Ashby. [*Illust.* 7: 437]

46 (1776): 463–464. L: "Peerages." John Duncombe. [Sig.: "Crito"]

46 (1776): 496. A: Benjamin Stillingfleet. John Loveday, Elder or Younger. [Sig.: "Academicus"]

46 (1776): 497. L: "Raymond Lully." Samuel Denne. [Sig.: "W. and D."]

46 (1776): 511–512. L: "Latin Jest-Book." Samuel Pegge the Elder. [*GM* 66–ii (1796): 1082]

46 (1776): 512. L: "Passage in *Hamlet*." Samuel Denne. [Sig.: "W. and D."]

46 (1776): 540. L: William King. Samuel Denne. [Sig.: "W. & D."]

46 (1776): 558–559. L: "Seasonable Reflections." Michael Wodhull. [Sig.: "L.L."]

46 (1776): 601–603. L: "Miscellaneous Observations." John Loveday, Elder or Younger. [Sig.: "Scrutator"]

47 (1777): 13. L: "Bishop Berkeley." John Loveday, Elder or Younger. [Sig.: "Academicus"]

47 (1777): 35. R: *Dissertation upon Phalaris.* John Duncombe. [*Lit. Anec.* 3: 250–251]

47 (1777): 58–59. L: "Constructing Glasses." Samuel Pegge the Elder. [*GM* 66–ii (1796): 1082]

47 (1777): 86–87. V: "Epitaphium." John Carr. [*Lit. Anec.* 8: 305]

47 (1777): 104. L: Cornua Ammonis. Michael Wodhull. [Sig.: "L.L."]

47 (1777): 115. L: "L'Estrange's *Josephus.*" John Duncombe. [Sig.: "Crito"]

47 (1777): 116–117. L. "Cromwell Family." John Loveday, Elder or Younger. [Sig.: "Scrutator"]

47 (1777): 124. L: "Anecdote." John Duncombe. [Sig.: "Crito."]

47 (1777): 165–167. L: "Scripture Chronology defended." John Loveday, Elder or Younger. [Sig.: "Academicus"]

47 (1777): 217–218. L: Supplement to Swift corrected. John Loveday, Elder or Younger. [Sig.: "Scrutator"]

47 (1777): 261–262. L: "St. Constantius." Samuel Denne. [Sig.: "W. & D."]

47 (1777): 262–263. L: More on St. Constantius. Samuel Denne. [Sig.: "W. & D."]

47 (1777): 304. L: "Goose-Grass." Samuel Ayscough [?]. [Sig.: "S.A."]

47 (1777): 314. L: "Pennant's 2d Tour to Scotland." John Loveday the Younger. [*Illust.* 3: 458]

47 (1777): 320–322. A: "Of the Crasis." Samuel Pegge the Elder. [*GM* 66–ii (1796): 1082]

47 (1777): 361–365. A: "Rowley's Poems." Michael Lort. [*Lit. Anec.* 2: 597]

47 (1777): 372. L: On Mr. Cromwell. John Duncombe. [Sig.: "Crito"]

47 (1777): 372–374. A: "Of the Crasis." Samuel Pegge the Elder. [*GM* 66–ii (1796): 1082]

47 (1777): 374–375. L: "Mr. Delany." John Duncombe. [Sig.: "Crito"]

47 (1777): 381. L: Dean Swift, etc. John Loveday, Elder or Younger. [Sig.: "Scrutator"]

47 (1777): 382. L: "Coin of Maximinus." Richard Gough. [Sig.: "D.H."]

47 (1777): 421–422. L: "Dodd's Publications." Richard Gough [?]. [Sig.: "Historicus"]

47 (1777): 431–432. L: "Dog-days." Richard Gough. [Sig.: "P.Q."]

47 (1777): 440. L: "Pennant's Eulogium." John Loveday, Elder or Younger. [Sig.: "Academicus"]

47 (1777): 470. L: "Mrs. Macaulay's Statue." John Duncombe. [Sig.: "Crito"]

47 (1777): 484. L: "Inscriptions discovered." David Henry [?]. [Sig.: "D.Y."]

47 (1777): 520–521. L: "National Society." Richard Gough. [Sig.: "P.Q."]

47 (1777): 527. L: "Of the Crasis." Samuel Pegge the Elder. [*GM* 66–ii (1796): 1082]

47 (1777): 544–546. R: *Doctrine of the Sphere.* Richard Gough. [Sig.: "Q."]

47 (1777): 567–568. L: "Method of developing Inscriptions." Samuel Pegge the Elder. [*GM* 66–ii (1796): 1082]

47 (1777): 589–590. A: "Of Briefs." John Duncombe. [Sig.: "Crito"]

47 (1777): 641. L: "Remarks on divers Passages." John Loveday, Elder or Younger. [Sig.: "Scrutator"]

ADDITIONS TO KUIST'S *NICHOLS FILE*:
SYNOPSIS BY CONTRIBUTOR

Ashby, Rev. George (1724–1808). 44 (1774): 553–554; 46 (1776): 105–106, 157–158, 461–463.

Ayscough, Rev. Samuel (1745–1804). 47 (1777): 304 [?].

Bartram, John. 35 (1765): 511–514.

Carr, John (1732–1807). 47 (1777): 86–87.

Cave, Edward (1691–1754). 2 (1732): 822; 5 (1735): 734–736; 19 (1749): 288, 413n; 22 (1752): iii.

Collinson, Peter (1694–1768). 21 (1751): 561; 25 (1755): 503–504, 550–551; 26 (1756): 16, 113–114; 35 (1765): 159–160, 212; 36 (1766): 331.

Cowper, John (1737–70). 31 (1761): 374.

Denne, Rev. Samuel (1730–99). 39 (1769): 252 [?]; 44 (1774): 508–510; 45 (1775): 178–180; 46 (1776): 57–59, 208–210, 497, 512, 540; 47 (1777): 261–262, 262–263.

Dodd, Rev. William (1729–77). 36 (1766): 203–204 [?].

Duncombe, Rev. John (1729–86). 23 (1753): 92, 412–413, 421–423; 29 (1759): 587, 593; 30 (1760): 337, 382 (2), 514–515; 31 (1761): 38, 125 [?]; 32 (1762): 35, 87; 34 (1764): 537 (2); 35 (1765): 6–7, 112–114; 37 (1767): 346–347, 453–456, 488; 38 (1768): 18–20, 57–61, 213–215, 373–376, 462–464; 39 (1769): 19–21, 122–126, 281–284, 345–348, 382–385, 576–579; 40 (1770): 12–16, 57–59, 70–71, 115–119, 168–171, 201–203, 203–204, 251–254, 262, 280 [?], 307–310, 310–311, 320, 353 [?], 355–357, 407, 415–416, 449–452, 454–457, 464, 479, 501–505, 505, 566–568; 41 (1771): 9–12, 73–76, 154–156, 166, 252–255, 344, 350–351, 439–443, 446, 547–548; 42 (1772): 60–61 [?], 219–221, 256, 273–275, 517–518; 43 (1773): 223–224, 369, 438, 484, 499–500 [?]; 44 (1774): 77, 249, 328 [?], 403–404, 459, 462; 45 (1775): 633–634; 46 (1776): 63–64, 64 [?], 210–211, 396, 463–464; 47 (1777): 35, 115, 124, 372, 374–375, 470, 589–590.

Duncombe, Sarah. 42 (1772): 257–258.

Farneworth, Rev. Ellis (d. 1763). 25 (1755): 59–61 [?].

Fothergill, Dr. John (1712–80). 21 (1751): 151, 195–196, 243–244, 293, 344, 390, 440, 488, 577–578; 22 (1752): 5–6, 56, 75, 102, 151–152, 202, 252, 300, 346, 396, 443–444, 497–498, 590–591; 23 (1753): 8, 63, 112, 158, 209, 260, 305, 354–355, 401, 453–454, 502, 553–554; 24 (1754): 8, 58, 106, 151–152, 204, 256, 303, 352, 400, 445–446, 493–494; 25 (1755): 6–7, 7, 55, 103, 152, 197 (2), 197–198, 246, 343, 439 (2).

Franklin, Benjamin (1706–90). 22 (1752): 560–561.

Gough, Richard (1735–1809). 37 (1767): 443–444, 549; 38 (1768): 5–6, 208, 327, 464, 515–516, 608–609; 39 (1769): 247–248, 345, 425–427, 443, 527; 40 (1770): 21–23, 183, 256–259, 259, 290–292, 468; 41 (1771): 30–31, 120–121, 257, 315–317, 459–460, 468, 496, 543–546; 42 (1772): 175, 185–186, 208, 255–256, 520, 523; 43 (1773): 8, 17, 182–184, 319, 581; 44 (1774): 247, 409, 456; 45 (1775): 24, 132, 273–274, 326, 327, 513–516, 632–633, 633; 46 (1776): 355, 356–357, 401, 446–447, 461; 47 (1777): 382, 421–422 [?], 431–432, 520–521, 544–546.

Greene, Rev. J. 46 (1776): 167–168 [?].

Weston, Rev. Stephen (1747–1830). 43 (1773): 283–284; 44 (1774): 409, 465; 45 (1775): 481.
Wodhull, Michael (1740–1816). 38 (1768): 355, 356; 46 (1776): 558–559; 47 (1777): 104.

A COLLABORATION IN LEARNING: *THE GENTLEMAN'S MAGAZINE* AND ITS INGENIOUS CONTRIBUTORS

by

JAMES M. KUIST

DURING the last fifty years of the eighteenth century and the first three decades of the nineteenth, *The Gentleman's Magazine* published thousands of articles, poems, and reviews submitted by writers in the public at large.[1] Before 1750 and after about 1830, the magazine was largely the product of a paid staff, but during the intervening eight decades—nearly a century of publication—this periodical took its character from qualities inherent in the ideas and opinions of the hundreds of writers who contributed to its pages each year on a volunteer basis. Although in its general format and informational features *The Gentleman's Magazine* perpetuated qualities which gave it popularity and wide circulation in its earliest years, the grounds on which it maintained its strength after 1750 were the intimacy and plenitude with which it represented the mind of its audience since it published work emanating from that audience itself. The leading feature of the magazine each month, the section of "Miscellaneous Essays," which ran to half or more of each number, was nearly exclusively the domain of contributing writers. The next featured section, the poetry, also was largely supplied by contributors.

The editors, of course, published selectively and maintained a discernible presence. They tended, however, to appear submerged in the identity of the fictitious proprietor Sylvanus Urban, and even Mr. Urban changed the manner in which he presided over the publication so widely recognized as his. In the beginning, he had served the public, city and country at once, by selecting from other periodicals the most readable essays and other literary works and by providing the most current information. With the years, however, his

---

1. Documentation for the following discussion of the magazine's history may be found in the introduction to my book, *The Nichols File of "The Gentleman's Magazine"* (Madison, WI: Univ. of Wisconsin Press, 1982), pp. 3–22, and in my earlier monograph, *The Works of John Nichols: An Introduction* (New York: Kraus Reprints, 1968).

presence grew avuncular: he served as an arbiter and genial host. Correspondents almost invariably addressed him among their opening remarks. This matter of form attended to, however, the contributing writers developed discourse almost entirely intended for one another. The pages of *The Gentleman's Magazine* became a forum in which many individual voices were to be heard, and each was to be given an equal hearing (or at least the opportunity for one). The value and significance of such an opportunity were not lost on several generations of literate men and women in England, continental Europe, and America.

To the cultural historian, *The Gentleman's Magazine* serves today as an authentic compendium of thought, opinion, and learning from the later eighteenth and early nineteenth centuries. If it is not encyclopedic in its nature, the magazine represents the times voluminously. It is also a fascinating record of the intellectual lives of individual persons. Insofar as it is possible to detect and isolate the work of individual writers, most of whom published anonymously or over pseudonyms in the magazine, we may learn much about the concerns, the habits of mind, and the evolving thought of the people of this age. Within the past decade, the recovery of files kept by the editors has made it possible to reconstruct the corpus of texts produced by each of several hundred writers in *The Gentleman's Magazine* during this period.

Such documentation may help to confirm, though it does not greatly extend, our knowledge about the lives and work of Samuel Johnson, William Cowper, Bishop Percy, and others who have attracted prior biographical and bibliographical attention. More compelling, however, is the opportunity now first readily available to us of reading as one corpus the various writings of George Bennett, a solicitor of Rolstone, Somerset; of the Rev. Samuel Denne, a vicar in Kent; of Mr. John Hodgson of Red Lion Square in London; of the Rev. Joseph Mills of Cowbit, Mrs. Jane West of Little Bowden, and Mr. John Roby in Ireland. The list of names might cover several pages. A common denominator exists among all those on such a list: largely, in some cases exclusively, *The Gentleman's Magazine* served as the medium by which their private learning became public discourse, and had the magazine not given them this opportunity much of their learning would never have achieved its articulation. For few people of any other age has such an opportunity existed.

More than any other factor inducing the magazine's conversion from reprocessing periodical literature to publishing original contributions was the sheer abundance of such materials. The printing of original work which correspondents might submit was within the scope of editorial policy as Edward Cave outlined it in the earliest numbers. But though the magazine carried occasional articles and poems supplied by writers beyond the staff, Cave seems to have intended to include only the most interesting or controversial within the regular monthly format, diverting such other pieces as came to hand into a series of supplementary pamphlets, a procedure he followed during the 1740s. By 1750, as the annual prefaces for that and the next year announced, the flow of work from the editor's correspondents had convinced Cave that the public at large was a more promising source of edification and entertainment for the magazine's readers than was the assortment of periodical literature already in the hands of this readership. That after Cave died in 1754 he was succeeded by proprietors with less aggressive instincts, ideally suited as editors to compile and to arrange, doubless helped to confirm Cave's redefinition of editorial policies which was their immediate inheritance.

By 1778, when John Nichols—a young printer who had already contributed several pieces to the magazine—bought part of the proprietorship, the partnership between *The Gentleman's Magazine* and a reading public which wrote for it had been firmly cemented through two decades of collaboration. The manner in which Nichols cultivated and extended an arrangement he inherited was characteristic of a man of his energies. Although the procedures of submission and selection functioned so well as to need little stimulation, he seems to have given considerable impetus to the practice of writing for the magazine. Through a column he instituted, he established public communication with correspondents, and he doubled the number of pages in each issue from 1783 onwards. Nichols remained in charge of the magazine's affairs until his death some fifty years later.

His son and grandson, both of whom worked with him in managing *The Gentleman's Magazine,* shared in the decision to limit the participation of contributing writers beyond a paid staff when the elder Nichols died in 1826. That decision apparently had more to do with contemporary publishing fashions and with the presence of strong editorial associates such as John Mitford than with disinclination to admit unsolicited work into the magazine. Nonetheless, between 1834, when they began to publish a New Series, and 1856, when the family sold the proprietorship, the policies of John Bowyer Nichols and John Gough Nichols effected only a limitation upon rather than the exclusion of contributions from writers in the public at large.

We may understand with greater immediacy the habits of mind and qualities of thought and the motives shared by the magazine's many contributors by looking closely at individual writers whose work appeared during this period. The two considered here are representative in many specific ways of the magazine's broad clientele. The Rev. William Tooke was a prolific author noted particularly for his works on Russia. Before he achieved wide public recognition, however, his frequent contribution to *The Gentleman's Magazine* served as a crucial means of development in his authorial practice. Tooke's articles nearly spanned the period of John Nichols' editorship. The second writer, Edward Phillips of Melksham, was ten years younger than Nichols and Tooke. His essays in the magazine, which he seems to have produced in his later years and which thus incorporate the reflections of a lifetime, reveal many of the preoccupations of educated people in this era as they attempted to come to terms with cultural change. Phillips' correspondence with the editors of *The Gentleman's Magazine* has recently come to light in the massive manuscript archives of the Nichols family.[2] His letters

2. The most extensive collections of archival materials on the Nichols family and their

there constitute perhaps the only remaining traces of the personal circumstances out of which his essays in the magazine emerged. Lasting well over a century, for insight into the literary lives of persons such as Edward Phillips, we have relied on the selected correspondence which Nichols and his son published in the *Literary Anecdotes* and the *Illustrations of the Literary History of the Eighteenth Century*. But Phillips' letters were not selected for either series, and even Tooke's correspondence, we can now see, was edited considerably. The treatment of Tooke and Phillips in the present study has been informed greatly by a reading of the letters which they and the many persons like them exchanged with members of the Nichols family and which today are available again to introduce us to the realities within which they lived.

I. WILLIAM TOOKE (1744–1820)

The Tooke family maintained friendships with the Nichols family through several generations. William Tooke and John Nichols were schoolboys together at the academy of John Shield in Islington. But while Nichols remained a quintessential Londoner, seldom straying far from the metropolis, the Tookes were for years a family of English exotics living far from their native shores. In 1771, five years after Nichols entered into the partnership with William Bowyer which launched his busy career in publishing, Tooke left England to become Chaplain in the English church at Cronstadt, in the Gulf of Finland, a position from which he moved to the Chaplaincy at the British Factory in St. Petersburg three years later. His two sons were born there, Thomas in 1774, William in 1777. Each of the three Tooke men made his mark in life and is the subject of an article in the *Dictionary of National Biography*. The elder William Tooke is identified as the "historian of Russia" whose many books on the history and culture of that country, as well as on a variety of theological and literary topics, made him a well-known author in his own day. Thomas Tooke is remembered as an economist whose theories had considerable impact on the formulation of monetary policy, the subject of his several books published during the earlier nineteenth century. The younger William Tooke, a solicitor by profession with a seat in Parliament for several terms, was one of the founding officers of London University and was active in the Royal Society and the Society of Arts. True to his name, he too was a contributor to the magazine.

In 1792, William Tooke and his family settled in London after he received a long-awaited inheritance from his uncle. Quite clearly, the two decades which the family spent abroad were powerfully formative years. They provided the Rev. Tooke, who had already published books on antiquarian

---

various enterprises are to be found today at the Folger Shakespeare Library, the Columbia University Library, the Bodleian Library, and the British Library. Manuscript letters and other documents are also to be found in the Osborn collection at Yale, at the John Rylands in Manchester, and at the Advocates Library in Edinburgh. *The Nichols File* contains a catalogue of materials at the Folger and includes a discussion of some of the materials available at other sites.

and theological subjects, immersion in the traditions of a fascinating foreign country and close access to contemporary Continental scholarship. Within this unusual general setting, his sons grew up in a richly cultured home where interesting, brilliant people visited and where books and bookishness were central in the daily routine. The very remoteness from England which members of the Tooke family shared during these years was undoubtedly a condition in which the seeds of their later achievements were given intense nourishment.

In his early twenties, William Tooke had demonstrated a proclivity for study and writing that was to be one of his characteristic traits. He published three works before leaving England. During the next twenty years, he found time to complete only two. Tooke had achieved sufficient notice to be elected a Fellow of the Royal Society in 1783. His duties as Chaplain to the British Factory, however, and his activities in the social and learned circles in which he moved, did not allow him time to produce the volume of writing which he would achieve later. In this period of his life, he seems to have been sorting out his interests, meeting and reading the work of Continental scholars, assimilating historical documents, studying the new French and German publications—it was the period in which he began the scholarship from which the great outpouring of printed volumes would emanate at the end of the century. During these years, *The Gentleman's Magazine* served Tooke as a clearing house, a place in which he could sketch out his observations and knowledge about Russia, a repository for information which he did not wish to delay conveying into print or for which he sensed there was an interested readership immediately at hand. In all, Tooke contributed twenty articles to *The Gentleman's Magazine* while he was living and working in St. Petersburg.[3]

In his situation a considerable distance from home (a distance made to seem much more considerable by the hazards of shipping) William Tooke read avidly the books which Nichols and other friends sent him. Among the products of the London press which Tooke received was *The Gentleman's Magazine*. Nichols had become a proprietor and the printer of the magazine several years after Tooke's departure from England, and Tooke noted with

---

3. I have not thus far identified articles written either by the Rev. William Tooke or by his son William beyond those in *The Nichols File*. I must here record that the assignment of work attributed to the two men in my book contains several errors. The handwritten attributions in the editorial file copy refer ambiguously to "Tooke" or to "W Tooke" or to "Mr Tooke" at each of the works included in my listing. Fairly arbitrarily, I assigned the installments of the long work on Horace to the younger Tooke: he was the first to use the initials "W. T." and he shared his father's interests both in literature and in Russia. I did not at the time consult the elder Tooke's obituary in the magazine in which, as I indicate later in this essay, reference is made to his authorship of the commentary in question. On the basis of place as indicated in the headings of the printed articles, I now assign to the younger Tooke only the following items listed in my catalogue: the first item; the nine items in the next column beginning with the note on Dr. Beadon; and the final three items in the listing. All others I now assign to the Rev. Tooke, though the two obituary notices (see hereafter) may have been written by either man.

pleasure the increasing traces he detected of his friend's presence in the text.[4] The magazine helped him keep abreast of the cultural issues currently engaging his English contemporaries, such as the 1782 controversy over authorship of the poetry claimed by Thomas Chatterton to have been written by a fifteenth-century priest named Rowley. Nichols was Tooke's publisher, and much of their correspondence through the early 1780s had to do with the progress of the two works which Tooke was publishing at a distance from the press that made him uncomfortable.

The personal letters he sent his boyhood friend are bathed in the consciousness of his situation. Unexcerpted, they are much more highly animated, more newsy, often more tenderly written than the texts which Nichols published in the *Literary Anecdotes*. Quite clearly, Tooke treasured his unusual locus, his place in a significant foreign capital which gave him entree into a most interesting society and brought him into contact with celebrated people. He knew how to value the opportunity to learn about aspects of his world with which few contemporary Englishmen were familiar, to explore realms which men and women like himself living throughout England would never directly experience. At the same time, he felt keenly what it is to live far from home and friends:

O if it were possible for you to be here!—my head turns round with the thought.—O if it were possible! But we may meet again. I say, we may. We must. We will. It is impossible but we must.—Nay, at present, there sits Mrs. Nichols with my wife in the parlour—they will both be up presently.—Here are you boring over some of my old books, with your great spectacles.—Nance at play with Betsy.—Mrs. Morris looking out at window upon the river.—Old Duncombe, and the dull doctor from the Spa fields sha'n't come.[5]

The twenty articles which Tooke wrote in Russia for *The Gentleman's Magazine* introduce a variety of matter. He enclosed the first in a letter to Nichols dated 9 August 1782 O.S.; the last appeared late in 1789. Though the sequence is a miscellaneous assortment as to subject—Nichols usually adopted the terms "Occasional Remarks" or "Original Correspondence" as running heads in the magazine—Tooke tended to write about specific places or curiosities of natural life in the earlier essays and to dwell at greater length on Russian history in the later ones. His accounts of the ancient city of Bolgari (LV, i, 15–18), of the "Burial place of the antient Khans, at Kazimof" (LV, i, 172–173), of the Russian muskrat Mus Jaculus (LV, i, 264–266) and Slepetz (LV, ii, 761) in 1785 were succeeded by topographical and naturalistic description of Pavlofsk (LVI, i, 455–457) and of the Crimea (LVI, ii, 643–648) and by an "Account of the Progress of Arts and Sciences in Russia" (LVII, i, 390–395) in 1786–87. In communicating these articles to Nichols, Tooke at times professed to be rather uninterested in what he wrote: ". . . I do not care one polushka about them, and . . . you may put them in any place you think

4. See among others his letter dated 20 July 1782 O. S. (Bodleian MS. Eng. lett. c. 366, f. 124): "I read the volume of the Gentleman's Magazine which is come over, and there discover numberless traces of J. N."

5. Letter dated 8 July 1784 O. S. (Bodleian MS. Eng. lett. c. 366, ff. 134–37).

fit."[6] He took Nichols to task, however, for what he considered carelessness in the reproduction of at least one of the earlier engraved plates which accompanied his work,[7] and as one article succeeded another in the magazine his allusions to them in personal letters reveal well enough the purposefulness with which the articles were produced.

From the first, Tooke's Russian articles were published over a pseudonymous signature, "M. M. M.," which possessed some significance for him: the initials are those of the Tooke family motto, *Militia Mea Multiplex*.[8] Out of this motto, apparently, the author created a distinct persona, a man vaguely military by profession whose duties require him to travel extensively throughout the Russian territories. He told Mr. Urban at the beginning of his first article that the notes on the antiquities he described were derived from his travels and that he thought of sending them through "the accident of my meeting with some numbers of your Magazine at the house of a German officer at Simbirsk. . . . If the engravings are executed with accuracy from the drawings I herewith transmit, and the narrative faithfully given, I may be occasionally induced to send you more, as often as my warfare in this world, which is very various, will allow me avocation" (LV [1785], i, 15).

Perhaps to aid Tooke in the objectification of this persona, Nichols subjoined a footnote to the writer's remark that he sends the article as "a favour": "That we do 'esteem it a favour,' our friendly correspondent will see by its being so early inserted; which is done, we will assure him, without the most distant view to 'the bear-skin boots,' or 'the pastilla,' or 'the sweet kloukva quass,' or 'the caviar,' he so liberally promises.—The invariable rule of this Magazine is, never to receive a bribe for what is either inserted or omitted" (LV, i, 15). The ideas and information which Tooke transmitted in the succeeding articles may well have been drawn from excursions he actually made, but his care in dating each article from a specific place and his scattered references to duties which called him from one encampment to another served to perpetuate and confirm his fictional authorial identity.

Mr. Urban's correspondent "M. M. M.," whose avocation was to share a knowledge of Russian antiquities and natural history with his fellow readers of *The Gentleman's Magazine*, was also a contemplative observer of the more general human scene. Tooke came to use the opportunity of writing about Russia for discourse on human nature and on books in the vein of the eighteenth-century periodical essayists. His account of the Don Cossaks and their region, in two articles dated 31 Oct. 1785 O. S. (from Tscherkask) and 5 Nov. 1785 O. S. (from Azof), is prefaced, for instance, by several paragraphs on literature as a source of our insight into human character. The pretext for these remarks, he says, is "the vexatious want of character throughout the

6. Letter of 8 Sept. 1785 O. S. (Bodleian MS. Eng. lett. c. 366, f. 169).
7. Letter of 25 Sept. 1785 O. S. (Bodleian MS. Eng. lett. c. 366, f. 173).
8. The motto is explained (without documentation) in the account of the younger William Tooke in the *DNB*. The Rev. Tooke's playful references to his manifold warfare, at various places in his articles, make the motto pretty accessible.

regions I am doomed to traverse" (LVI [1786], ii, 548). His real agenda, however, would seem to be a call for more attentive biographical analysis in
English literature. Attached to Tooke's long account of the Crimea is a
similar prefatory essay even less integral to his primary subject. He expatiates
on human tendency to rail against fate, when establishing self-control would
allow us to deal purposefully with the "common occurrences of life." This
leads him to compare the *Spectator* papers with Johnson's *Rambler* as guides
to self-knowledge.

We find in the articles which William Tooke wrote for *The Gentleman's
Magazine* during his sojourn in Russia the core of interests and play of mind
which were to be displayed so richly in the numerous works he published
after returning to England. Evidently he was all the while gathering documentary materials and storing observations that he wished to commit to publications of greater scope, and in his letters he indicates increasingly a desire
to exchange his present situation in the world for a place closer to his publisher and to the reading public. In 1791 he told Nichols:

I wish to return to England, but my uncle does not approve of it. He says, I am very
well where I am: (and that is very true.) and why should I wish to be a poor curate
in London?—But I do not intend to be a poor curate any where. I will sooner be
corrector to your press. What say you; suppose I put some of my money into your
house, and come and help you . . . A clergyman can be a corrector—it is his proper
business.[9]

But until he returned, he could in a sense practice. Writing about the
land and society within which he found himself, focusing from time to time
on authors and literary works, modern and ancient, in the course of his
reading, he prepared for an established periodical audience a series of articles
in which he exercised various authorial manners. He wrote description, developed scientific and historical evidence, shaped speculative opinions about
human nature, cultivated narratives faithful to a persona he created or, in
a more complex exercise, pretended to weave together the disorganized notes
of a fellow traveller.[10] A comparison of the books which Tooke published
after residence in Russia with those published before and during that period
would doubtless reveal a number of things, including simply a greater maturity. To the experience of writing articles for *The Gentleman's Magazine*,
however, we may understand that Tooke owed a certain measure of the development he attained towards his establishment as an author of recognized
importance among his contemporaries.

In the three decades of his life after he left Russia, Tooke continued to
be a contributing writer for the magazine, and in fact provided a more significant level of work—eighty articles, as compared with the twenty he sent to
Nichols from Russia. The preponderance of these were a group of sixty-
seven articles (perhaps best conceived as successive segments of one long work)

9. Bodleian MS. Eng. lett. c. 366, f. 168.
10. See, for instance, Tooke's remarks in the magazine in 1786 (LVI, ii. 552 and 648).

on Horace which appeared from the latter part of 1806 through 1811. He wrote one or two obituary articles.[11] Of the remainder, two articles (for both of which he used his Russian signature, "M. M. M.") appear to be leftovers from Russia, published soon after the resettlement in England: a biographical note on von Haller and a note on annotation in a copy of *Salmisii Exercitationes Plinianae*.[12] The rest concerned a variety of things Russian and appeared in 1812 and 1815–16. All of Tooke's work published after 1800 appeared either anonymously or over his actual initials.

Tooke's long commentary on Horace is a work unto itself in his canon. In its conception, it is essentially the experience of a learned eighteenth-century reader, exploring the text of Horace's epistles and satires sequentially and offering remarks of various kinds—exegetical, philological, amplificatory —in apparently random fashion, though his progress through the text advances nearly line by line. It is the schoolroom exercise carried forward in maturity, the summary explication of a text grown, through countless readings, as familiar as the lines on the hand. There is constant interplay between painstaking analysis of the particular and highly generalized notions about the poet. The earliest installments in the series are called "Observations" and "Remarks," but thereafter they bear the title "Illustrations of Horace," a use of the term "illustration" which appropriately connects Tooke's work with the content and manner of literary scholarship as it was conducted in his generation and in many generations preceding his. His long series of remarks was, therefore, perfectly tailored for an audience such as the subscribers to *The Gentleman's Magazine*, a body of readers who had been provided such readings of the standard authors in previous volumes and who perhaps kept journals full of such remarks of their own in the privacy of their studies.

As representative of the genre, Tooke's remarks on Horace are delivered with a stylistic elegance which many of his knowing readers might not have been able to achieve. He is rarely content with the perfunctory observation: "*Venafri*. The oil from the territory of Venafrum was reckoned the best. *Plin. lib xv. cap. 2.*" (LXXXI [1811], ii, 428). More characteristically, Tooke is given to broader periods:

The predominant idea in this poetical discourse, and the result of those reflections, which our Bard pursues in it respecting the inconsistency of mankind in matters that are of the last importance to them, forms, in some degree, the subject of the generality of his Satires and Epistles, and of some of his finest Odes. . . . That which we seek is always in our power; it is either here, or no where. Horace was so firmly persuaded of this truth, and of the whole practical theory of life, of which it is the principle, that

11. That on James Ward in 1806 (LXXVI, ii, 985–987) was doubtless by the senior Tooke, an old friend of Ward. He may also have written the obituary of Nathaniel Rix in 1820 (XC, ii, 375) since he appears to have been working actively up to the time of his own death later that autumn. Neither article bears a signature in print, and the marginal attributions in editorial records are ambiguous without other documentary evidence.

12. These appeared in the magazine in 1794 (LXIV, ii, 686–687) and 1795 (LXV, i, 204–205).

he could not expatiate, either in morals or in satire, without taking his departure from it, or recurring to it. (LXXIX [1809], 705–706)

In his obituary in *The Gentleman's Magazine*, we are told that Tooke was revising this series on Horace at the time of his death "for separate publication" (XC [1820], ii, 467). The revision must have consisted chiefly of new, more general introductory matter than Tooke wrote for the series as it originally appeared, for his remarks are highly polished in their original state and seem to represent decided opinions, a culminating rather than tentative reading of the Roman poet. His remarks on Horace are at the other end of the spectrum of composition from the early articles on Russian history, geography, and natural life. In them, Tooke introduced and rehearsed the subject matter of the major publications he projected. In the "Illustrations of Horace," Tooke delivered in the magazine a work of major scope very nearly in the finished state it would have possessed had he lived to publish it separately.

During the last three decades of his life, the Rev. William Tooke was not the only member of his family writing articles signed "W. T." in *The Gentleman's Magazine*. His son William—"that monkey Bill,"[13] as his father described him during boyhood in a letter to Nichols—began his own correspondence with Mr. Urban in a set of remarks on the current English passion for German literature in 1799 (LXIX, ii, 923–924). This was followed by an article entitled "Causes of Present Scarcity; and Remedies Proposed" in 1800 (LXX, ii, 918–920), by three articles on the distresses of chimney-sweeps in 1803–5,[14] and by a note on his own edition of Churchill's poetry (LXXIV [1804], ii, 1188–89). By now, the former little rascal was beginning a professional career, having served his apprenticeship to a solicitor in Gray's Inn with whom he entered into partnership in 1798. The claims of public life allowed little time for authorship during these years. Later, he was to republish his edition of Churchill in three volumes (1844), the two-volume *Monarchy of France, its Rise, Progress, and Fall* (1855), and a volume of verse (1860). His further work in the magazine included an article on Nicholas Rowe's will in 1822 (XCII, i, 207–208), one on the history of the Tooke family in 1839 (N. S. XII, 602–606), and several notes on literary and biographical matters in the early 1840s. His final contribution to *The Gentleman's Magazine* appears to have been an article signed "Vassili Vassilovich" entitled "The Chapters of 'Political Philosophy' on Russia" in 1843 (N. S. XIX, 40–42).

The younger William Tooke contributed more sporadically and less voluminously than his father did to the pages of Mr. Urban's miscellany. Like his father, who occasionally published in *The Monthly Review*, he also contributed to the *New Monthly Review* and the *Annual Register*. The work published by the two William Tookes in *The Gentleman's Magazine*, one hundred thirteen articles, constitutes, however, a special and distinctive body

13. Letter of 8 Sept. 1785 O. S. (Bodleian MS. Eng. lett. c. 366, f. 169).
14. LXXIII (1803), ii, 1028–30; LXXIV (1804), i, 27–28; and LXXV (1805), i, 535–536.

of writing, a utilization of opportunities which the *Gentleman's* held forth to them, as it did to many others like them, in a way which made this periodical important to its era. It provided the opportunity to organize and shape ideas, as in the Rev. Tooke's miscellaneous observations on Russia and his son's commentary on reading tastes in late eighteenth-century London. As in the younger Tooke's remarks on the plight of young chimney-sweeps, it provided an immediate audience for addressing issues which challenged the conscience. Also, as in the elder Tooke's extended discussion of Horace, the magazine was ready to carry the more fully rendered productions of learning pursued in the private study. The magazine stood ready at any time to broadcast the request for information, to gather in the piece of fugitive evidence, to transmit the reply to a critic, to disseminate a decided opinion. In surveying the writings of the William Tookes, father and son, published in *The Gentleman's Magazine*, one comes to understand the diverse ways in which this periodical participated in the lives of its literate and thoughtful audience.

II. EDWARD PHILLIPS, JR. (1754–1831)

Perhaps the only information about this man which is readily available in standard biographical resources is the following reference in the obituary columns of *The Gentleman's Magazine* for April 1831 (printed in the May number [CI, i, 476]): "GLOUCESTER.—In his 77th year, Mr. Edward Phillips, formerly of Melksham." No date of death is recorded, and no further details are provided, even editorially, about the life and work of one who contributed sixty-six articles, many of them substantial essays, to this periodical. He is not included in the *Dictionary of National Biography*, and the printed catalogues of the British Library contain no mention of his name. John and John Bowyer Nichols do not refer to him, even in passing, in the *Literary Anecdotes* and *Illustrations*, chronicles of the literary history of the eighteenth century but also a repository of countless details about those whose lives, like Phillips', extended into the nineteenth century. Perhaps he would have been included in the sequel which Bowyer Nichols appears to have planned on the literary history of the early nineteenth century.[15] As far as one can tell in the absence of personal and professional information about him, his contribution to the cultural life of his times seems to have consisted entirely of the essays he published in *The Gentleman's Magazine*.[16]

Since even in the magazine his work appeared not over his own name

---

15. See the "General Introduction" to *The Nichols File*, p. 15, and n. 26 to that section.

16. In searching for other works he may have published, the only one I have found over the signatures he used is an article in three installments entitled "The Science of Political Economy," signed "E. P.," in the *New Monthly Magazine* in 1821 (I, 329–335; 476–484; and 701–707). Although the expository style is similar to that of Phillips' essays in *The Gentleman's Magazine*, the subject is not one which he addressed even in passing in the *Gentleman's*, and it seems to me unlikely that he was the author of this article. In his correspondence that I have seen with the Nichols printing firm, he refers to a slim volume of his work for which the firm arranged publication. I do not know its title. The volume apparently found few buyers, and I have not found it in catalogues of the standard British and American repositories.

but over the pseudonymous signatures "E. P." or "Alciphron," his obscurity is perfectly understandable. Yet the corpus of his articles in this periodical alone is a substantial body of work which circulated among a significant readership for over a decade. His "Speculations on Literary Pleasures," which appeared in seventeen installments during 1827–29, ran to some 71 pages in length. His essay "On the Mutability of National Grandeur" in 1823 covered 14 pages of the magazine. He published essays long enough to need division into two or three installments on the "Progress of Literature in Different Ages," on nineteenth-century poetry, on Thomson and Young, on Johnson and Helvetius as moralists, on "Italy and the Italians," on Gibbon and Lardner, on the "Value and Importance of History," on the "Influence of Time and Place in Developing Genius," and on the Continental historian Niebuhr. His single essays cover a diverse and interesting array of topics: "On the Pleasures of Philosophic Contemplation," "On the Subjects of Epic Poems," and many others. The writings of Edward Phillips, Jr., of Melksham are well worth the attention of anyone seeking to understand the intellectual life of the early nineteenth century.

Phillips' first contact with those who were to print and circulate his work came in a letter (now first published) "To the Editor of the Gentlemans Magazine" dated 19 February 1817. His approach to Nichols was much the same as that of others who paused at the gateway between their private worlds and the realm of public discourse:

The Essays on miscellaneous subjects connected with literature which are frequently to be found in the Gentleman's Magazine, has induced me to think that a communication of a literary nature would not be deemed unacceptable, & that any performance which should aim at combining the useful with the pleasing would be willingly admitted to a place in your Monthly publication . . . if you are disposed, Mr. Editor, to receive some communications of the sort I have mentioned, I will be obliged by your earliest intimation by post. . . .[17]

The essays which Phillips apparently had immediately in mind were of a reflective nature in the manner of the eighteenth-century periodical essayists. The first two were published early in July[18]—one ("Essay on Greatness of Mind") in the June number of the magazine, the other ("On the Pleasures of Philosophic Contemplation") in the Supplement to Part I of the volume for 1817.[19] Another essay of this kind, "On the Appropriation of Hours of Leisure," came out in the October number. Whether he had these essays on hand when he wrote for editorial encouragement in February is not clear. In their published form, the essay in the June number is dated 2 June and

17. Bodleian MS. Eng. lett. c. 362, f. 10.

18. LXXXVII, i, 512–514. At this time, the June number and mid-year Supplement were published, probably together, at the beginning of the next month. As published, the "Essay on Greatness of Mind" is dated 2 June (with no indication of place). Both the note of salutation and the essay are signed "E. P."

19. LXXXVII, i, 582–584. No salutation is printed with this essay. It is undated and unsigned (but is attributed to Phillips in editorial annotation in the file copy of the magazine).

that in the October number 10 September. At any rate, beginning with his "Remarks on the Character and Genius of Johnson," which appeared in the January number for 1818, the sequence of Phillips' essays intermixed the treatment of more specifically focused subjects and the more speculative discourse with which his contributions to *The Gentleman's Magazine* had begun.

Phillips' essay on Johnson (LXXXVIII, i, 31–37) is a good example of his work. He obviously found the subject congenial, and he let his thoughts play out slowly and deliberately. Phillips realized that he was approaching Johnson's life and works at an interesting time, a little over three decades after Johnson's death, a quarter of a century after the decade in which so many recollections of the famous man, including Boswell's, had first been published. Phillips was thirty years old when Johnson died and presumably had read the essay on Shakespeare, the account of the journey to Scotland, and the *Lives of the Poets* when these works first came out. The reading public in 1818, however, included many persons of a generation after Phillips' who knew little of the Johnson canon but had read much about his personal eccentricity and frank opinions. "Casual readers," Phillips comments, "naturally recur to what, with most pleasure, is attended with least trouble; and hence, oftentimes form their estimate, and even their literary estimate, rather from these objectionable traits, which occupy a prominent feature in Johnson, than from the sterling weight and real excellence of his works." Although Phillips reviews Johnson's life to establish the consistency between his principles and actions and comments more broadly on Johnson's "fine discriminating powers and manliness of thought," much of the essay is commentary on specific works, including his lesser-known early biographies:

Although perhaps less nervous . . . than . . . the Lives of the English Poets, they yet exhibit greater simplicity and ease. Perspicuous and pure, these compositions unite in a high degree dignity with elegance; beauty of arrangement, and harmony of period, are so happily combined, that the reader at once feels his interest excited, and his approbation secured; concise, yet on the other hand sufficiently luminous, the Author in narration strikes at principal events, neglecting the review of subordinate matter; his chief aim, after having imparted requisite information on those points, seems rather to be to delineate character, than to heap together occurrences in the detail. These performances, in conjunction with the Lives of the English Poets, must long remain among the most finished biographical sketches in the language.

By and large, in his critical views about literature—his most frequent subject as an essayist—Edward Phillips showed himself to be very much a man of his generation. His tastes and principles of judgment were grounded in the literary values of the later eighteenth century. He was a Classicist attending the birth of Romanticism. This is not to say that his criticism of poetry in the early nineteenth century was a reactionary dismissal of the contemporary as viewed against a golden heritage. But he expected poets to assume a place within a tradition to which, it seemed, they necessarily belonged. He believed in the strength of this tradition. Along with his praise for Shakespeare and Milton and (less inevitably by then) for Dryden and Pope, Phillips could assert that "Collins, Gray, Armstrong, and Mason . . . Glover, Akenside,

Thomson, and Young, contributed by their labours to raise the dignity and character of metrical composition to a height not eclipsed by any other age or nation. . ." (LXXXIX [1819], ii, 400).

Phillips' long essay in 1819 "On the Poetry of the Nineteenth Century"[20] contains no mention of Shelley or Keats, and he had absolutely no use for Wordsworth and Coleridge ("littleness for which Literature has scarcely a name," "quaint conceit, splendid inanity . . . unintelligible sentiment"). Phillips was quite ready, however, to meet other writers on their own ground. He admired the poetry of Crabbe but ultimately found it limited. He shared with his contemporaries the feeling that Moore was a gifted poet, though he found the recent oriental style of this poet too mannered. Scott, he felt, had soaring creative powers, but in his view posterity would find Scott's interests too parochial. "Our poetical pretensions of equality, therefore, with several previous epochs during the long line of our literary history, may be justly a matter of question with the cool unprejudiced critick." The single great exception, Phillips felt, was Lord Byron. But he despaired for Byron even while admiring him.

It was difficult for Phillips to balance his attraction to Byron's poetry with his alienation from the poet's ideas.

Inheriting from nature some of the highest requisites of Poetry, the powerful appeal to the heart and to the human sympathies with which the Poems of his Lordship seldom fail in being accomplished, as they may be termed unique in his own day, are perhaps sufficient to place him on a rank with those of other times, who, in other respects, are certainly his superiors. . . . His diction and language are happily adapted to give force and grace of utterance to the variety and beauty of his thoughts, while the flow and general dignity of his numbers impart to his verse a life and energetic warmth of feeling rarely to be found, with equal effect, in any other writer. (LXXXIX, ii, 316–317)

On the other hand, he found Byron too often "gloomy and despondent in his views of life," a poet who "exhibits, in his intellectual speculations, a glaring licentiousness of principle, associated with the querulousness of a dark and brooding misanthrope. . . ." Such depression of mind and character led Byron often enough to "a negligence of speech, a quaintness and prettiness unworthy alike of his general style, and of an author who writes for a literary immortality." The fundamental problem for Phillips was that Byron "offers outrage to the correct principles of sober reason, while the imagination of the reader hangs with the liveliest interest and emotion on fine scenes of sentiment and of pathos. . . ."

Phillips' evident distress over this point of tension in his reading of Byron apparently led him in 1822 to write an essay, over nine thousand words in length, which he called "The Rhetoric of the Infidel School." Here, citing not only the kinds of criticism of Byron which he himself had previously made but also the noble poet's evident disdain for such arguments, Phillips ranges through the history of British letters to show how many writers, even of the

20. LXXXIX, ii, 315–317; 397–400; 498–502; 582–587.

first eminence in their own times, had passed into disregard because of their intellectual and moral flaws. He compares Byron chiefly with Lord Boling-broke, of the previous century, but refers also to the lives and works of Rochester, Herbert of Cherbury, Hobbes, Voltaire, Hume, and Gibbon. He reviews aspects of "Childe Harold" and "Don Juan" and other poems which he finds objectionable, particularly "Cain," the blasphemous character of which he distinguishes pointedly from the treatment of Satan in "Paradise Lost." He concludes:

The admirers of his Lordship's genius are as numerous as his readers, but does he think that the claims of Poetry, however transcendant, will do for him what it has denied to others? If the author of 'The Patriot King' could not preserve his reputa-tion, after impugning principles which the common consent of the greatest minds had decided to be propitious to the welfare of the human race, it is not probable that any new tale which the author of 'Manfred,' 'Don Juan,' or 'Cain,' can tell them, should induce them to alter their suffrage in his favour. (XCII [1822], ii, 586)

Although Phillips' principal subject as an essayist was the literary tradi-tion and history of his country, his work demonstrates considerable range. He wrote on Swedish and Italian literature and on the pleasures of historical research. When his subject was specifically literary, much of his attention was engrossed by moral or theological questions, by the larger cultural issues to which, he evidently believed, all learning should address itself. Given to generalization and abstract argument, he did not neglect the practical: his essays on the learned achievements of Locke (LXXXIX [1819], ii, 589–592) and the importance of Cook's exploits (XCVIII [1828], ii, 24–25) were written explicitly to lobby for the erection of public monuments. Within themselves, the essays often cover a broad spectrum of ideas and effects. His three-part discourse on Johnson and Helvetius is set as a narrative, his thoughts about these writers and the principles implicit in their work arising from his agita-tion of mind during a storm which he describes in rhapsodic detail. Similarly, an essay entitled "Reveries in Autumn" (XCV [1825], ii, 108–111), which begins with an account of his feelings as he observes the descent of evening on a wild rural landscape, becomes a long discussion of atmospheric phe-nomena based on the theories and observations of leading natural scientists.

Edward Phillips was perhaps most truly in his element in the long series he called "Speculations on Literary Pleasures." These essays form a chronicle of early nineteenth-century thought, ranging from commentary on Locke, Johnson, and Franklin to consideration of the ideas of various contemporary thinkers. Perhaps it was the summary chronicle of his own reflective life. He was free in this loosely structured discourse to allow his mind to rove along contours of thought which delighted and stimulated him. He let his mind play with the notions of writers who had captured his attention and had made him think. It is not too extravagant to claim that, in extending to Phillips the opportunity to publish, The Gentleman's Magazine allowed a man retiring from his public duties to compose and deliver his own intel-lectual legacy.

Within the pages of *The Gentleman's Magazine*, the writings of William Tooke and his son and of Edward Phillips, Jr., possess so many of the characteristics of the articles collected there that they blend seamlessly with their textual environment. In the personae which they each more or less developed, in the character and style of their discourse, in the kinds of subjects which they explored, these three writers are entirely representative of the magazine's family of contributors. We read an article by "M. M. M." or "Alciphron" and think of it as an extension of the views of "A Well-Wisher to Truth" or a correction of facts cited by "T. T." There is a linear quality to the learning spread out for us by those who contributed to *The Gentleman's Magazine* over the years in which Tooke and Phillips were contributors, and certainly these two participated busily in the creation of a collective text which we now look back upon as a document of cultural history.

All too easily, we may overlook the fact that Tooke and Phillips—that all of the contributors, indeed—were not members of a school, probably did not even know one another except as they read one another's work in the magazine, properly speaking were not even writers in a professional sense. They were coeval individuals, each living out a course of years with personal and professional commitments which identified them in terms distinct from those of a "literary" or "cultural" establishment. What they had in common was a private commitment to learning, an intellectual life informing and energizing the core of daily existence. They each pursued studies in which their interest never abated over the years, and they each took stock reflectively of the world in which they lived. In these qualities, too, the writers we have been considering were entirely representative. Every contributed item we find on the horizontal surface of the magazine's text is an element in a vertical process by which the learning of an individual mind has achieved its expression.

As divergent and separately constituted as were the lives of William Tooke and Edward Phillips—as different as they appear to have been personally—they each carried things worth saying into Mr. Urban's forum, an agenda of thought and opinion which derived from their own intellectual activity. As different as were the preoccupations and styles of the fascinated historian and the speculative essayist, they each had allotted places in this forum. Especially after the advent of more rigidly oriented journals in the early nineteenth century, it was a distinguishing feature of *The Gentleman's Magazine* that all persons who wished to write and whose writings could be conceived of as adding constructively to the discourse were provided a place on the printed page. It is not an overstatement to say that *The Gentleman's Magazine* in fact created many writers, for the major opportunity many men and women had to follow out their studies into publication, to complete their thoughts by carrying them into statement, was afforded by the policies and practice of this British periodical. Paralleled hundreds of times in the experiences of their fellow contributors, the personal attainments of Tooke and Phillips in their collaboration with the editors of *The Gentleman's Magazine* constitute a phenomenon of real significance in our cultural tradition.

JOHN NICHOLS'S NOTES IN THE
SCHOLARLY COMMENTARY OF OTHERS

by

ARTHUR SHERBO

THE contributions of John Nichols to the scholarly literature of the eighteenth and early nineteenth centuries are both invaluable and widely known. As is almost inevitable in vast editorial enterprises like his, he often drew on the help of others. One of the earliest of such contributors was Isaac Reed, the retiring and modest conveyancer who was a close friend of Nichols until Reed died in 1807. Already in 1775 he had assisted with Nichols's editions of the works of William King and of the twenty-fourth volume of Swift's works. Less recognized is how Nichols himself contributed to the scholarly editorial projects of others, many of which also involved Reed.

Although one will learn from the *Dictionary of National Biography* that George Colman, the elder, was the editor of the 1778 ten-volume edition of the plays of Beaumont and Fletcher, that same biographical compilation will not inform one that Reed helped Colman to the extent of over two hundred notes. Reed, it is known, signed his notes "R," but there are also fifteen notes signed "J.N." J.N. is John Nichols. Alexander Dyce, editor of the still indispensable edition of Beaumont and Fletcher because of the fullness of the commentary, so identifies him, i.e. "J.N[*ichols*]" in a note on *The Pilgrim* (VIII. 29), as does George B. Ferguson, editor of the critical edition of *The Woman's Prize* (1966, p. 223). In addition to the fifteen notes in the Beaumont and Fletcher edition, notes which exhibit him, early in his editorial career, as a commentator on the drama, a rarity for him, Nichols also aided in Reed's 1780 edition of Robert Dodsley's collection of *Old Plays*, as well as in the 1794 edition of Johnson's *Lives* of the English poets, a work to which Reed also contributed.

The Beaumont and Fletcher plays had been edited in 1750 by Lewis Theobald, Joseph Sympson, and Thomas Seward, and seven of Nichols's notes express disagreement with those of the editors of that edition. The principal differences are over emendations.[1] Only twice does Nichols agree with, in these instances, Mr. Seward;[2] twice he ventures upon emendations of his own, once to change "he" to "ye," explaining that "The corruption is very easy," and once to add a comma.[3] The first of these emendations is accepted in the Cam-

---

1. IV 231 (*Valentian*); V. 273–274 and 313 (*A Wife for a Month*); V. 477 (*The Pilgrim*); VIII. 193 (*The Island Princess*).
2. IV. 133 (*The False One*); V. 279 (*A Wife for a Month*).
3. IV. 402 (*Monsieur Thomas*) and V. 488 (*The Pilgrim*).

bridge *Beaumont and Fletcher* (1979, IV. 448); the second, silently, by Alexander Dyce (VIII. 40). Twice Nichols explains "obscure" expressions, explaining that "Great as your beauty scornful" means "As remarkable for your *scorn* and cruelty, as for your *beauty*" (III.265) and that "seal it with my service" means "put a period to my service" (III. 409). In his one gloss, he defines "brave" as "well-dress'd" (III. 457). His most interesting note is on the lines, "Let's remove our places. / Swear it again" in V.iii of *The Woman's Prize*, for it recalled Shakespeare to him: "This is plainly a sneer at the scene in Hamlet, where (on account of the Ghost calling under the stage) the Prince and his friends two or three times remove their situations.——Again, in this play, p. 317, Petruchio's saying, '*Something I'll do; but what it is, I know not!*' Seems to be meant as a ridicule on Lear's passionate exclamation, '——*I will do such things— / What they are, yet I know not!*'" Ferguson, editor of the critical edition of this play, gives Nichols credit for both parts of his note.

It remains only to complete the evaluation of these notes. Dyce quotes Nichols's notes three more times, identifying him only as "J.N."[4] And while Dyce does not quote or cite Nichols's other notes, he has no notes where Nichols has one (V. 313; VII. 379) and, most curiously, disagrees with Nichols's note on *The False One* (IV. 159), writing that "a correspondent whose signature is I.N." [sic] explained that passage; Dyce quotes Nichols's note and concludes that I. N.'s interpretation was "forced and far-fetched" (VI. 299), evidently forgetting or not yet making the identification with Nichols.

In the Preface to his 1780 edition of the collection of old plays originally edited by Robert Dodsley in 1744 Isaac Reed acknowledged that "those notes which have the letter N annexed to them, are such observations as occurred to the printer of the first six volumes in reading the proof sheets" (I. xxi). The volumes were "Printed by J. Nichols," Reed's friend. I have found only seven notes by N. in the first six volumes. Nichols invokes Dr. Johnson's *Dictionary* for the definition of "seat" meaning "situation"; explains that a "come-you-seven" (not in *OED*) is "a gambler, a dice-player"; and sees an allusion to "the sign called *The Saxon's Head*" in the words "the picture of Hector" in *The Hog hath Lost his Pearl*.[5] Of greater interest are his notes on "scotch boot" in *The Malcontent*, and on "Peter-man" and "figent" in *Eastward Hoe*. "The *torturing-boots*," he wrote, "are mentioned by Swift, vol. xiii. 1768, p. 314, to have been hung out *in terrorem* to Captain Creichton in 1689" (IV. 57). A "Peter-man" was "the common appellation of those who formerly used unlawful engines and arts in catching fish in the river Thames" (IV. 227), a much more informative note than the definition of the *OED*, "A fisherman; formerly app. one who practised a particular kind of fishing." The third note reads, "Figentia (in chemistry) are things which serve to fix volatile substances. *Figent*, therefore, as applied to memory ["figent memory"], may be synonymous with retentive" (IV. 246). *OED*, quoting the same passage from *Eastward Hoe*, defines "figent" as "Fidgety, reckless," but has no entry for

4. Respectively I. 188; IV. 139; VI. 398.
5. Modern editors have adopted the note.

"figentia." One note remains. Reference is made in *The Roaring Girl* to the "six wet towns" between the "*Lambith* workes" and "*Windsor-bridge*," and Nichols, native Londoner who lived all his life in that city, was ready with the identification, naming Fulham, Richmond, Kingston, Hampton, Chertsey, and Staines, and adding, for good measure, "The other intermediate towns are Chelsea, Battersea, Kew, Isleworth, Twickenham, and Walton" (VI, 116).[6]

There was also an appendix of "Additional Notes" in volume twelve; it contained eight more notes by Nichols. In the first of these he gave a biographical sketch of the heroine of *The Roaring Girl*: "Mrs. Mary Frith, alias Moll Cutpurse, born in Barbican, the daughter of a shoemaker, died at her house in Fleet-street, next the Globe Tavern, July 26, 1659, and was buried in the church of St. Bridget's. She left twenty pounds by her will, for the conduit to run wine when King Charles the 2d returned, which happened in a short time after. *From a MS. in the British Museum* (p. 398)."

He called upon two works he had recently edited for two notes, the first of which was on the words "he that farms the monuments" in James Shirley's *The Bird in a Cage*: "In a poem describing the tombs in Westminster Abbey in the last century (preserved in *Nichols's Select Collection of Poems*, vol. 4. p. 169) mention is made of the *master of the shew*. It there also appears, that the price of admission was *one penny*; it was afterwards raised to *three pence*; and, in 1779 (since the Earl of Chatham's effigies have been placed there) still further advanced to *six pence*. As a large sum must annually arise from the curiosity of individuals, it is to be lamented that the tombs in general are suffered to remain in so disgracefully dirty a condition (p. 417)." The second impressed into service was the works of William King, in an edition of which he had been helped by Reed. Here he quoted King on the "cittern" which he, Nichols, stated "began to be disused at the beginning of this century" (p. 432), a statement corroborated by the *OED*. His note on "love-locks" is much more detailed than that of the *OED*, which simply notes that a lovelock was "a curl of a particular form worn by courtiers in the time of Elizabeth and James I; later, any curl or tress of hair of a peculiar or striking character." Nichols wrote, "*The love-lock* was worn on the left side, and was considerably longer than the rest of the hair. King Charles and many of his courtiers wore them. The king cut his off in 1646. See *Granger*, vol. 2. p. 411" (p. 416), *Granger* being James Granger, whose *Biographical History of England, from Egbert the Great to the Revolution*, to give it its short title, was notable chiefly for its engravings.

The second definition of "sollar" in the *OED* is "A place exposed to the sun. *Obs.*" In Marlowe's *Jew of Malta* Barabas speaks of "Cellars of wine, and sollers full of wheat," and Steevens had correctly glossed a soller as "a loft or garret." Nichols volunteered that a "solarium, among the old Romans, was a

---

6. Cyrus Hoy, *Introductions, Notes, and Commentaries to Texts in 'The Dramatic Works of Thomas Dekker,'* ed. Fredson Bowers (1980), III. 71, reprints Nichols's note, citing "(Note in Reed's edition of Dodsley's *Old Plays*, quoted by Dyce)" as his source, unaware of the identity of "N."

level place at the top of their houses. . . . At Rome there was a *solarium* in some part of almost every public edifice; it being esteemed an essential requisite for health as well as pleasure" (pp. 417–418). The first example of "solarium" in the *OED* is dated 1891. The last of the eight notes, three in number, are on the same page (424). Thomas Warton, in a note on *Othello*, cited by Reed for the words "Batchelor whifflers" in Jasper Mayne's *The City Match*, had defined a "whiffler" as "a light, trivial character, a fellow hired to pipe at processions," to which Nichols objected. Batchelor whifflers were "*young men* free of the company" and were considered, "by the company they belong to, pretty nearly in the same point of view as a gentleman considers the upper servants he keeps *out of livery*." According to the *OED*, both definitions are acceptable, although "the sense of 'piper, fifer' found in Dicts. from Hersey's ed. of Phillips (1706) on is baseless." In the context of Mayne's lines, however, Nichols was right. He was able to state, in the second of those notes, that the "Topographical MSS." of William Habington, author of *The Queen of Arragon*, "are now in the hands of Dr. Nash, and will be made use of in his History of Worcestershire, two volumes, 1781 and 1782, "Printed by John Nichols," who knew whereof he wrote in his statement about the Habington MSS.[7] Nichols's last note is keyed to the headnote to Shakerley Marmion's play *The Antiquary*: "Mr. Samuel Gale told Dr. Ducarel, that this comedy was acted two nights in 1718, immediately after the revival of the Society of Antiquaries; and that therein had been introduced a ticket of a turnpike (then new) which was called a *Tessera*." If Samuel Gale, the antiquary, whose MSS. passed through the hands of Dr. Ducarel and then were bought by Richard Gough, and many of which were printed by Nichols in *Reliquiae Galeanea*, was right, the editors of the multi-volume *London Stage* have not recorded two rare performances.

The 1794 edition of Dr. Johnson's *Lives* of the poets contains notes by R, N, and H, i.e. Reed, Nichols, and Sir John Hawkins, the notes of the last having first appeared in his edition of Johnson's works. One of Nichols's notes, the last of the thirteen he contributed, is actually signed "J.N." (IV. 324). He is right in all his suggestions, being cited twice and quoted once in G. B. Hill's edition of the *Lives*. He noted, of Cowley, that he was unsuccessful in 1636 as candidate for election to Trinity College, Cambridge, and that his satire *Puritan and Papist* was added to Cowley's works "by the particular direction of Dr. Johnson," a practice, he also noted, that obtained with Edward Young's works in the edition of the English poets to which the *Lives* were prefatory.[8] He knew when Richard Duke entered Westminster school and then Trinity College, Cambridge (II. 250) and that Nicholas Rowe was not elected a King's scholar until 1688 (II. 293), in the first instance offering information not in Johnson's account and in the second correcting him. Johnson had written of Thomas Yalden that he had "been chosen, in 1698, preacher of Bridewell Hospital, upon the resignation of Dr. Atterbury";

7. See Nash, I. 585; the pedigree of the Habington family faces p. 588 of volume I.
8. Respectively, I. 5, 7; IV. 324.

Nichols pointed out that Atterbury became Bishop of Rochester in 1713, at which time Yalden succeeded him as preacher at Bridewell (III. 141). Of a partial quotation from one of Richard Savage's letters he remarked, "See this continued, *Gent. Mag.* vol. LVII, 1140 [read 1040]," a contribution to the *Gentleman's Magazine* which has a number of footnotes by "N," Nichols himself, of course (III. 319). Twice more he invoked the *Gentleman's Magazine*, of which he was editor, once for an attempt to ascertain the identity of Pope's "Unfortunate lady," by "J.N." (IV. 2), once to fix the date of the death of Major Bernardi, mentioned in the life of Pope. This second contribution, in the periodical for March, 1780, p. 125, was by "Crito," i.e. the Reverend Mr. John Duncombe, a regular contributor and one of Nichols's friends.

Nichols, with Bishop Percy and Dr. John Calder, was involved in the six-volume edition of *The Tatler*, published in 1786, and he went to it for two notes, giving precise references both times. In his account of Addison and *The Spectator* Johnson had stated that "when Dr. Fleetwood prefixed to some sermons a preface overflowing with whiggish opinions, that it might be read by the Queen, it was reprinted in *The Spectator*." Nichols wrote, "This particular number of the *Spectator*, it is said, was not published until twelve o'clock, that it might come out precisely at the hour of her Majesty's breakfast, and that no time might be left for deliberating about serving it up with that meal, as usual. See edit. of the Tatler with notes, vol. VI. N° 271, *note*, p. 452, etc." (II. 327). *The Tatler*, "ed. 1786, vol. VI. p. 452," was also invoked for the daily number of essays sold (II. 335). Matthew Prior's uncle was "a vintner near Charing-cross," wrote Dr. Johnson, to which Nichols added, "Samuel Prior kept the Rummer Tavern near Charing-cross in 1685. The annual feast of the nobility and gentry living in the parish of St. Martin in the Fields, was held at his house, Oct. 14, that year." [9]

Nichols produced an immense quantity of scholarly work, and the canon of his work will not be much increased by the thirty-five notes he contributed to the works of other scholars, but they deserve to be known, and they are further evidence of the close intimacy between him and Isaac Reed.

9. III. 2. Only the first part of the note is cited in G. B. Hill's edition of the *Lives*. Nichols made two identifications in the life of Savage, III. 320, 321.

TITLE-PAGES PRODUCED BY THE
WALTER SCOTT PUBLISHING CO LTD

by

JOHN R. TURNER

THE Walter Scott Publishing Co Ltd of Felling, Newcastle-upon-Tyne, began business in 1882. Until that date the proprietor, Walter Scott (1826–1910, made a baronet in 1907 but not related to Sir Walter Scott of Abbotsford) had been, and continued to be, a very successful builder and contractor, operating as a builder mainly in North-east England but undertaking extensive work on railway and dock construction throughout Britain. The printing and publishing business appears to have been acquired as a result of the impending bankruptcy of The Tyne Publishing Co, when Scott stepped in and took over.[1] Printing and publishing was therefore an unexpected and completely new line of business for Scott. Nevertheless, he almost immediately made a success of the venture and within a few years he had published several hundred titles. The publishing company continued in business until 1931 although steadily declining after Sir Walter's death in 1910.

The business was based on series of reprints: Camelot Classics edited by Ernest Rhys (who later became the editor of Dent's Everyman series), the Emerald Library, the Oxford Library, the Canterbury Poets, and so on. But far more than reprints were undertaken; for example, the company produced the Contemporary Science Series consisting of original works under the editorship of Havelock Ellis; they were the first to publish English translations of Ibsen and brought out early translations of Tolstoy's works; they were the first to publish some of Bernard Shaw's work, and some of George Moore's.

The great majority of the publications were perfectly normal books but a few copies survive which are unusual. The evidence seems to show that from his start as a publisher in 1882 Walter Scott printed and published certain popular titles and sold some of the copies to booksellers (and sometimes to other publishers) in which the title-pages made no mention of Scott. The

---

1. Accounts vary on the details of Scott's acquisition of the publishing company. On 15th August 1882 the *Publishers' circular* announced that the Tyne Publishing Co now belonged to Scott, but certainly the Tyne *Printing* Co continued in business after this date and they seem to have continued as publishers as well as printers. Furthermore, from the beginning, Scott's printing works was in Felling-on-Tyne and according to local and trade directories the Tyne Printing Co was never in Felling. James Clegg's *International directory of booksellers* . . . , Rochdale, 1910, asserts that The Walter Scott Publishing Co Ltd was founded in 1875 and presumably this information was supplied by Scott, but none of the other sources agrees with this date.

imprint on these title-pages was that of the particular customer who had bought the copies and thus made it appear that the book was published by the customer. The title-pages were printed by Scott, but the firm's own Walter Scott title leaf was cancelled and was replaced by the customer's title leaf. However, apart from the cancelled title leaves the rest of these copies was identical with the standard Scott copies; the books had Scott's colophon and could even include advertisements for other Scott publications. Copies were sometimes re-bound by the buyer but the books were also available complete in a standard Scott binding. Most of the names on these title-pages are not well known but single examples have been found which show that J. M. Dent and Mudie's Library were also involved.

The procedure of issuing books with tailor-made title-pages seems to have begun with the Tyne Publishing Co before Scott took over and was then continued by Scott. Unfortunately the history of the Tyne Publishing Co has proved to be even more obscure than that of Walter Scott and only one example from them has been found so far. In fact, it is quite possible that other publishers besides Tyne and Scott used the procedure.

The example from the Tyne Publishing Co is found in two copies of Lewis Apjohn's *William Ewart Gladstone*, one with a title-page with Tyne's imprint and the other with the imprint of J. M. Dent. The Tyne title leaf is normal but Dent's is a cancel; in all other respects apart from the bindings the two copies are identical. They have similar frontispieces and texts from the same plates, including the text on the upper parts of both title-pages above the imprints. Even the list of Tyne agents is present in both copies.

The title leaf in the Dent copy has been cancelled, not by binding the cancellans in with the sheets, but by removing the cancellandum (presumably an original Tyne title leaf) and pasting the Dent cancellans onto the stub. In all the following examples of books with cancelled title leaves it is this method of pasting the cancellans onto the stub of the cancellandum which has been used.

J. M. Dent mentions in his autobiography that he began his working life as a bookbinder and in about 1873 he had the idea of buying printed sheets direct from publishers. However, he says nothing about having his own title-pages printed.

I had noticed that booksellers had books bound in leather in their windows, and I knew that they bought the books in sheets from the publishers and had them bound by their own bookbinder. Now I thought if I could say to the publishers that I would buy their sheets if they would give me some work in contra account, I could then bind the sheets and sell to the bookseller, and so make work in two ways.[2]

The Tyne Publishing Co, however, seems to have gone one better than this in providing Dent with his own title-page so that he could sell the copies he had bound as his own publications. Before 1882 Dent had not yet published any-

2. J. M. Dent, *The House of Dent 1888–1938* (1938), pp. 34–35.

thing of his own, and a little later in his autobiography he notes: 'I had during 1886 and 1887 been dreaming of publishing—only a renewed dream of boyhood. Some years before I had compiled, with the help of my wife, one or two birthday books and others, and I had published them with an idea of selling them in my leather bindings.'[3] The Dent copy of *Gladstone* is half bound in leather on cloth boards with marbled end papers and all edges gilt so perhaps it was one of the 'birthday books and others'.

Thus, Tyne appears to have had a business agreement with Dent, and two other copies of Apjohn's *Gladstone* show the connexion between Tyne and Scott and the continuity of the procedure with title-pages. Apjohn's book contains a chronological table of the events in Gladstone's life which ends at 9th November 1880 in the Tyne and Dent copies. Those copies were followed by one with a title-page from James Askew of Preston since here the chronological table ends at May 1890 and this copy has an extra forty pages of text. Askew's title leaf is a cancel; the book was printed by Walter Scott and has his colophon. This Askew copy therefore seems to be similar to Dent's and would have been preceded by an issue from Walter Scott.

The only corresponding Scott issue so far discovered, however, is later than Askew's. The chronological table ends at Gladstone's death on 19th May 1898 and there are twenty more pages of text than in Askew's issue. It seems likely that there must have been an earlier Scott issue to provide the text for Askew. Scott had certainly published the book before May 1890 because he gave a copy to Newcastle Public Library[4] in March 1889. In any case Scott would have obtained the title when he acquired the Tyne Publishing Co since they had already published it. The bulk of the text, *ie* pp. [17]–301, is from the same plates in all four copies which again indicates the continuity from the Tyne Publishing Co.

Besides taking over the titles along with the Tyne Publishing Co, Scott seems also to have adopted from them the system of printing title-pages for named customers.[5] Since the firm was acquired as a going concern presumably including the staff, and since Scott was new to publishing, this is not very surprising.

The remaining examples discovered all involve Scott. There are six titles besides Apjohn's *Gladstone* and usually there is a pair of copies for each title, one printed and published by Scott with a normal title leaf, and the other printed from the same setting of type and with a cancelled title leaf bearing the imprint of someone else. All the copies have Scott's printer's colophon, and two copies with non-Scott titles (Harrop's issue of Hope, *Life of Gen-*

---

3. *Ibid.* p. 53.

4. Newcastle Public Library acquisitions ledger. The copy no longer exists.

5. Other possible examples are found in Harvard University Library, which has two copies of Howard Blackett's *Life of Giuseppe Garibaldi*, one published by the Tyne Publishing Co and the other by John McGready, and the University of British Columbia Library, which has a copy of J. T. Lloyd's *Henry Ward Beecher: his life and work*, a Tyne Publishing Co title which was also 'published' by John McGready.

eral Gordon, and Matthews and Brooke's issue of Brontë, *Shirley*) include advertisements for Scott publications after the main text.

Without surviving documentation it is not possible to reconstruct Scott's exact working practices. The procedures were likely to vary according to circumstances, but in all probability the following would have taken place in Scott's day-to-day work. The type for a particular title would have been set, stereos made from it, and the sheets printed from the stereos. Part of the print run would be bound for stock and the remainder stored as sheets until the bound stock ran low, when more copies would be bound from the sheets in stock. This process would continue until those sheets also ran low and then a reprint would be considered. If an order was received for copies with a bespoke title-page, the Scott title leaf would be removed from sufficient copies to fill the order, the customer's title-page would be printed, and the new title leaf pasted into the books. As mentioned, the new title leaves are always pasted onto the stubs of the old leaves.

As far as the printing of the cancellans title leaves is concerned, it is clear that this was done by Scott and not by his customers. The similar setting of the title-pages of Apjohn's *Gladstone* has already been mentioned and there are more similarities in other pairs of titles. For example, the only difference between the title-pages of the Scott and Askew issues of Hope's *Life of General Gordon* is the change in the imprint. These are simple typographic title-pages but the design of three other title-pages (the Scott and Dodgson issues of Dumas' *Twenty years after*, and the Matthews and Brooke issue of Brontë's *Shirley*) shows them to be from the same printer because they all follow the same layout and use the same ornaments in a similar way.[6]

The alternative explanations to the proposition that the non-Scott copies derived entirely from Scott are that either Scott sold sheets to his customers, or he sold stereos to them. Both alternatives are party refuted by the fact that some of the non-Scott copies have Scott advertisements. If the customers had had such control over the product before binding took place, presumably they would have removed Scott's advertisements.

In addition, copies exist in which not only the sheets and cancelled titles derive from Scott, but also the bindings. The Scott issue of *Twenty years after* is half-bound with dark green cloth spine-strip and corner pieces on light green cloth boards, and gold tooling has been applied to the front, spine and back. The binding on *Shirley* from Matthews and Brooke is exactly the same except for the colour of the cloth which is dark red on the spine and corner pieces and light red on the boards. The binding on the Dodgson issue is in a different style but, despite Dodgson's title-page, it even has the name 'Walter Scott' at the foot of the spine. Even more significant, the paper used for the linings of the hollow backs in *Shirley* and Dodgson's *Twenty years after* is exactly the same. Waste paper has been used and it is possible to see down the

---

6. The ornaments form two sides of a frame: along the head an ornament with spirals of leaves 11 x 97 mm; along the gutter an ornament with stylised leaves 141 x 18 mm. There are also two rows of eleven star ornaments, one above and one below the author's name.

hollows that the paper is printed or written on by hand in the same brown ink and in the same style of lettering. The non-Scott copies must have been supplied, if required, ready bound by Scott.

Another slightly unusual feature which helps to prove that Scott supplied bound books, or at least sewn book blocks, to these customers is that several of the copies are wire sewn (all the copies from Scott except the Coleridge; Apjohn, *Gladstone*, Hope, *General Gordon* and *New World heroes*, from Askew; *Shirley* from Matthews and Brooke; and *Twenty years after* from Dodgson).[7] Wire-sewn books, as opposed to pamphlets, were never common in Britain although there are a few examples still surviving. According to Bernard Middleton, 'wire staplers came into use in the 1870s, but within a few years they were discarded in favour of thread sewing machines'.[8] This is supported by Geoffrey Glaister: 'In 1877 August Brehmer brought from Philadelphia to London his patent machine which wire-stitched both pamphlets and books. The books were stapled to tapes across the backs, but as the wire tended to rust and disfigure the pages their use for books lapsed'.[9] Walter Scott must have owned a Brehmer machine or patronised a bookbinder who owned one because wire sewn copies of books which he printed and published besides those being discussed here are still occasionally found.[10] Tapes are used in the normal position across the spine of the book, and the gatherings are saddle stitched with wire. Each staple passes from the inside of the gathering around the top and bottom of the tape in a similar way to thread sewing, or alternatively each staple passes through the tape, with the cut ends of the wire meeting at the back of the tape.

Scott copies with variant issues from the same plates discovered to date are as follows:

TYNE/SCOTT TITLE-PAGES[11]

Lewis Apjohn, *William Ewart Gladstone* London: Tyne Publishing, no date. Title leaf normal; no printer's colophon; 'Chronology' ends 9 Nov 1880. Copy in the British Library.

OTHER TITLE-PAGES

Lewis Apjohn, *William Ewart Gladstone* London: J.M. Dent, no date. Title leaf cancelled; no printer's colophon; 'Chronology' ends 9 Nov 1880. Copy in University College of Wales, Aberystwyth.

7. All the Askew copies have similar bindings (red leather quarter bound on red cloth boards blocked on the front with the words 'Gems of Literature Series') with no indication that the cases were supplied by Scott. It is therefore possible that Scott sometimes supplied only the book blocks and the customer provided the cases.

8. *History of English craft bookbinding technique* (1963), p. 294.

9. *Glossary of the book*, 2nd ed (1979), p. 515.

10. The following are a few examples which I have seen: J. Arthur Bain, *Life and explorations of Fridtjof Nansen*, nd; Thomas Browne, *Religio Medici . . . and other essays*, 1886; Daniel C. Eddy, *The young woman's friend*, 1885; *English fairy and folk tales*, ed Edwin Sidney Hartland, nd; J. T. Lloyd, *Henry Ward Beecher: his life and work*, 1887; and Edward Bulwer Lytton, *Alice, or the mysteries*, nd. It does not follow, of course, that all copies of these books will be wire sewn, because one edition could be bound in a variety of ways. Routledge also sometimes used a wire sewing machine in their Morley's Universal Library Series.

11. The Scott copies which have been used to set against the non-Scott copies have

Lewis Apjohn, *William Ewart Gladstone*
London: Walter Scott, no date. Title leaf
normal; colophon: The Walter Scott
Press, Newcastle-on-Tyne; 'Chronology'
ends 19 May 1898; wire sewn. Copy in the
British Library.

[No copy of a corresponding Scott issue of
Shirley has been traced]

Samuel Taylor Coleridge, *Poems*
London: Scott, 1886. Title leaf normal;
colophon: Printed by Walter Scott, Felling, Newcastle-on-Tyne; thread sewn.
Copy in the National Library of Wales.

Alexandre Dumas, *Twenty years after*
London: Scott, no date. Title leaf cancelled; colophon: The Walter Scott Press,
Newcastle-on-Tyne; wire sewn. Copy in
the National Library of Wales.

Eva Hope, *Life of General Gordon*
London: Scott, no date. Title leaf normal; colophon: The Walter Scott Press,
Newcastle-on-Tyne; wire sewn. Copy in
the National Library of Wales.

Lewis Apjohn, *William Ewart Gladstone*
Preston: James Askew, no date. Title leaf
cancelled; colophon: The Walter Scott
Press, Newcastle-on-Tyne; 'Chronology'
ends May 1890; wire sewn. Copy in the
British Library.

Charlotte Brontë, *Shirley*
Bradford: Matthews and Brooke, no date.
Title leaf cancelled; colophon: The Walter Scott Press, Newcastle-on-Tyne; wire
sewn; Scott advertisements. Personal
copy.

Samuel Taylor Coleridge, *Poems*
London: Mudie's Select Library, no date.
Title leaf cancelled; colophon: The Walter Scott Publishing Co., Ltd., Newcastle-
on-Tyne; thread sewn; 'Mudie' advertisements. Copy in the National Library of
Wales.

Alexandre Dumas, *Twenty years after*
Leeds: Joseph Dodgson, no date. Title
leaf cancelled; colophon: The Walter
Scott Press, Newcastle-on-Tyne; wire
sewn. Copy in the British Library.

Eva Hope, *Life of General Gordon*
Preston: James Askew, no date. Title leaf
cancelled; colophon: The Walter Scott
Press, Newcastle-on-Tyne; wire sewn.
Copy owned by James Askew and Son
Ltd.

Eva Hope, *Life of General Gordon*
Edinburgh: Nimmo, Hay and Mitchell,
no date. Title leaf normal; colophon:
The Walter Scott Press, Newcastle-on-
Tyne; thread sewn. Copy in Cambridge
University Library.

Eva Hope, *Life of General Gordon*
Manchester: John Harrop, 1885. Colo-
phon: Printed by Walter Scott, The
Kenilworth Press, Felling, Newcastle-on-
Tyne; Scott advertisements. Copy in Uni-
versity of Georgia.[12]

been chosen simply for their accessibility, mainly because the bibliography of Scott reprints
is extremely obscure. All the Scott titles are from one or other of the reprint series but it
is almost impossible to say from which particular series. Scott's reprints are almost invariably undated, and individual copies seldom have any indication of the series to which
they belong. According to Scott's advertisements the same title could appear in several different series, still with no indication in the books themselves; *Oliver Twist* and *Pickwick
papers*, for instance, are each in seven different series.

    12. It has not been possible to examine this copy, and the Harrop state appears to be

Eva Hope, *Grace Darling, heroine of the Farne Islands*
London: Scott, no date. Title leaf normal; colophon: The Walter Scott Press, Newcastle-on-Tyne; wire sewn. Copy in Newcastle Public Library.

Eva Hope, *New World heroes: Lincoln and Garfield*
London: Scott, no date. Title leaf normal; colophon: The Walter Scott Press, Newcastle-on-Tyne; wire sewn. Copy in the British Library.

Eva Hope, *Grace Darling, heroine of the Farne Islands*
Glasgow; Sydney: John McGready, no date. Two title-pages present; colophon: Printed by Walter Scott, The Kenilworth Press, Felling, Newcastle-on-Tyne. Copy in University of British Columbia.[13]

Eva Hope, *New World heroes: Lincoln and Garfield*
Preston: James Askew, no date. Title leaf cancelled; colophon: Printed by Walter Scott, Felling, Newcastle-on-Tyne; wire sewn. Copy owned by James Askew and Son Ltd.

Other points which still need comment concern firstly the Scott issue of Dumas' *Twenty years after*. The book is a normal Scott publication printed throughout by him like the others, except that the title leaf even here is a cancel. Perhaps in this one title a mistake was discovered in the cancellandum. An alternative explanation, albeit not a very satisfactory one, is that title-pages were left blank in all books which Scott was promoting in this way and a customer's or Scott's own title-pages were added only when orders were received.

Secondly, an interesting variation on the presence of Scott's advertisements in non-Scott books is found in the Mudie issue of Coleridge. One leaf of advertisements has been added after the text with the heading 'Mudie's "Morris" Edition of the Favourite Canterbury Poets' which thus gives a half-hearted acknowledgement to Scott's Canterbury Poets Series. Certainly all the twenty-three titles listed are from Scott's series, but the intention seems to be to suggest that these are Mudie's publications—even if they are printed on a cancelled leaf facing Walter Scott's colophon.

Thirdly, the question of when all this took place can be answered to some extent. Only Harrop's *General Gordon* and Scott's Coleridge are dated (1885 and 1886 respectively) but despite this there are other indications of when the books appeared. The chronological table in the four copies of *Gladstone* provide three more dates: 1880 (for Tyne and Dent), 1890 (for Askew) and 1898 (for Scott).

Further deductions can be made from the addresses on the title-pages. Walter Scott moved from Paternoster Square to 24 Warwick Lane in late June 1885[14] and thus his issues of *General Gordon*, *New World heroes* and *Grace Darling* with Warwick Lane on the title-pages were all printed after this date. His issue of *Twenty years after* gives the address as Paternoster Square and consequently must have been printed before June 1885. Similarly,

---

rare. The *National union catalog pre-1956 imprints* lists only four copies and one of these (the copy claimed to be in the Library of the Department of the Navy) has proved to be a ghost. No copy has so far been located in Britain.

13. It has not been possible to examine this copy.
14. *The bookseller*, 4 July 1885, p. 647.

Askew's company history states that the firm moved to 96 Fishergate Hill in 'the early 1890s'; since all three Askew copies have the address, they all appeared after 1890.

John McGready began in business on his own and then from 1880 to 1885 he traded as McGready, Thomson and Nevin.[15] After 1885 the partnership appears to have been dissolved and he continued to operate under his own name only. Because McGready's *Grace Darling* makes no mention of McGready, Thomson and Nevin it would not have been produced during the five years of their partnership and therefore would have appeared before 1880 or after 1885. It could not be printed by Scott and also have appeared before 1880 because Scott was not a printer until 1882, so it must have been printed after 1885.

In the Canterbury Poets series the earliest volumes are dated but dating stops after 1888. Then in undated volumes the series style was changed. At first the books were printed in red and black, the title-page had a large red initial and every page had a red ruled border, and there were ornamental head and tail pieces. When the change occurred the ornaments and ruled borders were removed and the books printed throughout in black only. The change in style appears to have occurred in 1889 because *American sonnets* (entered in the *English catalogue* in 1889) is in the early style, while Landor's *Poems* (*English catalogue*, 1889), Owen Meredith's *Poems* (*English catalogue*, 1890), and *Women poets* (*English catalogue*, 1890) are all in the later style. Mudie's Coleridge is printed in the second style and therefore must have been printed in 1889 or later. Furthermore, Mudie's volume has what could be a date, '7–04' (= July 1904?), printed below Scott's colophon on page 294.

One final comment should be made about the Nimmo, Hay and Mitchell issue of *General Gordon*, which does not conform to the pattern and therefore seems to suggest a slightly different business agreement with Scott. The Nimmo copy was printed by Scott and has his colophon on the final page of text. However, the title leaf has not been cancelled and it was printed with the rest of the sheets on a leaf conjugate with the second leaf of the text. Secondly, although mostly from the same setting as the Scott issue, a correction has been made to change to roman an italic *o* used by mistake on page 368. Thirdly, the binding is thread sewn rather than wire sewn.

Of the businesses mentioned on the non-Scott title-pages, Nimmo, Hay and Mitchell were the nearest to a conventional publisher. The partnership was formed in 1883[16] and continued in business until the mid-1930s. They appear as publishers in the *English catalogue* from 1898, the first year to include the list of publishers' names and addresses. James Clegg in 1910 described the firm as a publisher of 'reward books, birthday books and non-copyright classics',[17] and they frequently advertised their publications in *Publishers' circular* and *The bookseller*.

15. *Industries of Glasgow* (1888), and Kelly's *Directory of stationers.*
16. *The bookseller,* 4 October 1883, p. 895.
17. James Clegg, *International directory of booksellers* (1910). Earlier editions list Nimmo, Hay and Mitchell as publishers without giving a description of the business.

It therefore appears that the Nimmo, Hay and Mitchell copy of *General Gordon* is actually what all the other non-Scott issues give the impression of being—a separately published book. It seems likely that Nimmo, Hay and Mitchell came to an agreement with Walter Scott and bought some form of right to publish, with Scott still retained as the printer.

To conclude, the evidence presented here is admittedly based on a small sample, it does not provide final proof, nor is it all present in one book or pair of Scott and non-Scott books. Short of the discovery of a written agreement between Scott and one of his customers the evidence is never likely to be conclusive. However, it seems reasonable speculation that Walter Scott offered bound books for sale in which the title-page was specially printed with the customer's name so that the customer appeared to be the publisher. The arrangement was flexible; for example, the books could be bought as bound copies but customers could also provide their own bindings. The titles were all taken from Scott's list of publications and both Scott's original publication and the customer's copies were in print at the same time. Apart from the title-page there was usually no attempt to disguise Scott's involvement, even to the extent of leaving advertisements for Scott publications in the volumes. Scott must have seen the method merely as a way of selling more books. He must have discounted keeping his own name before the public on the title-pages and regarded sales by James Askew, John Harrop and the others, quite rightly, as Scott sales.

Presumably there would have been a minimum order below which Scott would not supply tailor-made title-pages, but this must have been fairly low. It is hardly conceivable that even a bookseller like Matthews and Brooke who had a well established and profitable trade could have taken thousands of copies of Charlotte Brontë's *Shirley*. It is difficult to understand how Scott found the system worth while because the amount of work involved in printing and inserting individual title-pages in only a few copies at a time was considerable. Nevertheless the method was in operation for several years, it was inherited by Scott from the Tyne Publishing Co, it was being used by them in 1880 or '81 and Scott was still using it in 1904. Despite its long history these books were only a small part of Scott's output[18] and most of his publications were perfectly ordinary books which were sold in the normal way through bookshops.

18. I am in the process of compiling a list of Scott's publications which so far contains about 1200 titles.

A MIXED BAG FROM *THE BOOKMAN* OF NEW YORK

by

ARTHUR SHERBO

THE editors of the *Literary History of the United States* write that "One of the most distinguished literary and critical journals during the first quarter of the twentieth century was the *Bookman* (1895–1933)."[1] In *A History of American Magazines*, Frank Luther Mott devotes ten pages to his account of the *Bookman*; I quote the one sentence pertinent to this article: "There were some articles in these early years by English critics—Clement K. Shorter, George Saintsbury, Edmund Gosse, Andrew Lang—and much attention to British books and writers."[2] Despite the articles by the English critics named and by others not named, and despite the great attention to British books and other writers, a great deal of the matter pertaining to these writers and their works, or writings about them, lies buried and forgotten. I intend to resurrect some of this forgotten matter, confessing at the same time that I have not exhausted all the possibilities offered in these volumes. I should add that I have also gleaned some Henry James items that will appear in *The Henry James Review*. And while my primary concern is with matters British, I reprint poems by John Greenleaf Whittier and William Cullen Bryant and letters by Oliver Wendell Holmes and Ellen Glasgow, all also forgotten. As with others of my forays in the periodicals, I offer but little comment and proceed seriatim.

The first number of the *Bookman* (February 1895) contained an item with the title "From an Unpublished French Essay of Charlotte Brontë" (pp. 30–32) with the following headnote: "We are enabled to give the following extracts from an essay written by Charlotte Brontë, in French, on *The Death of Moses*. The essay, an exercise given her by M. Héger during her stay in Brussels, has not hitherto been published. After telling how Moses at the end of his life received the command of God to climb Mount Nebo, and how he blessed one by one the twelve tribes, the narrative proceeds:—" (1:30). One long paragraph in French is quoted, followed by this interpolation: "There comes an excursion into biblical criticism. Are we to interpret the narrative literally, and believe Moses to have been actually face to face with God, or as an allegory? Her answer is decisive," i.e. the account is not an allegory. The rest of the French is quoted and then there is an English "Translation of the Extracts." What is of more interest than the "unpublished French essay" is the light it throws on the regime in the *Maison d' Èducation Pour*

1. Fourth ed., rev. (1974), 2:62.
2. *A History of American Magazines, vol. 4 (1885–1905)* (1957), p. 433.

les Jeunes Demoiselles sous la direction de Madame Heger-Parent, Rue d'
Isabelle à Bruxelles where Charlotte and Emily were enrolled in 1842 and
where Charlotte fell in love with Constantin Heger, Madame Heger's husband.[3] There is one other work by Charlotte which attests to her fluency
in French, a translation into English verse of the first book of Voltaire's
Henriade.[4]

The fairly recent (1983) Twayne Publishers' *George du Maurier*, written
by Richard Kelly, does not list Shirley Brooks, editor of *Punch*, in the index,
nor any others named in the following letter, except for a passing reference
to William Frith. The letter has du Maurier's sketch of Calderon, Destouches,
and himself on the third page. All three originals are on one page of the
November 1896 number.

The following letter was written by George Du Maurier to Shirley Brooks when
he was editor of *Punch*, in which he mentions the artists Frith, Calderon, and
Destoches, Edmund Yates, and Bellew, the fashionable preacher of the day.

1 ALBION PLACE, RAMSGATE.
Wednesday.

DEAR SHIRLEY: Ave! I have been a long
time answering the last, but for the first few
days I felt seedy and out of sorts, the usual
effect of the first week of the seaside on me.

We are having a very jolly time with Frith,
Calderon, Destoches *et quibusdam aliis*; and
the sooner (the) Shirleys come the better;
there are to be Yates and *elle*, and Bellew
shall be hot i' the mouth, too. You and I will
leave the giddy throng and retire to some
solitary place where we can see the bathers; I
have no doubt Frith will join us and Bellew
(with an opera glass, which he will keep all to
himself, with the usual selfishness of his cloth).

I congratulate you on your lines about
Faraday. I am going to devote the rest of my
leisure here to a black-edge poem about myself, and if you like I will put in a word
for you.

I suppose that this will find you somewhere in Cornwall. Give my kind regards to
the Cuddleips if you are with them. I am
much afraid that your arrival here will be
after our departure, from what Mr. Frith said.
We stay here W. P. and D. V. for another
fortnight.

I have been working hard all day and am
more than usually idiotic, or I should write
you a longer letter and paint the fascination
of Ramsgate more glowingly.

P. H. C., E. O. D., & G. D. M.
looking at the bathers

---

3. See Clement Shorter, *The Brontës, Life and Letters*, 2 vols. (1908), I, Chapter 11,
"The Pensionnat Héger, Brussels," for this episode in Charlotte's life.

4. Published in 1917 with an introduction by Clement Shorter.

Leonée Ormond, in her definitive biography, *George du Maurier* (4:183) (1969), lists Calderon and Frith in her index, but not Destouches, Bellew, and the Cuddleips. The letter to Brooks may be dated August 1867, Ormond describing the Ramsgate holiday as of that date (pp. 191–192). There are four letters from Brooks to du Maurier quoted in George S. Layard, *Shirley Brooks of Punch. His Life, Letters, and Diaries* (1907); none from du Maurier to Brooks. Du Maurier had illustrated some of Brooks's works, the "Nursery Rhymes" in *Punch* being among those. I could not discover who the Cuddleips were. Should not a future biographer identify them?

James C. Johnson of Langley, Fairfax County, Virginia, wrote to the *Bookman* to make known that he had in his possession "the manuscript of a poem written by Thomas Moore during his visit to this country, which has never been published." Moore was hospitably treated by William Wischam, "a prominent figure in the State capitol of Virginia," and wrote the verses in Wischam's house. Johnson received the manuscript "from a grandchild of Mr. Wischam." He provided a facsimile of the manuscript and concluded his headnote by stating that the poem was now printed for the first time. The text of the facsimile is faithfully reprinted in the July 1898 number, and I have not found any subsequent printing of the poem.

> Yes! I did say on the pine barren view,
>   As weary I journeyed the wild road along,
> Virginia's rude soil I would glad bid adieu
>   And never remember Virginia in song.
>
> I had passed through her towns and no converse had met,
>   Though in converse my heart knew its fondest delight.
> And so firm in my breast had dear friendship been set,
>   That of friendship I thought I might challenge the right.
>
> But soon was the change when to Richmond I came,
>   For the stranger here met with a heart like his own,
> And he sighs that his verse will ne'er equal its fame,
>   And give it for friendship the highest renown.
>
> In the house on the hill a free welcome he found,
>   The welcome that told him its friendship was true,

And long shall the praise of its master resound,
  While gratitude claims from his heart the just due.

O woman, here too both in beauty and sense
  Thou are blest with the boon which art can not improve,
Thy looks and thy smiles such sweet favours dispense
  That the heart of the stranger is tempted to love.

Then, Richmond, accept a stranger's farewell!
  If the tear of regret of his love be the proof,
Long, long in his heart shall thy memory dwell,
  And in age be the theme of the days of his youth.

(7:386–387)

Nine poems in the known canon of Moore's poems begin with the word "Yes." The account of Moore's visit to Virginia in 1803 in Terence de Vere White's *Tom Moore, The Irish Poet* (1977) makes no mention of the Wischams or, of course, of these verses. Indeed, his account (pp. 40–41) does not gibe with Moore's poem or with Johnson's headnote which contains a reference to the cold reception accorded Moore in Norfolk.

The next two pieces are letters by Robert Browning and by Elizabeth Barrett Browning. The first, in the June 1899 number, is reprinted from Moscheles's *Fragments* 1899 (pp. 217–218) and has escaped the notice of Browning scholars, despite the fact that Moscheles, a very well-known portrait painter, had painted a portrait of Browning. I quote the headnote as well as the letter.

Mr. Felix Moscheles's *Fragments of an Autobiography*, reviewed on another page, contains a number of fine photogravures of his well-known portraits. One of these is his excellent painting of Robert Browning. It was Browning, by the way, who gave him the only letter of introduction, which he has carefully kept, at the time of the painter's visit to America in 1883. "To this day," he says, "when I read it, it seems more like music than like epistolary prose to me." The letter was characteristic of the "best and kindest of men"; and ran thus:

19 WARWICK CRESCENT, W.,
11th August, 1884.

To whomsoever it may concern:
    I have received such extraordinary kindness from Americans, and number so many of them among my friends, that it would seem invidious if I selected those whom I ventured to believe would oblige me were it possible. I shall therefore say, in the simplest of words, that should my dear friend, the Painter Moscheles, meet with any individual whose sympathy I have been privileged to obtain, whatever favour and assistance may be rendered to him, or his charming wife, will constitute one more claim to the gratitude of (9:309)[5]

Since Moscheles went to the United States in 1883, the date of Browning's letter should be 1883. Mrs. Browning's letter to Cornelius Matthews, editor of *Graham's Illustrated Magazine*, is one of a number of manuscript letters in the collection of William Harris Arnold, bibliophile and writer on bibliog-

---

5. *NCBEL* does not list Moschelles's work in the entry for Robert Browning, although there are eight letters from Browning to him in *New Letters of Robert Browning*, ed. William Clyde deVane and Kenneth Leslie Knickerbocker (1950) and a number of references to Browning in the *Fragments*.

raphy. Mrs. Browning's letter, writes the editor of the *Bookman* in the April 1901 issue, "is of especial interest, as in it she expresses her great admiration for Tennyson. It is believed to be unpublished."

For the future you shall have a better correspondent, if indeed my writing to you oftener can appear to you a better thing—and your indulgence will help you to understand, in the meantime, how a very weak hand, such as mine is, may be overworked in the preparation for the printing of a book, until it is forced to deny itself to the claims of private letters. Also from the latter part of January to April I am apt to be more shaken than usual by the visitations of our English climate and the influence of the east winds.—I have a heart which runs like a racehorse, leaps like a hunter, & stands still like a mule, all in the course of one morning—so that I am sometimes forced to be quiet, & think of life, death & the wind. Upon the whole, my health does improve, I think, and two summers now together might renew me, I fancy. But I live upon a point,—a spire of a church—liable to precipitation every instant—which is no reason, however, that I shd write so much about it.

Yes,—I will explain how impossible it was for me to escape the mortification of refusing to see your friend Mr. Belford. He wrote a very courteous letter to me when he found that I cd not see him, & amused me exceedingly by inquiring into the personal history of my relation Mr. Tennyson. Leigh Hunt, he said, had intimated somewhere that he was my relation!—Now I remember that Leigh Hunt in his 'Last of the Violets' (which, by the way, has just been republished by Moxon, together with his other collected poems) had the goodness to say of me

'I took her at first for a sister of Tennyson's,' and that poetical relationship which after all I have no better claim to, I fear, than lies in Mr. Hunt's 'gentilnesse,' is the only one existing between us. Indeed I never saw Mr. Tennyson in my life. So far in reply to your question—which made me smile again. And I have thanks upon thanks for you besides, for your kind words added to the mistake. As to the mistake, if I could make out a hundred & ninety-ninth cousinship a hundred & ninety-nine times removed from Alfred Tennyson, I would snatch at it, and frame my pedigree. (13:153)

Mrs. Browning wrote at least three other letters to Matthews, on August 28, 1843, and on October 1 and November 14, 1844.[6] The reference to Leigh Hunt's collected poems "republished by Moxon" makes it possible to date the letter in the *Bookman* as sometime in 1844, the year Edward Moxon republished Hunt's *Poetical Works*.

While there is much material for literary biographers in the pages of the *Bookman*—interviews, letters to periodicals, reminiscences—I have limited myself to extracts from two pages (326–327) on Wilkie Collins from the December 1901 number.

A short paper entitled "Reminiscences of Wilkie Collins," by Olive Logan, was recently submitted to THE BOOKMAN, and with the writer's consent we are reprinting extracts from it here, because they seem to be especially adapted to this department of our magazine. Mrs. Logan met the novelist at a London luncheon party, and led him to talk of his impressions of the United States and his methods in the making of his books. While there is biographical ephemera students of Collins may find of interest, what is of more general importance are his views on some aspects of novel writing and on Emile Zola and some other novelists.

6. *The Letters of Elizabeth Barrett Browning*, 2 vols., ed. Frederic G. Kenyon (1899), 1:132–135, 198–200, 213–215.

An extract from Mrs. Logan's account then follows:

The novelist was asked if he approved of beginning a story with a sensation.

"Yes, if the sensation be a good one, and one which belongs naturally at the beginning of the story. Then, too, however uncertain an author may be concerning the exact conduct of the middle of the tale, he should always know how it is going to finish; and steadily working toward a prearranged termination, should always keep the action moving; that should never lag. Another thing: when you have interested your readers in one set of characters, it is most unwise to drop them and begin another chapter with 'We must now return to,' etc. The reader is disappointed at losing the people in whose fate he has become interested, and only by an effort takes up the thread of the new peoples' destinies, again to feel the same rebuff when he is forced to quit these new friends with 'We must now go back to,' etc. Another characteristic I deem essential to good novel writing is always to introduce a poetical side in the midst of every-day practicalities. It does not do to grovel in the dirt too much."

"Zola?"

"True; but the taste is ephemeral. Victor Hugo, whom I esteem the greatest poet France ever produced, though not its greatest novelist, will be read a hundred years hence, when all the race of Zolas is forgotten."

"Do you read Daudet?"

"A little—not much. He is not so dreadful as Zola, but he is very bad. Both, and all their followers, are only imitators of the very worst features of Balzac, not one line of whose exquisite poetry and pathos they are capable of producing, however. I should like to see either Zola or Daudet try to write anything as beautiful as the death of Père Goriot, for instance. Oh, we have had these coarse writers in our English fiction, and they have had their day of success, too. Look at Smollett and Sterne; there is not a publisher in England who would risk the reproduction of their works, for they are dead, and nothing on earth can revive them, while edition after edition of *The Vicar of Wakefield* pours through the presses, and no novel of the day, even, is more widely read." (14:326–327)

Biographies of Collins would have been enriched by these reminiscences of Mrs. Logan's, actress and writer and lecturer on the theater. While Balzac is quite properly mentioned as Collins's hero, and Victor Hugo, another French writer whom Collins admired greatly, is also accorded mention, there is nothing in the biographies about Zola and Sterne. Collins's views of the dullness of Daudet's novels and the excellence of *The Vicar of Wakefield* are corroborated in Kenneth Robinson's *Wilkie Collins: A Biography* (1952), pp. 289 and 293–294. And then, of course, of much greater importance than these critical opinions, is Wilkie Collins on his methods of composing fiction.

One article in the October 1903 *Bookman* bears the eye-catching title "Confessions of a Literary Quill-Driver." The piece is an autobiographical sketch by Eugene Lemoine Didier (1838–1913), author, publisher, critic, bibliophile, and editor. Didier, not one to hide his light under a bushel, made the most of the occasion, being afforded some fourteen long columns of the periodical (pp. 135–142). What is germane, however, is the answer Oliver Wendell Holmes gave to Didier's youthful letter, "telling him [Holmes] with easy assurance, that I was well-fitted by my tastes, education and accomplishments —(I was a college-bred shorthand writer with literary aspirations) for the position of amanuensis to a literary man, and suggested that, perhaps, he might require my services; but, if he did not, would he be so kind as to recommend me to some one who did; also to use his influence to open a way for me to some good magazine that paid well," adding that he "did not expect to be treated with cold indifference, but with kindness and sympathy" (p. 135). He had the good grace to characterize Holmes's answer as "very kind." Holmes wrote,

BOSTON, December 6, 18—.

Dear Sir:—I regret that it is not in my power to direct you to any place of employment such as you desire. In a city like this the crowding to all such employments is very great and there are a very few situations to be divided among a great number of applicants. As for myself, I am not (as I am often supposed to be) an editor, and have no writing to do which I am not competent to do myself with a little occasional aid from members of my own family. I regret not to be able to give you encouragement as to employment in Boston, but the truth is there is next to none of the kind you mention, as most of our writers are as poor as rats themselves and no more able to keep an amanuensis than they are to set up a coach and six.

I do not even know how to advise you beyond this simple counsel which I have occasionally given to young aspirants:

If you think you have literary talents, write something for the best paper or magazine you can get into, keep to one signature, and you will be found out by a public which is ready to pay the highest price for almost every kind of literary ability. If you do not think you can make a reputation, why not become a reporter for a newspaper? At any rate you stand a much better chance of finding occupation at home, where you are known, than among strangers. I do not "turn from your petition with cold indifference," but it is utterly out of my power to do more than give you these few words of friendly advice.

Yours very truly,
O. W. HOLMES.
(18:135–136)

"As the good Doctor did not suggest the probability of getting an opening for me in any 'magazine that paid well,'" wrote Didier, quoting himself, "as I had requested him to do, I had to do the best I could for myself, which was what others have done before and since" (p. 136). He concluded his article by listing the periodical articles he had written and the sums he had earned for each ((pp. 141–142).

The August 1904 *Bookman* posed a number of questions to authors and to illustrators "about the value of illustrating novels" as "illustrators have in many cases been severely criticized because they do not seem to have read the text of the stories which they illustrate, and in consequence have made some queer 'breaks'" (p. 348). One of the authors asked to reply to the four questions posed to them was Ellen Glasgow. Her answer was brief and to the point, briefer than the answers of Winston Churchill, George Barr McCutcheon, Josephine Daskam Bacon, and Nancy Huston Banks:

To the Editors of THE BOOKMAN:

GENTLEMEN: In reply to the questions you ask in your letter of April the 6th, I would say that I care very little for illustrations in my books—or, for that matter, in any of my favourite books by other writers. The only novel I can recall which seemed to me perfectly interpreted by the pictures was the English edition of "Resurrection."

Whether or not illustrations add to the popularity of a book I am in no way able to judge. This is a question for a publisher. No, I have never found that an artist was able to reproduce my own mental image of a character, but it seems unreasonable to expect this since, of course, the same words convey totally different impressions to two different minds. To the last question I can answer "yes." So far as my experience permits me to express an opinion, I believe that the artist generally reads the book very carefully. Where he differs from the author is, after all, in a distinct—one may say diverging point of vision. Very truly yours,   ELLEN GLASGOW.
(19:349–350)

Resurrection is, of course, the novel by Tolstoi, a writer for whose works Miss Glasgow had the highest admiration. E. Stanley Godbold, Jr. writes that "before 1900 she [Miss Glasgow] discovered Leo Tolstoy's *War and Peace*, the book she quickly decided was the greatest novel ever written."[7] An illustrated edition of *Resurrection* was published by T. Y. Crowell of New York in 1899. I have not seen a copy.

The *Complete Verse* of Hilaire Belloc (1970) includes a poem simply titled "The Author" (pp. 224–226), which, bare of any comment, loses the cream of the jest. Part of a disparaging discussion of the American *Who's Who* in the July 1904 *Bookman* is the following, necessary for an appreciation of the joke.

In England also there is a tendency to take the people in *Who's Who* a little too seriously, and Mr. Belloc has hit them off in the following:

"DONE INTO VERSE."
A Suggestion for a Rhymed "Who's Who."

KEANES, HERBERT. B. 1846. The son of Lady Jane O'Hone and Henry Keanes, Esq., of 328, St. James's Square, and "The Nook," Albury. *Clubs*: Beagles, Blues, Pitt, Palmerston, the Walnut Box, the Two-and-Two's, etc. *Education*: Private tuition, Eton and Trinity College, Cambridge. Has sat for Putticombe, in Kent, 1885–1892. Nephew and heir of the Right Hon. the Earl of Ballycairn. *Occupation*: Literature, political work, management of estate, etc. Has written: "Problems of the Poor," "What, indeed, is Man?" "Flowers and Fruit" (a book of verse), "Is there a Clifford?" "The Future of Japan," "Musings by Killarney's Shore," "The Ethics of Jean-Paul," and "Nero." Is a strong Protectionist and a broad Churchman. *Recreations*: Social.
(19:444)

The poem follows, the text the same as that in the *Complete Verse*, but with marginal notations imitating the various sections of a typical *Who's Who* entry. Thus, the fifth stanza is labelled "Parentage"; the sixth, seventh and eighth, "Education"; the ninth, "Clubs"; the tenth, "Career"; the eleventh, "Occupation"; the twelfth, "Works"; and the last, "Recreations, etc." Only now can the poem be enjoyed as it was meant to be.

Walter Jerrold, who wrote on and edited much English literature (some fourteen columns in *NUC*), including literature of the eighteenth century, offered "A New Found Poem of Oliver Goldsmith's" to the editors of the *Bookman* who reprinted it in the November 1914 number. The article is not listed in the bibliography of secondary works on Goldsmith; the poem, Gold-

---

7. *Ellen Glasgow and the Woman Within* (1972), p. 43. See also *Ellen Glasgow and the Ironic Art of Fiction* (1960), p. 201, for Miss Glasgow on Tolstoy.

smith's or not, was either not known to Arthur Friedman, editor of Goldsmith's works, or rejected by him. I quote Jerrold's explanatory paragraph,
the poem, and Jerrold's concluding remarks.

The following lines have been found in an old close-packed scrap-book. This
scrap-book—the completion of which is noted as having been made on November
21, 1812—consists of an extraordinary medley of three or four thousand cuttings from
newspapers and magazines of the preceding sixty or seventy years, but the Goldsmith
item has no indication of the place or date of its appearance. It runs as follows:

VERSES

Written by the late Dr. Goldsmith
Addressed to A Friend

O Firm in virtue, as of soul sincere,
Lov'd by the muse, to friendship ever dear!
Amongst the thousand ills of thousand
　　climes,
To name the worst that loads the worst of
　　times,
Is sure a task unpleasing to pursue,
Trackless the maze, uncertain is the clue;
The Ruling Passion still by all confess'd,
The master key that opes each private breast
Here fails; this darling child of nature's
　　school
Submits to custom's more resistless rule.

Should I recount the vast unnumber'd train,
Subjects or Vice of Folly's motley reign;
A heedless multitude, a giddy throng,
The theme of satire, and the scorn of song!
To scan their wild excesses, or to name
Their crimes would put the modest muse to
　　shame.
What if we rove where rigid winter reigns,
O'er Zembla's wastes or Lapland's dreary
　　plains;
Where Lux'ry yet has no soft art displayed,
Where yet Refinement never raised her head;
Where no choice stores the steril lands af-
　　ford,
But rear alike the reindeer and his lord;
O'er moss-grown deserts *these* content to
　　stray,
Those wait in caves the wish'd return of
　　day;
Yet Nature feeds them, yet alike they prove
The gracious hand of all sustaining love:
How high joy sparkles on each savage face
When bright'ning ether calls them to the
　　chase,
Well may their hearts with purest transports
　　glow,

Few are their wants and small their source
    of woe;
Yet may her pow'r endeavour to controul
That leading vice which animates the whole.

While chief amongst the dissipated train,
The soft-ey'd Lux'ry holds her magic reign;
Alas! what refuge can fair Virtue find
The soul corrupt, what laws, what ties can
    [bind?]
Us'd to deceive and tutor'd to beguile,
Death in her charms and ruin in her smile;
Like some trim harlot, while the idle stands
And binds our youth in Philistean bands.
'Tis she that bids enervate arts arise,
That swells the dome to emulate the skies,
That fills the city and the crowded port,
That bids ten thousands to the mart resort;
While Want, that meagre looking fiend, in-
    vades
The rural seats and hospitable shades;
While the poor peasant the sad change de-
    plores,
In secret pines, or quits his native shores,
Seeks better seats in other climes to gain
Or sink at once beneath the whelming main.

Is not Refinement still the source of care,
Ev'n to the best that breathe the vital air?
Ev'n Learning's self corrupted by her art,
The mind enlarging oft depraves the heart;
How small the gain improvement can bestow,
When taste refin'd but brings refined woe.

O sweet Simplicity, celestial maid,
Still at thy shrine my artless vows are paid,
Do thou and Nature still direct my way,
Who follow Nature cannot go astray;
Nor let the great, nor let the grave despise
The humbler blessings from thy reign that
    rise:
No joys like thine from pomp or learning
    springs,
The boast of schoolmen, or the pride of
    kings!
Whilst our soft sons an hapless race remain,
In Lux'ry's lap condemned to every pain;
Ev'n in enjoyment pine their hours away,
And fall at last to anxious cares a prey.

Four rows of asterisks follow in the cutting from which this is copied, indicating either that the "Verses" ended thus abruptly or that but a portion of the whole
is given. Further search may reveal the periodical in which the lines appeared and
the date of their appearance. The scrap-book maker has trimmed his cuttings so close
to the type that he has rarely left any means by which bibliographical facts can be
ascertained. From the paper on which they are printed it can be gathered that the

"Verses" were published shortly after Goldsmith's death, and there seems no reason to doubt their genuineness. (40:253–254)

While there can be no certainty about the authorship of the poem, comparison with works, both poetry and prose, of the accepted canon make it highly probable that the poem is Goldsmith's. His views on luxury were somewhat ambiguous, but not in *The Deserted Village*, where he fiercely inveighed against it. In *Verses*, lines 19–36 paint the grimmest picture of luxury which, as in *The Deserted Village*, forces peasants to emigrate. Lines 37–42, condemnatory of Refinement, echo Goldsmith's views, as recourse to the index in volume five of Arthur Friedman's edition of Goldsmith's works clearly demonstrates. The following portion of the *Verses*, those on Simplicity (ll. 43–50), stress, as does Goldsmith in other works, the difference between it and Refinement. Indeed, the movement from refinement to simplicity is seen in the twenty-fifth letter of *The Citizen of the World*: "the inhabitants of the country, from primitive simplicity soon began to aim at elegance, and from elegance proceeded to refinement." The opening sentence of "The History of Carolan, the last Irish Bard" reads, "There can be perhaps no greater entertainment than to compare the rude Celtic simplicity with modern refinement" (*Works*, II. 105 and III. 118). Line 45 of *Verses*, "Do thou [Simplicity] and Nature still direct my way," is close to words in one of Goldsmith's Prefaces, "it finds nature in almost every instance acting with her usual simplicity" (*Works*, V. 231). The praise of the rigors of a northern existence (hard primitivism) of the last 18 lines of *Verses* finds its counterpart in lines 165–198 of *The Traveller*. Line 55 of *Verses*, "Where no choice stores the steril lands afford," is close to line 169 of *The Traveller*, "No product here the barren hills afford."

Much of the diction in the *Verses*, or what I have termed poetic diction, with all its perjorative connotation, is common to scores, even hundreds, of eighteenth-century poets and poetasters and cannot, therefore, be offered in evidence. The absence of some of the words in the *Verses*, among them "enervate," "emulate," "dissipated," "whelming," "trackless," from the canon of Goldsmith's poetry, while it should be mentioned, is of no real significance. The poetic canon is slight, some 2700 lines (about the number of lines in the first three Books of *Paradise Lost*). And a reading of Goldsmith's prose reveals his use of most of those words.[8]

Finally, for I arbitrarily limited myself to the first fifty volumes of the periodical, here are the unpublished poems by John Greenleaf Whittier and William Cullen Bryant in the February 1917 number. The title of the article in which they appear is "A Literary Discovery. Unpublished Poems by Bryant, Whittier, Holmes and Gerrit Smith." The author, Charles T. White, wrote much on Lincoln, and his *Bookman* piece is listed in the *NUC* by virtue of the fact that one copy is enclosed in a slipcase in the Stanford University Library. As the poems are not in the collected poems of Whittier or Bryant,

---

8. Martin Furey, doctoral candidate in English at Michigan State University, is completing a computer analysis of the "Goldsmith" poem.

I reprint them now with a brief extract from White's explanatory headnote.

A relative of John Pierpont submitted "unpublished poems by William Cullen Bryant, John Greenleaf Whittier, Oliver Wendell Holmes, and Gerrit Smith sent to John Pierpont, poet, Unitarian clergyman, anti-slavery and temperance reformer, on his eightieth birthday anniversary, April 6, 1865, in the city of Washington."

TO JOHN PIERPONT

Health to thee, Pierpont, tried and honest,
In Freedom's fight among the soonest,
Who still as Freedom's minstrel croonest
    Her triumph lays,
And like some hoary harper tunest
    Thy hymns of praise!

Where's now the ban ecclesiastic?
Where they who played their first and last trick
To clog thy Christian steps elastic
    And drown thy word
So keen, so trenchant and sarcastic,
    A two-edged sword!

Where now are all the "unco' good,"
The Canaan-cursing "Brotherhood"?
The mobs they raised, the storms they brewed,
    And pulpit thunder?
Sheer sunk like Pharaoh's multitude,
    They've all "gone under"!

And thou, our noblest and our oldest,
Our Priest and Poet first and boldest,
Crowned with thy fourscore years beholdest
    Thy country free.
O, sight to warm a heart the coldest,
    How much more thee!

All blessings from the bounteous Giver
Be thine, on either side the river;
And when thy sum of life forever
    The angels foot up,
Not vain shall seem thy long endeavour
    All wrong to root up!
                JOHN G. WHITTIER.
Amesbury, 3d mo., 1865

TO THE REVD. DR. JOHN PIERPONT, ON HIS EIGHTIETH BIRTHDAY, APRIL 6, 1865

The mightiest of the Hebrew seers,
Clear-eyed and hale at eighty years,
From Pisgah saw the hills and plains
Of Canaan, green with brooks and rains.

Our poet, strong in frame and mind,
Leaves eighty well-spent years behind,

And forward looks to fields more bright
Than Moses saw from Pisgah's height.

Yet be our Pierpont's voice and pen
Long potent with the sons of men,
And late his summons to the shore
Where he shall meet his youth once more.
April, 1865.   WILLIAM CULLEN BRYANT.

(44:633–634)

As a boy Whittier read Pierpont's *Airs of Palestine*; later he wished to see Pierpont run for governor of Massachusetts and for Congress; he wrote an earlier poem, "To J.P.," in 1883; and he was asked by Pierpont's widow to write her husband's biography.[9] Charles H. Brown's *William Cullen Bryant* (1971) does not mentoin Pierpont.

While it is admittedly anticlimactic, bibliographers, among them those of the old and new *CBEL*, would have done well to have included a number of articles in the *Bookman*. I list a *very* few: Chesterton on Matthew Arnold (16:116, 374), J.W. Hammerton on Barrie (6:116–123); Arthur Symons on Austin Dobson's poems (5:195), Arthur Waugh on Edmund Gosse (4:205–208), Edith Warton on Stephen Phillips's *Ulysses* (15:168–170); W.J. Dawson on Robert Louis Stevenson (4:35–39)—six among hundreds.

9. See Roland H. Woodwell, *John Greenleaf Whittier: A Biography* (1985), pp. 10, 136, 141, 147, and 344 respectively. The poem "To J. P." is on p. 177 of the Cambridge edition of the *Complete Poetical Works*.

A BIBLIOGRAPHICAL ANALYSIS OF THE MANUSCRIPT OF D. H. LAWRENCE'S *THE WHITE PEACOCK*

by

A. R. ATKINS*

B IBLIOGRAPHICAL analyses by Bruce Steele and Helen Baron of the manuscripts of D. H. Lawrence's second and third novels (*The Trespasser* and *Sons and Lovers* respectively) have shown that the final works can include

* I wish to thank George Lazarus for allowing me to consult the manuscript of *The White Peacock* and Hueffer's letter to Lawrence, and Dr. Helen Baron and Dr. John Worthen for advice concerning earlier versions of this article. Previously unpublished parts of the manuscript of *The White Peacock* are published here with the permission of the Estate of Frieda Lawrence Ravagli.

passages written up to two years earlier.[1] The history of Lawrence's first novel, *The White Peacock*, is just as complicated. The aim of the analysis offered here is to unravel the development of *The White Peacock* by establishing when each page of the final manuscript was written and when subsequent layers of revision were made. My hope is that this information will aid future scholars in their understanding of how the novel was put together and their interpretations of its constituent elements.

My account may be compared with Andrew Robertson's "Introduction" to the Cambridge Edition of *The White Peacock*.[2] Robertson sets out the historical background to the writing and revision of the novel, but he does not describe the detailed structure of the final manuscript. My analysis reveals that the revision and rewriting of *The White Peacock* was a more complex process than has hitherto been recognized, especially when one considers its relationship with the events of Lawrence's life and the writing of poems and other works through 1909–10. The first few pages of this paper outline the history of successive versions of *The White Peacock*; the major stages included the first two drafts called "Laetitia", two further drafts called "Nethermere", and the final novel *The White Peacock* which resulted after a revision to the proofs. The analysis in the rest of the paper identifies the components of the final manuscript, ignoring the proof revisions (which are listed in the Cambridge Edition) and those pages of the early drafts which were not incorporated into the final manuscript (most of them have been lost or were destroyed).

Historical Background

In 1908 Lawrence recalled his boredom in September 1906 with his teacher training course at University College, Nottingham: 'It was imperative that I should do something, so I began to write a novel—or rather, I resumed a work I had begun some months before—two years last Easter'.[3] The first draft ("Laetitia I") was completed by June 1907. Lawrence was, however, dissatisfied with it and immediately began to rewrite from the beginning. The second draft ("Laetitia II") was finished by May 1908. A forty-eight page and a ten-page fragment of the respective drafts have survived and have been published in an appendix to the Cambridge Edition.

Lawrence moved to Croydon to start work as a schoolteacher in October 1908, and began to rewrite his novel in January 1909, renaming it "Nether-

---

1. See Bruce Steele, 'The Manuscript of D. H. Lawrence's "Saga of Siegmund" ', *Studies in Bibliography*, 33 (1980), 193–205, Helen Baron's '*Sons and Lovers*: The Surviving Manuscripts from Three Drafts Dated by Paper Analysis', *Studies in Bibliography*, 38 (1985), 289–326, and her 'Jessie Chambers' plea for justice to "Miriam" ', *Archiv für das Studium der neueren Sprachen und Literatur*, 137 (1985), 63–84.

2. *The White Peacock*, edited by Andrew Robertson (Cambridge University Press, 1983). Hereafter *WP*. The manuscript of the novel is now in the possession of Mr. George Lazarus, and a microfilm copy is in the D. H. Lawrence Collection at Nottingham University Library (NUL).

3. *The Letters of D. H. Lawrence*, edited by James T. Boulton (Cambridge University Press, 1979), I, 49. Hereafter *Letters i*.

mere". It is difficult to determine his rate of progress with the new work because he rarely mentions it in his surviving letters of the period. On 19 August 1909, however, he told his teacher friend Louie Burrows, with whom he was collaborating on short stories: 'It will take you at least three years to write a novel—at school' (*Letters i* 136). Lawrence had begun his own novel three years earlier, at Easter 1906, so it seems likely that he had recently brought the work to some form of completion. This was probably before the end of July because he was away from Croydon on holiday in August (two weeks on the Isle of Wight, the rest in Eastwood).

In late August 1909 Lawrence heard that some of his poems had been accepted for publication by Ford Madox Hueffer (later Ford), the editor of the *English Review*. He met with Hueffer in London before 11 September, and it was probably at that meeting or in a letter that Hueffer said he would 'be glad to read any [prose] work' Lawrence sent him (*Letters i* 138). After revising parts of the manuscript, probably with the help of two friends, Lawrence submitted his novel to Hueffer just before 1 November (see *Letters i* 141). This completed draft is referred to as "Nethermere I" in the following analysis.

On 20 November Lawrence wrote: 'Hueffer is reading my novel. He says it's good, and is going to get it published for me' (*Letters i* 144). On 15 December Hueffer sent Lawrence a letter approving the work. Lawrence immediately sent a copy of the letter to the publisher William Heinemann, and asked if he could send him "Nethermere I" to be considered for publication (*Letters i* 148–149).[4]

The whereabouts of "Nethermere I" between 20 November and 15 December is unclear. Robertson suggests that Hueffer returned the manuscript before writing to Lawrence on 15 December; Lawrence would then have had time to revise the work before offering it to Heinemann (see *WP* xxvii). I believe, however, that Hueffer held onto the manuscript up to 15 December, discussing it with Lawrence when Lawrence visited his home in central London at weekends.[5] Hueffer's letter of 15 December told Lawrence: 'I have now read your novel, and have read it with a great deal of interest'. He gave his opinion of the book's faults and merits, and offered advice on how to improve it and approach a publisher, having decided it was too long for the *English Review*. Even if he had already told Lawrence, as seems probable, to forward a copy of his letter to Heinemann and had deliberately phrased it so as to

4. Letter from Ford Madox Hueffer to D. H. Lawrence, now in the possession of Mr. George Lazarus. The letter is in Lawrence's handwriting because he copied it out to send to Heinemann. It was not known to J. T. Boulton when he edited the Cambridge Edition of Lawrence's letters (see *Letters i* 149 n.1). The complete letter will appear for the first time in John Worthen's forthcoming Volume One of a new three-volume biography of Lawrence, to be published by Cambridge University Press.

5. Hueffer describes this revision process in *Mightier Than The Sword* (1938); repr. *D. H. Lawrence: A Composite Biography*, edited by Edward Nehls (University of Wisconsin Press, 1957–59), I, 120–121. Hereafter *Nehls i*. A shortened version may be found in *WP* xxvi. Hueffer is notorious however for 'embroidering' his memory, and it is unclear at what time these discussions, if any, took place.

arouse Heinemann's interest, it seems reasonable to accept his opening statement as a strong indication that the manuscript was still in his hands. The letter contains no suggestion that Hueffer was returning the manuscript to Lawrence for revision; the manuscript was delivered to Heinemann's office in central London at an unknown date after 15 December by Violet Hunt, who lived with Hueffer.[6]

Lawrence met Heinemann on 20 January 1910 and was informed that "Nethermere I" had been approved for publication, subject to a number of alterations. It is not known when the manuscript itself was returned to Lawrence, but Helen Corke remembers him unpacking it for her sometime in February, after asking her to look over it for him.[7] The manuscript has not survived intact. It was substantially redrafted over the following months into "Nethermere II", which is the surviving manuscript and was used as setting copy for the first edition of *The White Peacock*. "Nethermere II" was delivered to Heinemann on 11 April (see *Letters i* 158–159). Whilst Robertson surmises that "Nethermere I" was revised during late November and December 1909, I believe that all the revisions to "Nethermere I" were made after February 1910 and were in effect the writing of "Nethermere II".

The Manuscript "Nethermere II": *General Features*

Andrew Robertson states that "Nethermere II" is entirely written on Boot's exercise paper (see *WP* xxiv). The list of paper types in the Appendix shows that this is not the case. Robertson also says that the manuscript's pages were originally in 'gatherings of six pages folded once, but these have been cut at the fold; the resulting sections of twelve written pages (8 x 6.5 inches) are numbered consecutively by DHL in roman numerals' (*WP* xxiv n.19). This is true of the entirely rewritten Part III, but the earlier parts have quires of various sizes. The manuscript consists of long stretches of one particular paper type, interspersed with pages of different paper types which appear to have been written after the main body of the text. This suggests that Lawrence would tend to buy a batch of paper of a particular type, use it up, and then buy a new batch which was sometimes made by a different manufacturer.

One way of dating the pages would be to compare the paper with the types of paper used for Lawrence's letters between 1906 and 1910. Helen Baron's paper analysis of *Sons and Lovers* shows that during 1911–14 Lawrence often used the same paper for writing his novels and his letters. Comparatively few letters survive from 1906–10 but they show that Lawrence usually wrote his letters on special sheets of writing paper. He only occasionally used paper types similar to those used in "Nethermere II". These are recorded in the Appendix of this article, but in view of their scarcity there is insufficient evidence to establish that letters from a certain period were being written at the same time as certain pages of "Nethermere II".

---

6. See *Nehls i* 127.

7. Helen Corke, *D. H. Lawrence: The Croydon Years* (University of Texas Press, 1965), p. 6. Hereafter *CY*.

There are five different types of handwriting in "Nethermere II". Lawrence's hand forms the bulk of the script. Twelve pages are in an unknown hand. The hands of Agnes Mason, Agnes Holt and Helen Corke appear on pages which they copied out neatly, and Corke also wrote revisions throughout the manuscript. All three women were Croydon school-teachers. Mason worked at the same school as Lawrence and remained his friend throughout his Croydon years; Holt, whom Lawrence briefly contemplated marrying in the autumn of 1909, met him at an unknown date and continued their relationship until she moved to the Isle of Man in mid-1910; Corke met Lawrence briefly through Mason in late 1908, but was intimate with him only from September 1909 until he left Croydon in March 1912.

It is unclear exactly when Mason and Holt did their copying. Andrew Robertson suggests that Holt copied her seventy-six pages during the revision period which he believes Lawrence undertook in between Hueffer's appraisal of the novel during November 1909 and the manuscript being sent to Heinemann in December (see *WP xxvi–xxvii*). He dates Mason's writing in the final revision period of February–April 1910. John Worthen suggests, however, that

> although Agnes Holt had been DHL's unofficial fiancée in the autumn of 1909—she copied into his poetry notebook those of the poems published in the November 1909 *English Review*—they agreed not to marry sometime in the winter of 1909: almost certainly before Christmas. Although they remained friendly, this cooling of their relationship suggests that she might not thereafter have been so available (or willing) to copy, and that she may well have done her stint earlier. . . . As Agnes Mason's first 6 pages of copying (and some thereafter) clearly followed on from Agnes Holt's 76 pages, that part of their work almost certainly represents DHL's attempt to get the manuscript into a presentable form for Hueffer in the second half of 1909.[8]

Datings must remain tentative, owing to the lack of biographical evidence, but Worthen's judgment concerning the probabilities is persuasive. Agnes Mason's involvement appears to be more complicated than that of Holt's; her pages are not in a single block of text and may have been written at different times through the autumn of 1909 and spring of 1910.

Most of Helen Corke's accounts say that she became involved with the revision of the novel in 1910, when her relationship with Lawrence developed into a closer intimacy. Her diary of the period has an entry dated 25 March 1910 which refers to 'some folios of David's story which [she was] revising for him' (*CY 6*). She remembers that in February Lawrence asked her to 'read the manuscript and make suggestions, especially marking passages showing prolixity'.[9] They also worked together on the manuscript at her home, when she may have written corrections according to Lawrence's direct instructions, although she does not say who did the actual writing. Five pages of the final manuscript are in her hand, but there are also corrections and re-wordings

8. Letter to author dated 24 August 1989.
9. *In Our Infancy* (Cambridge University Press, 1975), p. 179. Hereafter *IOI*.

scattered throughout the work, confirming her memory of the extent of her involvement.

The Manuscript "Nethermere II": *Paper Analysis*

My analysis of "Nethermere II" accounted for the following features: the paper make, whether or not the tear marks down one side of a page or a torn watermark could be matched with that of another page elsewhere in a quire, evidence of stapling to indicate whether bound or unbound quires were used, the scribal style of the page and quire numbers, the principal scribe on each page, and the layers of revision in different scribal styles and ink types.

Page and quire numbers proved to be very unreliable as scribal indicators because even when characteristic features of a sequence of numbers could be listed, they could not be linked to any particular person. There was no apparent consistency to the way a given scribe would write his or her numbers. The numbers must, however, have been written quite late in the history of the manuscript, because although there are sections transferred from earlier drafts there are no sequences of re-numbered pages. It appears that in early drafts of the novel Lawrence did not number individual pages as he wrote them. The stapled and folded quires were simply numbered with roman numerals. A similar procedure was followed for Lawrence's 1909 play *A Collier's Friday Night*. The pages of this manuscript are unnumbered and grouped entirely by folded sections.[10] This system may also be seen in the surviving pages from "Laetitia I" and "Laetitia II" (see *WP* 328). When Lawrence realised the extent of his later revisions to the novel he must have decided to number each page; a page which needed copying out could then be easily identified by its number, torn out and thrown away, and the new page inserted into the quire at the correct location. Bruce Steele and Helen Baron show that Lawrence continued to use this system for *The Trespasser* and *Sons and Lovers*. The situation is complicated with *The White Peacock*, however, by the other people who helped Lawrence copy pages, as will be explained later.

I also paid attention to the content of the revisions; in both versions of "Laetitia", for example, George's family was named "Worthington". This name may be found corrected to "Saxton" in several places of "Nethermere I", which suggests that these pages belong to an earlier period of composition than other sections of the manuscript where Worthington is never used, but Saxton occurs instead in the body of the text. It is not known exactly when Lawrence decided to change the name from Worthington to Saxton. Since Holt and Mason's pages always use Saxton, the change must have occurred before about mid-September 1909, the earliest probable date at which they became involved in the revision process.

Six makes of paper were identified in the manuscript and labelled from A to F. Their details are listed in Table 2 in the Appendix. There are no noticeable differences in their colour, see-through and finishing features. All the

10. The manuscript is held in the D. H. Lawrence Collection at the Harry Ransome Humanities Research Center (HRHRC), University of Texas at Austin.

lines are printed front and back and there are no ruled left margins. Paper A and paper F are easy to distinguish at first because their top margins slope so differently. The slope of paper F pages, however, gradually decreases through Part III, owing to manufacturing variation, until the last pages are almost indistinguishable from paper A. The different layers of revision between Holt's A and Lawrence's Part III pages indicate, nevertheless, that papers A and F do belong to different periods of composition.

Table 1 shows the chronological development of the manuscript and identifies its various components by paper type, principal scribe and layers of revision. The page numbers refer to the manuscript (*MS*) and the Cambridge Edition of *The White Peacock* (*WP*). Dotted lines connecting the column for September–October 1909 to the column for February–April 1910 indicate those pages which were copied by Agnes Mason and cannot be firmly dated. Agnes Holt and Mason had very distinctive handwritings and made no revision marks to the manuscript. Corke's handwriting was noticeably rounded and she always used dark blue-black ink and a thick nib. Lawrence made revisions in three different styles: in pencil, in black ink with a fine nib (which I call the 'thin' style), and in a black ink written with a markedly thicker nib (which I call the 'thick' style).

Table 1: A Chronology of the Paper Types, Scribes and Layers of Revision in the Final Manuscript of The White Peacock

Page MS [WP]	1907–8 (Laetitia II)	Jan-July 1909 (Nethermere I)	Sep-Oct 1909 (Nethermere I)	Feb-April 1910 (Nethermere II)
Part I starts on page 1				
1–76 [1–29]			*A*-Holt; DHL thick	DHL pencil & thin; Corke
77–82 [30–32]			------*A*-Mason-----------	DHL pencil & thin; Corke
83–88 [33]		*B*-DHL	DHL thick	DHL pencil & Corke
89 [34]				*A*-Corke
90–91 [34]			--------*C*-Mason--------------------	
92–116 [35–45]		*B*-DHL	DHL thick	DHL pencil & Corke
117–119 [45]			*D*-Mason; DHL thick	
120–123 [46–47]		*B*-DHL	DHL thick	DHL pencil & Corke
124 [47]			*D*-Mason [Tear matches p. 117]	
125 [48]		*B*-DHL	DHL thick	
126 [48]			--------*C*-Mason---------DHL thin	
127–133 [49–51]		*B*-DHL	DHL thick	
134 [51]			--------*C*-Mason--------------------	
135 [51]			--------*D*-Mason--------------------	
136–159 [52–61]		*B*-DHL	DHL thick	Corke
160 [62]			--------*A*-Mason--------------------	
161–163 [62–63]		*B*-DHL	DHL thick	DHL pencil & Corke
164 [63]			--------*A*-Mason--------------------	
165–166 [64]		*B*-DHL	DHL thick	Corke
167 [64]			--------*A*-Mason--------------------	
			[Tear matches p. 164]	
168–170 [65]		*B*-DHL	DHL thick [Tears match pp. 161–163]	
171 [66]			*A*-Mason; DHL thick	DHL pencil & Corke
172–201 [66–78]		*B*-DHL	DHL thick	Corke

202 [78]		-------D-Mason---------------	
203–222 [79–85]	B-DHL	DHL thick	DHL pencil & Corke
223–271 [85–103]	E-DHL	DHL thick	DHL pencil & Corke
272–274 [104–105]		-------A-Mason-------------Corke?	
275–286 [107–110]		-------C-Mason-------------Corke	
287–289 [110–111]		-------A-Mason-------------------	
		[Tears match pp. 272–274]	
290–312 [112–121]		-------A-Mason-------------Corke	
Part II starts on page 316			
313–320 [121–126]		-------D-Mason-------------Corke	
321–326 [126–128]		-------A-Mason-------------------	
		[Tears match pp. 306–312]	
327–329 [129]	E-DHL	DHL thick	Corke
330 [130]		-------D-Mason-------------------	
331–350 [130–138]	E-DHL	DHL thick	Corke
		[Tears match]	
351–553 [138–225]	B-DHL	DHL thick	DHL pencil & Corke
554 [225]			D-Corke
555–564 [226–229]	B-DHL	DHL thick	Corke
565 [230]			D-Corke [W/m matches p. 554]
566 [230]	B-DHL	DHL thick	
567 [230]			A-Corke
568 [231]	B-DHL	DHL thick	Corke
569 [231]			A-Corke [Tear matches p. 567]
570–575 [231–233]	B-DHL	DHL thick	Corke
		[Tears and w/m match, as do pp. 568, 575]	
Part III starts on page 576			
576–737 [237–293]			F-DHL; DHL thin & Corke
738–749 [293–304]			F- unknown; DHL thin & **Corke**
750–802 [304–325]			F-DHL; DHL thin

In the remainder of this paper I justify in detail the datings made in Table 1. My evidence relies on two assumptions; firstly, that it is a strong possibility that Lawrence would use only one particular paper type over a given period; secondly, that revisions of a particular 'style' were all made at the same time. Some pages have as many as four levels of revision, but the styles may easily be distinguished.

The Final Manuscript: Material from "Laetitia II"

The E pages (223–271 and 327–350) are two sequences inserted into the large block of B pages extending from page 83 to 575 (which is uniform except for Corke and Mason's copied pages). The E and B pages must have been written and the insertion must have occurred before the revisions of September—October 1909 because both the E and the B pages use the name "Worthington" (subsequently changed to "Saxton"). The section linking the two E sequences (pages 272 to 326) was copied out by Agnes Mason in October 1909 or March 1910, always using "Saxton".

There is evidence that Lawrence removed some E pages from the surviving E sequences, either before they were incorporated into the B block before October 1909, or during the drafting of "Nethermere II" in February–April 1910. For example, some lines are deleted at the bottom of the page now numbered 259. If one reads the deleted sentences, and turns to page 260, the text does not run on in meaning. There must have been material in between pages 259 and 260; Lawrence inserted a chapter division at the top of page 260 to account for the change of subject matter (see Note to *WP* 100:16). The E quire headings were clearly written at the same time as the main text (the ink shade is the same). The pages were numbered individually at the same time as the 'thick' revisions. Furthermore, a large amount of 'thick' revision on page 237 was followed by pencil revision which deleted the whole page. The pages must therefore have been numbered before the 'pencil' revisions, otherwise page 237 would have been thrown away. It had to be kept to maintain the existing number order. The same is true of pages 213–215 of B paper.

The E pages appear to belong to an earlier period of composition than the B pages. The handwriting style on E pages is much more formal and 'copper-plate' than on B pages; it is akin to the neat handwriting used by Lawrence for his college essays from 1906–8 and for both drafts of "Laetitia".[11] Pierre Loti's *Pêcheur d'Islande* is mentioned on page 229, and since Lawrence is believed to have read this novel in August 1907 (see Note to *WP* 87:35 and *Letters i* 36) the reference probably indicates that these E pages were not written in 1906 or early 1907, and therefore did not belong to "Laetitia I".

Why did Lawrence transfer these particular E pages? Helen Baron and Bruce Steele have shown that when Lawrence transferred pages in *Sons and Lovers* and *The Trespasser*, he did so to save himself copying out material which he felt would need only minor revision (if any) in the new draft. The same conclusion may be reached here. In the first E section (pages 223–271) Cyril tells George that Lettie and Leslie have got engaged. Lettie subsequently broke the engagement in "Laetitia II", but for "Nethermere I" Lawrence decided: 'I don't believe Lettie ever did break her engagement to Leslie —she married him' (*Letters i* 92). George's self-pitying response to Cyril's news, and the prelude to the Christmas party of Chapter VIII (to page 271, *WP* 103), were appropriate to the plots of both "Laetitia II" and "Nethermere I". Subsequent events for "Nethermere I" (pages 272–326) were either written on B paper or on revised E pages; we cannot tell which because the pages were later copied out neatly by Agnes Mason.

Lawrence returned to E paper for pages 327–350. The events here include Annable's discovery of the lovers in the woods and his caustic comments about women, and Lettie's last farewell to George before she marries Leslie. All these events could have occurred in what we know of the plot of "Laetitia II" (Annable was first introduced into the novel in "Laetitia II", and Leslie jilted Lettie, who then married George), whilst also being acceptable for the

11. See NUL, D. H. Lawrence Collection, LaL 1 and 2. Surviving material from "Laetitia I" and "Laetitia II" is in the Bancroft Library, University of California at Berkeley. The paper type of these pages is quite different from type E. The paper is the same height, but each page is only 127 mm wide. I am indebted to Dr. Bonnie Hardwick of the Bancroft Library for this information.

revised plot of "Nethermere I". Lawrence stopped using E pages at page 350 because he decided in Section 3 of Part II Chapter I to change the character of Meg, whom George was now going to marry instead of Lettie. The extent of Meg's early relationship with George is unknown (she is briefly mentioned in a draft plot-plan of "Laetitia I" which will be published in John Worthen's forthcoming biography of Lawrence), but the new plot of "Nethermere I" clearly required Lawrence to increase her role in the novel.

Lawrence may have written these E pages as separate sections in early 1909 to accommodate the change of plot for "Nethermere I" and then incorporated them into a second version of the draft copied out later in the year on B paper. There is no evidence, however, for believing that he wrote "Nethermere I" in this way. The most likely hypothesis is that the E pages were simply transferred forward from "Laetitia II" to "Nethermere I" as the new draft was being written. The material on these E pages which existed before Lawrence's 1909 'thick' revision is therefore a fragment of "Laetitia II" and is in addition to the material printed in the appendix to the Cambridge Edition of *The White Peacock*.

The Final Manuscript: Principal Materials from "Nethermere I"

Most of "Nethermere I" was written on Type B paper. The quires are usually between twelve and fourteen pages long. Such consistency suggests that they were written as part of a regular routine, as Lawrence later remembered: 'I must have written most of ["Laetitia"] five or six times, but only in intervals. . . . But at Croydon I worked at ["Nethermere"] fairly steadily, in the evenings after school'.[12] The name Worthington (later corrected to Saxton) occurs frequently in these pages. A number of literary references help to date the writing. Page 461, for example, where reference is made to H. G. Wells's *Tono-Bungay*, cannot have been written before December 1908 to March 1909, because Wells's novel was first published as a serial in the *English Review* over that period. Similarly, Stephen Reynold's story *The Holy Mountain* (referred to on page 509) was published in the *English Review* over April–July 1909. Finally, the earliest that Lawrence is known to have read Dostoevsky (page 461) is May 1909.[13] The text written on the B pages is a mixture of new material and revised passages copied from "Laetitia II", as can be seen, for example, when pages 157:31–158:14 of the Cambridge Edition are compared with the extract of "Laetitia II" printed in the appendix (*WP* 348–349:5). Another example is the age of Mr. Saxton. On page 406 of the manuscript he is said to be forty-five years old, as his original Mr. Chambers would have been in 1908. Lawrence probably copied this detail from "Laetitia II" without correction, because during his 'thick' 1909 revision (see below) he updated Mr. Saxton's age to forty-six (see Note to *WP* 186:5).

12. 'Autobiographical Sketch', *Nehls i*, pp. 102–103.

13. See *Letters i* 126, and Rose Marie Burwell, 'A Checklist of Lawrence's Reading', in *A D. H. Lawrence Handbook*, ed. Keith Sagar, Barnes and Noble Books (1982), pp. 59–126, entry A140.

The Final Manuscript: 'Thick' Revision to B and E Pages and Agnes Holt's Copies

In the autumn of 1909 Lawrence tided up "Nethermere I" for submission to Hueffer. The earliest level of corrections appears to be those made with a thick-nibbed pen, in black ink, to the B and E pages. It is the 'thick' correction style which changed "Worthington" to "Saxton"; this particular change must have been made before Mason and Holt began copying, because they always used "Saxton" on their pages.[14] Lawrence continued to make 'thick' revisions after Mason and Holt's copying, however; numerous 'thick' corrections may be found on their pages. Further evidence that the 'thick' revisions were the first to be made is offered later in the paper.

Lawrence also numbered pages individually during this revision for Hueffer, and he took the opportunity to remove deleted pages from some quires. The similarity between the ink colours of the page numbers and the 'thick' revisions can clearly be seen, especially on pages 417, 519 and 526.

Agnes Holt copied out pages 1 to 76 on a new paper, Type A, probably between mid-September and the end of October 1909. She used the name Saxton and numbered the pages as she wrote them (the numbers are in the same ink as the main text). Lawrence numbered the quires afterwards, and inserted chapter divisions in a black ink which may easily be distinguished from Holt's ink. On page 44 Holt copied as far as the word 'hesitated' (*WP* 17:5). Lawrence then wrote a few sentences (*WP* 17:6–10) and Holt continued after leaving a space of three lines. This suggests that she was copying from Lawrence's revised (presumably in 'thick' style) B pages, which he then threw away; on page 44 she broke off for some reason, and Lawrence set her on her way again by writing a few lines. After she completed her pages Lawrence revised them again in 'thick' style.

The Final Manuscript: Agnes Mason's Contribution

It is difficult to identify precisely when Agnes Mason did her copying. Owing to the lack of detailed information about her from biographical sources, we have to concentrate on clues offered in the manuscript. Her pages have remarkably few further revisions by Lawrence, which suggests that she may have made her copies late in the revision process. All Mason pages with 'thick' revisions must, however, have been written in 1909. There are a few corrections by Corke, so those copies must have been made before Corke checked that part of the manuscript in March–April 1910. Any pages copied by Mason in Part III of "Nethermere I" would have been thrown away when Lawrence completely rewrote that section. In the following analysis I describe noticeable features of each surviving block of Mason's pages and attempt to draw conclusions about when they were written.

The first page in Mason's hand is on A paper (page 77), and continues on directly after Holt until the end of Chapter 3 on page 82. Mason uses the name Saxton throughout. She did not number the pages, and as the number

14. The change of 'Worthington' to 'Saxton' occurs on pages 130–133, 138–140, 149, 165, 242–243, 368, 420, 468, 508, 512, 564 and 566.

style is different from that on Holt's pages, it was probably done by Lawrence. This was definitely before Helen Corke's involvement, for on page 77 Mason mistakenly wrote: 'She played with of the book' (see *WP* 29:25), and Corke corrected it by adding 'the leaves'. Mason's A pages were presumably left over from the supply used by Holt. Papers A and D were also used by Corke, but never by Lawrence. He entered 'thick' revisions onto the existing manuscript pages rather than make fair copies, although he later rewrote Part III on a different paper type altogether.

Many of Mason's pages are single sheets inserted in a main block of B paper. Judging by her largest contribution (pages 272–326), she appears to have had papers A, C and D all to hand at the same time for these fair copies. In Quire XXIV, pages 275–286 (a twelve-sheet quire) of C paper lie between pages 272–274 and 287–289 of A paper. The tear of page 272 matches page 289, page 274 matches 287 and page 273 matches 288, whilst the cross of a 'T' on page 288 carries over onto the back of page 273 (the quire had not yet been torn into single sheets when she wrote the 'T'). Quire XXV (page 290–305) is all A paper (some tears match). Quire XXVI (page 306–326 plus one blank A page) consists of fourteen pages of A paper split into two groups of seven bracketing a central section of eight D pages.

It is difficult to date the writing of pages 272–326 and to say why they were copied out in the first place. The writing must have occurred before Corke's involvement, since on page 279, for example, Corke changed '[Marie's hair] lies wavily, to coil in her neck' to read 'lies low upon her neck in wavy coils' (*WP* 107:39). This time Mason did not write the page numbers, as she did with her single sheets. The new page numbers were written by Corke; the ink colour is the same as for her corrections. It seems likely that Lawrence simply gave Mason's pages to Corke to correct and number, although he did give them a final 'thin' revision. There is little revision on these pages, suggetsing that Mason copied them at a late stage in the manuscript's evolution. The text had certainly been revised since the E pages of "Laetitia II" because H. G. Wells's novel *Tono-Bungay*, which Lawrence had not read when he wrote the E pages (see *WP* 121:17), is mentioned. The plot content of these pages is not, however, sufficiently distinctive to tell whether the material copied by Mason had been largely transferred from "Laetitia II" or consisted of new work written for "Nethermere I". The plot deals with Lettie's birthday/engagement party; George's resentment seems appropriate for the plots of both "Laetitia II" and "Nethermere I", but the fact that Mason copied this large section suggests that Lawrence had heavily revised this scene at some time during or after the writing of "Nethermere I".

Mason's pages 90–91 have no corrections, and the page numbers have the same ink colour as the text, which is clearly different from the surrounding block of B paper in Lawrence's hand (pages 83–116). Mason must have copied out pages 90–91 after Lawrence numbered his B pages, which was some time after he had written the B text; the ink is different, and there are signs that B pages were left out before numbering began. At the bottom of page 146, for example, a sentence once continued onto the next page. During 'thick' revision, the sentence was deleted and the next page (and possibly others) was thrown away. Lawrence then numbered the pages individually for the first time; page 147 is the start of a new chapter.

Mason's pages 117–119 and 160 stop short of being full of text, indicating that although she was tidying up Lawrence's B pages, she was obliged to keep to an existing numbering system. Pages 134–135 are unrevised by Corke or Lawrence and, like page 126, are crowded at the bottom, presumably again because Mason was keeping to the numbering system. Page 202 is also crowded at the bottom, and unrevised. Her fair copy stands in dramatic contrast to the following page. Page 203 on B paper is covered with corrections in Lawrence's 'thick' style. For some reason she did not make a fair copy of this page.

Mason's pages 117 and 124 on D paper, and 164 and 167 on A paper, have clear matching tears, and so were probably written at the same time. The slope of the top margins of pages 164 and 167 also confirms that they originally formed one sheet of paper in a quire. Upside down on the reverse side of page 167 Mason began to copy out the text found in full on page 164, but stopped after a few words. She must have realised that she had started her new sheet the wrong way around, by writing in the small bottom margin. The tear patterns of Mason's other A pages (77–82 and 171) are not sufficiently distinctive to allow matching.

Mason's single pages of A, C and D paper are all numbered in a similar style and ink colour. This style and ink are noticeably different from the surrounding B pages written by Lawrence. It may seem probable that Mason's pages were all written after Lawrence numbered his B pages, and before the final revisions by Lawrence and Corke in March–April 1910. This conclusion is supported by an analysis of the revisions on Mason's page 171. Her text is cramped at the bottom, indicating that she was trying to squeeze a fixed amount of revised B material onto the new page. At some time after this Lawrence wrote in pencil on the back of page 170: ' "You'll mesh yourself up in a silk of dreams." ' (see *WP* 66:15). Helen Corke copied this correction onto Mason's page 171. Furthermore, page 171 has revisions in Lawrence's 'thick' style, indicating that it was copied in October 1909 and subsequently revised; the same is true of page 117.

The dating of these pages should not, however, be extended to include all of Mason's single sheets, judging from a fragment of "Nethermere I" which Helen Corke tore in half lengthways and used as a bookmark.[15] The fragment is of Type B paper, was once the start of quire 14 and was removed when Agnes Mason copied it out as page 135 of "Nethermere II". This dating is suggested by the levels of revision on the page. There is 'thick' revision and a pencil revision by Lawrence, and a minor blue-black revision by Helen Corke. Mason must therefore have copied out page 135 (which is unrevised) after Corke's involvement in March 1910. The same is therefore possible for Mason's other unrevised pages. It is simply not possible to tell. Mason's pages

15. See HRHRC, D. H. Lawrence Collection.

would therefore seem to have been copied at different times throughout the mid-September 1909 to March 1910 period.

The Final Manuscript: Revisions by Lawrence and Corke in 1910

The order in which various revision styles were made can often be established only by the evidence on a few pages where several styles occur and a later style revises an earlier one. There is evidence that Lawrence's 'thick' revisions were made before his 'pencil' ones, and the 'pencil' before Helen Corke's contribution. Whenever Lawrence made a 'pencil' correction, Corke later overwrote it with her characteristic blue-black ink and rounded handwriting. Lawrence replaced ' "you have not treated him kindly of late" ' on page 194 with ' "I suppose he is paying you back" ', in 'thick' black ink. He later crossed this out with a pencil and wrote ' "You have treated him badly" ', which Corke then wrote over in blue-black ink (the phrase was eventually deleted in proof). Pages 213–215 were corrected in 'thick' black ink and then deleted with diagonal pencil strokes across the page, after the pages had been numbered. The deletion in pencil was then confirmed by Corke's blue-black ink (see *WP* Notes to 82:33). The deleted pages were not thrown away because the deletions occurred after the pages were numbered; the manuscript would have had a jump in the text from page 212 to 216.

Because of the close relationship between Lawrence's pencil revisions and Corke's later over-writing, it seems likely that the pencil revisions were made in February or March 1910. Lawrence rarely used a pencil in his extant manuscripts from this period. The only other pencil writings occur in two significant sections of one of his poetry notebooks.[16] An unfinished and untitled poem may be found written in pencil inside one fly-leaf. It appears to be Lawrence's first response to reading Corke's "Freshwater Diary" in February 1910 (see *CY* 7). A completed poem (in ink) entitled "A Love Passage", found amongst the main body of the text, starts off like the pencil poem but then changes, indicating that it is a revised version. It is preceded by the prose-poem "Malade" which is in pencil and was probably written during Lawrence's illness in February; the poem has the same image of a flapping tassel of a window-blind as Lawrence's letter of 28 February (*Letters i* 155). Writings in pencil occur nowhere else in Lawrence's poetry notebook. It seems possible that Lawrence used a pencil when he was lying in bed convalescing (rather than a bottle of ink which could be spilled), writing the first version of "A Love Passage" and "Malade", and taking the opportunity to start the final revision of "Nethermere I", which he had just received from Heinemann. He may have done this before he thought of asking Helen Corke to look over the manuscript, or in the three days between asking her and personally delivering the manuscript to her home.[17]

The poetry notebook has very few poems written in this period of early 1910, in contrast to the large number that were written or copied into the

16. NUL, D. H. Lawrence Collection, LaL 2.
17. See *IOI* 177.

notebook around November 1909, probably in response to a suggestion by Hueffer that Lawrence should offer a volume of verse for publication (*Letters i* 144). Lawrence had plenty of time to write poetry through November to January whilst Hueffer was reading "Nethermere I" and Heinemann was considering it for publication, but had little time in February/March 1910 because he was intermittently ill and then busy revising his novel. He worked through the manuscript with Corke, sitting in her sitting-room in the evenings and 'discussing points of the revision' (*CY* 20).

Corke wrote in corrections and new sentence orderings, presumably with Lawrence's agreement. She also helped him correct the novel's proofs in September 1910, and believed that 'Lawrence took reasonable care in the reading of his proofs, and he would have fiercely resented any inaccuracy on the part of the compositor'.[18] Such resentment would presumably have also applied to Corke if she had tried to correct the manuscript without his permission. Her revisions either overwrite Lawrence's 'pencil' revisions or re-order sentences, as he had asked her to look for 'split infinitives and obscurities of phrase' (*CY* 50). On page 83, for example, she changed 'I put it away, the letter' to 'I put the letter away'. On page 279 she changed '[Marie] is a little below the fashion' to 'behind the fashion' (*WP* 108:1) and, on page 604, 'a jingle of a flat piano' to 'a jingle from an out-of-tune piano' (*WP* 247:17). On page 390 she changed the clumsy sentence 'It was decided that it was an accident' to 'They decided at the inquest that the death came by misadventure' (*WP* 154:37).

Corke also copied out a few pages neatly. On the back of page 88 Lawrence wrote some extra sentences in pencil (*WP* 34:19–26) to be inserted on page 89. Corke must have decided to copy out page 89 incorporating the new text, although for some reason she chose to leave out part of one of the new sentences. She began to copy it, and then crossed it out; the Cambridge Edition uses Lawrence's pencil version.

The Final Manuscript: Final Revision by Lawrence

On 9 March Lawrence believed that he had 'nearly finished the novel ready for the publisher' (*Letters i* 156). He must have decided to rewrite Part III after this date, for he spent another month finishing the novel. Part III was entirely rewritten on Type F paper; many of the page tears and watermarks match up within quires, and the page numbers are the same colour ink as the main text. There is evidence of rapid composition; the black ink was often not allowed to dry properly before the page was completed and turned over, so that an imprint was left on the back of the preceding page. The new text has incidents which appear to be based on events in Lawrence's life between November 1909 and January 1910 when "Nethermere I" was with Hueffer and Heinemann. Emily's letter from 'Old Brayford', for example, is full of details that suggest it was based on letters from Jessie Chambers after she moved to West Bridgeford in February 1910 (see Note to *WP* 261:32).

18. Letter to M. J. Bruccoli, printed in 'A Note to the Text', *The White Peacock*, ed. Harry T. Moore (1968), p. 357.

Lawrence also refers to George Moore's *Evelyn Innes* which he read in November 1909 (*Letters i* 142).[19]

Helen Corke looked through Lawrence's new pages as she had done with Parts I and II, making corrections and copying out four heavily revised pages, which she numbered. For example, on page 643 she corrected 'Meg and him' to 'Meg and he', and on page 756 she changed ' "I can hardly believe it is possible it is you" ' to ' "I can hardly believe it is really you." ' (*WP* 307:19). Pages 738–749 (quire LXI) were written by an unknown person. The style is similar in places to Lawrence's, but other features, such as a flowery 'Q' on page 739 are very uncharacteristic. Both Corke and Lawrence subsequently made corrections to these pages.

Corke remembered that when pages were copied out neatly by her, 'the original pages were destroyed, and the fair copies were incorporated in the manuscript, which then received the author's final personal revision'.[20] Lawrence's final revision across the whole manuscript was in black ink with a thin nib. There are only a few places where it is possible to confirm Corke's memory that the 'thin' revision followed her own. On page 40, for example, a Corke revision was crossed out by Lawrence in 'thin' style, and on page 752 there are two 'thin' deletions, including one of a phrase which Lawrence had previously revised in pencil and Corke had copied over.

Lawrence described the final revision and rewrite to Heinemann's co-director Sydney Pawling as follows: 'A good deal of it, including the whole of the third part, I have rewritten . . . I think I have removed all the offensive morsels, all the damns, devils and the sweat . . . I am sorry the manuscript is in such scandalous disarray, but I have done my best to keep it tidy. I am sorry, also, that I could not compress it any further. It is a pity, but I could not cut my man to fit your cloth. I have snipped him where I could, and have tried to make him solid' (*Letters i* 158, 11 April 1910).

Lawrence's account is largely confirmed by the paper analysis. We have seen above that pages were cut or 'snipped', even though this disrupted the page order and meant that the deleted pages had to be left in a disorganised manuscript. 'Offensive morsels' were indeed removed as Heinemann had requested on 20 January. The publisher was probably particularly sensitive to such matters after the decision of the Circulating Libraries' Assocation on 30 November 1909 to censor itself and withdraw 'objectionable' books.[21]

19. Other examples of real-life events which Lawrence appears to have referred to are recorded in the Cambridge Edition (see *WP*, Note to 282:38, 283:4, 284:24 and 305:14–18).

20. Corke's note accompanied the sale of *The White Peacock* manuscript in 1934, and is now in the possession of Mr. George Lazarus.

21. Brian Musgrove, referring to chapters seven and eight of Samuel Hynes' *The Edwardian Turn of Mind* (1968), notes that the CLA was formed in response to public pressure by such groups as the National Vigilance Association for censorship of books by the State. The CLA planned to 'screen works by secret, internal vote, with the support of the Council of Publishers' Association, which in turn recommended the co-operation of the Society of Authors'. See 'D. H. Lawrence's Travel Books', unpublished PhD dissertation (Cambridge University, 1989), p. 23, and A. H. Thompson's *Censorship in Public Libraries* (1975).

Lawrence changed 'damn' to 'dash', for example, on page 46, and the words 'belly' and 'devil' were deleted on pages 58 and 59. These changes again suggest that Holt wrote her pages (1–76) in October 1909 and that they were corrected by Lawrence in 1910. If Holt copied her pages in 1910, Lawrence would presumably have taken the opportunity to alter 'damn' to 'dash' and so on before she began to copy.

Lawrence's assertion that 'a good deal' of Parts I and II had been 'rewritten' presents problems however. It seems highly unlikely that the E and B pages analysed in this paper represent freshly written material like Part III. Lawrence may have been referring to the pages copied by Mason and Holt, especially if many of Mason's pages of uncertain dating were in fact copied in March 1910. The material on these pages may conceal extensive revision of the pages they replaced. These uncertainties do not, however, alter the order of events outlined in this paper; they affect only the rate at which those events occurred. If Holt and Mason did make their copies in February 1910, Lawrence would also have had to fit in all the extant layers of 'thick' and 'thin' revision, any revisions on the pages which were eventually copied, and write Part III before 11 April. This would indeed have been a 'labour of Hercules'. He may, admittedly, have been exaggerating the extent of his revision to account for the delay in the return of the manuscript. Another possibility is that he regarded his 'pencil' and 'thin' interlinear revision to Parts I and II as 'rewriting', even though the work was not nearly so extensive as the new Part III. Why might he have felt this? An answer is suggested by a consideration of the context and content of the final revision.

Since September 1909 Lawrence had been growing increasingly intimate with Helen Corke. She told him about the tragic events in her life in the summer of 1909, when her married admirer H. B. Macartney had killed himself. In February 1910 she showed Lawrence some of her writings, including the "Freshwater Diary".[22] Sometime after that Lawrence began to write "The Saga of Siegmund". This new novel was based on Corke's writings and Lawrence's understanding of her and Macartney, and told the story of the fatal passion between the musician Siegmund and the sexually reluctant Sieglinde (also called Helena). Jessie Chambers remembers that Lawrence wrote to her shortly before Easter (27 March) 1910, when he was still revising "Nethermere I": 'I have always believed it was the woman who paid the price in life. But I've made a discovery. It's the man who pays, not the woman' (*Letters i* 155). This is a discovery he might have made from the story of Siegmund, but it also describes one of the conclusions that could be drawn from the revised novel "Nethermere II". Siegmund kills himself after the failure of a relationship, and George's living-death at the end of "Nethermere II" can be seen as a form of suicide through alcoholism, after the failure of his relationship with Let-

---

22. "The Freshwater Diary" was originally published as an appendix to *IOI*, and was reprinted in an appendix to *The Trespasser*, ed. Elizabeth Mansfield (Cambridge University Press, 1981).

tie.[23] The overlap between the material of "The Saga of Siegmund" and "Nethermere II" is also suggested by the fact that Lawrence mistakenly used the name 'Siegmund' for Leslie three times in Part III (see *WP*, Note to 255:16).

If Lawrence regarded his revisions to Parts I and II as 'rewritings' it would be because he had adjusted the early parts to fit with his revised conception of one of the main themes of his novel. On 23 January 1910 he had believed all he had to do was 'alter in parts', as requested by Heinemann (*Letters i* 152). By March, however, Part III, which brought together and extended the themes of Parts I and II into the middle-age of the characters, had to be re-written to take account of the discovery that Lawrence had announced to Chambers. In Parts I and II Lettie was made less forward in her encouragement of George's attentions, perhaps to emphasize George's later failure to take the initiative and Lettie's willingness to take the easy route in life, so denying her deepest desires and contributing to George's self-destruction. Despite being told to remove potentially offensive phrases, Lawrence did add some relatively explicit descriptions of George's sensual response to Lettie. For example, in 'thin' revision style he added 'For the first time in his life [George] felt his heart heavy with concentrated passion' (*MS* 77, *WP* 29:29), and 'he shivered, so much did he want to take her and crush her bosom up to the hot parched open mouth of his breast' (*MS* 78, *WP* 29:35).

Space limitations prevent further analysis of connections between "The Saga of Siegmund" and "Nethermere II", or of the different thematic emphases of "Nethermere I" and "Nethermere II". Such analyses, which may lead to an increased understanding of Lawrence's early literary development, how he shaped his novels and moved between different possibilities and interpretations, cannot be undertaken by reference to any current published text. The general editorial policy of the Cambridge Edition, for example, has been to include variants between previously published texts, the final manuscript and the proofs. As a result, material deleted at earlier revision stages is rarely provided in either Andrew Robertson's edition of *The White Peacock* or Elizabeth Mansfield's *The Trespasser*. This article provides insights beyond those made possible by the apparatus of Robertson's edition. It should, one hopes, enable critics to undertake an 'archaeological' exploration of Lawrence's first novel in similar fashion to the possibilities opened up by the articles on *The Trespasser* and *Sons and Lovers* by Bruce Steele and Helen Baron, although analysis of these latter two novels will still require access to the texts of "The Saga of Siegmund" and the various versions of "Paul Morel".[24]

23. That Lawrence saw a connection between alcoholism and suicide is confirmed by his 1913 "Foreword" to *Sons and Lovers* (see *The Letters of D. H. Lawrence*, ed. Aldous Huxley [1932], p. 102).

24. The manuscripts of the various "Paul Morel"s are held in the D. H. Lawrence collection at the HRHRC. The substantially complete second draft of "Paul Morel" will be

The writing of "Nethermere II" may be summarised as follows:

Stage One: Lawrence wrote the E pages for "Laetitia II" in 1907–8.

Stage Two: Lawrence wrote the first version of "Nethermere I" on B paper between January and July 1909, incorporating the E pages of Stage One. He may have numbered the pages at the end of this writing.

Stage Three: Lawrence revised his novel in 'thick' style before the end of October 1909. The completed "Nethermere I" was considered for publication by Hueffer and Heinemann from 1 November 1909 to 20 January 1910. Lawrence called on Agnes Holt and Agnes Mason to copy out and number some pages neatly on Type A, C and D paper, either in September/October 1909 (the most likely option for Holt) or possibly in February–March 1910. In either case, he checked their copied pages for mistakes, made more 'thick' revisions to some of these pages, and continued to revise the remaining text.

Stage Four: "Nethermere I" was returned to Lawrence in February 1910. He began his final revision either straight away, or after he had completed his 'thick' revision and overseen pages copied by Holt and Mason. The work began with some revisions in pencil. Helen Corke later overwrote these in blue-black ink. The extent of her revisions are as described in her memoirs, namely new sentence structures and corrections to tense and names. She also rewrote five pages on Type A and D paper. Agnes Mason may have done some further copying, both before and after revision by Corke. The pages were being passed backwards and forwards between the various scribes. Mason then dropped out of the picture, probably from mid-March onwards as Lawrence entirely rewrote Part III on Type F paper with some help from an unknown amanuensis. He may also have already begun "The Saga of Siegmund" as his relationship with Corke and her writings grew closer. Corke made further revisions to Part III before Lawrence gave his final polish to the entire manuscript in 'thin' style.

APPENDIX: PAPER DESCRIPTIONS

I. "NETHERMERE II"

Paper A

   Dimensions: 200 mm long, 162.5 mm wide.

   Lines: 21, at different angles. The lines are an average of 8.5 mm apart. The 'front' top margin slopes left-right from 20 to 22 mm, whilst the 'back' top margin slopes left-right from 20–19. The bottom margin slopes too, but less consistently, varying between 8.5 and 10 mm in width. If the front of one page is placed against the back of another, so that they meet along the torn edges which had originally been joined, the top margin slopes consistently across both pages from 22 mm to 19 mm. This fact provides a useful and consistent check as to the identity of what appears to be a *Paper A* page, if the side-tears cannot be shown to match those of another page.

   Calendaring: Chain-and-wire

   Watermark: "Boot's Cash Stationers"

Paper B

   Dimensions: 202 mm long, 163 mm wide.

published by Cambridge University Press in 1991 or 1992 at the same time as Carl and Helen Baron's forthcoming Cambridge Edition of *Sons and Lovers*.

Lines: 21, at different angles, and an average of 8.5 mm apart. The front top margin slopes 19–20 mm, the back top 21–20, so the same matching as for *Paper A* can be done. The bottom margin is larger than for *Paper A*, varying between 10 and 11 mm in width. The lines are a very pale blue; this is the distinguishing feature of *Paper B*.

    Calendaring: Chain-and-wire
    Watermark: "Boot's Cash Stationers"

Paper C
    Dimensions: 202 mm long, 161 mm wide.
    Lines: 20, an average of 8.5 mm apart. The front top margin slopes 20–21 mm, the back top 21–20. The bottom margin is between 14 and 15 mm. The lines are noticeably finer than those of *Papers A* and *B*.

    Calendaring: Chain-and-wire
    Watermark: None

Paper D
    Dimensions: 202 mm long, 162 mm wide.
    Lines: 20, an average of 8.5 mm apart. The top margin is consistently 25 mm wide, so distinguishing this paper easily from *Paper C*. The bottom margin is between 10 and 11 mm. The lines are as fine as with *Paper C*.

    Calendaring: Chain-and-wire
    Watermark: None

Paper E
    Dimensions: 201 mm long, 162 mm wide.
    Lines: 20, an average of 8 mm apart. The front top margin slopes 28–29 mm; the back top margin slopes 29.5–29 mm. The bottom margin varies between 10 and 11 mm.

    Calendaring: None
    Watermark: A complex oval design reading: "HIERATICA (a vegetable Parchment) I. S & C."

Paper F
    Dimensions: 200 mm long, 162.5 mm wide.
    Lines: 21, an average of 8.5 mm apart. The first pages of this paper type in the manuscript have a very noticeable slope to their top and bottom margins. 'Front' and 'back' sides can be matched up with pages elsewhere in a given quire. For example page 577 measures as follows:

	Front (text)	Back (blank)
Top margin:	18.5 to 20 mm	20 to 17.5 mm
Bottom margin:	10 to 9 mm	9 to 11 mm

Page 586 (whose torn edge and watermark matches page 577) measures:

Top margin:	17.5 to 16 mm	18 to 18.5 mm
Bottom margin:	11 to 13 mm	12 to 10 mm

If these pages are placed together as above with *Paper A*, then the front side of page 577 lines up with the back of page 586, and vice-versa. However as Part III progresses this slope to the lines becomes increasingly less noticeable, until in the last quires the pages are indistinguishable from *Paper A* pages (a front top margin slope of 20–21 mm, and a back top margin of 20–19 mm).

    Calendaring: Chain-and-wire
    Watermark: "Boot's Cash Stationers"

II. LAWRENCE'S CORRESPONDENCE

    Lawrence usually used special small sheets of paper for his letters, especially for those to Louie Burrows and Blanche Jennings. Sometimes he used exercise book paper, but the sheet size was very different from the standard size used in "Nethermere". The following list of paper types only includes those which appear similar to

Types *A* to *F*.[25] I have also examined the paper of all other extant letters from this period which are written on exercise book paper, but none are of the types used in "Nethermere".

1) Second page of letter dated 30.6.09. Dimensions: 203 mm x 163 mm. Lines: 20, an average of 8.5 mm apart. Top margin 26 mm, bottom margin 15 mm. No watermark. Possibly *Type D* paper.

2) Double sheet used for letter dated 20.11.09. Dimensions: 203 mm x 164 mm. Lines: 21, an average of 8.5 mm apart. The lines are noticeably pale. Top margin is 20–21 mm at the front, 19–20 mm at the back. Bottom margin is 13–12 mm at the front, 14–13 mm at the back. Watermarked "Boot's Cash Stationers". Possibly *Type B* paper. The same paper was used for the poem "Absence" sent to Grace Crawford on 21.11.09.

3) Two single pages used for letter dated 23.1.10. Dimensions: 202 mm x 160 mm. Lines: 20, an average of 8.5 mm apart. Top margin 21.5 mm, bottom margin 10 mm. No watermark. Possibly *Type C* paper.

4) Second page of letter dated 9.3.10. Dimensions: 204 mm x 164 mm. Lines: 21, an average of 8.5 mm apart. Top margin 18 mm, bottom margin 14.5 mm. Watermarked "Boot's Cash Stationers". Possibly *Type F* paper.

5) All of letter dated 28.1.10. Dimensions: 200 mm x 160 mm. Lines: 20, an average of 8.5 mm apart. Top margin 22 mm, bottom margin 9 mm. No watermark. Possibly *Type C* paper.

Lawrence used a new type of paper for his letter to Florence Wood on 28 January 1910, and used this and one other type for most of his letters through the rest of 1910. The first paper type is watermarked with an oval design showing a lion holding a spear, surmounted by a crown and with the Letters 'F M L' underneath; the second type is watermarked "T. H. SAUNDERS".

25. Letters 1 to 4 to Louie Burrows are in NUL, D. H. Lawrence Collection, LaB53, LaB62, LaB67 and LaB68. The letter to Grace Crawford mentioned with letter 2 is in the HRHRC, D. H. Lawrence Collection. I am indebted to J. Clegg of Special Collections, Central Library, University of Liverpool for the information about Letter 5 to Blanche Jennings, which is in the D. H. Lawrence collection, MS.2.88(20).

DOCUMENT OR PROCESS AS THE SITE OF AUTHORITY: ESTABLISHING CHRONOLOGY OF REVISION IN COMPETING TYPESCRIPTS OF LAWRENCE'S *THE BOY IN THE BUSH*

by

PAUL EGGERT*

A N unusually thorny problem can arise in the preparation of a reading text of a critical edition if multiple printers' copies are extant which were originally prepared by the author for simultaneous publication (typically, in New York and London) and if the author revised the copies differently.

* This essay is a revised form of a paper given to an editing session at the 1989 MLA

Developing practices to deal with such a case—the typescript copies of *The Boy in the Bush*—has revealed a confusion which the usual formulation of the goal of scholarly editing glides over. 'Scholarly editors may disagree about many things', G. Thomas Tanselle observed in 1976, 'but they are in general agreement that their goal is to discover exactly what an author wrote and to determine what form of his work he wished his public to have'.[1] The editorial method described in the present essay is aimed at achieving that goal by satisfying Tanselle's attendant call for the critical judgment of textual cruxes on a case-by-case basis; and it accepts as a matter of course his clear implication that, often, no single document will fully represent the author's intention for the work. Consideration of *The Boy in the Bush* typescripts has, however, highlighted the need for a further editorial distinction beyond that of document and work: a distinction between the *process* of composition and revision on the one hand and the documentary *sites* of the inscription of the process on the other. This distinction, if accepted, can justify a provisional but potentially clarifying separation of the 'authorial function' from the 'production function' even where the evidence of the former and the requirements of the latter reside in the very same documents and where the same person—the author—discharged both.

It is first necessary to outline the particular textual problem.[2] *The Boy*

Conference in Washington, D. C. Thanks for helpful commentary are due to Fredson Bowers, Hans Walter Gabler, Peter Shillingsburg and David Vander Meulen. The essay has also benefited from the 'Afterword' to Gabler's Garland edition of Joyce's *Ulysses* (3 vols., New York, 1984), and his 'The Text as Process and the Problem of Intentionality', *Text*, 3 (1987), 107–116.

1. 'The Editorial Problem of Final Authorial Intention', *Studies in Bibliography*, 29 (1976), 167; cf. also his 'Recent Editorial Discussion and the Central Questions of Editing', *Studies in Bibliography*, 34 (1981), 23–65.

As a result of the impact of post-structuralist ideas and Continental styles of textual criticism upon Anglo-American editing, this agreement is less general than it formerly was. For a survey, see D. C. Greetham, 'Textual and Literary Theory: Redrawing the Matrix', *Studies in Bibliography*, 42 (1989), 1–24. For an account of editorial orientations which marginalise authorial intention, see Peter Shillingsburg: *Scholarly Editing in the Computer Age*, English Department Occasional Paper 3, Faculty of Military Studies, Duntroon, A.C.T., 1984 (2nd ed. Athens, Ga.: U. of Georgia P., 1986); and 'An Inquiry into the Social Status of Texts and Modes of Textual Criticism', *Studies in Bibliography*, 42 (1989), 55–78.

However, if Chris Tiffin's description of the ideal of 'recuperating final authorial intention' as a 'most venerable and tenacious' concept means that critical editions will continue to be prepared according to this goal for some time yet, then the present illustration of the dynamics of authorial intention in revision may be of some evolutionary value: Tiffin, 'Final Intention, Revision and the Genetic Text: Editing Rosa Praed's *My Australian Girlhood*' in *Editing in Australia*, ed. Paul Eggert, English Department Occasional Paper 17 (University College ADFA, Canberra, A.C.T. / New South Wales U. P., Kensington, N.S.W., 1990), p. 132. My own feeling is that the critically established reading text will continue to have a place but that its pre-eminence can no longer be assumed: see my 'Textual Product or Textual Process: Procedures and Assumptions of Critical Editing' in *Editing in Australia*, pp. 19–40.

2. Some complexities of the textual situation not relevant to the present discussion are ignored here; for these and for otherwise uncited factual observations made in this essay see the Cambridge U. P. edition of the novel (1990).

in the Bush is a collaborative novel, but all of the extant manuscript material is in the hand of D. H. Lawrence and none in that of Mollie Skinner, an Australian bush-nurse and amateur novelist whom he had met when he visited Western Australia in 1922 and who, at his encouragement, wrote and sent him for placement a novel about colonial life in the 1880s. He believed the novel was unpublishable and so, with her permission, rewrote it in September-November 1923 in California and Mexico, sending the manuscript on in two batches for professional typing and subsequently adding a new last chapter in January 1924 after returning to London and just prior to correcting the (by now) typed copies. Though widely dispersed, the autograph manuscript and two typescript copies are extant: the latter became the setting copies (known as TSIa and TSIb, respectively[3]) used by his American publisher, Thomas Seltzer and his English publisher, Martin Secker, both of whom published the novel in 1924.

Both TSIa and TSIb contain 543 pages, and bear Lawrence's revisions and corrections in the page range 167–528. The reason that his revisions do not appear on pages 1–166 is that in London he revised a now lost, earlier typescript—one copy only—of this section (which represents the first batch of manuscript). It was then re-typed (ribbon and carbon) while Lawrence got on with revising duplicate typescript copies of the rest of the novel (corresponding to the second batch). When he received the copies of the re-typed section he simply added them in without further revising them, thus constituting TSIa and TSIb.[4] In pages 167–528 there are approximately 180 substantive revisions consisting of about 100 single word changes, about 65 revisions of short phrases, with the remainder being quite substantial changes. As he revised TSIa and TSIb Lawrence had had to bring the novel into line with the new last chapter he had just added which had given the novel a significant shift in emphasis.

In the interests of producing a reading text of *The Boy in the Bush* as close as possible to the one Lawrence 'would have wished to see published',[5] the autograph manuscript was chosen as base text and a procedure envisaged of emending it from one of the typescripts wherever Lawrence himself had revised them—provided of course they copied the manuscript accurately.[6] This solution, relying on textual evidence unambiguously in the hand of the author, might have swept away the textual problems in one move were it not for a complicating factor which soon became evident. Although TSIa

---

3. Items E55f and E55e in Warren Roberts, *A Bibliography of D. H. Lawrence*, 2nd ed. (1982). The manuscript is made up of items E55a and E55b; Roberts gives locations.

4. Pp. 528–543 are the typing of the new last chapter of manuscript and received only spelling corrections.

5. General Editors' Preface, The Cambridge Edition of the Works of D. H. Lawrence (1980–).

6. No proofs survive, but in view of Lawrence's known correcting of the novel's proofs for Martin Secker it was also decided to take some readings from the first English edition; and because Lawrence corrected a duplicate set of Secker proofs for Seltzer (so that the latter could check his own independently set proofs against them), a few readings have also been taken from the first American edition.

and TSIb (destined to serve as printers' copies) had been typed profession-ally, no doubt originally as ribbon and carbon of one another, they had later been mixed up, becoming composites of ribbon and carbon—the form in which they are found today. Evidence gradually mounted indicating that Lawrence was responsible for the shuffling when revising the typescripts—*differently*.

Page 468 of both typescripts provides a striking example of the process (see illustrations; the handwriting is Lawrence's). On the sixth line of the first heavily revised paragraph in the TSIa page is the handwritten sentence starting: 'This had made her rebel . . .'. At first TSIa read 'so terribly against him' before 'him' was replaced by 'the thought of him'. Two sentences down a nearly illegible 'But' was replaced by 'Now'. At the same places in TSIb may be seen 'so dangerously against the thought of him' and 'Now': TSIb has no erasures of handwriting here. Lawrence may have revised TSIa, made the additional alterations, and *then* transcribed the whose passage to TSIb, changing 'terribly' to 'dangerously', and making a range of other changes further down the page as he went. *Or*, he could have transcribed first, de-veloping the passage in TSIb as he transcribed, and then, realising that the typescripts now read differently, made a rough attempt to match them up. Belated or half-successful matching-up occurs elsewhere in the typescripts, suggesting that Lawrence felt the tug of responsibility but lacked the iron will of consistency necessary to achieve the result. As an author in revision Lawrence could not help but take the opportunity presented by transcription to further shape his description of Monica's awed resentment of the novel's hero; but as a scribe Lawrence's qualities were only mediocre. His mind was not on *that* job; and anyway, he may have reasoned, if the English and American editions were not exactly the same, what would it matter?[7]

The evidence of page 468 alone suggests a convenient hypothesis: that Lawrence always worked on TSIa first and on TSIb second. If so, TSIb would have been the transcription copy throughout and would contain the last reading in most cases. But an editor, tempted to embrace such a simple solu-tion, is apt to be reminded of the situation of the donkey A. E. Housman describes, hesitating between two equally attractive bundles of hay;[8] would the editor have shown one typescript to be a superior source of emendation simply by walking away from the other one?

If that ignominious fate were to be avoided, closer inspection would be necessary. A textual collation showed that sometimes TSIa appeared to have the last reading and sometimes TSIb. An explanation of what must have happened readily suggested itself. In transcribing changes from TSIa to TSIb (or vice versa), Lawrence had frequently altered them. Evidently

7. Whether Lawrence consciously reasoned thus cannot be known, but he was aware that he was preparing copy for two separate typesettings and at this stage he did not know that Seltzer's proofs would be checked in-house against a duplicate, authorially corrected set of Secker's (see previous note).

8. 'The Editing of Manilius', in Housman's *Collected Poems and Prose*, ed. Christopher Ricks (1988), p. 377.

amused him, he would see it had fair play.

And he took Monica in his arms, glad to get into grips with his own fate again. And it was good. It was better perhaps, than his passionate desirings of earlier days had imagined. Because he didn't lose and scatter himself. He gathered, like a reaper at harvest gathering.

And Monica, who woke for her baby, looked at him as he slept soundly and she sat in bed suckling her child. *She saw in him the eternal* ~~She would never be able to get really near to him: that she knew. She could never be able to get from him that delicious but deadly intimacy which she craved, but which she knew was a sort of calamity. He had been willing to give it before. So she had taunted him with Esau.~~ *stranger. There he was, the eternal stranger, lying in her bed sleeping at her side. She rocked her baby slightly as she sat up in the night, still rocking in the last throes of rebellion. The eternal stranger, she must fear him, because she could never finally know him, and never entirely possess him. She would never belong to her. This had made her rebel so dangerously against the thought of him. Because she would have to belong to him. Now he had arrived*

~~And now he had turned away, to something that belonged to his own male self alone. He had turned to his own male god, and would never give final intimacy to any human being whatsoever. He had given his ultimate intimacy to his own male God, and she was powerless.~~ *again before her like a doom, a doom she still stiffened herself against, but could no longer withstand. Because the emptiness of the other men, Percy, Esau, all the men she knew, was worse than the doom of this man who would never give her his ultimate intimacy, but who would be able to hold her till the end of time. There was something enduring and changeless in him. But she would never hold him entirely. Never! She would have to resign herself to that.*

Well, so be it. At least it relieved her of the burden of responsibility for life. It took away *from her her own strange, fascinating female power, which she couldn't bear to part with. But at the same time she felt saved, because her own power frightened her, having brought her to a brink of nothingness that was like a madness. The nothingness* ~~her own strange, fascinating, but distracting responsibility. She was free of her own responsibility, even if she had lost her dangerous power.~~ *that fronted her with Percy was worse than submitting to this man. After all, this man was magical.*

She put her child in its cradle, and returning waked the man.

He put out his hand quickly for her, as if she were a new, ~~tremendous~~ *blind* discovery. She ~~laughed to herself~~ *quivered and thrilled,* and left it to him. It was his *mystery, since* ~~affair, if~~ he would have it so.

TSIa

Alfred M. Hellman Collection,
Rare Book and Manuscript Library,
Columbia University

amused him, he would see it had fair play.

And he took Monica in his arms, glad to get into grips with his own fate again. And it was good. It was better perhaps, than his passionate desirings of earlier days had imagined. Because he didn't lose and scatter himself. He gathered, like a reaper at harvest gathering.

And Monica, who woke for her baby, looked at him as he slept soundly and she sat in bed suckling her child. ~~She would never be~~ She saw in him the eternal stranger. There he was, the eternal stranger, lying in her bed sleeping at her side. She ~~able to get really near to him that she knew. She would never be~~ rocked her baby slightly as she sat up in the night, still rocking in the last throes of ~~able to get from him that delicious but deadly intimacy which she~~ rebellion. The eternal stranger, whom she feared, because she could never finally possess ~~craved, but which she knew was a sort of calamity. He had been~~ him, and never finally know him! She would never belong to her. This had made her rebel ~~willing to give it before. So she had taunted him with Ben.~~ so terribly against him. Because she would have to belong to him. Now he had arrived again before ~~And now he had turned away, to something that belonged to his own~~ her like a doom, a doom she still fought against, but could no longer withstand. Because the emptiness of the ~~male self alone. He had turned to his own male god, and would never~~ other men, Easu, Percy, all the men she knew, was worse than the doom of this man who would never give her ~~give fixed intimacy to any human being whatsoever. He had given~~ his ultimate intimacy, but who would be able to hold her till the end of time. There was something enduring ~~his ultimate intimacy to his own male God, and she was powerless~~ and changeless in him. But she would never hold him entirely. Never! She would have to resign herself to this.

Well, so be it. At least it relieved her of the burden of from her her own strange and fascinating female responsibility for life. It took away ~~her own strange, fascinating,~~ powers, which she couldn't bear to part with. But at the same time she felt saved, because her own ~~and distracting responsibility. She was free of her own responsi-~~ power frightened her, having brought her to a brink of nothingness that was her madness. The nothingness ~~bility, even if she had lost her dangerous power.~~ that fronted her with Percy was worse than submitting to this man beside her. After all, this man so magical

She put her child in its cradle, and returning waked the man.
Blind
He put out his hand quickly for her, as if she were a new, ~~discovery~~ quivered and thrilled, discovery. She ~~laughed to herself~~, and left it to him. It was his mystery, since ~~wait, if~~ he would have it so.

TSIb

Harry Ransom Humanities Research Center,
The University of Texas at Austin

pleased in some cases with the new reading, he then transferred it back to the first typescript (but not always); with some longer revised passages he transferred back only some parts of the new reading. And often he would enter a revised reading in one copy and fail to transcribe it to the other (or, possibly, decide not to). The inevitable result was that his publishers would not receive identical setting copy and that TSIa and TSIb would contain thirty-seven instances where emendations appear on only one typescript, and twenty-nine instances where both typescripts are revised, but revised differently.[9] The retrieval of a reading text from this unexpected textual tangle had begun to look decidedly problematic: would it be possible in relation to the last two-thirds of the typescripts where the variant revisions occur to discover the last-entered reading in each case?

To attempt to answer that question it would be necessary to reconstruct how Lawrence had physically treated the typescript copies as he revised. The typists had not paginated the last two-thirds of the typescript[10] and Lawrence's hand-written pagination of this section involved several attempts to get right. Had these paginations been carried out as Lawrence revised or after he had finished revising? Towards the end of the novel he discarded some pages when replacing them with some pages he typed (amateurishly) himself. Because the replacements contain exactly the same pattern of successive cancelled paginations as previous and succeeding pages the paginations must have succeeded the revision.[11] The alternation of ribbon and carbon copy in the two typescripts precisely at chapter-ends[12] further suggests that Lawrence had been trying to keep the typed sheets together in chapters as he revised, and in fact one of the cancelled paginations resulted from his having left chapter xi temporarily out of the count. These considerations made it possible to conclude that Lawrence was probably presented with the typescript copies either in one bundle (ribbon copy of a chapter followed

9. This exposes a fundamental flaw in the Romantic idea which Aldous Huxley circulated about Lawrence as an author who never revised but instead rewrote his works entirely —as of course he famously did with *Lady Chatterley's Lover*. (See Huxley's Introduction to his edition of *The Letters of D. H. Lawrence* [1932], p. xvii).

10. I.e. pp. 167–528: see note 4.

11. The cancelled paginations were occasioned by Lawrence's errors in paginating. The evidence at this point, together with the regularity of the pattern of cancelled paginations in TSIa, indicate that TSIa and TSIb had already been assembled into discrete bundles (see next paragraph) before being paginated and that therefore pagination-stage succeeded revision-stage. (The paginations are, moreover, in pencil whereas the revisions are in ink.) Lawrence paginated TSIa first: it has the bulk of the cancelled page-numberings. By the time he got to p. 468 of TSIb he had got the numbering right, and so it has only the one page number (see illustration). Thus the cancelled paginations do not assist in determining the sequence of revisions.

12. With the exception of 3 pages (pp. 315, 425, 524) plus 3 others, the result of carbon reversal. The typescripts of *Women in Love* (TSIa and TSIb: items E441d and E441e in Roberts, *A Bibliography*) follow a similar pattern (information from David Farmer). So does the surviving partial typescript, most of whose twin is lost, of *Aaron's Rod*: see L. D. Clark's Cambridge edition (1987), pp. xxxiv–xxxv.

by its carbon copy, then the ribbon copy of the next chapter followed by its carbon, and so on) *or* in complete, separate bundles.

However, this conclusion did not reveal the order in which Lawrence revised, for however he pulled the chapters off the pile or piles he went on to re-collate them pretty much at random. (And he must have known he had done this when he subsequently paginated; evidently it did not worry him.) He was not devoting much effort into getting the collation nice and tidy.[13] It would have served little purpose for an editor to have notionally re-sorted TSIa and TSIb into ribbon and carbon copy because textual evidence showed that while Lawrence frequently revised ribbon copy first and transcribed his revisions and corrections to the carbon copy, he did not always do so. (Even if he had meant to do so he could accidentally have pulled pages off the wrong pile—if there was more than one pile—or he could have shuffled the two copies of the particular chapter in his hands as he laid them down.)

Although it is likely that Lawrence revised a chapter at a time, he appears to have stopped to transcribe from one typescript to the other after each page. The evidence lies in his correction of a great number of misstruck and faint characters—up to ten per page. Where Lawrence corrects such mistyping on any page the proportion he transcribes to the other copy is high. If he had waited till he got to the end of a chapter, it is unlikely that he would have picked up so many by leafing back though. Moreover, *within* a chapter there is evidence Lawrence would occasionally swap from revising say, ribbon copy (and transcribing to carbon) to revising carbon copy (and transcribing to ribbon); he would even, on rare occasions, move from one copy to the other while working on a particular page. (After making an alteration he could have immediately transcribed, then continued to read down the page on which he had transcribed the alteration.)[14]

An editor confronting this criss-crossing trail of textual revision might try to simplify matters: he might decide to take a modified 'best text' approach and incorporate into MS those revisions appearing in only one of the typescripts, consigning those in the other to the textual apparatus. However there is no evidence with *The Boy in the Bush* that Lawrence preferred one typescript over the other, so that the editor's decision, like that of Housman's donkey, would be arbitrary. Another simplifying technique would be to try to establish a rough chronology of revision in the competing typescripts by counting all cases where Lawrence revised a reading in one type-

13. The psychology of a modern-day equivalent readily explains this inattentiveness: a teacher collating photocopies of a multipage handout he has prepared for his students is apt to feel that because he has already put the 'real' effort into writing the document, and because the collation of discrete copies is in comparison a merely mechanical matter, he can afford to let his attention wander. The results are usually unfortunate.

14. P. 2 of TSIa and TSIb of *Women in Love* furnish an earlier example of this: see photo-reproduction in Charles L. Ross, *The Composition of 'The Rainbow' and 'Women in Love': A History* (1979), pp. 157–158.

script, changed it immediately to another reading, and only entered *that* reading into the other typescript. So, for instance, on page 404 of TSIa, Len Ellis's age is typed 'not seventeen', which Lawrence changed first to 'not eighteen' and then to 'only seventeen'. TSIb has the second revised reading alone. At such points TSIa is clearly the correction copy, and TSIb is the transcription copy. Provided such examples outnumbered those where the contrary was true, the editor might be tempted to prefer TSIb as the source of emendation throughout.[15] But such evidence would not demonstrate the chronology of the documents as a whole, only the chronology of the revisions at those points. Is there an alternative to this sort of rough and ready calculation, or is it the best that can be done?

The answer must depend on the circumstances of the case, but with *The Boy in the Bush* it has, in fact, proved to be possible to establish the chronology of revision, though to do so is to thread back and forth between the typescript documents. The practice developed for the purpose made it possible to treat the revision stage as a single version which is witnessed in its entirety by neither typescript alone but by both. Taken together, the typescripts witness and can be made to yield a continuous stage of revision. To have chosen one of the typescripts as the source of emendation of the base text manuscript would have been to downgrade the importance of Lawrence's active engagement as an author in the revisional process. Arbitrarily to favour one document over a process that was actually witnessed by both documents would have been tantamount to ascribing textual authority to Lawrence's fallibilities as scribe and collator—functions which were clearly not uppermost in his mind.

To have chosen both typescripts and to have prepared a parallel text edition would not have produced an 'ideal text' either, for such an edition would also have been based on the extant documentary forms of the text rather than on the revisional process. This last observation points to the special significance of the textual situation of *The Boy in the Bush*: that it has been possible to distinguish the function of author-in-revision from his function as a participant in the production process, working to provide his publishers with copy which would allow the bookmaking to continue. Of course it was Lawrence's need to provide corrected copy which gave him the opportunity to engage in a process of revision, so to that extent the distinction does not hold; but, once he was involved in it, his dual functions—author-in-revision as against participant in the production process—may be usefully distinguished.

Two observations arise from the distinction. First, it may be found applicable in similar editing situations involving typescript or proof copies (i.e. where the author is sent two proof sets with one intended as copy for another publisher's separate type-setting).[16] Second, the distinction, if it is found to

15. Lindeth Vasey uses this method, but with additional evidence, in her Cambridge edition of Lawrence's *Mr Noon* (1984).

16. The problem may also have parallels with textual situations dating from before the invention of the typewriter. Washington Irving's *Conquest of Granada* (1829) is one

have a wider applicability, may help clarify those familiar disagreements about choice of manuscript or first edition as base text where the holograph manuscript is extant but the author is known to have read proof and approved them. Both sides in the debate believe the practice they advocate is aimed at establishing the authorial text; but my distinction suggests they may be invoking, unawares, different criteria under the same name. The distinction being proposed might help clarify matters by underlining the importance of going beyond the question of *whether* the author was involved at proof stage to conceptualise the kind and level of engagement he had. The editor would be asking himself whether it were possible in the particular case to distinguish between the author's compositional-revisional processes on the one hand and his participation in the commercial production processes on the other. This is not to claim that the two processes are separate and discrete for clearly they are not, only that a clarifying distinction may be able to be made. *Not* to ask the question may be to put oneself at risk of shifting inconsistently from one criterion to the other whenever a hard decision is faced.

A summary of the various sorts of evidence encountered and made use of in dealing with the typescripts of *The Boy in the Bush* may be of some interest, for in fact it proved possible to track Lawrence's zig-zag path of revision with sufficient confidence to allow the preference of a reading in one or other typescript in all but one case of variant revision. Taken singly, each sort of evidence is indicative rather than conclusive, and its relative importance will change depending on the condition of the documents an editor encounters. When, for comparison, I checked the typescript copies of Lawrence's travel book *Etruscan Places*, some chapters of which exist in three copies all revised by him, the kinds of evidence differed somewhat.[17] Because the preparation of three copies meant two lots of transcription from the

---

(ed. Miriam Shillingsburg, 1988). Irving wrote the autograph manuscript in Spain and gave it to Spanish scribes to copy. Because their uncertainties with the foreign language varied from slight to entire, the copying tended to be slavish rather than regularising in habit. Where the scribe could not recognise a word, a blank was left for Irving to fill in later: with the exception of one chapter his markings appear on almost every page. However, rather than just fill in the blanks by reference to the autograph, he sometimes thought of wordings he preferred and proceeded to alter the autograph to match. Sometimes he thought of a further improvement in this transcription and so had to return to the scribal copy to enter it. Occasionally the revisional track did not run to completion, leaving variant revised readings.

Irving sent the autograph to his American publisher via his nephew, Pierre Irving who, believing the manuscript was inadequately pointed, took upon himself the job of re-punctuating it in such a way that the original punctuation was frequently obliterated or at least made dubious so often as to prevent its use as base text. Thus the editor adopted the scribal copy as base text on the grounds that it more reliably transmitted the authorial punctuation than did the autograph manuscript. She emends the base text from the autograph wherever it has a later substantive reading than the scribal copy.

17. Roberts, *A Bibliography*, items E117b, E117c and E117d. The investigation of these typescripts was too brief to allow a conclusion to be reached as to the applicability of the present method to the editing of *Etruscan Places*.

correction copy, the likelihood of revisional development in the process of transcription increased dramatically. This process left the typescript copies with more than *The Boy in the Bush* yields of what is the best kind of evidence: an autograph revision in one typescript which was then cancelled and replaced by a second revision before the second revision only was transferred to the next copy. Such evidence on any one page of *The Boy in the Bush* suggests Lawrence was reading and revising the first copy and transcribing to the second, so that if a variant revision appears elsewhere on that page in the two typescripts there is prima facie (although not conclusive) evidence as to which one was chronologically later.

The next best evidence proved to be the tiny revisions—misstruck characters and marks of punctuation—which Lawrence was especially liable to overlook, particularly if he had a number of other and more obvious revisions and corrections to transcribe on the same page. If an editor were dealing with an author who transcribed chapter by chapter rather than page by page, then the job would be much easier, for many more transcriptional failures would be generated as some or many of the tiny corrections were overlooked. The present method would become relevant in such a case if, following revision, pages of the typescripts had been combined at random, thus destroying the integrity of each chapter's status as a first or second revised copy.

The state of the carbon copy also provided clues (although rarely in the case of *Etruscan Places* where the carbon was fairly evenly inked): poorly inked carbon copy will frequently fail to reproduce lightly struck characters, and, if the carbon paper itself was misaligned, ends of lines may have been cut off or the last line not transferred at all. Where Lawrence did not correct words rendered illegible in these ways on a carbon-copy page but did enter other revisions on it, it is likely that he was reading the legible ribbon-copy page and transcribing to carbon—and of course vice versa when he corrected them all, particularly if conveniently combined with, say, a spelling error which he corrected only on the carbon copy.

The size of the handwriting can also indicate the direction of revision: two sizes on the one page of one copy may indicate two-stage revision. Lawrence could have entered his revisions in that copy and put the page to one side; bringing the corresponding page of the other copy in front of him, he would then have transcribed the revisions. But if, in transcribing, he immediately saw the need for another alteration on the same page, this would mean returning to the first copy to enter the alteration there, his physical movement of hand and arm being liable to cause a different size (or slope) of handwriting from the correction he had originally entered. The ease with which lengthy interlinear revision is squeezed into the available space may also suggest on which copy the revised reading was entered first. Only when transcribing would Lawrence be aware of how much space the reading required to be easily legible and so be able to adjust the size of his writing and spacing to suit.

Once the correction copy has been provisionally distinguished from the transcription copy for a given page the evidence being relied upon must be tallied with evidence from surrounding pages (or part-pages), particularly in the same chapter (if the alternation of ribbon and carbon is by chapter). One assumes that Lawrence would tend to move from copy to copy in a regular rhythm of revision and transcription, but one must remain alert to any and every piece of physical evidence which suggests that, for whatever reason and at whatever point, he changed the direction. For pages which bear no variant revisions no decision need be made of course, although such pages may well have indicative evidence which may help with decisions having to be made about the chronology of revision on other pages nearby.[18] With *The Boy in the Bush* the assumption that Lawrence would naturally revise ribbon copy and transcribe to carbon proved to be unfounded, but that direction did seem more usual with the *Etruscan Places* typescripts.

Further specification of the method is probably unnecessary, especially given that the kinds of evidence and their relative weights will probably differ from author to author and case to case. The crux of the procedure may be summarised however as the need to pay attention not just to the readings normally thought textually significant but also to the apparently insignificant, to the accidents of typing and transcription, so as to recover the historical process of revision. It took the present writer a long while to see these kinds of evidence, even though he had been poring over the typescripts, pondering the patterns of revision he could see so much more obviously inscribed. The literary critic in him had to learn to take its cues from the textual detective. Certainty, he found, was rarely obtainable; but strong probability was, allowing a more finely honed way than alternative methods afford of approximating the text of final revision.[19]

While readers continue to require, and publishers demand, the finalising of such texts, the critically established reading text based upon a certain standard, typically that of the postulated recovery of authorial intention, remains a worthwhile goal. The goal is an idea, the perfect achievement of which would produce an 'idea-l' text. However the logic of the present argu-

18. A revision entered on only one copy presents other difficulties: the author may have forgotten to transcribe, decided not to, or only thought of the new wording while transcribing other revisions and then neglected to enter it back into the correction copy. These considerations—which necessarily lack textual evidence—are imponderable. But what such revisions certainly show is that the author did intend to, and did, make the change at some point in the revisional process. The fact that the autograph change appears in one document and not in the other does not give the document in which it appears any superior authority except at that point—where it witnesses *a* step in the revisional process absent in the other copy.

19. From typescript revision stage(s) onwards textual transmission characteristically takes divergent paths towards separate publication (although crossover at proof stage can occur: see note 6). These divergent routes might suggest that the techniques of editing medieval or ancient literature would be applicable. But the problem under discussion is not the winnowing out of scribal corruption, for the author himself is responsible for most of the variance. When transcribing revisions he is of course acting in a scribal mode, but being the author he is liable, in any act of transcription, to change suddenly from scribal to revisional mode.

ment, if extended, is that the 'ideal' text will be more closely approximated when the processes of composition and revision are, wherever possible, distinguished from and allowed to take precedence over the extant documentary forms in which the processes are inscribed. To define the goal of critical editing as establishing the text which fulfills (typically) the author's intentions is to elide two kinds of authority: authority deriving from the author-in-composition and -revision with authority deriving from the documents he was prepared to countenance or 'authorise' as sufficient for the production processes to continue. Although evidence for the first kind of authority can only be derived from the documents, the situation with the Lawrence texts described here demonstrates that a distinction between the two kinds of authority at least sometimes can—and, where possible, suggests that it should —be made.

Critical editing involves a determined attempt at an act of historical recovery of the diachronic processes of authorial inscription. I am simply urging that, where feasible, the editor should refine on the diachronics of revision and accept the consequences of the distinction I have proposed even if this means abandoning the integrity of two or more documents which witness a continous stage of revision. This is especially the case when, as with *The Boy in the Bush*, the so-called integrity of the documents depends on little more than where the pages and chapters happened to fall as their author finished with them: whether on the table, on the floor, or wherever he dropped them.

SIMMS'S FIRST PUBLISHED FICTION

by

JAMES E. KIBLER

A MONG the personal papers of American novelist and poet William Gilmore Simms (1806–1870) is a pencilled list of cryptic jottings of initials, names, and dates ranging from July 1824 to February 1825.[1] Investigation reveals that this page is a chart in the author's own hand of his publications in the Charleston *Courier* for this period—when he was but eighteen years old. There are seventeen entries which turn out to be for poems published under the initials or pseudonyms, "W. G. S.," "S. G. W.," "S.," "W******,"

---

1. General Manuscripts Collection, P 1540, South Caroliniana Library, University of South Carolina.

"Altamont," and "Mortimer." With the exception of "W******," all of these pseudonyms and the poems to which they are attached have already been identified.[2] Simms had been publishing poetry in the local Charleston newspapers since the age of fifteen;[3] his first proved verses date from early 1823 when they appeared in the Charleston *City Gazette* under the pseudonym "16."[4] The seventeen poetry listings in Simms's note, with the one exception, thus serve merely for corroboration.

An eighteenth very significant entry, however, is the line: "Octavian myself 27 July." This refers to a contribution to the *Courier* for 27 July 1824, signed "Octavian," and entitled "Light Reading." The "myself" identifies the piece as by Simms and thus provides yet another Simms pseudonym, number 230, to be exact. Even more importantly, it makes known for the first time Simms's earliest prose work, thus pushing back by a year the date accepted as the beginning of his career as fiction writer.[5]

"Light Reading" is a satiric prose sketch told from the first-person point of view. Its youthful narrator, in a Byronic manner typical of the early Simms, is a loner, a proud lad who goes his own way, having no "interest in the affairs of mankind." Though men have always treated him with disdain, he has at least been successful with the ladies, who have been his major solace. After the sad events detailed in this sketch, he forswears them also and becomes the "Eremite," particularly scorning the "pride of wealth" of the "purse-proud" and "the regular time-plodding mechanics of existence, whose only object in life is the attainment of . . . wealth." The contempt for materialism shown here in this first known prose work is directly in line with a theme in his recently discovered earliest letters of 1826, where he similarly expresses his scorn for the greed which he witnesses on the frontier, thus foreshadowing his mature work's concern over the destructive force of materialism on character, individual wholeness, and the formation of high culture.[6] In valuing wealth over the things of the spirit, mankind loses the things of most worth, a truth expressed as a major theme of much of the mature poetry and fiction. Thus, in this sketch in the *Courier* of 1824, he is already voicing (two years

2. Recorded in James Kibler, *The Pseudonymous Publications of William Gilmore Simms* (University of Georgia Press, 1976) and Kibler, *The Poetry of William Gilmore Simms: An Introduction and Bibliography* (Columbia, S. C.: Southern Studies Program, 1979). The poem signed W****** is "A Lock of Hair" in the Charleston *Courier*, 22 November 1824.

3. *The Letters of William Gilmore Simms*, ed. Mary C. Simms Oliphant, *et al.* (University of South Carolina Press, 1952–1982), I, 161, 285; II, 221.

4. His first poem under this pseudonym was "Sonnet—To My Books," Charleston *City Gazette* (20 March 1823). See also Kibler, *Pseudonymous Publications*, p. 91.

5. Previously thought to be 30 April 1825. Simms's first work of fiction was heretofore considered "The Wreck" (*New York Mirror*, vol. 2, pp. 313–314). For a list of Simms's short fiction, see Betty Jo Strickland's excellent "The Short Fiction of William Gilmore Simms: A Checklist," *Mississippi Quarterly*, 21 (1976), 591–608.

6. For these letters and a study of them, see James Kibler, "*The Album* (1826)—The Significance of the Recently Discovered Second Volume," *Studies in Bibliography*, 39 (1986), 62–78, and "Simms's First Letters: 'Letters from the West (1826),'" *Southern Literary Journal*, 19 (1987), 81–91.

in advance of his first letters) his unrelenting criticism of American materialism, which he was later to discern as the cardinal evil of his age.

Much of the sketch, however, satirizes the speaker himself. His aloofness
and highmindedness lead to both a literal and figurative "fall" involving
considerable discomfort and embarrassment. First his fiancée deserts him for
a "rich, clod-hopping burgher." Then his next intended inspires him to try
to elope with her. His rope ladder at her third-story window breaks, and he
falls into a Charleston sewer, much humbled. His "fair" but superficial mate
then breaks off the match, realizing that he is not the man of the "many and
superior qualities" of which he had at least temporarily convinced her. The
narration reveals that the speaker's highmindedness might stem from vanity
and arrogance. His artificial language characterizes him as foppish and superficial. While his values and actions seem honorable, the motives for them are
definitely subject to question. In telling his story, the speaker shows more
about himself than he knows; and his character becomes more important than
the story he tells. What saves him from being an insufferable prig is his sense
of humor and his ability finally to realize about himself at least something of
what the reader already knows. It is interesting to note that "Light Reading"
has some affinities with Simms's verse monologues of 1825–1835[7] in that both

7. For example, see his "The Broken Arrow," written in May 1825 and first published
in Charleston *Courier* (31 May 1826) and "The Modern Lion," Charleston *City Gazette* (22
Dec. 1830). The latter has particularly close similarities to "Light Reading" because also
spoken by a young dandy of the city:

THE MODERN LION

i

I am a pretty gentleman,
  I walk about at ease,
My habits are all pleasant ones,
  And very apt to please.
I dress with taste and tidyness,
  My coat's a purple brown;
And with a bamboo in my hand,
  I switch my way 'bout town.

ii

The ladies like me, terribly—
  And 'pon my soul, I'm sure,
My absence were a sad disease
  That I alone could cure.
To me they all refer at once
  My judgment, it is law;
I fill them all with love of me,
  And that begets their awe.

iii

'Twixt twelve and three I shop with them
  At four o'clock I dine—
And 'twixt the six and eight I loll,

prose and poetry share first-person narrators who reveal their own character through their narrations. In this first prose work, the eighteen-year-old author is thus experimenting with an effective form of which he would later make good use. Here follows the text from the *Courier* of 27 July 1824, without emendation. Octavian's parting statement that "You shall hear again from me anon" suggests that Simms intended writing a series of such sketches which would trace Octavian in his progress. No other sketches, however, have as yet been found in any of the Charleston papers.

[For the Courier]

LIGHT READING

Mr. Editor.—I am one of that unfortunate class of beings, whom Nature, in a sportive mood, has created apparently for her own amusement—a species of non descript, differing from the rest of the world; their superior, considering myself, and by them considered, an object of alternate scorn and pity. I have no interest in the affairs of mankind—alone—an Eremite amid the pressure of thousands. Such a char-

---

Or push about the wine.
Then for the evening coterie,
And for the evening chat,
I put my lilac breeches on,
And take my velvet hat.

iv

My visage is remarkable—
For so they all agree,—
At least, they're all in love with it,
And that's enough for me.
'Twould do you good to see my face,
And forehead, I declare;
One half the latter smooth and smack,
The other black with hair.

v

Two different pictures should you see;—
My right profile is grand;
The Brigand pattern, savage—sad—
Most admirably plann'd.
While, on the left—Adonis' self
Would much his fortune bless,
To own my style of countenance,
And steal my fav'rite tress.

vi

I have been painted many times—
But never to my mind;
I think to sit to Inman soon
As I can raise the wind.
I'll write a book to print with it,
And in a little while,
Employ the 'Mirror' and the 'Star'
To show me up in style.

acter can hardly be supposed to have any intimate connection with the regular time-plodding mechanics of existence, whose only object in life is the attainment of that wealth, which it is my only object to circulate. I was alone, while in company gay and reserved; cold, yet familiar. I felt myself independent of the world, and therefore scorned the opinions which I was confident would either originate in their selfishness of character, or exude from the feigned humility of aristocratic pride of wealth. I consoled myself for the want of riches by my contempt and scorn of its possessors. I considered the poor man, the animal who conquers the prey, whilst the purse-proud I likened to the kite who pilfers it. With such opinions it is hardly likely that my associates could be numerous, and it was, therefore, necessary that I should find some remedy for that lack of society without which, life is a void, and enjoyment *pain*. Possessing naturally an amorous constitution, I necessarily turned to the fair; and, to do justice to *their taste*, they seemed pretty generally to view me with a favorable eye. Although my comrades would attribute their kindness to the variety of woman's taste, perpetually changing, ever fickle and eager in the pursuit of the curious and eccentric. But this Mr. Editor, I considered sheer envy, resulting from my almost unparalleled success. I however, my dear sir, did not long remain untroubled with the contingencies of this species of pleasure. I experienced various degrees of alloy, extremely galling to one, so irritable and susceptible as myself. For instance: one lady, who had given me considerable encouragement, and whom I calculated in a short time to bring to my own terms, evaporated with a rich, clod-hopping burgher. Mrs. Pride, timely came to my assistance, and consoled me with the reflection, that I should congratulate myself on escaping from a connection with one so mercenary. But alas! Mr. Editor, that pride of soul, was soon to be humbled! That mind soon trampled upon—those hopes abortive. One fair who had seized my heart by surprise, and whom my amorous fancy had pictured divine, was, after a little perseverance, made acquainted with my many and superior qualifications, and had consented to smile. The time was fixed; the rope ladder prepared, and duly attached to her third story window, and I on its summit; my fancy exulting in the prospect of complete success. When, oh! most murderous hemp! one twist became undone, the others followed the neck-breaking example, and I was precipitated like another Phæton from the acme of enjoyment to the gloom and depth of Acheron, without even embracing the fair, who in consequence of my failure and subsequent appearance, refused to ratify her former vows. I had almost forgotten to state, that but for the polite foresight of her sire, who no doubt had some inkling of the future, I should not now be scrawling this epistle; nor recur with trembling to the twists of hemp! My fall was broken and my neck saved unbroken, by my descent to the pliable foundation of a sewer recently erected by her father. You shall hear again from me anon.   OCTAVIAN.

Notes on Contributors

D. C. Greetham is Executive Director of the Society for Textual Scholarship, co-editor of its journal *TEXT*, and teaches textual scholarship and textual and literary theory at the City University of New York Graduate Center. He is an editor of Trevisa and Hoccleve.

Peter L. Shillingsburg, Professor of English at Mississippi State University, is a former chairman of the Committee on Scholarly Editions, general editor of The William Makepeace Thackeray Edition being published by Garland, and author of *Scholarly Editing in the Computer Age* and articles on editorial theory and practice in *A&EB, PBSA, SB*, and *Bulletin of the Bibliographical Society of Australia and New Zealand*.

G. Thomas Tanselle, Vice President of the John Simon Guggenheim Memorial Foundation, teaches bibliography and editing in the Columbia University English Department and is co-editor of the Northwestern-Newberry edition of *The Writings of Herman Melville*. He has recently completed terms as president of the Grolier Club and of the Bibliographical Society of America. A new collection of his essays, many of which first appeared in *Studies in Bibliography*, is about to be published by the Bibliographical Society of the University of Virginia under the title *Textual Criticism and Scholarly Editing*.

Johan Gerritsen is professor emeritus of English Language and Medieval English Literature in the University of Groningen, Netherlands, having in early days been with the Royal Library at The Hague. His main work, besides lexicography, is in analytical and textual bibliography and codicology. In recent years he has published on various Old English manuscripts, on the backgrounds of the Swan drawing, on the printing of the Dutch poet and dramatist Vondel, and on Plantin at work in and after October 1563.

Joseph A. Dane, Professor of English at the University of Southern California, is the author of *The Critical Mythology of Irony* (1991) and numerous articles on medieval literature and Chaucer.

Adrian Weiss (Associate Professor) teaches Shakespearian drama, Renaissance literature, and history of criticism. His research progresses in several directions: identifying the sets of matrices comprising hybrid typefaces in Elizabethan/Jacobean printing; sorting out the printing histories of standing-type (*Malcontent, Eastward Hoe!, Fawne*) and shared plays; and developing programs for computer-assisted compositorial analysis and font analysis. Relocation closer to rare-books collections is critical to the continuation of his work.

KATHLEEN IRACE received her doctorate from the University of California, Los Angeles, in December 1990. She is currently finishing her book on six Shakespearean "bad" quartos.

JOHN JOWETT, formerly an editor of the Oxford Shakespeare, currently lectures in English Literature at the University of Waikato, New Zealand. As well as his contribution to the Oxford Shakespeare, he has published various articles, mainly on textual and related critical issues, and with Gary Taylor has co-authored the forthcoming book *Shakespeare Reshaped, 1606–1623*. He is working on the new Oxford edition of Thomas Middleton's works.

CLIVE PROBYN is Professor and Chairman of English at Monash University, Victoria, Australia. His last book was *English Fiction of the Eighteenth Century, 1700–89* (1987), and his next is *The Sociable Humanist: the Life and Works of James Harris (1709–80)*, to be published by Clarendon Press in 1990.

EMILY LORRAINE DE MONTLUZIN is Professor of History at Francis Marion College in Florence, South Carolina. She is the author of *The Anti-Jacobins, 1798–1800: The Early Contributors to the "Anti-Jacobin Review"* (London, 1988) as well as articles on eighteenth- and nineteenth-century British press history.

JAMES M. KUIST is a Professor in the Department of English and Comparative Literature at the University of Wisconsin-Milwaukee. He is the author of *The Nichols File of "The Gentleman's Magazine," The Works of John Nichols: An Introduction*, and various essays on this periodical and its publishers. He has also written on Gray, Chatterton, Malone, and Sterne.

ARTHUR SHERBO, Emeritus Professor of English at Michigan State University, is making a special study of periodicals.

JOHN R. TURNER is a Lecturer in the Department of Information and Library Studies at the University College of Wales, Aberystwyth. He was the Managing Editor of Scolar Press Ltd. in the late 1960s and early 1970s. At present he is working on a history of the Walter Scott Publishing Co. of Newcastle-on-Tyne.

A. R. ATKINS recently submitted his thesis entitled "Narrative Voice and Self-Representation in D. H. Lawrence's Fiction, 1906–12" to the University of Cambridge, after a year on a Fulbright and a Wingate Scholarship at the University of Texas, Austin.

PAUL EGGERT is senior lecturer in the English Department, University College ADFA, Canberra. His editions of *The Boy in the Bush* (for the Cambridge University Press series The Works of D. H. Lawrence) and the conference proceedings *Editing in Australia* (English Department Occasional Paper 17, New South Wales Univ. Press) both appeared in 1990.

JAMES E. KIBLER, JR., is Professor of English at the University of Georgia. He is the author of various articles on Southern literary figures and three books on William Gilmore Simms. His edition, *Selected Poems of William Gilmore Simms*, was published by the University of Georgia Press in 1990.

BIBLIOGRAPHICAL SOCIETY OF THE UNIVERSITY OF VIRGINIA

OFFICERS

President, IRBY B. CAUTHEN, JR., Wilson Hall, University of Virginia, Charlottesville, Virginia 22903

Vice President, KENDON L. STUBBS, University of Virginia Library, Charlottesville, Virginia 22903

Secretary-Treasurer, RAY W. FRANTZ, JR., University of Virginia Library, Charlottesville, Virginia 22903

Editor, FREDSON BOWERS, Route 14, Box 7, Charlottesville, Virginia 22901

Executive Secretary, PENELOPE F. WEISS, University of Virginia Library, Charlottesville, Virginia 22903

Hon. Secretary-Treasurer for the British Isles, MRS. DOUGLAS WYLLIE, Westbrae, 39 Libo Ave., Uplawmoor, G78 4AL Glasgow, Scotland

COUNCIL

DAVID L. VANDER MEULEN	(1991)	RUTHE R. BATTESTIN	(1994)
KENDON L. STUBBS	(1992)	VACANT	(1995)
NANCY ESSIG	(1993)	MRS. LINTON R. MASSEY	(1996)
	I. B. CAUTHEN, JR. (1997)		

PAST PRESIDENTS

CHALMERS L. GEMMILL, ATCHESON L. HENCH, LINTON R. MASSEY, KENDON L. STUBBS

Studies in Bibliography is issued annually by the Society in addition to various bibliographical pamphlets and monographs.

Membership in the Society is solicited according to the following categories:

Subscribing Members at $30.00 a year receive *Studies in Bibliography* and other bibliographical materials issued without charge by the Society. Institutions as well as private persons are accepted in this class of membership.

Student Members at $15.00 a year receive the benefits of *Subscribing Members.*

Contributing Members at $100 a year receive all publications and by their contributions assist in furthering the work of the Society. Institutions are accepted.

Articles and notes are invited by the Editor. Preferably these should conform to the recommendations of the Modern Language Association of America. All copy, *including quotations and notes,* should be double-spaced. The Society will consider the publication of bibliographical monographs for separate issue.

All matters pertaining to business affairs, including applications for membership, should be sent to the Executive Secretary, Penelope F. Weiss, University of Virginia Library, Charlottesville, Virginia 22903.

CONTRIBUTING MEMBERS FOR 1990

BODLEIAN LIBRARY, Oxford, England

UNIVERSITY LIBRARY, Cambridge, England

CARLETON UNIVERSITY, Ottawa, Canada

IRBY B. CAUTHEN, JR., Charlottesville, Virginia

JACK DALTON, New York City

PETER J. D. DEDEL, Suffern, New York

UNIVERSITY OF DELAWARE, Newark, Delaware

ROLF E. DU RIETZ, Upsala, Sweden

EMORY UNIVERSITY, Atlanta, Georgia

FREIE UNIVERSITAT, Berlin, Germany

GEROLD & Co., Vienna, Austria

JOHAN GERRITSEN, The Netherlands

ANTHONY HAMMOND, Ontario, Canada

UNIVERSITY OF HAWAII, Honolulu, Hawaii

INDIANA UNIVERSITY, Bloomington, Indiana

WALLACE KIRSOP, Victoria, Australia

MARK SAMUELS LASNER, Washington, D.C.

MELVIN M. McCOSH, Excelsior, Minnesota

PAUL MELLON, Upperville, Virginia

HARRISON T. MESEROLE, Bryan, Texas

DAVIS W. MOORE, Denver, Colorado

HOWARD S. MOTT, Sheffield, Massachusetts

MOUNT ALLISON UNIVERSITY, Sackville, Canada

CALVIN P. OTTO, Charlottesville, Virginia

PRINCETON UNIVERSITY, Princeton, New Jersey

UNIVERSITY OF PUGET SOUND, Tacoma, Washington

RICE UNIVERSITY, Houston, Texas

OTTO SCHAEFER, Schweinfurt, Germany

SOUTHERN ILLINOIS UNIVERSITY, Carbondale, Illinois

UNIVERSITY OF SUSSEX LIBRARY, Brighton, England

G. THOMAS TANSELLE, New York City

ROBERT A. TIBBETTS, Columbus, Ohio

WILLIAM M. TUCKER, Palo Alto, California

PETER TUMARKIN, New York City

CALHOUN WINTON, College Park, Maryland

STUART WRIGHT, Winston-Salem, North Carolina

PUBLICATIONS IN PRINT

Distributed by the University Press of Virginia

Former publications of the Society not listed here are out of print. Those wishing a complete list of them should see the annual lists in successive volumes of Studies. *Members will receive a 20 per cent discount on all publications. Orders should be addressed to the University Press of Virginia, Box 3608, University Station, Charlottesville, Virginia 22903, U.S.A.*

Blehl, Vincent Ferrer, S.J., JOHN HENRY NEWMAN, A BIBLIOGRAPHICAL CATALOGUE OF HIS WRITINGS. $25.00.

Bloomfield, B. C., and Mendelson, Edward, W. H. AUDEN, A BIBLIOGRAPHY, 1924–1969. $35.00.

Bristol, Roger P., INDEX TO SUPPLEMENT TO EVANS' *American Bibliography*. $20.00.

Bristol, Roger P., SUPPLEMENT TO EVANS' *American Bibliography*. $50.00.

Dameron, J. Lasley, and Cauthen, Irby B., Jr., EDGAR ALLAN POE: A BIBLIOGRAPHY OF CRITICISM 1827–1967. $35.00.

Evans, G. Blakemore, editor, SHAKESPEAREAN PROMPT-BOOKS OF THE SEVENTEENTH CENTURY. Vol. V: Text of the Smock Alley *Macbeth*. $35.00. Vol. VI: Text of the Smock Alley *Othello*. $35.00. Vol. VII: Text of the Smock Alley *A Midsummer Night's Dream*. $50.00.

Fry, Donald, *Beowulf* AND *The Fight at Finnsburh*: A BIBLIOGRAPHY. $25.00.

Gallup, Donald, EZRA POUND: A BIBLIOGRAPHY. (Published in conjunction with St. Paul's Bibliographies.) $50.00.

Grimshaw, James A., ROBERT PENN WARREN: A DESCRIPTIVE BIBLIOGRAPHY, 1922–1979. $40.00.

Guiliano, Edward, LEWIS CARROLL: AN ANNOTATED INTERNATIONAL BIBLIOGRAPHY, 1960–1977. $25.00.

Herring, Phillip F., editor, JOYCE'S NOTES AND EARLY DRAFTS FOR *Ulysses*: SELECTIONS FROM THE BUFFALO COLLECTION. $42.50.

Herring, Phillip F., editor, JOYCE'S *Ulysses* NOTESHEETS IN THE BRITISH MUSEUM. $42.50.

Hirsch, Rudolph, and Heaney, Howell, SELECTIVE CHECK LISTS OF BIBLIOGRAPHICAL SCHOLARSHIP, Series B, 1956–1962. $25.00.

Hodnett, Edward, AESOP IN ENGLAND. $20.00.

Johnson, Linck C., THOREAU'S COMPLEX WEAVE. The Writing of *A Week on the Concord and Merrimack Rivers* with the Text of the First Draft. $45.00.

Life, Page West, SIR THOMAS MALORY AND THE *Morte Darthur*: A SURVEY OF SCHOLARSHIP AND ANNOTATED BIBLIOGRAPHY. $28.50.

MacMahon, Candace W., ELIZABETH BISHOP, A BIBLIOGRAPHY, 1927–1979. $25.00.

Maynard, Joe, and Miles, Barry, WILLIAM S. BURROUGHS, A BIBLIOGRAPHY, 1953–73. $27.50.

Partridge, A. C., A SUBSTANTIVE GRAMMAR OF SHAKESPEARE'S NONDRAMATIC TEXTS. $27.50.

Polk, Noel, WILLIAM FAULKNER, *The Marionettes*. Trade edition. $17.50.

Pound, Ezra, A QUINZAINE FOR THIS YULE. $10.00.

Ross, Charles L., THE COMPOSITION OF *The Rainbow* AND *Women in Love*. $20.00.

Roth, Barry, AN ANNOTATED BIBLIOGRAPHY OF JANE AUSTEN STUDIES, 1973–83. $30.00.

Spalek, John M., GUIDE TO THE ARCHIVAL MATERIALS OF THE GERMAN-SPEAKING EMIGRATION TO THE UNITED STATES AFTER 1933. $50.00.

STUDIES IN BIBLIOGRAPHY, Volumes 1–44. $35.00 each. (Volume 10 out of print)

Tanselle, G. Thomas, SELECTED STUDIES IN BIBLIOGRAPHY. $35.00.

Tanselle, G. Thomas, TEXTUAL CRITICISM SINCE GREG: A CHRONICLE 1950–1985. $9.95.

Tanselle, G. Thomas, TEXTUAL CRITICISM AND SCHOLARLY EDITING. $40.00.

Tucker, Edward, THE SHAPING OF LONGFELLOW's *John Endicott*. A Textual History, Including Two Early Versions. $20.00.

Vander Meulen, David L., POPE'S DUNCIAD OF 1728: A HISTORY AND FACSIMILE. $40.00.

Weisenfarth, Joseph, GEORGE ELIOT: A WRITER'S NOTEBOOK, 1854–1879 AND UNCOLLECTED WRITINGS. $30.00.

West, James L. W., III, A SISTER CARRIE PORTFOLIO. $25.00.

Wright, Stuart, RANDALL JARRELL: A DESCRIPTIVE BIBLIOGRAPHY, 1929–1983. $35.00.

Wright, Stuart and West, James L. W., III, REYNOLDS PRICE: A BIBLIOGRAPHY, 1949–1984. $25.00.

Wright, Stuart and West, James L. W., III, PETER TAYLOR: A DESCRIPTIVE BIBLIOGRAPHY, 1934–87. $40.00.

WINNERS OF THE 1990 STUDENT AWARDS IN BOOK COLLECTING

John Piller (Contemporary Poetry)
Samuel Pyeatt Menefee (Manuscript Diaries)
David M. Seaman (Chaucer)

Honorable Mention

Kevin L. Blackwell
Diana Branscome
Stephanie J. L. Gertz
Sian M. Hunter
W. Russ Mayes, Jr.

Corinne McCutchan
Frederick A. Patterson
David Reed
Victoria C. Rowan
Theodore Wu

This book was printed by letterpress from type cast on the Linotype by Heritage Printers, Inc. of Charlotte, North Carolina. The typeface is Baskerville, a design by John Baskerville (1706–1775), English printer and typefounder. Linotype Baskerville is a weight-for-weight and curve-for-curve copy of Baskerville's celebrated printing type. The pattern for the cutting was a complete font of (approximately) 14 point, cast from Baskerville's own matrices—exhumed at Paris, France, in 1929. The paper is 70-pound Glatfelter, an acid-free paper with a useful life of 300 years.